FROM COCHISE TO GERONIMO

The Civilization of the American Indian Series

New Mexico MAGAZINE

1st gift Subscription $25.95
2nd Gift Subscription only $15

For Canadian & foreign subscriptions add $20 each

My Name ....

Address ....

City .... State ....

Zip .... Phone ....

☐ GIFT #1 ($25.95) TO: ....

Address ....

City .... State ....

Zip .... Phone ....

☐ GIFT #2 ($15.) TO: ....

Address ....

City .... State ....

Zip .... Phone ....

Total # of subs being ordered _____   71111S

FROM COCHISE TO GERONIMO

The Chiricahua Apaches, 1874–1886

EDWIN R. SWEENEY

University of Oklahoma Press : Norman

Also by Edwin R. Sweeney
Cochise: Chiricahua Apache Chief (Norman, Okla., 1991)
Merejildo Grijalva: Apache Captive, Army Scout (El Paso, 1992)
(ed.) *Making Peace with Cochise: The 1872 Journal of Captain Joseph Alton Sladen* (Norman, Okla., 1997)
Mangas Coloradas: Chief of the Chiricahua Apaches (Norman, Okla., 1998)

Library of Congress Cataloging-in-Publication Data

Sweeney, Edwin R. (Edwin Russell), 1950–
From Cochise to Geronimo : the Chiricahua Apaches, 1874-1886 / Edwin R. Sweeney.
    p. cm. — (The civilization of the American Indian series ; v. 268)
Includes bibliographical references and index.
ISBN 978-0-8061-4150-3 (hardcover : alk. paper)
1. Chiricahua Indians—History—19th century. 2. Chiricahua Indians—Wars.
    3. Chiricahua Indians—Kings and rulers—Biography. 4. Indians of North
    America—Wars—1866-1895. 5. Indians of North America—Wars—New
    Mexico. 6. Indians of North America—Wars—Arizona. 7. New Mexico—Ethnic
    relations—History—19th century. 8. Arizona—Ethnic relations—History—19th
    century. I. Title.
E99.C68S94 2010
305.897'2560789—dc22

                                                                2010019921

From Cochise to Geronimo: The Chiricahua Apaches, 1874–1886 is Volume 268 in
The Civilization of the American Indian Series.

The paper in this book meets the guidelines for permanence and durability of the
Committee on Production Guidelines for Book Longevity of the
Council on Library Resources, Inc. ∞

To a man I most admire, Mike Kwedor,
the consummate man of my times:
inspirational teammate, honorable Marine,
loving husband, proud father of three daughters,
and my friend of fifty years.

And to my beautiful daughter Courtney Arias Sweeney
(April 2, 1984–October 8, 2004).
"She left the way she came, Too soon, Too soon."
(From the poem "Too Soon" by
Tiffani Sweeney, October 9, 2004.)

CONTENTS

ILLUSTRATIONS

Maps

Maps created by Berndt Kuhn

ACKNOWLEDGMENTS

I was twelve years old when I was first introduced to Cochise in 1962. It changed my life. I was with a friend, Dale Samuels, in the library at the junior high school in Stoughton, Massachusetts, about twenty miles southwest of Boston. We had recently moved there from South Boston, or Southie, as we affectionately called it. Dale handed me a biography on the Apache chief Cochise. He had read the book and urged me to look at it. To this point in my life, the only books I had read were American Revolution histories and baseball biographies. My knowledge of American Indians was limited to what I had seen on television. But I liked the dust jacket and decided to scan the first chapter. From that time forward, I read everything on American Indians that I could get my hands on. Of course, Cochise has remained my favorite. Nothing can satisfy my desire to learn about him. Nine months ago, I met Dale Samuels at our high school's fortieth reunion and reminded him of the role he had played in my life. Thanks again, Dale.

Two writers profoundly affected my decision to research and write about the Chiricahua Apaches. The trailblazer in the study of Apache–military relations was Dan Thrapp, who began his research in the early 1950s and provided a blueprint for those who followed his example. A humble and magnanimous man, he was always ready to help and to listen. Though he always downplayed his role in my development as a researcher and writer, he was my mentor and my friend. I enjoyed a similar relationship with Eve Ball, whose works have given us a perspective on Chiricahua Apache history from informants who rode with Victorio and Geronimo.

I have made many friends during my thirty-five years of visiting historic sites and researching the Apaches in the Southwest. At the top of my list is Dan Aranda of Las Cruces, New Mexico. His knowledge of Apacheria in southern New Mexico is unsurpassed. He is truly a well-rounded historian. He understands nature, the desert, and the mountains and sees life through the eyes of a people who had to live off the land. Nearly every one of my field trips in New Mexico and Arizona has been with him. He is like a brother to me. In Arizona, my best friend is Al González of Tucson. Besides providing me with a place to stay, his charming personality and interesting conversations have opened my eyes on many subjects important to the borderlands. And he has always done it with a twinkle in his eye and genial laughter.

In Arizona, I would like to thank Larry Ludwig, ranger-in-charge at Fort Bowie, and his wife, Sandy; Bill Hoy of Bowie; Charles (Chuck) Collins, Rick Collins, Alicia Delgadillo, Bill and Mary De Stefano, Bill Gillespie, and Frank Puncer, all of Tucson; and Alan Ferg and Diana Hadley of the Arizona State Museum in Tucson. In addition, for their hospitality, my thanks go to George Robertson of Sunsites (George is a dear friend who, aided by a photo once owned by Joseph Sladen, found the rock formation where Cochise and General Howard discussed peace); Kathryn Plauster of Dragoon; Mary Beth and Roy Dawson near Cochise's East Stronghold; and Marjorie and Jerry Dixon at Cochise's West Stronghold, in St. David.

In New Mexico, I am grateful to Nick and Dolores Ortega of Chis; Emilio Tapila of Las Cruces (no one knows the Black Range and the San Mateo Mountains better), who has provided expertise and advice; Apache scholar Sherry Robinson of Albuquerque; and Lincoln County historian Lynda Sanchez. And special thanks to my Apache friends at Mescalero, Ellyn BigRope, Anita Lester and her late husband Parker, Jordan and Annette Torres, Claudina Saenz, the late Berle Kanseah, his son, James, and Silas Cochise. I have learned much from them.

Thanks also to Judy Walters of Summerville, South Carolina; Randy, Kelly, and Mathew Stevenson of Wildwood, Missouri; Jim and Gwen Ramatowski of O'Fallon, Missouri; Alexander Sudak, of Koscierzyna, Poland; Allan Radbourne of Taunton, England, who has always shared his vast knowledge of Apaches; and Miriam Perrett of Lampeter, Wales.

I consider myself extremely fortunate to have become friends with Berndt Kuhn, a fellow researcher from Sweden. Now, Berndt is no stranger to western historians in the Southwest. We have marveled at the nuggets he continues to mine, and the material that he has so graciously shared. In this respect, I owe

Berndt a hearty handshake, for I am grateful to be the recipient of his diligent efforts.

I would like to acknowledge the contributions of three persons who have helped to improve the final product. The first is Bud Shapard of Pisgah Forest, North Carolina. Bud has just written the definitive biography of Loco, chief of the Chihenne band of Chiricahuas. For the past decade, we have traded weekly phone calls about our common interest. Mostly I have broadened my vocabulary, learning his down-home southern phrases, which date to his childhood. In return, he has learned that tonic in Boston is a soft drink. The second man, Bob Utley, needs no introduction. When I met Bob a few years ago, he acted as though he was as impressed with me as I was with him. Naturally, I was, and still am, in awe of the greatest western historian in our country. Bob read my manuscript, and his suggestions have improved the final product. The third person is William Betts. Bill, a retired professor of English composition and literature from Indiana University of Pennsylvania, was kind enough to review my manuscript and correct its many flaws in punctuation and grammar. His help has been invaluable.

Finally, I must pay tribute to my wife, Joanne, and my daughters Tiffani, Caitlin, and Courtney. We lost our youngest daughter, Courtney, almost five years ago. She was twenty years old. The depths of our despair seemed bottomless. A few years later, we gained two sons-in-law, Drew DeManuele and Mike Wilson. They are the sons I never had. Drew and Tiffani gave us grandchildren, Cooper and Scout. Their endearing presence remind us that we have plenty of love to give, even after experiencing a period of inconsolable grief.

St. Charles, Missouri
July 23, 2009

FROM COCHISE TO GERONIMO

INTRODUCTION

The dawn of the 1870s brought dramatic changes for the Chiricahua Apaches. The American occupation of their territory had forced the four Chiricahua bands (Chihenne, Bedonkohe, Chokonen, and Nednhi) to accept the hard lesson that accommodation with Americans was necessary for their survival. Buoyed by a cautious optimism that their children would enjoy the benefits of peace while retaining their traditional ways, they agreed to settle on two reservations in their ancestral homelands in southern New Mexico and southeastern Arizona. For several years, times were good. The tribe's population, which had steadily declined between 1850 and 1870, had stabilized at some 1,250 members.

These idyllic times changed with little warning in 1876 and 1877, when the government closed both reservations and moved the Chiricahuas who were willing to the reviled San Carlos Reservation in Arizona. In retrospect, we can see that if the government had consolidated the Chiricahua bands at either Ojo Caliente in southern New Mexico or Chiricahua in southeastern Arizona, it might have averted the ensuing conflict that resulted in tremendous loss of life on all sides. Certainly, if the choice had been Ojo Caliente, the Victorio War would never have occurred. A progressive agent familiar with the Chiricahuas could have moved the Indians slowly on a path toward planting and raising stock. Their culture and political organization would have remained intact. The Victorio War of 1879–80 was a direct product of this ill-conceived government policy of concentration.

Of course, half the tribe initially refused to relocate to San Carlos. Thus, Apache outbreaks, military campaigns in which the army employed Apache scouts to track down Chiricahuas in New Mexico and Mexico, quick-striking Chiricahua raids into the United States from Mexico, and the inevitable return of the hostiles to the San Carlos Reservation marked relations over the next decade. With each surrender, because of Mexican campaigns and treachery, the Chiricahuas returned drastically reduced in numbers. After fifteen months of hostilities (the last outbreak occurred in May 1885), the United States government had had enough. It removed nearly all Chiricahuas from Arizona to Florida. But this decade of sporadic warfare had taken such a dramatic toll that by September 1886, only 540 Chiricahuas remained, a figure that reflects a 57 percent reduction in population. This book chronicles the heartbreaking story of a people who in about ten years lost nearly everything they valued.

Many readers are probably familiar with my earlier books on the Chiricahua tribal leaders Cochise and Mangas Coloradas, which are mainly biographical with a heavy dose of life and times as well. I see this volume as the third part of a trilogy, an extension of my earlier books, which cover nineteenth-century Chiricahua Apache history, through 1863 in Mangas Coloradas's case and through 1874 for Cochise. But this book differs from these earlier biographies in that it does not center on one man because the Chiricahuas lacked a dominant tribal chief after Cochise's death in 1874. Instead, its focus is on the men who provided direction to the four bands, two of which were rapidly losing their identity through loss of lives by the early 1880s.

From my knowledge of the preceding years and from the understanding that the cataclysmic events of the 1870s and 1880s had their genesis in incidents that occurred in 1861 and 1863, when the American military betrayed Cochise and treacherously murdered Mangas Coloradas, I hope to produce a proper view of this period. These reckless acts planted the seeds that sprouted after the closing of the Chiricahuas' reservations on ancestral lands and the subsequent removal of the Indians to San Carlos as part of the government's concentration policy.

The sons of these iconic chiefs, Naiche and Mangas, always remembered the American military's betrayal. At critical junctures, they made decisions based on what had happened to their fathers. Moreover, by the time Naiche and Mangas had reached the age of twenty, each had lost older siblings. Naiche's brother, Taza, died of pneumonia on a visit to Washington to meet the Great White Father in 1876. His death left a void in authority and catapulted Naiche into a premature leadership role. During the 1870s, Mangas would see three brothers fall in battle, one with Cochise, and two with Victorio. Mangas, who had married a daughter of Victorio, followed his father-in-law's cue until Mexicans entrapped them at Tres Castillos, where the patriot chief died in battle.

Naiche and Mangas grew up experiencing so many changes so rapidly that even the most sagacious of the Chiricahua shamans could not have anticipated them. Each man was pacific by nature, content to live on reservations if treated fairly. Nevertheless, each fled the agencies, Naiche in 1881 and 1885 and Mangas in 1877, 1879, and 1885, in part because of their well-grounded distrust of the American military. Naiche's two outbreaks were a direct result of this suspicion, but Mangas's actions, at least in 1877 and 1879, were motivated more by an abhorrence of the San Carlos Reservation and by a love for his ancestral country in New Mexico.

Contemporary chiefs who had fought alongside Cochise and Mangas Coloradas (Victorio, Nana, Juh, Chatto, and Chihuahua) would remain important leaders into the 1880s. And it is impossible to ignore the presence of Geronimo, who seemed to have a gift for being in the center, directly or indirectly, of virtually every important event in Chiricahua history between 1876 and 1886. The exception was the Victorio War of 1879–80, although he played a role in the events leading up to even that conflict. Geronimo, too, was a follower of Mangas Coloradas and an associate of Cochise. It comes as no surprise that in his autobiography, published in 1905, he emphasized the American military's treachery against these two chiefs. When threatened by troops, Geronimo would consult his Power, a kind of guardian spirit which came in the form of healing ability, clairvoyant powers, and superior skills in hunting and raiding, which usually told him to leave the reservation before the troops seized him. This advice corroborated his well-honed instincts, which led the shaman to flee the moment he felt his life or liberty to be in danger.

The period beginning with the closing of the Chiricahua Reservation in June 1876 and ending with the Geronimo War in September 1886 has been the subject of numerous monographs and books. These works focus on the military's campaigns and battles and the Chiricahuas' raids and reprisals. But just as important were the years in which the Indians settled on the reservations at San Carlos and near Fort Apache. This period has received limited attention, particularly the years 1876–81, when the Chokonens under Naiche were on the San Carlos Reservation. Taza and Naiche had made a deathbed promise to their father to keep the peace with Americans. This commitment guided Naiche until 1881, when, fearing for the safety of his people, he left the reservation. During the tumultuous decade ending in 1886, Naiche spent six and one-half years on reservations at San Carlos and at Turkey Creek, south of Fort Apache. In contrast, Geronimo chose the uncertainty of life in Mexico, where he lived for nearly five years during this decade. Mangas and Nana topped that record, spending six of the ten years off the reservations in a warlike attitude.

The Apache conflict of the 1870s and 1880s was entirely defensive. The Chiricahuas were not fighting to resist occupation; they knew that cause was lost. So why did they resist? Fear of punitive measures by the American military was uppermost on their minds. To be sure, some fought as a last resort for their way of life, the liberty to live in their ancestral homelands (at least in the case of Victorio, Mangas, and Nana), and the freedom to pursue happiness by honoring their own cultural beliefs. Others carried on the torch because they believed their precarious but free life in the Sierra Madre Mountains of Mexico was better than life on the San Carlos Reservation, where malaria, especially at the subagency, had reduced Naiche's Chokonens by half between 1878 and 1880. Others left the reservation involuntarily, forced out by militant leaders, destined for the same hardships and fate as their warlike brethren.

The Chiricahuas' final outbreak in 1885 sealed their fate. Mangas and Geronimo were the ringleaders. Naiche and Chihuahua joined up only after Geronimo lied to convince them to leave. Yet only 27 percent of the tribe (34 men and 110 women and children) left the reservation. During the fifteen months of hostilities, at least fifty-eight of the eighty men left on the reservation responded to General George Crook's call to serve as scouts against their kinfolk. They were more effective than Western Apache scouts, who, though superb trackers, did not know the Sierra Madres, which had been the homeland for the Nednhi band of Chiricahuas.

When the Geronimo War finally ended, in September 1886, the United States government played out the final act of perfidy. President Grover Cleveland authorized the removal from Arizona to Florida of every Chiricahua Apache, including nearly all who had remained on the reservation. Even the loyal scouts, who had helped the military pursue Geronimo and persuade him to surrender, suffered the same consequences as the hostiles who had killed and plundered in southeastern Arizona, southwestern New Mexico, and Mexico. For the next twenty-seven years, the tribe remained prisoners of war, under the control of the War Department. The government did not know what to do with them. And the people of Arizona wanted nothing to do with them.

Whenever possible in this book, I use the actual words of the Apaches to reflect their thoughts and feelings. For my biographies on Cochise and Mangas Coloradas, one of the difficult challenges was the scarcity of oral history before 1870. In contrast, significant information from the Chiricahua point of view is available from American and Mexican archives and, most importantly, from the Morris Opler Papers recently opened at Cornell University. Furthermore, in the Arizona State Museum on the University of Arizona campus, we have the invaluable accounts Grenville Goodwin collected from Western Apache scouts. They recall the military campaigns of the 1880s in the Sierra Madre Mountains through a different lens than that of the military men who wrote the reports.

Readers will find in this story the usual figures of the American Southwest: the celebrated Cochise and George Crook; the controversial Geronimo and Nelson A. Miles; the enigmatic Chatto and John Clum; the patriots Victorio and Captain Emmet Crawford; the bellicose Juh and Joaquin Terrazas; and the ubiquitous Bonito and Tom Jeffords. Perhaps new to the reader is the cast of lesser known characters, some obscure but all vital to the story: The charismatic Chief Chihuahua and assistant surgeon Leonard Wood; the selfless shaman She-neah and American Felix Knox; the honorable Jelikine and Lieutenant Britton Davis; the principled Taza and Lieutenant James Richards; the dignified Naiche and Captain Adna Chaffee; the daredevil warriors Tsedikizen and Lieutenant John Anthony (Tony) Rucker; the courageous Chiricahua warrior Fun and New Mexico rancher John Shy; the hardy White Mountain woman Mrs. Andrew Stanley and Chiricahua warrior Atelnietze; the defiant Kaetenae and Juan Mata Ortiz; the grandfather warriors Nana and Captain Wirt Davis; the peacemakers Loco and Lieutenant Charles Gatewood.

To their contemporaries, each was a hero or a villain depending on what side you were on. Most whites looked at Apaches as savages; most Chiricahuas looked at whites as faceless adversaries who wanted to take their land and destroy their culture. With the benefit of hindsight, I see individuals who were responding to serious threats to their way of life, affronts to their principles and ideals. Each had strengths and weaknesses, in some more deep-seated than in others. Here follows the story of a clash that would have been avoidable if the United States federal government had simply been more attentive to the needs of the Chiricahuas. The participants in this narrative were individuals whose actions, with some exceptions, were appropriate for the times in which they lived.

Maps

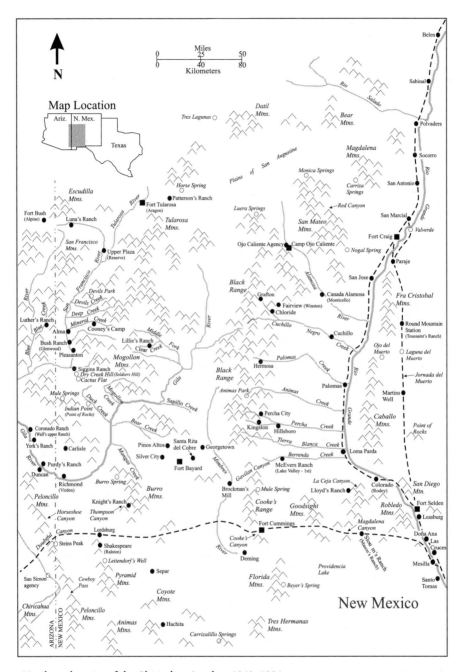

Northern domains of the Chiricahua Apaches, 1860–1886

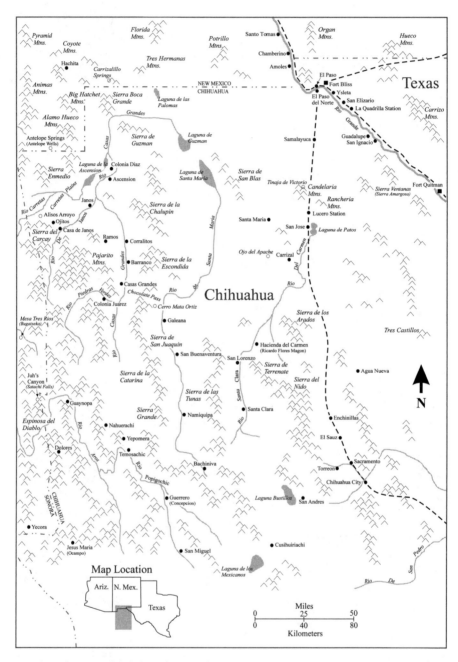

Southern domains of the Chiricahua Apaches, 1860–1886

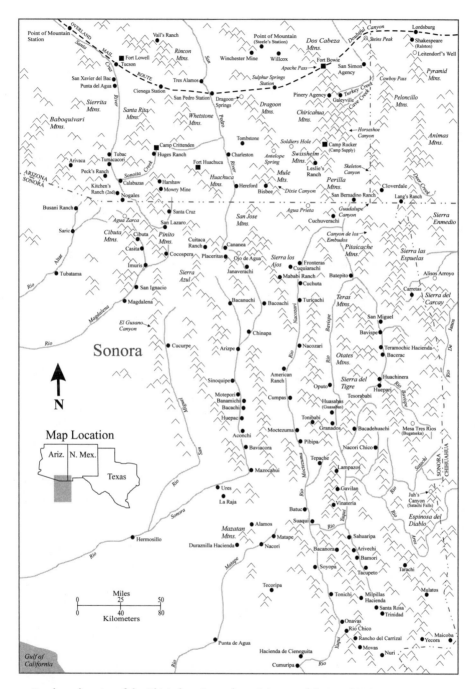

Point of Mountain
Station
OVERLAND
MAIL
Vail's Ranch
Point of Mountain
(Steele's Station)
Dos Cabeza
Mts.
Doubtful Canyon
Lordsburg
Steins Peak
Shakespeare
(Ralston)
Fort Lowell
Tucson
Rincon
Mts.
Winchester Mine
Willcox
Fort Bowie
San Simon
Agency
Leitendorf's Well
San Xavier del Bac
Punta del Agua
ROUTE
Tres Alamos
Apache Pass
Cowboy Pass
Pyramid
Mts.
Sierrita
Mts.
Cienega Station
San Pedro Station
Dragoon
Springs
Pinery Agency
Galeyville
Turkey Creek
Cave Creek
Peloncillo
Mts.
Baboquivari
Mts.
Santa Rita
Mts.
Whetstone
Mts.
Dragoon
Mts.
Chiricahua
Mts.
ARIZONA
SONORA
Tombstone
Soldiers Hole
Horseshoe
Canyon
Animas
Mts.
Camp Crittenden
Huges Ranch
Charleston
Antelope
Spring
Swisshelm
Mts.
Camp Rucker
(Camp Supply)
Tubac
Tumacacori
Fort Huachuca
Skeleton
Canyon
Arivaca
Peck's Ranch
Sonoita Creek
Harshaw
Mowry Mine
Huachuca
Mts.
Mule
Mts.
Leslie's
Ranch
Perilla
Mts.
Cloverdale
Deer Creek
Kitchen's
Ranch (2nd)
Calabazas
Nogales
Hereford
Bisbee
Dixie Canyon
San Bernadino Ranch
Lang's Ranch
Busani Ranch
Santa Cruz
Agua Prieta
Guadalupe
Canyon
Sierra
Enmedio
Agua Zarca
San Lazaro
San Jose
Mts.
Cuchuverachi
Saric
Cibuta
Mts.
Cibuta
Pinito
Mts.
Cuitaca
Ranch
Cananea
Canyon de los
Embudos
Casita
Cocospera
Placeritas
Ojo de Agua
Sierra los
Ajos
Fronteras
Cuquiarachi
Pitaicache
Mts.
Sierra las
Espuelas
Imuris
Sierra
Azul
Janaverachi
Mababi Ranch
Cuchuta
Batepito
Aliso Arroyo
Tubatama
Rio
San Ignacio
Bacanuchi
Bacoachi
Turicachi
Teras
Mts.
Carretas
Sierra del
Carcay
Magdalena
Rio
El Gusano
Canyon
Chinapa
San Miguel
Bavispe
Sonora
Cucurpe
Arizpe
Nacozari
Teramochic Hacienda
Bacerac
Otates
Mts.
Rio
N
Sinoquipe
American
Ranch
Oputo
Sierra del
Tigre
Huachinera
Huepari
Map Location
Motepori
Banamichi
Bacachi
Huepac
Cumpas
Huasabas
(Guasabas)
Tesorababi
Ariz.
N. Mex.
Aconchi
Tonibabi
Granados
Bacadehuachi
Mesa Tres Rios
(Bugatseka)
Texas
Moctezuma
Pibipa
Nacori Chico
Baviacora
Tepache
Mazocahui
Lampazos
SONORA
CHIHUAHUA
Ures
La Raja
Gavilan
Juh's
Canyon
(Satachi Falls)
Batuc
Vinateria
Suaqui
Espinosa del
Diablo
Mazatan
Mts.
Alamos
Rio
Sahuaripa
Miles
Duraznilla Hacienda
Matape
Nacori
Bacanora
Arivechi
Bamori
Tarachi
Hermosillo
Soyopa
Tacupeto
Rio
Matape
Tecoripa
Tonichi
Milpillas
Hacienda
Mulatos
Santa Rosa
Trinidad
Onavas
Rio Chico
Maicoba
Punta de Agua
Rancho del Carrizal
Yecora
Movas
Nuri
Gulf of
California
Hacienda de Cieneguita
Cumuripa
Rio

Southern domains of the Chiricahuas in southern Arizona and Sonora, Mexico

13

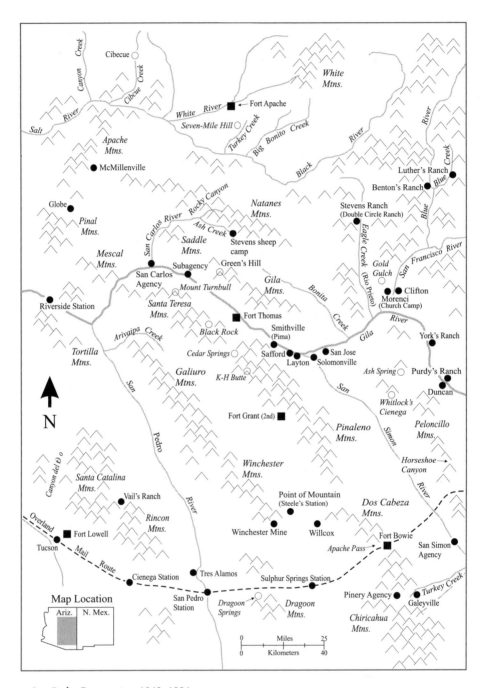

San Carlos Reservation, 1860–1886

1

THE FIRST CHIRICAHUA
RESERVATIONS

They [whites] told me when I was a boy that my mind and my
way of living was no good. Take ours [white men's,] that is the
kind of mind to have and the only way to live. Yours is no good.
Throw it away.
    Naiche to Major Hugh L. Scott, September 21, 1911

In October 1872, after waging a twelve-year war against the Americans, Cochise, the Chiricahua Apache chief of the Chokonen band, made a peace treaty
with General Oliver O. Howard. It was a historic moment. To memorialize
the treaty, Howard placed a rock on a mesa just south of the mouth of the
West Stronghold in the Dragoon Mountains of southeastern Arizona. Howard declared that "as long as the stone lasted the peace would remain unbro-
ken."[1] The terms of the treaty granted Cochise a reservation in his ancestral
country and an agent (Thomas J. Jeffords) chosen by him. Moreover, although
Fort Bowie adjoined the reservation, the soldiers had no jurisdiction over the
Indians, an important point to Cochise, who retained a profound distrust of
the military because of its mistreatment of him at Apache Pass (the Bascom
Affair in early 1861).[2]

Howard's acquiescence to Cochise's demands that Jeffords have complete
autonomy on the reservation (effectively obviating General George Crook's
intervention) would create enormous problems because the southern border
of the Chiricahua Reservation adjoined northern Sonora. As far as Cochise
was concerned, he had made peace with the Americans. The Mexicans were a
separate issue, and he did not intend to make a treaty with them. If anything,
Howard's failure to forbid the Chiricahuas from raiding in Sonora was an error

of omission. His inexperience with Apaches was evident here; he simply had no idea of the fanatical hatred that the Chiricahuas felt toward Sonora.

In any event, Cochise and Tom Jeffords took immediate steps to bring stability and organization to the new reservation. Cochise sent out runners to gather the remainder of his band and to inform the Bedonkohe and Nednhi bands of Chiricahuas living in southwestern New Mexico and northern Mexico of his decision. About October 20, Jeffords brought in the Steins Peak local group, which was probably under the leadership of Chihuahua, a forty-year-old self-assured chief who was the boldest Chokonen of his time. Next, on November 20, 1872, Jeffords and his assistant, Fred Hughes, made a treaty with some 325 Nednhis and Bedonkohes at Pinery Canyon in the Chiricahua Mountains. The Nednhis under Natiza, Juh, and Nolgee numbered about 225 individuals; the remainder were Bedonkohes under Esquine and Coha.[3]

The Tularosa Reservation in the Mogollon Mountains in New Mexico housed the fourth Chiricahua band, the Chihennes under Victorio and Loco, and a second group of Bedonkohes led by Chiva and Gordo. In the spring of 1872, the government had moved them there from Ojo Caliente (where they had settled in 1869), despite their vigorous objections. Though confinement to reservations was the price for peace, after the long period of warfare with Americans, the two Bedonkohe chiefs were somewhat content because the locations were in their ancestral grounds. But the Chihenne chiefs longed to return to their former reservation at Ojo Caliente, which Chiricahuas considered sacred grounds.

By late 1872, for the first time, every Chiricahua was on a reservation, giving us accurate population figures for the Chiricahua tribe. They numbered about 1,244 individuals, 544 at Tularosa, and about 700 at Chiricahua.[4]

Despite what most southwesterners thought, this new era of tranquillity pleased the Indians, for their chiefs realized that peace was necessary for the survival of their people. And if the government treated them well, honored its agreements, and allowed them to live on the grounds set aside by treaty, their days at war with Americans were over. Although the Chiricahua Reservation lasted less than four years, the rock that symbolized the commitment of the United States government to the Chiricahua Apaches remains today at the mouth of Cochise's pristine West Stronghold. It did not disappear, despite the whims of an institution that valued expediency over integrity when it came to honoring its agreements with Native Americans.

The Chiricahua Apaches have earned a reputation for being fierce, uncompromising, and unmerciful adversaries of Americans and Mexicans. But were they warlike by nature? One of my earliest statements in my Cochise biography makes that assertion, but I would now argue the reverse. Most nineteenth-century whites saw Apaches as cruel and merciless, warlike and incorrigible. These characterizations were certainly apt for describing their mode of warfare and their methods of dealing with their enemies. Yet, most Anglos and Mexicans failed to understand that Apaches were not intrinsically warlike. It may surprise some readers to learn that when Americans first arrived in New Mexico, the Chiricahuas did not consider them enemies because the former had not done anything to merit that designation. The evolution from friend to foe was earned only by systematic abuses of the relationship or by egregious acts of treachery that took Apache lives. Only when Americans betrayed the Chiricahuas' trust did they go to war.

They went to war, by their own definition, to avenge what they considered unlawful, unjustifiable, or treacherous acts carried out against them. That they sustained some warfare for prolonged periods, as in the Chiricahuas' hostilities against the Spanish and Mexicans, and in Cochise's case for over a decade against Americans, was a function of a self-perpetuating cycle of violence. Periods of prolonged warfare against Mexicans in the nineteenth century became a way of life from one generation to another. This insatiable hunger for revenge only spawned more vengeance and, even more important in the Chiricahua world, a deep and abiding distrust of whites.

Violence begot more violence. If the initial act was extreme, such as the betrayal of Cochise and the hanging of his relatives at Apache Pass in 1861, or the treacherous capture and brutal, premeditated execution of Mangas Coloradas in 1863, the impact on the Chiricahuas far transcended the loss of loved ones and respected tribesmen. They had to avenge the infamous abuses that had become seared in the memories of all Chiricahuas, particularly those of the leaders who succeeded Cochise and Mangas Coloradas. They had learned the hard lesson not to trust Americans, especially the military. These ingrained suspicions factored into the outbreaks of the 1870s and 1880s.

Apaches were a happy, proud, and fiercely independent people. Members of the Athapaskan linguistic family, they called themselves Tinneh or Inde, which, loosely translated, means "Man" or "People." Historians and anthropologists disagree about when they reached their historic homelands in the American Southwest, but they were probably well entrenched there by the mid-1500s.[5] Linguistically, the Apache nation consisted of seven major groupings: the Jicarillas, Lipans, and Kiowa-Apaches formed the eastern division, and the Navajos, Mescaleros, Western Apaches, and Chiricahuas formed the western division.[6] Besides a closely related language, these tribes shared several cultural traits. They lived in small mobile bands or groups, usually in mountainous areas. Gatherers and hunters, they were quick to adopt new technology from the people with whom they came into contact. A spiritual race, they believed that both animate and inanimate objects possessed power that they could hand over to tribal members. They usually went to war to protect their territory or their families, or to exact vengeance on enemies who had wronged them.[7]

The Chiricahua tribe consisted of four bands with each, at least before the reservation period in the early 1870s, inhabiting a well-defined area.[8] The easternmost band, called Chihennes ("red-paint people") by the Chiricahuas and Warm Springs, Mimbres, or Copper Mine Apaches by southwesterners, lived between the Rio Grande River and Silver City. This band consisted of at least three smaller units, called local groups, with the Mimbres River, Black Range, and Ojo Caliente among their favorite village sites. In the 1850s, their leaders were Delgadito, Cuchillo Negro, and Ponce. Upon their deaths in the 1850s and early 1860s, Victorio, Loco, and Nana succeeded them, though sons of those 1850s leaders remained prominent men in the Chihenne band through the Victorio War of 1879–1880.

The smallest band in numbers was the second Chiricahua band, the Bedonkohes, which enjoyed political strength within the tribe because of its influential chief, Mangas Coloradas, a powerful man standing nearly six and a half feet tall. A Bedonkohe by birth, he exercised enormous influence among the Chihennes throughout his lifetime. He held close ties to Victorio, who one informant claimed was born into Mangas Coloradas's local group, which consisted of Chihennes and Bedonkohes.[9] The Chiricahuas called this unit Ne-be-ke-yen-de, meaning "Country of People" or "Earth They Own It People," in reference to the large tribal gatherings at Santa Lucía Springs. This famous place was situated along the northeastern face of the Burro Mountains, a few miles below the Gila River, near today's Mangas, northwest of Silver City. One informant of Morris Opler said that Mangas Coloradas was chief of the Chihennes though he lived in a separate region. Another informant revealed that Mangas Coloradas was a tribal chief, "the head of all the Chiricahuas," during his lifetime, which agrees with the historical record. Chatto, the famous Chiricahua leader of the 1880s, was born into Mangas Coloradas's group. His father was Mangas's brother, perhaps the man known as José Mangas. In later years, Chatto waxed nostalgically about the exciting times during his formative years when the bands gathered to celebrate important events and to develop political and military strategies under the direction of Mangas Coloradas.[10]

Two local groups lived mainly in the Mogollon Mountains, considered by the Chiricahuas to be their sacred mountains.[11] After Mangas's death in 1863, the Bedonkohes' leaders were José Mangas, Chastine, Gordo, Chiva, and Esquine. Several sons of Mangas Coloradas were prominent men into the 1870s and 1880s. Mangas Coloradas also enjoyed tremendous influence among the Chokonens, the third Chiricahua band that called southeastern Arizona and northern Mexico its home range. His son-in-law, the legendary Cochise, led the Chokonen band from the mid-1850s until his death in 1874. His local group was called Cai-a-he-ne, "Sun Goes Down People," signifying their position as the group farthest west.[12] Other Chokonen groups were located in the Chiricahua Mountains (Tse-ga-ta-hen-de, or Rock Pocket People) and in the Dragoon Mountains (Dzil-dun-as-le-n, or Rocks At Foot Of Grass Expanse).[13] After Cochise's death in 1874, his two sons, Taza and Naiche, succeeded him. But neither possessed the charismatic leadership skills of Cochise. As a result, leaders such as Skinya, Chihuahua, Cathla, Nahilzay (known as Talking Chief for obvious reasons), and Chatto (whose mother was a Chokonen) shared leadership duties with Cochise's sons from 1874 to 1886.

The Nednhis were the fourth Chiricahua band. Before the reservation period, which for them began in 1872, they lived almost exclusively in the mountains of northern Mexico. Probably the most independent of the bands, they maintained close ties with the Chokonens, whose territory adjoined theirs, the Bedonkohes, who occasionally roamed into northern Mexico, and the Chihennes, for one Nednhi local group often camped in the Florida Mountains south of Deming, New Mexico. In 1840, they were the most numerous of the four bands, boasting between six and seven hundred members. Martine and Fatty, two of Morris Opler's principal informants, have shed some light on the political organization of the Nednhis, which in the late 1840s had two distinct divisions, each comprising two or three local groups.

The Chiricahuas called the Carrizaleno division Gol-ga-ene or Gul-ga-ki, "Open Place People" or "Prairie Dog People," referring to their penchant for camping in the Chihuahuan lowlands near El Carmen or Carrizal.[14] They also occasionally roamed north to Janos and southern New Mexico. Their main chiefs in the 1850s were Cojinillin and Felipe. From the mid-1840s through the early 1860s, Chihuahuan soldiers, aided by their counterparts from Sonora, systematically wiped them out. After killing Cojinillin in 1863, they convinced Felipe and forty-six Gol-ga-enes to surrender in early 1864. The chief capitulated only after soldiers captured his wife and children. His reward for wanting to be with his family was an all-expenses-paid trip to Chihuahua City, where officials hanged him before a cheering crowd in the town square.[15]

Only a few of the Gol-ga-enes survived. One was a young teenage boy named Fatty, who joined the Nednhi division for a while. His cousin, Martine, who went through his *dikohe,* or novice period, in the early 1860s, recalled these violent times in Sonora and Chihuahua: "There were so many raids [that] I got through in a hurry." It had taken him less than one month to complete the four raids necessary to become a warrior.[16]

Martine explained that his Nednhi division had two local groups: The Nde-nda-i, to which he belonged, inhabited the Carcay Mountains in northwestern Chihuahua and the Teras and El Tigre ranges in northeastern Sonora. The second was the Haiahende, who lived in the New Mexico panhandle and in the mountains in northeast Sonora and northwest Chihuahua. Both groups occasionally wandered north into southern Arizona and New Mexico and far south to Guaynopa, a stronghold deep in the Sierra Madre, to a mountain they called Dzil-da-na-tal, "Mountain Holding Head Up And Peering Out," just east of the Sonora boundary. This was the home of a small group called Tu-ntsa-nde, "Big Water People," an appellation referring to the Aros River, which sweeps around Guaynopa in a semicircle.[17]

The leaders for the Nde-nda-i were Soquilla (Chewing Rocks), Coleto Amarillo, Tuscaze, and Nolgee. Mexican troops killed the first two leaders in the Florida Mountains in southern New Mexico in 1849 and 1852, and Tuscaze in the Chiricahua Mountains in 1867.[18] Soquilla was Martine's grandfather, and Nolgee was Martine's father. The second main group, the Haiahende, was led by Láceris, sometimes called Pláceris. Upon his death in the late 1850s, Láceris's two sons, Galindo and Juh, succeeded him. When the former passed from the scene in the early 1860s, Juh took his rightful place as chief, for as Martine explained, Juh's father (Láceris) and grandfather had led the group since the 1830s.[19]

The Nednhi band showed great devotion to Juh, a powerfully built leader also called Tandinbilnojui, "He Brings Many Things With Him," a name likely referring to his prowess as a raider.[20] Born in the early 1820s, by 1860 he had forged a close alliance with Cochise, spurning contacts with Mexico and finding refuge in the remote high country of the Sierra Madre Mountains. He would lead the Nednhis until his death in 1883.

The Chiricahua people experienced tremendous disruptions to their way of life during these transitional years from war to peace. After all, reservation life with its inherent constraints affected the fabric of their traditional existence. Before this, their movements were contingent on which plants and fruits were coming into season and where they might best find game. Confined to a specific area, they found that much of their ancestral homeland was now off-limits, especially for the two bands in New Mexico, where it was too dangerous to leave the reservation to hunt or to gather at places now overrun by miners or claimed by ranchers. Suddenly they were supposed to transform their existence, in which gathering, hunting, and raiding were vital economic pursuits, to a life of government rations and eventually self-subsistence by raising crops and stock. Indian agents also expected them to exploit the reservation's natural food sources and to hunt game within its confines.

The Chiricahuas also faced another insidious problem—one that would continue into the 1880s. As part of the rations, Indian agents regularly issued corn, which the Apaches fermented into *tiswin*, or "gray water."[21] Also called *tulapai*, this beverage, a long-standing social drink, became more frequently used during the reservation years possibly to alleviate the boredom of their sedentary life. The Indians held tiswin parties that frequently degenerated into violent altercations that took Apache lives. Moreover, these flare-ups sometimes led to outbreaks.

Still, the Chiricahuas fondly remembered the early reservation years as an idyllic time, which had brought a semblance of stability to their lives after a decade of hostilities. Indian agents usually issued them rations of corn and beef, and they no longer had to worry about the incessant threat posed by American soldiers. Furthermore, in the first years of reservation life (1870–1876), they were free to continue raiding into Mexico, which provided their young men with training and status and afforded the veteran warriors the opportunity to exact vengeance and accumulate economic wealth.

The first year of the newly established Chiricahua Reservation was a success in many ways: it eventually attracted nearly 1,000 Chiricahuas to settle there, and these Apaches refrained from raiding in Arizona and New Mexico. The downside was the location of the reservation. Its southern boundary adjoined Sonora, and many of Cochise's young men, the Nednhis, and the Bedonkohes raided into Sonora with impunity. In addition, Chihennes and Bedonkohes from the Tularosa agency in New Mexico used the reservation as a thoroughfare to raid Sonora.

In early 1873, General George Crook, military commander of the Department of Arizona, ever disdainful of Howard's efforts, was eager to jump into the dispute. He went so far as to make plans for a military takeover of the reservation. But first he had to prove that Cochise had violated the terms of the armistice. And because Cochise and Howard had failed to sign a formal treaty (the pact was an oral agreement between two men of integrity), Crook was uncertain of the terms.

In late January 1873, Crook sent Captain William H. Brown, Lieutenant John G. Bourke, and a small escort to the reservation to obtain Cochise's understanding of the terms. Jeffords arranged the meeting, which took place on February 3, 1873, in Cochise's East Stronghold of the Dragoon Mountains. Bourke recorded the interview. Captain Brown asked Cochise "what stipulations, if any, were made in the treaty with regard to the people in Mexico?" Cochise responded that "the Mexicans are on one side in this matter and the Americans are on another." He did not deny that his young warriors "are liable to go down from time to time and do a little damage to the Mexicans." Cochise's comments must have disappointed Crook, for clearly Cochise believed that he had not violated the agreement.[22]

The next month Eskiminzin, the chief of the Arivaipa band of the San Carlos group of Western Apaches, paid Cochise a visit. Though they were probably the two best-known Apache chiefs in Arizona, they had reportedly never met, which seems odd because the territories of the two men were adjacent to each other. They enjoyed a productive meeting and worked out an agreement that visiting Indians on their reservations must have a pass signed by the agent. They agreed to arrest violators and return them to their proper reservation. As Eskiminzin's party departed, Cochise, in accordance with Apache manners, "gave Eskiminzin a horse, saddle, and bridle and to each of the Indians with him a horse."[23]

There is little doubt where the horses came from. During the first six months of Jeffords's reservation (October 1872–March 1873), Chiricahua Apache depredations in Sonora were just as severe as they had been during the same period a year before the peace treaty. Cochise and Jeffords asserted that they were stock raids, but they were much more serious than that. In fact, the Indians were cutting down anyone in their path. From January 1, 1873, through February 7, 1873, Apaches murdered seventeen Sonorans; by the end of June, this number had multiplied sixfold to one hundred, at least according to one informed estimate. The Sonoran press lashed out at the government of Sonora and the United States for not protecting defenseless people.

The attitude displayed by American officials outraged Sonora, though Cochise had pointed out to Crook's emissaries that when he lived in peace with Mexico at Fronteras and Janos, authorities there had encouraged him to raid into the United States. Undoubtedly, Apaches residing on the Chiricahua Reservation were responsible for most of the depredations. No Chiricahuas lived in Mexico at this time. Thus, Sonoran governor Ignacio Pesqueira'sassertion that his troops had followed the trails of Apaches to the Chiricahua Reservation was true. Yet, Sonora's claim that Howard had granted Cochise the right to raid into Sonora was ridiculous. Sonora's most prominent newspaper, *Estrella de Occidente*, reported this as fact and added that the Americans were also furnishing guns, saddles, and mounts. As calmer heads prevailed, Governor Pesqueira accepted that Howard had not given Cochise permission to raid his state. Yet, he astutely pointed out, "neither local, civil, or military authorities have attempted to impede these [incursions]. What if the situation was reversed? Would Americans tolerate it?"[24]

General Howard suggested that Sonora send a peace envoy to Cochise, who would then grant them a truce, or so Howard believed, thus revealing his naïve perceptions and simple solutions to an age-old and very complex problem. In March 1873, Sonora sent to the Chiricahua Reservation two prominent military officials from Fronteras, Juan Luna and Cayetano Silvas, both of whom had a long history in negotiating with and battling against Cochise (and their Indian fighting days were far from over). With Jeffords's help, they met Cochise, probably near his camp in the Dos Cabezas Mountains opposite Ewell Springs, and told him that Sonora wanted a permanent truce. Cochise dismissed their appeal, saying he would "not think of it." He denounced Sonora's treatment of his people. Several Chiricahuas were less than discreet about their raiding into Sonora. One warrior boasted that they killed every Mexican they encountered, and another admitted that a chief had been slain along the Sonora River the month before. Luna concluded that prospects for a truce were dim: "The Apaches showed me a profound hatred [and] were against peace." Cochise even had to restrain a warrior who wanted to take Luna's horse in payment for his brother, whom Mexicans had captured years before.[25]

A few months later, some 150 disenchanted Bedonkohes and Chihennes under Gordo, Chie, and Nana left Tularosa for the Chiricahua Reservation. Their appearance failed to surprise Jeffords, for a small group had relocated from Tularosa in February 1873 and had predicted that more would be coming when the weather improved. Benjamin Thomas had taken command of the Tularosa agency the previous January. A sincere man, he was a pragmatist who planned to begin the process of moving the Apaches from warriors to farmers. Although he had some experience with Indians (he was formerly employed as the doctor on the Navajo Reservation), he faced a culture shock, for his wards had yet to adopt his vision for their future. Thomas claimed that Nana's party had left on a social visit, hoping to return with presents of horses from the wealthy Indians at Chiricahua. Yet many went to join their kinfolk for a foray into Mexico. Nana's presence on these visits was customary considering that his wife was Nah-dos-te, Geronimo's sister.[26]

Once at Chiricahua, however, the disenchanted Chihennes and Bedonkohes saw another option—one they clearly planned to exercise. The newcomers quickly discovered that life under Tom Jeffords was more to their liking. In particular, they found the manner in which he managed his agency much less constraining than Agent Thomas's by-the-book methods at Tularosa. Gordo's group would remain at Chiricahua. Nana and Chie stayed for almost three months. Nana established his camp at Bonita and Pinery Canyon, where the Nednhis and Bedonkohes had their rancherías. Chie and his family likely moved to the Dragoon Mountains, where he would have spent time with his uncle, Cochise.[27]

The Chiricahua war party, which consisted of members from every Chiricahua band, invaded Mexico in June 1873. About a month later, they returned to the reservation with plunder and a captive boy from Chihuahua, Panteleon Rocha, who was with Geronimo (the earliest English reference to him that I have found).

Jeffords, knowing that he had the support of Cochise, immediately decided to rescue the youth, but it would not happen without incident. Hughes suggests that Jeffords simply rode into Geronimo's camp and seized the boy, but other accounts claim that he had to negotiate for his release. Anytime Mexican captives were involved, the Apaches always objected to releasing them, asserting, with some justification, that Mexicans never returned their Chiricahua hostages.

In a council with Jeffords at San Simon, the Chiricahuas agreed to release the boy if Americans would return a child whom they had captured during an attack on a ranchería in the Chiricahua Mountains in February 1871. Jeffords's promise to investigate failed to allay the pent-up anger of some Chiricahuas. One Chokonen named Tiscli, who was a member of Skinya's group, assumed an aggressive posture. Fred Hughes, who had been ill, rose from his sick bed, anticipating trouble. Tiscli reacted and tried to stab Hughes, but without success. After Jeffords restored order and tempers cooled, he may have given

Geronimo a small gift to calm the waters. Though one eyewitness interpreted that gesture as a sign of weakness, in reality it was a small price to pay, for it appeased the Indians and did not set a precedent. Jeffords knew that the Apaches, in accepting the gift, would consider the matter dropped even if he could not produce the boy captured by Americans over two years before. Jeffords held the boy for about a month until he learned that his parents had come to a settlement on the Mimbres, when he put the boy on a stage for a happy reunion with his parents.[28]

Nana left Geronimo's camp soon after. On August 5, 1873, he and a Chihenne leader, Rafael, with twenty warriors and their families, returned to Tularosa, where they encountered the tail end of a major crisis. It had erupted because of Sánchez (a noted raider of Ponce's group), Victorio's inability to deal with his son-in-law Pajarito, and the never-ending commotion from the Indians' continued use of tiswin. Nana promised Thomas that he "would put things in order."[29]

Sánchez had just returned to Tularosa after raiding Shedd's ranch near San Augustin Pass in the Organ Mountains. Captain George W. Chilson, with ten troopers of the Eighth Cavalry, overtook the Indians near Cañada Alamosa, recovered the stock, and in a brisk fight killed two Indians and wounded another. Sánchez returned to Tularosa and soon discovered that Agent Thomas planned to arrest him with the help of Victorio and Loco. What Thomas did not understand was that one of Victorio's nephews was a member of Sánchez's raiding party. So, when the agent outlined his plan, Victorio naturally and impertinently refused to cooperate. Clearly frustrated with Tularosa, Victorio challenged the agent: if the soldiers came, he would fight them.

Unbeknownst to Victorio, Major William R. Price, a no-nonsense officer, had arrived at Tularosa with three companies of the Eighth Cavalry and twenty-five Navajo scouts. His appearance abruptly frightened away the Chihennes and Bedonkohes. Price pursued them and, after a few days of negotiations, convinced most of the Chihennes to return to the agency. Yet the Bedonkohes under Chiva and a group of Chihennes under Sánchez, Raton, and Miguel Tuerto went straight to Jeffords's agency.

This development infuriated Major Price. His blood boiled even more when he interviewed three Indians who had just reached Tularosa from Cochise's reserve. Though they preferred the Tularosa location, they liked the informal administration of Jeffords better than Thomas's strict rules. At Chiricahua, they had enjoyed a tiswin feast every day. Price wrote to Captain Samuel S. Sumner at Bowie, urging him to drive the Tularosa Apaches to New Mexico.

Sumner demurred, noting that he had no orders to take such action. This reply incensed Price, who began a major smear campaign against Jeffords that, incredibly, would reach the level of Crook and Howard.[30]

Now that he had the support of Major Price, Thomas took the opportunity to assume control over the Indians. In recent weeks, the Indians had become more surly and belligerent, even shooting arrows at his employees and at the doctor as they tried to carry on their regular duties. In late May, Pajarito killed two Chihennes while on a tiswin drunk; as Thomas issued rations on June 12, Pajarito appeared and began firing at two or three of his enemies but wounded a woman instead, probably mortally. Then, supported by his three brothers (Turivio, Turivio Flojo, Pajarito Chiquito), all tiswin crazed, they "defied the whole tribe for nearly one-half hour." A military guard was present throughout the melee, and the sober Chihennes wanted the soldiers to intervene and kill the Pajarito brothers. But Agent Thomas told them to let Victorio handle it. After all, he could call upon fifty men against the "Parajito desperados." But the chief did nothing, and the four bullies left the reservation for about three weeks, returning in early July.

By the time they returned, the agent had two announcements to make. First, he promoted Loco to principal chief because of Victorio's conduct during the recent turmoil on the reservation. Second, because the commissioner of Indian affairs had approved Thomas's plan to issue corn only once a month, reducing the ration by 75 percent, he would increase the beef and flour ration to compensate for the reduction. On August 7, 1873, Pajarito met with Agent Thomas, promised to behave himself, and to prove his sincerity pledged to capture Sánchez if he returned to the agency.

Unfortunately, Pajarito's good behavior lasted for all of three weeks, or until the monthly issue of corn. On August 24, he and his brothers got drunk again in Victorio's camp about two miles from Tularosa. They decided to go on a raid, but Loco and Nana stepped in and "opposed it strongly." Turivio "to vent his spite" shot a woman, but not mortally. His older brother, Pajarito, then finished her off. According to Agent Thomas, Loco and Nana had had enough. "Feeling that they [Pajarito brothers] had already done too much of this," Loco got his rifle and joined by Nana and others attacked the Pajarito brothers, sons of the famous Cuchillo Negro, in Victorio's camp. The showdown "became very general at very close range, the length of a lance." When the battle ended, Loco and Nana's followers had slain Pajarito and his youngest brother, Pajarito Chiquito, and wounded Turivio and Turivio Flojo. Loco and Nana had several wounded, but none fatally: a bullet shattered Rafael's leg; one of the Pajaritos shot an arrow into the chest of Nana's nephew (a son of Horache); another young man had his elbow fractured by a bullet; and a woman was shot in the side with an arrow.

Victorio's role in the battle was unclear; one of Nana's party shot an arrow that struck him in the face. Overall, Thomas said, it was an "ugly fight" with three dead and seven wounded. Yet it was also a clear victory for Loco and Nana, "who seemed to make it their special business to rid the tribe of the four pests." The entire band, except for Victorio and about thirty followers, joined Loco at his camp.[31]

After this quarrel, some Chihennes, fearing more trouble, left for Jeffords's agency. Gordo and Chiva were already there, never to return to Tularosa. In 1873, the number of Indians at Tularosa had steadily declined from an average of 663 in January to 339 in July, to about 250 (all Chihennes) in early December.[32]

Those absent had gone to the Chiricahua agency. In October 1873, Indian Inspector William Vandever examined Jeffords's accounts and determined that he had issued rations to an average of 1,000 Chiricahuas.[33] In later years, some would suggest (John P. Clum in particular) that Jeffords habitually overstated the number of Indians on his reservation. Yet, with the able assistance of Fred Hughes, his records were always in order. His enrollment records included the names and number of dependents, and he verified them "by actual counts in the rancherías." The breakdown was as follows: Chokonens, 375; Nednhis, 250; Bedonkohes, 250; Chihennes, 125. If the census for the two reservations is totaled, we get about 1,250 Chiricahuas, for no Western Apaches were at either agency.[34]

The disparity in population at the two reservations caused Indian officials in Washington to consider consolidating the two agencies into one. Meanwhile, the coming year of 1874 would bring joy to one reservation and inconsolable sorrow to the other.

2

PRELUDE TO REMOVAL

Cochise was head chief. It has always been the right for the son
to have the same [title] as his father.
  Chatto to Major Hugh L. Scott, October 16, 1911

By early 1874, the government realized that having two reservations for the
four bands of the Chiricahua Apaches was unnecessary. To its credit, it had
taken the first step to convince the Indians that they must cease hostilities in
the United States. That part of the equation had worked, probably better than
anyone could have imagined. But the experiment at Tularosa was a dismal
failure. By the end of 1873, only 250 Chihennes remained on the reservation.
Although its location was a considerable distance from the Mexican border,
the easy ride to the Chiricahua Reservation encouraged many Indians to journey there to participate in social events and forays into Mexico.

At the Chiricahua Reservation, Jeffords had one serious problem left to
solve. Under Cochise's strong tutelage, the Apaches had not raided in U.S.
territory. The Chiricahuas, however, had depredated into Mexico with impunity. This major blemish justifiably shaped Washington's perception of the
Chiricahua agency. The raids had become an indelible stigma associated with
Tom Jeffords's reservation and would have led to a military intervention there
in late 1873 if Cochise and Jeffords had continued to ignore the issue.

Assailed from all sides, Jeffords had to use his influence with Cochise to
convince him to halt the raiding. At stake was the future of the reservation.
Commissioner of Indian Affairs Edward Smith made it clear to Jeffords that
he would turn the agency over to General Crook unless the raids stopped. He
ordered Jeffords to make certain that Cochise understood the consequences.
It was only then that Cochise decided to intervene and, according to Fred
Hughes, end the practice. In early November 1873, when Jeffords was relo-

cating his headquarters from San Simon to Pinery Canyon in the Chiricahua Mountains, Cochise summoned the warriors and headmen for a tribal council. Representatives of the four bands were present. He issued an edict: this was his agency, and those who wanted to live on it must cease the raiding into Mexico.[1]

Soon after Cochise issued his ultimatum, Juh took 150 Nednhis and returned to Mexico, where he would remain until the late summer of 1874. His son, Asa Daklugie, told Eve Ball that his father stayed for periods on the Chiricahua Reservation, but "he came and went as he pleased."[2] Although Juh may have resented Cochise's imperious order, in truth he may have left simply because he had always preferred life in the Sierra Madre Mountains. He was never comfortable among Americans. He evidently departed about mid-December 1873, judging from the *Arizona Citizen* report that "a party had left the reservation for Mexico." Jeffords's report of January 31, 1874, to Commissioner Smith tended to support the news of Juh's departure: "All of the Indians who did not belong to Cochise's band . . . have gone to their own reservation." One must read between the lines of Jeffords's statement, which was alluding only to the Nednhis' departure. In mid-May 1874, Cochise's band numbered about 375 persons. Another 425 Chiricahuas were on the reservation in the Chiricahua Mountains—most of whom were Bedonkohes, with the balance split between Chihennes and Nednhis.[3]

About the time that Juh left, Loco and Horache went to Cochise's reservation to convince members of their groups to return to Tularosa. In September 1873, a few Chihennes had returned to Tularosa from Chiricahua, telling Agent Thomas that Jeffords and Cochise "do not want them to visit [Chiricahua] agency so much. Cochise objects because he has to bear all the blame for the horse stealing in Sonora." After a short stay, Loco returned to Tularosa in December 1873, bringing Sánchez and about seventy-five Chihennes. By the end of December, Thomas reported about 325 Chihennes and Bedonkohes on the reservation.[4]

In February 1874, Fred Hughes wrote a seemingly innocuous letter to the *Las Cruces Borderer* suggesting that most of Cochise's people would be willing to join the Chihennes on a reservation in New Mexico. Hughes believed it would "settle our Sonoran difficulties." Moreover, he inexplicably claimed that only a "half-dozen warriors would object." In Santa Fe, New Mexico's superintendent of Indian affairs, Levi Edwin Dudley, happened to read the letter and promptly forwarded it to Commissioner Smith in Washington. Smith, fed up with the Sonora controversy, ordered Dudley to visit Cochise to determine his feelings about removal to Ojo Caliente. If Cochise would move, Dudley was considering replacing Jeffords with Jacob May, General Howard's interpreter during his mission to Cochise. On May 21, 1874, when Dudley met with Tom Jeffords at Pinery Canyon, he learned that Cochise lay seriously ill in the Dragoon Mountains and that "it was feared that he might die."[5]

The next day they went to Cochise's camp. Dudley met Cochise's eldest son, Taza, whose Apache name was Daza, meaning "Heavy," to describe his solid build.[6] Born about 1840, Taza had matured into a superb warrior. After seeing Cochise's condition, Dudley offered to return when the chief's health improved. Yet, Cochise "insisted upon hearing me then, and said that he would soon die and that I had also better talk with his sub chiefs." Dudley had spoken for about an hour about relocation to Ojo Caliente when Cochise lapsed into a coma. The superintendent returned to Fort Bowie. A few days later, when he retraced his steps to the Dragoons, he found Cochise "mounted on his horse in front of his wickiup, having been lifted there by his friends, showing his determination and strength of will." Cochise told his guest that he "wished to be mounted once more before he died." The chief opposed the move to New Mexico, but he would leave that decision to Taza. Jeffords declared that he could move 250 Bedonkohes and Chihennes to Ojo Caliente at a moment's notice, and Dudley thought the Chokonens and Nednhis would also go if he appointed Jeffords as agent for the new reservation.[7]

On June 8, 1874, Cochise died of natural causes (probably stomach cancer), in the East Stronghold of the Dragoon Mountains. According to Fred Hughes, "three prominent aspirants" were possible successors to Cochise. They were his oldest son, Taza; the head captain and medicine man, Skinya (Haske-ne-l-a), "Angry, He Stares at It"; and the war captain, Nahilzay. Hughes thought Nahilzay the "preferable" choice because of his friendship with Americans.[8]

Cochise had had other plans. Hoping to ensure a smooth transition and a continuation of his policies, he had named Taza, whom he had groomed to take his place, as chief. His last words to his people were "to forever live in peace" with the whites and to obey Tom Jeffords. Years later Naiche recalled that his father told Taza and him "to pursue peace with the whites as long as they could." Cochise's subchiefs, or captains, especially Skinya, initially agreed to support this decision, but Skinya eventually felt slighted. Although his daughter, Nah-de-yole, would marry Naiche, Cochise's youngest son, Skinya seemed to bristle at Cochise's rebuke.[9]

Taza faced a daunting challenge. Whites—ranchers and miners—had occupied more and more of the lands formerly inhabited by the Chiricahuas.

It was only a matter of time before covetous, land-hungry Americans would confiscate Cochise's reservation in the corner of southeastern Arizona. The Sulphur Springs Valley showed enormous potential for farming and ranching, and the Chiricahua and Dragoon mountains were undoubtedly depositories of great mineral wealth. Taza had no idea that his world was changing faster than he could imagine. He tried to keep his people in check. But, now in his early thirties, he had lived in his father's shadow and lacked Cochise's record of accomplishments and influence. It would soon become apparent that he would be unable to control the Chokonens as his father had. Months after Cochise's death, the Chokonens began to splinter. About one-half, or 180 people, remained loyal to Taza; the other half, under separate groups headed by Skinya, Cathla, Nahilzay, and perhaps Chihuahua, went their own way, though they remained on the reservation.

During the summer of 1874, Gordo took his Bedonkohes and joined Juh in Mexico. Their presence allowed Mexican officials to resurrect the subject of the Chiricahuas' raiding into their country. The previous spring, Juh had opened negotiations at Janos, Chihuahua, to make a treaty in exchange for rations and an end to hostilities. Juh was blunt about his dislike of Americans, saying, "He never wanted to live in the United States." If granted peace, he even pledged to protect the Janos frontier from hostile Apaches who made incursions from American reservations. Janos officials sent Juh's offer to the political chief of the district of Galeana, who wisely instructed Juh to send an envoy to the governor of Sonora. In early July a Nednhi woman named Juana left Bavispe bound for Ures, Sonora's state capital, to consummate a peace treaty with the governor. Evidently the discussions bore fruit because she returned to Bavispe and then set out to Janos with Eligio, one of Juh's trusted headman, and three other women to arrange the final details.[10]

While all this was going on a raiding party from the Chiricahua Reservation entered Sonora and left widespread destruction in its wake. The foray, in which a dozen men from Tularosa participated, included such notables as Sánchez, Ponce, Bonito, his cousin (the celebrated shaman She-neah), and Miguel Tuerto, a one-eyed war leader. They easily enlisted others at the Chiricahua agency and headed into Sonora, raiding ranches and attacking travelers in the district of Moctezuma. The war party killed at least ten persons; in addition, it captured a great deal of stock before returning to Arizona. Mexican troops followed them to the border, incorrectly assuming they were Juh's band.[11]

But Juh had remained in camp near Janos, awaiting the results of his peace offering. In late July Captain Jesús Escalante organized a campaign of one hundred National Guard soldiers from Bavispe, Bacerac, Granados, and Huá-sabas. With Escalante was Sonora's most noteworthy Indian fighter of the mid-eighteenth century, Eusebio Samaniego of Bavispe. Following a script that Sonoran military officials had carried out countless times, they crossed the border into Chihuahua, clandestinely entered Janos, and went to the home of the municipal president. With bayonets drawn, they abducted the five members of Juh's band, who were awaiting the arrival of the peace commissioner from Galeana.[12]

Escalante's army then left with their hostages, forcing them to guide his force to Juh's camp located southwest of Janos, probably in the Carcay Mountains. As they approached the ranchería, Juana heroically tried to warn her people, but the soldiers shot her down, which did alert the village. The Sonorans captured the deserted camp and confiscated its supplies, including eight horses and two mules recently stolen in Sonora, which Escalante cited as proof that the Indians intended to trade—a compelling argument that he knew would provide cover for his illegal actions at Janos. The fate of Eligio and the other three Chiricahua women was never in doubt. After the flight of Juh's band, Escalante's soldiers murdered them "in cold blood." They undoubtedly scalped their victims, for Sonora had recently increased the bounty on Apache hair to 300 pesos because of the severity of Apache depredations in 1873. Escalante's duplicitous report, published in *Estrella de Occidente*, implied that the five Apaches were slain during the capture of Juh's camp.[13]

It is ironic yet symptomatic of relations between the two races that Sonorans punished Juh's band when he wanted to make peace with Chihuahua. After Escalante's illegal seizure, a Mexican official from Janos or Casas Grandes wrote a letter to Juh that Sonoran troops apparently intercepted after the capture of his ranchería. The note provided details about Escalante's execution of Juana and Eligio, and offered Juh "aguardiente in exchange for the stock stolen in Sonora," an indication that this age-old traffic in contraband remained in place along Mexico's northern frontier. Juh, however, returned to the Chiricahua Reservation, followed soon after by Gordo after Chihuahuan troops attacked Gordo's ranchería of fourteen warriors and their families, capturing a woman, her baby, and thirty-six head of stock.[14]

Sonora's execution of Eligio's party would open a new round of hostilities, especially after Juh returned to the Chiricahua agency. As the governor of Chihuahua had predicted to his counterpart in Sonora, the Indians would avenge Escalante's wanton act. In mid-September 1874, Jeffords issued rations to 654 Indians, the lowest total of the year; a war party had gone to Sonora, where they launched several raids in the districts of Moctezuma and Sahuaripa. One Sonoran patrol came across tracks of more than 150 Apaches, prompting *Estrella de Occidente* to exaggerate that "300 Chiricahuas were absent from the [Chiricahua] agency, raiding and killing in Sonora."[15]

Meanwhile, Washington officials finally authorized Dudley to close the Tularosa reservation, "a failure from the beginning," and return the Chihennes to Ojo Caliente. Agent Thomas had expected enthusiastic support for the plan, but when he first broached the subject to Victorio in April 1874 (before Dudley's visit to Cochise), the chief had inexplicably reconsidered after two years of complaining. Victorio said that "Cochise and his Indians are bad, and if they went there he did not want to go." On June 20, 1874, Superintendent Dudley received the official notification that Tularosa would be closed and the Indians taken back to Ojo Caliente. He told Thomas, now that "Cochise is dead that should do away with any opposition." Loco simply said, "Give us some place and let us remain there."[16]

Benjamin Thomas completed the transfer of 325 Chihennes, which included about eighty men, in early September 1874. Over fifty years later, Kinzhuna recalled that they had attempted to plant corn at Tularosa, but even the valleys were 8,000 feet in altitude. "We couldn't raise anything. The corn would freeze." As for the government transferring his Apaches to Ojo Caliente, Jeffords ominously predicted that if anyone tried to coerce his Apaches to move, they would go to war.[17]

Yet, because whites were just beginning to understand the ranching and mining potential offered by the Sulphur Springs Valley and the Chiricahua Mountains, the issue would remain on center stage for the next eighteen months. In the late summer of 1874, J. T. Rothrock spent some time at Fort Bowie as a member of Lieutenant George M. Wheeler's corps of engineers. His comments were discerning and prophetic. He mentioned that the Apaches gathered acorns, which they traded to the post sutler, who in turn shipped them to Tucson, where they commanded top price. He also visited Jeffords at Pinery Canyon and observed that his herd of beef cattle "was grazing, all looking pretty good." Rothrock concluded his report by describing in glowing terms the potential for the Sulphur Springs Valley and the Dragoon Mountains: "The Sulphur Springs Valley is one of the most desirable cattle ranges in Arizona having the general character of the San Simon Valley but with more and better pasture. Water is abundant enough for herding purposes. . . . Without exception, this was the best location for this we have ever seen. The neighboring Dragoon Mountains are yet in the hands of the Indians but will someday offer desirable locations for stock ranches."[18] The Chiricahua Apaches remained the only obstacle to development, and they had no plans to vacate their ancestral grounds, which were as valuable to them as to the Americans who coveted their land.

Meanwhile, by early 1875, affairs at Chiricahua were beginning to get out of hand. Taza's influence extended to about half the Chokonens, whom he tried to keep in check. But without the powerful presence of Cochise, the other half of the Chokonens as well as the Nednhis and Bedonkohes were free to continue their incursions into Sonora. Jeffords, never sympathetic to Mexicans below the border, became even more indifferent. Perhaps he realized that he was fighting a losing battle over this issue, and he had grown weary of talking about the long-standing problem. But this matter had become the primary focus of his reservation, threatening to obscure the two years of peace in southeastern Arizona. To his credit, several times he confiscated stolen stock from the Indians after the owners had tracked it to his reservation. Yet his response to his superiors in Washington was to obfuscate and to tell half-truths. He would never concede that his wards were responsible for any killings in Mexico. He allowed that they did a little mischief, but he insisted that they were embarking on harmless stock raids.

His favorite explanation was to blame a band of Chiricahuas that lived in Sonora. Nonetheless, his assertions were undoubtedly pure rationalization, concocted in an attempt to justify his own shameful apathy. Sidney De Long, the post sutler at Bowie, who should have known better (his store was trading with the Chiricahuas for their loot taken in Sonora), echoed Jeffords's claim, telling the *Arizona Citizen* that the raiding in Sonora was the work of a band that lived in that country. Hiriam C. Hodge repeated the "spin," as we would call it today, claiming that Jeffords told him that part of the band never came to the reservation. Furthermore, the agent added a deceitful argument that he knew would be compelling if true. He told Hodge that he was "sure that since the Howard treaty not one of them has ever killed an American or Mexican." The agent, however, was parsing words. While it was true that the Chiricahuas had not slain anyone in Arizona, below the border was a far different story. He revealed his private feelings when he told a newspaper reporter that the Mexicans were getting what they deserved for past acts of treachery carried out against the Chiricahuas.[19]

Overall, it was a messy business for Jeffords. In the spring of 1875, he told one American that the Chiricahuas had modified their raiding strategy. Instead of hitting vulnerable ranches and towns along the border, where Mexican soldiers could trail them to the reservation, they had decided to concentrate on targets in the interior of the state. To be fair, he did not encourage their actions, but without Cochise's powerful presence, he was helpless to prevent these forays.[20]

Once the raiding began in earnest, both sides spilled more blood, and the inevitable cycle of revenge and counterstrikes only intensified the antipathy both races felt for each other. In early January 1875, National Guard soldiers battled twenty Apaches north of Bavispe, killed one Apache, and wounded a few others. The patrol returned to Bavispe with the scalp of the dead man. In mid-January, Chiricahuas captured a freight train of twelve persons near Huásabas in the Sierra Madre. The Mexicans inexplicably did not have one firearm among them (a systemic problem in the towns and villages of Sonora). Just as incredible, the Apache leader spared their lives—although he took the entire train and stripped the Mexicans of their clothing. A few days later, six Apaches armed with repeating rifles assaulted the Hacienda de Pivipa, the former home of José Téran y Tato, an old adversary from the late 1840s and early 1850s. They killed two unarmed men working their fields, riddling one man with bullet holes until one warrior shot him through the heart. On January 27, 1875, the municipal president of Tepache wrote the governor: "It is difficult to take pen in hand and write about these killings when all that can be heard is the wailing of mothers, fathers, and orphans."[21]

In mid-April, a war party of thirty-six to forty Chiricahuas left the reservation for Fronteras. Thursday, April 15, 1875, was ration day at the agency's headquarters in Pinery Canyon. Chihuahua likely led the war party, which numbered fourteen Chihennes from Ojo Caliente. They left for Sonora soon after Jeffords rationed them. By 8:00 A.M. on April 16, the confident Apaches had occupied positions in the Los Angeles hills east of the presidio.

The Indians were unaware that the Mexican troops had recently received a shipment of Henry rifles. These new arms would play the pivotal role in the hard-fought contest. Angel Elías and Juan Luna audaciously led their men from the security of the presidio to confront the Chiricahuas. Unfortunately, particulars about the actual fight are scarce, and no account from the Apache perspective exists. It was clear to all involved, however, that the Sonorans won the battle because of the firepower of the Henry rifles. Luna's men routed the Chiricahuas from the battlefield. He last saw the Indians carrying several wounded men into the hills. They left two corpses and much of their supplies in the hands of the Sonorans, including nine parfleches loaded with corn, coffee, and dried meat, undoubtedly received from Tom Jeffords the day before in Pinery Canyon. Most of the war party continued their raid into Sonora, striking at ranches near Ures and returning with a great quantity of stock. An American followed their return trail to within a few miles of Jeffords's headquarters.[22]

In late May 1875, soldiers from Bavispe killed two Apaches in a fight at Ojitos. The troops followed the other warriors to the Chiricahua Reservation. In June two war parties left the reservation, one for Sonora and the second, under Juh, for Chihuahua. These war parties were out for revenge and the blood of as many Mexicans as possible. The band in Sonora killed two men near Ures and Magdalena in early July. With Sonora's military involved in suppressing a Yaqui and Mayo uprising, and the government in chaos because of a disputed governor's election, the Apaches faced token opposition. The Sonoran press denounced the military presidios as "useless and unable to provide protection."[23]

Meanwhile in Chihuahua, Juh, perhaps to avenge the five members of his band whom Escalante had executed the previous summer, launched a series of fearsome attacks on travelers and ranches between Galeana and Chihuahua City. In July alone, his war party killed four men and wounded five others near Galeana, and killed three men outside of Temosachic. But Juh reserved his most deadly assaults for Encinillas (a hacienda owned by the powerful Luis Terrazas), whose inhabitants had historically been ruthless and inveterate enemies of the Nednhis. In a one-month stretch, his warriors killed twenty-three people in Chihuahua, which responded by reinstating the scalp bounty, increasing it to an unheard-of five hundred pesos. In August, as his war party returned to their rancherías at Pinery Canyon, Juh ambushed a party of five men at Ojitos, north of Bavispe, killing four while the fifth escaped to Casas Grandes.[24]

In September 1875 a Chiricahua war party returning north with stolen stock attacked the Vinateria de Peñasco near Tepache. Several Mexicans hidden behind a wall shot down the leader of the assault, who turned out to be a chief named Chaguanito. Later that day, the Indians skirmished with National Guard soldiers from Tepache. Secure in their mountain breastworks, the Chiricahuas boasted that they would return with another war party to avenge Chaguanito's death once they took their plunder to the Chiricahua Reservation.[25]

Two months later, the Indians would avenge their April defeat at Fronteras and the death of Chaguanito. Again, Chihuahua apparently led this band to avenge the two men whose bodies the Chiricahuas had left on the slopes of the

Los Angeles hills near the presidio. The audacious chief, who held a lifelong antipathy toward Mexicans, pledged not to leave the area until he had killed Juan Luna; no one else would satisfy him. Juan Luna was the same man who had met Cochise and perhaps Chihuahua on the Chiricahua Reservation in the spring of 1873, hoping to make peace between him and Sonora. According to Chihuahua's son Eugene Chihuahua, a Mexican officer—probably Luna—had met his father near Fort Bowie and, noticing his light skin, assumed that Chihuahua was a Mexican by birth. This insulted Chihuahua, who reviled Mexicans as much as Cochise had.[26]

Luna certainly meant no harm by his remark. Now in his early forties, Luna had been fighting Apaches for over twenty years. In November 1855, he was the sole survivor of a group of twelve men who had left Fronteras for Bacoachi when the Apaches had attacked them at Capulin; Luna somehow escaped on foot and made his way back to Fronteras. Over the years, he had become one of Sonora's toughest Indian fighters, giving no quarter and asking for none in return. Yet, by 1873 he conceded to Cochise that "we are tired and weary of war; nothing can be gained from it." The Chiricahuas were the aggressors during the April 1875 battle, but Luna had become the symbol of that defeat.[27]

The small group that decided to hunt down Juan Luna had come from the Chiricahua Reservation. The first hint that the Indians had targeted Luna came from a man whom the Apaches captured in early November and later released. Chihuahua told his prisoner that they were waiting for Luna, who had gone to Arispe with an escort of eight men. They planned to ambush him on his return trip to Fronteras. On November 13, 1875, at Mora Canyon, along the road between Bacoachi and Fronteras, they attacked his party, directing most of their gunfire at Luna, as though he had a bull's-eye painted on him. They were so close that one warrior shot an arrow into Luna's body. Another salvo seriously wounded his horse and then killed Luna. Five of the nine Mexicans fled through the canyon and rode to Fronteras to spread the alarm. Three brave men remained with Luna and returned the Apaches' fire. They fought them off but not before another man fell victim to an Apache sharpshooter. The next day, the two survivors brought the two corpses to Fronteras. Sonora's official newspaper, *Estrella de Occidente,* eulogized Luna, calling him a "brave patriot."[28]

Meanwhile, at the Chiricahua agency, Jeffords continued to overlook the raiding into Mexico. On August 21, 1875, he penned his third annual report on the "conditions of affairs at this agency." After addressing a variety of concerns, he took the offensive and complained that small parties of Mexicans were invading his reservation. Fortunately for these aggressors, the Apaches had followed Jeffords's orders not to attack unless in self-defense.

According to Jeffords's records, the number of Apaches on the reservation had increased from 930 in 1874 to 965 as of July 5, 1875:

	1874	1875	Difference
Northern Chiricahuas [Cochise's band]	365	182	(183)
Southern Chricahuas [Juh and Gordo]	290	293	3
Mimbres, Mogollons, Coyoteros [Esquine, Chiva]	275	490	215
Totals	930	965	35

This comparison tells us that Taza had retained control of one-half of Cochise's Chokonen band; the other half had left the Dragoons for the Chiricahua Mountains. These Chokonens were led by Nahilzay, Cathla (Cullah), Skinya, and possibly the independent-minded Chihuahua. The figure of 293 seems very high for the Nednhis. I suspect Jeffords included Gordo's Bedonkohes, who totaled about 80 individuals. Finally, the 490 "Mimbres, Mogollons, and Coyoteros" consisted of about 190 Chokonens who had split from Taza, 170 Bedonkohes under Esquine, and 130 Chihennes and White Mountain Apaches. It is also possible that the 4 percent increase in the numbers represents a net increase resulting from more births than deaths.[29]

Unfortunately, we do not have reliable figures for the Apaches at Ojo Caliente after the fall of 1874. In mid-November 1874, John M. Shaw replaced the competent Benjamin Thomas, who had accepted the position of agent at the Pueblo agency. Shaw, a former state representative and probate judge of Socorro County, immediately discontinued several of Thomas's policies—including the issuing of a ration ticket to each Indian. When Thomas left, he reported 335 Chihennes at Ojo Caliente. Shaw claimed 384 at his first issue on November 26; that number swelled to 500 on December 31, 1874, multiplied to 903 on May 27, 1875, and exploded to about 1,300 on July 8, 1875. Clearly, the agent calculated the numbers by taking the amount of beef issued and dividing this by the weight of a normal ration. He really had no idea how many Indians were on the reservation. Jeffords's figures are explainable and consistent. Again, if we assume that the total Chiricahua population may have grown during the reservation years to 1,300 and that no significant defection from the Chiricahua agency to Ojo Caliente had occurred by summer 1875, then Thomas's last count of 335 seems accurate because Jeffords was reporting 965 Apaches at Chiricahua.[30]

In 1875, the commissioner of Indian affairs unveiled a plan to concentrate the Western Apaches at the San Carlos Reservation in Arizona and the Chiricahua bands at Ojo Caliente in New Mexico. In mid-April 1875, Levi Edwin Dudley arrived at the Chiricahua agency to talk to the Chiricahua chiefs about moving to Ojo Caliente. Now a special commissioner for Indian affairs (the Bureau of Indian Affairs in Washington had eliminated his superintendent's position in New Mexico the year before), he had just implemented the first leg of the concentration policy by closing the Verde reservation and moving almost 1,400 Tontos and Yavapais to San Carlos.[31] Now, he hoped to close Jeffords's agency and consolidate the Indians living there with the Chihennes at Ojo Caliente. But the chiefs refused, declaring "we would sooner die here than live there." Their defiance convinced Dudley. About a week later he told the *Grant County Herald* in Silver City that his "better judgment advised him not to interfere with them for the reasons they are now peaceable and . . . that forcible removal might endanger our present happy relations with them." Although the editors of the *Herald* readily endorsed Dudley's decision, their counterparts of the *Estrella de Occidente* in Ures, Sonora, would have demurred, painting a stark picture of how precarious life was for its citizens living along Sonora's northeastern frontier.[32]

In the middle was one of Arizona's most controversial men, John P. Clum, a mature twenty-two-year old man whom Washington had appointed Indian agent at San Carlos. Clum, a former divinity student at Rutgers College in New Brunswick, New Jersey, was associated with the Dutch Reformed Church. In his first year Clum, a wiry five feet nine inches tall, joined the football team and participated in the second game ever played between archrivals Rutgers and Princeton. He would not return for his sophomore year. Instead, he joined the U.S. Army Signal Corps, which assigned him to Santa Fe as a weatherman. In early 1874 the Bureau of Indian Affairs needed an agent for San Carlos. As part of President Grant's "peace policy," the Dutch Reformed Church was responsible for filling the position. Its officials asked Rutgers College for a recommendation, and Clum, who was already out west, seemed to fit the bill. He reached San Carlos in August 1874 and set out to reform the Indian service with special attention to the Apaches.[33]

Clum had much in common with George Crook. Both were highly principled men who considered themselves omniscient; thus, their philosophies, their methods, and their decisions were correct. They would brook no dissent from their legion of critics, whose opinions they dismissed as irrelevant and partisan. Clum was highly intelligent, scrupulously honest, and incredibly fearless. He was willing to accept any responsibility assigned to him by the commissioner of Indian affairs. He also exhibited a cockiness that bordered on arrogance and a confrontational style that most military men perceived as disrespect for their profession. It was unclear whether he arrived with preconceived notions and contemptuous feelings toward the military; yet, it soon became obvious that he wanted the military completely removed from managing the Apaches of Arizona. The primary difference between Clum and Crook, who could barely stomach Indian agents, was that the latter was a mature and experienced man who knew when to use diplomacy and tact, two words not in Clum's playbook.

As a reformer, Clum would accomplish a great deal. His philosophy was to treat the Apaches with respect and trust, believing they would reciprocate. Naturally, he was right. He never showed fear, a characteristic greatly admired by Apaches. He employed an Indian police force and appointed Apache judges (of course, he was the chief justice) to decide punishment. Clum taught them better farming methods, which improved crop yields, and forbade the Apaches from producing tiswin. He insisted on regular roll calls. He hired his brother, George, to serve as teacher on the reservation. And one of his most important decisions was to employ as his assistant Martin A. Sweeney, a redheaded Irishman and former prizefighter from Massachusetts, who had been a sergeant in the Fourteenth Infantry. Finally, he felt his foremost accomplishment was ridding the reservation of the army's presence, whose officers, he believed, had their own agenda, one that was not in the best interest of the Apaches.[34]

As noted historian Dan Thrapp put it, Clum had not established the policy of closing reservations and consolidating the Apaches to San Carlos, but he "enthusiastically welcomed it." Thrapp also suggests that Clum "favored it because it would make him the most important Indian man in the Southwest."[35] Each removal brought new Apache bands under his control, and Clum naturally interpreted each action as a success from the government's perspective. Yet, those Indians affected went unwillingly. Placing these disparate Apache groups, many of them former enemies, at a site that had been home to four bands of the San Carlos Western Apache groups, which numbered about eight hundred souls, showed an utter disdain for the welfare of the Apaches.

The second leg of that concentration policy at San Carlos concerned the Apaches living near Fort Apache. On March 31, 1875, the commissioner of Indian affairs, John Smith, instructed Clum to take control of the agency at Fort Apache until he named a new agent.[36] The order affected the Eastern and Western bands of the White Mountain group, and the Carrizo, Cibecue, and

Canyon Creek bands of the Cibecue group. It stunned the Indians, who initially refused to go. After a few months of debate between Clum, the military officers at Fort Apache, and the commissioner of Indian Affairs in Washington, Clum, itching to assert his authority, arrived at Fort Apache on July 22, 1875, and immediately held talks with the confederated bands. The Indians opposed the decision, but after Clum loaded their rations and supplies in wagons and burned the agency's buildings, most reluctantly agreed to move to San Carlos.

Of the 1,800 White Mountain and Cibecue Apaches, Clum allowed over 1,100 to remain behind—600, mostly women and children, to gather their crops, and another 500, which included the Indian scouts at Apache, their families, and a part of the Eastern White Mountain band that had decided to defy the order. The balance of 700 Indians, under fifteen leaders, journeyed to San Carlos on July 26, 1875. Five days later, Clum could report that the operation was complete.[37]

Two hundred Eastern White Mountain Apaches under Esh-kel-dah-silah, the same group that had ventured to Tularosa in late 1872, opted to rejoin Chiva at the Chiricahua agency. They informed Jeffords that they could not go to San Carlos because of animosities between them and the Pinals. One woman, Mrs. Andrew Stanley, told anthropologist Grenville Goodwin that they went to the Chiricahua agency because they had heard that other Apaches and soldiers were "planning to attack our group and kill us all." They joined their *nadots-usn* relatives (Chiva's group) who were living on the reservation.[38] She recalled that the agent was Da-ya-ti-tci-dn (One Who Has Red Throat), obviously referring to the red beard of Tom Jeffords, who gave them "beef and blankets and told the people [Chiricahuas] to let us live there." Jeffords said that he fed them because they were starving.[39]

Jeffords may have decided to ration them to keep them under his control, but others on the reservation were concerned that trouble was brewing. On August 20, 1875, Lieutenant William M. Wallace, new to Fort Bowie, wrote a courteous letter to Jeffords. The day before, Taza's band had come in from the Dragoon Mountains to receive their rations from Jeffords's agency at Bowie. One chief, perhaps Taza, was concerned that these newcomers "will do some mischief that will be attributed to them." Wallace dutifully reported the conversation to Jeffords, whose response curtly implied that Wallace should let him worry about Indian affairs. Angry at this rebuke, Wallace requested clarification from the department commander, General August V. Kautz, who had replaced Crook. "Please advise me whether . . . I should under any circumstances have anything to do with the Indians on the Chiricahua Reservation." He ended his request by asking "whether it is the duty of the Indian Agent to furnish the Post Commander with any information relative to the Indians that may be asked for?" Kautz's curt response must have chagrined Wallace: "Agents on Military Reservations should furnish such information as is necessary." If the agent refused to respond, the military had no authority to force compliance.[40]

That the White Mountain people found refuge on Jeffords's reservation, when they should have been at San Carlos, bothered Clum. On Christmas Day, 1875, in an unfortunate case of mistaken identity, two White Mountain men, Cla-cu-lay and Klek-le-gun-hey, killed the Bedonkohe chief Coha, who had served under Mangas Coloradas. The two men erroneously believed that Coha was responsible for their brother's death. According to Mrs. Stanley, this is what actually happened: "That chief [Coha] had not really done it, we found out later. [The White Mountain man] had gone to a camp where there was tiswin and wanted some, but [his] brother, the owner of the drink, said 'no, this is not for your mouth,' so the boy went home crying. He got a gun and shot himself in the forehead. About that time that chief [Coha] rode away. So they thought he did it. His brother who had the tiswin came running out and stabbed the *hai-aha* [Chiricahua] chief because he thought he had killed his brother." Jeffords reported that the White Mountain Apaches left the Chiricahua agency to "escape the vengeance of the Southern Chricahuas."[41]

With the Eastern White Mountain band gone, Jeffords might have thought that affairs would settle down for a while, but he had no such luck. Commissioner Smith had already informed him that he was slashing the budget for the purchase of corn by 25 percent for the remainder of the fiscal year, which would end June 30, 1876.[42] And to compound matters, in late November 1875, Indian Inspector Edward C. Kemble, who had just inspected the San Carlos agency, was in Tucson when he heard that "affairs at the Chiricahua Reservation were not in good shape." He therefore decided to make an unannounced visit to investigate the agency.

Jeffords's detractors in Tucson, which included many in the local press, had shaped Kemble's perception of him. If Kemble wanted to call Commissioner Smith's attention to Jeffords's shortcomings, his report, or hatchet job, succeeded. Jeffords, never a bootlicker, always fiercely independent, and perhaps tired of three years of hard and thankless work as agent, effortlessly antagonized Kemble. Offended by Kemble's surprise visit, Jeffords adopted a cavalier attitude, characteristically not attempting to conceal his contempt of the inspector. He boasted about the unique influence and unrivaled control that he held over his wards, leading Kemble to brand him "conceited." Other inspectors and officials, most recently Dudley, had commented on Jeffords's unorthodox ways. But they recognized that he kept the Indians in check, and just as important, they trusted him. Kemble's bureaucratic approach in managing Indians may have worked at many Indian agencies. But the Chiricahuas had recently fought a decade-long war with Americans. Any attempt to convert them into sedentary farmers would probably have led to a resumption of hostilities. Jeffords realized this and was content to keep the status quo for the short run. In the end, perhaps he thought he could convince the younger leaders that their old way of life must change, but there was no concrete evidence that Jeffords had any long-term plans for himself or for the agency.

Kemble's contempt for Jeffords influenced the objectivity of his report. He watched as the Indians showed up to receive their food, well mounted and well armed as always—much to the dismay of an incredulous Kemble. Jeffords's clerk dispensed the rations. His system predictably disturbed Kemble, who informed his superiors that the clerk issued rations "with a rapidity [that] surpasses the lightning calculator." The issue clerk should carefully weigh each portion instead of using "guess-work." Even Jeffords would admit that his method was imprecise, but he knew every man, the number in his family, and on which of the eight rancherías, located from one-half mile to fifteen miles from Apache Pass, the family resided.[43]

The inspector also believed that Sonora had every right to complain about the raiding from the reservation. Jeffords of course fiercely denied it and he received an unexpected endorsement from Captain Curwen B. McLellan, the commander of Fort Bowie, who told Kemble "that very little, if any, raiding is done into Sonora" by the Chiricahuas. McLellan, a Scot by birth, had served the Union with distinction during the Civil War, winning a brevet for his actions at Gettysburg.[44] Yet, he had been at Bowie for only a month and likely did not realize the magnitude of the problem or the nature of the Chiricahuas' relationship with Sonora.

Kemble raised two other points. First, he implied that Jeffords had no control over his subjects, who he claimed roamed north to the White Mountains and east to the Ojo Caliente reserve in New Mexico. This was a half-truth, though born from Kemble's naïvete rather than intent to mislead. The White Mountain Apaches had sought refuge at the Chiricahua agency only after Clum had ordered them to San Carlos. The Bedonkohes and Chihennes had relocated from Tularosa to Chiricahua more than two years before. To be sure,

Jeffords allowed the agency Apaches to visit relatives or to attend social events at Ojo Caliente. So, Kemble's claim that Jeffords's Indians were roaming off the reservation was invalid and misleading. Secondly, Kemble asserted that the government could easily replace Jeffords because he was not influencing the Indians to abandon their traditional ways. A new agent will "gradually disarm them, break them of their tiswin drunks, introduce cattle and sheep herding among them, and if need be prepare for their removal to another Reservation."

And where should the government send the Indians on the Chiricahua Reservation? Kemble had the solution: the Chiricahuas must advance from their traditional and uncivilized ways to raising crops and stock. Using John Clum's policies as a model, Kemble advised the commissioner, "I think the San Carlos Reservation will prove to be the best place suited to these Indians." One has to wonder how he arrived at this solution. Clum may have proposed this when Kemble had inspected San Carlos. During Kemble's visit in Tucson, several prominent persons had lobbied him to open the reservation to ranching and mining, individuals who convinced him that affairs at Jeffords's agency were "not in good shape." Yet, these reasons, Clum's quest for power, whites' coveting Chiricahua land for ranching and mining operations, and Kemble's ethnocentrism and dislike of Jeffords, obscured the only legitimate reason to find the Apaches a new home. That, of course, was the continued raiding from the reservation into Sonora.[45]

In any event, Kemble's report planted the seeds in the mind of Indian Commissioner Smith, who needed only a good reason to justify the nullification of General Howard's treaty with Cochise. He would not have to wait long.

3

REMOVAL TO SAN CARLOS

I would like to be allowed to remain on the present reservation.
[It] was here that my ancestors lived and died.
Taza to John P. Clum, June 6, 1876

About the time of Inspector Kemble's visit to the Chiricahua agency, Daniel W. Jones, a Mormon lay member anxious to preach to the Indians about his religion, arrived at Fort Bowie. Jeffords was predictably cool to his ideas, but Jones had a letter of introduction from Governor Anson P. K. Safford, so the agent permitted him to converse with the Indians. Jones told the Apaches that the Mormons were planning to settle in their country and wanted to be friends. The incident would not be noteworthy except for a warning Jeffords gave to Jones: "We were safe enough if we did not happen to run across any drunken Indians on the road."[1] Though Jones's party did not encounter any problems, Jeffords's statement would be prescient, an eerie harbinger of things to come. The incident that would disrupt the stability on the reservation would have its genesis in white man's whiskey.

On December 22, 1875, less than a month after Kemble's visit, Jeffords received a disconcerting letter from newly appointed commissioner of Indian affairs John Quincy Smith, who eleven days earlier had replaced Edward P. Smith. The new Smith was responding to Jeffords's letter of December 6, in which the agent had requested permission to purchase flour, coffee, and sugar. Jeffords informed his superior that he would exhaust his supply of flour by the end of December and noted that his coffee ration would last only to January 19, 1876. He had enough corn on hand to issue instead of flour, but he was reluctant to do so for they would use most of the ration to make tiswin. Smith reviewed the letter and told Jeffords he would approve a contract for 100,000 pounds of flour but that his budget would not allow for any salt or sugar. In closing, he ordered Jeffords to reduce his contract for corn by 25 percent. He explained that his budget for the Indians in Arizona until June 30, 1876, "will require the greatest economy on the part of agents."[2] Smith's order was the beginning in a chain of related events that would culminate in the dissolution of the Chiricahua Reservation.

On January 19, 1876, Jeffords informed Smith that his supply of beef would last until the end of February. He requested permission to contract for 300,000 pounds of beef; otherwise, he warned that his Indians would raid into Mexico "to procure cattle unless they are supplied with the rations as promised by Special Commissioner O. O. Howard when peace was made." His pleas failed to sway Smith. On March 4, 1876, Jeffords reported that his Indians had moved into the mountains "where they could obtain game." But, he warned, "I will not be able to exercise the same supervision over the Indians as I have done [for] it is impossible for these Indians to live without meat." Eight days later, Commissioner Smith, probably concerned that hostilities might erupt, decided to divert 150,000 pounds of beef from the Colorado Indian agency to Chiricahua.[3]

By that time, at least two war parties had left the reservation to raid into Mexico. Besides the shortage of beef, which compelled some to desert the agency for higher country, a smallpox outbreak in New Mexico had left the Indians fearful that whites could transmit it to them. Many older Apaches were remembering the epidemics of 1843–44 and 1861–62 that took the lives of seventy-five to one hundred Chiricahuas at Janos and Fronteras.[4] In response to the shortage and outbreak, Juh took a war party of Bedonkohes and Nednhis into Chihuahua, and Skinya led a raiding party of fourteen men into Sonora.[5] Taza moved his 180 Chokonen followers back to the Dragoon Mountains.

On February 8, 1876, Skinya's group espied a supply train heading for Cocóspera, Sonora. They waylaid the party, their first volley resulting in the deaths of three Mexicans and the capture of another. The fifth man, though wounded, escaped with most of the Apaches in pursuit. After a nine-mile flight, the Indians overtook and killed him. Meanwhile, an "old chief . . . who wore a headdress with a single mirror in the fore part of it" held the Mexican captive. This was probably Skinya, who inexplicably "pointed out the road to Imuris" and released his prisoner. A few days later, they headed for their ranchería in the Dragoon Mountains. At the San Pedro River, they stopped at the ranch of Gideon Lewis and requested flour, which he gave to them. After they left, one Indian returned and warned Lewis's partner, a man named O'Brien, to leave, for "the Indians were planning attacks." Skinya's party rejoined their families and discovered that Taza's group had returned to the Dragoons.[6]

Buoyed by their success, Skinya and Kushkla tried to persuade Cochise's sons to leave the reservation. Skinya, still disappointed that Cochise had named Taza as his successor, had hoped to convince Naiche, his son-in-law, to leave, knowing that if successful, Taza would follow. Yet despite the strong bond between a son-in-law and father-in-law, Cochise's deathbed words still echoed in the ears of Naiche and Taza. They spurned Skinya's proposal, and a fight erupted during a tiswin party, which left dead one man from each band and a young grandson of Cochise. The boy was likely the son of Cochise's daughter Naithlotonz and Shui-eet, or Sheta, who was a son of Chiva. Taza and Naiche, with their followers, immediately returned to the agency and bivouacked near Apache Pass. Soon after the intraband fight, Pionsenay and Kushkla took five men on a raid into Sonora. By early April they were back on the reservation, with thirteen horses and loot, including a supply of gold dust worth about one hundred dollars.[7]

About this time, Juh and Nulah returned to the reservation with a string of horses and mules. Once Jeffords found out that Juh had stolen stock from Chihuahua, he proceeded to his camp and dutifully confiscated eleven of the stolen animals.[8] Now Jeffords would face his most important crisis since the death of Cochise.

In March 1876, Nicholas M. Rogers, owner of a ranch at Sulphur Springs, which the Chiricahuas called Tut-sose, "Narrow Water," had purchased a keg of whiskey in Tucson and brought it to his ranch, despite Jeffords's warnings that it could very well lead to his death.[9] Somehow the Indians learned of his purchase, and on April 6, 1876, Pionsenay and Piarhel (Kushkla's brother) came to Rogers' ranch with gold dust or money from their recent raid into Sonora. Rogers sold them several bottles of whiskey for ten dollars each. The next day Pionsenay returned with his nephew, Nazarzee, and purchased more whiskey before leaving for their camp in the Dragoons. Now intoxicated, Pionsenay wanted to fight his brother, Skinya, and when their two sisters tried to intervene, he killed them. Pionsenay and Nazarzee then left camp and returned to Rogers' ranch, arriving there about an hour after sundown, about 6:00 P.M. on April 7.[10]

Earlier that afternoon, Rogers's partner, Orizoba O. Spence, had returned to the ranch after a successful pursuit of three men who had stolen a mule and a horse from Rogers a week before. A former cavalryman who had won a medal of honor for "gallantry in action" during an 1869 fight against Cochise in the Chiricahua Mountains, Spence had joined Rogers after his discharge from the service in 1874. Both men were sitting in chairs outside their ranch, unarmed. Pionsenay wanted more whiskey, but this time Rogers refused. Pionsenay immediately opened fire, killing Rogers. Spence ran into the house and managed to get his Henry rifle, but one Indian, likely Pionsenay, shot him before he could discharge a round. Next, they ransacked the station and carried away a horse loaded with whiskey, cartridges, and provisions before returning to their camp in the Dragoons.[11]

One hour later, a Mr. Brosier arrived at Sulphur Springs and discovered the grisly scene. He immediately dashed back to Fort Bowie, arriving there shortly after midnight. His report corroborated what Jeffords had heard about an hour before.[12] Taza had sent in Teese, who had served as a bodyguard for his father, with the news.[13] Jeffords requested help from Captain McLellan, who ordered Lieutenant Austin Henely to take forty-four men of Company H, Sixth Cavalry, with five days' rations to accompany the agent to Sulphur Springs station. Two citizens from Fort Bowie joined the soldiers.[14] They left at daybreak on April 8, 1876, heading first for Taza's camp, located about twelve miles from the fort, probably near today's Bonita Canyon in the Chiricahua Mountains.

As they approached the ranchería, Jeffords discovered that the Indians had retired "to the summits of the mountains." Jeffords then asked Henely to take his detachment on to Sulphur Springs; Teese and Jeffords approached the camp. The agent convinced Taza that they were safe "as long as they remained where they were." He also suggested that the Apaches move nearer to Apache Pass to distance themselves from Skinya's band. Taza and three Chokonens joined Jeffords as guides. Before leaving, Taza asked Chiva to assume control and keep the others in check until he returned. At dusk they reached Sulphur Springs station, where Henely's command was waiting for them.[15]

That evening Lieutenant Henely and Jeffords found the keg of whiskey that was the source of the problem. Rogers had spiked it with "a quantity of tobacco and other materials to give strength to the liquor."[16] Years later, Jeffords told historian Thomas E. Farish that the "other material" added to the whiskey was a "lot of chili," which, when mixed with the "plugs of tobacco[, resulted in a] decoction that would make any man crazy."[17]

Early the next morning (April 9), a messenger arrived with the news that Pionsenay's followers had killed one man and wounded another in two attacks on isolated ranches along the San Pedro River.[18] Apparently Pionsenay and Nazarzee had returned to camp with their plunder during the evening of April 7 and had informed Skinya of their deed. At once Skinya's group of about fifty people, including twelve men, broke camp and headed toward Sonora. Pionsenay took seven men (Kushkla, Piarhel, Nazarzee, Broaches, Tiscli, and two others) to the ranch of Gideon Lewis, a forty-two-year-old native of New York, who was planting potatoes in his field. Lewis's partner, O'Brien (the recipient of the warning two months before that fighting could erupt), was off hunting in the hills. He had urged his friend never to go unarmed when working his crops, but Lewis had disregarded this advice. He realized something was amiss when he saw the Indians rounding up his horses. When he and a Mexican boy went to investigate, the Indians ambushed them. Tiscli shot Lewis, killing him instantly, while several bullets riddled the boy's clothes. Despite this, the youth escaped into the brush, having seen seven or eight Apaches.

Next, they went to the ranch of Mr. Brown, who was irrigating his field. Broaches shot him in the leg, seriously wounding him. Brown crawled into the brush and lay low until a relief party found him the next morning. The Indians destroyed his house, taking rifles and ammunition. In their haste to rejoin Skinya, they left four of Brown's mules because they had trouble capturing them.[19]

After hearing about the depredations along the San Pedro, Lieutenant Henely decided to pursue Skinya's party. Leaving a detail of eight men with the bodies, Henely took the rest of his command, rations stuffed in their saddle bags, and, accompanied by Jeffords, Taza, and three other Chokonens, followed the trail into the Dragoons. It is not clear whether they followed the trail or, based on Taza's feelings, headed directly south to the San Jose Mountains, today known as the Mule Mountains. Taza believed Skinya would use this range to get into Sonora. In any event, at 10:00 A.M. on April 10, after an eighty-mile march with only two hours' rest, Taza found Skinya's band, on "top of a high peak approached only through deep canyons and narrow ridges." As they approached Skinya's position, the hostiles opened fire with a "terrible fusillade."

Despite the surprise, the ambush failed to inflict any casualties. During the midst of the volleys, Taza displayed the same courage and leadership qualities of his celebrated father. He "stood up on a rock in the middle of the firing and made a speech to the foe." Skinya's followers, who were so well concealed that Henely's command could not see them, responded with a second salvo that forced the soldiers to retreat and take cover. Taza offered to take his three warriors to drive the aggressors from the mountains if Henely would give him soldiers to support him. Henely, who had "shown much coolness and personal bravery," thought the situation was hopeless for assault. Finally, after the two-hour skirmish, he withdrew his men and decided to return to the fort. Skinya and Pionsenay slipped into Sonora.[20]

Jeffords at once set about to allay the Indians' concerns. Taza continued to exert his influence, supporting Jeffords and advising the other chiefs to remain on the reservation. To separate them from Skinya's band, the agent moved them to the eastern side of the Chiricahuas. During this unsettled time, rumors reached Tucson that every Apache had left the reservation except a chief named Ka-cheez (possibly referring to Chihuahua, whose Apache name was Kla-esch, or Tlai-heez), who had come into Fort Bowie. Another report from Bowie stated that a band of about fifty Chihennes and some "Coyoteros" (the White Mountain Apaches) had reinforced Skinya's band.[21]

Neither was true. Not one Indian from any Chiricahua band on the reservation had joined Skinya. Estevan Ochoa, the noted Tucson merchant whom the Chiricahuas knew well, arrived at Camp Grant at 9:00 P.M. on April 9 and reported that he had heard that Delgadito and Esquine had left the reservation with their Chihenne and Bedonkohe followers (44 men and 126 women and children, according to Jeffords). A later report suggested that their followers consisted of 32 men and about 100 women and children in all.[22] And in early May, two New Mexican citizens returned to Mesilla from Apache Pass and reported that Jeffords had told them that two hundred Apaches had left the reservation for Ojo Caliente. Apparently between 150 and 200 Apaches did leave the reservation for New Mexico only a few days after Pionsenay's uprising. In light of future controversy, this was an important development.[23]

Whatever their numbers, one small raiding party struck north, stealing nineteen mules from a mine near Clifton before going east to Ojo Caliente, where an advance group arrived by mid-April. The Bedonkohes, after a three-year absence, were uninvited intruders. They found affairs at Ojo Caliente almost as chaotic as the situation they had left.[24] Like Jeffords, the Chihennes' agent, John Shaw, had exhausted his beef supply. After a month without beef in their rations, the Chihennes, sullen and morose, talked about fleeing to Mexico and making a treaty there. The commander of the District of New Mexico, Colonel Edward Hatch, left Santa Fe for Ojo Caliente to placate the Indians and assure them that the military would provide for them until Shaw received funds from the Indian Bureau. Hatch found them "extremely defiant, the men all armed with Springfield, Winchester, or Sharps rifles."

He correctly noted that some Indians had just arrived from the Chiricahua Reservation, but he was wrong when he said they had a hand "in the murder of Spence and Rogers." Shortly after Hatch's arrival, two brawls broke out between the new arrivals from Chiricahua and Victorio's people. The first erupted on April 20, 1876, and the second the following day. "In a heated debate on the question of taking the warpath," Victorio's party killed three men from the Chiricahua Reservation. Victorio's only loss was the death of General Howard's good-natured guide Chisito, or Chie. Several men were wounded. As a result, Esquine's Bedonkohes, "the Arizona Indians, a portion of the Cochise band," as Hatch called them, retired to the uninhabited parts of southwestern New Mexico and the mountains of northern Chihuahua. From here they resumed some raiding for stock in New Mexico and in Mexico.[25]

Meanwhile, the top civil official in Arizona, Governor Anson P. K. Safford, devised plans to quell the uprising and to begin the process for the ultimate dissolution of the Chiricahua agency. In retrospect, it is amazing how quickly the usually deliberate bureaucracy of the Bureau of Indian Affairs responded to the crisis. Though the commissioner of Indian affairs had based his decision partly on erroneous information furnished by Governor Safford, in truth officials of the Bureau of Indian Affairs had grown tired of Mexico's complaints about the raiding carried out from the reservation. From the commissioner's perspective, it was immaterial that one intoxicated man, who convinced seven others to accompany him in raids that cost the lives of three Americans, had incited the uprising. The government now had cause to close the reservation and uproot some seven hundred Chiricahuas (considering that Esquine's and Skinya's 200–225 followers had already left) because of the actions of one psychotic man, Pionsenay.

On April 12, 1876, five days after the deaths of Rogers and Spence, Governor Safford met the ubiquitous John Clum, who just happened to be in Tucson. Together they formulated plans for dealing with the Chiricahuas. Clum viewed this as their third opportunity to eliminate another Indian reservation. He returned to San Carlos, and on April 14, 1876, fired off a telegram to Safford reporting that he had organized a "Special Police Force" of 235 Apaches who were "very impatient to join an expedition against the Chiricahuas." The next day Safford telegraphed Clum important news: "I learn today that a part of the band has not left." Though he possessed these new details, two days later Safford sent an ambiguous if not misleading telegram to the commissioner of Indian affairs in Washington. He reported that the Chiricahuas had "revolted in a body except Taza and a few followers." Safford must have believed that he could justify a little white lie if it led to the development of the rich agricultural lands and mineral deposits of southeastern Arizona.

Finally, two days later, on April 19, 1876, the governor telegraphed John Wasson, former editor of the *Arizona Citizen*, who was in Washington, D.C., recommending that the government close the Chiricahua Reservation and remove the Indians to either San Carlos or Ojo Caliente. And who was his choice for the job? Well, John Clum of course: "The only man with the nerve, ability, and confidence to do it." Safford's power play worked. The next day Congress set aside the funds to relocate the Chiricahuas, and on May 3, 1876, the commissioner of Indian affairs, John Quincy Smith, wired Clum to take charge of the Chiricahua Reservation and, if "practicable," to transfer the Indians to San Carlos. With the third leg of the concentration policy now officially approved, Clum eagerly accepted the assignment but insisted that he must be "properly supported," implying that he required military support. Governor Safford, after conferring with General August V. Kautz, the military commander of the Department of Arizona, asked Commissioner Smith "to see the Secretary of War at once and have him order General Kautz to render all needful assistance." On May 15, 1876, the secretary of war issued orders authorizing Kautz to support the removal. Kautz wired Washington that his forces would be ready by June 2.[26]

While Safford sealed the fate of his agency and Clum planned for the takeover, Jeffords was in the cross hairs of two other important Anglo institutions: the press and the military. The *Citizen* especially whipped up public opinion with an April 15, 1876, editorial that claimed that "999 out of 1000 people [believed] that the kind of war needed against the Chiricahuas was steady, unrelenting, hopeless, and undiscriminating war slaying men, women, and children." The editors of the *Citizen* had criticized Jeffords ever since he'd admitted to them in a "private" conversation that the Chiricahuas' raids into Sonora were a legitimate response to avenge past acts of Mexican treachery.

It was an insensitive and foolish remark, the type that would come back to haunt him, though there was no record that Jeffords encouraged any of the killings in Sonora. On May 20, 1876, the *Citizen* hurled another missile at Jeffords, writing a scathing editorial replete with lies and unfounded accusations, supposedly based on the testimony of someone who had lived at Fort Bowie during the previous few years. According to their anonymous source, the agent was "helplessly drunk at least one-half of the time"; traded liquor, guns, and ammunition to his wards; and permitted them to retain captive Mexican children. Jeffords was known to take a drink, but no evidence exists to suggest it ever interfered with his duty as agent. The other accusations were patently false. About the same time, General August Kautz ordered the commanding officer at Fort Bowie to "tell Jeffords that there is a very bitter feeling against his agency in the southeastern portion of the territory."[27]

Although he had received no formal notification from Washington, Jeffords undoubtedly heard about the decision when the *Citizen* published the news on May 6. The Indians got wind of it, but he could only tell them that he had not heard anything officially.[28]

To confound matters further, on May 10, 1876, Skinya sent an emissary to request a meeting with Jeffords, which he agreed to.[29] Between April 20 and May 2, 1876, Skinya's band of twelve men had attacked two supply trains and other travelers in the districts of Moctezuma and Arispe, killing at least nine men and taking over one hundred head of cattle, horses, and mules.[30]

Jeffords met Skinya about five miles from the agency. Skinya explained that he had fled the reservation after Pionsenay's attacks because he feared that "the military would be brought down upon them all and that their women and children would be killed in the fight." Skinya insisted that only three men (Pionsenay, Broaches, and Nazarzee) of the twelve men in his band had participated in the killings of the three Americans. The other nine men, including Tiscli, who had killed Lewis, had bivouacked about twenty-three miles south of Apache Pass, probably at Turkey Creek Canyon. Jeffords accompanied Skinya to his camp and to his dismay discovered that Pionsenay and the other two "outlaws" were also there. Though Pionsenay might have sobered up, he was still as ruthless. According to the agent, Pionsenay and his two followers "loaded their guns and threatened to kill Jeffords [hoping] that would drive all the Indians out." Skinya faced off with his brother. He and his men prevented the attack by shielding the agent, who returned to Apache Pass.[31]

The next day Skinya's band came to the agency without Pionsenay and his two accomplices, who had retired to the southern end of the Chiricahuas. With the help of his son-in-law Naiche, Skinya agreed to place himself "under the surveillance of Taza." Meanwhile Jeffords told Captain McLellan that he refused to "hold any communications" with Pionsenay's group and suggested that the military take the appropriate steps to capture them. After members of Skinya's band purchased supplies at the sutler's store, the clerk wrote the *Arizona Citizen* that one of his customers had murdered Rogers and Spence. He was confused, possibly referring to Piarhel, who had been with Pionsenay the first time they bought whiskey at Rogers's ranch, or Tiscli, who had shot Lewis. As Jeffords's luck would have it, Clum happened to read the erroneous charge and immediately reported the allegation to the commissioner of Indian affairs. In his letter, the self-serving agent also vowed to bring the murderers to justice.[32]

While Clum was assembling his San Carlos Apache police, General Kautz was marshalling troops and supplies to undertake a delicate mission that, according to the reports he was receiving from Fort Bowie, could touch off another Apache war. Therefore, to convince the Indians to go peacefully to San Carlos, he decided to make a show of force and ordered all the cavalry in his department to participate in the operation. And in case the Indians were thinking of resisting, he and Governor Safford had devised a three-pronged approach. First, they advised the governor of Sonora and Colonel Hatch in New Mexico to place troops along their Arizona borders. Second, Kautz would concentrate 550 troops and 100 Indian scouts near the Chiricahua Reservation, broken down as follows: seven companies of cavalry, with two companies of Indian scouts, to guard the east and west borders of the reservation, while five companies of cavalry marched to Fort Bowie at the time of removal. Third, Governor Safford, who clearly distrusted Jeffords and thus kept him out of the information loop, hired Jeffords's former assistant, Fred Hughes, to serve as his liaison to the Chiricahuas.[33]

Clum reported from Tucson on May 23, 1876, that his preparations for the removal were complete. He had fifty-four Apache police, with Merejildo Grijalva, former captive of the Chiricahuas, as interpreter.[34] Three days later, while waiting for General Kautz to arrive from Prescott, Clum's Apaches donned their "feathers and war paint" and put on a dance for the people of Tucson with Grijalva acting as the "master of ceremonies."[35]

The same night that Clum was entertaining his Tucson audience, Taza summoned Tom Jeffords for a serious talk. The young chief told Jeffords to leave the agency to avoid seeing "him and his brother killed, for [Taza] said they were not going to leave the Chiricahua Mountains." Jeffords reminded Taza of his own promise to Cochise: "If I ever left his people, I must see them to a place where they could live in safety." Jeffords had pledged his word, and Taza had promised his father that he would always obey Jeffords. After hearing Jeffords's arguments, Taza reluctantly consented to go.[36]

About this time, Governor Safford sent Fred Hughes to Apache Pass to get the latest intelligence about the Indians' intentions. Hughes spoke to Taza and Naiche about the plans to relocate them to San Carlos. They told Hughes that though "bitterly opposed to removal [they] are for peace under all circumstances." Instead of San Carlos, they asked Hughes to negotiate on their behalf with Clum for a place separate from the Western Apaches, "above the reservation near Pueblo Viejo," located about seven miles east of today's town of Safford. Hughes, realizing this area was not part of the reservation, agreed to pass on their request to Agent Clum. Afterwards, Hughes met Skinya, who refused to leave his homelands, vowing to "die rather then be removed." The two principal Nednhi leaders, Juh and Nolgee, also objected to San Carlos. Gordo, the Bedonkohe chief, had already removed his followers to Steins Peak, preparing to return to Ojo Caliente if fighting broke out.

Hughes, hitching a ride with the mail carrier, returned to Tucson on June 2, 1876, and met Safford and Clum. As Hughes expected, Clum turned down Taza's request for Pueblo Viejo but did consent to assign the Indians to the former site of Camp Goodwin, which at least addressed Taza's concerns about living some distance from the Western Apache groups. The next day, June 3, Hughes left for Apache Pass to tell Taza what Clum had offered.[37]

As civil officials worked feverishly to prevent bloodshed, the military was preparing for war—though General Kautz hoped to avoid fighting. His expeditionary force had reached Tucson on May 31. He telegraphed Captain McLellan at Bowie, asking "whether there is a possibility of effecting this [removal] without a collision." Kautz feared that his large force "might have the effect of frightening the Indians away from the agency." He asked McLellan to explain to the Chiricahuas that this "force is only to be used in case they resist or run away." Kautz also asked for advice on how to best position his troops. McLellan's answer was foreboding. He believed that the Chiricahuas would fight, especially because Taza had vowed "to die before he will remove." This prediction contradicted what Taza had recently told Fred Hughes, although it corroborated what Skinya had told Hughes. So it would appear that McLellan either had outdated information or was confusing Taza's former defiance with that of Skinya or Juh.[38]

Following McLellan's recommendation, Kautz decided to divide his force into three detachments. His command of five troops of the Sixth Cavalry, accompanied by Clum and his Apache police force, left Tucson on June 3, 1876, bound for Fort Bowie. Next, he directed the seven troops of cavalry at Camp Grant to take up positions east and west of the reservation. He sent Major Charles E. Compton with four companies of the Sixth Cavalry and one company of Indian scouts from Fort Apache (then at Camp Grant) to San Simon, about twenty miles northeast of Apache Pass. He ordered the second command, under Captain George M. Brayton with three companies of the Sixth Cavalry and one company of Indian scouts from Camp Verde (then at Grant), to Sulphur Springs. Inexplicably, Kautz had left a clear path to Mexico. Kautz planned to reach Fort Bowie on June 5, when he would find out what course, war or peace, the Chiricahuas had chosen.[39]

Meanwhile, Fred Hughes was about a half-day's ride ahead of the main body of troops. Reaching Jeffords's agency in the late evening of June 4, Hughes "had just barely shaken the dust from [his] clothing when an Indian runner arrived at the agency" from Taza's camp. He announced that a fight had broken out between Taza's and Skinya's groups. Apparently, during the day, Skinya's men and many Nednhis had become disturbed about the concentration of troops around the reservation. Skinya tried to persuade Taza and other Chokonen leaders to leave the reservation for Mexico. The older, experienced war chief, who espoused traditional ways and resistance, was pitted against the younger, more pragmatic leader, who deferentially tried to follow his father's deathbed advice to remain at peace. With Skinya's followers probably under the influence of tiswin, the seething animosities that had existed between the two factions since the February quarrel again exploded into violence. According to the emissary dispatched by Taza to Jeffords, Skinya's party was the aggressor, "having attacked their ranchería." If true, it would appear that Taza and Naiche were more than prepared to defend their village against, as Taza later explained, "our enemies."[40]

About an hour before midnight, gunfire reverberated throughout the recesses of Bonita Canyon in the Chiricahua Mountains.[41] It was a firefight at close range: the two sons of Cochise, their relatives, and loyal followers against Skinya, Pionsenay, and about a dozen of their men. Once it erupted, the twenty-year-old Naiche sent a bullet through the head of his father-in-law, Skinya, killing him instantly. Taza killed Kushkla and wounded Pionsenay with a bullet through his shoulder. Taza's followers also killed three men who had been active in the April outbreak (Tiscli, Piarhel, and Nazarzee) and wounded Broaches and two others. Taza thought he had mortally wounded Pionsenay, for he had last seen the murderer crawling away into the rocks, with "blood gushing from his mouth." Taza lost two men killed in the fight, including his brother-in-law Sheta (son of Chiva), and two of his men were wounded. The participants could measure in minutes the bloody conflict for control of Cochise's band. The actions of his boys would have made the celebrated chief proud. They had displayed unsurpassed courage and fighting ability, decisive leadership, and indomitable will in carrying out their promises to their father.[42]

Fearing that the few survivors of Skinya's band might return with the Nednhis, who were sympathetic to Skinya and Pionsenay, Taza had sent Teese to request help from Jeffords. The agent explained the situation to Captain McLellan, who dispatched Lieutenant Henely and thirty troopers to Taza's camp. Tom Jeffords and Fred Hughes went along to help Taza. Arriving in the early morning of June 5, 1876, they encountered Nolgee, who had come with his Nednhi group "with the evident intent of joining the party against Taza." Henely's troops fired a warning volley over their heads, "and they scattered like chalk in the wind." Then Jeffords, as usual, took control and met with Nolgee and Geronimo. Both leaders agreed to come in with Taza to meet Clum and General Kautz.[43]

About 9:00 A.M. June 5, 1876, Taza led his followers, 200 according to Clum, and 250 according to Kautz, to Fort Bowie, arriving there only one hour before Clum, Kautz, and his five companies of the Sixth Cavalry. They must have heaved a sigh of relief when they heard that Taza's group had prevailed in the fight with the militant followers of Skinya. Clum "handed [Jeffords] a copy of a telegram authorizing him to take charge of the Indians and the agency [and] suspend me." Jeffords, perhaps stung by the rebuke, justifiably lamented, "although I had not received the slightest intimation of such a course from the commissioner, I turned over the agency to him, and he took charge." That was the only official notice that Jeffords received. His controversial but, on the whole, successful tenure of three years and nine months was over. He was probably relieved that the Chiricahuas were now someone else's responsibility.[44]

The next day, June 6, 1876, Taza and three other Chokonen leaders, probably Chihuahua, Cathla, and Nahilzay, met with Clum and General Kautz. Chiva was also present with his small group of Bedonkohes. Fred Hughes recorded a summary of Taza's poignant speech:

> Taza told Clum that he would like to be allowed to remain on the present reservation; that it was here that his ancestors had lived and died; he said he was in no way to blame for the present outrages and cited that he had accompanied the troops sent out to chastise the renegade Indians and that he had at last succeeded in killing the Indians engaged in the outbreak. He said that he had always kept the treaty made by his father with General Howard, and that he always would. But he said, if it was our wish that he should go to San Carlos, then he would go; that we had treated him and his people well, and [he] would not forget that. He also called into mind the last words of his father, telling him to always live in peace with the whites. Then pointing to the little band around him, he exclaimed: That little band will always live

in peace with you. If they should, by some misfortune, be all killed off or die but one, that last one will never forget what you have done for us and will be your friend.

Hughes said that Taza's words touched everyone present.[45]

Clum agreed to assign them Camp Goodwin as their home, which satisfied Taza, who conceded to Clum that some twenty men of Cochise's old band had no intention of going to San Carlos. The Chokonen chief "took exception to being required to work, saying they knew nothing of planting and were evidently averse to labor." Clum and Kautz also decided not to push their luck and accordingly made "no effort to disarm them; it was thought best to leave that issue for another day."[46] To this point the operation had gone as smoothly as possible. Juh and Nolgee wanted a separate council and said they would be in the next day, June 7, 1876.[47]

As promised, the Nednhi leaders came in to Bowie the next day with Geronimo. They agreed to move to San Carlos but said they needed twenty days to round up their people. Hughes, feeling that Juh had no intention of going, had told Clum not to negotiate. Naturally, the omniscient agent disregarded the warning and countered with an offer of four days, which they accepted. After the parley, Hughes held a private meeting with General Kautz and expressed his reservations about the Nednhis' intentions. Kautz then ordered Compton to take his command to the southern end of the Chiricahua Mountains. "But in military affairs there is always too much red tape to permit prompt action," lamented Hughes. As he predicted, the Nednhi leaders returned to their camp, promptly rounded up their followers and stock, and abandoned everything that would impede a hasty flight into Sonora. Clum, always quick to blame others, never explained his questionable decision.

The next day Pionsenay sent Es-Tash (a "dark, mean looking Indian," according to Clum) to Fort Bowie, asking that Pionsenay be allowed to come in "to die of his wounds." Clum disarmed the messenger, taking his Winchester rifle and a revolver, and sent him back to Pionsenay's camp with twenty of his Apache police. They found the camp in the Chiricahuas and returned that evening with the wounded Pionsenay, one old man, and thirty-eight women and children. They were all that remained of Skinya's old band except for Broaches and a few men who had slipped into Sonora with the Nednhis.

Clum's Apache police also discovered the deserted Nednhi rancherías: "Kettles, axes, hatchets, cowhide, corn, dead dogs and horses etc. were strewn about the camp and a large trail heading from the camp in the direction of

Sonora." Brayton's and Compton's commands had combed the foothills on both sides of the Chiricahua Mountains, but the Nednhis had already slipped through the net into Sonora. Captain Brayton's command came upon four Chiricahuas returning from a raid into Sonora, and "quite a little skirmish occurred" in which his Indian scouts killed two men, one of whom was a "notorious raider called Dandy Jim."[48]

Monday, June 12, 1876, Clum, accompanied by Jeffords, Hughes, fifty-four Apache police, and Colonel James Oakes, with three companies of cavalry, departed Apache Pass with 322 Apaches. Taza, Naiche, Chihuahua, Nahilzay, and Cathla led the 300 Chokonens, and Chiva took twenty-two Bedonkohes. All told, only forty-two men were present. Taza left four Chokonens behind, including one who was mortally ill. They would rejoin their people at San Carlos in mid-July. John Rope, a Western White Mountain Apache, recalled that the military had provided "big army wagons with high sides" to transport those Indians without mounts. That night the "caravan" encamped at Ewell Springs, about fifteen miles northwest of Apache Pass. Clum and his police force guarded Pionsenay, whose wound the surgeon at Bowie had "carefully dressed." Clum expected to turn him over to civil authorities in Tucson.[49]

The next day, as Clum headed for Tucson, he unexpectedly met Sheriff Charles Shibell and his deputy, Ad Linn, at Point of Mountain. Shibell had a warrant for Pionsenay's arrest. At 2:00 P.M. Clum turned the outlaw over to Shibell and then rejoined the Chiricahuas on their march. Shibell tied Pionsenay's hands and feet and placed him in the back of the wagon. Approaching the San Pedro River about 9:00 P.M., they turned to check on their hostage and to their wonder discovered that he had, in the words of the *Arizona Citizen*, "vanished, evanesced, skedaddled, fluked, woodblued, escaped as it were." Whatever the appropriate term, Pionsenay managed to overtake Taza's dispirited cavalcade and convince two men (one was probably Es-Tash), one boy, and four women to leave with him for Mexico. By the time Clum told Jeffords, either it was too late for pursuit or Clum refused to allow Taza and a few men to join Jeffords in pursuit. Jeffords blamed Clum for Pionsenay's survival. He pointed out that if Clum had immediately informed him, Taza's men "would have retaken [Pionsenay] before sunrise the next day."[50]

On June 18, 1876, Clum "quietly located" the Chokonens at their new homes, selected by Taza, about two miles below the former site of Camp Goodwin in the Gila Valley. The third leg in the concentration policy was complete. Clum, elated over this happy outcome, telegraphed Washington that "the move is a great success and I think the terrible shade of Chiricahua has been passed away forever," thus proving that he was a far better agent than forecaster. His attitude of self-congratulation was somewhat tempered by Pionsenay's escape, which he conceded was "a very unfortunate affair." But he was quick to point out, "I am not responsible." Finally, he openly questioned the integrity of Tom Jeffords, declaring that the number of Indians at Chiricahua "has been very much overestimated."[51]

Clum calculated that at best, Jeffords had had between 415 and 445 Indians on the reservation. He began with Taza's 325 and then added the Nednhis, whom he estimated at 60, and Gordo's band, 30 to 60 members. Kautz also questioned Jeffords's totals (though his numbers were higher than Clum's figures), and concluded that Jeffords's counts "had been greatly exaggerated." He started with Taza's 325, and added to it the Nednhis at 209 and Gordo's at 30–60, and "summing them up, I could not make more than 550." These allegations, which Jeffords, in his typically reticent manner, failed to address, allowed Clum to discredit him. And when Kautz's and Clum's charges became public, they provided fodder for the territorial press to harm the reputation of Jeffords and justify the government's imminent land swindle—opening the Chiricahua Reservation for settlement and development to ranchers and miners.[52]

The main problem with Clum's and Kautz's statements regarding the Indians at the Chiricahua agency was that neither was in position to explain the differences in census figures between those on the reservation in June 1876 and the totals that Jeffords had submitted to the commissioner of Indian affairs, which it published in the 1875 Annual Report. Jeffords reported that he was feeding 965 Indians, which corresponds exactly to the number of Indians he rationed on July 5, 1875. But when Clum and Kautz arrived on June 5, 1876, only the Nednhis (209), Chokonens (300), and Chiva's mixed group of Bedonkohes and White Mountain Apaches (25) were on the reservation, or 534 Indians. In addition, seven Chiricahuas had joined Pionsenay, thus bringing the totals to 542 souls. We can also assume that the deaths and births pretty much offset each other, for we know that at least thirteen Chokonens were victims of infighting because of the Pionsenay trouble, and that other warriors were killed in Mexico. Thus, 422 Apaches were absent from the reservation between July 5, 1875 and June 12, 1876.

In the fall of 1875, Raton and Naliya left Chiricahua for Ojo Caliente, taking about 12 people with them. Jeffords's 1875 census included about 54 "Coyoteros" who were visiting Chiva and who left the reservation by the end of the year, thereby reducing the number to account for to 356. Jeffords, in his final report dated June 30, 1876, explained what happened to the missing Chiricahuas. Esquine and Delgadito had led one group of Bedonkohes and Chihennes that bolted the agency within days of the Pionsenay outbreak. Jeffords placed their numbers at 171, including 45 men. They had headed for Ojo Caliente but had met a chilly reception from Victorio and Loco. The third and last group to leave was that of Gordo, who departed in early June when he saw the initial concentration of troops (Kautz's Sixth Cavalry) taking up positions on the reservation. According to Jeffords, Gordo's group contained 176 Indians, including 36 men, most of them bound for Ojo Caliente. But Gordo's Bedonkohes amounted to only 85 members. The remainder included about 40 Chihennes and some 50 Chokonens who had refused to follow Taza's lead; these included a young leader named Chatto, of whom we will hear more, and Zele, who would be an important chief in the 1880s. According to the surviving reports of Indian Agent Shaw, some 140 Indians came to Ojo Caliente from the Chiricahua Reservation. Likely there were more, perhaps most of the 176 Apaches with Gordo, because his records were incomplete.[53] All told, Esquine's and Gordo's groups totaled 347 persons, nine fewer than the 356 persons we need to account for.[54]

Formerly a chief under Mangas Coloradas, Gordo led a group that included several of the fighting men who would figure prominently in the years to come. They arrived at Ojo Caliente in two parties, on June 14, 1876, and on June 18, 1876. The Indian Agent, John Shaw, reported the arrivals as Gordo; his son, Perico (Geronimo's second cousin); Bonito, the White Mountain Apache who had married into the Bedonkohe band; and Chinche, another leading man in the 1885 outbreak with Geronimo.

Tom Jeffords was an honest Indian agent. There is no evidence of any corruption or graft. Unlike other agents who sold the Indians' rations and pocketed the proceeds, Jeffords at times purchased provisions out of his own pocket. About the time Commissioner Smith suspended him from duty, he commented, "I am now poorer than when I was first appointed."[55] During his tenure, three Indian Inspectors had examined his accounts, census lists, vouchers, and other accounting records. Each auditor found them in order.[56] After his dismissal, Jeffords sent his final accounts to the commissioner of Indian affairs, who forwarded them to the second auditor for final review. The examiner found one discrepancy, a voucher for $4.50 that Jeffords had paid to advertise in a Tucson newspaper for a flour contract. The department later found the necessary documentation to support Jeffords's expenditure, closed his accounts, and gave Jeffords a clean bill of financial health.[57]

But if you were a resident of Tucson and a regular reader of the *Arizona Citizen*, you believed that Jeffords ranked just above the devil himself. After the paper's scathing May 20, 1876, editorial, Jeffords wrote a letter telling his side of the controversy to his friend Charles O. Brown in Tucson. The *Citizen* refused to publish it, explaining that Jeffords "is an aider and abettor of thieves and murderers [who] can under no circumstances use the pages of the *Citizen* to pardon the flimsy falsehoods of denial."[58]

But on June 9, 1876, the *Arizona Miner* in Prescott did publish Jeffords's rebuttal, in which he denied the *Citizen's* charges as "untrue from the commencement to the end." He refuted each assertion. He concluded his letter by suggesting that in the future, it should try to get "its information from reliable sources."[59] The *Citizen* chastised the *Miner* for printing Jeffords's explanation.[60] Soon after, the *Grant County Herald* in Silver City published a letter signed by twenty-six men that extolled Jeffords's virtues and his record as agent. After all, "not a single murder by Indians has been committed in our section of the country." In addition, the article pointed out that on several occasions, Jeffords had returned stolen stock to its rightful owners on both sides of the border. "These were the actions of a man [whose] heart is in the right place," concluded Jeffords's supporters.[61]

In its editorial dated June 24, 1876, the *Citizen*, bored of the controversy, got right to the point about the significance of the removal. No longer would Jeffords be the issue. It editorialized: "Henceforth the Chiricahua [Reservation] drops out of sight as a nursery for bad Indians." It explained:

> The [former] home of the Chiricahua Apaches . . . is a rich domain of mountain and valley embracing some of the best mineral and agriculture features of the Territory. And while the thought of opening this great region to settlement formed no part of the motives which led to the removal of the Apaches from San Carlos, nevertheless the securing of this tract of land to the prospector and farmer will ultimately result from the removal. Some of the valleys are said to be the best watered, and the stock ranges the finest in southern Arizona. . . . The region will probably soon be thrown open to settlers. Those who have been on the reservation say it is impossible to give one who has never seen it an adequate idea of the beauty and varied wealth of [a] large portion of it.[62]

These are the real reasons the government abolished the Chiricahua Reservation. It was only a matter of time, and Pionsenay's two murders at Sulphur Springs provided the excuse. Even if the Indians had ceased their raiding into Sonora (the only legitimate reason to remove them), the government would have found another reason to close the reservation. The Indians were obstacles in the path of Anglo prosperity and capitalism. Why should the fate of a handful of Indians hinder the development of the rich mining and agricultural regions of southeastern Arizona just because they happened to lie in the ancestral homes of the Chokonens? The Indians could certainly adapt to the low country in the Gila Valley at San Carlos, where most the other Arizona Apaches were living, or so the rationale went.

Even the most sagacious of Americans or Chiricahua Apaches could not have envisioned the impact that the closing of the reservation would play in the violent drama between whites and Apaches that would unfold over the next decade. In June 1876, the four bands of Chiricahuas totaled about 1,275 members. A decade later, when the Geronimo War ended in September 1886, their numbers would be decreased to 525, and the Bedonkohes and Nednhis would no longer be distinct bands.

4

GERONIMO'S AND CLUM'S TRAVELS

The first thing we knew, without no trouble, all the cavalry surrounded us at [Ojo Caliente] and took us out there to Arizona [San Carlos].

Sam Haozous, grandson of Mangas Coloradas

The reservation life between 1870 and 1876 had ended the tribe's population drain after the decade-long war with the United States and Mexico. Times were good, perhaps prosperous, as the government regularly fed the Apaches, who must have felt content and secure because they had no worries about enemies looking to attack them. The closing of the Chiricahua Reservation disrupted their world. Less than half the Apaches, mainly Chokonens, moved to San Carlos. The Nednhis slipped into Sonora, and the Bedonkohes and a few Chihennes returned to southwestern New Mexico. Perhaps half of them settled at Ojo Caliente; the other half remained in the mountains of southwestern New Mexico and northern Mexico.

The leaders of each band had adopted courses, based on philosophy and recent history, that they believed suited the needs for their followers. The Chokonens tried to adapt to their unfamiliar surroundings at San Carlos and the inherent constraints of reservation life. The Chihennes were happy at Ojo Caliente, but they had Bedonkohe and Chokonen refugees from the Chiricahua Reservation settling with them. And that did not bode well. Those Nednhis and Bedonkohes attempting to live in traditional ways, as free Apaches, faced military forces of two nations determined to vanquish them. The Americans' objective was to force the hostile Chiricahuas to settle at San Carlos; the Mexicans sought to wipe them out. But whether isolated on reservations or roaming in their mountain homes, they were unaware of how rapidly the world around them was changing.

Ensnared by these two divergent options, the Chiricahua bands needed progressive leadership—pragmatic men who could convince their followers that they must consider new ideas. Yet their leaders, except Cochise's two sons, remained men who had earned status and achieved prominence by guiding their people through the bellicose times of the 1860s. There were no tribal leaders in the mold of Mangas Coloradas or Cochise. Instead, chiefs such as Victorio, Esquine, Gordo, and Juh were provincial leaders who looked out for their own followers and reached solutions based on their own circumstances. The one chief already committed to peace was Loco, the farsighted Chihenne who had accepted by 1869 that accommodation with Americans was the only correct course. Trapped in the middle, making choices based on their own life experiences, these leaders found themselves caught in a vice with virtually no chance of survival if they clung to traditional ways and solutions. The lesson was this: remain on reservations and your people might live to an old age if free from disease; take refuge in Mexico and face Mexican troops or villagers seeking your destruction by any possible means.

Those Apaches who had fled the Chiricahua agency hoping to live as they had from time immemorial faced staggering odds. Esquine's Bedonkohes and a small group of Chihennes under Miguel Tuerto and Raton had decided to return to the mountains in extreme southwestern New Mexico, an area that had provided safe refuge in years past. But they soon encountered another problem, perhaps one they considered the most insidious—the army had recruited Western Apaches and Navajos as scouts to hunt them down. Serving under energetic American officers, these scouts would prove effective allies of Americans against the Chiricahuas.

Meanwhile, in Mexico, Juh faced equally overwhelming odds. Once there, his people had to raid to survive, which meant the inevitable clashes with Mexican troops from towns along the foothills of the Sierra Madre Mountains. But their downfall was in their own willingness to negotiate with Mexican authorities in Chihuahua, a pattern that went back over a century. No longer dealing from a position of strength, Juh soon understood that Mexico's only remaining Apache policy was extermination.

Safely ensconced at San Carlos, the Chokonens, taken from their healthy canyon and valley homes at Chiricahua, struggled to adapt to their new homes in the Gila Valley, near the site of the former Camp Goodwin, which was just south of the Gila River about seven miles west of today's Fort Thomas. On

June 19, 1876, Clum telegraphed Commissioner Smith: "the Chiricahuas are in and quietly located."[1]

Yet, Clum neglected to mention that their new location was decidedly unhealthy. They were camped along the Gila lowlands where the summers were unbearably hot and infectious diseases such as malaria thrived. In fact, the army had closed Goodwin in 1871 because the year before "almost every soldier and family was hit by fever."[2] Another account was more specific: "It was considered too malarial—indeed the most unhealthy [post] in the territory."[3] Three years earlier, Governor Safford had said that the swamp near Goodwin was responsible for malaria, a "fever-hole," he called it, that gave Arizona a "bad name" because the soldiers at Goodwin were "constantly sick."[4]

Taza's people knew about this quandary. Seven years earlier Cochise had refused to go to Goodwin, telling an army officer, "it is no place for Indians. They die after being here for a short time."[5] The White Mountain Apaches had refused to relocate to San Carlos in 1875 because of its reputation. Even the commander at Fort Apache concurred, saying they seemed to have good cause for their objection. Eugene Chihuahua, son of Chief Chihuahua, told Eve Ball that their new location was a "hot, bad place. There was no water fit to drink, no wood, no game, no shade; there was nothing but stickers and insects. It was the worst place in all the land claimed by Apaches. Daklugie [son of Juh] says they put us there to die. I think so, too, when I think of it."[6] Though no one put them there to die, it is understandable that the Apaches thought that to be the case. Eventually, it must have seemed like a death sentence to the Chiricahuas, though the available census data indicate that they were healthy the first few years at Goodwin. Still, given these conditions at the camp, it was a wonder that Taza agreed to live there; and the indifference displayed by Safford and Clum is perplexing.

According to Clum, the Chokonens were "unusually intelligent" Apaches who would remain peaceable if he furnished sufficient rations. He claimed to have taught Taza's people how to make adobes, "and they developed into good Apache citizens." This idyllic picture was not quite true. None of the men worked, for that was part of their agreement to move to San Carlos. Moreover, neither Clum nor the military had disarmed them, allowing them to enjoy a status separate from that of the Western Apaches. In mid-July Clum had a talk with the Chokonen chiefs. All went so well that he did "not have the least fear regarding the Chiricahuas' conduct."[7] Yet, a few days later, Nahilzay left the reservation with twenty-five Chokonens and joined Pionsenay in Mexico.[8] A few weeks later, General Kautz ordered the establishment of Camp Thomas, seven miles east of Goodwin. The garrison would provide support for the Indian agent at San Carlos.[9]

By this time Clum was getting, as he put it, "restless." He had fallen in love with a young woman from Ohio and had devised a "scheme" to raise cash for his trip east to marry his "courageous girl." He was so arrogant that he first asked the Bureau of Indian Affairs to provide the funding, but it turned him down flat. The resourceful agent, recalling the success of the performance that he and his Apache police force had staged in Tucson a few months before, decided to organize his own "Wild Apache" show to finance his trip to Washington, D.C. He convinced two friends to bankroll the tour. Together, with Clum of course, they raised five thousand dollars. "We clearly envisioned a vast throng, besieging the theaters where we were advertised to appear and speedily advancing [us] into the millionaire class [as] a result of the amazing returns at the box office."

The agent selected twenty-two Apaches to accompany him, including two Chokonen leaders, Taza and Cathla. According to the agent, every Indian on the reservation wanted to go. He based his selection on influence and "the acting ability required to assure the success of our proposed entertainments." Besides the Chokonen chiefs, several Western Apache leaders, including Eskiminzin, whose followers were survivors of the ignominious Camp Grant massacre five years before, joined Clum's thespians. To help out, Eskiminzin brought four civilians, the renowned Merejildo Grijalva, S. B. Chaping, and two teamsters.[10]

On July 29, 1876, Clum's party left San Carlos in three wagons, bound for the train depot at El Moro, Colorado. Their progress was slow. Three weeks later, they passed Albuquerque before they finally reached El Moro in late August. A few days before embarking by train for their adventure east, Grijalva told Clum he was concerned about Taza. It seems that Taza had boasted to his fellow Apaches about his father's victories won in battle over Americans. According to him, the Americans were fortunate that his father had consented to make peace, "otherwise there would be very few white people left alive." Clum told Grijalva, "Don't be alarmed [for] in two days we will be on the railroad," and Taza would see the fallacy of his beliefs. Clum was right.

At El Moro, they boarded the train and headed toward Washington. At St. Louis on September 8, 1876, they gave their first of three unsuccessful performances. The next day their aspiring acting careers ended; Clum's Wild West Show was over.

His entourage went on to Washington. The president was out of town, but they did meet the commissioner of Indian affairs, who agreed to pay for their return trip to Arizona. They also toured the White House, took a cruise on the Potomac, and attended Barnum's circus. But Sunday, September 18, 1876, torrential rains engulfed the city. The desert Apaches "shivered in the damp and storm." Soon afterwards, Taza came down with pneumonia. Despite the best medical attention, the honorable chief, in the prime of life, died on September 26, 1876. The next day, he was buried in the Congressional Cemetery. General Howard and Commissioner Smith attended the funeral. The narcissistic Clum's arrogance knowing no bounds, he saw some benefit to the tragedy. Taza's death had "afforded the Indians with an opportunity to observe the civilized methods and customs of caring for the sick and preparing the dead for burial." The Apaches then returned to Arizona in the care of Merejildo Grijalva, while Clum left to get married. He would not return to San Carlos until late December 1876.[11] Katharine C. Turner sums up the futility of Taza's tragic trip: "Taza's is the most fruitless trip to the Great White Father on record. He traveled two thousand miles for no reason except to help pay a white man's traveling expenses to his bride-to-be; he called when his Great White Father was not in; and he could not linger for his return, since he was bound on a longer journey to a far higher Potentate."[12]

During Clum's absence, Acting Agent Martin Sweeney was forced to deal with a few problems of his own. About a month after Clum left, he reported that the Apaches were "peaceable and getting along contentedly." Yet, addressing reports of Apache depredations along the border, specifically the killing on July 14, 1876, of two miners in the Chiricahua Mountains by either Pionsenay's or Juh's followers, he declared that a lack of pack mules was the only reason he was unable to send a detail of scouts "to clear that country of hostiles."[13] He also implied that the Chokonens would be willing to help since "they had tendered their services" against Skinya and Pionsenay.[14] Even when Sweeney faced a shortage of food that fall, compelling him to reduce the ration by half, the Indians "continued to behave well and seem contented," a testament to his managerial abilities. The Chokonens liked Sweeney and were comfortable with Ezra Hoag, whom Clum had appointed agent for the subagency. To compensate for the decreased rations, Hoag and Sweeney allowed the Chokonens and the White Mountain Apaches to move to the nearby Santa Teresa Mountains to hunt game and gather acorns and mescal.[15]

Naiche first heard the news of his brother's death when Merejildo Grijalva and Cathla returned to the reservation, probably in early December. Clum and his bride reached San Carlos a few days before January 1, 1877. Shortly after, he met Naiche and explained what had happened to Taza. Naiche was understandably distraught and blamed the agent for his brother's death, suggesting that Clum had employed witchcraft to poison Taza—a belief shared by some of Eve Ball's Chiricahua informants. Then Eskiminzin, the Arivaipa leader, spoke up in defense of Clum. He assured Naiche that the agent "had done everything that was good and right for Tahzay [Taza] while he was sick and after he had died." Eskiminzin's words seemed to mollify Naiche.[16]

Meanwhile, during the five months (August–December 1876) that Clum was absent from San Carlos, those Chiricahuas who had refused to move to San Carlos found it difficult to live as traditional Apaches. Furthermore, Mexico, distrustful of American expansionism, refused to allow American troops to cross the border.

After fleeing from the Chiricahua Reservation, Juh had hoped to make a truce in Mexico. Yet, both Sonora and Chihuahua were facing distressing economic and political times. Juh first tested the waters at Janos, but authorities there were unable to get a commitment from Chihuahua City because Terrazas's forces were fighting Díaz's forces for control of the state. Disillusioned with prospects at Janos, Juh opted to make a rare overture to Sonora. In late July, he solicited peace at Fronteras, while Geronimo, perhaps with Juh's blessings, went to Ojo Caliente to find out what kind of treatment they might receive if Juh brought his followers there.[17]

Juh waited for a time, but Sonora was just coming off the disputed governor's election of 1875 that had triggered intense fighting between the forces of Ignacio Pesqueira and those of Francisco Serna, whose followers believed he had won the election. Finally, in March 1876, Mexico's president Lerdo de Tejada sent General Vicente Mariscal to restore civil order. Mariscal's concerns were not then with the frontier, so he took no action in response to Juh's solicitations.[18]

Having heard nothing from Fronteras, Juh headed for his old strongholds in the Sierra Madre, passing by the Teras Mountains in late August.[19] Meanwhile, Pionsenay's and Nahilzay's Chokonens and Nolgee's small Nednhi group, each with about fifteen men, had recently raided Bacoachi and Cumpas in the Moctezuma district. These depredations ended any thoughts that Sonora had of peace. Juh met with Geronimo, who had returned after a brief stay at Ojo Caliente. Though Geronimo had many relatives at Ojo Caliente, and may have favored relocating there, he was unable to persuade Juh.[20]

Next, a truly extraordinary development took place. In early October, Juh and Geronimo sent Zebina N. Streeter, also known as the White Apache, to open negotiations with the prefect of Moctezuma for their 209 followers. Streeter asserted that he had joined the Nednhis to save his own life after he had exposed corruption at the San Carlos agency.[21] While Streeter was negotiating, Geronimo and a chief named José María Elías, whose Apache name was Nat-cul-ba-ye, split from Juh and sent feelers to Bavispe and Janos. Their group numbered fifty-three people. Obviously, they hoped to delay any Mexican campaigns while Streeter was negotiating on their behalf.[22]

General Mariscal, now the governor of Sonora, was cautiously optimistic about the Chiricahuas' proposal. He instructed officials at Moctezuma:

> As such is the conduct that this tribe always shows, there is no guaranty of their faith and promises. The Governor wishes to make peace but he counsels that experience has taught us not to be tricked. The conditions are: They can live in peace with this state at any of the five military colonies at a distance of one league from the presidio; they must surrender their arms; they will be counted daily; they cannot leave the area without permission from the agent that will be assigned to them. The Governor agrees to feed and clothe them; if they want to plant, he will protect them against all attacks. For their part, they only have to live in peace with Mexicans and all other inhabitants of this state, and are prohibited from passing into another country to commit depredations.[23]

Streeter remained in the area for a few weeks. He spoke to Colonel Elías, the military commander of the northern presidios, who told the American that he would offer the Apaches a reservation at either Santa Cruz or Bacoachi. Elías allowed the Indians eight days to come in, but they never showed. Streeter next went to Ures and from here to Guaymas, where he met Governor Mariscal in early December.

But, unbeknownst to Streeter, Juh's patience had worn thin. He decided to retire south to a safe haven in the high country along the Aros River in the Sierra Madre Mountains, a place where Mexican troops were disinclined to conduct operations. The previous month his followers had killed ten Sonorans and wounded four people in the district of Sahuaripa. In response, in mid-November a patrol from that district surprised Juh's camp at Chamada, which overlooked the Aros River about thirty miles due east from Sahuaripa, near the Chihuahua border. The soldiers killed two Apaches and recovered a large amount of material and seven animals. Still, Mariscal told Streeter, he would make a treaty if Juh complied with the terms as outlined in October. Streeter returned to Juh's camp with the offer, but the Nednhi chief decided against further talks.[24]

Meanwhile, in southern New Mexico, small groups of Chihennes led by Miguel Tuerto and Raton, and Bedonkohes under Esquine, continued to live in the mountains of southwestern New Mexico, mainly from the Florida Mountains south and west to the panhandle that extended to the southeast border of Arizona. These parties had engaged in some minor raiding in New Mexico and northern Chihuahua. In mid-August ranchers reported that a band of 150 Apaches was camped on the headwaters of the Gila. But after stealing some stock along the Mimbres River and near Silver City, they headed south toward the Florida Mountains.

Americans were soon on their trail. The first was a party of ranchers from the Mimbres River, which, in early September, pursued the raiders to the Tres Hermanas (Three Sisters) range some ten miles northwest of today's Colombus. The Chiricahuas called this low range, which runs north to south, Dziltai, meaning "Three Mountains." Besides being a sacred mountain, where many Chihennes had received their source of supernatural power, this conspicuous landmark was a resting place for Indians before they moved south into Mexico or headed north to the Florida Mountains. Along its slopes, they harvested mescal in the spring, and in the higher country, they gathered walnuts and acorns in the fall. On this occasion, a raiding party of some twenty-five warriors had stopped to rest when Americans discovered their camp. Approaching to within one hundred yards, four citizens "drew a bead" and shot the Indian sentry, probably killing him. The enemies exchanged some seventy shots before the Apaches fled the scene.[25]

Captain Henry Carroll led another group of Americans, which consisted of twenty-five men of the Ninth Cavalry, the all African American unit whom Plains Indians knew as Buffalo Soldiers, on a patrol from Fort Selden.[26] He followed a trail of Apaches that led to the Florida Mountains, where he found an Apache camp on September 15, 1876. "The Indians were sleeping and resting their horses" when Carroll's command surprised them. One trooper sent a salvo that struck the chief, leaving "one arm shot to pieces." He continued to fire at the soldiers with his "rifle by holding it on the stub of his broken arm until the soldiers gave him a special volley and he fell dead pierced with twenty bullets." Carroll's men "fought nobly," wounding at least three other Apaches and recovering eleven ponies. The Indians were supposed to be "Chiricahuas from Arizona" and were probably members of Esquine's group.[27]

Meanwhile, the situation at Ojo Caliente had become unsettled after the closing of the Chiricahua Reservation. Gordo's Bedonkohe followers, some Chihennes under Delgadito, and some Chokonens under Chatto and Zele went to Ojo Caliente. Gordo's group arrived first, bringing news of the deadly fight between the followers of Taza and Skinya. Later that month Zele and a few of his followers came in. With him was the Tissnolthos family, consisting of three brothers, one of whom would be with Geronimo in the final surrender in September 1886. After Gordo's arrival, Shaw requested instructions from Washington. On June 21, 1876, Commissioner Smith authorized him to issue rations until the Indian Bureau reached a permanent solution. Smith also told Shaw to do all in his power to keep the newcomers on the reservation. Shaw, pleased with the decision, declared that he "did not anticipate any trouble in managing them."[28]

Yet these refugees threatened to disrupt affairs at Ojo Caliente. Jeffords ran his agency differently than other agents did, exercising control through personal relationships with the Chiricahua leaders. At Ojo Caliente, however, the Indians, once they discovered that they could intimidate the agent, held sway. A month later Shaw warned that some of these "Chiricahua Indians are young warriors who carry good arms, are well mounted, [and] are very haughty, difficult to manage, and may cause serious trouble."

Violence erupted while his employees were issuing rations on July 13, 1876. A Chiricahua chief was disrupting the process, demanding "a larger issue of rations than they were allowed." Fortunately, the no-nonsense "Loco, my reliable chief," ever anxious to preserve peace, responded decisively (as he had during the brawl with the Pajarito brothers). He rushed to the scene, hoping to prevent trouble. Instead, the Chiricahua attacked Loco, who responded by shooting him "in self-defense." The slain man's relatives grabbed their arms, and for a moment it looked like a general melee would break out. Cooler heads finally prevailed, and the chiefs held a council and ruled that Loco should pay to the family of the deceased man merchandise that totaled $57.50. Agent Shaw furnished the goods.[29]

On July 22, 1876, Indian Commissioner Smith, with the blessings of the secretary of the interior, issued a formal ruling that granted asylum to those Chiricahuas who had relocated to Ojo Caliente instead of moving to San Carlos. By this time John Shaw had resigned (he would have been fired for incompetence because of the recommendations of Indian Inspector Edward Kemble) and was awaiting the arrival of his replacement.[30] On August 15, 1876, Commissioner Smith named James Davis of Pennsylvania as the new agent. But Davis would not relieve Shaw until October 15.[31]

Meanwhile, the lame-duck agent soon had more problems. The Ninth Cavalry was in the field conducting operations against Chiricahuas. They were sometimes unconcerned whether the Indians were peaceful or hostile, a distinction that, admittedly, was always difficult to make when Apaches lurked on the outskirts of a reservation.

In early September, an American patrol left Camp Vincent, a tent outpost established by a company of the Ninth Cavalry in the northeast part of the Black Range, "near the junction of Taylor and Beaver Creeks."[32] Lieutenant Henry H. Wright, with several Navajo scouts, including Barboncito, who had formerly lived with the Chihennes, went to the aid of a citizen who had recently had stock stolen by Indians. Wright admitted that he had no idea of the boundaries of the Ojo Caliente Reservation because "they don't appear on any of our military maps." Guided by Barboncito, they followed the trail of a mounted Apache, probably Washington, Victorio's eldest son. As the troopers approached the ranchería, his men opened fire, which caused the women and children to flee the camp. One warrior tried to insult the Americans as he "defiantly patted his posterior in derision." When the Indians in great haste abandoned their camp, Wright's men occupied and burned it.

Kinzhuna was a young teenager who had left camp with two young men to hunt deer that day. When they saw the Navajo scouts, they returned to camp to spread the alarm. Victorio ordered everyone to "break camp and go into the mountains." Kinzhuna and his mother rode a horse away from the village. "In order to hide their trail, they scattered out, made back turns, before they all met in the mountains again."[33] Though Wright failed to identify the exact site, the *Grant County Herald* placed the ranchería on the Cuchillo Negro River, about twenty miles southwest of the agency. Agent Shaw protested to Colonel Hatch, declaring that Wright's actions were unprovoked and had left Victorio's followers destitute. Since the troops had not spilled any blood, this deplorable affair failed to arouse the Indians to retaliate.[34]

As his tenure ended, Shaw made important observations to his superiors in Washington. Wright's recent attack on Victorio's camp and the clashes between Apaches and troops in southern New Mexico had left the reservation Indians nervous and agitated. Moreover, new Chiricahuas continued to arrive. These "strange Indians," had been in the recent "fight south of here" (either the one at Tres Hermanas or the one in the Florida Mountains), and he feared that they "would cause trouble." Fortunately for him, on October 15, 1876, his replacement, James Davis, arrived at the agency and relieved Shaw from duty the next morning.[35]

Davis was woefully unprepared for his new assignment. During the next few weeks, fifty Chiricahuas arrived and requested rations. He conceded to the commissioner of Indian affairs, "[When I] took charge of the agency I had no rule to guide me in the issue of rations." Though the Indians claimed "to number about one thousand," Davis correctly believed there were no more than "500–600 Indians on the reservation." The Apaches also wanted the beef cattle delivered to them, but Davis instructed his employees to butcher the cattle and issue the meat at the clerk's window. The Chiricahuas disagreed and in early November brazenly took four head of cattle "in the presence of the herders and employees." Davis decided he had to take firm steps to control these "insolent and overbearing" Indians.[36]

He asked the chiefs to "bring in their families and bands" for enrollment. They flatly objected, claiming that many of their followers were too sick to come in. They asked Davis to defer his request until next summer, but he refused. Now determined to show that he was serious, Davis sent a note to Colonel Hatch, asking for cavalry to protect the agency and its employees.[37]

He made this request because Loco was concerned that the Bedonkohes and Chokonens at Ojo Caliente had "many unruly young men inclined to go on raids." In response, Hatch ordered Captain Charles Steelhammer at Fort Craig to investigate affairs at the agency. Taking fifteen cavalrymen, he reached Ojo Caliente on November 22, 1876, a day before the next scheduled issue. Though he found the Apaches "were on their good behavior," Steelhammer corroborated Davis's concerns. Not only did the Indians "strongly object to being counted," but during a parley with four chiefs, Loco urged him to furnish more troops because he could not control those "coming in from other reservations." Steelhammer, mixing some saber rattling with diplomacy, told the chiefs that if they failed to exercise control, then Colonel Hatch would ensure "that they got all the soldiers they wanted as [he] was determined to make them all good Indians. They understood perfectly and seemed to enjoy the hidden meaning of my reply."

Steelhammer digressed to point out that the Apaches were well armed (mainly Springfield breechloaders) and liberally supplied with ammunition. He even saw one of "our latest cavalry carbines in their hands." In conclusion, he put his finger on the most significant problem that led to instability on Apache reservations in the Southwest—inexperienced agents, usually from the East, whom the Indian Bureau appointed because of religious affiliations. Steelhammer remarked that Davis "appears to be a good and honest man but from a lack of experience is overawed by all the difficulties."[38] The captain returned to Fort Craig, hoping that his appearance had restored order to the agency. Davis, however, remained apprehensive, expecting a confrontation.

Despite Steelhammer's warnings, the Chiricahua leaders remained insolent, refusing to allow Davis to enroll them. On December 2, 1876, he telegraphed the commissioner of Indian affairs in Washington: "It is necessary immediately to locate one company of cavalry at the Southern Apache Agency to be kept there until I get the enrollment and count of the Indians and establish a system of issuing rations at the window accordingly. The chiefs refuse to be counted and take the cattle killed. I intend to make enrollment and count on next Thursday [December 7] and issue [rations] accordingly. . . . The commanding officer at Fort Craig needs instructions to do so."[39]

Davis must have had some success with this approach, for on January 6, 1877, he reported that he had rationed 521 Apaches; a week later, that number had increased to 672, likely suggesting that other Chiricahuas, probably Geronimo and Esquine, had come to the agency.[40] If we add the 300 Chokonens at San Carlos, some 972 Chiricahuas were then apparently on reservations. That would mean that about 275 were roaming, about 225 in Mexico under Juh, Nolgee, and Pionsenay, and a small band in northern Chihuahua and southwestern New Mexico under the inveterate Chihenne hostile, Miguel Tuerto.

Many of these newcomers, including Geronimo, had come in after an American patrol had destroyed their winter camp. About November 1876, Geronimo had split from Juh, who had decided to remain in Mexico. The shaman took his family and a few followers and rejoined Esquine in southwestern New Mexico. Several Bedonkohes, probably led by Geronimo, decided to go on a raid into southern Arizona. On December 2, 1876, Samuel Hughes wired General Kautz that Indians had stolen twenty-one horses from his brother's ranch near old Camp Crittenden. Kautz sent the report to Fort Bowie, which was then a base for the operations of Second Lieutenant John Anthony (Tony) Rucker and Company C Apache scouts.[41]

Although Congress did not authorize the hiring of Indian scouts until 1866, the army had frequently employed Indian guides and scouts before this time. Crook began using Apache scouts during his first stint in Arizona (1871–1875). The army paid the scouts, who usually enlisted for three months, at the same rate as an enlisted man. An army officer commanded the scout companies with the assistance of a chief of scout, usually a frontiersman familiar to the Apaches. Army officials had designated two companies of forty Indians to serve the Department of Arizona. In September 1876, General Kautz received permission to enlist a third scout company because of the raiding in southern Arizona after the closing of the Chiricahua agency. The performance of the Apache scouts impressed the general, who noted that they are "more efficient than double the number of soldiers."[42]

The scout companies in Arizona consisted of Company A, at Fort Apache; Company B, at Camp Verde; and the newly formed Company C, whose sole mission was to patrol southeastern Arizona and pursue hostile Chiricahuas who had refused to relocate to San Carlos. All the scouts were Western Apaches, and Company C consisted of Pinals, one of the four bands of the San Carlos group of Western Apaches.

This combination of Apache scouts with indefatigable and dedicated officers would eventually counteract the Chiricahuas' inherent advantages in their ancestral mountain homes. The equation was no longer unbalanced. Apaches learned the hard way that their formerly safe havens in New Mexico lay vulnerable to attack by the Apache scout companies. Though the Indians may not have then realized it, a new paradigm had emerged: the presence of these scouts forced Chiricahuas, who had formerly called southeastern Arizona and southwestern New Mexico home, to seek refuge in Mexico.[43]

Rucker, ten troopers, and thirty-four Apache scouts of Company C left Fort Bowie on December 11, 1876. He reached Crittenden six days later and picked up the Apache trail, vowing to "follow it to the end no matter where or to what country it led." His pledge impressed the editors of the *Arizona Weekly Citizen*: "Everyone who knows him says he will do it." His scouts followed the tracks east through the Huachucas, across the San Pedro, and turned northeast across the Chiricahua Mountains. Hoping to throw off pursuit, the Apaches headed north toward Steins Peak, and then abruptly reversed course to the south. To replenish supplies, Rucker returned to Bowie on December 30, 1876.[44]

The Indians probably felt that Rucker had abandoned his pursuit, but the tenacious officer had no such thoughts. On January 4, 1877, he left Bowie with a surgeon, seventeen troopers of the Sixth Cavalry, and his thirty-four Indian scouts in command of Chief of Scouts Jack Dunn. Returning to Steins Peak, the scouts cut the trail and followed it south into the Pyramid Mountains. Here Rucker received a message from Dunn that he had found the Apaches' ranchería, probably near the northern part of the Animas Mountains. Rucker dismounted his troopers, leaving six men with the horses and taking the balance to rendezvous with Dunn and his scouts. After Dunn described the camp's location, Rucker sent him and the Apache scouts to occupy a hill about 150 yards west from the village; he took his eleven troopers to a hill about three hundred yards north of the camp. Dunn's command was to launch the attack at daybreak, January 9, 1877.

According to Rucker's succinct report, at the first volley the Apaches "rushed from their lodges and took positions behind rocks, and returned fire briskly." According to two Apache scouts involved in the attack, the Indians had just finished an all-night dance and several were making their way back to their wickiups. Regardless, the assault so shocked the Apaches that, in their haste to escape, many left behind their possessions and weapons. Those Chiricahuas with arms fought a stubborn rearguard action, twice driving back Dunn's Apache scouts. Dunn lost his corporal Eshin-e-car, mortally wounded during one assault. Finally, the third charge by Rucker's troopers and Dunn's scouts captured the village of sixteen lodges and drove the Indians from the field.

Rucker estimated that the village contained thirty-five men, which, if true, suggests that he had attacked Geronimo and Esquine's winter camp. In their abrupt flight, the Apaches had left behind seven Springfield rifles, two Winchesters, one Sharps carbine, and other material that linked them to the abolished Chiricahua agency. Rucker's men also found the bodies of ten Indians in camp and captured a nephew of Geronimo, a boy thought to be five and one-half years old. In addition, during the battle, three scouts had seized most of the Indians' herd, forty-six horses, and mules. Fifty-five years later, Perico, who had been in the camp at the time, bitterly remembered the role of the San Carlos scouts.[45]

Rucker received well-earned praise from his superiors. From Fort Bowie, Captain McLellan applauded the lieutenant for the "indefatigable manner in which he has performed the duties assigned him."[46] It was a milestone if not a watershed moment. For in this patrol, Western Apache scouts, who outnumbered the troopers two to one, had proved their mettle against the Chiricahuas. This trend would continue for the duration of the Apache campaigns.

There are good reasons to believe that Geronimo was describing this event in his autobiography. He recalled one incident when "United States troops surprised and attacked our camp. They killed seven children, five women, and four warriors, captured all our supplies, blankets, horses, and clothing, and destroyed our tepees. We had nothing left; winter was beginning, and it was the coldest winter I ever knew. After the soldiers left I took three warriors and trailed them back toward San Carlos." His number of casualties exceeded Rucker's estimate of ten, but we can assume that Rucker reported only the number of bodies left in the Indian village. The Indians possibly carried off other victims who later perished from their wounds.

Other elements of his story (though Geronimo's chronology is confusing) tend to point toward Rucker's tenacious campaign. The accounts concur in noting that the attackers completely destroyed the village and confiscated its contents. The time of year seems right, for Ghost Face, the Apache designation for winter, appeared in early January. Finally, Geronimo remembered that "we had heard that Victorio . . . was holding a council with the white men near Hot Springs. We easily found Victorio and his band, and they gave us supplies for the winter. We had not the least trouble with Mexicans, white men, or Indians."[47]

His brother-in-law, the Chihenne chief Nana, was there as was the family of Jason Betzinez, whose father, Nonithian, was Geronimo's first cousin. Apaches are by nature generous people, and we can assume, as Geronimo said, that his friends and relatives welcomed them, shared their belongings and provisions, and provided sanctuary for him and his followers.

While it was true that Victorio welcomed Geronimo, not everyone, including Nana, was happy with his arrival. Some Chiricahuas, especially those who only wanted to live in peace at Ojo Caliente, disapproved of Geronimo's presence, fearing that trouble would soon follow. Almost eighty years later, Sam Haozous recalled that the Chihennes and Bedonkohes at Ojo Caliente lived in peace with their neighbors.[48] According to Haozous, Geronimo's arrival in 1877 changed everything and led directly to the tragic events of the next decade.[49] Another Chiricahua described what happened when Geronimo settled at Ojo Caliente: the Chihennes "were on friendly terms with the towns around us and we were causing no trouble here." Then Chokonens and Bedonkohes arrived, bringing plunder from their recent raids. Duncan Balatchu, a boy at the time in Loco's group, remembered that Loco and Nana warned Victorio that these newcomers "will get us into trouble. But Victorio wouldn't do anything about it." He said, "These people are not bothering us."[50]

Yet, Geronimo longed to avenge Rucker's attack, which had inflicted so much loss of life and property. After a short rest at Ojo Caliente, he had persuaded Gordo and some forty to fifty warriors—Bedonkohes, Chihennes and Chokonens, evidently led by Ponce and Chatto—to join him on a raid into southern Arizona. The band slipped into Mexico and apparently joined a second band of Chokonens and Nednhis under Pionsenay, Juh, and their white friend Zebina N. Streeter, fresh from his failed peace mission to Governor Mariscal. By early February the war party crossed into Arizona via the Huachuca Mountains.

This would be more than just a raid for stock, for the Chiricahuas were also out for blood. Daybreak, February 4, 1877, one band struck Thomas Hughes's ranch along the Sonoita River. Hughes lost fifteen horses, and one man was wounded at his ranch. Later that day he reported that the Apaches, who he believed were led by Juh, had killed ten men in the Sonoita Valley alone, though that seems to have been based on rumors. Hughes thought he might have to "pick up his traps and get out of the country."[51] His neighbor, Englishman Herbert R. Hislop, who owned the Empire ranch, agreed: "It is an awful country to live in . . . as really there is no safety for life or property. When one gets up in the morning he does not know whether he will be killed during the day by these murdering, plundering Apache Indians or Mexicans."[52]

The war party then split up; one group continued west, resting in the Santa Rita Mountains near Tubac. Here, shortly before dawn on February 7, they discovered three Mexicans sleeping and "shot them dead in their blankets." Later that day they killed another man and wounded two others, one being William Devers, who died a year later from his wounds. Meanwhile, the larger party had continued south along the Sonoita River and on February 7 raided the San Rafael ranch, a few miles southeast of Sonoita Creek and the Santa Cruz River, killing one man and capturing forty-five head of stock. Both parties were safely across the line into Sonora by February 8. In two days they had killed at least seven men (various accounts place the dead between ten and fifteen) and stolen about one hundred head of stock.[53]

Meanwhile, on February 8, 1877, Arizona's governor Anson Safford, in Tucson to address the ninth territorial legislature the month before, received news of the depredations and decided to take action. In his address, Safford had stressed the need for law and order and vigorously advocated a message of unbridled war against Apache hostiles. He criticized the military, believing that it had been too passive. He and the legislature decided to take aggressive action. The representatives appropriated ten thousand dollars to enroll sixty men into a territorial militia to pursue hostiles. This symbolic measure made the politicians feel better. But would it help?[54]

A kind and magnanimous man who led by example, Safford believed passionately that his territory would not reach its social and economic potential until the military pacified the Apache. These raids reinforced his conviction that General Kautz's policies were to blame. Safford uncharitably concluded that the War Department should replace Kautz. With him in charge, it would take twenty years to defeat the Apaches, asserted Safford. Naturally, John Clum supported the governor. Rebuking Kautz's policies, Clum charged that one company of Indian scouts remained holed up at Fort Apache, doing nothing more than drawing "wages, rations, and [getting] drunk." Kautz' negligence "cleared the way for murder and is so declared by the blood of . . . our citizens."[55]

In truth, Safford's and Clum's allegations were unfair. Clum had lashed out at the Apache scouts at Fort Apache because the military had not forced them and their families to San Carlos after Clum had relocated part of the White

Mountain people in spring 1875. But this complaint exposed Clum for what he was all about—power. The Apaches still at Fort Apache were led by Pedro, a forty-year-old chief of the Carrizo band of the Cibecue group. They had become self-sufficient raising 250,000 pounds of corn and other vegetables. According to Corydon E. Cooley, who had married Pedro's daughter, Pedro's people had not received rations in two years. They were prospering, and Clum and Safford should have embraced this turn of events.[56]

Kautz was not negligent; if anything, he lacked an ability to play the politics mastered by Safford. No hostiles lived permanently in Arizona, and their raids had originated from their sanctuaries in northern Mexico and the reservation at Ojo Caliente. Kautz had deployed his troops as he thought best. After all, he had only one regiment of cavalry, and the concentration of Apaches at San Carlos had mandated that he keep most of his soldiers in central Arizona. Though southeastern Arizona remained sparsely populated, he did have two capable lieutenants, Rucker and Henely, with their Apache scout companies, patrolling the border.

After receiving authorization to form a sixty-man militia, Governor Safford turned to the boy agent, John Clum, requesting that he enroll sixty Apaches from San Carlos. Clum agreed but wanted his chief of police, Clay Beauford, a former sergeant in the Sixth Cavalry, named captain.[57] By February 20, 1877, Beauford was in Tucson with a company of fifty-four Apache police, ready for enrollment in the Arizona militia. Two days later, Safford gave Beauford his marching orders: take Company A, Arizona volunteers, to southeastern Arizona and follow the raiders' trail to wherever it leads, even into Mexico. If their trail leads to a "reservation, you will cooperate with the agent . . . rescue the stolen property, [and] arrest or punish said hostile Indians." The governor's order would soon make him look prophetic.[58]

By this time Kautz had sent a representative to investigate affairs at Ojo Caliente. In late January, he had written Agent Davis at Ojo Caliente for information about hostile Chiricahuas who had sought refuge there. Davis, fed up with unruly and uncooperative Indians, had apparently left the agency, though his resignation would not take effect until early April. Acting Agent Walter Whitney responded that 250 Chiricahuas had sought refuge at Ojo Caliente, but about 100 were now present. After he received Whitney's letter, Kautz ordered Lieutenant Austin Henely to Ojo Caliente to investigate.[59]

On March 16, 1877, Henely, after meeting Whitney at the agency headquarters, recognized an Indian he had known from his days at Fort Bowie. This man was none other than Geronimo, who was "indignant because he could not draw rations for the time he was out." He, Gordo, Chatto, and Ponce (Howard's guide) had returned to the reservation with a herd of one hundred stolen horses. Henely believed there "were about 35 Chiricahua renegades [Bedonkohes and Chokonens] and the rest, some fifteen men, Warm Springs [Chihennes], had formed part of the war party that had killed nine men in southern Arizona the previous month."

Kautz dutifully wired Governor Safford, who at once telegraphed the commissioner of Indian affairs in Washington. After reciting Henely's letter, the governor, sensing an opportunity to tie up the loose ends resulting from the closing of Chiricahua, could not resist firing one last salvo at the Apache agent at Ojo Caliente. Safford charged that the agent "has no control over the Indians and they do as they please. The Indians should be removed and all concentrated at San Carlos or an agent should be appointed, in place of the current one, who has the will, courage, and capacity to organize an Indian police and compel a daily count." One has to wonder whether Safford used Clum as his ghostwriter, for in this last passage, he was laying the foundation for a Clum takeover, just as he had in the case of the Chiricahua Reservation the year before.[60]

Commissioner Smith, tired of the unsettled state of affairs at Ojo Caliente, responded quickly. On March 20, 1877, he telegraphed Clum, giving him a set of specific instructions: "If practicable, take Indian Police and arrest renegade Chiricahuas at Southern Apache Agency. Seize stolen horses in their possession; restore the property to rightful owners; remove renegades to San Carlos and hold them in confinement for murder and robbery. Call on military for aid if needed." Smith's measured response seems appropriate. He had authorized Clum to apprehend the guilty parties and bring them to justice.[61]

Naturally, Clum eagerly accepted the challenge—even if it involved only the "renegade" Chiricahuas. But he was probably confident that he could persuade Indian officials in Washington that it might be best to extend the parameters to include all Chiricahuas at Ojo Caliente. He knew that Washington would give him the jurisdiction he needed without bothering to ask the Indians how they felt. Dan Thrapp believed that Clum "exulted" in the prospect of placing all Apaches west of the Rio Grande "under his control at San Carlos, and this pleased his ambition and his vanity."[62]

It would take Clum about a month to make the necessary preparations. By this time Clum and Kautz had become embroiled in a bitter feud concerning the manner in which each carried out his responsibilities. Clum realized he could not fight a two-front war. He decided to forge civil relations with the military in New Mexico, who had received orders from Washington through General John Pope and the Department of the Missouri, to cooperate with him in arresting Geronimo. By mid-April Clum, with his one hundred police, had reached Fort Bayard, ten miles east of Silver City. From here, he sent a message to Major James Franklin Wade, who, with three companies of cavalry, was to meet him at Ojo Caliente on April 21, 1877. Clum had learned from one of his "dependable" scouts that Geronimo, with 80 to 100, followers had received rations on April 14. According to Whitney's count, he had rationed 599 Indians.[63] On April 15, 1877, Clum wired Commissioner Smith, hoping to receive authorization to expand his mission: "I advise movement of all to San Carlos." Two days later, Smith approved Clum's suggestion if the military authorities concurred.[64]

Clum never bothered to discuss the removal with the military. At noon, April 20, 1877, his police camped twenty miles west of Ojo Caliente. Here he wrote a hasty note to Acting Agent Whitney, asking two questions: How many Apaches were at Ojo Caliente, and what was his opinion about removing every Indian to San Carlos? Whitney responded that the Apaches "will naturally object strongly to being removed from their old homes." Although he believed they would go without a fight, he thought that some would leave the reservation before removal. Despite this, he agreed that this was the most "favorable" opportunity to carry out the revised plan. Clum decided to take his mounted police, who numbered twenty-two, on to Ojo Caliente, where he arrived on the evening of April 20. Beauford, with the remainder, about eighty men on foot, would follow with orders to reach the agency before daybreak, April 21, 1877.[65]

Meanwhile, at Ojo Caliente, Clum received a message from Major Wade, which informed the agent that he would not reach the agency until April 22. Knowing that Wade's arrival might frighten the nervous Apaches, Clum decided to carry out his orders without the major.[66]

The story of Clum's celebrated capture of Geronimo has been told many times and thus needs no in-depth recounting here. At daybreak April 21, 1877, with Beauford's detachment of police safely concealed in the commissary building next to the agency headquarters, Clum sent a messenger to Geronimo's camp, about three miles away (probably in a canyon in the lower San Mateo Mountains), inviting him and other chiefs in for a talk. Geronimo later said that he thought it was a friendly invitation.[67] His actions support this statement, for he would not have come in if he had suspected a trap of any kind, especially in light of what had happened to Cochise and Mangas Coloradas. It was also ration day, so the Indians had planned to come in that morning. Shortly after sunrise, he approached the agency with some fifty men, women, and children. With him were the Bedonkohes, Gordo and Francisco, the Chihenne leader, Ponce, and the Chokonen chief Chatto. What happened next caught the Apaches off guard.

Geronimo's warriors gathered in front of the agency headquarters to hear out Clum. At this point, they could see only Clum's twenty-two Apache police. They had no idea that Beauford's eighty men lay in wait if Clum needed them. Clum penned several accounts of this tense meeting, and he enhanced later versions to produce additional drama even though it needed no hyperbole. He began by telling the Apaches that if they listened carefully, "no serious harm would be done to them." Then, according to these later versions, Geronimo responded with defiance. Clum wrote: "The situation demanded action—prompt action—and very promptly the signal was given." Beauford's Apache police emerged at "top speed" from the commissary building. The Western Apaches "completely surprised and surrounded the Hot Springs gentry."[68]

But this sequence of events in these later accounts was apocryphal and at variance with Clum's letter dated April 24, 1877, to the *Arizona Weekly Citizen,* three days after the encounter. In it, Clum clearly says that he gave the signal to Beauford once the Indians had assembled to hear his talk.[69] How much Clum may have fabricated the rest of his encounter with Geronimo is unclear. After Beauford's scouts had surrounded the Chiricahuas, Clum reminded Geronimo that he had broken his promise made the previous June at Apache Pass. To ensure that this would not happen again, Clum ordered him to the blacksmith shop, where an agency employee riveted shackles to his ankles. Clum also arrested Fatty and Ponce, who had just returned from an early April raid in Arizona. That afternoon Clum met with Victorio and Loco and counted 434 Apaches. He also arrested Jatu (sometimes called Tado, who was either a son or son-in-law of Nana), who had joined Ponce on the recent Arizona raid. He now had four men in shackles under the watchful eyes of his police.[70]

Major Wade and his cavalry force reached the agency the next day, April 22. Again, Clum ordered the Indians to appear for a count; this time only 175 were present. Four prominent chiefs, including the pacific Loco and the Bedonkohe Esquine, had removed their camps several miles east of the agency. The next day, most of the Indians returned, including Loco and Esquine. Clum finally held talks with the Indians on April 24, when they agreed to move to

San Carlos. It was that or flee, and with the presence of Wade's three companies of the Ninth Cavalry and Clum's Apache police, the chiefs decided not to
resist. Before going, they cached some of their weapons in a cave for future
use.[71] Years later Sam Haozous, who was present at the conference, recalled
that they really had no choice in the matter. He related that his people had
come in innocently to talk with Clum: "And the first thing we knew, without
no trouble, all the cavalry horses surrounded us all in that reservation, in that
camp. [Then] they took us out there to Arizona."[72]

By this time Clum had arrested either sixteen or seventeen prominent leaders and warriors who had been involved in the February and early April raids
in southern Arizona. Besides the four in shackles (Geronimo, Fatty, Ponce,
and Jatu), he had taken into custody Gordo; Francisco; Kenaszi (Putting on
Lots of Pollen), who had married a Mexican girl raised by Mangas Coloradas;
Nulah (a Bedonkohe who on April 25 had challenged Clum's right to shackle
Geronimo and fell victim to the butt of Clum's rifle); Chatto; Cooney; Lopez
and Patecas, both wanted for a raid months before; and five unidentified
men.[73] On May 1, 1877, 453 Chiricahuas, consisting of some 300 Chihennes
and 153 Bedonkohes and Chokonens began their unhappy trek toward San
Carlos, where they arrived on May 20, 1877. A smallpox outbreak took the
lives of several Apaches, perhaps as many as eight, before they reached their
new reservation. About 150 Chiricahuas had avoided removal. Some joined
the Mescaleros, some went north to Navajo country, some may have joined
Juh in Mexico, and others lurked in the mountains along the border.[74]

The fourth leg of concentration at San Carlos was complete. The Apaches
west of the Rio Grande were now on one reservation. Just as Taza's band had
paid the price for Pionsenay's actions, Loco and Victorio's people had suffered
the consequences for allowing Geronimo's raiding party refuge on their reservation. Though the vain Clum, who anointed himself the "great and good,"
after the *Arizona Miner* referred to him in those terms, was satisfied, the Chihennes felt betrayed.[75] Southern New Mexico had enjoyed relative peace from
Apache raids for most of the 1870s, but the last years of the decade, because
of the government's cavalier treatment of the Chihennes, would experience
incessant Apache warfare that far exceeded any of the brutal fighting in the
1860s. And Geronimo would forever remember Clum's trap and his period
in shackles. He now distrusted American civil and military officials. In the future, rather than face possible punishment, his first instinct was always to run
before Americans took action against him.

If Clum had carried out his original mission, and not expanded it to satisfy his own ego and designs, the Chihennes could have conceivably remained at Ojo Caliente. Loco, Victorio, and Nana had kept their people in line. Raiding from Ojo Caliente into Mexico by their followers had decreased significantly. They were more prepared to adopt more progressive ways than were their counterparts at Chiricahua agency. Unfortunately, the refugees from the Chiricahua agency, joined by a few Chihennes from Ojo Caliente, furnished Clum and the Bureau of Indian Affairs with the excuse, the bloody raid into Arizona, to close down another reservation and consolidate the Apaches at San Carlos. Clum, with the misguided approval of Washington Indian officials, changed the equation. He may have solved a temporary problem, but the removal of all Apaches from Ojo Caliente exacerbated relations and created fresh turmoil for southern New Mexico. And his reliance on Western Apache police caused future problems between the two tribes.

In the end, the Chihennes were the ones who suffered the most, experiencing a tremendous loss of life and a complete loss of country. And what of Clum? He was too arrogant and self-absorbed to understand his complicity.

5

NEW TROUBLES AT SAN CARLOS

In the future we don't want to tread over any more thorns. We want to die from old age or disease and not from fighting and trouble.

Nana, October 24, 1877

General August Kautz had exercised restraint during Clum's and Safford's incessant campaign to discredit him. According to them, he was an incompetent military leader who had remained passive while hostiles had raided at will since the breakup of the Chiricahua Reservation. Kautz's patience reached its breaking point after he read their unjust criticism in the newspapers. He decided to strike back against his accusers. But his methods were subtler than the confrontational style of Clum and Safford.

On April 9, 1877, as Clum began his trip to Ojo Caliente, Kautz wrote his superiors in Washington, D.C., asking permission to station an officer at San Carlos for the dual purpose of gathering Indian intelligence and of observing and inspecting the issuing of rations. His explanation for making this request was simple: Safford and Clum had criticized him for not paying attention to the movements of hostile Chiricahuas, who had found sanctuary at the Ojo Caliente agency in New Mexico. To remedy this, he wanted one of his men on the ground to provide him with intelligence since Clum was uncooperative. On April 28, 1877, the secretary of the interior approved his request.

The underlying reason that Washington officials adopted his suggestion was the universal belief that many Indian agents were eager to line their own pockets by graft. After all, an agent's authority was virtually autonomous. In 1874, when the Bureau of Indian Affairs had centralized control by eliminating local superintendents and consolidating authority in Washington, the Indian agent had virtually no local supervision. The bureau relied on regular audits of reservations to prevent corruption. Yet, by the time Indian inspectors investigated alleged acts of graft, the Indian agent, if corrupt, had carried out his plan, cooked the books, and, if he was smart, covered his tracks.

One can imagine the reaction of the egotistical Clum when he heard that one of Kautz's officers was at *his* agency to check on *his* activities. The day after Clum returned to San Carlos from Ojo Caliente, Lieutenant Lemuel A. Abbot, a Vermont native who had been wounded five times in the Civil War, reached the agency with a detachment of soldiers. Abbot explained that his orders called for him to inspect Indian supplies and to witness the distribution of rations. As Kautz expected, the feisty Clum decided to fight fire with fire. On June 5, 1877, he sent a defiant telegram to the commissioner of Indian affairs, refusing to "submit to an inspection by the Army. I am ready to transfer my property. How soon can I be relieved?" By the next day he had calmed down, but he remained steadfast: "It is an insult to the honor, integrity, and manhood of an agent, and I should resent it as such."

Clum had actually resigned twice during the prior six months. The Interior Department had accepted his resignation on April 28, 1877. He would remain until they found a replacement. With the removal of the Apaches from Ojo Caliente to San Carlos, the Bureau of Indian Affairs dragged its feet, probably hoping to defer filling the position until this crisis was over. But Clum was impatient. On June 9, 1877, having heard nothing from the commissioner, he suggested a revolutionary idea. He graciously agreed to remain as agent if authorized to enroll two more companies of Indian police, thus allowing the War Department to withdraw the troops from Arizona. Clum's Apache police would provide security. And Arizona would be rid of General Kautz.

The commissioner did not consider Clum's proposal. This time Clum was unable to bully his superiors in Washington, and even his most ardent supporter, Governor Safford, could do nothing. Try as they might, they could not get the order rescinded. The two men had underestimated the political muscle that a commanding general of a military department possessed. The pragmatic Kautz had won. The sanctimonious Clum, as Kautz expected, had interpreted the edict as a slap in the face. To the agent, this was a matter of principle, and Washington officials were questioning his integrity. Clum, like Tom Jeffords, was scrupulously honest, but he had backed himself into a corner. He resigned, effective July 1, 1877.[1]

In the meantime, some 150 Chihennes and Bedonkohes had scattered rather than move to San Carlos with Clum. One family left behind at Ojo Caliente was that of Jatu, whom Clum had arrested and then shackled for leading a raid into Arizona. Before leaving for Arizona with Clum, Perico and others had looked for them but could not find any trace. Perico recalled: "After four or five days most of them came back to the agency. But one woman was lost. She was a big, fat woman, the wife of Jatu. With her, she had three children, a baby in a cradle, a girl about seven years of age, and a boy a little bigger. She thought that the people were all gone and she stayed in the mountains with her children. Then she got a notion to come out to Mescalero country."[2]

The story, narrated by Jatu's son, continues: before they crossed the Rio Grande, a bear surprised them near Mount Cuchillo. Placing her boy and girl in a tree, his mother confronted the bear, who killed the brave woman and then grabbed the baby's cradle and swung "it against a rock," killing the baby. The bear could have reached the two children but inexplicably sat there for a while before leaving the area. The children came down the tree. They didn't know what to do. As they sat there crying, they had a supernatural experience. Suddenly, "Grey One, the clown [a mountain spirit], came from this holy mountain and approached them. He carried a sword, not a stick. 'What are you crying about, he asked the children?' They told him all that had happened. 'We don't know what to do. Come with me,' said the clown. He got to a cliff at the foot of the mountains. 'We are going in here . . . don't be afraid.' Then Clown turned and hit the cliff with his sword. A door opened."[3]

The children followed the Clown into the mountain, where they remained for four days at a special tipi, feasting on an abundance of food, watching continuous dances, and being reassured by the presence of Nana, who was likely their grandfather. After four days Clown gave them a choice of remaining in this idyllic setting or going back to Ojo Caliente. The children chose the latter, obviously wanting to join their father. Clown said, "Everyone is at San Carlos now. Your father has a chain around his neck and is in prison right now, . . . It was the truth too, what Clown was saying . . . . There is a white man over at the agency. I will lead you to him. You can stay in his house with him. Next year your father and all your relatives will be back in Hot Springs. . . . I am going to watch over you."

The Clown escorted them to Ojo Caliente, where their former agent took them in, just as he had foretold. Later that year, when they reunited with their father, they told this incredible story. The boy served as the narrator. Before he began, he "would pray, and after he finished he would pray."[4]

Mrs. Andrew Stanley mentions these two children in her account to ethnologist Grenville Goodwin. An Eastern White Mountain Apache, she had resided on the Chiricahua Reservation in late 1875. She left there after her people killed Coha and after her brother-in-law had fatally wounded her husband during a tiswin party. In the summer of 1876, to escape the attentions of an older man who was courting her, she agreed to go to Ojo Caliente with a White Mountain woman who was in love with a Chiricahua man. Mrs. Stanley's brother had married a Chiricahua woman and was also at Ojo Caliente. They left the Graham Mountains and traveled through the Mogollons, eventually finding their way to a Bedonkohe camp, probably Gordo's, near Ojo Caliente. With customary Apache etiquette, they were warmly welcomed. Her companion soon married the Chiricahua man; Mrs. Stanley had a joyful reunion with her brother and joined his wife's extended family group.

Her happiness was ephemeral as her brother suffered the same fate as her husband, slain by an intoxicated friend during a tiswin party. Shortly after (apparently in early April 1877), Mrs. Stanley left Ojo Caliente with four or five others for the Mogollon Mountains. After a short stay, two men returned to Ojo Caliente to find "the wickiups of the people all still there, the canvas still on them, and the dogs still there. But all the people had been taken away from there by the Whites. So they went to the house where the White men stayed, and that was how they got caught." They were prisoners for one day until they broke a window and escaped during the second night. But, Mrs. Stanley lamented, "the little boy and little girl [Jatu's children] who had got caught there did not get away. They were too small."[5]

Contemporary accounts corroborate Mrs. Stanley's story. On May 4, 1877, only three days after Clum left, two Chokonens, later identified as members of Pionsenay's band, came to the headquarters of Whitney, the former acting agent. He sent word to Lieutenant Wright, who arrested them at 2:00 A.M. on May 5. Wright also captured their arms, provisions, and six animals. He put the prisoners in the guardhouse, but they escaped around 3:00 A.M. on May 6, 1877, when the guard "probably" fell asleep.[6]

The two men returned to Mrs. Stanley's small group. Leaving the women in camp, they left on a raid. They first killed three Mexican women at a ranch before ambushing William Wilson and another man at Ash Springs. The two men had left Silver City with a wagonload of potatoes, bound for Camp Grant, when the Chiricahuas opened fire, killing them both, crushing their skulls with the yoke, then carrying off the team, bridles, blankets, and supplies. The report claimed that three Apaches had carried out the attack; yet, in reality, only the two men with Mrs. Stanley were responsible.[7]

Her party then went to the branch agency at San Carlos, where the Chokonens were camped. Here Mrs. Stanley saw Chihuahua, the Chokonen chief, who invited her to visit his camp. But the two men in her party decided to head south toward the border. According to Mrs. Stanley's account, they were "not afraid that anyone would follow them because they thought they were great fighters." En route, the small party, which numbered five or six in all, probably ambushed and killed two mail riders near Apache Pass, one on May 29 (Jackson Tait) and the other on May 31 (Sam Ward). Early accounts suggested that fifty Apaches were involved; later accounts mentioned twelve, and finally five or six, which is exactly the number of Mrs. Stanley's party. She also mentioned that the men had killed two Americans who were traveling to the Animas Mountains, which also concurs with the Apaches' route, according to the Indian scouts.[8]

One reason Mrs. Stanley's party had gone to San Carlos was to find out what had happened to Pionsenay's followers, who had apparently split from Juh after an April 15, 1877, raid against Thomas Hughes's ranch. Hughes, Manuel Soto, Martin Sánchez, and Jesús Robles had followed the trail of nine Indians, who later united with another party of twenty-seven warriors that ambushed Hughes's party, killing Sánchez and Robles. Hughes escaped narrowly, and Soto found safety behind some rocks. Soto counted thirty-six Indians and one white man, undoubtedly Streeter, who "directed the movements of the party."[9] The Nednhis returned to Mexico, but the Chokonens decided to head to San Carlos. Around May 6 part of Pionsenay's band, nine men and eighteen women and children, showed up at the subagency and agreed to surrender to Ezra Hoag. But their chief, Pionsenay ("the devil unchained"), had second thoughts and left with one young man, a Mexican captive whom the Apaches had reared. The Indian police from San Carlos, under Acting Agent Morgan L. Neville, escorted the prisoners to the guardhouse at the main agency.[10]

The attacks on the mail riders and the leadership void at San Carlos prompted Indian Inspector William Vandever to return there. The previous month he had reviewed Clum's operations at San Carlos and had come away much impressed with the agent, who had convinced Vandever that the military's presence at San Carlos was a "hindrance rather than a help." Yet the inspector also recognized that the agent's timeworn threats to resign each time he disapproved of an order or policy had left a sour taste among federal Indian officials in the capital. The commissioner of Indian affairs, John Q. Smith, though unsympathetic to Vandever's perceived bias against the military, asked him to oversee the agency and to provide status reports until the commissioner could appoint a new agent.[11]

Soon after reaching San Carlos, the inspector made some important decisions. His first act was to ensure that all were on the reservation. On June 19, 1877, he reported that all "here are accounted for." He had learned that Juh, Nolgee, Pionsenay, and one Chihenne chief, whose "name I have not learned," led the bands responsible for the April raids in southern Arizona. Vandever informed the commissioner that he had "offered 100 dollars for the head of the four ringleaders—dead or alive, and amnesty to the rest." Next, he appointed Martin Sweeney as the interim agent. Sweeney, who had acted in this capacity during the months that Clum was absent the previous year, immediately requested permission from the commissioner to hire Merejildo Grijalva as interpreter for the Chiricahua bands ("who require more attention and talking to than the other Indians") living at Goodwin.[12]

In mid-July, Vandever also requested authorization, undoubtedly prompted by his meetings with the Chiricahuas, to release from bondage the seventeen Chiricahuas whom Clum had captured at Ojo Caliente. Clum had kept them locked up in the San Carlos guardhouse. Some men remained in shackles, including Geronimo and Chatto, and all were required to work. Vandever thought that they were "thoroughly subdued." Moreover, he believed that Geronimo and other prominent men might be helpful in "forcing the renegades to come on."[13] Evidently the commissioner agreed to this proposal, for Vandever set them free. Geronimo clearly never forgot his humiliating experience. Few Americans truly understood the effect of Clum's imprisonment of him and how "strongly it entered into his subsequent flights."[14]

Vandever remained at San Carlos as an adviser to Sweeney until the new agent arrived. Sweeney continued to issue rations every Friday (twenty-one pounds of beef, five pounds of flour, five ounces of sugar, two ounces of coffee, and one ounce of salt), but eventually he reduced rations to accommodate reduced levels of inventories.[15] The Chihennes, particularly Victorio, were dissatisfied with their new home a few miles west of Fort Thomas, near today's town of Geronimo. To begin with, smallpox remained a problem, and several Chihennes perished from this contagious disease. Moreover, according to Jason Betzinez, they "were completely downcast over the prospect of having to live in this hot, desolate country."[16]

Lieutenant Abbot placed the blame for running out of rations squarely on Vandever's shoulders. He implied that fraudulent practices had been ongoing for the past year, thus indicting Clum's regime. Since Clum's departure, the Apaches had left the reservation to gather "nuts, fruits and other indigenous products to satisfy their hunger." Vandever had slashed rations in July and

August. On July 26, 1877, he admitted that he had nothing to issue, and he blamed contractors for failing to deliver on their contracts. Lieutenant Abbot charged that Vandever was "gravely negligent [and] wholly unworthy of the trust as an officer in the civil service."

Moreover, Abbot thought the Indian official was "criminally inefficient." Though he conceded that he did not have all the records of the agency, he believed that "only half of the contracted supplies were furnished." And much of the food furnished was of poor quality. Vandever even admitted that suppliers had spilled a large shipment of rice before it reached the reservation, and that contractors had added water to a shipment of nearly 18,000 pounds of sugar to compensate for quantities sold en route.[17]

During this instability, the Chiricahuas' old friend Tom Jeffords renewed acquaintances with the Chokonen and Chihenne leaders. He had come to the reservation as a broker for the beef contractor. He would have been unwelcome if Clum had been there, and Vandever was apparently in Tucson to meet the new agent. After spending the night at Camp Thomas, Jeffords went to the Chiricahua camp and ostensibly met Naiche's people for the first time since June of the previous year. He also spoke with Victorio, and perhaps Geronimo. Weeks later, Vandever accused him of drinking whiskey with his friends, which would not have been out of the question since Jeffords and Cochise shared a bottle from time to time. Regardless, Jeffords, as only he could, gained important intelligence. He learned that the Chihennes, frustrated with their living quarters and conditions, lack of food, and difficulties with the White Mountain Apaches, were ready to jump the reservation. Jeffords was displaying no perspicacity in making this warning. Even General Kautz, distant in Prescott, felt the same way, though he made his feelings known only in hindsight. Recognizing their love for their homeland, Kautz felt they would leave unless surrounded by military force.[18]

Lieutenant Abbot was hearing the same rumors, but he hoped that the arrival of Clum's replacement, Henry Lyman Hart, with several wagonloads of supplies, would placate the Apaches. Nonetheless, on August 29, 1877, Kautz ordered commanders at Apache, Grant, and Thomas to send out patrols that would "be seen by the Indians" to display the military's preparedness. Hart and Vandever reached the reservation that very same day. According to Vandever, the Indians "were well pleased" after meeting their new agent. Lieutenant Abbot concurred, remarking on August 31, 1877, that the "temper of Indians [is] improving." Hart impressed Abbot, who had received orders "to establish cordial relations with the new agent." Abbot described Hart as a "gentleman and a man of sense with whom relations will be amicable." The new agent from Ohio was just as eager to cooperate with Lieutenant Abbot. Both wanted to avoid the rancor that had characterized the regimes of Clum and then Vandever, who had left the agency about August 30, much to the delight of Abbot.[19]

Before Hart had a chance to settle into his quarters, he faced two situations that tested his resolve. The first involved Chiricahuas who had had their fill of living as traditional Apaches and now wanted to live on the reservation. The second episode centered on the disenchanted Chihennes who despised San Carlos and yearned to return to their native country.

On August 30, 1877, Hart's second day on the job, Nolgee, Pionsenay, and sixteen warriors were near the subagency, looking to surrender, but were "afraid of being punished." Fresh from Mexico, they had come in two groups: Nolgee and Nahilzay, with the larger band of about fifteen Nednhis and Chokonens, had probably killed a mail rider about twenty miles east of Fort Bowie; Pionsenay and two others (including a "renegade Mexican boy who usually accompanied him") had crossed into Arizona west of the Huachucas and run off a horse from a rancher on the Sonoita. Troops and Indian scouts followed him through the Dragoons, Chiricahuas, north into the Peloncillos, and then onto the reservation. According to one report, Zebina Streeter may have been with Pionsenay.

Nolgee and Nahilzay, promising to behave, surrendered to Lieutenant Gilbert Raymond Overton on August 31, 1877. Nolgee agreed to send one man with Overton and the agency police force to bring in the rest of his group. Pionsenay, with a price on his head, fled with his two followers. Overton returned with nine others and turned them over to Subagent Ezra Hoag. Indian Inspector Vandever, then preparing to leave the agency in Hart's hands, happened to be present. Having placed a bounty on Nolgee's head a few months before, he was probably not in a hospitable mood. Consequently, he informed the Nednhi chief, "whatever offenses could be proved against any of his party . . . [those] guilty would be punished." These ominous words ensured a short stay at San Carlos for Nolgee.[20]

Nolgee evidently joined Bonito and Chiva, who were apparently living near an Eastern White Mountain ranchería headed by George, a Chiricahua who had married into that band. Pionsenay entered the camp the night of September 1, 1877. He quickly convinced Nolgee and several other men (a few, according to Agent Hoag; several according to Lieutenant Abbot), and some twenty of their women and children, to leave the reservation. Nahilzay, whose followers had joined Naiche's band, remained. To speed up their escape, Pionsenay's party helped themselves to several horses belonging to the White Mountain Apaches.[21]

The morning of September 2, Subagent Ezra Hoag alerted Captain Clarence M. Bailey at Camp Thomas. Nolgee, he believed, "came in good faith [but] they have a great many enemies here" and left because they feared that "others might implicate them in their killing scrapes," a clear reference to Vandever's warning. Hoag blamed Pionsenay: "He wields a great influence over them and they fear him more than the devil," a clear indication that the Chiricahuas believed he possessed supernatural powers that he employed for malevolent purposes. A Western Apache scout was more direct, simply declaring that Pionsenay "belongs to a family that kills." Despite Pionsenay's well-earned reputation, a band of White Mountain Apaches cut the trail of his fugitives and overtook them on September 3, 1877, recapturing thirteen Chiricahuas and twenty-eight horses. But by the next day, Pionsenay and Nolgee had made their way to Steins Peak. From here, they struck east into New Mexico, where they killed two Americans and eleven Mexicans at ranches on the Gila and the Burro mountains, before dashing to their camp in Mexico.[22]

As the White Mountain Apaches returned with their prisoners, they unexpectedly encountered a large body of troops and Indian scouts under Captain Tullius Cicero Tupper. His detail, which included two scout companies headed by Rucker and Lieutenant Robert Hanna, augmented by seventeen Apache police from San Carlos, were on the trail of the Chihennes who had bolted from the reservation during the evening of September 2, 1877, one night after Nolgee's exodus.[23]

The long-predicted outbreak had occurred, and it was hardly a spontaneous decision by the Chihenne leaders. Instead, it was a well-conceived operation, unrelated to Nolgee and Pionsenay's movements, inspired solely by the Chihennes' love of their homeland at Ojo Caliente. From their first day at San Carlos, it was never a question of if they would leave but only a matter of when.

Several other factors accelerated their decision to leave. First, problems had erupted between them and the "Coyoteros," or White Mountain Apaches. The latter were unhappy that the Chihennes were living in their country. Their presence further depleted the game and natural food supplies and perhaps reduced potential farming areas. This bad blood had apparently led to an encounter with the Chihennes, who felt outgunned because they had cached most of their weapons before leaving Ojo Caliente. The chiefs had other concerns: the water was bad, the location unhealthy, and their rations insufficient—all of which was true.[24]

Meanwhile, Vandever, perhaps to obscure his own culpability, pointed the finger at Tom Jeffords, who was always a convenient scapegoat. Ten days after the outbreak, on September 12, 1877, the inspector, then at the Mescalero reservation near Fort Stanton, charged that that Jeffords, after furnishing the Indians with whiskey, had "stirred up insubordination." The allegation was sheer nonsense, undoubtedly concocted to rationalize or to justify his own conduct. When Kautz heard of the charge, he asked Lieutenant Abbot to investigate.

Abbot believed the accusation was "false and malicious. Vandever is very bitter against Jeffords and it is quite likely that his prejudice has affected his judgment." Abbot continued: "I do not suspect Jeffords in the least of influencing the Warm Springs [Chihennes] to leave the reservation but on the contrast think his conduct has been commendable." If anyone should shoulder responsibility, it was Vandever, claimed Abbot. He was "astonishingly negligent in not providing these Indians with sufficient and proper food during the entire time they were at the San Carlos reservation." Six weeks later, Vandever, realizing the controversy he had started, backed off from his indictment of Jeffords, now charging that Jeffords had only "excited the Indians." He conceded that the Indians left because of "trouble with the Coyoteros and they did not like the water supply."[25]

The main reason for leaving was their love for Ojo Caliente, which must have seemed like heaven compared with the barren and inhospitable San Carlos. As Sam Haozous simply explained, "We got our homes there [Ojo Caliente]. No one wanted to stay away from our reservation."[26]

Agent Hart had no way of knowing that the Chihenne leaders had made their ultimate decision to leave shortly after he issued their first complete ration in several weeks, Thursday, September 1, 1877. At first, the pragmatic Loco, who had worked for solutions to avert bloodshed over the previous decade, objected to leaving. But he acquiesced when most of his band said they were going, with or without him. As dusk gave way to darkness on September 2, 1877, some 310 Chiricahuas, in four groups, started for New Mexico. Victorio, Loco, Nana, Mangas, and Tomaso Coloradas led the Chihennes, and Esquine and Francisco commanded the small Bedonkohe contingent. Conspicuously absent was the balance of those transferred from Ojo Caliente— some 145 Bedonkohes and Chokonens under Geronimo, Bonito, Gordo, and Chatto. As far as the Chihenne chiefs were concerned, these troublemakers, or "bad Indians" as Victorio, Loco, and Nana later called them, were responsible for their transfer to San Carlos in the first place.[27]

The Chihennes crossed the Gila River near old Camp Goodwin and headed north toward the Gila Mountains. By the next morning, September 3, they had dropped into Ash Flat, where Palmer Valor, one-time member of the San Carlos police force, was surprised to see a "long column of Indians moving along with their horses . . . headed in the direction of Eagle Creek." Valor was returning from Nantanes Plateau with his wife and four other women. He was escorting an in-law, injured during a recent scrape with a bear, to San Carlos for treatment. Unaware of the outbreak, Valor fired two shots into the air to attract the Chihennes' attention. Shortly after, two men came to investigate. They met the women in a canyon (Palmer Valor was above them on a ridge). The men revealed that Victorio's band had left the reservation. Victorio was not with the main body; he commanded the rearguard of warriors who would protect them from soldiers and scouts. The two men returned to their people.

At dawn the next morning, Palmer Valor's party heard gunfire, which increased in volume and intensity. Victorio's rearguard had rejoined the main body, and they were fighting the soldiers and Apache scouts. At sunrise, four Western Apaches rode into Valor's camp. One of the men was Valor's father-in-law; another was Bylas, the uncle of Richard Bylas. They were in pursuit of Victorio. Suddenly, they saw the Chihennes emerge from a draw near Arsenic Springs with soldiers and scouts on their trail.

The four mounted Apaches immediately followed Victorio. Valor "ran after them fast—my legs were like an automobile in those days." Victorio's men then set fire to the grass to give the rest of the band time to climb a prominent yellow bluff. The Chihennes occupied the ridge and began firing from concealed positions on the soldiers and scouts below. Then Palmer Valor was astonished to hear "my father-in-law calling me by my real name even though I was his son-in-law [your father-in-law doesn't call you by your true name unless under stress]. 'You are enlisted as a scout so go to the Chiricahuas now and fight them . . . .' I got up and started to run for the bluff toward the Chiricahuas. There were little winds under my legs as I ran." He joined his father-in-law and Bylas in a position below a bluff. Here they found seven horses, which Palmer Valor drove across the canyon, out of range. Victorio was incredulous that the three men had taken his horses. He called down to Bylas, "Is that you doing that?" Bylas responded, "Yes, that is me doing that." Victorio vowed, "All right, you will hear about this some day." And he meant it.[28]

The army happened to have plenty of troops available to follow Victorio. Tupper's command, which featured the indefatigable Rucker, did overtake the Chihennes along the San Francisco River and Mogollon Mountains on September 8 and 10, 1877. In the first skirmish, the Apache police force from San Carlos, consisting of seventeen warriors, with five of Rucker's Apache scouts, did nearly all the fighting. Hanna's scouts battled the Chihennes on the 10th. All told, the two commands captured thirteen Chihennes and killed eleven others, most of them women and children.[29] One Western Apache scout named Chapeau exemplified the barbarous hatred between his people and the Chihennes when he boasted that he dispassionately put a bullet through the head of a baby rather than care for it.[30] Among the killed and captured were several members of Loco's band. A few months later, the chief pleaded for the return of his people: "Those that are dead cannot be brought back to life; but we ask earnestly for the living."[31]

After these attacks the Chihennes split into smaller groups. Although Victorio and Loco realized that a return to Ojo Caliente was not then a prudent move, a small party headed toward the Black Range and the San Mateo Mountains. Another group, between fifty and sixty, crossed the Rio Grande and found refuge at the Mescalero Reservation. The main body, under Loco, Victorio, Tomaso Coloradas, Mangas, and Nana, continued north to the high country in the upper Mogollons. From here, they moved north into Navajo country, where Loco, Victorio, and Mangas had friends and relatives by marriage.

In mid-September the Chihennes ran into Navajos who were farming about fifty miles southwest of Acoma. Fortunately for the Chihennes, with the Navajos was Jesús Arvizu, an old acquaintance of Mangas and Tomaso Coloradas. Their father, Mangas Coloradas, had captured Arvizu at Bacoachi, Sonora, in January 1851. About a year later, the chief had traded the boy to the Navajos for a horse.[32] Arvizu had remained with his adopted people through his adult years, when he served as interpreter. After a brief reunion, he agreed to take a message from the Chihennes to the commander of Fort Wingate, located eleven miles east of today's Gallup, New Mexico. Wingate's commander, Captain Horace Jewett, informed Colonel Hatch, who authorized Jewett to open negotiations with the Chihennes. Jewett dispatched a few Navajo scouts with Arvizu to bring in the Apaches.[33]

Victorio, Loco, and Tomaso Coloradas came to Fort Wingate on September 24, 1877. Representing 144 people camped in the Gallo Mountains, just north of their old reservation at Tularosa, they requested permission from

Jewett to settle near Acoma. After a five-day stay, they left to bring in their people. Accompanied by Thomas Keam, former agent for the Navajos who was now interpreter at Fort Wingate, and five Navajos, the three chiefs crossed the lava beds and, after a ninety-mile march, found the Indian camps in the Gallo Mountains. The Chihennes told Keam that they would accept a reservation near Fort Wingate but would not "willingly go back to San Carlos." Keam escorted the band, which had increased to 187, to Fort Wingate, where they arrived about October 5. Sixteen days later, a group of 46 Chihennes, probably led by Nana, came in. Captain Jewett sent them two miles west to a place called the Milk Ranch, a fertile area with good water and grass. Each morning the three chiefs checked in at Wingate to meet Captain Jewett.[34]

New Mexico's military and civil authorities debated the Chihennes' fate. Colonel Hatch, fearing they would be an unsettling influence among the peaceful Navajos, decided that they could not remain at Fort Wingate. Then Indian Inspector Vandever arrived at the fort. Naturally he chimed in with his two cents, suggesting that a "bad precedent would be set" if the bureau sent the Indians back to Ojo Caliente. Vandever concluded that the government had two options: return them to San Carlos or remove them to the Indian Territory, meaning Oklahoma.

Both solutions were remarkably insensitive if not pointless. Dan Thrapp summed up the dilemma: "The fact was that no one had any idea what to do with the Apaches except move them somewhere." Hatch's superiors, including General John Pope, military commander of the Department of the Missouri, intelligently concluded to return them temporarily to Ojo Caliente, "a favorable point at which to assemble them." In Chicago, General Philip H. Sheridan concurred, and Hatch made plans to move them back to their ancestral homes.[35]

The Chihenne chiefs were delighted. On October 24, 1877, their three principal leaders, Victorio, Loco, and Nana, expressed their feelings to Captain Jewett at Fort Wingate. Blaming their problems on "bad Indians" (referring to Geronimo and other refugees from the Chiricahua Reservation), each man unequivocally stated his desire to live at Ojo Caliente, where they would be content.

Statement of Chief Victorio:

> When we came here, I informed the Commanding officer that we wanted to stay here, but if we went to Ojo Caliente, we did not want to go to any other place. We want to stay at Ojo Caliente. In case we

do go to Ojo Caliente, we do not want any other Indians to interfere with us. . . . We want to die there. There we have plenty of water, and plenty of rain, and we want to go to work. . . . The words that he has spoken have been spoken before God and he wishes it distinctly understood that his tribe does not wish to be removed from Ojo Caliente. His thoughts are scattered and he asks that no blame be attached to them on account of the bad Apache Indians. What he has said, he hopes will not be rubbed out. He had spoken the truth.

Statement of Chief Nana:

We will be pleased to work and see our crops come out of the ground so that we can have something to eat when we go to Ojo Caliente. When we have no trouble among us, it will be a pleasure to get up in the morning and hear the birds singing merrily. We want to live happily and contented until there is nothing left of us from old age. We want to die from old age or disease and not from fighting and trouble. We wish to remain in the same place so the sun will shine on the same side, the rain from the same side, and the wind from the quarter it wants to come. We want to have plenty of children and increase our tribe. He is getting old and his flesh is getting soft. . . . In the future we do not wish to tread on any more thorns.

Statement of Chief Loco:

He asks all to do what they can for himself and his family. A portion is at San Carlos also with the Coyotero Indians and he does not want them to remain there. . . . We want all of them sent to us at Ojo Caliente. Those that are dead cannot be brought to life and we earnestly ask for the living . . . . What we want to do is plant, raise corn, vegetables, and melons so we can look on with pleasure while it is growing. These are all the words he can think of at present and can get out of his head.[36]

On October 31, 1877, the Chihennes, "almost naked . . . without arms and dispossessed of everything," left Fort Wingate with an escort of troops bound for Ojo Caliente. Before their departure, the sympathetic post commander distributed a bedsack "to each Indian to make clothing [and] one condemned blanket to each Indian without one." They finally reached their old homes about November 10, 1877. Indian officials appointed Thomas Keam as agent for as long as "necessary." Helping him was Jesús Arvizu as interpreter. The Indians' fate would be the subject of countless debates in the months to come.[37]

Back at San Carlos, Agent Hart, aided by a liberal supply of food, a common sense approach to diplomacy, and the welcome departure of Vandever, had restored order to the agency, which had appeared on the verge of a full-scale rebellion. Three days after the Chihenne outbreak, Hart contemplated moving the Chiricahuas closer to San Carlos. Clearly, they did not want to move. Lieutenant Abbot agreed with Hart but warned that the Chiricahuas were "sulky and may leave if moved."

Furthermore, Abbot was pessimistic about the Chiricahuas' future on the reservation even if Hart permitted them to stay put: "It is only a matter of time as to whether these Indians will leave." Hart apparently had second thoughts on removal, and four days later, Abbot telegraphed his superiors that the Chiricahuas would remain put. Almost two weeks later, on September 23, 1877, Agent Hart held a formal council with the Chiricahua leaders. Though he mentioned only Geronimo, undoubtedly Naiche, Chihuahua, Chatto, and Gordo were present. Hart named Geronimo "captain" of those Chiricahuas, some 145, whom Clum had removed from Ojo Caliente with Victorio's people. They had stayed on the reservation because the Chihennes wanted nothing to do with them. Geronimo and Naiche said they would remain on the reservation. Geronimo's pledge, undoubtedly made in good faith, was just as sincere as the government's promises contained in various agreements, treaties, and executive orders.[38]

Hart did restore stability at San Carlos. In early October he described the Indians as peaceable and predicted they would remain on the reservation. About a month later, he wrote the editor of the *Arizona Weekly Citizen* that his warehouse was now fully stocked with supplies, including three hundred thousand pounds of flour and large quantities of sugar, rice, salt, and soap. Suppliers were delivering beef as promised, and he had recently distributed annuity goods. The *Citizen* could not resist commenting on this idyllic picture: the Indians "present a plump and handsome appearance," having everything necessary to "prolong their material existence."[39]

During this time, the agent, after hearing that Nolgee and Pionsenay were eager to come in, decided to open negotiations. In late November Hart sent a small band of Chiricahuas to Ash Creek, where they established contact with Nolgee and, surprisingly, Juh. Both Nednhi chiefs were concerned about

Mexican patrols.[40] The presence of the intractable Juh had initially raised Hart's spirits. Though he had never met the Nednhi chief, the agent knew that the reservation Chiricahuas considered him the key to bringing in the hostiles who had eluded Clum's grasp in June 1876.

After his spring raids into Arizona, Juh moved his base camp from the Animas Mountains, where his people had gathered and harvested the agave plant, to the Sierra Madre Mountains. His ultimate destination was Guaynopa, tucked several miles inside Chihuahua, east of the Sátachi River, in incredibly rough and remote country.[41] Guaynopa was near the site of an old silver mine that had been worked by the Spanish in the eighteenth century.[42] It was about thirty miles southeast of Nácori Chico, Sonora, seventy-five miles south of Casas Grandes, and some sixty miles northeast of Sahuaripa.

Jason Betzinez and Asa Daklugie called this place the Great Canyon. It had historically been a favorite sanctuary of Nednhis, especially Láceris, Juh's father. It was virtually impregnable to access, for the ranchería was on the rim, and it would take their enemies all day to get to the top, which they could reach only by a dangerous zigzag trail. The Nednhis also knew of a trail that crossed to the western side of the canyon, down a zigzag course, which led "down the precipitous walls of the gorge." From this time forward, it would become Juh's safety net, affording him equal opportunities to raid west into Sonora or east into Chihuahua.[43]

Although Nácori Chico was the closest town, Juh worried most about the Chihuahuan towns located sixty to seventy-five miles to the east at Namiquipa, Yepómera, and Temosachic. These villagers, mostly Tarahumara Indians, had fought Apaches for generations. As vaqueros, they had honed such skills as riding, tracking, roping, and herding, leaving them well suited to confront the Apache in his terrain. These towns were "independent, self sufficient, and open to individual achievement." This atmosphere fostered an emphasis on duty, bravery, and honor, turning "peasants into warriors," in the words of one borderland's historian. "Masculine valor and military prowess became a source of rights and privileges as well as status and honor." From these opportunities, natural leaders emerged, men eager to receive recognition, rights, and privileges. The Tarahumaras, inveterate foes of the Apaches, earned prestige by waging punitive campaigns. When their tribal members encountered Apaches, fierce fighting usually resulted because neither side gave any quarter.[44]

The battleground in the late 1870s was the district of Sahuaripa, which was the center of Juh's activity. The town lay in the middle of a fertile valley surrounded by fields of corn with a stream running through its center. It boasted a population of about two thousand people and a public school of seventy-eight students. It was also the political and military headquarters for the district. Its national troops, however, faced a constant problem endemic to all of Sonora's frontier communities—inadequate arms and ammunition. The small towns, ranches, and mines in this mountainous district proved to be lucrative Nednhi raiding targets through the years. Consequently, the town could report only four working ranches; five were deserted because of "Apache incursions."[45]

Juh had several advantages: ever vigilant in his mountain fastness, he was fighting a guerilla war on his terms using the element of surprise, superior weapons, and better mounts. It is easy to imagine how a band of forty to fifty men and young warriors could terrorize a sparsely settled area. In the last two weeks of May 1877, a raiding party attacked travelers and ranches in the district of Sahuaripa, killing fifteen persons. By the first week of June, the raiders had returned to their ranchería at Guaynopa.[46] From this base two weeks later, Juh launched another deadly assault against the district of Sahuaripa.

On June 21, 1877, a war party of twenty-five Apaches, armed with "rifles and carbines," assaulted six people near Guadalupe, a mining town forty miles south of Sahuaripa. They took fourteen mules, killed three men, and wounded two women. By the next morning, the Nednhis, now reported at thirty men, had moved northeast about twenty-five miles to Tarichi, an agricultural center of five hundred residents. About 9:00 A.M., they ambushed a wagon train of thirty people and wounded several during a two-hour fight. To save themselves, the Sonorans abandoned everything, leaving thirty head of stock and their wagons in the hands of the Indians. A week later Juh's war party, now estimated at forty men, had secreted themselves northeast of Sahuaripa along a trail that led to Nácori Chico. Here they hit their third group of travelers, a seventeen-person caravan destined for Sahuaripa from Nácori Chico. Two men and one woman were slain in the assault, and the Indians took everything, stock and provisions.[47] Satisfied with their booty, the Nednhis returned to their rancherías at Guaynopa. Considering they were flush with supplies and stock, and living as free Apaches with freedom's inherent risks, one wonders if they would have traded positions with their brethren, who were then living on half-rations at San Carlos.

A short time after the last attack, the prefect of Sahuaripa, Señor M. Cuen, lamented to the governor that he had to delay his pursuit for a day until he could round up enough serviceable weapons to arm his national troops. The Apaches' weapons were far superior to those of his men. He pleaded: "We need help and better arms, especially repeating rifles." For the next two months,

Juh left the district of Sahuaripa alone. On August 3, 1877, Cuen informed his superiors that the Apaches "have not been seen in this district the previous month."[48]

After a quiet July in the Sierra Madre, Juh made plans for an incursion against Chihuahua. Details are sparse, but piecing together various accounts suggests that his war party, which may have included Pionsenay's and Nolgee's groups, killed twenty citizens and stole "a great deal of stock" in the district of Galeana. When one hundred soldiers pursued them in mid-August, Juh's war party waylaid them, slaying twenty-seven and putting the balance to flight.[49]

The Chiricahuas again divided: Nolgee and Pionsenay headed north and crossed into Arizona, destined for San Carlos. Juh returned to Guaynopa and lay low for a while. In mid-September, he sent raiding parties into the districts of Moctezuma and Sahuaripa. Their objective was stock and loot for the coming winter. After a two-and-a-half month period of no raiding in Sahuaripa, the prefect received news that Apaches had attacked and wounded two men near the Chipajora ranch, about fifteen miles north of Sahuaripa. At once Prefect Cuen sent a party of thirty-two nationals under Lieutenant Francisco Quijada, with orders to pursue the trail unless the Indians outnumbered his force. In that event, he was to return to Sahuaripa for reinforcements. Then the prefect would lead the campaign. Quijada found out that one survivor, Manuel Hurtado, had seen only six Apaches, but he believed others had remained hidden. Quijada easily followed the trail, which was marked by butchered cattle, before returning to Sahuaripa. Meanwhile, Cuen, anticipating another reign of Apache terror, had given the governor an ominous prediction: the raids of the previous June had terrorized the citizens in his district; if the state was unable to protect them, many settlers were prepared to abandon the district for safer parts.[50]

A week later Cuen sent another pressing appeal: "These savages have invaded this district from all directions." Cuen summoned the military and political leaders from the towns in his district to a meeting scheduled at Sahuaripa for October 5, 1877. They resolved to ask the governor for troops, arms, and provisions. Even before the conference took place, more reports of Apache atrocities had filtered in to the prefect. On September 29, 1877, Apaches had assaulted a ranch near Tarichi. Three Indians were involved in a hand-to-hand fight with Antonio Cruz and his wife, Dolores. While the latter was wrestling with one Apache, a second Indian shot her in the head. Other vaqueros hastened to the ranch and drove off the Indians. The initial reports praised the brave Dolores Cruz, saying that the bullet "did not seem to affect her brain and we hope she will live." Her husband sent two messengers to warn a nearby ranch, but the Nednhis ambushed them, killing both. They also discovered the body of a third man, Antonio Coronado. Two days later, Apaches, perhaps the same party, assaulted a group of eleven travelers about thirty-five miles south of Sahuaripa, killing one and seriously wounding two others.[51]

Between October 1876 and October 1877, Juh's band killed thirty-nine men and wounded twenty-one in the district of Sahuaripa alone. This represented 63 percent of those killed by Apaches in Sonora during this one-year period.[52]

Cuen's appeals stirred Sonora's governor into action. He passed Cuen's note along to Jesús García Morales, a veteran commander of the Cochise Wars. By this time, Morales had decided to launch a campaign, but, according to Sonora's vice governor Francisco Serna, it would be against Apaches who had invaded Sonora from the San Carlos Reservation.[53]

This statement reflected the common sentiment among Sonora's political leaders living in Hermosillo and Ures. After 1870 they always blamed their Apache problems on the United States, even when it was undeniable that those who had carried out these depredations were living within Sonora's borders. In fact, after the closing of the Chiricahua and Ojo Caliente reservations in 1876 and 1877, Apaches never used any Arizona reservations as a base for raids into Mexico. Local officials in Sonora's northeastern frontier understood this. American military leaders felt hamstrung because there was no agreement between the United States and Mexico allowing them to hunt down those Chiricahuas who had sought refuge in Mexico rather than go to San Carlos.

On October 22, 1877, a small Mexican patrol found an abandoned ranchería (its wickiups still standing), undoubtedly Juh's, northeast of Nácori Chico. From the signs, the commander concluded that the Nednhis had left two or three days before. On October 23, 1877, another patrol of forty-five troops left Bavispe bound for Guaynopa. En route, the commander cut a large trail of Apaches moving north. It divided into several trails, all converging near the Carcay Mountains, twenty-five miles southwest of Janos. North of Guaynopa, Captain Adrian Maldoñado, another Apache-wise commander who had fought Cochise in the Dragoon Mountains in 1870, also picked up a trail of two hundred Indians who were driving cattle toward the Carcay Mountains.[54] It appears that most of the hostile Chiricahuas, between 250 and 300 Nednhis, Chokonens, and Bedonkohes under Juh, Nolgee, and Pionsenay, had joined forces and opened negotiations at Janos.[55]

Nolgee and Pionsenay probably made their first contacts at Janos in October. The people of Janos knew both chiefs, and Pionsenay had served as a peace envoy for Cochise in 1872.[56] Chihuahua's governor, Angel Trias, Jr., whose father had been governor in the early 1850s, named Ramon Lujan as peace commissioner. Trias gave him full discretion either to make war or to make peace, "if it is possible."[57]

Meanwhile, on November 10, 1877, the large Chiricahua village had moved from the Carcay Mountains to a canyon near Casa de Janos, a long-deserted ranch, eighteen miles southwest of Janos. The next morning most of the men went to Janos, undoubtedly bringing stock and other Sonoran loot to barter with their longtime trading partners. What happened next at Janos is unclear. Lujan, the peace commissioner, had apparently not yet arrived. After a conference with local officials, the Chiricahuas suspended talks and headed for their camp.

As they approached their village, however, they espied Mexican troops from Sonora, poised to strike their village. The commander, José Vasquez, with forty men from Bavispe, had followed a fresh trail of forty Apaches driving one hundred head of cattle to the mouth of the canyon. From eight hundred yards away, he could see wickiups and the stock grazing nearby. As he prepared to strike the Apache camp, a sentry saw them and alerted the camp. The Apaches fled to the nearby hills. Before Vasquez could occupy the camp, he saw a cloud of dust and riders coming from the east. Assuming they were troops from Janos, he delayed his assault, took one man, and rode out to meet them. He got more than he had bargained for. The horsemen turned out to be fifty to sixty Chiricahuas led by Pionsenay, Juh, and Nolgee.

The Indians fired on Vasquez and his companion, who reversed direction and galloped back to their men. While he was in flight, an Indian bullet shredded Vasquez's reins, forcing him to dismount. His men joined him, and a general skirmish followed with heavy shooting but few casualties. Vasquez said that he drove the warriors into the hills.

The Chiricahuas' concern was their women and children. They had outflanked the Sonorans, gathered up their camp possessions, stock, and families, and headed northeast toward the Espuelas Mountains (Spur Mountains). Vasquez's only consolation came after the battle, when his men found the body of a Chiricahua left on the battleground.[58] Although he did not know the identity of his victim, this was likely the corpse of Pionsenay, the incorrigible fugitive and murderer who had caused so much trouble the previous twenty months. Vasquez's men took his scalp. The Chiricahuas later admitted to a loss of two men, including Pionsenay.[59]

Juh, Nolgee, and Broaches, Pionsenay's successor, took their people to Espuelas Mountains, which the Apaches called Dzilnde-z, "Long Mountain" because of its narrow length, which ran from northeast to southwest. They referred to one stronghold on the eastern side of this range as Tsesl-ja-si-kaat, "Rocks Brown in a Bunch," which lay on a high mesa protected by rocky ridges. This range also afforded the Indians easy access to Guadalupe Canyon if they needed to cross the border to avoid Mexican patrols. The chiefs decided to find out how their relatives at San Carlos were faring.

At San Carlos, Agent Hart was eager to get the hostiles onto the reservation, but he needed a liaison, and much to his delight, he had discovered that two Chiricahua leaders were just as eager to help bring their kinfolk in. In early December, Hart sent two Chiricahua chiefs, possibly Nahilzay and Gordo, a relative of Juh, to make contact with the hostiles. At Ash Springs they found a party of thirty-five Chiricahuas (eight Chokonens and twenty-seven Nednhis), led by Broaches, Juh, and Nolgee. At first all agreed to surrender if Hart would meet them at Ash Springs. Elated over this positive development, Hart left the agency on December 10, 1877; when he arrived at the springs, however, he found that only Broaches and seven Chokonens had remained. Juh and Nolgee had returned to Mexico.[60] This was the third time in the previous six months that Nolgee had flirted with the idea of surrendering at San Carlos. Why he never consummated these impulses remains a mystery; likely, he feared the Americans would imprison him as they had other captives. Though the Nednhis remained free, their independence would come at a tremendous toll.

6

THE COST OF FREEDOM

Chief Juh knew more about those mountains [Sierra Madre] than any other man.

Jason Betzinez, second cousin of Geronimo

After reneging on their agreement to meet Agent Hart at Ash Springs, Juh, Nolgee, and twenty-five warriors headed south toward their ranchería in the Guadalupe Mountains. About December 10, 1877, near Ash Springs, they captured a wagon train of supplies that had left Fort Bayard for Globe City. While looting the train, which consisted of clothing, flour, and liquor, Nolgee killed one teenage Mexican boy because he "would not stop howling." He released the others. Then his band divided. One group raided ranches along the Gila for horses; others continued south and killed a mail rider near Steins Peak.[1]

Hart had telegraphed the particulars to General Kautz, suggesting that he dispatch troops to intercept the Nednhis. The agent had already ordered Sweeney and Dan Ming to take his sixteen-man Apache police force to pursue the hostiles. They followed the trail south, reaching Fort Bowie by December 13, 1877. With them was one Chiricahua, identified only as Juh's brother, who had agreed to serve as guide. By this time Kautz had ordered troops from Grant and Thomas to unite with Sweeney's force. But their efforts fell flat. That same day Lieutenant Tony Rucker had picked up a trail of three Nednhis at Ralston Flats, about fifty miles east of Bowie.[2]

The persistent Rucker had left Bowie on November 27, 1877. He vowed to punish the Apaches, even if it meant crossing the border, where he thought, "the renegade Chiricahuas had their homes." Taking a pack train with forty days' rations, and twenty troopers from the Sixth Cavalry, his Indian scouts, and Lieutenant Timothy A. Touey from Camp Grant, Rucker headed south

107

toward San Bernardino, and then crossed the border into Sonora. At Alisos Canyon, he met Mexican troops from Fronteras under Colonel Angel Elías, who told Rucker that his force had followed a fresh trail of Chiricahuas north along the east side of the Guadalupe Mountains.

Rucker invited Elías to join his command, but the dutiful Sonoran commander "decided not to, saying that he had no orders to cross the border." Elías disregarded Rucker's illegal presence in northeastern Sonora. Military and civil officials living along the frontier were indifferent to the national controversy brewing between federal officials in Mexico City and Washington. Elías understood that any success achieved by Rucker would weaken the Chiricahuas and thus save Sonoran lives. Therefore, Colonel Elías tacitly supported their presence.[3]

Moving north into New Mexico, Rucker's Apache scouts picked up Juh's trail, "thought to be 5 or 6 days old." A week later near Ralston Flats, a few miles south of today's Lordsburg, the scouts discovered three Chiricahuas "preparing dinner and endeavoring to dry out their plunder, which was spread about near the water-hole." The scouts immediately attacked, killing one and wounding another. The two Chiricahuas fled south while the scouts collected the plunder: two mules, one horse, saddles, and merchandise from the looted wagon train. Rucker was unhappy that his scouts were more concerned with gathering plunder than following the two escaped warriors; their avarice, ironically, would pay dividends.

Rucker's scouts easily found the trail, which led to the Animas Mountains and to San Luis Pass. South lay Mexico, but that failed to deter Rucker. He forged south into the Espuelas Mountains, where the scouts found the Nednhi camp during the afternoon of December 17. After leaving a detail to protect his pack train, Rucker, a few soldiers, Jack Dunn, and twenty-five Apache scouts armed with Springfield rifles and fifty rounds of ammunition "toiled forward all night over the roughest country imaginable." By dawn, December 18, 1877, the command was in position. They had surrounded the ranchería as "completely as possible."

As the village began to stir, Rucker's men poured a devastating fire on Juh's village, which contained thirty-nine wickiups and about 150 persons. Pandemonium ruled the camp, as the Apaches swarmed out from their wickiups, their weapons in hand, trying to find cover. They fought valiantly until they evacuated their woman and children, who seemed to melt into the rocks, escaping through ravines and canyons. After occupying the ranchería, Rucker's force found fifteen bodies and captured one young girl left behind in the confusion. They confiscated all the Indians' possessions, including sixty horses and mules, fifty saddles, food, clothing, and other property. Rucker's scouts, who kept the stock and plunder, had inflicted a demoralizing loss on Juh.[4]

For the second time in less than a year, Rucker, with the invaluable service of the Western Apache scouts, had defeated the Chiricahuas. This time he had struck them in a stronghold they had long considered secure, a canyon on the eastern side of the Espuelas Mountains of northern Sonora, about ten or twelve miles south of the border. The victory was a tribute to Rucker's leadership ability, his determination, and his faith in his Western Apache scouts. Juh and Nolgee had not realized that an American force had illegally crossed the border in pursuit. And the Western Apache scouts deserved enormous credit. Though unfamiliar with the area, they were experts at reading sign and following a trail. These are the reasons Rucker was successful. Campaigns such as these earned him the reputation of a dogged and fearless commander—a man admired by his contemporaries, including the Apache scouts who served with him. Unfortunately, eight months later, Rucker, making a valiant attempt to rescue his friend Lieutenant Austin Henely from raging waters, drowned (with Henely) in a flash flood in a canyon in the southern part of the Chiricahua Mountains that today bears his name.

Meanwhile, the Chokonens that Mrs. Stanley was with had seen Rucker's command as they passed through the Animas Mountains. Many of his scouts were White Mountain Apaches, kinfolk of Mrs. Stanley, who had enlisted to free her. The two Chokonen men with her had "circled about [Rucker's] camp, but they were not seen at all." They overheard the White Mountain sergeant addressing his scouts: "If you shoot some Chiricahuas be sure and call out the name of that woman, she might be around there and be sure not to shoot her, please." When the two men returned, they told Mrs. Stanley that if the scouts attacked their camp, "then you will be shot by us first."

Her small group contemplated joining Juh's band in the Espuelas Mountains, but fortunately for them, they had had second thoughts and stayed in the Animas Mountains for a while. By doing so, they had avoided Rucker's attack on Juh's camp. Mrs. Stanley recalled,

> If we had gone down to the other place, we would have been killed [for] sure, for all those Chiricahuas were killed down there. When we finally did go there, they were all gone. We passed through where those people had been killed. Their clothes were still piled up there. The men said that they wanted to see the place where all the people

had been killed so they told us to go to one side while they went there. When they got back they told us, "there are a lot of dead people still lying there."

They called the names of the dead ones and said this man, and that man, and so on.[5] Then while we camped there those two men went back over there to where the place was and buried just their own kin, taking them up in the crevices of the rock and laying them there; but the rest, not kin to them, they just left the way they were.[6]

After Rucker's attack, the Nednhis met at some predetermined location before beginning their journey south into the Sierra Madre. Juh had to exercise care in moving his women and children to a secure place, and Guaynopa was the logical choice. A patrol from Bavispe followed two trails of Nednhis (one of thirty-five persons and another much larger) from Espuelas Mountains through Huergas Canyon to the Teras range. Elías sent a second patrol toward the Carcay Mountains to see whether Juh had retired there to open negotiations at Janos. Not finding any fresh signs, Lieutenant Jesús Escalante was confident the Indians were returning to Guaynopa. Colonel Angel Elías informed the governor that he would assemble a force of seventy men to examine Guaynopa. And, in case Juh reversed directions and headed for the border, Elías decided to station troops near Carretas and Ojitos to wait in ambush.[7]

Juh dispatched raiding parties to replace the stock, provisions, and camp equipment lost during Rucker's attack. On January 15, 1878, his warriors jumped a freight train, killing one man and wounding two others near Oputo. But the supply train eventually arrived at Bacadéhuachi with the supplies Juh's people needed. A week later they killed a man and wounded the son of Colonel Cayetano Sánchez near Moctezuma. On February 1, 1878, two Nednhi raiding parties struck on the same day, though some sixty miles apart. Southeast of Tepache, Indians attacked a convoy of fifteen persons who were returning with supplies to Batuc from Huásabas. During the attack, the Nednhis killed Julian Peralta, captured three mules, and burned the wagons after emptying their contents. Peralta's friends watched helplessly from their positions behind breastworks. That same day, another Nednhi raiding party assaulted the isolated Teópare ranch, some thirty miles southwest of Guaynopa. Located on the site of an old Spanish mission, the ranch stood on a mesa overlooking the west bank of the Teópare River, which flowed north into the Aros River. Below the ranch stretched a large valley of palm trees. The Indians burned the ranch, killing José Torres and two vaqueros. Juh now had much needed supplies.[8]

Two Nednhi raiding parties left Guaynopa in March. The first band, after establishing a base camp some twenty-five miles northeast of Tepache, crossed the Moctezuma River and headed southwest toward Ures. Streeter may have also been along, for eyewitnesses saw an American with the Apaches during this foray. About mid-March 1878, they struck two ranches near Ures, carrying away two boys, one about five and the second about seven. Hoping to lure out a rescue party in each case, they took their captives one hundred yards from the ranch. Yet no one dared come to their aid, so the Indians simply killed them. Next they assaulted the Tierras Negras hacienda, killing one man.

Toward the end of March, Chiricahuas surprised two vaqueros at a ranch near Mazacahui, twenty miles northeast of Ures. Less than one-quarter mile away, the vaqueros' partner, Jesús Delgado, who had taken cover in the grass, felt powerless while he watched the Indians slay his two friends. Suddenly, one Apache spotted a cow near Delgado and rode straight toward him. As the Apache flourished a lance in his free hand and approached the cow, Delgado ambushed him, but his first shot missed his target. The Chiricahua then charged Delgado, whose second bullet ripped into the Indian's stomach, knocking him from the horse. Delgado then hastened to the ranch, gathered reinforcements, and returned to the scene later that day, where they unexpectedly found the corpse of the Indian. Delgado took the scalp and proudly brought the trophy to Ures, where the governor rewarded him with fifty pesos. *La Era Nueva* lauded Delgado's "tremendous bravery," describing it as a "very good act."[9]

Meanwhile, in the last two weeks of March, a second group of raiders killed twelve people (though details are sparse), most of them from Oputo and Nácori Chico, in the district of Moctezuma.[10] These two towns, which lay in fertile valleys surrounded by the Sierra Madre, had populations of 508 and 276 respectively. Its residents were trying to eke out an existence despite the mortal fear. But the citizens of Nácori Chico, where most families had suffered a loss of at least one male during the Apache Wars, were ready to call it quits and abandon the town.[11]

In mid-April, two raiding parties struck the districts of Ures and Sahuaripa. On April 15 Indians assaulted a ranch near Mátape, killing two men and wounding a woman, who claimed that she saw an American directing the movements. If so, this was undoubtedly Streeter. A few days later, this party attacked a ranch north of Ures, making off with several head of stock. National Guard troops followed their trail, which led north along the Sonora River, but were unable to overtake them. Simultaneous to this raid, on April 21, 1878, near Tacupeto, seventeen miles south of Sahuaripa, Indians "in considerable numbers" attacked a mule train, taking most of the mules and provisions. Six days later, this band stole forty to fifty mules from another ranch, between Tacupeto and Tarichi.[12]

Sonora's military was active that winter, though with mixed results. García Morales led a patrol from Bavispe that searched the country between there and Janos, scouting Carretas, Casa de Janos, and the Carcay Mountains, but found only a horse abandoned by the Indians the previous November. It became clear to him that the Apaches were farther south in the Sierra Madre. Meanwhile, National Guard soldiers from Aconchi achieved a minor victory in mid-April when they located a temporary Apache camp some twenty-five miles northeast of Tepache. This was a holding area, to which the raiders returned with their stolen stock and loot. About April 20, 1878, the Aconchi nationals surprised the village of seven wickiups and killed one woman, captured a boy about four years old, and recovered some stock.[13]

This victory, small as it was, buoyed the spirits and confidence of General García Morales, even though Sonora's politicians and press were beginning to question his tactics. Timely intelligence and accurate information were his two pressing concerns. The Apaches' guerilla warfare had forced him to assume a defensive posture. It was unlikely that his troops would ever celebrate a victory such as the one Rucker and his Apache scouts had enjoyed. The only way to catch Juh's resourceful band was to surprise them in camp. The playing field was not equal, and Juh had the advantage. A good offense could usually exploit the weakness of a good defense because the former knew where it was going and thus could avoid the latter's strategy.

But the venerated García Morales did respond to the intelligence at hand, partially restoring the confidence of Sonora's frontier leaders and the editors of the state's press. In late March he had announced plans to move troops from the northern frontier to Sahuaripa. In May, responding to warnings that the citizens of Nácori Chico were thinking of abandoning their town, he moved his most capable officer, Colonel Angel Elías, and thirty-four dragoons to that town. Authorities at Nácori Chico postponed the mass exodus, at least for then.[14]

At this time *Boletin Oficial* published an editorial entitled "The Apache War," which not only was an honest appraisal of the current situation but also included progressive recommendations to solve the problem. The Apaches, as they had a century before, remained impediments to progress, especially to those towns in and around the Sierra Madre Mountains, "where their rancherías are probably located." This was a revealing admission. For the first time since the establishment of the Chiricahua Reservation in October 1872, Sonoran officials were acknowledging that their enemies were the Apaches living in the Sierra Madre rather than those residing on reservations in the United States. In conclusion, the editors recommended two important changes: first, relocate the border presidios from Santa Cruz and Fronteras (formerly thought to be the first line of defense against Arizona Apaches) to Sahuaripa and Carretas; second, permit the troops along the northeastern border to cooperate with United States forces stationed at Guadalupe Canyon and San Bernardino.[15]

This editorial was the work of Sonora's Ismael S. Quiroga, who spoke for many Sonorans when he pointed out to federal officials in Mexico City that Sonora, not the federal government, was responsible for defeating the Apaches. Because Sonoran officials understood Apaches, it should set its own policies based on what worked along its frontier. Moreover, Quiroga pushed for closer ties with Arizona as a means to achieve victory. Of course, federal officials in Mexico City probably choked when they heard that proposal. The United States had dragged its feet in recognizing the new administration of Porfirio Díaz. Most Mexican officials remained dubious of American motives, believing that their avaricious Yankee neighbors wished only to annex more of Mexico's northern regions.[16]

On March 5, 1878, General Orlando B. Willcox, Twelfth Infantry, relieved General Kautz from command of the military department of Arizona. Almost immediately, Willcox set out two priorities. First, he established Camp Supply in the lower Chiricahuas as a base from which the Apache scout companies (Rucker's and Henely's units) could patrol the border. Second, he wrote Governor Mariscal in Sonora, using as liaison the noted Tucson merchant Estevan Ochoa. Willcox outlined his plans to secure the border, and Mariscal responded with a pledge to keep him informed about Apache activities in Sonora. On April 27, 1878, Willcox lamented to Ochoa, who passed the letter on to Mariscal, that the "Indians are like pirates and I am only sorry that in driving them from our soil such as we have we cannot pursue them across the line to either capture or kill them . . . and so rid both nations of the bandits and murderers."[17]

At this time a similar situation along the Rio Grande in Texas threatened to explode into war with Mexico, but the local commanders, General Edward Ord and General Geronimo Trevino, worked diligently with each other to prevent an international incident. After the United States (in the summer of 1878) recognized Porfirio Díaz as the legitimate ruler of Mexico, he revealed that the senate had authorized him the previous May to sign a reciprocal crossing agreement with the United States. But he refused to make it law until the United States revoked an order signed by President Rutherford B. Hayes authorizing General Ord to pursue bandits and Indians into Mexico to protect American citizens, property, or interests. Díaz opposed this on principle, seeing it as a violation of Mexico's sovereignty.[18] Sonoran political leaders feared Apaches more than they feared Americans; federal officials in Mexico City feared American expansionism more than Apache raids.

In the late spring of 1878, the Nednhis continued to raid Sonoran settlements. On May 22, one war party, generously estimated at one hundred warriors (probably thirty to forty at most), attacked two men herding two hundred cattle near Mulatos, a mining town about seventy-five miles southeast of Sahuaripa near the Chihuahua border. They stole the herd and, before leaving, killed Antonio Arenas and wounded Jesús Monge. Two weeks later, on June 5, 1878, six Apaches ambushed Raphael Corona near Bacanora, ten miles southeast of Sahuaripa. After killing him, they retired to the hills near the town. Fifteen nationals, most unarmed, went on a fruitless pursuit. In mid-June, another raiding party, probably unaware that García Morales had ordered Colonel Elías and one company of presidio troops to garrison Nácori Chico, harassed the town. Elías, with forty-six men and six pack mules, found the tracks that led south about twenty-five miles before turning east. Elías crossed the Aros River and continued his march east toward Guaynopa, where on June 20 he came upon a trail of seventy to eighty Apaches with their families. Short of provisions, he returned to Nácori Chico, vowing to launch another campaign to Guaynopa.[19]

As usual, Juh was one move ahead of his Sonoran counterparts. In mid-1878 he left his stronghold at Guaynopa. His followers had slain seventeen people in the district of Sahuaripa that year. Though Prefect Cuen at Sahuaripa could not have known, Juh would leave his district alone until the fall. It was undoubtedly a welcome respite. In July, Juh rejoined Nolgee in the mountains west of Janos. They soon sent emissaries to Janos, requesting a truce with Chihuahua. Perhaps they meant it; likely, they wanted to trade some of their stock and loot taken in Sonora. They hoped their overtures had delayed any campaigns from Chihuahua while they gathered much needed seeds, nuts, fruits, and berries. They encamped near the Carcay Mountains and at Casa de Janos.[20]

Meanwhile, at San Carlos, despite his good intentions and promising start, Agent Hart was not devoting sufficient time and effort to the Apaches there. Instead, much of his focus, which should have been directed at carrying out his responsibility as agent for some 5,000 Apaches (which included the Yavapais who were not Athapaskans), was spent in acquiring and then developing mines that were either on the reservation or near its boundary. Before coming to Arizona, he lived near Socorro, New Mexico, where he had been involved in several mining ventures with a man called the Professor, whose real name was Percival Stockman. Within a few months of accepting the position as agent, Hart hired Stockman and his own brother as employees of the agency. His brother did little, if any, work, and Stockman concentrated on developing mining interests for him and Hart, even though he was on the payroll as issue clerk. Hart clandestinely furnished him supplies (corn, sugar, flour, and coffee) from the warehouse at San Carlos so he could carry out their joint ventures.[21]

By early 1878 Hart began to complain about insufficient food and inadequate funding. When E. B. French, who worked in the Second Auditor's Office, the agency empowered to review vouchers and expenses of Indian agents, questioned several of Hart's expenditures, the commissioner of Indian affairs responded that he regarded Hart "as an honest and careful official." Another visitor, E. F. Ferry, the brother of Senator T. W. Ferry, praised Hart, believing he was a man of "efficiency, integrity, sobriety, and Christian principles." Yet he was unaware that Hart made decisions to protect his interests and to improve his own finances. For instance, Hart bragged that several hundred Indians were always off the reservation, foraging in the mountains for native foods. To Hart, this meant extras he could sell to mining camps or use to support his own ventures. The interests of the Apaches had become secondary to his own insidious greed.[22]

In January 1878 Lieutenant Abbot, the honorable officer who had defended Jeffords from Vandever's charges, had an argument with Agent Hart. Abbot accused Hart of making "libelous statements" about him and requested that his superiors release him "from duties at San Carlos on account of their disagreeable nature." He also requested a court of inquiry, though his commander may not have seen any reason to clear his impeccable reputation. Within a day, Abbot's superiors relieved him from duty at San Carlos. Lieutenant Austin Henely replaced Abbot on February 8. Moreover, when the War Department transferred General Kautz in March, the military began to assume a less conspicuous role as inspector at San Carlos. On March 10, Henely reported that contractors had furnished their last supplies for the fiscal year (except beef) and asked permission to return to Camp Thomas.[23]

That winter Hart convinced some Apaches, including one hundred Chiricahuas under Geronimo and Naiche, to dig irrigation ditches. Yet, the Indians lacked tools, and the few that Hart supplied, along with the seeds, came too late for the planting season. One traveler who had observed the Chiricahuas was impressed with their behavior and efforts to farm despite "working under great disadvantages." Because the Indian department had not authorized Hart to purchase tools, the Chiricahuas were forced to dig "with sticks, and with baskets of their own making are carrying and throwing the dirt and gravel out of ditches."[24]

In early April, Indian Inspector E. C. Watkins arrived at San Carlos and visited the Chiricahuas, whose diligence and hard work impressed him:

> I came to a band of Chiricahua Indians at work opening up a large ditch from the Gila River for irrigation purposes. Men, women, and children were at work. Many of them with their hands scraped the dirt into baskets. I found three shovels among the entire party [which] consisted of at least 100. . . . I had a talk with them. They tell of the stone which General Howard planted on the mesa when they made peace and how he told them as long as the stone lasted the peace should remain unbroken. They speak in high terms of their new agent [and] ask for more farming tools.[25]

When General Willcox met Hart at Camp Thomas, he heard the same complaint from the agent. The Apaches needed tools, but Hart had no authorization to purchase them. Willcox cut through the bureaucracy and ordered the post commander to give the Indians any farming equipment that the army had condemned.[26]

Hart also faced the inevitable problem of undependable suppliers and inadequate rations. In February he was forced to put the Indians on half-rations; he also inaugurated a system by which he would issue rations only to those Indians who were present at the agency. A man could no longer receive rations for his family; each member had to be present. To make amends for this reduction in food, Hart issued passes that allowed Indians to move into the mountains to hunt and gather, which gave the agent less control over his wards. In the third week of July, Hart advised Governor John P. Hoyt, General Willcox, and the commissioner of Indian affairs, Ezra A. Hayt, that he was "out of supplies." He therefore requested authority to purchase food on the open market. The commanding officer at Camp Grant warned that the Indians were "uneasy and restless." Willcox again stepped in and authorized the release of fourteen thousand pounds of flour to the agent. And Hart's superiors in Washington immediately wired funds so that Hart could purchase beef.[27]

These measures helped to avert a minor crisis, but a potentially larger one loomed on the horizon. A rumor circulated in mid-June that one hundred Apaches had left the reservation, but the *Arizona Silver Belt*, published in Globe, discounted it: "The pets were never more friendly to the white man than now."[28]

Yet the newspaper had no way of knowing that one band of "pets," namely the Chokonens under Naiche, were then confronting a major epidemic brought on by an invisible assailant. Despite the unhealthy reputation of the Gila lowlands near the subagency and at Goodwin Wash, often called a "black hole" because of stagnant water and mosquitoes, it appears, based on the scant available census information, that the Chokonens had miraculously avoided catastrophic illness during their first two years at San Carlos. In fact, the records suggest they incurred no significant loss of life attributable to disease during this time span. The 322 individuals brought to the reservation by Taza in 1876 had increased to about 360 in the spring of 1878, when they faced a deadly enemy, malaria, for the first time.

Scientists had not yet discovered the relationship between mosquitoes and malaria, which struck the Chokonens living along the low-level marshes of the Gila flats, which were havens for the disease-infested mosquito larvae. With no immunity and little or no experience with the disease, the Apaches succumbed quickly. They naturally preferred treatment from their own medicine man. Yet, they had no means of dealing with a disease that attacked the red blood cells and left victims with flulike symptoms such as fevers, chills, headaches, and frequent vomiting. Without treatment, the infected person usually died within a few weeks. Eve Ball's Apache informants saw relatives and friends die of malaria at San Carlos.[29] As Asa Daklugie described it,

> At San Carlos for the first time within the memory of any of my people, the Apaches experienced the shaking sickness. Our Medicine Men knew of herbs that would reduce bodily temperature but had nothing effective against the strange and weakening attacks that caused people to alternately suffer from heat and cold. At times attacks came that caused people with high temperatures to feel cold and shake uncontrollably while covered with blankets. And this sickness sometimes lasted for weeks unless the patient died.[30]

Agent Hart addressed this problem in an October 1878 letter, when he conceded that he had permitted some four hundred to six hundred Indians

(Chiricahuas and White Mountain) to move into the mountains to gather wild foods and "recover from sickness caused by malaria in the valleys."[31] Yet he minimized the toll, especially the cost in lives incurred by the Apaches from the "shaking sickness." Of course, as agent he was not about to admit that the population of his wards was falling because he feared that his superiors would cut his budget accordingly. This would not be the last time that Naiche's people would confront this lethal disease, which took the lives of some fifty to sixty Chokonens in the late spring of 1878.

A result of Hart's permitting the Indians to leave the subagency to gather wild fruits and vegetables and to hunt game was a newfound independence for the Chiricahuas. Many moved about fifteen miles southwest to Black Rock in the Santa Teresa Mountains. From this secluded area, with little oversight by the subagent, they were free to conduct their business as they saw fit. And once they obtained corn, either by trade or as part of their rations, they began making tiswin. To his credit, Clum had virtually eliminated this practice during his regime. His Indian police had actively "sought out and destroyed tiswin stills, arrested the makers of the tiswin, and put them in the guardhouse." By late summer 1878, Eskiminzin admitted to former agent John Clum that the practice had again become widespread: "Now tiswin is freely made and freely drunk and much drunkenness prevails among the Indians." Hart, refuting Clum's assertion, said that Eskiminzin denied making the statement to Clum. According to the agent, "no tiswin is allowed to be made or drunk."[32] Of course, Hart neglected to mention the role that tiswin had played in Geronimo's escape two months before.

The Apaches' right to make tiswin, and the problems that often resulted, inevitably led to trouble. It was the reason Geronimo left San Carlos in the summer of 1878. Jason Betzinez, who was not there (he was at Ojo Caliente with Victorio and Loco), heard about the affair. By combining his account with a report written five days later by George Smerdon, the acting agent at San Carlos in Hart's absence, we can reconstruct the events of the evening of August 1, 1878.

Both accounts agree that one of Geronimo's party became inebriated and then committed suicide. Betzinez erroneously believed that Geronimo's camp was north of Camp Thomas; actually, it was at Black Rock, southwest of the subagency. Smerdon simply wrote, "One Indian being drunk committed suicide." Betzinez was more specific: "While they were drinking intoxicating liquor, Geronimo began scolding his nephew, for no reason at all. This disturbed the nephew so much that he killed himself." Angie Debo thought that the boy was a son of Nana, but he and his family were under guard at Ojo Caliente with most of the Chihennes.[33] In any event, Betzinez and Smerdon both said that Geronimo left after the death. The date was August 2, 1878.[34]

Betzinez believed that Geronimo was remorseful; Smerdon concluded that Geronimo, knowing "that he could not hide the fact of his having made tiswin and was afraid of being put in the guard house here, he concluded to leave the reserve, and done so, taking with him his three wives and two children, *but no men*. The party only numbering six in all." His Chiricahua sources told him that Geronimo "was not likely to join the Bronchos [Nednhis] for some time, his idea being to keep away . . . until the tiswin trouble has passed." But Clum's incarceration remained indelibly etched in his mind. As usual, he consulted his Power, and it told him to run rather than trust American justice. He would not chance his freedom.[35]

Once Geronimo made his decision, he led his family into the Peloncillo Mountains and took the old Apache corridor south into Mexico. As luck would have it, he found Juh in the Carcay Mountains. It must have been a joyful reunion. The two men had much to discuss, for they had not seen each other for almost eighteen months. Geronimo brought the Nednhi leaders up to date with affairs at San Carlos.[36]

At this time, Juh was waiting to hear from the Mexicans at Janos. He had sent emissaries to Janos in early August. The military commander met the envoys, whose sincerity impressed him, so he recommended to Angel Trias, Chihuahua's governor, that they conclude a treaty.[37] Mexico's federal Indian policy prohibited the establishment of reservations. Its goal was assimilation for those Indians open to changing their ways and extermination for those who refused. Governor Trias's administration had just begun to fall out of favor. Hurt by a poor crop harvest in 1877 and Apache raids in the northwestern frontier, he had angered the business community by imposing new taxes, eliminating opposition in the state legislature, and imprisoning his former political opponent.[38] Thus conditions were ripe for another ascent to power of Luis Terrazas, whose cousin Joaquin was the state's premier Indian fighter. In response to Juh's offer, Trias made a counterproposal, which, in effect, doomed any hopes for peace.

The terms first negotiated at Janos mirrored those armistices of previous years. Chihuahua had made formal agreements with Chiricahuas in 1842, 1850, 1857, 1860–61, and 1872. Juh's father, Láceris, had been a part of the first three agreements, and Juh had had a leading role in every treaty beginning in 1857.[39] Familiar with past negotiations and conditions, he proposed a simple arrangement: he would make peace with Sonora and Chihuahua and even agree to join forces with Mexicans in case of war with Americans. He did not request rations. Apparently the Nednhis just wanted to be left alone, to "live in the country where they were born." Of course, Juh said nothing about not raiding into the United States.[40]

About September 1, 1878, federal forces came to Janos and held a council with Juh and his leading men, Nolgee, Geronimo, Nat-cul-baye, and the fearless Mexican-born Jelikine, whom the Mexicans called Chino because of his wavy hair. Chihuahua's conditions, however, were in stark contrast to those offered by Juh. The state would grant peace only if the Nednhis agreed to relocate to Ojinaga, some 250 miles southeast of Janos along the Texas border. Stunned at this proposal, Juh requested time to consider it. The Nednhis returned to their ranchería in the Carcay Mountains. Distrustful of federal troops, they avoided Janos, going instead to Casas Grandes and Corralitos on trading expeditions.

Meanwhile, in mid-September Sonoran captain Jesús Escalante had left Bavispe to meet with officials at Janos. He agreed to defer action against Juh until September 25, 1878, which was Chihuahua's deadline for the Nednhis to consummate the treaty. If no treaty was agreed to, then both states would begin operations. Escalante readied his two companies of presidio troops from Fronteras and Bavispe for a campaign into the Sierra Madre.[41]

As expected, the Nednhis moved farther south into the Sierra Madre to avoid the federal and presidio troops. During the cease-fire, they debated their next step. Geronimo had brought them current news about affairs at San Carlos, especially regarding the paucity of rations and the malaria epidemic. On the one hand, Hart's liberal philosophy of allowing the Apaches to move into the foothills to gather and hunt would have been an attractive option to the skittish Nednhis. On the other hand, the presence of the mysterious shaking sickness was a powerful deterrent. Before leaving Carcay, either Juh or Nolgee, or perhaps both, sent three men to gather intelligence at San Carlos. The rest of the band (about 175 in all) decided to retaliate against Chihuahua.

They would waylay travelers at Chocolate Pass, a narrow defile located midway between Galeana and Casas Grandes. Because of the number of ambushes Juh had carried out here, and the appalling number of casualties, it remained the most dangerous canyon in northwestern Chihuahua. On September 26, 1878, one day after Chihuahua's deadline to Juh, a freight train loaded with beans for Silver City, with twenty-five men, women, and children, rode into Chocolate Pass. We will never know how vigilant they may have been or whether it would have even mattered, for that day, not one of them would survive the Apaches' assault. Nepuneruno Acosta and another man reached the grisly scene shortly after the attack. Debris and bodies littered the ground, the air pungent with the smell of death. They watched helplessly as a few victims gasped their last dying breaths. Remaining only a few minutes, they hastened back to Galeana and returned with a force of one hundred men, who followed the Indians to their ranchería, which, they reported, contained five hundred Indians, an obvious exaggeration. According to one account, during their return to Galeana they jumped a party of five Chiricahuas, killing four.[42]

Meanwhile, at San Carlos, the Nednhis' emissaries found the situation disturbing. Hart had left the agency on a trip east (leaving his brother in charge), and his replacement had furnished some beef, but he had no flour on hand. In late August Indian officials at San Carlos reported that the flour contractor was missing. Accordingly, General Willcox again interceded and ordered the post commander at Camp Thomas to supply the agency with flour. But wagons could not cross the Gila, which was swollen by recent rains. Finally, Lieutenant Abbot came up with an idea to load the flour on a raft and ferry it across the river. His ingenuity temporarily solved the problem, but supplies remained insufficient. The Chiricahua chiefs talked to the subagent, who gave them passes to visit the upper Gila country to hunt and gather acorns and mesquite beans.[43]

Two respected army officers criticized Hart for the condition of the agency. Major Charles Compton, commanding Camp Grant, explained that "trouble both in the past and present can be attributed to gross negligence and mismanagement regarding supplies on the part of persons who have absolute and entire control of the Indians on the reservation." Lieutenant Abbot at Camp Thomas seconded Compton's assessment: "It is my belief that the Indians are hungry and that they procured passes to go foraging." As Naiche was moving his campsite, two Nednhis from Mexico visited him. Shortly before midnight, September 10, 1878, they appeared near his village, inquiring about conditions at the reservation. A few days later, the Chokonen chief gathered 150 of his band and headed for Pueblo Viejo. Abbot, unaware of the size of the Nednhi party from Mexico, was concerned that the Chiricahuas were moving "nearer to the renegades and cannot result in good." They fell in with their old friend Merejildo Grijalva, the former interpreter at San Carlos, whom Hart had recently fired after a disagreement. According to one man, Hart had fired Grijalva after the interpreter questioned Hart's illegal activities.[44]

In the meantime, the Nednhis had not heard from their envoys to San Carlos. In early October, they sent eight men north to the border, hoping to rendezvous with them.[45] Only one of the original three envoys returned, and his report about conditions at San Carlos was far from encouraging. The surviving Nednhi, who may have been Martine, explained that American soldiers had overtaken the three Apaches and killed two. Lieutenant Henry Pratt Perrine led this command, which followed the Chiricahuas into New Mexico to Bear Creek, seventeen miles northeast of old Fort West. Here his Apache scouts overtook and killed two of the three Nednhis, who were either attempting to reach the Chihennes at Ojo Caliente or hoping to retrieve a hidden cache of weapons. Perrine's command, which lost one Indian scout in the skirmish, recovered four horses and one mule. The nine Nednhis returned to Nolgee and Juh with the news. The current instability at San Carlos (short rations and malaria) was enough to convince them to risk the perilous life in northern Mexico.[46]

The three Nednhi chiefs separated. Nolgee with fifty followers returned to the Janos area and resumed negotiations there; Geronimo and forty followers went to a stronghold about one hundred miles south of Janos, which would place him north of Guaynopa; and Juh with the largest party, some eighty to one hundred in all, went deep into the Sierra Madre, to the Tarahumara Mountains, some one hundred miles south of Geronimo.[47]

The first news of Juh's presence came on October 25, 1878, when a man near Tacupeto saw a band of Apaches traveling south along the Sahuaripa River. Three days later this party raided Trinidad, killing two men and wounding two others. Then, on October 29, they headed east toward Maycoba, where they assaulted two men, killing Candelario Duarte and wounding his brother-in-law, Marcial Apodaca. The municipal president of Trinidad reflected on how dispirited his citizens were: "If nothing is done, they [Apaches] will finish us. We are without arms, powder, and lead." Then he sent an urgent appeal to the governor: "Every inhabitant of this frontier cries out for your paternal protection . . . send us arms and provisions so we [can] tenaciously pursue this ferocious enemy." Political leaders at Trinidad enlisted forty men from the miners at Yecora, Maycoba, and Trinidad. It left on a campaign but found no Apaches. Juh had moved his camp farther north to avoid any pursuit.[48]

Chiricahua antipathy toward Mexico was soon compounded by the deadly events of November 12, 1878, a disastrous day for the Nednhis. Two separate attacks, one by federal forces near Janos and the second by Sonoran troops north of Guaynopa, wiped out one-fourth of the band.

One Chiricahua eyewitness described to Lieutenant Abbot at Camp Thomas the chicanery employed by Mexicans at Janos. Unfortunately, surviving evidence is silent on the events leading up to the disaster of November 12,

1878. This is what likely happened. In early November, Nolgee sent a message to Janos that he wanted to make peace. Local officials lured him in with promises.

Nolgee, however, was unaware that federal troops were in the area. These Mexican soldiers recalled vividly the massacre of twenty-five men, women, and children at Chocolate Pass just six weeks earlier. And they wanted Apache blood. On November 12, 1878, Nolgee brought his group of forty-four persons to Janos to celebrate the new armistice. The Mexicans served a feast in which mescal flowed freely. Many adults became intoxicated. Then the soldiers surrounded the inebriated Apaches. They massacred two-thirds of Nolgee's group, thirty-three in all, including Nolgee and nine men.

Residents at Janos would not have considered this operation, not as long as Juh was still in the mountains, but the federals had no fear of Juh and undoubtedly felt that the more Indians they could kill today, the fewer they would have to kill tomorrow. One thing seems certain: Nolgee had let his guard down. The Nednhis had long-standing relationships with the residents of Janos. They were cautious, always on guard at the first hint of treachery. To strangers, they were always suspicious if not fearful. The presence of the federal troops must have surprised Nolgee. Ah-dis and a few women and children, survivors of the treachery, arrived at the subagency after a twenty-two-day journey, and told the story to Lieutenant Abbot at Camp Thomas. Martine and a few others joined Juh at Guaynopa and related the dreadful news.[49]

That very same day Sonoran presidio troops scored an important victory over Geronimo's party. A force under Lieutenant Jesús Escalante followed the trail of a raiding party from Bacadéhuachi into the Sierra Madre to the San Pedro Mountains just north of Guaynopa. They surprised the Nednhi camp and killed ten Apaches. Geronimo may have referred to this assault in his memoirs. Though he erroneously places the year as 1880 (he was at San Carlos that entire year), Geronimo correctly recalled that "we were in the mountains south of Casas Grandes" when twenty-four Mexican soldiers attacked our camp, which contained forty Indians. He was close regarding the number of Mexicans involved and remembered exactly the number of Apaches in camp. Escalante had caught the sentinels napping, and Geronimo was puzzled: "I do not know how they were able to find our camp unless they had excellent scouts and our guards were careless, but they were shooting at us before we knew they were near." Geronimo mixed up the rest of the event with another fight in Chihuahua, but he did admit that he had lost twelve warriors in the attack, though Escalante's report claimed that his men had slain ten Indians.[50]

Meanwhile, the same day that Mexican forces destroyed Nolgee's followers and defeated Geronimo's group, American troops were herding two-thirds of the Chihennes from Ojo Caliente to San Carlos. It was another in a series of incredibly stupid decisions made by federal officials in Washington. Loco, the peace chief, led his band back to Arizona. Victorio, a reluctant patriot chief, had resolved never to return to San Carlos. His reasons were simple: "This is my country. I don't want to go. We have not done anything [wrong]."[51] Though not as eloquent a speech as that of his contemporary, Chief Joseph of the Nez Perce Indians, his words were impressive. And he was obviously prepared to assert that "he would fight no more forever" if the government would permit him to remain at Ojo Caliente. Loco would go, but not him. He had pledged to die fighting rather than return to San Carlos.

7

RESISTANCE, SURVIVAL, MISERY

My father and another man were told to go out and get Ho's
[Juh's] band, make peace, and bring them to the reservation.
Sam Kenoi

Since their return to Ojo Caliente in November 1877, Victorio and Loco, living under the watchful eyes of United States troops stationed at Ojo Caliente,
had kept their followers in check. They asked only that the government assign
them permanent homes in the hills and canyons near their sacred spring and
box canyon. To some Chihennes, it seemed as though they had never left, their
experiences at San Carlos simply a bad dream. One Chihenne said: "When
we got over there [Ojo Caliente], why we are in the same way. They gave
us rations [and] everything [was] all right."[1] As the Clown had foretold, Jatu
joined his two children. Hoping for a favorable decision from a distant government, they remained in limbo for nearly a year. They also pleaded with their
agent, Thomas Keam, to unite them with their kinfolk who had remained at
San Carlos. Accordingly, the chiefs asked Keam to prepare an itemized list of
their relatives still at Hart's agency, requesting that they "be restored to them."
Their poignant appeals touched Keam: "I would state that it is an almost daily
occurrence of one or two coming to me, and begging in tears, to have either a
father, mother, or children restored to them."[2]

Omniscient federal officials in Washington debated their fate. The Interior Department, which included the commissioner of Indian affairs, Ezra A.
Hayt, suggested transferring the Chihennes to Fort Sill, Oklahoma; the War
Department demurred, believing that Fort Sill was overloaded with Southern
Plains tribes and thus unable to accommodate the Apaches. Therefore, during the summer of 1878, while Naiche's Chokonens wondered whether they
would receive their weekly rations at San Carlos, and Juh's Nednhis struggled
to survive in the Sierra Madre, Victorio and Loco patiently waited to hear

125

the government's decision. General Philip H. Sheridan, frustrated at the delay (and the twelve thousand dollars' annual cost for Indian rations paid by the War Department), recommended that the War Department simply stop caring for the Chihennes, which would force the Interior Department to assume its rightful responsibility.[3]

Sheridan's proposal spurred the Indian department into action. The first week of June 1878, Indian Inspector E. C. Watkins, fresh from an inspection of San Carlos, reached Ojo Caliente. He was unmoved by the Chihennes' appeals to remain there: "They told the same old story about this being the homes of their fathers." He recommended that the government exile them to Fort Sill, Oklahoma Territory. But, if Indian officials decided to return them to San Carlos, he suggested that Agent Hart, with his Apache police, could easily escort the Chihennes to San Carlos once the army had moved them to the Arizona border.[4] On July 22, 1878, General William Tecumseh Sherman ordered the military to assist in the removal of the Chihennes back to San Carlos. Dan Thrapp sums up the Chihennes' hapless situation: They were "enmeshed in heartless bureaucratic processes determined to return them to the one place above all others they dreaded to go."[5]

On October 25, 1878, Captain Frank T. Bennett, Ninth Cavalry, left Ojo Caliente for San Carlos with Loco and arrived at San Carlos on November 25, 1878, with 172 Chihennes, but only 20 men in all.[6] Loco protested the unjust decision but decided to go because he loved his children and did not want to see "them killed in the wilds."[7] With Loco was a chief named Kisalchilly, shown as Sis-es-chole on the agent's rolls, and other men such as the "noted warrior" Stalosh, the famous shaman Ramon, and future scout, train jumper, and Apache survivalist Massai, whose Apache name meant "Crazy."[8] Two young Chihennes, Jason Betzinez and Sam Haozous, were also among the entourage. Victorio, as he had vowed, with some forty-four men and eighty-five to ninety persons in all, scattered to the mountains. With him were his sons-in-law Turivio and Mangas; two more sons of the mighty Mangas Coloradas, Lopez and his brother Tomaso Coloradas (Tomascito); Nana, his son-in-law Horache, and his nephew or son-in-law Jatu; the inveterate raider Sánchez; the war chief Showano and his brother Choneska (Ghun-sta, or Big Tooth), and the Bedonkohes Francisco, Vicente, and Esquine.

This time, perhaps at Loco's request, Agent Hart had the Indians build their wickiups on a high bluff a few miles from the San Carlos agency, east of San Carlos River and just north of the Gila. They were about fifteen miles west of their Chokonen and Bedonkohe relatives at the subagency and far enough removed from the White Mountain people, who Loco claimed had mistreated them during their first stay. The location was much healthier than the Gila lowlands near the subagency. But it was hardly an oasis in the desert, especially during the summer months, when temperatures often reached the century mark or higher. Moreover, it was almost bare of vegetation. Many years later, Jason Betzinez remembered, "Dust storms were common the year round, and in all seasons except the summer the locality swarmed with flies, mosquitoes, gnats, and other pesky insects." Yet, Betzinez saw a silver lining because they "were untroubled by attacks of enemies and the Government did feed us after a fashion." And they were away from the Goodwin marshes, where malaria had done its deadly work on Naiche's band.[9]

Sam Haozous agreed with Betzinez, because for the next forty-one months they lived in peace, which "the people liked." Still, they had little to do. Nothing would grow there, and they had to get permission to hunt in the mountains. And because they had once fled the reservation, authorities were ever vigilant, keeping a close watch over them. So they gambled and told stories at the evening campfires.[10]

Loco found affairs at San Carlos almost as unsettled as when he had left fifteen months earlier. Agent Hart had apparently lost all interest in the Indians and instead devoted most of his time and energy to lining his own pockets. Graft and corruption became normal, insidiously finding their way into virtually every transaction. Shady contractors, dishonest employees, and other whites looking to profit from their association with the Indian agent became customary. In early 1879, Commissioner Hayt received word of Hart's mismanagement of San Carlos and sent Indian Inspector John H. Hammond, who had replaced Vandever, to investigate.[11]

Hammond concluded that the rumors were true. His investigation revealed that Hart had sold Apache rations to nearby mining stores and camps, which forced him to issue half allotments of flour, coffee, sugar, and tobacco to the Indians. After his employees inspected and received the beef cattle, Hart permitted the contractors to retain possession until he was ready to issue to the Indians. Because Hart had essentially ignored long-standing practices of internal controls, he was left vulnerable to ethics charges. Some of his employees were also dishonest. And to top it all off, Hammond found that Hart carried at least one "ghost" employee on the agency's rolls (Percival Stockman) who was prospecting on the reservation. While Hammond was taking testimony, Agent Hart resigned on March 22, 1879, though for some peculiar reason the inspector allowed him to remain until a replacement arrived. Then, inexplicably, Hammond suspended his investigation. His reasons would soon become clear.[12]

Meanwhile, the Apaches were getting restless because of the scarcity of food. A mounting discontent was brewing among the Apaches at the agency, at least according to the warnings coming from Archie McIntosh, one-time scout and confidant of General George Crook. Many army officers believed that the Scot-Chippewa Indian frontiersman was not only a pernicious influence among the Apaches but also a man of questionable integrity. Regardless, in early February 1879, he had spent a day with the Arivaipa chief Eskiminzin, who was perhaps related to McIntosh's wife, Dominga. According to McIntosh, the chief had told him that every Apache band on the reservation, except the Yumas, had decided to "go on the warpath as soon as the snow on the mountains melts." McIntosh also claimed that Pedro, the important White Mountain chief, was "cognizant of the scheme."[13]

The report drew the immediate attention of General Willcox, who, recognizing that controversy about Indian affairs at San Carlos had cost his predecessor his job, had a stake in keeping the Apaches at San Carlos quiet. He had suspected that matters on the reservation were less than satisfactory. Hearing that Indian Inspector Hammond was then en route to San Carlos to investigate Agent Hart confirmed his feelings. Though Willcox admitted, "McIntosh's reputation is not good," he understood the importance of keeping the Indians at San Carlos content. Therefore, he dispatched two trusted officers, Major Charles E. Compton (from Fort Apache) and Captain Adna Chaffee (from Camp McDowell), to find out whether McIntosh's version had any credibility. After investigating, they were to meet with Inspector Hammond.[14]

On March 6, 1879, Major Compton reported to General Willcox:

> I had a long talk with Agent Hart about Archie McIntosh's report that the Indians are about to break out. Hart says there is not a word of truth in the report of McIntosh. Eskiminzin says that he talked to McIntosh 29 days ago at his house and said nothing [for McIntosh] to make such a report. Eskiminzin says all are contented and satisfied. Mr. Hart informs me that all the bands, excepting the Chiricahuas are engaged in planting and getting ready to farm. The Chiricahuas do not work but are content and give no trouble. I feel satisfied that Mr. McIntosh has made a false report.[15]

Three days later Compton reiterated that every band "except the Chiricahuas are busy digging ditches, building fences, and working." He ended with a seemingly benign statement, though it was one that literally could have sent chills through the bodies of Naiche's people: "The Chiricahuas are at the Sub

Agency 15 miles above San Carlos on the Gila." This meant that the subagent had relocated them from the mountains to the Gila Flats, the scene of their first bout with malaria the previous year. And, though details are vague, Naiche's people would face a second battle with malaria during the spring and early summer of 1879, which would take at least fifty more lives.[16]

But Inspector Hammond, after talking to the Apaches, believed that McIntosh had stumbled onto something, for he sensed a stiff resentment stemming from their hunger. Though the inspector did not expect a general uprising, he sent word to General Willcox to prepare for trouble.[17] In mid-March the *Arizona Weekly Citizen* reported that the "San Carlos Indians are having a rough time of it. Last week no flour was served to them [and] the week before they had one half of their usual ration." To compensate for the reduction, Hart issued corn, from which they made tiswin, and a "wholesome drunk" resulted in the death of one Indian at the subagency.[18]

Meanwhile, at Prescott, General Willcox made plans to discourage any Apache outbreak. He explained the brittle situation at San Carlos to his superiors: "Indians have been short of food so many times since the beginning of the fiscal year, hostilities might well be expected." He continued:

> Inspector Hammond reports indications of trouble at San Carlos. Messengers coming in with intelligence from which Hammond does not fear any large movement but precautionary measures are being taken. The Coyoteros, 800 strong, [are] increasing number of guns. Hammond has applied for authority to disarm dangerous bands [Chokonens]. I have ordered out some troops from McDowell, Verde, [and] Apache, and all the cavalry are ordered to be in readiness for field service at once.[19]

Charles Harlow, who attended Hammond's council at San Carlos, reported that the Chihennes, Chokonens, and White Mountain Apaches were "disaffected but have been straightened out again" by the inspector's blunt and serious warning. According to Harlow, Hammond had warned the Apaches that if an outbreak occurred, "not one would return alive." Though Hammond's harsh rhetoric appears incongruous with the policies of the Indian Bureau, he probably meant what he said, at least when it came to intimidating Apaches. After all, Hammond proudly referred to himself as a "son of a bitch on wheels."[20]

Matters at San Carlos could not have been much worse, it seemed, but they soon became so. In mid-May, Willcox braced for yet another threat to the stability there when he received a report from Lieutenant Charles Gatewood, then at Ojo Caliente with a company of Apache scouts, that Victorio and thirty men were headed to San Carlos to retrieve his women and children from the reservation.[21] After splitting from Loco, Victorio and Nana had begun to raid in New Mexico, but apparently they decided to confine their efforts to livestock to avoid killing Americans. In early December, Nana, Sánchez, and Raton led a group of fifty-nine Chihennes, which included twenty-three men, across the Rio Grande into the Caballo Mountains and then to the Mescalero agency. On January 23, 1879, Tomaso Coloradas and eight others joined Nana's party. Nana spoke for his followers. They wanted to remain at Mescalero (until they heard from Victorio) but would not consider going to San Carlos. Victorio, with the balance of men, about twenty-two, had left on a raid into Mexico. There is no record that he met any Nednhis, who were then 175 miles south in the Sierra Madre near Guaynopa.[22]

In early February Victorio had returned from Mexico and opened negotiations with Americans at Ojo Caliente. After a few months of talking, to the chagrin of the agent at Mescalero, Washington officials decided to allow Victorio to join Nana there. But when told of this concession, Victorio vowed to "die first" and immediately fled into the mountains. Victorio's biographer, Dan Thrapp, believed that the chief had "misunderstood" the specifics of the new orders, in which the government had actually acquiesced to his wishes. Instead, Victorio inferred or actually heard that "he was to be returned to San Carlos." Colonel Hatch visited Nana and Tomaso Coloradas at Mescalero and the latter agreed to try to find Victorio and explain the new offer. But Tomaso could not locate Victorio, who by then had left for San Carlos.[23]

On the way, Victorio killed four herders near Silver City and stole eighty mules near Clifton. By the evening of May 18, 1879, his party was near the subagency, trying to convince the Chokonens to join him, but without success. Yet, two women and two children joined Victorio from the mixed Chiricahua band (formerly under Geronimo) that had not bolted during the September 1877 exodus.[24]

Victorio returned to New Mexico. Near the San Francisco settlement at today's Glenwood, several ranchers, having heard that Indians were in the vicinity, set up a trap. They tied a horse to a tree, hoping that Apaches would take the bait. Then three Americans staked out the position. Four Apaches, including Turivio, approached the horse to investigate. Jim Keller, John Morris, and Robert Coulter opened fire, killing three of the four Indians, including Turivio. Victorio vowed to retaliate. Several months later, Apaches told a Mexican at Tularosa that they would kill twenty men to avenge Turivio's death.[25]

Victorio swept east, crossed the Rio Grande, and resumed negotiations with the new Mescalero agent, Samuel A. Russell, who informed the chief that the government would permit him to remain at the Mescalero agency. By the end of June, the reluctant chief brought his followers there, hoping that the government would transfer his kinfolk at San Carlos to Mescalero. Indian affairs at San Carlos, however, were still in a state of disorder.[26]

To begin with, Inspector Hammond, who had temporarily assumed command of the agency after Hart's resignation, was spending most of his time inspecting mines, some of which were within the limits of the reservation. Then in May, he traveled to New York and Washington, D.C, to line up potential investors and to confer with Commissioner Hayt. He then returned to San Carlos and entered into a conspiracy to shift the reservation boundary to exclude a mine that Agent Hart had recently sold to Edward Knapp. Knapp happened to be Edward Knapp Hayt, son of the commissioner of Indian affairs. When it became public that Hammond, ostensibly with Hayt's tacit blessing, had dropped the investigation of Hart's activities, General Clinton B. Fisk, the president of the Board of Indian Commissioners, ordered a thorough review of activities at San Carlos. Sickened at what he learned, Fisk leaked the report to the press in fall 1879, thus forcing the secretary of the interior, Carl Schurz, to fire Commissioner Hayt in late January 1880.[27]

Meanwhile, Commissioner Hayt had asked the War Department to appoint an army officer until he could find a substitute for Hart. General Irvin McDowell, commander of the Division of the Pacific, asked General Willcox to suggest a replacement. Willcox first asked Captain May Humphreys Stacey, Twelfth Infantry, at Fort Thomas to take the position, but he wanted no part of it, citing health reasons (he had lost twenty pounds in the previous six months and was not up to the challenge).[28] Stacey nominated Captain Adna R. Chaffee of the Sixth Cavalry. A Civil War veteran of Gettysburg (where he was wounded) and Sheridan's raid on Richmond, Chaffee was a veteran cavalryman with a fine reputation among his contemporaries. Willcox suggested Chaffee, and General McDowell forwarded Chaffee's name to the commissioner of Indian affairs, who made the appointment.[29]

Chaffee was the antithesis of his two predecessors. He had not sought the job and apparently did not want it. He accepted the assignment because he knew that the agency was in disrepute. To the job he brought clear scruples and a military code of ethics, which the agency sorely needed. Moreover, he was sincerely concerned about the Indians' welfare, and he planned to gain their confidence by addressing their concerns in an honest and systematic manner.

On July 1, 1879, Willcox telegraphed Chaffee at Fort McDowell to go to San Carlos and relieve Agent Hart. It took Chaffee five days to reach San Carlos, where he found Hart and Inspector Hammond. Hart was uncooperative, as Willcox had predicted a few weeks earlier, and refused to turn over the agency records and property until he received orders from Commissioner Hayt. Hart also wanted his bondsman relieved from any financial responsibility. Chaffee reported these details to Willcox, who wired the Indian Bureau in Washington for instructions.[30]

While affairs were on hold, John Walker, an American married to a Western Apache woman, passed along information to Captain Stacey that added fuel to an already volatile situation. On July 11, 1879, a White Mountain Indian had come to Walker's ranch above Fort Thomas with ominous tidings, similar to those heard by Archie McIntosh five months before: "The Indians without regard to tribe or band on the San Carlos Reservation had recently held three councils to consider whether they should go on the war path or not. The older men advised prudence and wanted the rest to wait to see if the government intended to give them any rations or not." The allied Apaches planned to draw the military away from their posts by making simultaneous raids along the frontier. Then they would launch assaults against the skeleton garrisons at forts Apache, Thomas, and Grant. And who was the man the Apaches chose to lead this war? Naiche, then called Young Cochise, whose band had faced smallpox, malaria, and irregular rations.[31]

John Walker believed that the councils and debates had taken place. While Hart was paying attention to acquiring mines and selling the Apaches' rations, the Apaches had met in council to discuss an appropriate response. Clearly, the lack of food was their primary concern. But a secondary issue, as mentioned in Inspector Hammond's report of April 18, was the "diseased conditions . . . of the San Carlos Indians. Many little children are born in disease and the evil is spreading."[32]

Walker's report sent shock waves though the minds of Arizona's military and civil hierarchies. That same day, Indian officials, perhaps Hart himself, questioned Naiche, who denied "any knowledge of any such movement." Yet, according to Walker's Apache source, Naiche, then in his early twenties, was not yet prepared to assume the mantle of war chief. His explanation was simple: "When his father died he had enjoined him to preserve peace with the whites as long as he could." Naiche evidently was ready to give Americans another chance to prove they wanted peace as much as Apaches did. If conditions remained unsettled, and his people continued to die of disease and starvation, then, in good conscience, he could go to war.[33]

On July 15, 1879, two days after Walker's report, Inspector Hammond (Indian officials had not yet uncovered his conspiracy with Hart) and the new agent, Captain Chaffee, held a council with the "chiefs of the tribes on the reservation." Each leader took turns to deny the rumors of an alliance and potential uprising. Naiche received close scrutiny. Hammond "closely questioned [him] and he denied all knowledge of any such purpose." His response convinced both Chaffee and Hammonds that "there was nothing to the Walker report."[34] Yet the commander of Fort Grant, Major Abraham K. Arnold, analyzed the situation succinctly: "Whether we have peace or not depends upon whether or not we provide proper subsistence." Fortunately for all parties concerned, Chaffee officially relieved Hart on July 19, 1879, and began the process of restoring credibility to his office.[35]

He soon bid good riddance to Hart, a "damned scoundrel" according to Chaffee.[36] Before leaving, the disgraced agent suggested that Chaffee, just to survive, would be forced to operate within the framework that had epitomized Hart's tenure at San Carlos: inefficient, corrupt, with ghost employees, unbridled waste, spoilage, and graft, and overbearing, intimidating, and sometimes dishonest contractors. Chaffee quickly realized that the only way to control affairs at San Carlos was to establish clear policies and procedures. He imposed internal controls with pragmatic solutions and closely supervised his employees, whom he forced to work instead of "sitting in the shade." He reorganized the agency warehouse, carefully storing annuity goods and rations. To ensure conformity to his rules, he had "to direct, in person, as well as post myself in the office, and receive many stores. The traders tell their stories, the contractors theirs, and the agency folks of course are not far behind."[37]

Chaffee also listened to the Apaches' concerns and reinstated the Apache police force, hiring forty of the influential men and chiefs to serve, including Zele and Chihuahua. When his first allotments in mid-July contained only an issue of beef, many Apaches complained.[38] He therefore gave passes to Nahilzay, Naiche, Chatto, and several White Mountain Apaches so they could gather natural foods in the mountains and plant crops at various sites. Nahilzay took his group to Cottonwood Mountain, just south of Black Rock in the Santa Teresa Mountains.[39] Naiche and Chatto went to George Stevens's ranch on Eagle Creek. Stevens's wife, Francesca, the daughter of a White Mountain Apache chief, had been close to Cochise, who had called her sister.[40] Consequently,

Naiche felt comfortable at Stevens's ranch, which was also a much healthier site than the Gila lowlands that had infected his people with malaria.

Besides the problem of rations, which Chaffee had restored to full issues by August, Washington authorities had resurrected the debate about which reservation should house the Chihennes. Chaffee believed they should be together, and that was his only concern. On July 26, 1879, he wrote the commissioner of Indian affairs to recommend such a course. Either send the Chihennes at San Carlos to Mescalero or move those at Mescalero to San Carlos, he suggested. Hayt chose the former course, and on August 11 Chaffee informed him that he needed fifteen hundred dollars to transfer his wards to Mescalero. Unfortunately, that soon became a moot point. Ten days later, on August 21, 1879, Victorio, fearing that civil officials in New Mexico were going to arrest him for horse stealing and murder, left Mescalero with about 145 Chihennes and Bedonkohes.[41]

News of Victorio's activities, and recent raids by the Nednhis in southern Arizona and New Mexico, prompted Chaffee to recall the Chokonens from the mountains to the branch agency. By this time, Chatto, Cathla, and Gordo had merged into one group of 55; Bonito and Chiva had joined to form another of 104; and malaria had reduced Naiche's band to 183.[42] That left Zele and 80 to 90 Chokonens, Chihennes, and Bedonkohes whom Clum had moved from Ojo Caliente in the spring of 1877. They joined Loco's band at the main agency. Ezra Hoag dispatched Palmer Valor to bring in Nahilzay from Cottonwood Mountain. Three days later, on August 28, Chaffee learned that Victorio had jumped the Mescalero Reservation. He at once ordered the subagent at the branch agency to "bring to the vicinity of the Branch all the Chiricahuas and Southern Apache." Furthermore, Chaffee directed, "keep your scouts well in hand about the Branch" until hearing about Victorio's movements. What Chaffee could not have known is that the Nednhis were responsible for the raids in early August in Arizona and the August 13 stock raid in New Mexico.[43]

Although Juh and Geronimo had kept a relatively low profile in the Sierra Madre for most of 1879, General Willcox, in Prescott, had been thinking about them since the survivors of Nolgee's band had come to San Carlos. Willcox knew that as long as the Nednhis remained in Mexico, citizens living in southern Arizona would be at risk. And he understood that the raiding done from Mexico had derailed his predecessor, General Kautz. Though most of their depredations were against the citizens of Mexico, he logically felt that bringing them to San Carlos would benefit all parties—Americans, Mexicans, and Apaches.

Willcox knew he was exploring a new paradigm that, were he to fail, would open him to ridicule from all sides. The idea of sending peace envoys to convince hostile Apaches living in another country to relocate to a reservation in Arizona, where the United States government would then sustain them, was an unconventional, bold, and problematic decision. But, if successful, he would save lives on both sides of the border.

The Chiricahua chiefs offered to send envoys to the Nednhis. Hart agreed, and in early February 1879 sounded out Major Compton at Fort Apache. After giving the matter "much thought and consideration," Compton urged Hart to take the Chiricahuas up on their offer: "If some of the relatives and friends—now at San Carlos, of the Indians now roaming at large, could be induced to visit the bands of Geronimo, Whoo [Juh], and Nolgee, if the latter is still alive, and inform them of the benefits which would accrue to them . . . successful accomplishment of this undertaking would result in incalculable good to Southeastern Arizona as well as to the safety and comfort of the Indians themselves."[44] Six weeks later, on March 24, Compton announced that he and Hart had a party of four Chiricahuas ready to go to Chihuahua to make contact with the Nednhis.[45] Yet, either General Willcox or General McDowell at division headquarters put the plan on hold.[46]

The emissaries might have had a difficult time finding Juh and Geronimo. In January and February, two reports from the districts of Moctezuma and Sahuaripa revealed that the Nednhis had left them alone. As it turned out, Juh and Geronimo were then raiding in Chihuahua. For the third consecutive winter, Juh had made camp deep in the Sierra Madre near Guaynopa. From this base, he and Geronimo had raided several ranches in western Chihuahua near Yepómera and Guerrero. In response, from Guerrero, Captain Mauricio Corredor, a Tarahumara Indian who lived in the neighboring village of Arisiachic, and Commander J. Francisco Marquez organized a force of 150 "peasant soldiers" to follow the Apaches.

By January 29, 1879, their army had reached Basoloachic, a few miles south of Yepómera. For the next nine days, Marquez's command had to wait out heavy snows and rain, which made it impossible to move out. Finally, on February 7, 1879, they headed west into the mountains. One week later, they found three recently abandoned rancherías (about eight days before, said Marquez's scouts) that formed a triangle. The first two camps contained thirty-five and fifty wickiups; the third, apparently used by the sentinels, was smaller. Marquez noted that the Apaches had located one camp in a "very rough arroyo that was very favorable" for the Indians.

This was Juh's camp in the Arroyo de Guaynopa. The size of the camp also suggests that some Chihennes and Bedonkohes, who had fled from Ojo Caliente during the May 1877 removal, had probably joined him for the winter. The Chiricahua chiefs, after their raiding parties from Chihuahua returned, had anticipated that the soldiers from Chihuahua would come after them. So they had broken camp and headed southwest into Sonora.[47] But the mission had served a purpose. The Chihuahuans had gained important knowledge on Juh's winter base, an advantage they would use four years later to launch a devastating attack on Juh while he was camped in the very region they had just explored.

Juh likely led the band that followed the Aros River south to the mining settlements. On February 15, 1879, fifteen or twenty of Juh's men attacked a party from Tarachi en route to Mulatos, killing the municipal president of Tarachi, Gregorio Anaya, and two other men "known for their honor," Santos Anaya and Jesús Villaneal. From Mulatos, authorities dispatched sixteen men led by Jesús Quinteros. As he was collecting the corpses, he could see the Apaches on a nearby ridge. He yearned to retaliate, but he knew the situation was hopeless, for an assault would certainly take more Sonoran blood. Five days later, the same band attacked two parties near Tacupeto, killing at least one man.[48]

Juh and Geronimo returned to their base camp and decided to strike Nácori Chico. On March 26, six men left the pueblo to bring provisions from Granados and Bacadéhuachi. That same day, Apaches ambushed them at El Collote. Slain in the assault were three men, Anselmo Coronado, Candelario Lucero, and Santos Lucero. Juan Coronado was left severely wounded. A relief party went to their aid, but before the party reached El Collote, the Apaches attacked them and five more men "died heroically." This disaster left Nácori Chico's citizens demoralized, and nearly shattered the will of its inhabitants. Again, the prefect of Nácori Chico warned that "the situation is very bad [here] and it may be necessary for us to leave unless we are provided protection." The prefect of Moctezuma immediately sent thirty-two men to provide security. Eight days later, a band estimated at between thirty and thirty-five warriors stole fourteen mules at Lampazos, near Tepache. In June, Sonora sent troops to Guaynopa, which action led Juh and Geronimo to move north to solicit peace at Casas Grandes and Janos.[49]

The first report of Juh and Geronimo's presence at Casas Grandes came from Bavispe on June 18, 1879, when the commander reported that a band of one hundred warriors had solicited peace.[50] They were apparently at Janos in late May, for the customs officer wrote to Mexico City to complain about Juh's band. As usual, however, he had his facts wrong, implying that Juh and his band were fugitives from San Carlos who only came to Mexico to depredate before returning to Arizona to trade their spoils for more arms and ammunition at San Carlos. For the past three years, Juh had lived exclusively in Mexico.[51]

Juh's proposals went unanswered by state officials. Though Governor Angel Trias enjoyed the support of Mexico's president Porfirio Díaz, his administration was self-destructing because of a severe economic depression brought on by another poor crop harvest, this time in 1879. Furthermore, Apache raids had compelled him to impose a new, burdensome tax, which alienated even his own supporters. Trias's opponents, sensing his vulnerability, issued the Plan of Guerrero in August 1879, which was effectively a coup to allow the Terrazas family to regain power.

Without federal support, the ranchers in the northwestern frontier decided to appease the Nednhis, giving them some blankets and a few hundred dollars' worth of presents. For the time being, the ranchers agreed to leave Juh alone as long as he left their district alone. By the time General Geronimo Trevino arrived with five hundred federal troops, the Terrazas administration was firmly entrenched in power.[52]

With the news of the Nednhis seeking peace with Chihuahua, General Willcox thought again about bringing Juh's people to San Carlos. On August 26, 1879, he ordered Lieutenant Guy Howard (then at Fort Huachuca), son of General Howard, to take dispatches to Fronteras "to procure all the news you can in regard to Indian raiders in Mexico."[53] And Captain Chaffee decided to find out whether the Chiricahuas at San Carlos were still interested in helping to bring their kinfolk to the reservation. Willcox, on September 2, 1879, wrote his counterpart in New Mexico, Colonel Hatch, that Juh's band "may be brought in by a chief from San Carlos if it can be well managed."[54] Three days later, Willcox sent a dispatch to General McDowell at division headquarters marked "Confidential":

> I am in receipt of information from the head chiefs of the Chiricahua Indians that the remnants of the tribe . . . may now be prevailed upon to join the Agency at San Carlos. These chiefs have offered to give any

assistance in their power to this end. It is reported that about 25 families are now at Casas Grandes, Chihuahua. The balance are scattered
through various parts of the state of Chihuahua. Yesterday, my aide-
de-camp, Lt. Haskell, started via San Carlos under special instructions
from me to secure this desirable end.[55]

Lieutenant Harry L. Haskell, Twelfth Infantry, a native of Maine, had
fought with distinction in the Civil War. Assisted by Archie McIntosh, Haskell
met the Chiricahua chiefs at San Carlos. They were ready to help. It was evident to all that emissaries would have to enter Mexico to find Juh. According
to Eve Ball's informants, the two messengers who agreed to undertake this
hazardous mission were Gordo, the Bedonkohe chief, and Ah-dis, the survivor
of Nolgee's local group, who was now living with Naiche's people. In addition, George, the Chiricahua chief who had married into the White Mountain
band, apparently went along, and Chihuahua, a relative of Archie McIntosh's
wife, and whose son was destined to marry Juh's daughter, may have added
his powerful influence. Finally, Haskell asked Tom Jeffords to help, thus suggesting that he had modeled his bold plan after Jeffords's celebrated mission to
Cochise with General Howard.[56]

Just as Haskell's party was ready to depart, General McDowell had second
thoughts and ordered Willcox to "to suspend movement for Chiricahua renegades and await further instructions at San Carlos." Willcox wired McDowell
that he had placed the mission on hold while suggesting that "careful action
[was necessary] to prevent misunderstanding and disappointment on the part
of Chiricahua chiefs." But he remained convinced that this mission should be
carried out. Thus, he urged McDowell to consider requesting that the commissioner of Indian affairs issue orders that would allow Captain Chaffee to
pursue this matter. And, subtly addressing the main sticking point (the delicate
issue of Mexico's sovereignty), he summarized a recent letter that he had received from Angel Elías, the commander of Fronteras. Elías had promised to
cooperate in punishing "these evil doers who commit depredations on both
sides of the line." After all, Willcox logically concluded, "Mexican authorities
along the frontier would be as glad as ourselves" if Americans could persuade
Juh to leave Mexico and settle on San Carlos.[57]

Willcox's persistence paid dividends. The next day, September 14, 1879,
McDowell acquiesced, telegraphing Willcox the conditions of the mission. He
insisted that Haskell's peace party must "have nothing to do" with the Nednhis
while they are in Mexico. Yet, Haskell could communicate with Mexican offi-

cials informally "to secure their cooperation." Again, recognizing the sensitive aspect of the mission, Willcox instructed Haskell to emphasize to the Mexicans that this "movement is one originating with the Indians themselves, and one which is sanctioned by our military authorities, believing it to be in the best interests of both Governments and for the Indians." These restrictions, however, which expressly prohibited any Americans to cross the border into Mexico, did not apply to the two Chiricahua emissaries, who were Haskell's ace in the hole and his best chance at establishing contact with Juh.[58]

By mid-September Haskell's peace party, consisting of Archie McIntosh, Atzebee (a sergeant on the agency police force), and four other men (Gordo, Ah-dis, George, and perhaps Chihuahua), headed south to Camp Rucker in the southern Chiricahua Mountains, which would be their base of operations. They arrived about September 20, and three days later, Gordo and Ah-dis slipped into Mexico. The ancestors of Gordo recalled the circumstances: "They were issued an army rife, Springfield 45-70, with belt and cartridges and plenty of ammunition. The two men were told to go and get Ho's [Juh's] band, make peace with them and bring them in." At Rucker, Haskell met Tom Jeffords, who had just come in from inspecting a few mining claims in the Chiricahua Mountains. Jeffords soon had the unexpected pleasure of meeting Lieutenant Guy Howard, who had just arrived at Rucker with Company D Apache scouts. The two men immediately warmed to each other, with Jeffords giving the son details of his father's dangerous mission to Cochise.[59]

The emissaries would have more trouble than anticipated trying to find Juh and Geronimo. On July 18, 1879, Lieutenant Charles Gatewood, who commanded a company of Apache scouts at Fort Bayard, passed on intelligence that Geronimo had left Juh "and was expected to turn up somewhere." The source for this information was probably John Ayers, former agent at Tularosa, who had met Geronimo and twenty-five Apaches at either Janos or Casas Grandes. Employed by the beef contractor at San Carlos, Ayers had recently returned from business in Chihuahua. Geronimo boasted that he was planning a raid into the United States.[60]

In late July, a raiding party of sixteen warriors, likely led by Geronimo, entered southern Arizona. On July 30, 1879, one group of six warriors raided Pete Kitchen's ranch and captured a twelve-year-old boy; the next day, another band ran off eleven mules and one horse from O. E. Shaw, who had delivered a load of barley the day before to Fort Huachuca. Shaw raced back to Huachuca, where the commanding officer sent out a patrol to follow the Apaches. A few days later, Americans opened fire on the band that the boy was with, which angered the Apaches. Shortly after, they came across three men and ambushed them, firing two volleys of six shots, slaying two brothers named Schellanbach and wounding the third man, T. B. Merchant. Then the Indians released the boy, revealing to him that they were from Ojo Caliente, which suggests they were Bedonkohes or Chihennes who had not gone to San Carlos. Another report claimed that witnesses had seen a white man with the Indians. If true, Zebina Streeter may have resurfaced after a long absence.[61]

This group later joined another raiding party and continued east toward San Bernardino, where they killed two mules before proceeding into Chihuahua. On August 15, 1879, Lieutenant Augustus Perry Blockson, a graduate of West Point two years earlier, with Company C Apache scouts found a deserted ranchería along the border that had housed about sixty Apaches. Meanwhile, another raiding party of twenty-four warriors, under Juh, had entered New Mexico and on August 13, 1879, stole some stock near Fort Cummings. They apparently continued into the Black Range and united with Victorio. Thus began the exasperated chief's tragic yearlong journey to meet his fate, for he would never return to any reservation.[62]

According to what Louis Scott, the American consul in Chihuahua City, had heard, Victorio and Juh "have not been able to agree for years and personally are not friends," which may have been true because the Nednhis, during the previous two decades, had enjoyed closer ties with the Chokonens and Bedonkohes.[63] Regardless, on September 4, 1879, Juh and Victorio joined forces for a quick-striking raid against the horse herd of Captain Ambrose Eugene Hooker's Company E at Ojo Caliente. Within five minutes, the Indians, numbering between forty and sixty men, had slain five soldiers of the Ninth Cavalry and three citizens. They also took the entire herd of sixty-eight horses and mules.[64] Six days later, a party of fifty-seven warriors appeared at Gregorio Chavez's ranch on Animas Creek northeast of Hillsboro. At the ranch were his wife, seven children, and a few vaqueros. Chavez first assumed they were soldiers or scouts because they rode in single file. And then he saw Victorio, who cautioned him not to run, for he was a friend. A dozen warriors under Sánchez went inside Chavez's ranch, looking for weapons and cartridges, but Chavez had none, so in frustration they destroyed his furniture and carried away his bedding. One Apache pulled his wife's gold ring from her finger, and several whipped and kicked one of his vaqueros. They were gone by mid-morning, taking a few horses, nineteen cows, and a few lambs with them.[65]

The next day they raided McEver's ranch, about ten miles south of Hillsboro, killing either six or seven men and stealing most of its horses. Later that day they attacked a group of Mexicans at Jaralosa Cienega, three miles from McEver's ranch, brutally slaying at least ten Mexicans (men, women, and children), who were "horribly and disgustingly mutilated [with] iron bars." Among the dead were the widow and son-in-law of the celebrated guide of the 1860s Juan Arroyo.[66]

Yet the Chiricahuas did not escape unscathed. The cowboys at McEver's ranch reportedly wounded several Indians; and Manuel Stapleton claimed to have shot two Apaches while he was taking a bullet in the leg. The *Grant County Herald* reported the raiders were "Southern Chiricahuas . . . belonging to Hoomos [Juh's] band in Mexico." In mid-September, the Nednhi chief left Victorio and returned to the Casas Grandes area, where Juh admitted to Mexicans that he had raided into the United States, killing every person in a wagon train massacre and several Negroes, thus implicating him in the raid on Hooker's command at Ojo Caliente. Expecting pursuit, he moved his camp away from Casas Grandes and then took his fighting men on a second foray into New Mexico, just missing the arrival of Gordo and Ah-dis by a few days.[67]

During Juh's one-month absence, American troops had given Victorio no rest, battling his people in two major engagements on Animas Creek and near Ojo Caliente.[68] The two Chiricahua band chiefs reunited in mid-October.[69] On October 10, 1879, Apaches burned Lloyd's ranch, about ten miles west of today's Hatch. Six men from nearby El Colorado, today known as Rodey, went to investigate. About a mile west of the ranch, Apaches waylaid them, killing four men while the other two returned to Rodey for help. In response, a group of thirty-five men from El Colorado and Santa Barbara rushed to the scene. Again, the Indians ambushed them at La Ceja Canyon, killing an unknown number and putting the rest to flight. Meanwhile, on October 13, 1879, another relief party from Mesilla, seventeen men led by Eugene F. van Patten, ran headlong into Victorio and Juh. The allied Chiricahuas routed them, killing another five men, including William T. Jones, the county clerk for Doña Ana. Later that day, the war party captured several abandoned, well-stocked wagons and wiped out a Mexican train of thirteen wagons (twelve Mexicans, one American) at Flat Top Mountain. These three days were among the most sanguinary of the Victorio War in New Mexico in 1879–80.[70]

The allied Chiricahuas now headed south toward the Florida Mountains and then straight as an arrow into Chihuahua. Major Albert P. Morrow, with members of his Ninth Cavalry and Lieutenant Charles Gatewood's Apache scouts, trailed them into Chihuahua, where he skirmished with the Chiricahuas on the evening of October 27, 1879, suffering the loss of one Apache scout killed and two more wounded. From here Victorio and Juh struck east about one hundred miles and encamped in the Candelaria range. Safe there, they sprang back-to-back ambushes on two parties from Carrizal, killing over thirty of that town's men. Afterwards, Victorio headed north to New Mexico; Juh and Geronimo decided to return to the Sierra Madre, raiding, plundering, and killing as they made the 150-mile trek back to camp. En route, Juh admitted to a Mexican near Casas Grandes that his band had lost two important leaders during the fierce fighting in New Mexico. Victorio had also lost several warriors, including Tomaso Coloradas.[71]

About November 25, 1879, Juh reached his camp, where he found Gordo and Ah-dis. They had had trouble locating the camp, though recent reports had placed Juh near Casas Grandes. And when they finally did find it in mid-October, although they had just missed Juh and Geronimo, they did convince seven Nednhis (two men and five women and children) to head north for the border, where Haskell's sergeant of police, Atzebee, was waiting. The others would not leave until Juh and his warriors returned from their foray into New Mexico.[72]

At first, Juh summarily rejected Gordo's overture. Defiantly waving his rifle, he declared, "I am not going in. . . . If they get me they kill me." Gordo reasoned with his friend, pointing out that Juh's band had many children: "I don't see why you run like a wild man—no sleep and food, no water." Martine recalled that the messengers told Juh about the advantages of the reservation, urging him to come to San Carlos, where he would at least have peace of mind. And, because of General Willcox's involvement, Gordo could assure Juh and Geronimo that the Americans would not hold them accountable for previous depredations. "Nobody [is] going to hang you," declared the Bedonkohe chief to his Nednhi counterpart. One can imagine the two close friends, sitting at a campfire, smoking and drinking, as they reminisced about the old days and discussed the dramatic changes affecting their world. It was a hard sell, for Gordo must have addressed the deaths from malaria. Nonetheless, by morning, Juh came to see the wisdom in Gordo's words and agreed to consider moving to the reservation. After all, if his people disliked conditions there, they could always return to Mexico in the spring.[73]

Meanwhile, on October 31, 1879, Sergeant Atzebee arrived at San Carlos with seven Nednhis; they admitted that they were concerned about Mexican campaigns and revealed that the balance of the band would be in by December 10. In late November, Haskell sent Archie McIntosh, Atzebee, and one of the surrendered Nednhi men to try to make contact with Juh. After an absence of thirteen days, they returned without having seen Indians. Soon after, Haskell left, "intending to go through the Guadalupe Mountains into the Sierra Madre, taking two men and two Indians." The Indians were probably Chiricahuas. The second day out, after they had crossed into Mexico below San Bernardino hacienda, the scouts saw smoke signals from the Guadalupe Mountains, some "fifty or sixty miles to the eastward." Haskell dispatched George and another scout to find out what the signals "might mean."[74]

The Nednhis had sent the signals. As Daklugie recalled, once Juh had determined to move to San Carlos, his men "would have to acquire horses and other items needed for the trip." So, the chiefs sent out raiders to steal the "necessary mounts and supplies."[75] They struck the new mining town of Nacozari, where in a two-week period they stole over twenty mules and horses. The war party killed four Americans and two Mexicans near Tepache and Granados. Then they continued their march north toward the border to rendezvous with Haskell.[76]

During the night of December 12, one of Haskell's Apaches returned bringing news that the Nednhi would see him, but only if he came to their secluded camp without soldiers. Undaunted, Haskell left immediately, taking only his interpreter. At twilight on December 13, his party rode into a deep canyon and finally met the subjects of his search, a group of eighty Indians of the "most restless and suspicious tempers," led by Juh and Geronimo. The Indians had just lit their campfires. Gordo accompanied Haskell to Juh's wickiup to discuss the terms of surrender. A few days earlier, the band had held a council to discuss the offer brought by Gordo and Ah-dis. The decision to surrender was nearly unanimous. But the "third chief" of the band objected, and "in the heat of a most angry discussion, was shot dead by Johronimo [Geronimo]."

Juh (and Geronimo) had one simple concern: "Will my people have to go to jail if [we] surrender?" Haskell assured them that the agent would treat them well if they lived in peace. The lieutenant also promised to escort them to the reservation and to remain until Juh felt comfortable with the arrangements. Early one morning, Juh showed up at Haskell's tent. He explained, "Here is my wife and little boys. It is too cold in the mountains. I will stay with my friend." Haskell was euphoric; he knew that the Nednhiş would go to San Carlos.[77]

The two Nednhi chiefs denied any involvement with Victorio. They wanted to rest their stock and wait for the balance of their people before going to the reservation. They also asked that Chaffee send Nahilzay from San Carlos to them. Chaffee thought they were asking for Nolgee. On December 18, he cleared up the mistaken identity, writing that Nolgee was not at San Carlos.

But Nahilzay, "the man I think the Indians want, refuses to come to them." Yet, Chaffee must have impressed on Nahilzay the importance of this mission, for in three days he was on the move to Camp Rucker.[78]

Why they requested Nahilzay would soon become apparent. To begin with, he had surrendered at San Carlos in late August 1877. They probably wanted assurances that Americans had refrained from taking punitive action against him for his past raids. Furthermore, his half-brother, the Bedonkohe chief Esquine, was with the Nednhis. Esquine had first left San Carlos with Victorio and Loco in September 1877. In October 1878, he had remained with Victorio instead of returning to San Carlos. Most of his followers, who had numbered 175 three and a half years before, were either dead, at San Carlos with Chatto, or with Victorio. He had recently split from Victorio and joined the Nednhis after several hundred Mexican troops under General Trevino had attacked his village at Lake Guzman, killing or wounding eighty Chiricahuas on December 5, 1879. Though Trevino had certainly exaggerated the number of casualties, he had struck another dreadful blow to the Chiricahuas.[79]

Nahilzay arrived at Camp Rucker about December 24, and four days later Haskell's party, which included 102 Nednhis and 17 agency Apaches, threaded their way through the Chiricahuas, the Swisshelms, and then north toward Turkey Creek and Fort Bowie. On December 30, 1879, a "big talk was held," which included Tom Jeffords, whom they greeted with great fondness. Geronimo did most of the talking, as was customary because of Juh's tendency to stutter. Juh said he wanted a stable treaty. Willcox had written Haskell that the Nednhis "should be required to deliver up their arms unless there was a specific promise to the contrary." But this difficult undertaking would have been impossible to carry out. Juh had never been comfortable with Americans and, after three and one-half years in Mexico, was suspicious and skittish. He hoped that Agent Chaffee would permit them to live at the subagency with the Chokonens, a request that Chaffee granted.[80]

After the talk at Fort Bowie, the Nednhi warrior Jelikine and his wife paid a visit to the White Mountain scouts who had encamped near the fort. He joined them for a meal. John Rope, one of the scouts, who knew Jelikine well, watched carefully as a heavy-set Nednhi walked over to join them. This was Juh, whom, Jelikine said, even his own "people were afraid of," for he was a powerful shaman. The scouts invited Juh to sit down and eat, placing coffee and a plate of bread in front of him. He said, "All right, I like to try the scouts' food and see what it is like." After a satisfactory meal, the chief said, "It is good food and tastes well." That evening the Nednhis held a dance.

They invited the scouts to attend. Has-ke-na-dil-tla (Esquine), an "old, lame Nednhi," was the shaman who led the men in singing the songs for the social dances that lasted all night. The next day the Nednhis played the hoop and pole game with the scouts. The Chiricahua warrior, Nat-cul-baye, also known as José María Elías, wagered a white mule against John Rope's Navajo blanket. After the two men split the first four games, John Rope called off the fifth game over a misunderstanding.[81]

Haskell's cavalcade left Bowie in early January 1880, reaching San Carlos on January 7. Chaffee assigned them an area next to the Chokonens at the subagency. According to him, Juh's band numbered 103 individuals, of whom 21 were men.[82]

Lieutenant Harry Haskell, with the support of his superior, General Willcox, had carried out a demanding, if not dangerous assignment with patience, diplomacy, and courage. The controversial Archie McIntosh had also played an important, if not decisive, role. He may have known Geronimo during the latter's first stay at San Carlos, and McIntosh's influence among the Chiricahuas would grow stronger. Yet Haskell was the leader of the mission, the one who believed strongly in the long-term benefits for Chiricahuas, Americans, and Mexicans. Tom Jeffords was quick to praise his efforts, citing his "good judgment" and pointing out that Haskell had treated the Nednhis with respect, one of the basic doctrines in establishing good relations between former enemies.[83] General Willcox applauded Haskell for "the high order of military merit evinced by [him] in the patience, skill, and energy displayed in the execution of this important duty."[84] When Lieutenant Haskell returned to Prescott, he provided Arizona governor John C. Fremont a firsthand account of the mission. Fremont's daughter Lily succinctly summed up the operation in her diary entry: "Everyone thought it impossible he should succeed."[85]

If Haskell had failed, Juh would have faced grave danger in Mexico and possibly fatal consequences to his band. Mexico eventually would have exterminated them, just as they had Nolgee's group. Haskell's undertaking had not only saved Apache lives, but it had also brought peace to Sonora for the first time in almost a half-century. Few, if any, Apache raids occurred there between January 1880 and October 1881. Chihuahua, however, was not so fortunate, with Victorio lurking on its frontier.

As the new decade dawned, the four Chiricahua bands were now at San Carlos. They numbered about 700 people; only Victorio's Chihennes and a small band of Bedonkohes remained free, and together they totaled no more than 150 individuals (Victorio, however, had many Mescaleros with him).

Thus, since the dissolution of the two reservations in 1876 and 1877, the tribe had suffered a net loss of some 400 members. And, when one considers the probable number of births during this period, it is more likely that nearly 450 Chiricahuas had lost their lives to malaria and other diseases on the reservation, attacks from American troops led by Apache scouts, assaults by Mexican soldiers, and Mexican chicanery at Janos and Casas Grandes. The hardest hit were the Chokonens and Nednhis, each having endured a loss of about 150; in contrast, the Bedonkohes lost perhaps 75, and the Chihennes about 50.

Surprisingly, the Chihennes were the band least affected during this period. Yet, Victorio had a destiny, and it was gaping.

8

NAICHE SPEAKS,
AND FATE FINDS VICTORIO

Naiche says he has lost 125 of his band to sickness since 1876.
Thomas Jeffords to Colonel Eugene Asa Carr

After living the previous three and one-half years in Mexico, surviving by his wits, determination, and luck, Juh appreciated the tranquillity at San Carlos. He had settled his people at the subagency next to Naiche's Chokonens. A bond between the two men developed; the young Chokonen chief was drawn to the Nednhi chief, who had been a strong ally of his father. Agent Chaffee continued diligently to oversee affairs on the reservation. Despite the positive developments, several unforeseen events threatened their ability to endure the daily challenges of reservation life.

Shortly after Juh's arrival at San Carlos, General Willcox, recognizing the importance of attending to their needs, reminded Chaffee to pay special attention to Juh. The next day, on January 13, 1880, Chaffee assured Willcox that "so far the Chiricahuas [Nednhis] are contented with the late change of locality and mode of life. I think they will remain with us. I issue blankets to them in the morning."[1]

Willcox urged Chaffee to fulfill the promises made to the Nednhis. A month later, however, Chaffee reported that he had depleted his supply of flour. Severe winter weather had prevented the contractor from delivering on his contract. Instead of waiting to hear from the Bureau of Indian Affairs in Washington, Chaffee immediately sent a telegram to General Willcox, explaining the crisis. Willcox at once ordered the commander of Camp Thomas to provide the necessary flour so that Chaffee could issue the weekly ration. That minor emergency dissipated, Chaffee soon faced another problem: Juh's people were unhappy with the quality of the water near the subagency. To remedy this, Chaffee permitted the Chiricahuas to move their camps to the foothills, where the water was less stagnant and fit for consumption.[2]

Willcox then faced another situation. Mexican officials had protested Juh's return to Arizona. Willcox assured the Mexican consul at Tucson, Francisco Prieto, that Juh's followers "will be kept at San Carlos, where they can harm neither Americans nor Mexicans." Willcox even suggested that Juh might furnish men as scouts against hostiles, referring, of course, to Victorio's band. But Prieto remained concerned, suggesting that unless authorities kept Juh under scrutiny, he could leave the reservation and slip away into Mexico. Willcox downplayed that possibility, though he explained that to treat them as prisoners would be a "breach of faith" of their terms of surrender.[3]

This response failed to mollify Chihuahua's governor, Luis Terrazas, who was well acquainted with Juh. Terrazas demanded that Governor Fremont turn over Juh's band to Mexican officials. Fremont requested a response from General Willcox, who wrote a well-reasoned explanation that recited in chronological order the few known movements of Juh since he had left the Chiricahua Reservation in June 1876. He diplomatically pointed out that Juh had been in Mexico from that time until he requested peace with Chihuahua in the summer of 1879. But, because of that state's reluctance to provide economic assistance, negotiations had stalled. In conclusion, Willcox summarized,

> Since their surrender they have conducted themselves in a satisfactory manner. Juh, Geronimo, and their followers are not Mexican Indians. Their delivery [to Mexico] . . . is therefore disapproved for the following reasons: First, the Indians are American Indians; second, they returned based on our promise that they would be received and protected; third, these Indians were raiding in the United States and Mexico. Mexicans did nothing about either act; fourth, we have effected the separation of Juh and Geronimo from Victorio.[4]

Although he overplayed the alliance between Juh and Victorio, most of Willcox's points were valid. He probably had no way of knowing that the Nednhis' historic band territory lay primarily in northern Mexico. In contrast, the editor of the *Grant County Herald* reported that New Mexico's governor Lew Wallace would have "immediately complied with the request."[5]

Perhaps Juh had heard this talk, or was unhappy with the amount of rations, or simply longed to return to his former homes in the Sierra Madre, but by early spring 1880, rumors began to swirl that he was planning a breakout.

Chaffee had reduced by half the Chiricahuas' coffee and sugar rations because he had information that they had been trading them away. But this decision had angered the Chiricahuas because many were using coffee to prevent malaria.[6] On March 24, 1880, Colonel Eugene Asa Carr, in Tucson to give a speech to influential citizens, warned the commanding officer at Fort Bowie to prepare for a possible "break out" by Juh's band, who were reportedly dissatisfied.[7] Some three weeks later, department headquarters messaged Colonel Carr that the "trouble with Chiricahuas may be serious."[8] And in May 1880, Willcox ordered Lieutenant Cruse to take position near Ash Creek "to keep an eye on some malcontents" from Juh's band "who were threatening trouble." Cruse was also to watch out for Victorio, who had recently sent a war party to attack the families of Apache scouts allied with the military.[9] With uncertainty in the air, Geronimo, after an argument with Juh, joined Esquine, who had assumed leadership of Chatto's and Gordo's group.[10]

Victorio's activities in New Mexico and the danger he posed to the reservation had left military and civil officials concerned that he might invade the hallowed ground at San Carlos to liberate Loco's band or to incite other Chiricahuas. After all, many of Victorio's dependents were then living with Loco. And many Americans automatically assumed that Juh, who had joined forces with Victorio in late 1879, might again want to cast his lot with his fellow warrior. American troops, aided by Apache scouts, a few of them possibly Chiricahuas, had been chasing Victorio on both sides of the Rio Grande since late1879. With a large body of Mexican troops patrolling Chihuahua's northern frontier, the Chihenne chief's best options remained his ancestral strongholds in the Black Range and the San Mateo Mountains that guarded his beloved Ojo Caliente.

On January 12, 1880, Major Albert P. Morrow, with a large force, including artillery, overtook Victorio on Percha Creek, west of Hillsboro. Victorio escaped to the north, but not before the troops had slain several warriors. One sheepherder reported that Nana had held him prisoner. The chief had conceded that Morrow's artillery, or "big guns" as the chief called them, had killed six warriors. Morrow's loss was one sergeant killed and one scout wounded.[11] Morrow pursued Victorio along the eastern face of the Black Range until the chief crossed a grassy plain into the San Mateo Mountains, about fifteen miles north of Ojo Caliente.

Next, Victorio approached Cañada Alamosa and asked Andy Kelley about terms.[12] According to an unofficial account included in Karl Laumbach's seminal work on the battle at Hembrillo Canyon, Kelley probably remained in Victorio's camp as a hostage while the chief went to Ojo Caliente to discuss terms with Captain Hooker on January 16. After the parley, Hooker allowed Victorio to leave. When the chief reached camp, he released Kelley, and the conflict continued.[13]

Morrow's force caught up with Victorio the next day. His Apaches had taken positions near the top of "the highest peak," probably either Vics or San Mateo Peak, "when they displayed a white flag to talk." Victorio was there, "mounted on a white horse, a fine powerful animal which he had ridden on all of his recent raids." He wanted to go to Ojo Caliente, if Morrow "could assure him of protection." Morrow, naturally, insisted that Victorio's followers would first "have to give up their horses and weapons." Victorio had reportedly told Mexicans that he would go on a reservation if the "whites would deliver up his women and children now held at San Carlos."[14] After the parley, Morrow tried to dislodge the Apaches, but without success. The Indians shot and killed Lieutenant James French and wounded two scouts. Victorio escaped without loss.[15]

Colonel Hatch informed his counterpart in Arizona, General Willcox, to brace for another attempt by Victorio to liberate his relatives at San Carlos. He also passed along Victorio's offer to surrender if the government allowed his people at San Carlos to join him at Ojo Caliente.[16] Hatch endorsed the idea, as did his superiors, General John Pope, commander of the Department of the Missouri, and General Sherman in Washington. The Interior Department, however, rebuffed the proposal. Victorio's biographer Dan Thrapp concluded, "The Indians must meet Interior's terms or fight to the death."[17]

In February 1880 the homeless Chihennes forded the Rio Grande, crossed the Jornada del Muerto, and went into the San Andres Mountains. Three separate commands followed, one under the indefatigable Morrow and his Buffalo Soldiers, forcing the Chihennes to make one stand on February 3 and another six days later. Both fights were brisk engagements. Morrow claimed that he routed Victorio on the third, and Victorio drove Captain Louis H. Rucker from the field on the ninth. The troop's losses were one dead and four wounded. Morrow believed he had wounded or killed several Apaches. By the end of February, two of Victorio's men appeared near the Mescalero agency. But they would not deal with the military, and the agent, James Russell, refused to negotiate without authorization. Thus, the Americans squandered another chance to resolve this tragic and unnecessary war.

While Victorio rested in the San Andres Mountains, Colonel Hatch was organizing a three-pronged expedition to rout him from the mountains and then engage him in a climactic fight. The commander had assembled thirteen companies of cavalry (twelve of the Ninth and one of the Sixth), a detachment from the Fifteenth Infantry, a company of Navajo scouts from New Mexico, and three companies of Apache scouts from San Carlos under Lieutenant Charles B. Gatewood. This was the most formidable force organized against hostile Chiricahuas since the Bonneville Campaign of 1857. The plan was to trap Victorio in the San Andres Mountains, force him into a pivotal battle, and prevent the survivors from escaping to the south or west. Hatch's command outnumbered Victorio's fighting force, which included some fifty Mescaleros, by about five to one. But the troops were in three columns, and Victorio did not intend to make a stand against those odds unless absolutely forced to fight.

While Hatch was making these preparations, Victorio had been raiding settlements along the Rio Grande. Many Mescaleros (generously estimated at between 200 and 250, according to the Indian agent), concerned about the number of troops lurking near the reservation, left to join Victorio. In late March a Mescalero chief returned to the reservation with word from Nana that the Chihennes would settle at Ojo Caliente if permitted by the government. Unfortunately, this was not to be. In early April, Hatch's army began its offensive toward the San Andres Mountains.

On April 6, 1880, Captain Henry Carroll, with two companies of the Ninth Cavalry, went into Hembrillo Canyon with seventy-one troopers and a few civilian guides. Though he knew that Victorio was near (the day before, troops had skirmished with him), this knowledge did not prevent him from falling into a "V-shaped defensive trap" according to Karl Laumbach. About one hundred Apaches, equally divided between Mescaleros and Chiricahuas (mostly Chihennes with perhaps a few Bedonkohes), sprang the trap, unleashing a withering fusillade that surprised Carroll's command.[18] Surveying the situation, Carroll decided to occupy the nearest ridge in front of his men. Fortunately for the troopers, night was approaching, and the Indian positions were too distant to inflict any damage.

That evening Carroll faced two challenges: his thirsty men and mounts needed water, and the Apaches, he supposed, would take advantage of the darkness to assume closer positions. Carroll decided to lead a detachment to reach the springs that lay about 350 yards away. But Victorio and his men were waiting for Carroll's parched-mouth troopers. From their concealed positions, they picked off several of the brave captain's troopers, wounding a good number, including Captain Carroll. Because only a few men had been able to fill canteens from the spring, most of Carroll's troopers went thirsty.

The Apaches were so close that the entrenched soldiers used their revolvers to keep them at bay.

The first detail to arrive the morning of April 7, 1880, was Lieutenant Patrick Cusack's two companies of Ninth Cavalry, which had followed Carroll's trail into Hembrillo Canyon. Although Victorio's warriors launched several volleys at Cusack's command, the cavalry rendezvoused with Carroll without suffering any loss. The second command, under Captain Curwen McLellan, which consisted of one company of the Sixth Cavalry and three companies of Apache scouts from San Carlos led by Lieutenants Charles Gatewood, Stephen C. Mills, and James A. Maney, reached the scene shortly after Cusack. Laumbach believes Chiricahua scouts were present, perhaps for the first time in combat as American allies against their kinfolk.[19] Even though the Americans and their Apache allies outnumbered Victorio's force three to one, Victorio remained on the battlefield. Later that day the combined forces assaulted Victorio's positions and finally drove him from his fortified entrenchments. Apache scouts played an important role during the flanking movements that forced the chief to abandon his village. One Western Apache scout, Harvey Nashkin, recalled that the fight ended when American forces shot a Chiricahua chief, likely Miguel Tuerto, in the late afternoon. Tuerto, a leader noted for his bravery and disdain for reservation life, died soon after. The Apaches left three bodies on the field of action. The soldiers lost eight men wounded of Carroll's command (two fatally).[20]

The allied Apaches made their escape. Some Mescaleros headed toward their reservation but discovered that a large American force had surrounded the agency and disarmed their people. Thus, they left for the mountains. Victorio, joined by several Mescaleros, crossed the Rio Grande and headed back to his beloved Black Range. En route, on April 20, 1880, Sánchez, an inveterate raider well known to residents of Cañada Alamosa, and Vicente, a relative of Geronimo (perhaps a brother), led a mixed band of Mescaleros and Chihennes on a raid against the herd at Cañada Alamosa. The next day Victorio and Cavio, probably Caballo, a noted shaman, talked to Andy Kelley and warned him that hostilities would continue unless Loco's band was sent to Ojo Caliente from San Carlos.[21]

Running out of patience, the Chihenne patriot chief decided to take matters into his own hands: a foray to San Carlos to liberate his women and children still confined at San Carlos. This would serve two purposes. First, his route would take them through the Mogollon country, and he owed the settlers there for their ambush of Turivio's party the previous year. Second, he wanted to exact revenge on the Western Apaches for their active role at Hembrillo Canyon and on the White Mountain chief Bylas for stealing his horses during his breakout from San Carlos in 1877.

On April 28 a party of warriors, led by the Bedonkohe Francisco, approached a sheep camp manned by eight Mexicans. José María Sánchez owned the herd, which totaled about ten thousand. Seeing the Apaches approaching from the mountains, Sánchez sent Teodoso Sánchez to take a position overlooking camp. Francisco approached in peace, asking for something to eat. A hospitable Sánchez invited them to come in: "Help yourselves, there is plenty of meat, corn, flour, coffee, and sugar." Once the Indians had surrounded the camp, "Francisco ordered the band to fire," which was the signal for Victorio to rush in with more warriors. "A general fire opened all around" as the Apaches slaughtered Sánchez, six Mexicans, and hundreds of sheep in the cross fire. The lookout, Teodoso Sánchez, though shot in the abdomen, was able to mount his horse and escape.[22]

The next day the war party lay siege to the mining settlement in Keller's Valley, today known as Alma. Victorio's party ambushed two men before they could make it to their cabins. Their horses returned to Alma without James Cooney, the leading miner in the region, and Jack Chick. Immediately the settlement of thirty-two miners with their families prepared to fight. Many families took shelter at the Roberts place, a fortress the miners had built to withstand an Apache attack. About 10:00 A.M. Victorio's warriors opened fire. That afternoon one brave Chihenne approached so close that a miner from inside the cabin was able to send a shot into his body, killing him instantly. This proved to be Manuelito, one of Victorio's most prominent warriors.[23] Roman Sarecena, who knew Manuelito, helped bury the corpse. That night the Apaches burned several unoccupied log cabins. The fighting continued the next day with no known casualties before Victorio withdrew the evening of April 30, 1880. All told, Victorio's men had killed four miners. He had avenged Turivio's death, but it had come with a cost.[24]

In early May Colonel Hatch warned his counterpart in Arizona, General Willcox, to brace for Victorio, who was "en route to San Carlos." Willcox forwarded this information to Chaffee, who prepared to thwart Victorio's plans. First, he sent his agency police to patrol the eastern section of the reservation; next, he ordered the Chokonens and Nednhis to return to the subagency. They had likely been living near Black Rock or perhaps in the Gila Mountains, north of today's Sánchez, a favorite campsite of Geronimo. Regardless, Chaffee's decree came as a disappointment to Juh and especially Naiche, who recalled the malaria outbreaks that had devastated his people the previous two springs while they were living near the subagency, along the Gila lowlands.[25]

Chaffee and Willcox were uneasy, awaiting the explosion. On May 7, 1880, a band of Chihennes emerged from the hills near George Stevens's ranch on Eagle Creek. They "cleaned out" the ranch's cattle and horses. Victorio led them, and he clearly planned to continue the bloody cycle of revenge and retaliation. Some accounts state that Washington, Victorio's son, was the leader, and that Nana assisted him. It seems likely that each man was present. Regardless, their motive remained clear to all. As summed up by new agent Joseph C. Tiffany, "The raid was to get their squaws [and children] and have revenge on the scouts who fought them."

According to one report, Victorio first surprised two White Mountain men who were playing cards, telling them he had "come to fight the scouts." Next, according to the reliable John Rope, Victorio forced one man to divulge the whereabouts of Bylas, who had gone to the subagency but was due to return. The chief then set up a trap and slaughtered Bylas and "all his family." The *Arizona Silver Belt* placed the dead at nineteen men, women, and children, but that report may have been premature or exaggerated. George had seen Victorio. Charles Connell, an American well acquainted with the Chiricahuas who worked at San Carlos, confirmed Victorio's presence. And Jimmie Stevens, son of George Stevens, told author Ross Santee that Victorio was responsible. Moreover, though two Apaches told George Stevens that they had seen Victorio, for some reason Tom Jeffords, whom Carr had called on to investigate, was not so sure. In any event, the White Mountain Apaches would forever remember this act. In the months and years to come, the army would have no trouble enlisting scouts to serve against the Chiricahuas. In particular, Richard Bylas, the nephew of the slain Bylas, never forgot the affair.[26]

American troops and Apache scouts responded quickly to the Chihennes, who numbered thirty-six according to Chaffee, and ninety according to the first report of Colonel Carr.[27] Chaffee's estimate was closer to the mark. Though Victorio had accomplished one objective, he was unable to achieve his second goal. It was too dangerous to approach his relatives with Loco, for their village was near the San Carlos agency, where they were under the watchful eyes of the agency police and scouts. Before leaving, however, he did succeed in getting a messenger to the Nednhis, but they wanted no part of his cause.[28] Just as he decided to retreat, Captain Adam Kramer, with a detachment of the Sixth Cavalry and Apache scouts, overtook the Chihennes at Rocky Canyon near Ash Creek. After a brisk engagement, the Apaches withdrew, but not before they had killed one soldier and wounded an Apache scout.[29]

The Chihenne raiding party in Arizona inspired Willcox to take action. He telegraphed Colonel Carr in Tucson, ordering him to move out in full force to pursue Victorio "to the bitter end." One day later, on May 9, 1880, Willcox fretted that Victorio might get away before troops could punish him.[30] Finally, as Victorio faded back to the mountains of New Mexico, an agitated Willcox decided to turn his full attention to the Chihenne chief. He revealed his thoughts in a letter to Colonel Carr:

> It appears as Victorio is trying to do in Arizona as he has done in New Mexico. The general wishes you to prevent this, if possible, and will for that purpose place the resources of this department at your disposal. He hopes that you may be able to give the old scoundrel a good thrashing. . . . The fact that the old fellow has been able to do pretty much as he pleased in New Mexico has been pretty much attributed to the color of his opponents in that country.[31]

The last assertion, a direct condemnation of black soldiers of the Ninth and Tenth Cavalry, is illustrative of the inherent contempt, disrespect, and outright bigotry manifested by some military officers toward the Buffalo Soldiers. Many white officers who commanded black soldiers did not share this opinion, however. And, in fact, Willcox's disparaging comment about the performance of the black regiments in New Mexico was completely spurious and unwarranted. White soldiers would not have fared any better than the Buffalo Soldiers; the qualities that made a good soldier—obedience, discipline, and courage—were, of course, color blind. But it remained a controversial subject during the Apache Wars, almost on a par with the military's use of so-called treacherous Apache scouts. One newspaper, *Thirty-Four*, published in Las Cruces, blamed the black soldiers for the military's inability to subdue Victorio. It repeated the racist impression that these soldiers lacked courage and pride.[32]

While Victorio occupied Willcox's thoughts, Agent Chaffee reported a disturbing rumor to him. The word was that Juh was restless, perhaps over rations or living conditions at the subagency, and planned to leave the reservation and join Victorio, if "he gets the opportunity."[33] This news jolted the department commander, for he had thought that Juh was content. At once he telegraphed Colonel Carr, ordering him to move troops to the vicinity of San Carlos in case of an outbreak. Then he ordered Naiche's and Juh's people to return to the subagency from their mountain homes even though they had no intention of joining Victorio.

The two chiefs returned grudgingly. Each time rumors placed Victorio near the agency, Indian officials ordered those Chiricahuas living a healthy lifestyle in the nearby mountains back to the subagency near the malaria-infested Gila marshes. Within weeks of returning, Naiche's and Juh's followers faced yet another epidemic of malaria that would claim many lives. By June 1880 a smoldering animosity had taken hold of the two chiefs, especially Naiche, whose medicine men felt impotent against this insidious disease. Naiche had had enough. This was the third consecutive year of malaria, and he knew the plague was related to their living conditions. He was ready to leave the reservation.

Willcox was focused on bringing Victorio to San Carlos. Recalling the success of Haskell's mission in bringing in the Nednhis, he thought the opportunity might be ripe to convince Victorio to come in. Thus, he decided to try to enlist Juh's and Naiche's services as emissaries to Victorio. After all, he reasoned, the "best way to keep Juh [on the reservation] is to employ him on our side, watch him, pay him well, and act accordingly."[34]

The plan was to send Tom Jeffords and Archie McIntosh to solicit advice from the Chiricahuas about bringing in Victorio. Willcox wanted Juh and Naiche to take a message to Victorio to tell him that he "has been out long enough and must come in" to San Carlos. Willcox even offered to pay Juh and Naiche sixty dollars a month and lesser chiefs, specifically Nahilzay, forty-five dollars per month. Both Willcox and Carr recognized the unique influence Jeffords enjoyed with the Chiricahuas who had the "utmost confidence" in their former agent. Carr maintained that the Chiricahuas "will do more for him [Jeffords] than for anybody [else]." Carr planned to send Jeffords and McIntosh to San Carlos before he moved his troops near the agency. They could assure Juh that Carr's visit was to promote peace and understanding. This promise was necessary because the Nednhis were extremely skittish, and they may have misinterpreted the presence of troops, thinking they were "about to be captured, dismounted, or disarmed."[35]

Willcox asked Colonel Carr to arrange matters with the agent. On May 13, Carr telegraphed Chaffee, enclosing copies of correspondence between him and Willcox, assuming that the agent would acquiesce to Willcox's wishes. Both Carr and Willcox thought that Chaffee was "suspicious of Hoo [Juh] and company."[36] Even so, Chaffee's reaction to their plan must have surprised them. The scrupulously honest Chaffee, whose term as agent was ending, was in no mood to adopt a policy that he thought was unwise, even though it was popular with officers who outranked him. Not only did Carr's suggestion fall flat, but Chaffee, his explosion point now attached to a very short fuse because he felt Willcox and Carr were overstepping their authority, solely to appease Juh, refused to allow either McIntosh or Jeffords on the reservation.

Chaffee telegraphed Carr:

> I have no respect for their opinion. As to their influence, it is bane-ful in the extreme. Juh is now here and I have talked with him for an hour. He professes the best friendship and says he has no wish to leave further. He pretends to speak for his whole band. The other Chiricahua captains have been here today and state their feelings to be like those of Juh. If Victorio stays away, I have no fear and will retain Juh and his band here and hope to do so even though Victorio should come. I have ever treated him kindly the same as all the rest but no better and under all circumstances require obedience from the rest. . . . I [will] continue to do so is one reason why I do not want the presence of both McIntosh and Jeffords on the reservation. They can have no authority. Neither would they adopt my view of the case. Jef-fords was once ordered off this reservation. [McIntosh], I do not want about me at all. With due respect for the wishes of General Willcox and proper appreciation of his great desire to assist me in every way possible, I must still decline the services of these men and their pres-ence also. All quiet [here].[37]

Carr, who had sent Jeffords by stage to Camp Thomas, wired him to remain there to "await further orders." Yet he saw a silver lining to the situation: "One good thing, Chaffee will not send for Archie McIntosh so when you get at them you will do everything your own way." That suited the independent nature of Jeffords.[38] Meanwhile, at Camp Thomas, Captain Stacey, whom Carr had taken into his confidence, apparently helped Jeffords with logistics. Jeffords, who remained at Camp Thomas for about a month, gathered intel-ligence for Carr, who conceded that he did so under "rather difficult circum-stances." Jeffords discovered that the Chiricahuas were reluctant to bring in Victorio. He did meet Naiche, who begged off because "he has two wives, etc." He predicted that Juh would come to the fort and see him the moment he heard of Jeffords's presence.[39]

By May 23, 1880, Jeffords had met both Geronimo and Juh and had care-fully explained the situation to them. They complained about Chaffee "shut-ting them up" along the Gila after Victorio's raid on May 7. According to

Jeffords, they were "very near leaving the reservation on account of confinement and sickness." He persuaded them to remain until the arrival of new agent, Joseph C. Tiffany, who was due to replace Chaffee within the week. Jeffords also talked to the Chiricahuas about Victorio but admitted they had no specific information on his movements. For now, Jeffords believed that "Juh and the rest are all right."[40]

Joseph C. Tiffany arrived at San Carlos on June 1, 1880. He would be the last agent nominated by the Reformed Church as part of the policy first established by President Grant in the early 1870s. Honest, deeply religious, and a sincere humanitarian, Tiffany seemed the ideal candidate for the position. But, like most government-appointed agents to the Apaches, he had neither experience nor any knowledge of them. Contemporary opinion suggested that Tiffany's tenure was marked by failure, graft, and disaster. Yet, John Bret Harte argues persuasively that contemporaries and historians have besmirched Tiffany's character and misrepresented his record. Though somewhat portly in stature (the Chiricahuas called him Big Belly), Tiffany was an energetic man with progressive ideas, and he was accustomed to getting things done.[41]

Tiffany actually received the appointment despite the efforts of two former Chiricahua agents who again wanted the job: John Clum and Tom Jeffords. In December 1879, Clum naturally wrote his own letter of recommendation to the commissioner of Indian affairs. After all, was there a mortal alive who could have properly understood the nuances of the man and his unsurpassed accomplishments as agent? He reminded the commissioner, "I did good work for the government during my administration and could do more. Will you consider my application?" He crowed about his record of accomplishment: "You know who I am and what I am." This ominous statement must have annoyed Commissioner Hayt, then embroiled in a controversy because of Hart and Hammond at San Carlos, a conspiracy that would cost him his job. Clum's arrogant assertion reminded the commissioner of why he could never consider Clum, whose antagonism toward the military was well known.[42]

Jeffords was another matter. Sometime in early 1880, he had decided that he would take the job if offered to him. This was probably not his idea but instead the notion of well-meaning friends. Unlike Clum, Jeffords rarely tooted his own horn. Military men were his strongest supporters; perhaps they realized that Jeffords could make their job easier. Arizona governor John C. Fremont, the old Pathfinder who understood the importance of a good scout or frontiersman, wrote the first letter of recommendation on January 24, 1880. It was no coincidence that Fremont composed the letter the day after he and his daughter had entertained Lieutenant Haskell and learned of Jeffords's role in bringing Juh's band from Mexico.[43] Haskell and General Willcox were likely behind his dispatch, which the governor laced with a good dose of fact along with the obligatory hyperbole inherent in most letters of recommendation. He wrote:

> I write to ask from you the appointment [of] Mr. Jeffords, former agent for the Chiricahua [Apaches] with whom he has a very peculiar influence. Those Indians seek his advice on all important occasions and might be relied on always to be guided by it. In a recent visit to them he was received with demonstrations of extraordinary affection such as Indians most rarely bestow on any white man. According to what I have learned there could not be found at the moment a man so singularly well qualified for the post as he is. The Chiricahuas are the ruling element among the Indians at the agency and I believe that his appointment would secure the certainty of continued peace among these Indians. . . . I am satisfied that General Howard, General Willcox, and other officers would strongly unite in my request for Jeffords' appointment.

One day later, Fremont added a few more details about the nature of the fascinating relationship between Tom Jeffords and Cochise:

> In continuation of my letter from yesterday . . . I write to say that the chief Cochise died in Mr. Jeffords' arms. I mention this as giving to show Mr. Jeffords' fitness because of his friendly relations with the Chiricahuas. . . . I would add to Mr. Jeffords' efficiency that he would have friendly cooperation from the military officers of the Territory who remember and recognize the value of his former services.[44]

It hardly mattered that Cochise did not take his last breaths in the arms of Jeffords, for the former agent did have more influence among the Chiricahuas than any other white man had.

About a month later General Willcox added his two cents' worth. He pointed out that Jeffords enjoyed the "confidence of Governor Fremont, General Stoneman, and General Howard." For that reason, Willcox, after making his own inquiries, also endorsed Jeffords: "The importance of having an experienced, able, and honest man at San Carlos is so great that the question of peace or war in Arizona depends on it."[45] Even Lieutenant Guy Howard, son of General Howard, had concluded that Jeffords was "by far the best man, civilian, to take charge of the various tribes collected at San Carlos." He asked his father to "write in Jeffords' favor to the Secretary of the Interior."[46]

Given these important endorsements, we must ask the question, why was Jeffords apparently not considered? There is no "smoking gun" or memorandum that could provide us with some insight into the minds of those making the decisions in Washington. Likely, Indian officials, fed up with the endless criticism and incessant controversy at San Carlos, simply wanted a fresh start. The responsibility for nominating agents for Arizona rested with the missionary board of the Reformed Church. Thus, when Brigadier General Clinton B. Fisk, a member of the Board of Indian Commissioners, proposed Joseph Tiffany, the deal was struck.[47]

Unfortunately, no one seems to have considered that Jeffords could still have served an important role on the reservation, perhaps as Tiffany's assistant or, more importantly, as subagent for the Chiricahuas. Though he would not have adopted a progressive program like Tiffany (building a school and overseeing the digging of irrigation ditches), Jeffords might well have provided the trusting counsel to avert the two major outbreaks from the reservation in 1881 and 1885. In retrospect, the two men might have been a good mix: Tiffany lacked knowledge and experience with the Apaches; Jeffords lacked the vision and organizational skills of Tiffany. If they could have worked with each other, perhaps—just perhaps—they could have put egos aside, and together may have brought stability to Indian affairs at San Carlos.

Willcox was disappointed in Tiffany's appointment. He was skeptical. When he heard the news, he urged Governor Fremont to use his influence to reverse the decision. He feared an outbreak that "would be infinitely worse than Victorio in New Mexico [and] would stop all mining in this Territory for years to come." Fortunately for all concerned, his doomsday prophecy failed to occur, and on June 1, 1880, Joseph C. Tiffany arrived at San Carlos. One of his first actions was to restore the coffee and sugar rations, cut in half by Chaffee, to full issues.[48]

Two days after Tiffany assumed his new position, General Willcox instructed Colonel Carr to visit San Carlos. The department commander had several issues on his mind. He wanted Carr's thoughts on the new agent, the mood of Juh and Naiche, and a prognosis for getting the Chiricahuas' help in organizing a peace party to bring Victorio in to San Carlos. A seasoned veteran of almost a quarter of a century of service in the West, Carr thought the "nation owes it to itself to treat the poor, miserable savages with justice and humanity."[49]

He reached San Carlos in late June. To guarantee that he would find a warm welcome with the Chiricahuas, he had Tom Jeffords as his interpreter, liaison, and advisor (at 150 dollars per month), and the help of Frank Bennett, chief of police at San Carlos. Jeffords's presence comforted Naiche and Juh, who both spoke freely and candidly. For Naiche, it would be the most revealing interview during his years at San Carlos.

Carr first paid a courtesy call to Agent Tiffany at San Carlos on June 30, 1880. For two days Carr sized up the fifty-two-year-old civil servant. Tiffany impressed Carr, who described the agent as an "excellent gentleman, determined to do what is right, and having the ability to carry out his intentions at least as well as any man could do under the circumstances in which he is placed. . . . He has already acquired respect and regard from his wards." He praised Tiffany's plans for building schools to educate children and to increase the amount of tillable land by "making dams and acequias."

Next, he and Jeffords followed the Gila east about fifteen miles to the sub-agency, where Chaffee had confined the Chiricahuas since Victorio's raid in early May. Carr held a powwow with Juh, Geronimo, and Naiche. But Nahilzay was ominously absent because his daughter had just died from malaria. With the trusted Jeffords by their side, Juh and Naiche felt comfortable enough to voice their displeasure at their living conditions along the malaria-infested Gila lowlands. Both chiefs complained "that they were kept more closely confined than other Indians." Juh pointed out that he had come in voluntarily, and Naiche reminded Carr that he had lived peacefully at San Carlos for the past four years.

Naiche, noting that "there were many deaths," wondered why they could not return to their ancestral homes in the Chiricahua Mountains, where "they were always well." Jeffords believed "they were very near leaving the reservation a short time since because of confinement and sickness." But he persuaded them to remain until the arrival of the new agent, who "might give them more liberty."

This travesty was equally apparent to Carr:

> The subject of sickness and death at San Carlos is a painful one and is apt to be shirked. I suppose it is now impossible to change their location and they must submit to what is in store for them palliated only by such sanitary and medical provisions as can be made available and

by the gradual acclimation of those who survive. . . . Of all the bands
on the San Carlos Reservation, I believe that only part of the White
Mountain Apaches [who are] allowed to live in the mountains and the
Arivaipas are born healthy.[50]

Carr also observed that the Apaches' medicine men had no measures with
which to counter malaria. Moreover, most of the Chiricahuas "do not like to
use white man's medicine," a statement confirmed by the Apaches.

The chief's passionate appeals for common consideration touched Carr,
particularly after Naiche stated that he had lost one-third of his band (which
had numbered 325) to sickness (primarily malaria) "since they came to the
reservation in 1876." A few days later, Naiche must have made a count of
those victims, for he told Jeffords to tell Carr that some 125 Chokonens had
perished from sickness, a figure that seems about right given the scant census
data from 1876 to 1880. The significance of Naiche's admission is that one
cannot find any reference to these fatalities among the records of the San Carlos agency. Most occurred on Hart's watch.

Carr's third objective was to learn what he could from the Chiricahuas
about Victorio, and whether he would be receptive to emissaries from San
Carlos. He summarized what he had learned from the chiefs:

> Several of his friends have spoken about going to see him. They think
> he would not come in while pressed by our troops. . . . He [is] now
> in Mexico . . . [and] would no doubt come in to San Carlos on assur-
> ances of safe conduct. When [here] it would depend on how he felt
> upon seeing his family etc. whether he would be willing to bring in
> his band. He is about sixty years old and is said to be very fond of his
> wife and children now at the agency. Reports differ as to whether he
> has a younger wife with him or [not]. . . . Colonel Tiffany is will-
> ing to have Victorio's band on the Reservation, and would cooperate
> cordially.

In wrapping up his discussion of Victorio, Carr passed along Jeffords's belief that "nothing could be done with Victorio either to ask him in to treat
[for peace] or to treat with him in the field without the presence of a white
man in whom he has confidence." And who could carry out this assignment?
According to Jeffords, only he and "another man now in Mexico," clearly a
reference to Zebina Streeter, "could or would fill that bill." Jeffords obviously

envisioned organizing a peace party to duplicate his remarkable mission to Cochise. Unfortunately, his former guides, Chie and Ponce, were now dead. But he had enough influence among the Chiricahuas to enlist either a relative or a close friend of Victorio. The mission would remain under consideration for the rest of the summer of 1880.

Carr's report is noteworthy for two other observations. First, he noted that if "Congress would support a sufficient force to put down the first show of hostility, I think that the Indians would be allowed to live and roam in their native mountains without danger to whites and without dying from bullets or malaria." Second, he informed Tiffany of the Chiricahuas' concern that "there was a difficulty about his interpreter [Mickey Free] conveying what was said to or by them" during their first meeting with Tiffany. This would not be the last time they would complain about Free's integrity or capabilities.[51]

After General Willcox read Carr's report, he quickly realized that the government must take action to transfer the Chiricahuas from the Gila lowlands to the mountains. If forced to remain at the present location, a bust-out was almost sure to follow. On July 8, he telegraphed Carr to ask Tiffany for "the best measures possible for the health" of Juh's and Naiche's bands.[52] Tiffany, to his credit, responded immediately. He dropped everything to visit the camps of the Chiricahuas. He saw firsthand the sickly conditions and was much moved. Tiffany counted fifty-nine sick persons in the Chokonen and Nednhi rancherías. Moreover, within the past month, ten persons had perished from the shaking sickness. Though Tiffany did not mention the specific cause of death, he attributed the sickness to "living in the low lands along the Gila River . . . [and to drinking] the water which is very different from mountain springs."

Tiffany also spoke to the chiefs, particularly Juh and Geronimo, who admitted that they had thought about leaving the reservation because they were not getting enough to eat. They explained to Tiffany that "they had been wild . . . and had to live on things obtained in the mountains." But the confinement at the subagency deprived them of gathering natural food such as mescal, nuts, and berries. And without these staples to supplement their rations, they were often hungry. Tiffany had seen enough. By the end of the visit, he gave the chiefs the good news: they could move their people from the death camps into the mountains and live in a fifteen-mile strip between Mount Turnbull and Black Rock in the Santa Teresa Mountains. The chiefs were "happy and pleased" with their new locations. The news also delighted Willcox, who expressed his appreciation to Tiffany for the decision.[53] A few weeks later Tiffany could report that all "is quiet on the reservation. The Indians are peaceable."[54]

Now Carr turned to another urgent problem. At the urging of General Willcox, he wrote to Colonel Edward Hatch, the commander of the District of New Mexico, to explain their plan to bring Victorio to San Carlos:

> I am not in favor of proposing peace to hostile Indians but I think that communication with Victorio could be opened, if deemed desirable, by sending some Indians from San Carlos with a white man. There are Indians at San Carlos who are friends of Victorio and who have proposed to open communication with him. Capt. T. J. Jeffords, formerly agent with Cochise's band, and now Post Trader at Camp Huachuca, would be willing to go with them.[55]

Meanwhile, after the May raid at San Carlos, Victorio had returned to his beloved Black Range. Here, at daybreak on May 24, 1880, Chief of Scouts Henry K. Parker and sixty Apache scouts, having surrounded Victorio's group during the night, poured a deadly fire into the camp, which was in a draw on a ridge at the head of Palomas Creek. Anticipating the Apaches' response to the first volley, Parker had divided his scouts into three divisions and positioned them to cover Victorio's expected route of escape. Within minutes, Victorio realized that he was "hemmed in [on] all sides." Surrounded by the scouts, his people sought refuge between two large rocks. For the rest of that day, the two sides continued to snipe at each other. Victorio, whom the scouts had wounded in the leg, maintained a lively exchange with his enemies, who remained in the high country overlooking the village until the afternoon of the second day. Now, his ammunition nearly depleted, Parker withdrew his force. The Western Apache scouts, with no help from regular troops, had won a stunning victory. Victorio had lost at least thirty killed (perhaps as many as fifty-five), including several of his best fighters. Parker had not lost a man.[56] Shortly after the battle, a party from Paraje came upon the scene and later described the grisly battlefield as "awful . . . the rocks and ground for a mile are covered with blood and the remains of Indians."[57]

Dan Thrapp concludes that this was a turning point in the Victorio War of 1879–80. After all, he points out, the Chihenne chief had "never been trapped, never clearly defeated" before Parker's decisive blow. "But from this time forward his star was on the decline."[58] Two weeks later, Apache scouts overtook a small party of Chihennes near Cookes Canyon and killed several, including Washington, Victorio's son. By then, the chief was harboring no illusions about his fate. With most of his family at San Carlos and his eldest son recently slain fighting for a cause he now knew was hopeless, he raced for Chihuahua to escape the troops and scouts. Before leaving, he released a Mexican captive who claimed that Victorio told him he "would not surrender until the last man was killed."[59]

Victorio headed for Chihuahua.[60] He had shown too much strength to have drawn from only his own Chihennes and Bedonkohe followers. Clearly, a large group of Mescaleros, disenchanted with the military control of their reservation, had remained out with him. His band numbered about 250 followers, split between Chiricahuas and Mescaleros. But there was dissension in the ranks. One Mescalero chief, Caballero, wanted to take his followers back to the reservation; Victorio promptly put an end to this defiance, killing the Mescalero chief to discourage further defections. By August, he had returned to the Candelaria Mountains. Twice he crossed the border into Texas, apparently trying to find sanctuary at the Mescalero agency, but both times troops turned him back.[61]

Before much longer, in mid-October 1880, Mexican troops under Lieutenant Colonel Joaquin Terrazas succeeded in cornering Victorio and most of his followers at Tres Castillos in east-central Chihuahua. Over a two-day battle, which ended on October 15, 1880, when the Apaches ran out of ammunition, Terrazas's force annihilated Victorio's band, killing seventy-eight, of whom sixty-one were warriors, at least according to Terrazas, but Apache accounts are at variance. The Mescaleros admitted that they lost forty-four dead, and that fewer than ten were men. If true, the Chiricahua fatalities totaled thirty-four, which included Victorio and many of his prominent men. Terrazas simply states that his men discovered Victorio's body after the battle; his corpse was identified by the "scar on his face near his mouth and broken incisive teeth." The Chiricahuas claim that Victorio took his own life when he realized all was lost. In addition, Terrazas had captured sixty-eight Apaches— twenty Mescaleros and forty-eight Chiricahuas.

Turquoise, a Mescalero with Victorio the night before the final battle, said that Victorio knew the end was near because he had run out of ammunition. Victorio said: "You are a man, but the end will be at sunrise." During the final battle, as several women and children were surrendering, Turquoise and a few others "ran like the wind [and] outran the bullets." They made their way back to the Mescalero agency.[62]

Of the 145 Chihennes with Victorio when he broke from Mescalero on August 1879, perhaps 60 to 70 survived Tres Castillos. They were led by Nana, a seventy-year-old grandfather, Mangas, Kaetenae, Jatu, Showano, and

Sánchez. These six leaders could boast but fifteen fighting men and a few boys capable of bearing arms. Among these survivors were Choneska; Bacutla and Nezulkide (two brothers of Kaetenae); Frijole, whose Apache name was Pet-zahn; Guydelkon; As-ka-do-del-ges, also known as Charley, Mahgado, and Chobegoza.

Some thirty-five Chihenne and Bedonkohe warriors had fallen with Victorio during the war of 1879–80. The important leaders, besides the chief (who apparently lost three sons, including Washington), were Turivio, last surviving son of Cuchillo Negro; the brothers Lopez and Tomaso Coloradas, sons of Mangas Coloradas; Horache, son-in-law of Nana; Vicente, a brother or brother-in-law of Geronimo; Francisco, a Bedonkohe chief; two warlike Chihenne chiefs, Miguel Tuerto and Raton, who were inflexible opponents of reservation life; Sathtin, a noted warrior; and Ponce, the good-natured guide of General Howard.

Terrazas's victory, the greatest disaster to befall the Chihenne band since Carrasco's surprise attack at Janos in 1851, provided a tragic climax to Victorio's fight for basic justice and his homeland. It would be normal to conclude that his death broke the spirit of his followers who outlived him. Yet, exactly the opposite resulted, and the coming year of 1881 would be a pivotal one. Nana would see to it that a bloody cycle of revenge and retaliation would follow. And old memories and distrust of the American military would force the Chokonens and Nednhis to make a decision about reservation life.

9

SUSPICION AND FEAR LEAD TO OUTBREAK

The talk of troops made Geronimo nervous. He was like a wild animal.

Chatto, 1931

The attitude of the Chiricahua Apaches at San Carlos in late 1880 was mixed. To be sure, once they confirmed the rumors of Victorio's death and that of most of his principal men, many of Loco's band went into mourning. After all, many of Victorio's men had sent their dependents to San Carlos with Loco. Even though one Chihenne, José Chanez, claimed that he had seen the chief after Tres Castillos, Agent Joseph Tiffany believed the news of his death. Charles Connell, at San Carlos in early 1881, believed that a few of Victorio's followers did return to the reservation, and, if so, Chanez could have been among them.[1] Agent Tiffany had heard that Victorio's widow at San Carlos, following the customs of her people, had cut her hair, likely to about ear length, after hearing of her husband's death.[2] But now she claimed that Victorio was alive and that she had cut her hair because of an illness.[3]

The other Chiricahua bands, though disheartened over the news, realized that Victorio had died in the manner he had sought. Those living at the subagency may have even felt relieved, for without his presence, there would be no more threats from him, thus no more relocations to the malarious lowlands of the Gila. Years later, writing from memory, Charles Connell recalled that in early 1881, the "Chiricahuas were seemingly content, and no indication of an outbreak by [them] was evident."[4]

Yet, in 1881, Victorio's successor, the seventy-year-old arthritic Nana, assisted by two capable assistants, Mangas and Jatu, led several raids into New

167

Mexico. The Apaches believed that Nana could call on his Power. He possessed two sources of supernatural help: Power over rattlesnakes, and Power over ammunition, for he had been able to lead raids that provided ammunition to his followers, which was a welcome addition because cartridges were always scarce.[5] Nana's reassuring presence rallied the survivors of Tres Castillos.

After Tres Castillos, Nana promptly clashed with both Mexicans and Americans, slaying five troopers of the Tenth Cavalry in Texas at Ojo Caliente below Fort Quitman on October 28, 1880.[6] In mid-November, his band intercepted and killed nine Mexican soldiers south of Carrizal and then moved north toward Santa Maria Lake, where American officials reported he had established his camp. In early December, Nana sent a small party into New Mexico. Though they apparently did no raiding, news of their presence soon reached San Carlos. With Nana's movements then shrouded in mystery, American officials made their timeworn assumption that the hostiles might have come from San Carlos.[7]

Juh and Geronimo happened to be absent (with permission) from the subagency when General Willcox received news of Apaches in southern New Mexico. He at once sent a telegram to Lieutenant Colonel William Price (formerly major) at Fort Apache, requesting that he investigate whether Juh and Geronimo were involved. If he discovered that they were off the reservation, Willcox ordered Price to "seize the families of the renegades and place them in close confinement." Though Tiffany denied that they were off the reservation, Willcox suggested that Price order Geronimo to return immediately to the subagency, even though his pass had not expired. They were likely encamped northeast of Fort Thomas in the Gila Mountains, north of today's Sánchez. According to Lieutenant Colonel Price, who always assumed the worst scenario with the Chiricahuas, Juh's request to leave the subagency to hunt was simply a ruse so that he could join forces with Nana. Price's suspicions were unfounded, and both chiefs returned to the subagency.[8]

Whether they were within the confines of the reservation was unclear. As far as Tiffany was concerned, however, this was a moot point, for the Nednhi chief "is so badly hurt that he cannot leave." He thought that Juh had suffered the injury in a brawl in which one of his wives stabbed him, but the agent did not disclose the nature of Juh's malady. Yet, Lieutenant Augustus G. Tassin, stationed at Fort Thomas between October 1880 and February 1881, recalled that he had met the "physically magnificent [Nednhi chief] who was suffering from a bone felon on his right middle finger." Tassin "lanced it for him." A grateful Juh responded with a gift of four Navajo blankets.[9]

In early January, Nana ended his stay in northern Chihuahua. Hoping to return to his beloved Black Range, he decided to probe the American lines.[10] But his presence would not go unnoticed. En route, his men would fight if the opportunity was right. During the afternoon of January 14, 1881, a Chihenne raiding party, reportedly led by Mangas, built eight "mounds of rocks" near the abandoned stage station at Good Sight Mountains, about thirteen miles east of Fort Cummings. Their first targets were two merchants (accounts differ on whether a woman was with them) transporting a wagonload of fish to Silver City. At sundown, they began to descend the trail toward Good Sight Station when the Apaches ambushed them, killing instantly both men and, according to one account, capturing a woman. The Apaches were disappointed with their plunder, for they detested fish.

Next, they waited two hours for a westbound stagecoach and killed both men, the driver, either James Swiney or Sweeny, and his passenger Thomas White. From the tracks, the relief party estimated that the Apaches numbered between thirty-five and forty. They had either women and children or Mescalero warriors with them. In any event, Mangas led the raiders north toward the Mimbres Mountains and then into their old haunts in the San Mateo range. Lieutenant Colonel Nathan A. Dudley, commander of Fort Cummings, led two companies of the Ninth Cavalry to the grisly scene and found that the Indians had burned two bodies, mutilated the other two, and smashed in their skulls.[11]

Though the Black Range was a cold place in which to winter, Nana's followers would find secluded canyons and plentiful game. They also recovered several caches of food and other provisions. And, naturally, his men, who had split up into two or three parties, had several encounters with whites. On January 19, 1881, Chihennes shot at a buckboard near Cuchillo Negro, but without effect. That same day they ambushed and killed two miners named McDaniel and Overton; they wounded a third man, but he escaped. Reports suggested that Nana then crossed the Rio Grande, but these proved false. Instead, one band of Chihennes raced north of the San Mateos, where on January 21, 1881, they espied a Mexican family of five that had left Fort Craig bound for Arizona. The Indians spared none.[12]

Nana's band crossed the border into Chihuahua in early February. Close on his heels was Lieutenant James Allison Maney, veteran of the Hembrillo Canyon fight, who was leading a company of Ninth Cavalry and Apache scouts. After an eight-day scout of 150 miles, under grueling conditions (his men had only "the worst kind of alkali water"), his scouts found Nana's camp in the

Candelaria Mountains on February 12, 1881. But the chief had deserted the village just before the arrival of Maney's detachment. Maney, however, succeeded in capturing thirty-three horses, and "all their camp including provisions, blankets and cooking utensils."[13] Although a remarkable achievement by Maney's command, Nana could always replace what he had left behind.

Nana decided to leave Chihuahua's eastern desert and return to the Sierra Madre Mountains, where Mexican troops would be unable to corner his people as they had Victorio at Tres Castillos. Along the way, he restored his supplies by intercepting a wagon train at Chocolate Pass, north of Galeana. He showed no mercy, permitting his warriors to slaughter the entire group of thirty persons and making off with the contents of nineteen wagons. Meanwhile, he sent his war chief, Showano, with two men, one woman, and a child to the Mescalero Reservation. His purpose may have been to sound out the agent about sanctuary for the surviving Chihennes. But it all became academic when ranchers tracked them down and killed four of the five Apaches (including Showano) in the Sacramento Mountains.[14]

Because of Nana's hostilities in January, Lieutenant Guy Howard formed a company of thirty Chiricahua and Western Apache scouts at San Carlos. About half were Chokonens from Naiche's band; the rest were Bedonkohes, Nednhis, and a few Western Apaches. Understandably, not one Chihenne from Loco's band enlisted. Chihuahua, the boldest and most respected Chiricahua chief of this time, was the sergeant of scouts.[15] Joining him was his brother Ulzana, his son-in-law Benectinay, and several men destined to play important roles as scouts in the 1885–86 Geronimo War: Tuzzone (Red Water Resting), Martine, Toosigah, Juan Segotset. Also with him were Tissnolthos, Nezegochin (Speckled Face), and Perico (White Horse), warriors who would ride with Geronimo in the final outbreak.[16]

What motivated them to become scouts against their own people was unclear. The informants of Eve Ball claimed that they simply wanted to escape the boredom of reservation life. Another reason frequently given was that the military issued rifles and ammunition to all scouts, which pleased them immensely. But the military had never disarmed either Naiche's or Juh's bands, so that explanation does not seem to hold water. Likely a man joined to earn some money, to escape the monotony of day-to-day reservation life, and to revisit his former homelands. And, in this case, most of the Chiricahua scouts who volunteered came from the Chokonens, and they had not enjoyed close relations with the Chihennes for almost a decade. Despite this, it was unlikely that Chihuahua intended to harm any of Nana's band unless in self-defense.[17]

That they enlisted as scouts suggests that the Chiricahuas were reasonably satisfied with conditions at San Carlos. During Tiffany's first year on the job, he could honestly say that he had achieved several goals. To begin with, he had maintained the stability established by Chaffee. He dispensed rations regularly, and the Indians seemed content. To promote self-sufficiency, he urged his wards to maintain fixed residences so that they could plant and care for their own fields. By the end of 1880, he could boast that nine bands, mainly the Arivaipa and the Cibecue, had taken him up on his offer. He also noted with great satisfaction that for the first time, most Apaches on the reservation were at work. With their help, he built new buildings, corrals, and a school for the children. He employed Indians as teamsters, herders, and laborers, showing them how to make adobe bricks and to dig irrigation ditches. Just as impressive, he had persuaded the Bureau of Indian Affairs in Washington to approve an investment in farming implements for the Indians' use.[18]

But the Chiricahuas still refused to work even though several headmen, notably Chatto, Naiche, and Zele, were serving on the agency police force headed by Chief of Police Albert Sterling. An Ohio native in his late twenties, Sterling had a sincere and sympathetic interest in Indians, and many Apaches, including Jason Betzinez, then a member of Loco's band at the main agency, liked and respected him.[19] The Chiricahuas were also pleased because Tiffany had no reason either to restrict their movements or to confine them along the Gila at the subagency. Free to live in the mountains, they escaped the malaria outbreaks that had infested Naiche's band the previous three springs. When not in the mountains hunting and gathering, they appeared at the subagency every Thursday to receive their ration tickets. On Fridays, the issue clerk distributed the weekly allotments of beef, flour, beans, sugar, coffee, salt, and soap to every person, regardless of age.[20]

But the matter of tiswin had become an ongoing problem, notably among the Chiricahuas: Chief Sterling had carried out an aggressive plan to control the making of tiswin. Between January and early June 1881, Sterling and his Apache police force arrested twenty Chiricahuas, six men (two for drunkenness and four for being absent without permission) and fourteen women, all for making tiswin.[21] Many prominent Chiricahuas disapproved of the government's interference in activities conducted within their camp. Chihuahua, who was not involved at this time because he was absent on service as scout, was especially upset. But interference was becoming the rule. The Indian police also arrested a young man destined to play a vital role in Crook's campaign into the Sierra Madre in the spring of 1883, a young man of the Canyon

Creek band of the Cibecue group of Western Apaches. His Apache name was Tsoe, but Americans called him Peaches. He had married a Chihenne woman of Loco's band. According to him, Sterling had mistreated him, ordering the Apache police to "string [me] up by the thumbs." His wife's relatives were so angry about Sterling's treatment that they vowed to "kill Sterling for what he had done."[22]

As he began his second year of service, Tiffany faced unforeseen challenges that, if ignored, threatened to undermine his accomplishments during his first year. It all began innocuously, when Nock-ay-det-klinne, a chief of the Cibecue Apache band, asked Tiffany for permission to relocate his followers to Cibecue Creek, a remote area about fifty-five miles north of San Carlos. Inasmuch as the agent had been all along encouraging the Indians to become self-sufficient, he issued the pass in mid-May. About a month later, Tiffany received disturbing reports that Nock-ay-det-klinne had held dances in which he had raised the spirits of two dead chiefs, Diablo and Es-ki-ole, to their knees.[23] They would return with divine powers from their God and lead the Apaches to victory over the Americans. The agent, hearing that tiswin had flowed freely at the dances, did not take the reports seriously; in fact, he seemed more disturbed about a recent visit by a Navajo who reportedly had tried to induce the White Mountain Apaches to go to war.[24]

In late July, Tiffany saw many months of work go down the drain when a series of heavy thunderstorms damaged several buildings at the subagency and obliterated his just completed irrigation project. He had little time to dwell on this misfortune, however, for Nock-ay-det-klinne's dances had begun to attract large numbers of disenchanted Apaches who were eager to hear his message. In June, Tiffany had sent Chief of Police Sterling and his Apache police to the medicine man's village; but the chief easily avoided the emissary and retired into the mountains. In mid-July Nock-ay-det-klinne moved his camp near Fort Apache, where he tried to summon the spirits. Though unsuccessful in his attempts to resurrect the spirits of the dead chiefs' bodies, he claimed that he had communicated with his supernatural Power.[25]

From Fort Apache, Nock-ay-det-klinne headed to San Carlos to meet Tiffany, who warned the charismatic chief to stop the dances. So, one week later, the chief returned to his country and made an ominous declaration that he could not "raise the dead until the whites had left the country." For two nights beginning on August 4, Nock-ay-det-klinne presided at dances that drew tremendous crowds of passionate followers. Again, he claimed that he could not raise the dead chiefs unless the whites were gone. With these distressing reports on his mind, Tiffany received other disquieting information, that Nana was raiding in New Mexico, which fueled the usual rumors that he might try to visit the reservation. He at once ordered a guard of thirty Western Apaches to watch over Loco's people.[26]

But Nana had no thoughts of going to San Carlos. Instead, he left his strongholds in the Sierra Madre with about fifteen men (among whom were Mangas, Bacutla, Kaetenae, Jatu, Sánchez, and Suldeen) and struck east through the parched Chihuahuan desert country that Victorio had traveled the year before. Along the way he attacked several parties, killing and looting, until he crossed into Texas near Fort Quitman on July 13, 1881. Four days later, Nana ambushed a small pack train—two men with four mules south of the Mescalero Reservation. They wounded one man, but both escaped. Nana's band slaughtered one mule for food (mule meat was an Apache delicacy) and took the other three. Yet, Nana had unwittingly assaulted two packers from the detail of Lieutenant John F. Guilfoyle, Ninth Cavalry, who was in command of Company B, Indian scouts, which also included Frank Bennett as chief of scouts and the Chokonen chief Chihuahua as sergeant.[27]

Most recently, Company B Indian scouts had called Fort Cummings their home; they had been there since leaving San Carlos on April 30, 1881. In mid-May, Guilfoyle received his assignment to move his scouts into Mescalero country, where a band of fifty Mescaleros (fourteen warriors under Manzanita) had been at large since Hatch's army had invaded the reservation and disarmed them in March 1880.[28] Guilfoyle assumed that the Mescaleros were responsible for the attack on his two men. He raced to the agency and picked up twenty troopers of the Ninth Cavalry, which, when added to his Apache scouts, strengthened his force to about fifty. At some point in his pursuit, Guilfoyle learned that a party of Mescaleros had reinforced Nana's party. His scout sergeant, Chihuahua, was undoubtedly the source of this information.

Chihuahua cut the trail east of the Sacramento Mountains and then rounded White Sands toward the San Andres Mountains. En route Chihuahua, Nezegochin, and Tissnolthos, who were scouting ahead of the troops, encountered Kaetenae, acting as Nana's scout in the rear. Years later, they enjoyed a hearty laugh about the confrontation, for they let Kaetenae go.[29] Finally, after a grueling eight-day march, on July 25 Guilfoyle and his scouts engaged Nana in a secluded canyon in the northern part of the San Andres Mountains. It was a quick, indecisive contest, with Nana, in classic guerilla warfare, abandoning his supplies and some stock before fleeing into the high country. Reports differ about casualties, but according to one account, the fearless Chihuahua had proved his worth by shooting one Indian.[30] The whirlwind pursuit had taken a toll on the troopers. Two prospectors arrived at Las Cruces to report they had run into Guilfoyle's command after the fight. They described Guilfoyle, his horses spent and his supplies depleted, as "hatless, coatless, weary, and worn," while Frank Bennett could "hardly sit up" after his horse had thrown him.[31]

On August 1 a group of thirty-six citizens, made up of miners and ranchers, rode into Red Canyon on the southwest side of the San Mateo Mountains. They were seeking Apache blood to equal the score, for Nana's war party had just slain eight miners, ranchers, and sheepherders en route to the San Mateo range. At mid-afternoon, on August 2, 1881, while the men enjoyed a siesta near a spring, the seventy-five-year-old arthritic war-party leader opened a deadly cross fire from outcrops on both sides of the canyon. Simultaneous to this volley, a group of Apaches, waving blankets, captured the horses, driving them down the canyon. The first fusillade killed one man and wounded seven others, and the dumbfounded party fled on foot without their horses, in great confusion and panic, to their homes in the Black Range. According to one eyewitness, the militiamen had managed to get off only a few rounds at their attackers, and now Nana had their horses. His stock replenished, he continued to the northwestern part of the range.[32]

The next day, August 3, in the midst of the raiding, killing, and fighting, in which Nana had spared no one, the chief and thirteen followers exited Red Canyon and headed north toward Mount Withington, a prominent peak that soared to over ten thousand feet in the northern San Mateos. In a canyon below lay a sawmill owned by Robert Stapleton, a fifty-three-year-old frontiersman who had come to New Mexico in 1850 with the Second Dragoons. After his discharge in the spring of 1854, Stapleton settled in the Socorro area and helped build Fort Craig.[33] During the early 1870s, he found employment at Ojo Caliente and Tularosa, where he became well acquainted with many Chihennes, including Nana.

En route to Stapleton's place, Nana and Jatu had stopped at Frank Pierce's ranch, captured him, and then went to Joseph Ware's ranch, a mile below Stapleton's sawmill. Here one warrior, Suldeen, surprised Ware, whom they marched back to his house where his brother and family were inside. Nana promised not to harm them as long as they followed his orders, but he told Ware that he would take whatever supplies he needed. When it began to rain, Nana considerately allowed Ware's wife and children to go into the house for cover. But after she complained that one of the young men had physically harmed her, Nana scolded the warrior, and she and her children stayed out in the rain with her husband. According to Ware, Nana had twenty Indians with him—eleven Chihennes, seven Mescaleros, and two Navajos. After a five-hour stay, they left.[34]

Nana led his men in single file as he rode to Stapleton's ranch for a meeting between two men who had been friendly in the reservation days. They talked for a brief time, probably less than thirty minutes. Stapleton suggested peace; Nana, however, like Victorio, seemed resigned to his fate—death, preferably in battle.

This meeting is important, for Nana, who lived another fifteen years, never talked much about his whirlwind raid, probably feeling that Americans would hold him accountable if he admitted too much. Stapleton's firsthand account is therefore revealing. He said that Nana came to his ranch between 2:00 and 3:00 P.M. on August 2, though it was almost certainly August 3, 1881. Stapleton saw twelve Indians and a Mexican boy, whom Nana claimed they had taken in a raid below the border. Actually, the boy was Sylvester Sisneros, and he had been herding sheep in the San Mateos with two other Mexicans when Nana attacked them, killing both men. Sisneros would remain with Nana for over three years. Nana mentioned to Stapleton that his followers consisted of ten Mescaleros and two Navajos, which, if true, suggests that his Chihenne warriors had separated from him after leaving Ware's ranch. Stapleton commented that Nana owned "a fine telescope glass, the best I ever looked through," which helped the chief to keep one step ahead of his pursuers, and that Nana's men carried army carbines and Winchester rifles.

Stapleton asked Nana about the prospects for peace:

> He [Nana] was sitting on his horse and turning, half around in his saddle, and waving his hand around to where two young warriors sat on their ponies.

> Nana: This is all that I have left of my once powerful band. Here are two of my nephews. All have been wiped out but myself and these two.
> Stapleton: I have authority from Captain [John W.] Bean [probably at Fort Craig] to talk to you about coming back to the reservation and living in peace.
> Nana: To live in peace! What kind of peace do you offer? Where in all these homes of my father is there one spot where [I] can place my foot and rest from strife. No. No. No matter where I am—here,

there, everywhere, they shoot at me. Where am I to go that I could live? You tell me that I am to be offered peace but within one hour I will be shot at.

Stapleton: What do you want? To come back to the reservation? Now, I am authorized to talk to you.

Nana: I know it, and I know that you would not lie to me.

Stapleton (I then asked him straight up and down): Do you want to come back to your reservation?

Nana: Yes, providing that we may live in peace as we did before, and that we may bring back our people from the San Carlos reservation to join and live with us.

Stapleton: Such a thing is possible. I will make known your desires to the commander. Nana, when will I see you again?

Nana: Maybe soon, maybe long time, maybe never this side of the happy hunting ground.[35] I am ready to die and when my time comes—it is near—I can feel it, but I will die with my face to my bitter foes, fighting and dying all the same. We have killed everyone we have come across thus far below [here] and after we leave here we will kill everyone we meet again. We had a fight below here three days ago and the Apaches are good yet. If night had not come so close I would have [killed all] white or Mexicans to tell of it [his ambush in Red Canyon]. They try to wipe me out, and I wipe them out, for I must kill to live. I am now going up to Navajo country. I want to try and get some Navajos with me. Soldiers, miners, ranchers, everyone is against me, and I must get help or they will get me soon.

Then Nana turned to his followers and said: "Come, there are bloodhounds on our trail." His men left in single file. Nana asked to borrow two of Stapleton's mules, saying that "he needed them and that he would return them," and, Stapleton believed him: "He has always kept his word to me."[36]

Less than two hours later, Nana battled Lieutenant Guilfoyle and his scouts at Monica Canyon. Then the chief continued north, where some ten Navajos, led by Margacito and Cibusto, joined him.[37] He resumed his raid, attacking ranchers, travelers, and soldiers, killing as many as possible in his bloody wake. He spared only those he captured. During his two-month foray, his small band traveled some two thousand miles, contested the cavalry seven times, and raided at least a dozen ranches and towns. Because he fought on his terms, usually from concealed positions, he suffered few casualties. His two raiding bands had killed between thirty and fifty whites, captured eight or nine New Mexicans and hundreds of head of stock, and eluded the efforts of over one thousand troops and scouts.[38] His guerilla warfare was a foreshadowing of the forays that would characterize hostilities in the Southwest during the remaining Apache Wars. He finally crossed the line into Mexico about August 23, 1881, the same time that Nock-ay-det-klinne's exhortations had created a volatile atmosphere at San Carlos that threatened to explode into war.

By this time, Agent Joseph Tiffany had concluded that he had to do something with the medicine man, whose influence now extended to the White Mountain Apaches. On August 10, he had written Colonel Eugene Carr that it "would be well to arrest Nock-ay-det-klinne and send him off or have him killed without arresting him." This seemed like an extreme measure given that the Apaches had neither spilled any blood nor committed any hostile acts. Tiffany thought that he had the support of the Yumas and Mohaves but was uncertain about the Chiricahuas. To find out their feelings, he sent a message to Naiche's and Chatto's camps to "see if they are disaffected." Three days later Carr, probably relying on information from Jeffords, messaged Tiffany that he heard the Chiricahuas were to attend the dance scheduled for Saturday, August 20. Yet, the chiefs assured Tiffany that they wanted nothing to do with the White Mountain Apaches and would not attend the dances. Just to be sure, Tiffany sent "scouts to their camps to see if they went; they did not go . . . except Bonito and two men who had gone to plant corn with George on Eagle Creek." Suspecting danger from the Americans, the prophet postponed the dance.[39]

On August 22, 1881, Pedro, aging chief of the White Mountain Apaches, arrived at Fort Apache to reassure Colonel Carr that his people had no intentions of going to war. With him was his son Alchesay, U-clen-ay, and Sergeant Mose, a scout. Pedro reminded Carr that he had been a staunch friend of Americans and denied the rumors of an uprising. He let U-clen-ay, who had just returned from the medicine man's camp, do most of the talking. U-clen-ay explained:

> When he has a dance he wants to have it without being disturbed; it is to bring the dead back and he don't want to be disturbed. When he was to come here, he was afraid he would be put in the guardhouse; he wanted to dance and not have any trouble; he was for the poor. The medicine man told me [U-clen-ay] that the Whites danced for their

own amusement and so did the Indians. They were friendly to the
Whites and intended to come up here and cultivate friendly relations.
The Medicine man himself has no bad intentions nor hostile inten-
tions; anything he does he gets on orders from the higher spirits.[40]

One week later, on August 29, 1881, Colonel Carr left Fort Apache with
eighty-four troopers, twenty-three Cibecue and White Mountain scouts, and
nine civilians, intending to arrest Nock-ay-det-klinne, hopefully without a
fight. Unfortunately, on August 30, 1881, after Carr took the chief hostage,
every one of his scouts except Sergeant Mose (twenty-two in all) deserted,
and several opened fire. A group of some thirty Cibecue Apaches joined their
brethren, killing several Americans, including Captain Edmund C. Hentig,
in the first minutes of the engagement. One soldier shot the medicine man;
another one bludgeoned him to death. As Carr's command retraced its steps to
Fort Apache, warriors from nearby camps, perhaps as many as one hundred,
joined the fray and harassed the soldiers until they reached the safety of the fort.
By the time the fight ended, the Apaches had slain seven soldiers and wounded
three others. The next two days, the enraged Cibecue and White Mountain
Apaches displayed their fury as they ambushed travelers, killing three soldiers
and four civilians near Fort Apache. And, on September 1, 1881, in a rare open
show of force, they boldly appeared near Fort Apache and skirmished with the
garrison until the soldiers, led by Colonel Carr, drove them off. Among the attackers were the formerly friendly Alchesay, U-clen-ay, George, and Bonito,
along with several of the mutinous scouts.[41]

Agent Tiffany's preliminary estimates were that fourteen Apache bands
comprising 220 men from the Cibecue and White Mountain bands had participated in the outbreak at Cibecue and in the hostilities afterwards.[42] The only
Chiricahuas involved were Bonito and two of his band (Ni-Natchy, Tal-e-cha-
a), who joined George and their White Mountain friends in the fighting after
Cibecue. Bonito, with twenty of his band, had camped at Eagle Creek with
George, the Chiricahua who had married into the White Mountain Apaches.
Tiffany noted that the balance of Bonito's band, about seventy in all, had remained at the subagency under his brother (actually his cousin), the celebrated
shaman She-neah. No other Chiricahuas joined in the hostilities, though the
hostiles had dispatched envoys seeking their help.[43]

All the contemporary evidence supports this impression that the few men
with Bonito were the only men associated with the Chiricahuas who took
up arms during the chaotic days after Cibecue.[44] This view disagrees with the

recollections of Asa Daklugie, the son of Juh, who claimed that his father, Naiche, Chihuahua, Nana, and Kaetenae had become convinced of the power of Nock-ay-det-klinne after they saw him raise the spirits of Cochise, Mangas Coloradas, and Victorio. But there is no record of either Juh or Naiche travel- ing north to attend these revivals. Nor was there any indication that they had any sympathy for the medicine man's prophecies. We know unequivocally that Chihuahua was absent from the reservation on scout duty from April 30 until early September 1881, the time when Nock-ay-det-klinne held all his dances. And Nana and Kaetenae, except for the six weeks they were raiding in New Mexico, were in Mexico. It would have been difficult for Nana to enter the reservation undetected by the White Mountain people, who considered the Chihennes their enemies after Victorio had brutally slain Bylas and his family. To sum up: No Chiricahuas were at Cibecue, and only Bonito (White Moun- tain by birth) and two others participated in the hostilities that followed.[45]

The Chiricahuas' initial response was to stay clear of the hostiles. The sub- agent, Ezra Hoag, had given a pass to Juh, Geronimo, and seventy-four others so that they could hunt and gather mescal north of Ash Creek, where they ex- pected to meet Naiche and his band. Connell remembered that Geronimo was a frequent visitor at the subagency that summer, loafing around and not doing much of anything.[46] Perico mentioned that he saw Geronimo use his healing power to cure a seriously ill man by singing over him for several days be- fore.[47] On August 28 the Chiricahuas stopped at Fort Thomas and spoke with their friend Lieutenant Haskell, who remarked that Juh was "very friendly." Haskell opined, "the Chiricahuas would not be drawn into complications with the White Mountain Indians." He was right, for on September 1, two days after the fight at Cibecue, Naiche visited Fort Thomas and spoke to Captain John L. Viven. The captain recalled the chief admitting that "he knew of the troubles and told me that he and the other chiefs are friends [and] that he would not allow any of his men to participate in the present trouble." Tiffany ordered Hoag to send runners to bring Juh and Geronimo back to the sub- agency, where they soon joined Naiche.[48]

General Willcox and Agent Tiffany hoped to enlist scouts from those bands who had not joined the hostiles. The Chiricahuas were their first "choice." Haskell summoned Archie McIntosh and Tom Jeffords (then in Tucson) to Fort Thomas, hoping they would use their influence to persuade Naiche and Juh to contribute men to the scout company. Naiche at first seemed willing to cooperate. And because Lieutenant Guilfoyle was then discharging Company B, Apache Scouts, with Chihuahua as sergeant, on September 6, 1881, Jeffords and Lieutenant Charles Gatewood entertained thoughts that several principal men might reenlist. On September 9, they and Lieutenant Haskell went to the subagency to "hire twenty-five Chiricahuas." Yet, upon reaching there, they discovered that Naiche's people were having second thoughts because they were concerned about the safety of their families. Even Jeffords could not persuade Naiche, probably because the Chokonens had enjoyed close relations with the White Mountain people as far back as Cochise's time and did not relish the idea of bringing in Bonito and his two or three followers, whom Americans now considered hostile. Naiche, however, vowed to fight the hostiles if they threatened his people.[49]

Though Tiffany and Carr could not have realized it, the major fighting was over, at least for several months. By mid-September, many hostiles began filtering into the reservation to surrender. Bonito and George were among the first, followed by five Cibecue chiefs on September 21, 1881. Despite this good fortune, affairs between Apaches and Americans remained fragile. Charles Collins, in his authoritative work on Cibecue, argues convincingly that General Sherman, in charge of the army in Washington, overreacted to the fight at Cibecue. Willcox was providing detailed reports to his commander sitting in San Francisco, Major General Irvin McDowell, in charge of the Division of the Pacific. McDowell was passing these along to Sherman, who originally misread the situation and concluded that he had on his hands an Indian War on the scale of the Sioux-Cheyenne Wars of the mid-1870s. Sherman telegraphed McDowell that he wanted "the renegades destroyed" and only wanted to hear results. The plans and logistics they left up to Willcox.

When Willcox received this information, he interpreted it literally and decided he would report only when he had something of interest. This vacuum in correspondence, which was less than a week, bothered the impetuous Sherman, who assumed that Willcox was inactive, when actually the commander had already transferred his headquarters to the nearest post in the field, Fort Thomas. Thus, Sherman reiterated his wishes to McDowell: "I want this annual Apache stampede to end right now, and to effect this result will send every available man in the whole Army if necessary."

Unfortunately, the Apaches at San Carlos, particularly the Chiricahuas (especially the skittish Juh and Geronimo), must have thought that indeed every soldier in the United States Army had congregated at San Carlos. Troops had converged on the reservation from every direction. Mainly because of unconfirmed reports and rumors, Willcox had transferred the entire regiment of the Sixth Cavalry to the vicinity of the reservation and had requested reinforce-

ments from the Division of the Pacific. They came in the form of two companies of cavalry and six companies of infantry, all rushed to southern Arizona
via the Southern Pacific Railroad, which ran through Willcox. Other troops
arrived from the District of New Mexico, led by Colonel Ranald Slidell Mackenzie, but all they did was further compound a confusing situation. It was a
classic case of overkill, for by late September this large concentration of troops
had no hostiles to fight. Fewer than sixty warriors remained absent, and they
were not anxious to reveal their positions.[50]

About September 23, 1881, several Chiricahuas rode to the main agency
at San Carlos to talk to Agent Tiffany. The large number of troops around
the agency concerned them. Juh asked whether "the troop movements were
related to their activities in Mexico." He admitted "they had been on the warpath [but] had come in good faith and were contented [and] did not want war
or to fight." Tiffany assured them that the army had come only to punish those
who had taken part in the fighting at Cibecue and afterwards. This apparently
satisfied the Chiricahuas, for they "shook hands much delighted" and returned
to the subagency.[51]

To Tiffany it must have seemed that the crisis was over, but one week later,
the situation took an abrupt turn for the worse. Friday, September 30, 1881,
was ration day, when most of the Apaches would be present to receive their
weekly allotment. Military officials made formal plans to arrest the Cibecue
Apaches who had surrendered at San Carlos, George and his followers, and Bonito. The operation at the main agency went well (though Natiosh and about
fifteen men had left the night before the roundup), and the military placed
some forty-five Apaches in confinement in the schoolhouse. Unfortunately,
their strategy to arrest George and Bonito at the subagency failed when the
former reneged on his promise to surrender to Major James Biddle at 3:00 P.M.
George, who had participated in the fighting after Cibecue, had broken his
word and was running. Biddle faced a thankless task. He dispatched the scout
company under Lieutenant Albert S. Bailey to George's ranchería, which they
reached about 6:00 P.M. His scouts took into custody those in George's village,
about thirty in all, mostly women and children and a few men.[52]

Biddle's decision evoked much criticism from contemporary civil officials,
and a few months later, from General Willcox himself, who later apologized
to Biddle "in the light of additional evidence which has come to my notice."[53]
These men, believing that Biddle had ignited the unfortunate chain of events
that followed, wrongly condemned him. Yet, Biddle had made a reasonable response; it was not his fault that the Chiricahuas had misinterpreted his actions.

The resulting backlash was the responsibility of one man—Chief George, who had run away rather than honor his promise.

Biddle's act had incensed and frightened George. He and Bonito fled to the Chiricahua camps of Naiche, Chatto, and Juh. George, defiant and scared, now vowed to fight, telling the Chiricahuas that American troops were coming to "murder their women and children." To further arouse their suspicions, according to the testimony of Naiche, Chihuahua, and Geronimo, George claimed that the soldiers planned to arrest the Chiricahua chiefs and deport them to a distant place. And, according to Naiche, George insisted that the Americans planned to place shackles on the chiefs, which image brought back unpalatable memories of Clum's treatment of Geronimo and Chatto. This discussion made Geronimo "wild as an animal," for any mention of "troops made him nervous."[54] Even the presence of Tom Jeffords, who claimed he was in their camp that night, could not allay their fears.[55] A few years later, a pragmatic Chihuahua said that he believed what George was saying: "He must [have] known because he was related to a white man."[56]

During this frenzied moment, the Chiricahua leaders held a council, and according to Geronimo, after recounting the betrayal of Cochise at Apache Pass and the execution of Mangas Coloradas at Fort McLane, they vowed to leave to avoid falling victim to American injustice. The older leaders, Juh and Geronimo, dominated the council, and the bravest Nednhi fighter, Jelikine, known to some whites as Little Chief because of his diminutive stature, supported them. Chihuahua corroborated Geronimo's account, saying that Juh had become "very much excited and [had] decided to leave." Years later, Geronimo explained that he thought "it more manly to die on the warpath than to be killed in prison."[57] Chatto's and Bonito's group of Chokonens and Bedonkohes, with a few White Mountain Apaches, followed in step.[58]

The Chokonens under Naiche, who had lived at San Carlos since June 1876, also decided to leave. Normally a cautious man who avoided risk, Naiche also had to weigh his father's death-bed wishes that he should remain at peace as long as possible. But this night, Juh's determination, memories of American treachery against his father and grandfather, and George's insistence that the military was planning to kill his women and children and imprison the chiefs convinced him. The aggregate of these factors led him to make an impulsive decision, one which in later years he would come to regret, believing that he had misread the situation and had made an irrational response owing to the confusion and paranoia of the time.[59] Two leaders in his band, however, were not as caught up in the emotions of that night and were reluctant to make a spontaneous judgment. The first was the forty-five-year-old Nahilzay, Cochise's brother-in-law, who was hesitant to join in the exodus. He left only after Juh and Naiche had compelled "his women and children to leave."[60] The second was the bravest and most flamboyant Chokonen of his time, Chihuahua. Though reputed to be a close friend of Juh, he was not eager to leave. He decided to flee only after he saw what he believed were troops heading toward his camp (Biddle's scout company went no farther than George's village). His followers were the last to leave.[61]

In all, about 375 Chiricahuas (including seventy-four men), consisting of 200 Chokonens, 89 Bedonkohes, and 86 Nednhis, busted out of the reservation at 10:30 P.M. on September 30, 1881.[62] Loco's and Zele's bands, which numbered 270 in all, remained at the agency. And what of George, the instigator, who had defiantly told the Chiricahuas he was leaving even before they met to discuss their options? As he had done with Biddle, he double-crossed the Chiricahuas and remained on the reservation.

Indians and military officials espoused several theories for the Chiricahuas' exodus. White Mountain Apaches, who were either bitter at Tiffany or were trying to minimize George's involvement, blamed the agent for not fulfilling promises to Naiche and Juh to complete an irrigation project.[63] The Cibecue Apache, Peaches, who had married a Chihenne woman and was living with Loco's band at the agency, claimed that Tiffany had mistreated them and "threatened to have them removed from San Carlos to a far distant country, so the Chiricahuas broke out." Yet these men were not in the Chiricahuas' camp that confusing night, and when we examine the evidence, it is obvious that their decision to leave was a spontaneous one, made chiefly because George had spread wild rumors about their fate if they remained. And, to add fuel to these yarns, the concentration of some six to seven hundred troops around the agency's perimeter exacerbated their apprehensions. In the Chiricahuas' minds, when soldiers came, trouble followed. From their perspective, the soldiers were there to round them up and move them elsewhere, just as they had at the reservations at Chiricahua and Ojo Caliente. Fatty lamented that the military had come after the innocent Chiricahuas instead of holding the guilty White Mountain responsible.[64]

The euphoric feeling those who left must have felt, no matter how exhilarating, would come at a severe cost. In the short term, their newfound freedom must have felt good. But it also meant that they would be following Juh's way of life in Mexico, where they were constantly exposed to enemies and had to raid for subsistence. Though Juh's band had survived, Mexican and

American campaigns had reduced it by half by the late 1870s. Naiche knew this, but his band had endured a similar loss from malaria on the reservation. Still, the son of Cochise would have preferred to remain on the reservation. In later years Naiche would declare that "I have always been sorry that I left for [we] have suffered a great deal."[65] Many Chiricahuas would come to share his view, for some 25 percent of those who left the reservation would perish in Mexico from chicanery or battle in the next two years.

10

JUH TAKES CHARGE

Juh was a great medicine man. This man was war chief, and
[we] all thought he was great.

Perico, Geronimo's second cousin

By 10:30 P.M., on September 30, 1881, the Chiricahua Apaches had gathered their belongings, rounded up their stock, and prepared themselves for their race south to Mexico. They understood, of course, that soldiers would follow. But they had supreme confidence in the ability of their leaders and fighting men to get them safely into the Sierra Madre Mountains. And with good reason. When Juh and Geronimo traveled together, the latter took charge of the advance guard. Juh took control of the main body and rearguard, which followed a few miles behind.[1] To these stalwart warriors we can add the presence of Naiche, Chihuahua, Chatto, and Bonito, whose leadership, fighting ability, and courage must have come as a great comfort to the women and children. Though fewer than one-third of the 375 Chiricahuas had horses, they were confident they could steal enough stock along the way to mount the entire band. Furthermore, because Indian officials had permitted the Chokonens and Nednhis to retain their arms, most of the seventy-four men and twenty-two teenage boys owned Springfield rifles. And, according to Geronimo, they had acquired plenty of ammunition during their stay at San Carlos and from the White Mountain Apaches before leaving the agency.[2]

Charles Collins, in his thorough study *The Great Escape*, points out that the Chiricahuas also enjoyed several advantages. Earlier that day, Ezra Hoag had issued rations to them, the rainy season had ended, the half-moon aided their movements in the dark, and they found temperatures perfect for night travel.[3]

Their usual route to Mexico would have taken them to the northeast, where they would strike Eagle Creek, follow it to the Gila, and then angle off

185

southeast toward the Peloncillo Mountains, which served as a corridor south to the Mexican border. This time, however, hundreds of troops were scouting that country, looking for hostiles involved in Cibecue. Thus, the leaders selected another more direct but less mountainous route. Sweeping past the subagency, they followed the road parallel to the Gila River toward Fort Thomas for about twelve miles. Then they pivoted to the south, dividing into four groups (under the band chiefs Juh, Naiche, Chatto, and Bonito) before they rendezvoused at Black Rock, a prominent landmark that stands 900 feet above the plains near the foothills of the eastern Santa Teresa Mountains. Before reaching there, Geronimo led one band that stole fifty horses and mules during three raids against two freighters and a rancher. From Black Rock, they moved about ten miles southeast, where they encamped along the foothills of the Santa Teresa Mountains in the late afternoon of October 1.

Meanwhile an Apache had informed Ezra Hoag, the subagent, of the breakout. He at once sent Mickey Free and an Apache scout to inform Tiffany, who heard the news at 1:00 A.M., October 1. Tiffany dispatched a messenger to Captain Stacey, then at the agency with one company of the Twelfth Infantry. The captain informed Colonel Carr, who, inexplicably, took no action. The next morning rumors of the uprising reached Fort Thomas. These were confirmed when Hoag arrived at the post and advised General Willcox. He immediately sent out Lieutenant Albert S. Bailey with his Apache scouts to ferret out the Chiricahuas' trail. They returned early in the afternoon to report that the tracks led to Black Rock. Within an hour, at 2:00 P.M., Willcox ordered Lieutenant Overton to take two troops of cavalry and Bailey, with ten Apache scouts, to follow the Chiricahuas. Bailey's scout company included eight Chihennes and Chokonens who remained at Fort Thomas because the military distrusted them. They would desert the evening of October 6 after they killed a Western Apache scout of their company. Overton's command spent the night near Black Rock.[4]

Before daybreak on October 2, Juh and Naiche led the main body of warriors south while the women and children traversed through the Pinaleño foothills, perhaps a mile east of the men. At 10:00 A.M., the warriors came upon Meregildo Sisneros, who was hunting in the Pinaleños, and chased him to Cedar Springs Station. They fired an ineffective volley at him, but then retired, for their advance scouts had reported that a large mule train was approaching the station. This was the cargo of Mariano Samaniego, who had a government contract to freight supplies from Willcox to the San Carlos agency. Samaniego would have led the train, but because he had important business in Tucson, he had assigned that task to his younger brother Bartolo, who left Willcox on

September 27 with twelve wagons and 108 mules carrying 14,000 pounds of goods for San Carlos. About a half-mile from Cedar Springs Station, he saw Apaches ahead. Samaniego had not heard of the outbreak and had no reason to be suspicious. He assumed they were Apache scouts, especially when the Apaches allowed a woman to drive a wagon through their lines. As it turned out, the presence of Samaniego's freight train probably had saved her life.

A few minutes later, Samaniego saw the Apaches spreading out and taking positions, "nearly surrounding the whole train." Then he became incredulous when they opened fire on the teamsters in the lead wagon. Bartolo Samaniego reacted quickly; he and the trailing three men rushed to the aid of the teamsters with the lead wagon, where he found one man dead and the other wounded. Then his four men got into a "little rut, almost beneath the wagon." For the next ninety minutes they returned fire, holding the Indians at bay. Finally, Samaniego, thinking all was lost, decided to charge the Indian positions. His men, inspired by his bravery, agreed to follow him. Samaniego headed directly for a rocky knoll occupied by Apaches. It was over quickly; one by one they fell, with the brave Bartolo the first one killed. The warriors rushed to the wagons, cut the harnesses from the mules, and took 102 prized possessions. They had killed six mules in the fighting. Before leaving, they plundered the wagons in a businesslike manner, taking eight Winchester rifles, eight revolvers, and about three hundred cartridges from the six brave men. After the warriors had looted for about thirty minutes, a few sentries perched on a high hill overlooking Cedar Springs Station fired several volleys—a warning that enemies were approaching. The warriors left immediately with their stock and loot.

But one man, Sosteños Estrada, who had followed the lead of Bartolo and charged the Indian positions had taken a bullet through the knee, falling to the ground. He later explained what happened next: knowing that escape "was impossible, I fell down and feigned death." Then a Chiricahua man "came to me as I lay on my face, turned me over and took off my cartridge belt, and struck me in the back with his gun." Estrada remained in that position for over an hour until he heard American troops arriving.[5]

The Chiricahuas continued down the road toward Fort Grant. Soon after, they came upon John Moulds, who was carrying supplies to Cedar Springs Station. They quickly killed him, taking four horses and his provisions. Twenty minutes later, they ambushed four soldiers from Fort Grant who were repairing the telegraph line. The soldiers never knew what hit them. The Indians took their horses and arms. Shortly after, American troops arrived at the scene. While they were examining the bodies, the Indians opened fire on them, thus beginning a battle that would become known as K-H Butte. The engagement lasted for some six hours and involved Cochise's former adversary Captain Reuben F. Bernard, some one hundred cavalry troopers, and thirty to forty Western Apache scouts. Early in the fight, the main body of women and children arrived in the hills behind the warriors, who occupied the high ground east of the main road.[6]

The chiefs held a council to decide how to get their dependents across the road below the troops' positions so that they could escape west toward the Galiuro Mountains. The reliable Jason Betzinez offers the only account available from the Chiricahuas' point of view. Though not present (he was with Loco's band, which had remained at San Carlos), he later heard that one older Chiricahua, frustrated at the stalemate, suggested that they make a charge against the right flank of the soldiers in front of them. This would create a diversion to allow the women and children to cross the road a few miles below the battle site.[7]

Betzinez does not reveal this man's name, but we can make a strong case for Jelikine, Geronimo's Mexican-born father-in-law. Captured as a boy by the Western Apaches, he was not a chief, but he was a natural leader during a crisis, a man the tribe counted on to make decisions. The diminutive Jelikine ("as tall as an old fashioned musket," said John Rope) had the heart of a lion. He thought nothing of defying the chiefs if he disagreed with them. Thus, it was likely he who proposed and led the night charge, which occurred about 8:00 P.M. and ended only after the warriors had advanced to within ten feet of Bernard's positions. Now, their mission accomplished without losses, the Apaches withdrew. For the next hour the warriors maintained sporadic gunfire until they received a signal that the main body had safely crossed below. Then they abandoned their post and rejoined their people, whom they found near the Galiuro Mountains that evening of October 2, 1881. Bernard's men continued south to Fort Grant with a loss of one dead and two wounded.[8]

The Chiricahuas were now in the Upper Sulphur Springs Valley, with few settlements and no forts between them and the border. Early morning October 3, they broke camp, the women and children hugging the foothills as they rode south. The warriors fanned out, taking 135 of Henry Hooker's horses from his famous Sierra Bonita ranch and fifty-one horses and mules from a rancher and a freight train. That evening they encamped at Point of Mountains (seven or eight miles northwest of Willcox), where they killed an old man named Vance. Though they had not seen any troops that day, General Willcox was making plans to pursue them.

At 2:00 A.M. October 4, the Chiricahuas left Point of Mountains and made a beeline toward their former homes in the Dragoon Mountains. About 6:30 A.M. they crossed the railroad tracks in Dragoon Pass and went directly for Cochise's East Stronghold, camping south of there in Grapevine Canyon, which they reached before mid-morning. Coming across a herd of cattle owned by Mike Noonan, they killed seventy-nine steers, butchered them, and packed about half the meat on horses. Just as they were completing this work, the cavalry suddenly appeared and opened fire within two hundred yards of their encampment.

Strange to say, they had not seen the three troops of the Ninth Cavalry led by Captain Henry Carroll, whose courage at Hembrillo Canyon had left Victorio in awe. Carroll's detachment was on loan from the District of New Mexico. And on his heels were two troops of the First Cavalry and two troops of the Sixth Cavalry, under the indefatigable Captain Bernard. The chiefs evidently had logically assumed pursuit would come from either Willcox or Fort Bowie; they had not seen troops following them from the north, and their scouts had not seen any soldiers coming west across Sulphur Springs Valley from Bowie, or south between them and the border. Of course they had no idea that General Willcox and Captain Bernard would play their trump card: transporting their cavalry, including horses, from Willcox to Dragoon Springs by railroad cars. Carroll's command had actually reached Dragoon Summit about 4:00 A.M., some two hours before the Chiricahuas crossed the tracks. His scouts missed the trail because the main body had crossed five miles east of Carroll's position. Consequently, this interrupted his pursuit for some five hours. By the time he pulled out, the Indians were going into camp south of the stronghold and would have been unable to see his movements from Dragoon Springs because of a high mountain between them and the troops.

Thus, Carroll's surprise volley absolutely stunned the Chiricahuas, who broke camp in a panic, abandoning stock and provisions, and fleeing south along the eastern foothills. For the next several hours a running fight was carried on until the Indians made such a stand at South Pass that the soldiers were kept at bay until dark, when they bivouacked. During the night, while the soldiers rested, the main body continued their escape, most fleeing east across the Sulphur Springs Valley for a pass between the Swisshelms and Pedregosas on their way to Mexico via Guadalupe Canyon or San Luis Pass.

During the confusion of October 4, a small group of Chiricahuas split from the main body and headed southwest toward the Huachuca Mountains.[9] It is not clear whether troops from Bernard's detail or troops from Fort Huachuca were involved (probably the latter), but one of these commands did overtake a small group of Chiricahuas between the Babocomari ranch and the Huachuca Mountains, killing two, including one man.[10] On October 7, the resourceful band crossed the border, making their escape; American troops could not enter the country because Mexico and the United States still had no agreement that allowed for reciprocal crossing.[11]

The escape of the Indians from San Carlos was a remarkable accomplishment and a testament to their capable leaders. The Chiricahua chiefs had led some 375 Indians, which included seventy-four men and twenty-two older boys capable of fighting, and had traveled 216 miles on their flight to freedom.[12] Along the way they kept to the foothills of southern Arizona's mountain ranges, which ran north to south, while attacking nearly every party they encountered. They were also fortunate that the military, which responded slowly and was out of position because its cavalry was deployed north of the Gila in the aftermath of Cibecue, was unable to redirect enough horse soldiers to get between them and the border and thus impede their forward progress during the week-long exodus. Moreover, pursued by twelve troops of cavalry, they had fought two rearguard actions against them, each time neutralizing the soldiers so that their women and children could further advance toward their destination. En route, their raids had supplied additional weapons, ammunition, and sufficient horses and mules to mount the entire band. They entered Mexico with 350 to 500 head of stolen horses and mules after abandoning over one hundred head during their flight through the Dragoons.

Their known losses were meager—Bernard's soldiers and scouts had slain one woman at K-H Butte and captured one woman and three children in the running fight in the Dragoon Mountains.[13] The Indian scouts claimed to have killed one warrior in the fight at South Pass, proudly displaying his discharge papers signed by Lieutenant Guilfoyle. But because they did not find a body, Bernard discounted their claims.[14] And, as mentioned, troops had slain one warrior between that post and the Babocomari ranch. No doubt the soldiers had wounded several men, perhaps including Bonito.

Now in Mexico, Juh led the band to his mountain sanctuary east of Casas Grandes, where they came across Nana's trail, which they thought to be two weeks old, leading into the Carcay Mountains. Nana would undoubtedly welcome his brethren, for his small group was facing overwhelming forces in northwest Chihuahua. About September 25, 1881, Nana and eight warriors had a fight with Mexican citizens near Casa de Janos, killing one man and wounding another.[15] Then Nana headed south into the Sierra Madre Mountains, planning to join his son-in-law, Jatu, who at daybreak of the same day, September 25, 1881, had stolen horses from a ranch six miles east of San Buenaventura. A force of sixty men followed the trail to Cristo Canyon in the Sierra Madre and skirmished with the Indians for nine hours. The Apaches wounded one soldier and killed eight horses before the Mexicans withdrew. During the battle, a twenty-five-year-old New Mexican woman and her son escaped from the Indians and found safety with the Mexican soldiers.

Her name was Placida Romero, and she had an interesting story to tell. She had gone through a terrible ordeal, suffering much physical abuse during her time in captivity, which she correctly recalled lasted for one month and eighteen days. On August 8, 1881, less than a week after Nana's interview with Robert Stapleton, his band, now reinforced by ten Navajos, had attacked her ranch at Cebolla, about forty miles south of Cubero. She sat dumbfounded, absolutely paralyzed as one Apache and one Navajo, a man named Cibusto, who had formerly visited their ranch in friendship, shot her husband in the back at the doorway of her ranch. Then they burned it down. The Chihennes took her and two children prisoner. The Navajos took her baby, while she and her son remained with Nana, who, she said, had led the warriors.

She described Nana as a "good-sized man, fat, and stout." She explained that during a raid or engagement the men ignored the captives, usually placing them in the rear. In the midst of the fighting, she took advantage of the confusion to take her son and flee to the Mexicans. In any event, Placida Romero told the Mexicans that this was Jatu's camp, and that he had twelve warriors and their families with him and five other captives taken during Nana's raid into New Mexico. Jatu told her that he meant to trade his captives for the Indians captured at Tres Castillos.[16]

Juh, back in his country and more comfortable dealing with Mexicans (he always claimed that he was a Mexican Apache), took control. Daklugie felt that his father dominated Naiche, who, he believed, was reluctant to lead after Taza's death, but the facts simply do not bear this out.[17] After all, Naiche had no trouble leading his band during the three and a half years that Juh was in Mexico after the closing of the Chiricahua Reservation. The two men developed a close relationship when Juh came to San Carlos in January 1880. Once in Mexico, every Chiricahua chief deferred to Juh, for he had survived in Mexico by his wits, his ingenuity, and his instinctive strategic decisions.

American military authorities fretted about the potential consequences of 450 Chiricahuas living below the border. Consequently, on October 13, 1881, Colonel Ranald Mackenzie, commander, District of New Mexico, authorized hiring Van N. C. Smith, a noted frontiersman who first came to central Arizona in 1863 before founding Roswell, New Mexico, in 1869. He had been a guide for Indian Inspector William Vandever in 1873 and chief of scouts for Lieutenant Guy Howard in late 1879. Moreover, he was a logical choice because he had frequently traveled to northern Chihuahua on business.[18]

By October 23, he was at Ascencion, fifty-five miles southwest of today's Columbus, New Mexico, when an American named Pacheco arrived from Janos. He told Smith the Chiricahuas were trading stolen stock at Janos. Soon after, an American officer stationed near the border interviewed an American, who said that at Janos he saw the "Indians and Mexicans drinking together and having a merry time." The *Grant County Herald* declared, based on a letter probably from Van Smith, that Juh had "made a personal visit to one of the towns" in northern Chihuahua, referring to Janos. According to what Pacheco had reported, Smith assumed that Juh and Nana had joined forces.[19] And, according to what four Chiricahuas told Lieutenant David N. McDonald in January 1882, the two chiefs did meet before Juh went to Janos to trade stolen stock. Furthermore, McDonald learned, Nana had traded much of "the property captured in the George Smith fight" to the Chiricahuas for much needed ammunition.[20]

After arriving at Silver City, Pacheco furnished additional details. He claimed that 450 Chiricahuas had encamped near the old presidio under the chiefs Juh, Nana, and Chino (Jelikine). He watched as the Apaches traded their stolen stock from Arizona to townspeople in exchange for corn, from which they made tiswin. Pacheco discounted rumors that the authorities planned to "take advantage of the unsuspecting savages, lure them into a trap, massacre them, and take the [rest] prisoners."[21]

Mackenzie received more intelligence on October 31, 1881, when George Zimpleman, one of the owners of the Corralitos Mining Company, arrived in Deming en route to his ranch at Corralitos. Zimpleman informed Mackenzie that he had received a letter from his son informing him that Juh "was trying to make peace with Mexican authorities at the same time swearing vengeance against the Americans and declaring that he cannot live on the [San Carlos] reservation." Zimpleman promised to "cooperate in any way" with Mackenzie, who could now call on two important sources for information.[22]

Chiricahua oral history corroborates a meeting between Juh and Nana, likely in the Carcay Mountains. Nana and Juh agreed to cooperate with each other. That evening the allied bands held a dance to celebrate.[23]

Early November 1881, Juh opened negotiations at Casas Grandes with Joaquin Terrazas, whose cousin Luis was governor of the state. Juh's intermediary was José Varela, the bilingual former captive whom Juh's mother had nursed back to health when the Nednhis had captured him as a baby. Varela had enjoyed a close relationship with Juh and often served as interpreter for the Nednhi chief, who called him brother. Though Terrazas had recently deployed 350 state troops at Casas Grandes, 100 at Janos, and 100 at Carrizal, he agreed to talk peace because he wanted no part of pursuing Juh in the Sierra Madre. He knew that General Carlos Fuero, commander of federal troops for Chihuahua and Durango, was coming north with 200 more soldiers. Fuero arrived with a goal of gaining the confidence of state leaders (essentially the Terrazas family) so that they could pose an effective fighting force against the Apaches.[24] Several times in 1881, Terrazas's troops had gone out in pursuit of Nana's Chihennes, only to return empty handed. Unsuccessful at defeating them in war, Fuero now felt that extermination was the only solution, even if carried out by treacherous means.[25]

The peace conference with Juh, Geronimo, and thirty warriors occurred on November 9, 1881, about three miles east of Casas Grandes on the banks of an arroyo. Here the Apaches met the man whose forces had defeated Victorio at Tres Castillos, Joaquin Terrazas. Juh said that his people were tired of war and asked the state to put aside land for them. He requested that Chihuahua designate the Carcay Mountains and the plains and valleys on both sides as his country, where his people could raise stock, gather wild foods, hunt, and plant. Terrazas explained that he would send this request to the governor. After a two-hour conference, Juh consented to return with his Indians to receive rations from Terrazas. The next day Terrazas issued beef cattle, sugar, flour, and other items, a procedure that he repeated two or three times over the next two weeks. He had hoped to persuade Juh and Geronimo to come into Casas Grandes, but so far, he had had no success. They were just too suspicious of Terrazas.[26]

Meanwhile, both of Mackenzie's informants kept him apprised of Juh's activities at Casas Grandes. On November 14, 1881, George Zimpleman wrote him that Juh's band, numbering some three or four hundred Apaches, was visiting Casas Grandes nearly every day. They had, he said, recently sold a "good many" horses and mules taken from their raids in Arizona. He also revealed that the Mexican government continued to concentrate troops with the objective of capturing the entire band to "transport them to the interior of Mexico under guard." Van Smith's report was just as informative as Zimpleman's. On November 14, 1881, he had left Casas Grandes to return to New Mexico. Before departing, he had observed the Chiricahuas trading over fifty of Hooker's horses and Samaniego's mules to Mexican citizens and officers. He mentioned

Terrazas's meeting of November 9 with Juh. Since then, the Mexican officer had tried to persuade Juh to come to town, but the chief remained apprehensive. Finally, Terrazas sent three barrels of mescal to Mexicans at Casas Grandes, directing them to dispense the beverage but only in exchange for the Apaches' arms and ammunition.

Smith did succeed in interviewing a few Chiricahuas in a cantina, but as they "get drunk as soon as they enter town," it was difficult to gather any information. They had not met Nana, they claimed, which was either disingenuous or a misunderstanding, for Nana had just separated from Juh and headed to eastern Chihuahua. Smith also spoke with Terrazas, who revealed his plan was "to gain their confidence and get them all in, with a view of entrapping them." He was waiting for General Fuero before carrying out the double cross.[27]

Juh and Nana foiled Terrazas's plans for chicanery when they abandoned the area. They distrusted Terrazas and had heard rumors from their friendly trading partners of his intentions. About November 27, 1881, Juh led the Chiricahuas south to his favorite winter home at Guaynopa.[28] Nana was not with him. In early November, he and his Chihennes had rounded Corralitos to the north and struck across the Chihuahua desert toward Presidio del Norte, where they hoped to find information about their people captured at Tres Castillos. The two chiefs agreed to meet in March, when the "weather was warm and the grass good."[29]

The first news of the Chiricahuas leaving Casas Grandes was heard when George Berry arrived in Tombstone from Chihuahua on December 8. Lieutenant Frederick A. Smith, accompanied by Tom Jeffords, interviewed Berry, who told them that the Apaches had left Casas Grandes, some said for the Chiricahua Mountains. Jeffords disagreed, predicting that Juh had moved south into the Sierra Madre Mountains.[30]

Controversy had dogged Jeffords since the Chiricahua outbreak from San Carlos, though his reputation with General Willcox and his aide-de-camp, Lieutenant Haskell, remained unblemished. They continued to rely on him for information and advice. In the days following the breakout, he had brought twelve Chiricahuas (mostly women and one old man, who may have been Chiva) to Fort Thomas. On October 17 Willcox hired him as interpreter. Six days later he and George Stevens left Fort Thomas for Safford, hoping to meet some Chiricahuas. But they returned a few days later, unsuccessful in their attempts to establish contact. Jeffords reported that the Chiricahuas were now in Mexico, beyond his reach.[31]

Jeffords's venture caught the attention of several Arizonans, who were looking for a scapegoat, and he was always a convenient target. First, his former
tormentors, the editors of the *Arizona Citizen,* mocked the military for having
confidence in him: "The valiant Captain Jeffords, whose great influence with
the wild and murderous Apaches . . . has at last been heard from, and bright
laurels are cut and dried awaiting the proper moment to descend majestically
upon his brow."[32]

Even men who should have known better were critical of Jeffords. Agent
Tiffany questioned Jeffords's usefulness, implying that the military overestimated his sway with the Chiricahuas because he had failed to persuade any of
them to serve as scouts after Cibecue. Tiffany concluded, "I do not place much
confidence in his opinion."[33] Arizona cattle baron Henry Hooker, who had
lost 135 horses to the raiding Apaches (15 belonging to Jeffords), believed that
Jeffords had unduly convinced the military that they "would get whipped" if
they fought the hostiles. If present in Naiche's camp during the chaotic times
after George gave his Paul Revere warning, Jeffords probably realized that
nothing he could say would make a difference. By then, he had developed a
thick hide and continued to march to his own beat, oblivious to and unaffected
by the expectations of others.[34]

Meanwhile, after several days of social dances and feasts at Guaynopa, the
Chiricahua leaders mapped a strategy for the coming months. Besides sending raiding parties against Chihuahua and Sonora, they also discussed Loco's,
Zele's, and Chiva's bands at San Carlos. They concluded to send a party to the
reservation to determine the prospects of liberating those bands. They were
probably confident of success, given their remarkable flight in early October. Geronimo's rationale was simple: they needed reinforcements to fight the
large concentration of Mexican troops. The Chiricahuas at San Carlos numbered about three hundred, of whom fifty were warriors.[35]

Kaywaykla's impression was simply that more of Loco's band would perish from malaria and starvation than if they were fighting for freedom in the
Sierra Madre.[36] Yet, they had enough to eat and had avoided malaria. Hart had
assigned Loco's people an area near the agency so that his Indian police could
keep a close watch over them. Although exceedingly hot in the summer, it was
dry and free from malaria. The malaria that struck the Chokonens and Nednhis
at the subagency was never a problem with the Chihennes at the main agency.

Historian Bud Shapard heard a different version from Loco's descendants.
They felt that those in Mexico were jealous because Loco was adjusting to the
white man's world. The idea to force them from the reservation came from

Kaetenae's wife, an excitable woman who noted, "Here we are, hungry and chased by the army, while Loco is sitting on the reservation, fat and comfortable." Betzinez blamed Kaetenae for convincing Geronimo to undertake this endeavor.[37]

They were probably unaware that the Chihennes had suffered another setback. Nana and Jatu had fallen in with some Mescaleros, for Terrazas had also captured many of their people at Tres Castillos. Late in the third week of November, they sent an emissary to Presidio del Norte, about fifty miles southeast of Tres Castillos, to find out about their people held by Chihuahua. The Mexicans feigned interest in negotiations before carrying out the official policy of Chihuahua. Kill as many Apaches as possible, even under the auspices of talking peace. Mexican soldiers surprised their camp, capturing and killing many. Reports place the casualties at forty, but this seems too high unless many Mescaleros were included. But Nana and most of the women and children escaped. Tragically, his son-in-law or nephew Jatu was among the dead. This event effectively ended the alliance between the Chihennes and the Mescaleros. Nana rejoined Juh in the Sierra Madre Mountains.[38]

In mid-December the Chiricahua leaders had decided to send Bonito and seven warriors to infiltrate the San Carlos Reservation. Bonito was a logical choice. Not only was he known for his courage and leadership (a half-century later Perico, Geronimo's second cousin, would rank him behind only Mangas Coloradas and Cochise as a leader), but he also had many relatives among the White Mountain people.[39] Moreover, part of his band, thirty persons in all, was still on the reservation with Chiva. To safeguard the small group, his cousin She-neah, a powerful shaman, likely accompanied the party. Bonito led his men into Arizona in late December, about the same time that one band of Chiricahuas was battling Mexican troops in the Sierra Madre.

In the past, the Chiricahuas had sent out many raiding parties in different directions. This time, however, recognizing that Mexican troops were patrolling on each side of the Sierra Madre and in the northern part of the range, they divided their forces into two parties. Juh's raiding patterns suggest that he, perhaps with Naiche and Chatto, took about forty warriors (leaving their dependents at Guaynopa) farther south into the Sierra Madre. His first encounter with Sonorans took place on December 13, 1881, when he killed three men between Sahuaripa and Mulatos. From here the band continued south into the mining districts, where they attacked the Trinidad mines at the end of December.[40]

Geronimo, who never forgot that Sonoran troops had killed his first wife and children, always sought vengeance against that state. Likely Chihuahua and Jelikine accompanied him as they led a band of forty warriors, who left their dependents at Guaynopa, and struck for the Sonoran settlements along the western foothills of the Sierra Madre. On the afternoon of December 19, 1881, they attacked a mule train between Tepache and Moctezuma. Later that day they ambushed and killed two mail riders near a deserted ranch. From Granados, twenty soldiers under Sergeant Evan Duraza hastened to the site of the attack, and then followed the Apaches' trail. At 8:00 A.M. the next day (December 20), at Cecalate, the Chiricahuas ambushed his command, killing five soldiers and wounding a sergeant and three others. The war party continued east toward the Sierra Madre foothills, where they routed a party of twenty nationals from Tepache, killing three men and seriously wounding the leader, the municipal president of the town. Over three days the Indians had slain fifteen persons, wounded five others, and captured two children.[41]

Two days later, on December 22, 1881, the same band surprised a mescal camp about twenty miles north of Sahuaripa at Criadora Canyon, slaying five more men. A rider came in with the horrifying news about 6 P.M. on December 22, 1881. Only one hour before, Manuel Valencia, the prefect of Sahuaripa, had sent out a well-armed force of fifty men under Jesús Quiroz, "known to be a thoughtful and brave commander," to scout the region between Sahuaripa and the Chihuahua border, particularly Chamada and Teópare a rugged thirty-mile stretch of mountainous country. Valencia had to strip his town of weapons, arming Quiroz's men with Remington rifles and carbines. The messenger from the mescal ranch claimed that seventy to eighty Apaches had attacked them. Valencia sent eleven mounted men, armed only with revolvers, under José María Cordova to the ranch. He also requested help from Arivechi, but their nationals had no weapons.

When Quiroz, encamped at Chipajora Canyon, received news of the raid he immediately went to the rescue, arriving at Criadora at 10:00 A.M. on December 23. Finding five corpses, Quiroz declared, "There was no time to mourn their deaths," and led his eighty-six men on the Chiricahuas' trail. The Apaches were driving a considerable herd of stolen stock toward Chamada, about thirty-five miles southwest of Guaynopa. Near there, on Christmas Day, he sent a force of twenty-four cavalry under Francisco Valencia to examine tracks that led into Soledada Canyon.

The Chiricahuas were waiting behind breastworks along the rim of the canyon. As Valencia's men approached to within one hundred feet, the Apaches sprung their trap, wounding Valencia and four other men. In minutes, they had killed fourteen horses and compelled the Mexicans to retreat before "they were all killed." Quiroz returned to Sahuaripa, where Prefect Valencia summed up their situation: "This district is facing a calamity because of a lack of useful firearms. Our people are determined to fight these savages but they lack arms while the Indians have repeating rifles [Winchesters]."[42]

After returning to Guaynopa with his stock and booty, Geronimo led a second foray. He crossed the crest of the Sierra Madre to the Bavispe River below Granados. Here the band stole 139 head of stock and crossed the valley northeast to the Moctezuma River, heading for the road between Cumpas and Bacoachi, where they ambushed a pack train. The eight teamsters escaped with a loss of two men slightly wounded. They claimed that the Apaches numbered thirty or forty and were under two renegade whites, suggesting the presence of Zebina Streeter.[43]

Juh's war party was also active. He led forty warriors across the southeastern slope of the Sierra Madre and on January 18, 1882, assaulted Dolores, a mining settlement in the extreme western district of Guerrero that had just reopened after years of inactivity. The Apaches killed two men and wounded three more during the first fire. Juh fought for five hours before calling off the engagement. The next day his men captured a thirty-mule train going to Dolores. The eight teamsters abandoned everything to save their lives.

Luis Terrazas, the governor of Chihuahua, authorized a bounty for every Apache captured or killed. He also agreed to finance the recruitment of one hundred Tarahumaras from Temosachic, "where the best Indian fighters in Mexico are said to come from."[44] He informed General Fuero, who vowed to avenge these outrages. Terrazas's actions contrasted starkly with those of Governor Carlos Ortiz in Sonora. The prefects of the frontier districts at Moctezuma, Arispe, and Sahuaripa had to beg the governor to send assistance. And if he could not send troops, they asked for firearms and ammunition to protect their families and launch campaigns against the Apaches.

By early February, Juh had returned to Guaynopa and decided to attack Nácori Chico, situated on the west bank of the Rio Nácori in a narrow valley in the center of the northern Sierra Madre. Both Cochise and Juh had targeted this outpost in the 1860s and 1870s; several times the three hundred isolated but brave citizens considered leaving it to the Apaches, who found it a convenient target because it was "located between the lowland ranches and [their] mountain hideouts."[45] By the evening of February 14, 1882, the war party of one hundred Chiricahuas had assumed their positions for an assault on the town at dawn.

At 7:00 A.M., on February 15, 1882, they attacked the sleepy village, but the battle-tested farmers of Nácori Chico responded. Details are sparse, but

according to the reports, the "valiant citizens of Nácori resisted them and repulsed their attack. They saw five warriors fall during the battle; the Apaches
carried off four." The Chiricahuas lurked on the outskirts all day because they
had left a fallen warrior near the town. That night they recovered his body and
rode away. According to one report, the Indian assault had taken the lives of
three Mexicans.[46]

About this time, Bonito and his seven warriors returned from their visit
to San Carlos. On New Year's Day, 1882, his party had stolen twenty-eight
horses from the Helms ranch in the Sulphur Springs Valley west of the Swiss-
shelms. One American saw the raiders after they stopped to eat in a canyon
near the Swisshelms; he counted seven warriors in camp and one with the
stock. Ranchers followed the trail, coming across the three dead colts and five
horses that the Indians had abandoned before crossing into Mexico via Guadalupe Canyon.[47]

Bonito left the stock in the care of a few younger warriors. Then he and five
men, silently and seemingly invisible, filtered north through the Peloncillo
mountain corridor to the Gila, when they turned abruptly west toward San
Carlos. Whether his party was on foot or mounted is not clear. Undoubtedly
he traveled by night and rested by day. By January 20, 1882, he was on the San
Carlos Reservation.[48]

That day the Chiricahuas stole some ponies from a Yuma (Yavapais) Apache
whose camp was a few miles north of the main agency. To thwart pursuers,
Bonito, who was about ten miles north of Loco's camp, took the ponies east
toward the Gila Mountains north of Fort Thomas. He then circled back toward the subagency, where the remnants of his old band, four warriors and
twenty-six women and children, all under Chiva, were living. After meeting
Chiva, and leaving two of his men there, Bonito and three men went to Loco's
camp near the San Carlos agency, where the four men stayed for a few days.
They told Loco that a large force of warriors would return in forty days to
carry away the whole band. They would kill any who refused to leave, warned
Bonito. Apparently they had received a mixed reception, for the dependents
of some of Nana's men were still at San Carlos with Loco, and Victorio's wife,
whose daughter had married Mangas, was reportedly eager to leave. Loco
wanted no part of the plan. About one week later, on February 6, 1882, a
woman of Loco's camp, who was married to a Western Apache, revealed this
information to the military.[49]

At department headquarters, General Willcox, already on edge and expecting more trouble from Juh, responded immediately, for this was the first

specific news of the Chiricahuas' intentions. He first wanted to be sure that military officials had advised Tiffany of the threat. He also asked Captain Daniel Madden for the identity of the Apache informant. On February 15, 1882, Madden responded to Willcox's request: "The Department Commander [Willcox] evidently forgets or overlooks the fact that I am pledged to secrecy on this subject, and that the name can only be given conditionally. When these conditions are complied with, I shall be at liberty to give the name, and will cheerfully."[50] This rebuke undoubtedly rankled Willcox, who shortly after received confirmation of Bonito's visit from another source: Indian Inspector Charles H. Howard, former brigadier general during the Civil War and brother of the famous Oliver.

Howard reached San Carlos a few days after American officials learned of Bonito's threat. The secretary of the interior, Samuel J. Kirkland, had sent him to study the situation at San Carlos, especially in light of Cibecue and the Chiricahua outbreak.[51] In mid-February, he met Loco, whose band the military had relocated closer to the agency a few days after hearing of Bonito's threat. The Chihenne chief admitted that Bonito "tried to induce them to go, but now the chiefs say they will stay." But they preferred a transfer to the Navajo Reservation.[52]

Bonito's undetected invasion of the reservation disturbed Willcox. No one knew by which route the Indians had taken their trip to and from Mexico. They likely returned to Mexico via Guadalupe Canyon after following the same route that they had used the previous October. A teamster, crossing the Sulphur Springs Valley on February 6, spotted the party moving south. This scare prompted an editorial from the *Tombstone Epitaph* suggesting that business and mining interests establish funding for twenty-five scouts to patrol the border "to exterminate renegades." Willcox ordered his post commanders to be vigilant for a Chiricahua raid into Arizona. On March 22, 1882, General Willcox dispatched Major David Perry with two troops and one company of Indian scouts to establish a base camp in the southern part of the Chiricahua Mountains. Remembering Bonito's warning, Willcox would send scouting parties along the border. But they would not trespass into Mexico because of two recent intrusions by overeager American lieutenants.[53]

The first event occurred in early November when Lieutenant Thomas Garvey, First Cavalry, crossed into Sonora near Agua Prieta with thirty troopers and eight Apache scouts. In all likelihood, he probably had no idea that he was in Mexico. If it were left to local Sonoran authorities along the frontier, who usually welcomed any force that would fight Apaches, the transgression would not have caused a ripple. But because it drew the attention of federal forces under Colonel Nicolas España, the colonel's superior, General José Otero, commander of the federal forces in Sonora, sent a formal complaint to General Willcox.[54]

The second incident was more serious and developed into a minor diplomatic snafu with Chihuahua. In mid-January 1882, Lieutenant David N. McDonald crossed the border with seven packers, seventeen Apache scouts, and two citizens after his scouts picked up an Apache trail. McDonald had left Fort Cummings on December 31, 1881. By January 4, 1882, he was at the border, camping at Carrizalillo Springs. The next day, his scouts discovered an Apache trail, which was perhaps that of Nana, then returning to the Sierra Madre Mountains after the double cross at Presidio del Norte. Running out of forage for his mules, McDonald decided to replenish supplies at Ascencion. He was an unwelcome intruder, especially with his seventeen Apache scouts. To his dismay, "Mexican troops surrounded his camp" and arrested him on January 8. His captors escorted his command to Casas Grandes, where he remained for several days until Colonel Santiago Nieto received the order from General Fuero authorizing the release of the Americans. On January 16, McDonald went to Corralitos and met George Zimpleman and four Chiricahuas (three old women and one old man). They had not accompanied the band into Sonora and were living off "the charity of Zimpleman's employees."[55]

McDonald, with the aid of his Apache scouts, "gave them money and food so as to create a friendly impression and get them to talk." They provided information about Nana's and Juh's activities. He also learned that Van Smith's usefulness as a scout had ended. Smith had written a letter to Mackenzie from Deming on January 11, 1882, in which he provided the latest news. In ending his letter, he claimed that he had curtailed his mission at Janos because a "wild horse" had kicked him on the knee. "Unable to ride on horseback" and needing medicine, he had left Mexico "to fix himself up." By that, he meant to get sober, as McDonald soon found out. Mexicans had told the lieutenant that Smith "was drunk much of the time" and that a civil official at Janos had "knocked him down."[56]

Colonel Mackenzie was furious at McDonald's actions (though the colonel's record as a field commander in Texas suggests that he would have taken the same course of action). As commander of the military District of New Mexico, he was doing all he could to establish amicable relations with Mexican military authorities in Chihuahua. In fact, after thanking General Carlos Fuero for the quick release of McDonald's command, he unequivocally condemned McDonald's actions, declaring that he had "ordered him detained and his conduct investigated." Mackenzie was not kidding. He wanted a piece of McDonald's hide, uncharitably recommending that the lieutenant be brought up on court-martial charges. Cooler heads prevailed, however, and Mackenzie dropped the charges.[57]

Meanwhile Willcox and Mackenzie prepared for the Chiricahua invasion that they felt was imminent. The first week of March, Frank Bennett returned from Galeana with the news that the Chiricahuas remained 150 miles south of there.[58] But they were then moving north, hoping to make a temporary truce at Janos or Casas Grandes to protect their women and children while most of the men went north to San Carlos.

About 11:00 A.M. on March 14, 1882, they stole eighty-three horses and mules from the Ramos hacienda, which was located midway between the Carcay Mountains and George Zimpleman's Corralitos ranch. The animals were grazing on a prairie west of the ranch when forty or fifty Chiricahuas swooped down from a hill and ran off part of the herd. George Zimpleman, Jack Williams, and five Mexicans pursued until the Apaches' rearguard opened fire, wounding three men, including Williams, and killing several horses. That same day another party stole ten horses from Janos. Juh and Geronimo's next move must have surprised Zimpleman. The following morning (March 15), they sent two women, one of whom was Geronimo's wife, to Ramos, riding horses that had been stolen the day before at Janos. They told Thomas Zimpleman, George's son, that they wanted to make a treaty. Zimpleman released the older woman with instructions to tell Juh that he would keep the other woman until the Apaches returned the stock stolen on March 14.[59]

Zimpleman's justice had an effect opposite from what he had intended. On March 17 Juh's warriors captured four sheepherders tending to Zimpleman's herd about thirty miles northwest of Corralitos. The Indians charged the herd, running off an estimated seven thousand head. Zimpleman sent William Crosby to the scene, where he found the remaining employees, some "twenty in number, in a demoralized state, huddled together, fearing another attack by the Apaches." But Juh still wanted to work out a private arrangement with Zimpleman, just as he had when José María Zuloaga owned the ranch. On March 18, the chief released one of his captives, who suddenly appeared at Janos with a message: bring the Apache woman to Casa de Janos or Juh would kill his three hostages.

The next day Francisco Mapula, a civil official at Janos, sent two Apaches who lived at Janos to establish contact with Juh. Meanwhile, a force of about thirty soldiers and eleven citizens went to Casa de Janos to meet the Apaches. When they arrived, they could see the Chiricahuas lurking in the foothills of the Carcay Mountains. Jack Kyle recalled that the Mexicans found "the Indians a little too thick and wouldn't go any further." Thus Zimpleman, Kyle, Crosby, and a man named Wilcox rode across the plain for several miles. When they saw about thirty Apaches two hundred yards away, Zimpleman told them that he wanted to talk, and five chiefs came forward: Juh, Geronimo, Naiche, Nahilzay, and Jelikine, who served as the interpreter. Zimpleman's party called him Chino (Wavy Hair) or Little Chief.

Juh asked Zimpleman for permission to camp on his land, pledging that his people "would not molest the people or the property of the ranch any further and would return the herders, sheep, and horses in exchange for Geronimo's wife." Zimpleman agreed to return the next day with the Indian woman and mescal to consummate the agreement. This time Mapula and a few citizens from Janos joined Zimpleman's party. From a distance, Richard Hudson watched the meeting with his binoculars. The Americans provided tobacco and both sides enjoyed a smoke. The same chiefs, and Bonito, were present. Mapula had a talk with Juh, who admitted that Nana was in his camp. He also declared that he wanted a "lasting peace." The two sides exchanged hostages, but the Apaches failed to return Zimpleman's horses and mules. One ransomed sheepherder said that the Apaches had not mistreated him. At night, however, they had tied his hands behind his back to prevent him from escaping. Yet, Mapula was wary of Juh's statement disavowing hostilities "because they always say the same thing."[60]

The next day, March 21, 1882, Juh sent his wife and another woman, with the ten horses and mules stolen earlier, to Janos. They spoke with Richard Hudson and George Zimpleman, promising to return his stock next. Hudson believed the Apaches wanted to make peace because they had some five hundred animals stolen in Sonora that they wished to barter for ammunition, which they needed before sending a raiding party into the United States.[61] This brief period of goodwill almost ended a few days later. A rumor reached Casas Grandes that the Chiricahuas had killed George Zimpleman near Casa de Janos. Colonel Santiago Nieto gathered a force from Casas Grandes and hastened to the scene. About one hundred warriors under Juh exhibited a white flag, yelling out that they did not wish to fight. They wanted peace and had already held discussions with civil officials at Janos, claimed Juh. Realizing the report of Zimpleman's death was false, Nieto went to Janos, where he spent several days attempting to persuade Juh to come with him to Casas

Grandes. On March 29, 1882, Juh sent an emissary to Nieto with the message that the chief would be in the next day. Yet Juh remained suspicious, recalling the betrayal by federal troops of Nolgee in November 1878. Richard Hudson confirmed that Juh was uneasy for "the Mexicans at Janos had several times got them in for a peace talk and murdered them."[62]

On the same day that he heard from Juh, Nieto received a message from Casas Grandes that Sánchez, the Chihenne leader in Nana's band, had requested peace at Casas Grandes.[63] It was no secret among the Chihennes that Sánchez's need for mescal clouded his judgment. The oldest surviving Chihenne in Mexico besides Nana, Sánchez was his logical successor. But Nana had decided that he could not trust him to lead because of his weakness for liquor. Indeed, it soon became clear to all that Nana was grooming Kaetenae as his successor.[64]

Meanwhile, Major George A. Forsyth at Fort Cummings had hired Lorenzo Carrasco to report on Apache affairs at Janos and Casas Grandes. He arrived at Janos on March 27 and learned that 450 Chiricahuas were camped at Casa de Janos. He said four Apaches had come into town that day, trading "stock for liquor and provisions." Carrasco also heard that the Chiricahuas were expecting the return of a party of forty Indians, who had gone north to the mountains near Fort Cummings to retrieve a cache of ammunition. According to Carrasco's sources, General Fuero would take no action against the Chiricahuas until Terrazas arrived from the south, where Fuero had sent him after Juh's raid at Dolores. The general expected Terrazas to reach Casas Grandes within days.

Carrasco had gathered important information about General Fuero's plans. The Apaches had outwitted him the previous fall, and he vowed that it would not happen again. Their assaults on Sonora and the raid at Dolores had not only incensed him but also convinced him that the ends justified the means. He looked at the Chiricahuas' return to Janos as an opportunity to settle forever Mexico's Apache problem. Correctly assuming that he would be unable to coax the entire band into Janos or Casas Grandes (where he could get them drunk and then slaughter them), he made plans to defeat them in battle. Though Fuero could call on six hundred troops within forty miles of Janos, he would not begin to implement his plan until Terrazas arrived with his Tarahumara Indian fighters.

Even before he received Carrasco's report, Mackenzie had written General Fuero to ask about Juh and Geronimo. Fuero freely admitted that they had requested peace at Janos but that it would "not be granted them." The general unveiled his duplicitous plan. When certain that the federal troops in Sonora had taken positions in the Carretas plains, he would "order a vigorous pursuit until a complete extermination is accomplished." He projected operations to begin on April 20 when "troops from Sonora will be in position." Until then, he "ordered that the Indians not be molested on any account, with the object of gaining their confidence."[65]

On April 5, 1882, George Zimpleman wrote Mackenzie to keep him informed of Indian affairs at Janos. The attitude of "cowardly Mexicans," who were indifferent to his stock losses and tolerated the traffic in stolen stock at Janos, had frustrated the capitalist. After Colonel Nieto advised him to accept the Chiricahuas' offer to return his stock for ten bolts of cloth and a barrel of mescal, he nearly exploded. Zimpleman was incredulous: Nieto's job was "to fight these scoundrels, wherever he finds them, and he advises me to pay them for robbing me and perhaps next week [they will] do the same all over again." Zimpleman could not comprehend that these practices had been a way of life at Janos for the past fifty years. A man who believed in swift retribution, he was itching to fight the Chiricahuas after exchanging his sheepherders, but Mexican officials prevented him from taking action. Worn out by Chihuahua's Indian policy, he conceded that "I have lost all my religion and patience."[66]

At the time Zimpleman was writing to Mackenzie, Colonel Joaquin Terrazas, who had reached Casas Grandes on March 30, left about April 5 in search of Juh and Geronimo. General Fuero had authorized him to take any measures either to kill or to capture the two men. Fuero told Terrazas to tell the Indians that if they wanted peace, they had to capitulate and give up their arms—essentially an unconditional surrender. On April 8, 1882, Terrazas met Juh (who "spoke in stuttering Spanish") and Geronimo, probably near Casa de Janos. They evidently did not discuss terms, for the two leaders promised to return two days later with other chiefs. They came back as scheduled. Terrazas, however, refused to allow Juh to speak because he had reneged on his promise to return the previous November. He would mediate terms with Geronimo, whom the other chiefs appointed as their spokesman. Terrazas, having concluded that an attack was not in his best interests, turned to his second plan—the carrot and stick approach. He promised to issue rations of flour, meat, sugar, and tobacco. Furthermore, he agreed to furnish mescal, if they so wished. Of course, his plan had a devious ulterior motive: gain their confidence, ply them with liquor, and when they were sufficiently inebriated, slaughter all regardless of age or gender.[67]

The next morning, April 11, Geronimo, with most of the warriors, headed north to San Carlos. With him was a cast of superb fighting men:

the Chokonens Naiche, Chatto, Chihuahua, and Cathla; the Bedonkohes Bonito and She-neah; the Chihennes Kaetenae, Mangas, and Sánchez; and the Nednhi Jelikine. Juh, Nana, and about thirty warriors remained in Mexico with some 325 women and children, including 15 teenage boys capable of fighting. Two days later, on the afternoon of April 13, Juh's wife and six other Apaches entered Janos and stayed until noon of the following day. Before leaving, they said that Juh would be in the next day. He would send a smoke signal to announce that he would meet with Mexican authorities.

Subsequent developments would force Juh to change these plans. That same day his wife returned to camp, two hundred troops from Sonora, under General Bernardo Reyes, had encamped at Casa de Janos. Reyes, however, had become seriously ill during the trip and was unable to ride. Colonel Lorenzo García dispatched two soldiers to Janos with a note requesting to borrow a wagon to take Reyes back to Bavispe. Meanwhile, General Fuero arrived at Janos on April 16, expecting to meet General Reyes. Fuero learned that Juh had seen the Sonoran army and left the Carcay Mountains for the Sierra Madre about thirty-five miles southeast of Casas Grandes.

Before leaving, Juh sent a small group of warriors to find Geronimo's war party and warn him about the presence of Colonel García's force at Casa de Janos. Then, on April 18, he sent a man and two women to Casas Grandes, hoping to determine the intentions of García's force. An American, C. F. Bottom, who was at Corralitos on April 19, 1882, said that George Zimpleman received a message from Casas Grandes that Juh was in the vicinity. This is an important fact because it establishes his location on that date and adds more to the mountain of evidence that Juh was not present in the events that were unfolding that very day on the San Carlos Reservation.[68]

11

LOCO HAS NO CHOICE

The Apache will perhaps learn to his sorrow that Sonora of today is not the Sonora of years gone by.

Tombstone Epitaph, January 23, 1882

Between sixty and seventy Chiricahua Apache men stealthily crossed the border into the United States in the early morning on or about April 12, 1882.[1] Contemporary opinions differ about where they entered because the military commanders of Arizona and New Mexico each provided evidence that the Apaches had crossed on the other's watch. This issue was crucial to Willcox (fighting to retain his command after Cibecue), who stated, even before he knew the facts, that the Apaches "did not come up through the Arizona frontier."[2] Mackenzie understood that it mattered little where they had infiltrated. Whatever their route, they apparently crossed the line between San Luis Pass, in southwestern New Mexico, and San Bernardino, in southeastern Arizona.

Opinions also vary about which mountain corridor they traversed en route to their final destination. Charles Connell believed they had moved north via the Animas Mountains to the Burro range, where they struck the Gila, following it into Arizona.[3] Noted scout Al Sieber claimed he picked up their trail in the northern Animas Mountains, which means they entered by San Luis Pass and went north through the Animas Mountains before breaking abruptly west into the Peloncillos.[4] A White Mountain woman told John Walker that the Chiricahuas came north between Guadalupe Pass and San Bernardino, thus placing their entry in southeastern Arizona.[5] The most accepted version has Geronimo's party (in two groups, forty mounted and twenty on foot) following the Peloncillo Mountains north to the San Simon Valley, which they crossed, probably in the early morning of April 13, 1882. The two parties united at Doubtful Canyon, near Steins, before continuing north to the Gila.[6]

Thus, it would appear that the Chiricahuas had set foot in both territories on their way to the reservation.

During the afternoon of April 16, 1882, a White Mountain Apache raced into George Stevens's sheep camp at Ash Flat, fifteen miles northeast of to-day's Bryce. He had seen Chiricahuas (the first notice that they were in Arizona) and believed they intended to raid the camp. Victoriano Mestas was in charge of the outfit that employed between seven and ten Mexican herders and several Apaches, including Richard Bylas and several others. Mestas and Bylas immediately "moved the camp to higher ground and all that afternoon they made fortifications." Mestas was a former captive of the Chiricahuas and knew Geronimo well. Thus, he recognized the voice that rang out from the darkness a few hours before dawn on April 17, 1882: "It is me, Mestas; it is Geronimo. I have many men and they are hungry. We will not harm you for I am Geronimo, your friend." Bylas warned Mestas not to let Geronimo in, "or they will kill you." And then Bylas, the White Mountain chief whose uncle Victorio had killed, derided the notion of trusting the shaman: "You lie, Geronimo, you want to kill us. Always you are a liar."

Geronimo ignored Bylas and repeated his request, which prompted Bylas to counter with his same warning. But Mestas's resolve was weakening. He was remembering that Geronimo had once given him a pony and saddle when he was a captive. Bylas countered, reminding Mestas that the gesture "was a long time ago. You were living with the Chiricahuas then. Now you work for the white man, George Stevens." For the third time, Bylas warned Mestas: "Don't let them come for they will kill you." But Mestas disagreed and after daybreak invited Geronimo to bring his band in. His wife prepared a meal of tortillas and mutton. Geronimo, however, disliked mutton and ordered Mestas's wife to cook a "two-year-old sorrel pony" that belonged to Jimmie Stevens. After the Indians finished the meal, Geronimo gave a signal and the warriors "disarmed the [six] herders and tied their hands behind their backs." Turning his attention to Mestas, Geronimo ordered him to remove his shirt ("a Mexican shirt with fine embroidery" that he did not want blood stained), which he would wear during the raid at San Carlos. Then he ordered his men to tie up Mestas, his wife, and two of their children.

Bylas, who was sitting with Naiche and Chatto, berated Geronimo: "Why do you want to kill these people after they have fed you and you promised to harm no one?" Naiche intervened and suggested that Geronimo pay Mestas's woman for the meal. Chatto, agreeing with Naiche, asked Geronimo why he would kill these people "when you promised to do them no harm? We would have lost many men if we had tried to attack this camp." Their words compelled Geronimo to back down. But only until he knew that he had an ally in the fearless Chihuahua, who reminded him: "These people are Mexicans and they are our enemies. Always the Mexicans have lied to us and killed our people." Emboldened by Chihuahua's support, Geronimo ordered his warriors to run "a long rope through the thongs" which bound each prisoner's hands and to lead them up a hill (today known as Deadman Tank) away from camp. The Chiricahuas shot and stabbed the defenseless Mexicans until nearly all were dead—six herders, Mestas, his wife, and two little children. One man somehow freed himself from the rope and tried to flee to safety. The warriors shot him down, though a few stray bullets almost hit Geronimo.

After the massacre, an agitated Geronimo stormed over to Chatto and Naiche, who were sitting with Richard Bylas. In later years, Bylas told Charles Connell that Geronimo wanted to kill him. The son of Cochise, however, would not allow this to happen. Naiche, in a voice loud enough for Geronimo to hear, told his two nephews to kill him "if he says anything." Geronimo lost his voice.

Naiche and Chatto were not the only Chiricahuas who abhorred Geronimo's treachery. The Mexican-born Jelikine said nothing as the ghastly slaughter took place. And when Geronimo returned, he kept silent, at least until the Chiricahuas noticed that they had overlooked a nine-year-old boy. He had just witnessed the killing of his mother and two brothers as the Indians had "beat their brains out with stones." Then they had tortured his father before putting him out of his misery with a hatchet blow to his skull. Stanislaus Mestas mentioned that Bylas's wife had begged Geronimo to spare the boy. When the Chiricahuas first saw him, one warrior said, "Here is one we missed," and Geronimo simply said, "Kill him too." But Jelikine would have none of that. Though Jimmie Stevens does not mention him by name, it is clear from his description that this was Jelikine:

> That was when the Chiricahua warrior threatened Geronimo. This warrior was a Mexican who had been captured as a little boy and raised by the Chiricahuas [actually the Western Apaches]. He was a small man, but he was a great warrior and very brave. Seizing a spear, he held it at Geronimo's heart as he spoke: "I am a warrior, Geronimo, always I have obeyed your orders. The people you have killed today are my people but something—I think it is their God—has spared the little one's life. Do not harm him or I will kill you, Geronimo." Then

[Jelikine] faced the entire band: "I will kill any man who harms the little boy. You are many. I am alone, but I will take many with me when I go."

The boy was spared.[7]

A few days later, Bylas's wife brought Mestas's son to Safford, where they were met by a White Mountain Apache who had escaped from the Chiricahuas. They told George Stevens of the grisly massacre. They reported that Naiche, Geronimo, and several of Victorio's old band, including Katoronny, probably meaning Kaetenae, were at the sheep camp. There was no equivocation about Juh; according to them, he was not present. The Chiricahuas had revealed they were going to San Carlos to get their people and would kill anyone in their way. Stevens sent a courier with a note to the commanding officer at Fort Thomas. He arrived there at 3:30 P.M. on April 19, too late to prevent the hostiles from carrying off Loco's band.[8]

The warriors had exercised great care to avoid detection in their movements. After the massacre, they forced Bylas and the White Mountain Apaches to go along (though they released Bylas a few days later). They stopped near Ash Flat for the rest of April 17. Then Geronimo, whose strength as a leader was rooted in his strong Power, sang four songs. His Power assured him that "all was going to be well on their way to San Carlos." That night and early the next morning (April 18, 1882), they followed the southern foothills of the Gila Mountains before taking cover on the ridges north of the subagency, where they went into camp not far from the Gila. The military and Indian agents remained unaware of their presence. About 7:00 P.M. on April 18, 1882, the warriors crossed the Gila near Calva. Bonito took a handful of men and sneaked into Chiva's camp. Chiva's small band (four men and thirty women and children) willingly left.[9]

Geronimo then started for the main agency at San Carlos, about eighteen miles west of the subagency, near the junction of the San Carlos and Gila rivers. About 9:00 P.M. Chihuahua, whose wife had tried to dissuade him from attempting such a risky mission, and seven warriors cut the telegraph wire about one-half mile west of the subagency.[10] Three hours later, a Western Apache scout appeared at the subagency's telegraph station with the news that the Chiricahuas were going to San Carlos. The operator, Ed Pierson, tried in vain to notify his counterpart at San Carlos. With the help of a few Apache scouts, Pierson found and repaired the down line. Throughout the night he tried to warn the main agency that the Chiricahuas were coming, but Stumpy

Hunter, the San Carlos operator, was sleeping and did not hear the emergency signal.[11]

Geronimo's men reached San Carlos about 1:00 A.M. on April 19. The chiefs decided to send important leaders to the wickiups of Zele and Loco. Jason Betzinez recalled that the evening was mild, and that the elders in camp had just finished an evening of telling stories. The stillness of the night was broken when a "rider trotted up to the front of our lodge and stopped." He asked directions to Zele's lodge, and Betzinez pointed out his camp, about five hundred yards to the southwest. But the warrior's clandestine visit had alarmed Betzinez, for he had not recognized the man and knew from his accent that he was a Nednhi, perhaps Jelikine.[12] About the same time, according to the testimony of Loco's daughter, Naiche and Chatto entered Loco's camp.[13] Loco, who had been a close friend of Cochise, probably welcomed Naiche. Chatto, however, was another story. Soon after, Zele arrived with his Nednhi guard. Zele later said that "his own people told them to [leave] or they would kill them both [him and Loco]."[14] Zele's version finds support from Loco's descendants, who told Bud Shapard that Chatto pointed a rifle at Loco and threatened to kill him if he refused to leave.[15]

Shortly before sunrise, Loco's village awoke to shouts coming from the Gila River. Betzinez ran out from his wickiup and saw a bewildering site. Geronimo had spread out fifty mounted warriors in a line between the village and the San Carlos River. As they came forward, Betzinez could hear one leader exclaim, "Take them all. . . . Shoot down anyone who refuses to go with us."[16] Sam Haozous corroborated Betzinez. He declared that Geronimo had ordered his men to shoot them "right there," referring to anyone who refused to leave. "We were prisoners."[17] Peaches, a Cibecue Apache who had married into the Chihennes, had no choice. They said: "You are one of us. You have two wives from our people and your little child is a Chiricahua."[18] Initially the village was in chaos, the surprise so sudden that Loco's people had time to gather only a few belongings. According to Acting Agent Stanley D. Pangburn, Loco's, Zele's, and Chiva's bands numbered three hundred, which included about forty-five men. About ninety of the women and children were the dependents of men who had ridden with Victorio, most of these men now dead.[19] Geronimo, Chiva, and Jelikine, with about thirty warriors, led the villagers from their camp and followed the Gila River east. Chihuahua and other chiefs stayed behind to form the rear guard.[20]

Meanwhile, while the Chihennes were leaving, the Americans and Indian police at the agency began to awaken, oblivious to events one mile away at

Loco's village. Stumpy Hunter went to his office when he heard the emergency signal from the subagency. Rushing to his station, he learned that Naiche and sixty warriors were en route to San Carlos. Immediately he told Chief of Police Albert Sterling (Tiffany was not at the agency). As they were talking, Chihuahua's party fired two shots into the air, knowing the gunfire would bring Sterling and perhaps other Americans to Loco's camp. When Sterling heard the shots, he and Sagotal, the sergeant of the Indian police, mounted their horses and rode off toward Loco's camp. The rest of the Apache police force had not yet assembled.[21]

Sterling crossed the San Carlos River and galloped over an open mesa for almost a mile; where the trail ran between two small hills, the Chiricahuas lay in ambush. As he rode between the hills, the Chiricahuas opened a cross fire, killing his horse and wounding him in the hand. Sterling tried to escape, but Chihuahua's party shot him two more times, killing the brave and respected scout. Sagotal, meanwhile, had separated from Sterling before the first fire, opting for a flanking movement around one hill. When he saw his friend killed, he returned to the agency to assemble the Apache police force.[22]

Apache and American accounts vary about who were involved. Sam Haozous simply said that one of Geronimo's warriors shot Sterling. John Rope, who was at the subagency, identified Na-guji (a brother of Nezegochin) as the slayer of Sterling. Rope claimed that after Na-guji killed Sterling, he "pulled off [Sterling's] pair of beaded moccasins" and wore them during the rest of the raid. Charles Lummis heard that three men were involved: Chihuahua, Na-guji, and Trataloris. He said that Trataloris shot Sterling off his horse and that Chihuahua and Na-guji finished him off. Chihuahua later admitted to his involvement. The slaying of Sterling served two purposes: first, it was an effective strategic move because it demoralized and temporarily crippled the Apache police force at San Carlos, eliminating them as a concern to Geronimo's fleeing party; second, it satisfied the Apaches' desire for vengeance, for those involved felt that Sterling got what he deserved for interfering with their right to make tiswin.[23]

During the past year, Sterling's police force had broken up tiswin parties and arrested many Chiricahuas for various offenses. Charles Connell, one of six Americans at the agency, claimed that the Chiricahuas shot Sterling to avenge an accidental death of a Chiricahua child the year before, when Sterling was firing at a Chiricahua at the subagency, probably while breaking up a tiswin party. We do not know whether he ever arrested Chihuahua. What is clear, however, is that the self-assured Chokonen chief always objected on principle to Americans meddling in the customs of his people. Years later Peaches revealed to Grenville Goodwin that the Chiricahuas had killed Sterling for stringing Peaches up by his thumbs.[24] This implies that a few of Loco's Chihennes participated in the ambush, which contradicts Betzinez's view that none of Loco's men fought at the agency. Eve Ball's informants claimed that Stalosh, a Chihenne, shot Sterling. A noted Chihenne warrior, Stalosh, if involved, may have been Peaches's father-in-law. James Kaywaykla, who was not there, told Ball that Stalosh had killed Sterling to prevent the scout from killing Loco. Yet, this scenario is certainly wrong because the Chiricahuas ambushed Sterling, who never saw Loco, for he had already left the village with Geronimo. Thus, Chihuahua, Trataloris, and Na-guji were involved in the killing (it took three bullets to kill the scout) to avenge some perceived wrong inflicted on them by Sterling in the course of duty, and Stalosh, if involved, fired on Sterling not to save Loco's life but to avenge the mistreatment of Peaches.[25]

Once Sagotal made it back to the agency, he found the San Carlos police ready to go. Charles Connell, a close friend of Sterling, agreed to take command. He and Sagotal led the Indian police to the scene and found Sterling's body, still warm and horribly mutilated. His attackers had severed his head (according to one account, they had kicked it around like a football).[26] Not wanting to harm Sagotal, the Chiricahuas told him to leave. But he was defiant. Chihuahua's warriors began firing, and Sagotal's police responded in kind. Connell had taken cover behind Sterling's corpse. Finally, a Chiricahua sharpshooter sent a bullet that ripped through Sagotal's head, killing him instantly. Without their leader, the San Carlos Apache police retreated to the agency.[27]

Geronimo led the band along a northeasterly route between the Gila Mountains and the Gila River. About midway to the subagency, they came across some wagons owned by a man named Gilson.[28] He and his two companions abandoned everything to save their lives, and the Indians captured the wagons, which were loaded with whiskey and clothes. The Chiricahua chiefs "said they did not want to fight, but had only come through to take their relatives away." The White Mountain Apaches wanted no part of a fight. They abandoned their village and moved south to Mount Turnbull. Only Navajo Bill and twenty-five Apache scouts remained behind to fight if necessary.[29]

Navajo Bill recognized Geronimo, Chiva, and Chino (Jelikine) at the front of the cavalcade. From here, the scouts saw "a long line of the Chiricahuas and Warm Springs people moving northeast north of the Gila River."[30] Near the subagency they changed directions, pivoting north toward the Gila Mountains and Ash Creek. Along the way the advance guard, led by Naiche, Chatto, and Kaetenae, killed three men near Green's Hill.[31] The Apaches reached Ash Creek after dark, when they again altered course, moving east through the Gila Mountains before stopping at a spring about midnight. Here the chiefs held a council to decide their next move. It was clear to Betzinez that Geronimo was in overall charge. They decided to send out a raiding party to bring in some of Stevens's sheep that were near. Then they continued the night march, finally stopping at dawn near the eastern part of Ash Flat, about twenty miles north of Fort Thomas. The band, which had traveled for almost twenty-four hours, needed rest and food. The warriors returned with several hundred sheep, allowing the hungry band to gorge on roast mutton.[32]

While the main body rested and feasted on mutton, one band of warriors skirmished with troops and scouts at Ash Creek Valley on April 20, 1882. Lieutenant George H. Sands believed his command "killed or wounded severely" one Indian and forced them to abandon about a dozen horses before the Indians found safety in the Gila Mountains.[33] The Chiricahuas rested the entire day, planning to resume their flight after sundown. Continuing their march east, they crossed Eagle Creek about eighteen miles north of the Gila in the early morning of April 21. Then they again changed direction, moving southeast along the eastern bank of Eagle Creek before veering east to the junction of the San Francisco and Gila rivers. Near here the band crossed the Gila to the south to await the return of their raiding parties. That morning they killed five men at Gold Gulch, between Eagle Creek and Clifton; later that day they killed nine men in two attacks near Church's Smelter, on the San Francisco River about five miles south of Clifton. Late that afternoon the band forded the Gila, where Geronimo and Loco located their camp on a high plateau, awaiting the return of their triumphant warriors.[34]

Betzinez recalled that they remained there for a "day or two." But, for one of the few times in his book, his memory was at fault, for the band left early the next morning, following the Gila northeast toward today's Guthrie. En route, they attacked the Coronado ranch, killing four Mexicans who evidently mistook the Chiricahuas for Apache scouts. Later that day, three more Americans fell victim to their onslaught.[35] North of York's ranch, Naiche, leading the advance guard of warriors, spotted a buckboard drawn by four mules. The people aboard were Felix Knox (a former soldier), his wife, two children, and a Mexican employee. Knox immediately reversed directions, hoping to reach York's ranch before the Indians. He soon realized that would be impossible, for the Apaches had gained ground and slightly wounded one mule. Turning over the reins to the Mexican, Knox kissed his wife and children goodbye and, with rifle in one hand and cartridges in the other, jumped from the buckboard. Turning to the oncoming Indians, he opened fire, getting off several shots before the Apaches cut him down. Yet he had saved his family. Naiche, like his father, Cochise, respected courage. Instead of mutilating Knox's body, he covered it with a blanket.[36]

Shortly after, the main body joined Naiche's advance guard and passed by York's ranch. Lola York looked on in amazement as she began to count the Chiricahuas. "She counted 236 men, women, and children, and this was after at least one hundred had passed."[37] South of York's ranch they raided Hill's ranch before circling "around to the north of the ranch houses where [they] would be out of sight behind a little hill." While there, a White Mountain Apache who had married a Chihenne woman held a puberty ceremony for his daughter, who had "reached womanhood." The parents held the abbreviated celebration, normally a four-day affair, even as "shooting was heard on the other side of the hill." A little below there, and a few miles northwest of Duncan, the band forded the Gila and waited for the warriors to return from their raids. Here the chiefs held another conference, concluding to make a night march south along the upper San Simon Valley, which ran parallel to the foothills of the Peloncillo Mountains. By daybreak they hoped to be near Steins, where they would find water and secure positions to rest.[38]

Betzinez recalled the difficult all-night journey. He, his mother, and his sister rode one mule as the warriors flanked the band on both sides, calling "softly to each other in the darkness." Despite these precautions, Betzinez reported that some of Loco's band escaped the vigilance and went north to Navajo country. About May 10 this group reached Fort Wingate and told authorities they wished to live on the Navajo Reservation. The refugees consisted of twenty-eight Indians, but only two men. Seventeen Chihennes were with Ast-tee-wah-lah, a man in his mid-forties "so far gone in consumption that he is unable to do anything." He was listed on Loco's 1880 census as Hos-te-wal-la. Twelve Navajos were with Che-wo-neg-ahu, a man in his mid-twenties. He had married into Loco's band and was probably enrolled as Ti-cho-no-ga on the 1880 census. On May 18, 1882, Mackenzie ordered them transferred to Fort Union, where the military placed the two men under guard. Hos-te-wal-la passed away shortly after, and his group remained at Fort Union for the next three years.[39]

Meanwhile, at dawn, April 23, 1882, the Chiricahuas turned east to the Peloncillos, where they went into camp on the rim of a high mountain north

of Steins. That morning Lieutenant Colonel George Forsyth had dispatched
Lieutenant McDonald, one enlisted man, and six Indian scouts to scout the
Steins range. At 8:00 A.M. McDonald's scouts found the trail of a dozen warriors who were returning to the main band at Doubtful Canyon. After he
followed the trail for a few hours, the Chiricahuas, perhaps under Chatto,
ambushed him about three miles north of Steins. Within minutes, they had
slain four of McDonald's scouts. McDonald, who had been under heavy fire,
retired with two scouts. Minutes later, six Yavapai scouts joined him. After
digging rifle pits and sending a courier to find Forsyth, McDonald carefully
made his way back to the scene of the ambush. Seeing the Chiricahuas dancing
and celebrating over the bodies of his scouts, he took careful aim and shot a
warrior, who was the only Chiricahua man killed that day.

Meanwhile, McDonald's messenger found Forsyth, who was then about
sixteen miles north en route to the Gila. Forsyth's command at once reversed
directions. His five companies of cavalry and Indian scouts galloped the entire
distance to McDonald's rescue. Arriving a little after noon, he prepared an assault against the Chiricahuas who had occupied the south and west ridges of
Horseshoe Canyon, about four miles north of Steins.[40]

Betzinez described the scene:

> Those of us who were watching the skirmishing from high up on the
> mountainside were getting restless. . . . When the soldiers had reached
> a point about a mile from our hiding place our warriors stripped off
> their shirts and prepared for action. I heard the leaders calling all able-
> bodied men to assemble for battle. Of course, the way the Indians
> fought was all voluntary. The chiefs were not able to order any man
> to fight, as the officers could do the soldiers. But the Indians would go
> into battle to keep from being shamed and to protect their families.
>
> Soon we saw our warriors moving down toward a deep U-shaped
> ravine. The soldiers were approaching up the canyon while our men
> were on the rim. The fighting began. Three of our men who were
> wounded were carried back up the mountainside. Maybe some were
> killed but I did not see any. The fighting grew very heavy, almost
> continuous. The soldiers fired ferocious volleys. Those of us who
> were watching were shivering with excitement as our men slowly
> withdrew under this fire.[41]

Betzinez's version agrees in general with Forsyth's account. The engagement began about 1:00 P.M., when the troopers opened fire on the position

of the Indians, who he correctly estimated numbered between sixty and one hundred men. For the next two and one-half hours, a brisk fight did take place, with the soldiers doing most of the shooting at Chiricahuas who had entrenched themselves behind rocks along the west and south ridges of Horseshoe Canyon. Hoyt Sanford Vandenberg, Jr., who has written a comprehensive account based on his careful examination of the battlefield and military reports, has concluded that Forsyth's report was "somewhat embellished." Vandenberg believes that Forsyth deployed the skirmish line outside the canyon and that the Chiricahuas "simply faded back and away" as the troopers advanced. Yet, on the left flank, a hot contest ensued for several minutes before the troopers' superior firepower compelled the Indians to melt away into the heart of the range.[42]

Forsyth thought his men had killed two warriors and wounded several others. But a year later, the Chiricahuas admitted to General Crook the loss of one man, likely the man shot by Lieutenant McDonald. Forsyth lost two men killed and four wounded as well as four scouts killed with McDonald.

Forsyth's next action confounded everyone. Instead of pursuing a party that he estimated contained as many as one hundred warriors, Forsyth inexplicably abandoned the chase and decided to return to the Gila, a decision that contemporaries and historians have criticized him for, and with abundant justification.[43] He later conceded that he had misread the situation, believing that McDonald had pursued hostiles from Mexico who planned to reinforce Geronimo's war party. Thus he felt that his troopers had fought Apaches fresh from Mexico instead of the main body.[44]

When darkness came to the San Simon Valley, the Chiricahua leaders led their people "down the mountainside" out of West Doubtful Canyon. Unsure of Forsyth's movements, they cautioned their people "to move very quietly."[45] They crossed the railroad near Vanar, west of Steins, en route to a spring the Chiricahuas called Bi-tu-gu-line (His Water Lives), known to Americans as Dunn Springs, in the northeastern part of the Chiricahua Mountains, about fifteen miles southeast of Fort Bowie.[46] They reached there before dawn on April 24, 1882, quenched their thirst, and then moved farther south to the north side of Blue Mountain, where they found more water and a place to rest. That day, raiders killed Deputy Sheriff Hugh Goodman near Galeyville.[47] They also rode to Galeyville, stole some horses, and tore down a few tents. Sam Haozous, who was thirteen years old at the time, may have been with this raiding party. The warriors rode "through that little town, killing anything they see, taking anything they wish."[48] There was no killing at Galeyville, but several miles west, at Ayres Mining Camp, the Indians killed two men.[49] Rumors, paranoia, and someone's wild imagination turned this into the Galeyville Massacre, resulting in an apocryphal report that Apaches had slaughtered thirty-five of its citizens.[50] Though the Indians had camped some six miles north of Galeyville, the troops at Fort Bowie were their main concern. Betzinez recalled that we "half expected to see troops come out toward us but none did."[51]

Late afternoon of April 24, 1882, perhaps as early as 3:00 P.M., the villagers hastily gathered their stock and embarked on another night march.[52] They were in familiar country, Cochise's former domain, which extended south into Mexico and Nednhi country. The chiefs, seeing daylight to the border, pushed their people over the next thirty-six hours, taking only a few brief stops, entering Mexico south of Cloverdale early the morning of April 26.

Here they cut a new trail over the roughest part of the Espuelas Mountains, before they dropped into a valley that separated that range from the Enmedio Mountains. To their amazement, they had not seen any American troops since Horseshoe Canyon. Feeling they were now safe, they decided to relax, enjoying "cheerful conversation . . . talking, laughing, and singing love songs." They made camp near the base of a "rocky butte" that stood by itself a short distance from the western face of the Enmedio Mountains, about seventeen miles below the border. West of camp was a *cienega* where they could water their stock. The chiefs decided they would rest for a few days before they joined Juh in the Sierra Madre. Even Loco seemed relieved at having escaped from the Apache scouts and American troops. This premature euphoria and the faulty assumptions, however, led to carelessness and disaster.[53]

Just as Forsyth had miscalculated at Horseshoe Canyon, the Chiricahua chiefs' complacency would turn a remarkable achievement into an unmitigated disaster. For the next two days and nights, they "gave themselves up to merriment and dancing," according to Betzinez. The women, however, had no time for such frivolity. They were in agave country, and the "mescal sheets were growing up green," making it a prime time to harvest and bake the important staple that was unavailable to them at San Carlos. They were so confident, they did not bother placing sentinels around camp their second night (April 27) at Enmedio Mountains. So they had no idea that American troops and Apache scouts, who had entered Mexico without permission, were in position to attack their camp at dawn the morning of April 28, 1882.

Major David Perry, commanding field operations in southern Arizona, had ordered Captain William A. Rafferty and Captain Tullius C. Tupper to follow the Chiricahuas after a messenger from Galeyville reached San Simon station at 8:00 P.M. on April 24. Tupper, knowing that the eagle-eyed Chiricahuas would see the dust kicked up by his cavalry, decided to remain at Galeyville until early evening April 25. He had made a good decision. His command consisted of two companies of the Sixth Cavalry (his and Rafferty's) and two companies of Indian scouts, one led by Lieutenant Francis J. A. Darr and the second by Lieutenant Stephen C. Mills. To top it off, they had the incomparable services of Chief of Scouts Al Sieber. Tupper began the pursuit with about 110 men.[54]

The scouts easily ferreted out the broad trail, which traveled through the eastern foothills of the Chiricahua Mountains and sliced across the valley to the Peloncillo Mountains and south to Cloverdale. Late afternoon on April 26, they entered Mexico. The pack train joined them, and the soldiers stopped to eat. Leaving the pack train in camp, Rafferty's command of eighty-seven troops and scouts left at 8:00 P.M., moving south over a difficult trail. Sherman Curley remembered that the "moonlight [made] the night like day." Yet, though the tracks were obvious, it was a challenging march because the country was overgrown with manzanita and chaparral. In two hours they had marched seven miles south along a trail that had begun to descend into a valley. Here the command halted because Sieber knew the Chiricahuas were near. At 10:00 P.M. he and ten scouts left the Espuelas Mountains and cautiously made their way into the valley that separated that range from the Enmedio Mountains. Sieber heard the beating of drums and could see Indians dancing around the bonfire. One scout crawled close to camp and estimated that 115 warriors were in camp, which must have included teenage boys. Armed with this intelligence, Sieber, Rafferty, and Tupper drew up a plan of attack.[55]

They counted on the element of surprise, sending lieutenants Darr and Mills with their scouts to a low ridge in the Enmedio Mountains about four hundred yards east of the Indian encampment. This tactic would remove the Apaches' best option of fleeing to the mountains. Rafferty and Tupper led the thirty-nine troopers west of the ranchería, some eight hundred yards away. If the jaws of the vice closed, and the strategy unfolded as they planned, their deadly cross fire would inflict tremendous carnage on the Indians. Darr's command was to open the battle at daybreak.

Fortunately for the Chiricahuas, the Apache scouts prematurely revealed the trap when they opened fire on three women and a young man (Talbot Gooday, a grandson of Mangas Coloradas) as they approached the scouts' positions while checking on mescal baking in a pit near them.[56] Sherman Curley was with the scout who opened the engagement. Curley wanted to capture the two girls, who had raced ahead of the older woman and Gooday. But, unfortunately for them, the sergeant next to him wanted vengeance.

Curley described the events of the morning of April 28, 1882, to Grenville Goodwin:

> When it was pretty near dawn, four Hai-a [Chiricahua] women came out on a little bluff right in front of where I was hidden in the rocks. They were going to a little pit where they were roasting mescal stalk. One of them was a girl, and she wore a lot of beads around her neck. This girl was walking in front. The sergeant was with me. The women were getting pretty close now and I said not to shoot the girl, that we would catch her alive. But this sergeant with me shot her anyway and killed her. I think he did this because his brother, who was chief of police [Sagotal], got killed there along with Sterling while in a Hai-a camp at San Carlos. The other women ran back in the rocks and got away.[57]

Though military reports claim that the scouts' first volley killed four Chiricahuas, one being a son of Loco, Apache reports disagreed. What was evident from Sherman Curley's account was that the first shot was not part of a coordinated volley but was simply an impetuous act of revenge that started the battle before Tupper's command was ready to assault the village. Curley implied that at least two Chiricahuas escaped, which agrees with Gooday's account.[58] Sam Haozous remembered only one fatality at the mescal pits.[59] Nevertheless, the remaining scouts sent several volleys into the Apache camp, killing six men and a few women. Tupper and Rafferty, surprised at the timing, led the cavalry on a mad charge toward the village from the west.

The first salvo shocked the village. Some men and women were already awake; some might not have slept at all because they had danced most of the night. While several men and women kicked dirt over their campfires, other confused villagers fled to a rocky hill south of camp. Jason Betzinez had gone to the herd to get his mule. After hearing the gunfire, he ran to the rocky butte south of camp where most of the villagers had taken refuge. From the outcrops the warriors made a stand, forcing the troopers, who had approached to within one hundred yards, to dismount and take cover. It could have been disastrous for the cavalry. Tupper expected that the Apaches' "volley aimed at Rafferty's troop" would empty "half the saddles [but] it was aimed too high and did little or no execution." Then the Chiricahuas, armed with Springfield, Winchester, and Sharps rifles, concentrated their fire against the soldiers, "temporarily pinning them down and forcing a retreat under fire." As the troopers retired out of range, the Indians killed one man and wounded another.[60]

By this time the chiefs had restored order. The warriors "stripped off their shirts, ready for action." Loco, whose son was killed early in the fight, tried to convince the scouts to defect to his side. They scorned his proposal, responding with a hail of bullets that slightly wounded him. Geronimo was active, trying to inspire his men. Sam Haozous said: "Well, Geronimo, he holler, he call the men, his fighting men, so there is soldiers on the west side there; more soldiers on that side [with the Indian's stock]. . . . Then, on the east side Indian scouts." Groups of young warriors, eager to help their people and to display their courage, heeded his call. Curley admired the bravery of Na-guji (one of Sterling's slayers), who led three charges to recapture the herd until he was "shot in the thigh" within fifteen yards of the rocky butte. Some warriors rounded up stock overlooked by soldiers. One older woman "climbed to the highest part of the butte" and called for her son Toclanny, thinking he might be with the scouts. But he and six other Chiricahuas were then on duty in New Mexico. A Western Apache scout responded by killing her. By late morning several daredevil warriors made a flanking movement from the south and east, gaining the high ground behind the scouts. Now, with the scouts' attention diverted to face the brave warriors, Loco led the main body from the rocky butte into the foothills of the Enmedio Mountains. They left their possessions in the village and most of their valuable stock in the hands of the soldiers.[61]

The flanking movement by the warriors stemmed the onslaught and saved many lives. The scouts abandoned their positions and rejoined the soldiers. Sherman Curley recalled the dilemma facing the scouts because they had expended most of their ammunition. He thought they were lucky, for "we just got out in time." In fact, Chatto may have been referring to this battle when he recalled leading an assault against Yavapai scouts who had killed a relative. He remembered gathering a small group of kinfolk to prepare for a charge against them. A shaman, perhaps the Bedonkohe She-neah, had prayed and turned to the four directions, blessing each man. Then he'd ordered Chatto and the warriors to charge the scouts' positions, forcing them to withdraw. According to Gooday, warriors who distinguished themselves were Kaetenae and a young, unidentified Navajo warrior. Another was Fun, a second cousin of Geronimo. Fun's Apache name was Yahe-chul, or Yiy-joll (Smoke Comes Out), which probably refers to the aftereffects of the rapid fire of his rifle.[62]

The Americans and scouts, who had fired about four thousand rounds during the seven-hour fight and skirmish, left the battlefield with a loss of one dead and two wounded. Apache losses were at variance. Betzinez reported only three women killed and four wounded, but he was confused. The next day scouts captured a wounded woman who admitted they had lost six men in Tupper's fight and thirteen at Horseshoe Canyon, but she seems to have reversed the numbers, or the interpreter was confused. Six months later General Crook began an investigation when Eskebenti, one of the White Mountain herders captured at Stevens's sheep camp, arrived at San Carlos after escaping from the Chiricahuas. He cleared up the confusion by revealing that the Chiricahuas had lost fourteen men in the Tupper fight. Crook confirmed this with Chiricahuas when they returned to the reservation in 1883. Both Rafferty and Tupper placed the dead at twelve men and several women.[63] Besides losing most of their herd, the Indians lost fifteen horses killed. Tupper also reported the site of the battle as the Hatchet Mountains in southwestern New Mexico, not wanting to admit they had entered Mexico.[64]

At sundown, the Chiricahuas assembled for another night march. By morning they hoped to reach the foothills of the Sierra Madre Mountains, where they planned to rest the next day before resuming the last leg of their journey to Juh's camp. Everyone had a long drink at a spring, and all shared the little food they had. The country they passed over was "level, flat, and grassy." As they were leaving, the warriors came in with a few horses (perhaps thirty or forty), which they had recaptured from the soldiers. Betzinez admired the accomplishments "of these brave young men, who were some of the best fighters of the Apache tribe." They transported the wounded, who included Naguji and one older woman, on wicker stretchers. It was an arduous trip because most of the women and children walked, protected by the mounted warriors in the front and rear. Yet they stoically moved south, crossing a wide valley occasionally intersected by washes and dominated by sotol, a plant that the Chiricahuas, if not pressed for time, would have harvested in much the same manner as the agave. Of course, they had no time for that, for every step brought them closer to safety and Juh's camp.[65]

Because the march went slower than planned, the chiefs remained concerned about the Americans. Thus, Geronimo deployed most of the fighting men at the rear of the column. Moreover, because they had received no warning from Juh, the leaders had not anticipated that a Mexican army was lying in wait to ambush them at Alisos Creek, one mile northeast of their rendezvous site in the Sierra Madre Mountains.

How did the Mexican army know where to set up the ambush? Though there is no confirmation of the following event from the Chiricahuas, John Rope seems to have heard about it from an undisclosed source, probably a fellow Apache scout. He explained that Mexicans had captured two Chiricahuas who had left Geronimo's war party after they had stolen four horses from a ranch near San Simon. Instead of continuing to San Carlos, they decided to return to Sonora and leave the horses in a safe place before rejoining Geronimo. Rope goes so far as to name the two men, Go-ya-bn and Gi-nas-zi-hn, the first man likely a warrior in Bonito's band. According to Rope, the captives told the Mexican commander Colonel Lorenzo García the route by which Geronimo would return. Armed with this intelligence, García set up the ambush.[66]

Rope's version seems correct with one exception: it is doubtful that Geronimo, whose party had crossed the border in secret and wanted to approach the reservation covertly, would have allowed any raids that could inevitably call attention to their presence. Therefore, it seems likely that these two men were not part of his group. Instead, I believe they were a separate party sent by Juh to warn Geronimo about García's army lurking along the Carretas plains. While waiting for Geronimo's band, they killed two unsuspecting Americans in the Mule Mountains. On April 18, 1882, as they returned to Sonora, troops from Bavispe and Bacerac captured them and their stolen stock north of Fronteras, killing nine according to Sonoran accounts.[67] The commander turned them over to García, who promised to spare their lives in exchange for information. Once they gave García what he wanted, it is likely that he had them executed. Those were the "nine" Indians reported killed on Sonora. But it was only two, and they had given up vital information.[68]

Dispatched by direction of the secretary of war in Mexico City, García was a career military man with clear scruples and a devotion to duty. He had an army of two hundred men, federal soldiers and Sonoran nationals, waiting at Alisos Creek, about one mile northeast of the Sierra Madre foothills. It was near dawn as the Chiricahuas approached the Mexican positions. The country was flat though interspersed with ravines and washes. The Indians were strung out in a column about a half-mile long. The rear guard, led by Geronimo and Chihuahua, had formed a skirmish line. One group, led by Mangas, had already passed the Mexican positions over an hour before. García allowed a second party—the advance group of some fifteen warriors under Chatto, Kaetenae, and Naiche—to ride past because he wanted to launch his ambush on the main body. About 5:00 A.M. on April 29, the Chiricahuas, following the creek as it wound its way to the southeast, came into plain view. The women in front accelerated their pace because they smelled coffee ahead and assumed that the advance guard had gone into camp. But the source of the pleasant aroma came from an enemy who wanted Apache blood. García, now satisfied that he had about half the band within his sights, gave the order to attack. From concealed positions, his soldiers poured indiscriminate fire on these unfortunate people.[69]

The first volleys, some from within one hundred yards, tore into the vulnerable women and children, who never knew what hit them. The opening fusillade of lead wiped out entire families. Peaches was hit, and then lost his two wives and baby during this volley.[70] Only a few men were then present, and they tried to restore order and fight off the attack. Then the Mexicans emerged from their hiding places and charged, bayoneting and "shooting down women and children right and left. . . . People were falling and bleeding, and dying on all sides of us," lamented Jason Betzinez. Much of the early fighting was hand-to-hand. The Apaches had difficulty standing up to a bayonet, and the infantrymen slew several warriors along the creek bottom where, after the fight, the Mexicans found twenty-one corpses. Many women and children tried to escape to the foothills about a mile away. In a "sloping" gully near there, they made a stand, but the infantry overtook them and killed many. García's men found nine corpses here, including that of an old gray-haired man, perhaps Gordo, who had killed at least two soldiers before the Mexicans overwhelmed him. Sam Haozous recalled the ghastly picture as "Oh, just fighting, fighting, fighting. Too many shootings out there." This first assault caused the most carnage, resulting in the deaths of a half-dozen warriors along with some fifty women and children.[71]

James Nicholas, a grandson of Chiva, also remembered the chaos. He had been walking along when he had heard gunfire that sent dirt and little rocks shooting through the air. When he saw an arrow fly by him, he realized they were under attack. He was to the rear of the women and children and heard people in front of him yelling, "Go back." Next, he heard women crying and shrieking while they tried to turn their mules around and escape to the rear. He grabbed the back of a horse's tail, but people were falling all around him. Into this chaos rode the younger warriors whom Nicholas called the "big boys." Racing into the confusion, they saved his life and that of many others. Trying to restore order, Geronimo and Chihuahua ran from the rearguard into the killing field, which halted the Mexicans' advance and probably saved the group from total annihilation.[72]

Within minutes of the ambush, Betzinez and Sam Haozous could hear Geronimo's voice as he and Chihuahua crashed forward from the rear with thirty-two warriors on a countercharge that drove the Mexicans back. García ordered another assault. By this time the warriors had gathered around Geronimo in a draw to "make a stand and protect the women and children." As the men swung into action, several women began furiously cutting out positions along the banks of the arroyo and digging rifle pits, making a large depression some six feet deep for the noncombatants. Two Apache sharpshooters, one a well-built young man in his early twenties, entrenched themselves under a tree near the lip of the bank and carefully picked off Mexicans who had no idea where the shots were coming from.[73] Geronimo's son Chappo and two of his second cousins, Perico and Fun, his father-in-law, Jelikine, and other relatives joined him. Chihuahua and his nephew Espida were there, as was Loco. From this arroyo, they began to fight back, and Mexicans paid in blood.[74]

Betzinez remarked, "Not all the heroes were warriors." A sack of five hundred cartridges was lying on the ground about fifty feet away from the arroyo. Loco had dropped it when he came under heavy fire. An old woman volunteered to retrieve the sack. Covered by Chihuahua, who was lying on his side, and the inspirational teenage warrior Fun, she successfully carried out her mission and dragged the sack to the arroyo. Some authors, including Ball, have identified this brave woman as Lozen. But they are wrong, for Apache accounts insist that an "old" unidentified woman merits the badge of honor, a description that does not fit Lozen who, in any event, was not even present. Geronimo's war party contained only men; Lozen was in the village with Juh and Nana.[75]

About 10:00 A.M. García recalled his men and decided to send his federal troops of the Sixth Battalion on a bold bayonet charge to dislodge Geronimo's group from the ditch. Geronimo could hear the officers imploring their men to kill him, the devil himself. As they charged, they screamed, "Geronimo, this is your last day." Captain Antonio Rada led the assault, but the Apaches responded with deadly volleys. Fun seemed to be ubiquitous as he dodged bullets and held cartridges between his fingers. More than one Mexican fell victim to his deadly Springfield rifle. Several warriors supported Fun. Among them was his half-brother, Perico, who was confident that his beneficent Power would keep him safe. A mighty warrior, Perico was never wounded in battle, a testament, he thought, to his Power.[76] Besides Perico, there was the fearless Chihuahua, who lay on his side methodically firing at the Mexicans even though they peppered him with bullets. The soldiers charged halfway to the Apache position before Geronimo shot Rada, if we are to believe the account in his autobiography.

During the bloody battle, one young Chiricahua expert shooter, whose name is lost to history, picked off five Mexicans, each dying from a bullet to the head. Finally, García directed his soldiers to concentrate their fire on his position, which silenced the brave warrior forever. Meanwhile, after Captain Rada fell, the Chiricahuas' volleys cut down many others. The battered and bruised survivors hastened a quick retreat. If they had continued to advance, the Apaches would have demolished the entire platoon. Though the retreat saved many lives, the Apaches had slain nine of the twenty-five attackers, wounded several others, and stopped them dead in their tracks.

It was now about 11:00 A.M., and, according to García's report, the major combat was over. Both sides were low on ammunition. The chiefs had no idea that García was done fighting. And García had no idea of the Chiricahuas' desperate position. If they could hold out until dark, then they would make their escape across the level plains to the foothills about a mile to the southwest. During the stalemate, the Chiricahuas became concerned that the fighting might begin anew when a detachment of sixty cavalry returned from a patrol to the northeast. García had his battle-fatigued men turn their ammunition over to the fresh troops, who launched a halfhearted charge, but the Apaches beat them back. As dusk approached, the chiefs made plans to evacuate the bloody arroyo under the cover of darkness. They would leave a few at a time, under total silence. As they began their escape, Geronimo said the Indians set fire to the grass to obscure further their retreat. Other Apache accounts, notably those of Betzinez and Gooday, suggest that the Mexicans lit the blaze to smoke out the Apaches. Regardless, García may not have realized that most of the Chiricahuas had fled the arroyo; a small group, led by the intrepid Fun, continued to fire sporadically to cover the retreat.

Indian accounts are also at variance about their decision to retire from the arroyo. As usual, the controversy centers on Geronimo's actions—his character and his courage. According to Talbot Gooday, Geronimo suggested that the men could escape if they left the women and children behind. His recommendation fell flat, especially when the hero of the battle, Fun, threatened to kill Geronimo if he repeated that thought. Angie Debo, Geronimo's biographer, was skeptical of this scenario (as am I), pointing out that Gooday and many Chihennes despised Geronimo because of his role in the exodus from the reservation that had led to so many innocent deaths and prisoners.

Gooday's version finds no support from Betzinez or Haozous; neither mentions that Geronimo wanted to save his hide at the expense of the women and children. Jason Betzinez, who was safely in the mountains, heard that "the warriors asked the consent of a few women who were there to let them choke the small children so they wouldn't give away their movements by crying." But he does not name Geronimo as one of those advocates. Sam Haozous, who was not in the pit, said the women in the arroyo needed no encouragement and that several willingly abandoned their babies. In fact, he notes, one mother choked her baby to death because she did not "want her baby to be a slave for those Mexicans." Furthermore, Haozous, no admirer of Geronimo, credited him with rallying the men to prevent a wholesale slaughter.

As for Geronimo's actions in the arroyo, several independent accounts charge him with cowardice during the battle. These versions are difficult to reconcile given that he led the charge of warriors into the teeth of the fighting during the most ferocious part of the battle. Two Chiricahuas who were in Juh's camp at the time, Eugene Chihuahua (the son of Chief Chihuahua) and Sam Kenoi (stepson of Fatty), claim that he hid with the women and children during the battle. Western Apache scout Sherman Curley examined the battleground the day after the fight and talked to several Chiricahua prisoners held by García's command. Curley, whose reminiscences are scrupulously honest and reliable, adds fuel to the fire of those who believed the Bedonkohe shaman acted cowardly. He said, "Geronimo was in this fight, but he hid himself and got away after dark. He was the one responsible for all this trouble." The story of Geronimo's alleged cowardice also reached the Mescalero Reservation, perhaps by Choneska, a Chihenne warrior captured by the agency police force in August 1882. Likely dispatched by Nana in an attempt to round up more followers, Choneska may have been in the fight at Alisos Canyon.[77] In any event, Solon Sombrero, a grandson of the Mescalero chief Natzili, was referring to the García fight when he told Ball that Geronimo "was in a hole where he stayed and gave orders from there. They could not get him out. They were out of ammunition."

Perhaps a reasonable explanation is possible. As the Apaches waited for darkness during the tense six-hour standoff, everyone worked feverishly to dig foxholes to provide more protection from Mexican snipers. Perhaps Geronimo, who had his teenage son Chappo with him, assisted in the digging and for this some warriors chided him. Geronimo had his detractors, but he also had a loyal core of staunch supporters. Most vocal was Asa Daklugie, Juh's son. Daklugie, who was not there, abruptly dismissed and strongly condemned any talk disparaging Geronimo's courage. Jaspar Kanseah, a Chiricahua leader into the twentieth century, agreed with Daklugie. And, we must remember the words of Geronimo, who believed that his Power had promised to protect him in battle—a belief he held for his adult life.[78] Given all this, I would suspect that his critics either misinterpreted his actions or, for reasons of their own, tarnished his reputation for bravery during the siege.

Before leaving the García fight, we must examine one other issue that looms large in Chiricahua history. Colonel García clearly allowed the vanguard of fifteen warriors to cross Alisos Creek and enter the foothills unmolested. According to Jason Betzinez, these men, led by Naiche, Chatto, and Kaetenae, inexplicably remained in camp, casually smoking, while the fierce fighting raged less than a mile away. This inexcusable behavior while their enemy slaughtered innocent women and children horrified Betzinez: "Here they were sitting well armed and with plenty of ammunition, yet doing nothing. I felt dreadfully ashamed of them. They never fired a shot, while half a mile away beyond the hill their fellow tribesmen and their women and children were being butchered." Kaywaykla justified their conduct by claiming the three chiefs felt compelled to protect their families. But their families had not accompanied them to San Carlos and were sitting in Juh's camp thirty miles to the south. Kaywaykla was clearly rationalizing the odd behavior of Kaetenae, his stepfather, and Naiche, his father-in-law. Al Sieber, who heard a version of this story said, "The young bucks put spurs to their horses and made [their] escape." Betzinez was right in condemning their actions.[79]

This was a major catastrophe for the Chihennes, for Loco had lost 40 percent of his band. García's army had killed seventy-eight Chiricahuas, nearly all of them Chihennes. Only a dozen or so were men, four of whom were former scouts. The Mexicans had captured thirty-three women and children, including Loco's daughter and Toclanny's wife. They had also confiscated fifty-eight horses and mules, showing that Rafferty had captured fewer than half their herd.

García's victory came at a heavy cost: four officers (Lieutenant Jesús García died from his wounds almost four months later) and nineteen soldiers killed; one officer and fifteen men wounded (six seriously), though it would appear as though they underreported the wounded, because one eyewitness saw considerably more, perhaps thirty to forty in all. To show their appreciation, the federal government in Mexico City awarded pensions to the families of the dead and disabled soldiers "for their heroic sacrifices."[80]

Many Chihenne survivors rightly blamed Geronimo and never forgave him for causing the death of so many innocent people. One has to question the validity of James Kaywaykla's statement, reported by Eve Ball, that Loco told

Nana "costly as the fight had proved, a summer at San Carlos would have been more disastrous," especially because Loco's band had actually increased in population since their return to San Carlos in late 1878. Bud Shapard, who married Loco's great granddaughter, has completed a biography on Loco with the help of Loco's descendants. He doubts that Loco made this statement because he was never happy in Mexico and had left so many of his people butchered or captured on the bloody field (including his son and his beloved teenage daughter in the hands of Mexican troops). After all, Loco had not left the reservation willingly, and Tupper's and García's fights had left him devastated by the loss of his family and followers.[81]

Now every Chiricahua except seven scouts then on duty at Fort Stanton was in Mexico.[82] Geronimo, Nana, and Juh may have had more fighting men, but at what cost to the tribe? For while they had gained forty warriors from Loco's and Chiva's bands, they had lost between twenty and twenty-five men in the process. Whether they had enhanced their position in their quest to live as free Apaches in the Sierra Madre was debatable. As we shall see, the remaining 650 Chiricahuas were anything but a cohesive tribe. And Chihuahua troops, after hearing about Sonora's victory, were desperate for a crack at Juh and Geronimo.

12

LIFE IN THE SIERRA MADRE

I saw the Mexicans were grinning as they cut the throats of the
[intoxicated] warriors.

Kayitah

The morning after the calamity at Alisos Creek, the Chiricahua survivors looked on in amazement at a perplexing scene unfolding on the Carretas plains. A large American army, five times the size of the one they had battled only two days earlier, had met García's troops near the battlefield. The Chiricahuas were disappointed at the outcome, for they "expected a fight to occur, but nothing like that happened."[1] Lieutenant Colonel George Forsyth led the army, which consisted of nine companies of cavalry and three companies of Apache scouts. Included in this body were the Apache scouts and troopers of Rafferty's and Tupper's commands, whom Forsyth had met the evening of their fight northeast of the Enmedio Mountains. Early the next morning, Forsyth led his men to Rafferty's battlefield, which they examined along with the deserted Indian camp. As the scouts gathered plunder from the abandoned village, the soldiers buried the body of the brave Private Goodrich, the trooper killed the previous day.

That day Forsyth's command easily followed the Chiricahuas' trail south, oblivious to the sanguinary events at Alisos Creek. Along the way, the scouts and soldiers found the bodies of eight Apaches (five men and three women) and captured a wounded elderly woman whom the Indians had left behind. About 5:00 P.M. they came to a creek bed "covered with boulders and a little water." Red willows had sprouted along its banks. Here Forsyth's army encamped, unaware that García's army was only a mile to the east.[2]

Near here, the scouts had earlier interrupted a few Chiricahuas preparing a body for burial. Nearby was a wicker stretcher that had carried the wounded man thirty miles in one day. Sherman Curley described the corpse: "His hair

230

was all combed out, his face was painted red, he had on a black coat, and on his feet were some beaded moccasins." The scouts recognized the moccasins and clothing as belonging to Albert Sterling. The dead man was Na-guji, the intrepid warrior whom troops had shot through the thigh during his attempt to recapture their herd at Enmedio. The Western Apache scouts were upset because of his involvement in Sterling's death. A dispassionate Curley simply recalled, "We took the moccasins off him, stripped him, and threw his body in a hole."[3]

Early the next morning, a bugle call awakened Forsyth's camp, but they did not recognize the signal, for it was a Mexican reveille. Forsyth then realized that Mexican troops were near, and with that a potential diplomatic nightmare. Lieutenant Charles A. P. Hatfield, of the famous Hatfield clan, was at the head of the column when Colonel García and his adjutant crossed a ravine and approached him. Hatfield, fluent in Spanish, served as interpreter. Though he thought the Mexican army "a sorry looking outfit," the no-nonsense Lorenzo García impressed Hatfield. "He was a soldier: Looked it, acted it, and meant what he said."[4] García asked Forsyth why he was in Mexico. The American explained that he was in pursuit of hostiles who had committed depredations in the United States. García, though sympathetic to Forsyth's mission, explained that he had entered Mexico illegally. Furthermore, García smugly pointed out that his army had destroyed the Apaches the day before, leaving Forsyth's force with no Indians to fight.

Forsyth asked for a tour of the battlefield, which the Mexican officers proudly conducted. The ghastly scene horrified the Americans. Not only were Apache corpses, mostly women and children, lying everywhere, but the Mexicans had not even bothered to bury their own dead, who were still in uniform, lying where they had fallen. García's command was also short of food and lacked medicine and doctors. Forsyth magnanimously offered the services of his doctors, which García happily accepted and appreciated. The surgeons performed two amputations that likely saved the lives of two men. Forsyth even allowed one doctor to remain with the Mexicans to administer to their wounded until they reached Bavispe.[5]

The plight of the thirty-three women and children prisoners touched the Americans and Indian scouts. The Mexicans admonished the scouts to stay clear, but that failed to deter them. Years later Curley recalled,

> Here there was a little canyon with water running in it just above us. . . . A little ways apart, on the ridge, the Mexicans were holding a bunch of Chiricahua women [and children] whom they had captured.

There were guards around them. We went over to these women, and
the Mexicans told us to get back but we went and talked to them
anyway. The women wanted us to give the Mexicans money to ran-
som them, as they wanted to go back with us. They were afraid to be
taken off with the Mexicans as captives. We did not have any money
so could not do anything.[6]

Most prominent among the captives was Loco's sixteen-year-old daughter,
a "beautiful girl," whom the Americans tried to convince the Mexicans to
release, but without success. Unfortunately, Loco's family never heard a word
of her fate; her loss devastated the old chief.

Despite the indiscriminate slaughter, American and Mexican officials applauded García's victory. Arizona's governor Frederick Tritle congratulated
his counterpart in Sonora "for the most illustrious achievements of the Mexican troops in so severely punishing the enemy of civilization, the savage
Apaches." But his letter had another purpose. He hoped to begin diplomatic
negotiations for a treaty that would allow troops from both countries to pursue Apaches, regardless of borders.[7] As Forsyth headed home toward New
Mexico, his command skirted Janos, where they heard church bells ringing in
celebration of García's victory.[8] García took a pragmatic view of his "noble
campaign." He wrote, "We are fighting against the sworn enemy of civilization, against an avid vampire which draws the blood of humanity on the
march of progress."[9] García's statement supports the conclusions of Ana María
Alonso, who wrote that most nineteenth-century Mexicans thought Apaches,
who lived in the hinterlands, were culturally somewhere between wild animals and humanity.[10]

Meanwhile, disappointed that Americans and Mexicans had not fought
each other, the morning of May 1, 1882, the Chiricahua refugees regrouped
and began their trek toward Juh's camp, some forty miles south. A dispirited
group descended from their mountain fastness. But the arrival of Geronimo
and those warriors who had escaped from Alisos Creek raised their spirits.
Betzinez praised these patriots, again noting that those who "had stayed in the
hills without fighting a shot stood silent." As Geronimo had during the raid,
he again took command, guiding the survivors south through the mountains.
He sent out a foraging party with orders to steal cattle and drive them to the
next rendezvous site, a favorite camping site with a spring about eight miles
southeast of Carretas, which they called Bent-ci-iye (Plentiful Pine Trees).[11]
Encumbered by many wounded and hungry people, they moved slowly on the
arduous trip higher into the mountains.

Later that day, the warriors drove in some cattle, and the band stopped to eat for the first time since the night before Tupper's attack at Enmedio Mountains. Knowing they were worn out, Geronimo decided to rest for two days before resuming their exodus on the morning of May 4, 1882. The main body finally reached Juh's village high in the Sierra Madre at Bugatseka about May 5, 1882. Though Betzinez called them Nednhis, the village contained members of the four Chiricahua bands plus several White Mountain Apaches, a few Navajos, and Mescaleros. Here the Chihennes met friends and relatives who in the fall of 1878 had followed Victorio rather than move to San Carlos with Loco. They shared food and blankets and talked about happier times in New Mexico. Years later Betzinez recalled, "Several hundred people were assembled in this one camp, seventy-five of them being first-line warriors. This was the largest number of Apaches that had come together in many years." In the mid-1930s, Yahnozha, a Chokonen related to Naiche and Geronimo, took Helge Ingstad to this camping site. Ingstad was impressed: "A better place to camp could hardly be found. We found a grassy field surrounded by large pine trees with a rippling brook winding through the green fauna." Yahnozha told Ingstad that the camp, often containing over one hundred wickiups, was a lively place: "We gambled, hunted, and ate. There was always plenty of food."[12]

Yet this concentration of a once formidable tribe, now broken down into small bands, two of which were on the verge of extinction, was not always harmonious. Betzinez observed, "When they couldn't find anyone else to mistreat, they fought among themselves." The Nednhis, especially, were a tough group, accustomed to the demanding life in the Sierra Madre.[13] Loco was never happy in Mexico, and even the relationship between Juh and Geronimo sometimes became strained.

Apache accounts vary, but most agree that the Indians wanted a treaty because of the concentration of troops in northwest Chihuahua. Chiricahuas later told General Crook that they were anxious for peace and opened negotiations, perhaps through some "semi-Mexicanized" Chiricahuas who were living at Janos, according to Eskebenti, a White Mountain Apache then with the hostiles.[14] Betzinez simply said that he believed "Geronimo was responsible for this, his motive being to get whiskey." Perhaps he was right. Haozous remembered correctly that after a stay "in the mountains," the leaders decided "to go down to a Mexican town somewhere, so they started off." One might speculate that they were interested in learning about the fate of their people captured by García. But Terrazas, who met Juh and Geronimo at Casas Grandes, seemed surprised that Geronimo said nothing about the battle at Alisos Creek. About one-third of the band, between 200 and 250 in all, established a camp along the San Miguel River, about three miles southwest of Casas Grandes. East of the creek stood a thicket that gave the place its name: Bosque San Diego. They soon regretted this foolhardy act.[15]

About May 18, 1882, Geronimo and Juh "shook hands" with civil officials of Casas Grandes, who declared the town open to Apaches. Geronimo recalled that the old foes promised "to be brothers. Then we began to trade." Groups of Indians entered the town with stock to trade to the inhabitants. Betzinez helped an older woman sell a horse in Casas Grandes. For a few days everything seemed to go well. Little did they realize that their "true friends," as Betzinez caustically called them, had prepared an elaborate trap. Even on the day they shook hands, five hundred troops were near Casas Grandes, waiting for the order to carry out the oldest trick in their play book: they hoped to get the entire band in town, furnish them with liquor, and slaughter indiscriminately as many as possible.[16]

Terrazas had postponed his first attack, planned for May 19, because he hoped to gain the Indians' confidence and entrap as many as possible in Casas Grandes. More Chiricahuas were arriving, and on May 21, he again delayed the attack, setting May 24 as the day his soldiers would execute their plan. But the day before the planned massacre, townspeople began to behave strangely, arousing the suspicions of the Chiricahuas. Fearing that Juh and Geronimo would flee to the mountains, Terrazas exercised his second option: his army would surround the village during the early hours of May 25, 1882, and attack at dawn.[17]

Hoping to allay the Apaches' concerns, the morning of May 24 officials at Casas Grandes sent two wagons to the Chiricahua camp. The first was loaded with bottles of whiskey or mescal; the second contained shelled corn, which they knew the Apaches would use to make tiswin. By early afternoon, the entire camp "was singing away and running around," drunk from the whiskey. Sam Haozous, who was present, said those inebriated "were happy but they didn't know what is coming to them." His wise mother, Nah-ke-de-sah, a daughter of Mangas Coloradas, had seen this Mexican perfidy before. She convinced her relatives, about fifteen men, women, and children, to leave camp before sundown.[18] The binge in the village went on all night; Betzinez, who had the foresight to bed down several hundred yards from the main camp, could hear the "drunken Indians in their camp, howling and dancing."[19] The village comprised families from Naiche's, Geronimo's, Zele's, Chatto's, and Juh's groups. In addition, a few Chihennes under Sánchez were present.

The first part of his strategy a success, Terrazas's army of 560 men began their march from Casas Grandes about 2:00 A.M., May 25. Juan Mata Ortiz was to take 200 men to positions northwest of the river; Terrazas would lead another 300 men and march around Moctezuma Hills, to a position southwest of the camp. A third force of sixty men from Casas Grandes was to assume concealed positions in a wooded area directly east of the village. By daybreak, Terrazas's forces would have surrounded the village, which Terrazas estimated accommodated 250 Apaches. His division would lead the assault at dawn.

Shortly before dawn, an hour before Terrazas was in position to seal the open area southwest of the village, several "raw recruits" from Mata Ortiz's command opened fire on some imaginary target. Other soldiers followed their lead, awakening the village—and those men and women not in a drunken stupor picked up their arms, grabbed their children, and abandoned camp, leaving their horses behind. Juh and Geronimo led the villagers southwest, hoping to make a stand on higher ground away from the village. A disappointed Terrazas reported that the Apaches, "protected by the cover of darkness, fled to liberty without being seen by my men." But at the village, the soldiers had killed or captured forty-three Chiricahuas, most too inebriated to understand what had happened, and had taken fifty-eight horses.[20]

The Indians put up a token resistance. Chiricahua oral history credits Nahilzay for leading a brief stand before Mexican troops either captured or killed him. Chatto, Kanseah, and Kayitah barely escaped with their lives. Sahn-uh-shlu, Kayitah's wife, saved him from certain death after Mexicans had wounded him. She dragged him into the weeds along the riverbank. From here, he could see the soldiers "grinning as they slit the throats of the adult men." It was a memory that haunted him for fifty years. In a recurring dream, Kayitah was always running away from Mexican soldiers.[21]

Nahilzay's wife, E-nah-dez-le, and young son escaped to a hill where Geronimo and Juh had rallied the warriors. From this incident the boy took the name Doaskada, "Didn't Come Up The Hill," a phrase which refers to Terrazas' decision not to storm the Chiricahuas' entrenched positions.[22] He and Mata Ortiz followed the trail to a hill where the Apaches were waiting. Juh, incensed at their betrayal, was defiant, charging in "stuttering Spanish because he could not speak clearly, that Joaquin [Terrazas] was a treacherous man." And he vowed to burn at the stake Juan Mata Ortiz. The Chiricahuas, retiring to another hill, seemed to disappear from Terrazas's radar screen.[23]

Terrazas and Mata Ortiz never lacked for courage. It therefore seems strange that they failed to assault the dug-in Chiricahuas, even with the Apaches' clear advantage of terrain and position. According to two Chiricahuas, they may have avoided a pitched fight because of Juh's strong medicine. Both Martine and Perico remembered a time when Juh had used his Power to confound Mexicans. Martine described how Juh had once performed a "ceremony to fool the enemy." He had spread some pollen on the ground, and the next thing Martine saw was a "company of cavalry and infantry" marching around the hill they were hiding on even though the trail was clear.[24] Perico, who may have been referring to the same incident, was in awe of Juh's Power:

> One time we all saw the enemy coming, and the enemy saw them. [Juh] said to the people: I am going to make [them] disappear, and we shall disappear from their view, too. Then Juh told the people to go behind a hill so they could not see the enemy. He alone stood on top of the hill. After about twenty minutes, [Juh] told them to come up again. When they came up, there were only cattle grazing around where the enemy had been. Juh told the men to go herd the cattle (but not to kill or eat them) and to take them to a river and shoot them all and then eat them. [I] was there and helped eat the cattle.[25]

The massacre was another devastating loss for the Chiricahuas. Mexicans had slain about ten in the village, including the Chihenne leader Sánchez, whose Apache name was Tah-ho-klisn, meaning "Falls in the Water," during the assault on the camp.[26] They captured the rest, thirty-seven men and women mostly too inebriated to resist. Apaches told General Crook that the Mexicans had bound the prisoners "head and foot, and carried [them] off."[27] Sam Haozous, watching from a distance with binoculars, corroborated this. He saw Mexican troops just pick up men and women, place them in three wagons, and haul them off to Casas Grandes, where they locked them in a house that night.[28] A few days later, Sonoran troops under General Bernardo Reyes and Colonel García arrived at Janos. Still smarting from their heavy losses at Alisos Creek, and knowing that many of the male captives were in the fight, Reyes likely issued the order for the final act of betrayal of the Chiricahua prisoners. Terrazas turned over to García about twenty-five of the thirty-seven prisoners.[29] Sam Haozous heard the story of Mexican justice from an eyewitness:

> There were guards on each side [of the jail], when they opened the door. The guards told these men and women, anybody who wants to try to escape to run out across the creek. Some of them [tried] to get

away [when] the Mexicans shot them. All of them [men] and women, just like that. Oh, they say, just three wagonloads of Indians. They kill all of them out there. He said that is what they done. The whole camp began to cry.[30]

Betzinez recalled that this witness, whom the Mexicans had shot in the leg, "jumped into the river and hid under some driftwood and thus escaped being found."[31]

Geronimo put their loss at twenty dead and several captured; Betzinez remembered that the Mexicans had slain "quite a few warriors" and captured many women and children. Two Western Apaches, then living with the Chiricahuas, had similar estimates but differed in the breakdown. Peaches believed that the Mexicans had slain eight men and captured thirty women and children; Eskebenti declared that Mexicans captured thirty-five, twenty-four men and eleven women.[32] The Chiricahuas recalled the names of thirteen men whom Terrazas's command had seized at Bosque San Diego. We can identify many from the San Carlos census of 1880. Naiche, Chatto, and Chihuahua lost relatives, the latter a brother, perhaps named Is-pie-de, one of the few who avoided death when Terrazas shipped him and nine others to the prison in Chihuahua City, where authorities fed them a Spartan diet of bread, meat, and soup, which they boiled from "beef heads."[33] Juh lost an important warrior named Esude. Zele lost three men from his group, and Mexicans captured Geronimo's fourth wife, Nah-no, whose name has previously been lost to history. She never rejoined him, likely perishing in the Chihuahua City prison.[34]

The survivors of the attack returned to the base camp southeast of Casas Grandes. After four days of waiting, the leaders decided to move southwest to Juh's stronghold at Guaynopa, which they reached about June 2, 1882. They camped on the eastern brink of Great Canyon, completely safe from enemies. The men arranged a hunt for deer and wild horses, while Juh sent out raiding parties to steal cattle from ranches in Chihuahua and Sonora. About June 10, 1882, the camp's sentries announced in astonishment that a solitary rider was approaching. The man turned out to be Massai, and he was looking for his wife Nah-go-tsieh and his two children, who had left San Carlos with Loco. The legendary Apache, who would become known for his survival skills, had been serving as a scout in New Mexico at the time of the outbreak.[35]

Less than a month before Loco's abduction, Second Lieutenant James R. Richards, commanding Company C, Indian Scouts, had come to San Carlos to recruit scouts. Operating under a mandate to enlist scouts "who had served before (except Yumas and Mohaves)," Richards met Agent Joseph Tiffany and Chief of Police Albert Sterling. Both recommended that he select Toclanny for his sergeant, a position Toclanny had held under Lieutenant Charles C. Hall. Agent Tiffany thought the Chiricahua was a "splendid man," and Sterling described him "as the best trailer on the reservation." In later years Toclanny boasted that he had never fought Americans, one of the few Chiricahuas of his generation who could make that claim. Richards enrolled six other Chiricahuas besides Toclanny: Ahnandia, a second cousin of Geronimo and a first cousin of Betzinez; José First; Tsedikizen (also known as Sundayman, who had married Loco's granddaughter); Nogusea (also known as Massai); Thlagodumas; and Dutchy, the only Chokonen in the group from Chiva's band. The day before they left for New Mexico, Loco met Lieutenant Richards and with great pride assured the officer that he "was taking some of the best young men of his tribe." And the chief boasted that whatever the circumstances, his men would "stand by me against all enemies."[36]

Soon after Loco left San Carlos, Colonel Ranald Mackenzie, the commander of the District of New Mexico, ordered Richards to discharge the seven Chiricahua scouts. The move made sense to Mackenzie, who feared a repeat of what had happened in the wake of the Chiricahua uprising on September 30, 1881, when several of Lieutenant Bailey's Chiricahua scouts had deserted and joined their people.[37] Richards, a young and highly principled officer, disagreed, feeling that this decision was simply another in a long line of American betrayals of a people whom he had come to trust and respect:

> Of course, it cannot be expected that my Indians would fight their own tribe. . . . Against any other hostiles, I believe that they [can] be thoroughly relied upon. I can offer no stronger proof of my belief in them by saying that I would follow where they lead without fear (for in case of treachery my life would be the first sacrificed) and that I am willing to stake my reputation as a soldier upon their fidelity. I wish to express myself strongly, but respectfully, in this matter and it is difficult for me to select exact terms in which to say so. . . . In their turn, they have come to trust and believe in me. When I disarm them, as your endorsement requires, I must do so without explanation. I then become in their eyes, as faithless as the typical white man.[38]

Despite Richards's compelling arguments, Mackenzie refused to revoke his order, admitting that he had "no confidence" in the Chiricahua scouts.

On May 9, 1882, troops escorted the scouts from Fort Stanton to Fort Craig. From here, they traveled to San Marcial, where they boarded a train for Willcox. About May 12, 1882, as they moved along the rails east of Deming, one scout, Thlagodumas, jumped from the train after a soldier foolishly threatened the scouts with death. When the train stopped, an officer sent Massai after Thlagodumas. He followed the trail but was unable to overtake his friend, who probably joined the Chiricahuas in Mexico. Massai rejoined the scouts and went on to San Carlos, where military officials discharged them on May 19, 1882.[39]

Ten days later Massai left the reservation for Mexico, where he found his family at the Great Canyon, or Guaynopa, about June 10, 1882. He stayed only a short time. Within ten days the restive Massai stole Betzinez's mule and took his family back to San Carlos. He apparently took his time, for his return trip to the agency took about two months. On September 1, 1882, Indian officials at San Carlos arrested a "renegade" Chiricahua, likely Massai.[40]

About the time that Massai left Guaynopa, Juh and Geronimo began to get restless. Though their camp was safe from Sonoran troops, they knew that their raids on Chihuahua would eventually bring a response from the Tarahumaras. The chiefs decided to move toward the Yaqui River in Sonora. They were a few days ahead of soldiers from Guerrero, Chihuahua, who scouted the Great Canyon in late June but found only eighteen head of stock and a large Indian trail going west. They placed the village near the Chico River, a tributary of the Aros River, just north of Guaynopa.[41]

The Chiricahuas had left Guaynopa between June 20 and June 23. Their first day's march took them along a "rough route through canyon after canyon" until they pitched camp about fifteen miles southeast of the confluence of the Bavispe and Aros rivers, some fifteen miles north of Sahuaripa. The chiefs decided to send out an advance party of warriors to scout several targets. When they returned a few days later, they reported the presence of Mexican troops at their targets, either Sahuaripa or Tepache. Again, the chiefs met to discuss strategy and concluded to split up. "There was no hard feeling about it," wrote Betzinez. Juh was uncomfortable near settlements and "wanted to retreat back into the heart of the Sierra Madre where there was good shelter and refuge." Most felt safer with Juh, including the followers of Loco, Nana, Naiche, Chatto, and Bonito; perhaps five hundred people in all went with him. Geronimo, joined by Chihuahua and Kaetenae, planned to launch two raids against Sonora—an initial one to the west and a second to the northwest. About eighty in all went with Geronimo, including his second cousin Jason Betzinez.

Juh and Geronimo would not reunite for almost four months. We can follow Geronimo's activities by correlating Jason Betzinez's narrative with his
accurate map to arrive at a good estimate of the movements of Geronimo's
group that summer of 1882. Of particular importance was a skirmish with
Mexicans that Betzinez said took place a half-dozen miles northeast of Moctezuma in the late summer of 1882. Contemporary reports from Moctezuma
confirm his account, agreeing as to the time of day, location, and results as
they knew them. They place the encounter on July 26, 1882. Using this date,
we can fill in the actions of Geronimo's group for most of that exciting summer, at least through the eyes of a twenty-year-old.[42]

After leaving the main band, Geronimo led his followers across the Yaqui
River, where they established a base camp on a mountaintop. Here they prepared for their raid, "making extra pairs of moccasins, cleaning our hair, sharpening knives, and cleaning and greasing guns. We had no tomahawks, arrows,
or spears. . . . By 1882 arrows and spears were rarely used." All the warriors,
some thirty in all, left camp about July 6, 1882. No women went along, which
corroborates what one informant told anthropologist Morris Opler, that a war
party consisted of "men only. Women never go on raids."[43] Betzinez remained
with the women and children in their mountain stronghold. Two days later,
the Chiricahuas attacked a ranch near Mátape, killing a man and stealing some
stock. On July 10, 1882, they swept by Álamos, whose men were unable to resist because the town had but three firearms. For the next ten days, Geronimo
and Chihuahua led attacks on ranches, pack trains, and travelers before returning to base camp on July 22, 1882, with great "quantities of dry goods, bolts
of cloth, and wearing apparel."[44]

Ironically, one of their attacks was on a party of Mexicans in which their
former friend Zebina N. Streeter was traveling. He had remained in Sonora
after Juh and Geronimo had moved to San Carlos in early 1880. On May 18,
1881, officials at Mulatos had arrested him for his involvement with Apaches.
Authorities sent him under guard to Hermosillo, where Governor Luis Torres
wrote a letter to Arizona's governor, offering to extradite Streeter.[45] Nothing
came of this, and Torres apparently released him. In July 1882, Streeter accompanied an escort of troops under Colonel Lorenzo Torres, which Chiricahuas ambushed somewhere between Sahuaripa and Moctezuma about July 8,
1882. The Apaches wiped out the seven soldiers and shot Torres in the thigh.
Torres, with Streeter, escaped to Moctezuma.[46] The only member of the party
not killed or wounded was Streeter. Though Streeter was a shadowy frontier

character, no direct evidence points to his collaborating with Geronimo; however, Chiricahuas recall that Streeter was with them on occasions during 1882 and 1883.[47]

Geronimo and Chihuahua decided to move north along the west bank of the Yaqui River, toward its confluence with the Bavispe River. Here they left their stock behind to graze in a hidden valley and stored their gear, loot, and saddles in caves. Taking only one mule, which Geronimo's wife and baby rode, they left camp in the early morning of July 25, 1882. At dawn they rounded Tepache, a small fortified village situated in a canyon, and headed north along the foothills. They traveled all day. They did no raiding; their purpose was to reach their rendezvous point undetected—a small clump of hills located north of the road between Moctezuma and Huásabas. By late afternoon they had crossed the road and "carefully covered their tracks" before making camp at the foot of these hills. They knew that troops garrisoned these towns, though they were probably unaware that General Reyes had moved his headquarters from Bavispe to Moctezuma, where he had arrived on July 16.[48]

Jason Betzinez has described what occurred the next day, July 26, 1882. That morning Geronimo dispatched his men to steal horses and mules to mount the band for the next leg of their journey. About noon the warriors returned with a herd of stock. The men and older boys "had a great time, roping them and breaking them for the women and children to ride." Betzinez was with his cousin Beneactinay, who had roped a mule that broke free and galloped into the valley. Betzinez impetuously chased it for two miles before he realized that a group of Mexican vaqueros from Caraverachi hacienda was on the trail of the stolen stock. Seeing Betzinez, they opened fire, but their aim was bad. Meanwhile, Beneactinay and other warriors, one with three cartridge belts crisscrossing his chest, charged the vaqueros "so fast that they failed to notice one soldier who was hiding in the bushes." This was José Aragon, and he picked off the last "Apache to ride by him." The mounted warriors, "hearing the shot, came dashing back just in time to shoot the Mexican." The band felt "dreadfully sad about losing a warrior," a Chihenne with Kaetenae.

Betzinez's memory was perfect, for he recalled that the skirmish occurred shortly after noon, about eight miles northeast of Moctezuma. He said Aragon had fired from a concealed position in the brush. Mexican reports concur with him as to the fight's location and time (1:00 P.M.), and in noting that they found Aragon behind brush in an arroyo. The only difference between the Mexican report and Betzinez's recollections was that the Mexicans had no idea that the brave Aragon had slain an Apache, for there were no Mexican eyewitnesses. Aragon's associates had fled, and the Apaches had carried off the body of their warrior.

When Reyes received news of the skirmish, he immediately sent out a force under Lieutenant Enrique Rivera, who encamped near the arroyo where they had found Aragon's body. Next morning, Rivera easily followed the trail toward the foothills, where the Chiricahuas were waiting to fight. But Rivera thought better of it. Betzinez said that the warriors finally realized that the Mexicans were not going to fight. Weary of waiting, "they moved on, traveling very fast right into the night." As they left, raiders hit a ranch near Cumpas and took thirty-nine horses. George Parsons, an American from Tombstone, claimed that one "bold Apache came into town" looking for stock before he rode away. Reyes dispatched another party of fifty men under Captain Francisco de Munoz. He joined Lieutenant Rivera, but they returned to Moctezuma on July 29, reporting that they were unable to overtake the Indians because of the difficult terrain.

Parsons saw the soldiers and remarked that "though clad in almost nothing, with rawhide sandals to walk with and *pinole* and jerky to eat," the Mexican soldier battles the Apaches and "generally whips him." Parsons's admiration for the Mexican fighting man was not one generally shared by most Anglos, but he recognized how dangerous the missions were and how challenging the tasks. General Reyes believed the Apaches were heading for the Teras Mountains, a longtime favorite stronghold of Geronimo. He messaged Major Luis Ceron at Bavispe to send a patrol there. But the major did nothing, for Betzinez makes no mention of encountering Mexican troops when encamped there.[49]

Meanwhile, the scouts reported to Geronimo and Chihuahua that the Mexican soldiers had abandoned the pursuit. The confident Chiricahuas "traveled slowly, enjoying the trip and the pleasant surroundings" as they returned to the Sierra Madre a few miles north of Oputo. The morning of July 29, 1882, they traversed an old Indian trail north along the Bavispe River toward the Teras Mountains, just northeast of the El Tigre range. It was a new adventure for Betzinez, who was proud to be with his relative Geronimo. He remarked "that the country was full of deer and other game" that just stood their ground. Little hunting had been done in this country, for Mexicans had no reason to venture so far from settlements, and no Apaches had lived in that part of the Sierra Madre for at least three years. Still, they took no game, for the band had plenty of dried meat, and Geronimo thought gunfire might alert

Mexican troops. That evening they reached the grounds that would serve as their new base camp, near the Teras Mountains. They were about thirty miles southeast of Fronteras, and fifty miles below the Arizona border.[50]

The Chiricahuas settled in for an "indefinite stay." Betzinez remembered fondly, perhaps idyllically, this period living as traditional Apaches. Vast stores of natural foods, like yucca fruit, acorns, and berries that had come into season, supplemented their diet. While the chiefs discussed their next foray, a raid into southern Arizona for ammunition (the warriors were short on cartridges), a White Mountain Apache named Na-nod-di (He Trots), who had married a Chihenne from Loco's band, deserted them. This occurred in mid-August 1882, and he took his wife with him, much to the disgust of his father-in-law, who sent a party after them with instructions to "hunt them down." Na-nod-di and his wife eluded their pursuers, eventually finding their way to the subagency, where military officials promptly arrested him in late August. They soon released him, for he had valuable information that military officials desired. And he had agreed to serve as a scout when called on.[51]

The war party of twenty-eight men left camp about August 23, 1882. It was a good time to raid because recent rains had replenished springs, and a full moon made nighttime travel possible. They took only seasoned fighters, for the band would be moving at "great speed and in constant danger from the troops." Betzinez had volunteered, but Beneactinay assured him that he had an equally important responsibility to remain in camp and look out for his sister and mother.[52]

Their first target was Turicachi, a settlement that the Spanish had abandoned before 1780. It lay on the west side of the main thoroughfare between Fronteras and Moctezuma. The morning of August 24, 1882, two Mexicans and two Americans were conducting a supply wagon for the Tajo mine. Geronimo's party ambushed the unsuspecting party, killing one American and wounding the other. Luiso Dominguez, who escaped to Fronteras with the news, said that he had seen fourteen Apaches. The next day the wounded American reached Fronteras with Jesús Granillo. They claimed to have killed one warrior, which may have been true. Betzinez recalled that two warriors returned to base camp with a wounded man who had died along the way. Manuel Gallegos, a thirty-year veteran who had fought Cochise, followed their trail from Turicachi to Pilares, where he recovered fifteen head of stock and saw the Apaches' camp in a strong position across the Bavispe River. He returned to Bacoachi with the information.[53]

Soon after the raid at Turicachi, the raiders divided into two groups, the first containing sixteen warriors, under Geronimo and Kaetenae, and the second consisting of nine warriors, under Chihuahua. For the first week they operated independently of each other. Geronimo's intent was to cross into Arizona and probably raid ranches along the Sonoita Valley, a favorite target of his. As it turned out, his raiders approached to within two miles of the border, but they never crossed into Arizona. Chihuahua's smaller party took positions along the well-traveled road between Bacanuchi and Cananea, which then led north to the border and the Mexican custom house at Palominas, about ten miles west of today's Naco. They would find no shortage of American prospectors and Mexican pack trains going to Tombstone.

Chihuahua's and Geronimo's raiders wasted no time. On August 25, 1882, Chihuahua's group raided the ranch at El Ojito, probably northeast of Chinapa, and made off with ten horses and mules. Then he led his eight battle-tested warriors north, ambushing a party of Mexicans north of Cananea, killing six of the eight men. Shortly before midnight, he launched a rare night attack against the Janaverachi ranch. Having surrounding the ranch, Chihuahua's men opened fire, sending several volleys through windows into the house. The cowboys had been sleeping, and they stumbled about in confusion, looking for their weapons to respond. Fortunately, no one was hurt.[54]

Meanwhile, Geronimo's band, after leaving Turicachi, went west, crossing the Ajos Mountains and the San Pedro River. At dawn, on August 26, 1882, they assaulted the Cuitaco ranch, some eight to ten miles north of Cocóspera, slaying Jesús Carbajal and José Altamiento and taking an undetermined number of stock. Sonoran reports claimed seventy Apaches were present; in reality, Geronimo had fifteen warriors with him, and they were moving rapidly toward the Arizona border. Later that day, a Mexican near Santa Cruz spotted the Apaches riding toward the Desviadero ranch, just south of the border. The commander dispatched thirty men, but they arrived too late. Geronimo's party had killed everyone on the ranch, two men, a woman, and her children. They had taken everything they could carry, including horses.[55]

Their presence near the border alarmed American authorities, who braced for Apache raids. Initial accounts stated that Juh led the war party and that it numbered between 120 and 200 men. One report suggested that their destination was San Carlos. A breathless rider galloped into Fort Huachuca with the news that the Apaches had raided the Sonoita Valley, forcing the inhabitants to abandon their ranches and move to Calabasas for protection. According to the messenger, "Men, women and children were ruthlessly slaughtered, houses burned and vandalized." These wild rumors, of course, trumped everything, drowning out the facts.[56]

Captain Daniel Madden had already sent a patrol under Lieutenant John N. Glass to examine the area along the border. Glass's command, which included five Western Apache scouts, entered Sonora and met troops from Santa Cruz, who "hailed the advent of our troops with joy." To this point the Sonorans had shown no appetite to pursue, "stopping for the inevitable cigarettes and consultation." Together they followed Geronimo's trail west, skirting the northern foothills of the San Antonio Mountains toward Nogales. Glass then abandoned pursuit, returning to Arizona, where he sent five Apache scouts to the Sonoita Creek to look for signs. Thus, Madden concluded that he had solved the mystery of the deadly Apache raid; someone had mistaken the scouts for hostiles and started the stampede. He calmly reported to head-quarters that the Chiricahuas had remained in Sonora. Moreover, he dismissed the notion that the raiders numbered two hundred. Instead, two small raiding parties, one of sixteen warriors and the other of nine, were operating in northern Sonora.[57]

Geronimo, once he discovered that Apache scouts were guiding American troops, pivoted south. Sweeping by the Buena Vista ranch, he and his party had a brief skirmish with the soldiers from Santa Cruz before changing course to the southeast. In the early evening of August 27, they surrounded a ranch while its occupants, three generations of the Castillo family, were eating dinner. To the Chiricahuas, they were faceless symbols that shared the same heritage of those who had carried out the massacre at Alisos Creek and the treachery at Casas Grandes. The results mirrored Geronimo's brutal massacre at Stevens's sheep camp. One young man, a cousin of the family inside the ranch, witnessed the grotesque slaughter. He had come in from the fields for dinner when he saw sixteen Apaches approaching the ranch. He watched in horror as four warriors entered the house and opened fire with their repeating rifles, probably Winchesters, slaughtering at the kitchen table the grandfather, grandmother, their son and daughter-in-law, and five children. Their barbarism sickened him: "When the hellish deed was done, the fiends raised a shout and cheered themselves and then mutilated the bodies." Before leaving, they burned the house and corral.[58]

The next day (August 28) they continued southeast toward their rendezvous point with Chihuahua's party, who, after their midnight attack on the

Janaverachi ranch, had ambushed several parties between Palominas, the customs house on the Sonora side of the border, and Cananea. Over three days (August 26–August 28), they had killed another half-dozen people, all of them well-armed travelers. One American, a man named Tom Johnson, was traveling north with two men when Indians, concealed in willows along the road, shot him in the back. The other two Americans, one of whom was John Hohstadt (of whom we will hear more in 1886), barely escaped with their lives. The Chiricahuas took Johnson's horse and rifle.[59]

The war party now decided to head home. Yet, plenty of good targets remained along the way. On August 29 they surprised the Bado Seco ranch, killing two people and taking more stock. By early the next morning, they had reached Cocóspera ranch, where the twenty-five warriors killed two more people. They also ransacked the ranch, taking what they could use, and rounded up more horses and mules. A company of troops from Magdalena followed them, but the Apaches easily out-distanced the soldiers. Eighteen hours later, after riding fifty miles during the day and throughout the moonlit night, they reached Bacanuchi before dawn on August 31.

This was the hacienda of Ignacio Pesqueira, the hero of the 1851 Pozo Hediondo fight and former governor of Sonora; it was on a mesa a few hundred feet above the floor of the valley. That morning Geronimo and Chihuahua led the attack, with the main resistance coming from two American miners who happened to be at the hacienda. Though Pesqueira employed sixty hands, they apparently remained holed up while the Americans did the bulk of the fighting. The Apaches' firepower finally took care of the two men, but not before the latter killed a warrior, or so the story goes.[60] By mid-morning the chiefs headed east toward the Pinito Mountains and to their base camp in the Teras Mountains, which they reached about September 2 or 3. Absent for ten or eleven days, the war party returned with "great quantities of ammunition [and] many articles useful for camp life." They had spared no one during the foray, killing everyone in their path (between forty and fifty people) and traveling some three hundred miles.[61]

Despite the loss of one warrior, the chiefs "planned" a victory dance. Betzinez recalled: "Soon we heard the beating of tom-toms and saw the women and girls gathering on the outer circle. The men were singing at the top of their voices rejoicing over their victories." After an all-night celebration, the men distributed the spoils of war to their partners and other members of the band. After resting for several days, they broke camp about September 10 and forged south, following the Bavispe River toward Oputo. In mid-September Geronimo and Chihuahua's band split—the former moving south toward Oputo and the latter heading east into the El Tigre Mountains. Geronimo's Power had warned him that Mexican troops were near. No one questioned his statement. All expected the Mexicans to appear at the time and place that Geronimo had foretold. And they did. After a brief skirmish, the band decided to rejoin Juh at Guaynopa. In early October, the reunion occurred.[62]

At this time, Betzinez met his cousin Ahnandia, who with three other scouts (Dutchy, Tsedikizen, and José First) had bolted from San Carlos on July 19, 1882. After their discharge in May 1882, the agent turned them over to Lieutenant Gatewood, who assigned them a place to live at San Carlos. But their families were in Mexico, and they felt threatened by enemies at the agency. So they had to leave. Dutchy, whose Apache name was My-klitz-so (Yellow Coyote), was the ringleader in a treacherous attack on four teamsters camped on the Gila, four miles from the San Carlos agency. As the teamsters were having supper, the Indians approached the camp, pretending to be friendly. Dutchy then seized the rifles of the unsuspecting men and opened fire, killing Jacob Ferrin and slightly wounding Kit Reynolds, whom Dutchy would have killed had he not fallen into the Gila. The other two teamsters escaped into the brush. The Apaches took sixteen head of stock and headed for the subagency; en route they took more animals from Nathan Appel's wagons, cut the telegraph wire between there and Fort Thomas, and went north toward Ash Creek, the route taken by Geronimo a few months before. In late July, they found Loco's band near the Aros River. Juh, with most of the men from Naiche's, Chatto's, and Bonito's bands, was then raiding ranches and fighting Mexican troops south of Sahuaripa.[63]

Despite the absence of an informant in Juh's camp, his activities are easy to document by following the blood of his victims. In late June 1882 Chiricahuas struck Tarachi, killing four citizens and taking stock. A party from Arivechi pursued them east, found two more corpses, and followed the trail to the Agua Blanca Mountains, where they found an abandoned ranchería that had housed eighty people and fifty wickiups. The Indian trail led north into the Sierra Madre and then divided.[64] Two weeks later, at daybreak July 20, 1882, Juh led a large war party, between fifty and seventy-five warriors, and burned the Carrisal ranch, located about twenty miles northeast of the Trinidad mines. Here they avenged García's massacre of their women and children, killing nine women and one child. They also made off with two hundred head of stock.

Two days later, the Chiricahuas killed two vaqueros near Onavas, and then waylaid a party of ten men who were going to reinforce Onavas, killing three and wounding three others.[65]

These sanguinary raids drew the attention of military commanders in the district. A force of nationals followed the hostiles to Rio Chico, where on July 27, 1882, they found the Indians well posted in the hills near La Cruz. Again Juh attacked, and another eight men paid the ultimate sacrifice with their own blood.[66] Soon after this engagement, Juh's warriors moved north. On his trail were thirty federal troops of the Sixth Battalion, led by Captain Aberto. Near Milpias, southeast of the Carrisal ranch that the Apaches had burned eleven days before, Aberto's men followed the Chiricahuas to a summit of a steep hill. Jason Betzinez described what one participant had told him:

> On this occasion the warriors had been skirmishing with Mexican troops for two days. Finally, their ammunition was about exhausted. The soldiers still followed them, so the Indians made a plain zigzag trail up a steep mountain. . . . Juh had the men roll a line of big rocks into place along the trail, ready to be dislodged down the mountain-side. . . . The [Mexicans] confidently marched up the zigzag trail. When they reached the summit the Apache warriors sprang out and attacked them. The Mexicans started to withdraw down the mountainside whereupon, at Juh's command, the Indians began rolling the great boulders down upon them. Many solders were crushed by the tumbling boulders and falling trees. Not many escaped.[67]

In reality, Aberto lost three dead and five wounded in the battle. In a ten-day period, Juh's followers had slain more than fifty Sonorans. Military officials believed that Juh had returned to his ranchería at Guaynopa. They were wrong.[68]

In August General Reyes planned a three-pronged assault into the Sierra Madre north and east of Sahuaripa. Juh's stronghold at Guaynopa was their objective, but in mid-August, Colonel García found the large encampment empty.[69] The chiefs had quarreled and separated. Juh, always independent, drifted back to Sonora. Naiche and Chatto remained together, moving their village south to the Aros River, about ten miles east of its junction with the Mulatos River. Loco established his camp near them.[70]

In early September, Juh and a large party of warriors began raiding near Mulatos, which they harassed until mid-month, killing a half-dozen people.

The mining town, lacking serviceable weapons, appealed for help to the prefect of Sahuaripa, who petitioned General Reyes at Moctezuma. He redeployed troops to provide protection for the mining district. Yet, when they reached the area in early October, Juh had gone. If Sonoran and Chihuahuan military officials had shared intelligence, Reyes would have known that in late September 1882, Joaquin Terrazas had captured one of Juh's men, who admitted that he was returning to the village at Guaynopa. He was the only man Juh lost during the summer's raiding.[71]

Betzinez remembered with pride the camaraderie felt by the Indians who were attempting to live as their ancestors had: "It was a very happy time for us all. We could hear their tom-toms at night across the canyon and I expect they could hear ours." A few days later, Geronimo's group decided to cross the canyon to Juh's camp on the brink opposite them. They remained there for quite a while, exchanging presents and reminiscences. The chiefs opted for a tribal venture against Chihuahua, undoubtedly to avenge the massacre at Casas Grandes the previous spring.[72]

Betzinez recalled that excitement erupted when She-neah suddenly shot and killed a Navajo man who had accompanied Geronimo's group the past several months in Sonora. This unidentified man may have been Cloh-neh, who had married Jah-ken-ish-ishn (Black Girl), a Bedonkohe woman who was the sister of Fun and half-sister of Perico.[73] The man had slain a relative of She-neah years before when serving as a scout for the army. "As usual, the Apaches never forgot, nor forgave," lamented Betzinez. "We were all sorry that this happened but no one did anything about it."[74] She-neah was a powerful war shaman who enjoyed the support of Bonito. It was also feasible that She-neah's guardian spirit may have caused him to act the way he did, as we shall soon see.

Although Betzinez fails to mention that a war party left the village, apparently the leaders decided to send two bands of warriors against Chihuahuan towns south and southeast of Guaynopa. They struck between October 19 and October 21, 1882, one ambushing a party of Americans and Mexicans near the Dolores mines, between the Aros and Tutuaca rivers, about seventy-five miles east of Sahuaripa. Here they killed two Americans, John and Patrick Walker, and one Mexican. Five Mexicans fought off the attackers before making their way to high ground. Meanwhile, the second war party raided as far east as San Isidoro, a hacienda near Guerrero, and along the Concepcion River between Temosachic and Matachic. They succeeded in slaying another eighteen people and taking a great deal of stock.[75]

The victorious war parties returned to Guaynopa. The chiefs, expecting a punitive campaign from Chihuahua, decided to abandon their stronghold and move north. Years later, Yahnozha passed along his recollections to Norwegian anthropologist Helge Ingstad: "We held many talks and would decide what each man do. . . . No leader can order over Apaches. All Indians have their say and make decisions together."[76] Their objective, by consensus, was Galeana, chosen because of its role in the attack near Casas Grandes the previous May. The entire tribe was together, and vengeance was on their mind. The Chiricahuas could muster about 130–140 fighters, including teenage boys. They left Guaynopa in late October, marching leisurely to the northeast. By early November, they had encamped about thirty miles southeast of Galeana. Here the tribe held a fire dance, a ceremony usually performed to fend off illness or epidemics. Betzinez watched intently as the dancers circled the encampment, warding off sickness by "gesticulating and blowing." The villagers prayed to the masked dancers, calling them "Men of the Mountain," imploring them to protect the people. Like the war dance, this event also lasted four days.[77]

Afterwards, the large camp moved northeast ten miles, where the "tom-toms started up again." The chiefs decided to hold a war dance to prepare the warriors for the challenges that lay ahead. "Young Indian boys who wanted to become warriors had to practice the dance as if it were a real battle." Also known as "fierce dancing," the war dance was a solemn ceremony in which the participants prayed for good fortune and vengeance. One informant told Morris Opler that they sometimes asked "our supernatural power to let us have the Mexican general or president. We called him by name for four days so that we could capture or kill him."[78] This time their targets were Joaquin Terrazas and Juan Mata Ortiz, the slayers of Victorio and their betrayers at Casas Grandes six months earlier. The medicine men sang and prayed, seeking confirmation from their Power that all was well.[79]

But all was not well with She-neah, the revered shaman and mighty warrior of the Bedonkohes. Renowned as a "war shaman," before a battle he customarily assembled his men in a circle and prayed for their safety. His advice had always proved to be right; his men believed his Power was strong and reliable. But as She-neah talked to his spirit, his men could sense that something had gone awry. They could hear him arguing with his Power during the ceremony. This was unsettling to all, for She-neah's Power had always been a beneficent source. The Chiricahuas felt that supernatural power can be "used for good or evil, depending on the character and design of the shaman." If a shaman allowed his Power to use him for harmful purposes, the Apaches branded him *enti*, meaning witch or sorcerer. If, however, he had the willpower and character to reject the evil use of Power, then malevolent events normally would not occur.

She-neah's Power had requested a "favor" in return for the help he had bestowed on the shaman. The story continues:

> His Power said, "In a day or so you are going to get into action against the enemy. I have helped you in many ways with beneficial power; now you have to do it the way I want it. I want the bravest man in your group. I want you to give that man to me to be killed."
>
> She-neah answered: "I will do no such thing. . . . I like to see my people increase in population with what power you gave us to help me along. I love all my men, my warriors. They want to live in this world as long as they can. . . . If you were a witch from the beginning, why didn't you tell me? I don't like witch people; I won't have witches talk to me. You promised me that it was all good for my people and myself. You didn't say that I would have to give my people every now and then."
>
> The Power told him, "I have helped you a lot. I have gotten you out of danger and helped in many other ways. And now I merely ask for a man to pay for that and you will not let me have one!"
>
> [She-neah] said, "My habit is not that way, and I am not going to do it. If you want to take anyone or have anyone killed, just take me. . . . Power said, Well, then I will take you."

She-neah's only chance to live was to avoid the battle. But he would not consider abandoning the men he loved.[80]

It was not by chance that Juh and Geronimo chose Galeana as the target, for Mata Ortiz owned a ranch near there. They sent a small party to steal stock at San Buenaventura on November 6, 1882. They hoped the Mexicans would follow the raiders into Chocolate Pass, where they planned to waylay them. Although the warriors accomplished their first goal and retired north to the San Joaquin Mountains, the troops had not dared to venture into the hills. Two days later, the Indians raided a ranch near Galeana and headed northeast toward the America Mountains and Chocolate Pass. Again, no troops followed, but local officials sent messengers to Joaquin Terrazas and Juan Mata Ortiz. Finally on the morning of November 12, Chiricahuas assaulted Mata Ortiz's ranch, killing a vaquero and taking stock. Mata Ortiz, instead of waiting for Terrazas to arrive from the south, opted to take matters into his own hands.

On November 13, 1882, he rode at the forefront of a party of twenty-two citizens from Galeana. By mid-morning he was at the mouth of the notorious Chocolate Pass. The trail was fresh. Although he was following only a handful of warriors, Mata Ortiz realized the perils of entering the canyon. He assembled his men and said, "If anyone has any misgivings about going on, they should return to the petticoats of their women." His men met his words with a defiant and resounding cry, vowing to die fighting if necessary. Mata Ortiz had no idea that the entire fighting force of Chiricahuas was waiting for him in the canyon ahead.[81]

The decoy tactic, a strategy often employed by the Plains Indians, was not a practice normally adopted by Apaches, whose favorite plan was to ambush their enemy. Yet, in reality, the Chiricahuas, because of their patience and mode of warfare, carried out this tactic more effectively than the Plains Indians, whose warrior culture encouraged individual acts of bravery with the highest honors awarded to those men who counted coup, touching or striking a live enemy. Consequently, the decoy strategy usually failed because the warriors lacked the discipline to wait until their enemies had swallowed the bait. Warfare was no game to Apaches; they wanted to dispatch their enemies quickly, with as little risk as possible. Consequently, when they employed this maneuver, it was usually with lethal results.

Juh and Geronimo had deployed their men in two positions. They concealed one body of warriors in a ravine to the left of the trail. The second force—the main body of warriors—hid in a "depression" a mile or two up the road. The first force was to launch the ambush once the Mexicans passed their positions. They hoped that Mata Ortiz would try to ride through the pass and run directly into the second body of warriors—a perfect trap. But, after the opening volleys, Mata Ortiz immediately led his command to a high hill on his right, where he ordered the survivors to dig in. The initial salvos had killed or wounded several of his men and many of his horses. Geronimo, Juh, and several older warriors took positions near a cedar tree at the foot of the hill. Betzinez and a handful of younger warriors served as horse holders behind a knoll about four hundred yards away.[82]

Two groups of Chiricahuas began to move systematically up the slopes toward the Mexicans' positions. Juh and Geronimo's group near the cedar tree provided cover. The frontal thrust came from the largest group, as they rolled rocks in front of them to protect their heads and bodies from the Mexican fire.

Bonito, whose Apache name means "He Stirs up the Earth," likely referring to his daredevil nature, volunteered to lead a group of eight warriors, "who always fought together as a group," to circle behind Mata Ortiz. In the rear of Bonito's party, according to Chiricahua custom, was its medicine man, She-neah.[83] As Bonito was approaching the crest of the hill, he turned around to see how his men were doing. He saw She-neah "raise up to fire through an opening between two rocks. As he did so, a Mexican bullet struck [him] on top of the head making a furrow from front to rear in his scalp and skull." Bonito became so "enraged that he screamed the order for the final attack." Both groups jumped up and charged to the top, with the brave Beneactinay among the first to the crest.[84] The warriors dove headlong into the Mexicans, fighting them "hand-to-hand" until they had killed or captured all except one man, who mounted a horse and escaped to Galeana. Geronimo shouted, "Let him go," for he would bring reinforcements from Galeana who could share Mata Ortiz's fate.[85]

The brave and principled shaman's prophecy had come true. He knew that if he fought, "he would not live more than a few days more."[86] Opler's description of this event perfectly fits the fight in Chocolate Pass. She-neah was in the rear of the group, precisely where the shaman was supposed to be; it was a hand-to-hand battle with guns (putting it in the late 1870s or 1880s); many Mexicans were killed; and the shaman was shot through the forehead, fitting Betzinez's eyewitness account. During the assault, the Mexicans had also killed a "promising" Chihenne warrior named She-sauson. The only part of the story at odds with the facts was the loss of two men in the battle instead of one. Yet Opler had two sources for this story, with one saying that She-neah's Power demanded one man, and the other saying it demanded two men.

As for the battle, Betzinez simply said, without boasting, that "everything went according to plan." The Chiricahuas had slain Mata Ortiz and twenty-one of his men. Mexican reports claim that the Apaches captured Mata Ortiz and that Juh burned him at the stake, thus fulfilling Juh's vow to Mata Ortiz after the treachery at Casas Grandes. One account even suggests that Mata Ortiz, a devout Catholic, asked God to forgive Juh for his actions. His friends found his body horribly mutilated and partially burnt. Apocryphal or not, Juh had his revenge. And in this bloody saga of staccato warfare, Chihuahua would soon avenge Mata Ortiz's death.[87]

And what of the Chiricahuas? Their primary concerns since leaving San Carlos were troops from Sonora and Chihuahua. Now they would face a new paradigm, one that would change the nature of Apache warfare in Mexico.

General George Crook had returned to command the Department of Arizona, bringing with him innovative tactics and pragmatic policies designed to seize the initiative and move the American military from defense to offense. Even the most sagacious Chiricahua shaman could not have predicted how Crook's presence would change the balance of power.

The big rock a few feet south of the "Cathedral" where Captain said you and Cochise had many a talk over peace making. Captain calls it the rock on which peace was made as he says it was here that Cochise first began to really and seriously consider the matter with you.

-- Alice Rollins Crane, 1895,
handwritten note to Gen. Howard

According to Tom Jeffords, in 1895, this rock formation near the West Stronghold is where General Howard and Cochise agreed to terms. Courtesy George Robertson.

Apache Pass, in the heart of Cochise's country. Photograph courtesy Kathryn Plauster.

Naiche, youngest son of Cochise, 1882. Courtesy Arizona Historical Society, Tucson (30385).

John P. Clum, San Carlos Apache agent, with unidentified men, 1874. Courtesy Arizona Historical Society, Tucson (15748).

Chihuahua, one of the bravest and most decisive Chokonen leaders. Courtesy Arizona Historical Society, Tucson (949).

Mangas, son of Mangas Coloradas. Courtesy National Archives and Records Administration (111-SC-82352).

Chatto, whom Lieutenant Britton Davis considered "one of the finest men, red or white, I have ever known." Courtesy National Archives and Records Administration (111-SC-82364).

Geronimo, a resourceful, determined, and brave man who made decisions based on personal
experiences and his spirit adviser. Courtesy National Archives and Records Administration
(83726).

Bonito, a White Mountain Apache by birth who married a Bedonkohe woman and led the charge against Mata Ortiz at Chocolate Pass. Courtesy Western History Collection, Denver Public Library (X-32868).

Nana, leader of the fighting Chihennes after Victorio's death. Courtesy National Archives and Records Administration (ARC ID: 530800).

Kaetenae, able successor to Victorio and Nana. He was sentenced to Alcatraz by Crawford. Courtesy National Archives and Records Administration (165-AI-8; ARC ID: 533047).

Peaches, Crook's indispensable guide into the Sierra Madre in 1883. Courtesy National Archives and Records Administration (111-SC-82346).

General George Crook, 1885. Courtesy Arizona Historical Society, Tucson (25624).

88217

Captain Emmet Crawford, Crook's right-hand man in Arizona. His military peers and the Chiricahuas respected him. Courtesy National Archives and Records Administration (111-SC-88217).

Noche, in a photograph often misidentified as that of Taza. Noche was Britton Davis's and Crawford's trusted scout in 1885–86. Courtesy Arizona Historical Society, Tucson (894).

Lieutenant Britton Davis, the Chiricahuas' agent at Fort Apache and Turkey Creek. Courtesy Arizona Historical Society, Tucson (19621).

Lieutenant Marion Maus, able successor to Crawford. Maus responded to every challenge and navigated his command out of the Sierra Madre. Courtesy Arizona Historical Society (16010).

Standing left to right: La-zi-eh, Atelinietze, Tisna, Geronimo, Naiche. None of those sitting or kneeling in back can be definitely identified. Photograph taken by C. S. Fly at Embudos Canyon. Courtesy Western History Collections, University of Oklahoma Libraries (Rose Collection, 857).

Mounted from left: Geronimo and Naiche. *Standing: (left, holding child)* Perico, *(right)* Tisna. Photograph taken by C. S. Fly at Embudos Canyon, 1886. Courtesy Western History Collections, University of Oklahoma Libraries (Rose Collection, 853).

From left: Yahnozha, Chappo, Fun, and Geronimo. Photograph taken by C. S. Fly at Embudos Canyon. Courtesy Western History Collections, University of Oklahoma Libraries (Rose Collection, 858).

General Nelson A. Miles. He wanted the Chiricahuas removed from Arizona but not to Florida. Courtesy National Archives and Records Administration (111-B-4187).

Captain Henry Lawton. General Miles counted on him to bring Geronimo in. Courtesy National Archives and Records Administration (111-SC-87410).

Geronimo's group during a train stop en route to San Antonio. *Seated front, from left:* Fun, Perico, Naiche, Geronimo, Chappo, Garditha. *Back row:* Kanseah, Yahnozha, Tissnolthos, Ahnandia, Nah-bay, La-zi-yah, two women, Beshe. (Four people remain unidentified.) Courtesy National Archives and Records Administration (111-SC-82320).

Juh, Nednhi chief, the one Chiricahua chief who preferred life in Mexico, as depicted by Mary P. G. Devereux in January 1881. Courtesy Arizona Historical Society, Tucson (43838).

13

JUH FALLS FROM GRACE

[Juh] has lost his prestige and influence with the Indians. I regard Geronimo as the ablest chieftain the Chiricahuas have.

General George Crook

Geronimo was never really a chief but became one because of all the trouble.

Kayitah

As summer ushered in its oppressive heat and humidity to our nation's capital, the men entrusted with setting policy on Indian and military affairs in Arizona met in council. The Apache unrest that had resulted from Cibecue and continued with the Chiricahua outbreaks in September 1881 and April 1882 confounded them. Unfortunately, logistical problems and serious misconceptions clouded their perception of events in distant Arizona. They knew only that changes must occur in the Indian and military control of Arizona, and the sooner the better. The Apache troubles had drawn national attention, for it was the only conflict remaining, and the past decade of instability at San Carlos frustrated the two cabinet secretaries in charge of the Indian Bureau and the War Department.

On June 30, 1882, Joseph Tiffany resigned as agent. His health had failed him, and he had spent much of 1882 absent from his post. He had come to symbolize everything that was wrong at San Carlos, the stereotype of the corrupt Indian agent. Of course, he had made mistakes, but nobody seemed to remember the energy, innovations, and progress that had marked his first year. Following his resignation, he became the convenient scapegoat for the disorder at San Carlos.[1]

The paradox was that the government's decisions seemed to guarantee a repeat of its mistakes at that reservation. It failed to understand that firsthand experience, practical knowledge, and genuine empathy for Apaches remained vital to the success of the agency. Without these qualities, the inherent obstacles overwhelmed the agent. Washington's policy of appointing agents based on patronage and Eastern elitist ideology only guaranteed more failure at San Carlos.

Fortunately, the War Department was free to take steps that made sense. On July 14, 1882, General William Tecumseh Sherman reassigned Brigadier General George Crook to the command of the Department of Arizona. General Willcox had devoted more attention to San Carlos than to any other matter during his four and a half years in command. Like Tiffany, he had not failed. Yet Sherman recognized that the problems at San Carlos, for which Willcox was in "no manner" responsible, required Crook's steadying presence. Willcox had "done his best," and in the long term, conditions at San Carlos were bound to improve because of his efforts. For the short term, however, Sherman believed that the government must provide a psychological stimulus to improve matters. Fortunately, he had at his disposal the perfect man for the job, George Crook, "for the Apaches know and fear him." Actually, Sherman confused fear with respect, for respect was the term that best described the Apaches' feelings toward Crook.[2]

Crook assumed command of the department on September 4, 1882. Wasting no time, he immediately underscored two issues essential to his operations: he requested permission to double his department's allocation of Indian scouts from 125 to 250, for, he reasoned, catching Apaches "must be done through their own people." And then he issued orders for a pack train to join him for a tour of the department, specifically to San Carlos and Fort Apache.[3] He hoped to renew relations with the Apaches whom he had known during his first tour in Arizona. Accompanied by Lieutenant John G. Bourke, Corydon Cooley, Al Sieber, and a surgeon, J. O. Skinner, Crook, mounted on his mule named Apache, went first to Fort Apache and then to San Carlos to hear "all that has happened since I left here to bring about this trouble."[4]

His party's arrival at Fort Apache settled down the atmosphere almost overnight. Will C. Barnes, an enlisted man at the post, described Crook's entrance: "At the head of the line rode Crook on a large, gray mule, his usual mount. A yellow canvas coat and a pair of blue soldier trousers, much the worse for wear, was his uniform. On his head he wore one of those white East Indian pyramidical hats. . . . At the pommel of his saddle he carried a double-barreled shotgun—his favorite weapon. He had a rather full, grizzly beard, and his hair was long. A most unmilitary figure, indeed!"[5] At once, he sought out his former Apache friends. Between September 22 and September 29, 1882, Crook met Western Apache leaders near Fort Apache and the Indian agency at San Carlos. Their comments troubled him. The Apaches believed that the troops had betrayed them at Cibecue. They complained that most agents focused on lining their own pockets than attending to their welfare. Alchesay, a White Mountain leader who had been close to Crook, succinctly summed up the situation as the Apaches saw it: Indian agents "talk to [us] in one way and act in another." They claim that this "man is bad and that man is bad. I think the trouble is that they themselves are bad." Certainly some agents were corrupt, some were self-serving, and some were indifferent. The Apaches at Fort Apache were most concerned about corruption and the concentration policy that had forced the White Mountain and Cibecue groups to abandon their ancestral farms near Fort Apache and relocate to the subagency. Crook concluded that they had clearly lost confidence in most American officials, especially those civilians involved with the agency.

He also interviewed military men. To those officers who did not know Crook, he came across as brusque, aloof, and taciturn. Lieutenant Thomas Cruse, who had commanded a company of Apache scouts, was unsettled some by his reception in Crook's tent where Lieutenant John Bourke cross-examined him like "a prosecution attorney." But he soon realized that his first impression was wrong: "Crook was interested only in getting the whole situation clear in his mind."[6] First, the general set out to restore trust. On October 5 he issued Orders Number 43, in which he reminded his officers that one of "the fundamental principles of the military character is justice to all—Indians as well as white men." He pointed out the frightful consequences to those who ignored this rule. He also stressed another point: address Apache grievances quickly and fairly, and promise only what you can deliver.[7]

Crook also vowed to end the sea of corruption, graft, and apathy that had become so ingrained in the culture at San Carlos. The new Indian agent, Philip P. Wilcox, a patronage appointment because of his friendship with the secretary of the interior, Henry M. Teller, initially gave his blessings. A former judge and U.S. Marshal, Wilcox happened to be visiting Teller in Washington, D.C., when the position at San Carlos opened. To his astonishment, his friend selected him as the new agent.[8] He admitted to Lieutenant Britton Davis that he accepted the job because "of the salary when he could get nothing better."[9]

He had been on duty for only a few weeks before he met Crook. An initial honeymoon period followed in which the two men worked together and became allies, especially when it came to besmirching Tiffany's reputation and efforts.[10] Toward the end of September, Crook made two significant appointments, detailing Captain Emmet Crawford and Lieutenant Charles Gatewood to assume control of the Apache scouts and the Indian police at San Carlos and Fort Apache respectively. Devoted to Crook, principled and fair, both men would serve with honor over the next three years.[11] With them came a permanent garrison at San Carlos and a shared responsibility for the administration of the Apaches, a situation unlike that on any other reservation in Arizona or anywhere else in the country. Regretfully, this dual control was inevitably bound to cause problems with the civil Indian agent.[12]

Crook also asked Wilcox to allow the White Mountain and Cibecue Apaches to return to their old country around Fort Apache. His suggestion came at a good time. Acting Agent Pangburn had recently fired Ezra Hoag, charging "Crooked Nose" with drunkenness and graft. Thus, Pangburn eliminated the subagency, which required the Apaches to move nearer to San Carlos to receive their weekly issues.[13] Crook's recommendation was an important step toward self-sufficiency for the White Mountain and Cibecue groups, for they again would begin to plant at their former farms. Wilcox agreed, providing the Apaches picked up their rations at the agency.[14]

Wilcox told the *Denver Tribune* that Crook "was doing splendid work and I will aid him all I can." Furthermore, he boasted, this "was the first time in the history of Indian affairs that such a thing [cooperation between military officials and Indian agents] has occurred." According to him, their unparalleled alliance had turned San Carlos into an Apache utopia, a vacation haven that the Chiricahuas in Mexico, once they learned of it, would come posthaste to live the easy life: "They are well fed, and all they have to do is hunt and lie about their tents and sun themselves and gamble for tobacco and blankets."[15] After all, a little white lie never hurt anyone. Wilcox seemed determined to do as little as possible while earning as much as possible. Though the two ideas seem incongruous, they had become natural partners when it came to Indian agents at San Carlos. And speaking of partners, the agent's first priority in lining his own pockets was to appoint his son-in-law, John A. Showalter, as the sole trader on the reservation, a lucrative position that would bring in several times the amount of Wilcox's salary as agent.[16]

Wilcox called Denver home, and it was clear from the beginning that he preferred the mile-high city to Arizona, which to the public he euphemistically described as "a very pleasant place to live if it wasn't so hot."[17] His private sentiments were the same, simply more blunt: he informed Lieutenant Britton Davis that "Arizona [was] a hole not fit for a dog." He would carry out his sentence to live there, but only for the minimum time "necessary in order to hold the job." Davis tersely observed: "He was from Colorado and kept his word."[18]

Crook's contingent remained at San Carlos to observe the issuance of rations on Friday, October 13. While there, they met eight Chiricahuas, which surprised both Bourke and Crook. Agent Wilcox had no idea that any Chiricahuas were on the reservation. These were probably Toclanny, the Bedonkohe scout who had remained on the reservation, and several Chiricahuas who had left the hostiles' camp in the Sierra Madre and returned to San Carlos: Massai and his family, Na-nod-di and his wife, and two Chiricahua women who had come to the reservation with Eskebenti, a White Mountain Apache.[19] Whatever they told Crook must have persuaded him that some Chiricahuas in Mexico yearned to return to the reservation. He decided to extend an olive branch.

He quickly organized a small party of scouts led by Navajo Bill, with two Chiricahua women (one was a Bedonkohe named Nah-je-ke or Nat-Tzuck-ei-eu) who had been with the hostiles a few months before, to enter Mexico and establish contact with the Chiricahuas.[20] Crook and Bourke had to coax Navajo Bill into crossing the border. In early November, he and another scout claimed to have met two Chiricahuas some five miles north of the Alisos Creek battleground. The two hostiles would not approach within two hundred yards. And they were belligerent, threatening to kill the scouts if they came any closer. Furthermore, they wanted no part of San Carlos, claiming they would return with a war party at some point. On November 8, 1882, Navajo Bill returned to Arizona, his mission a failure. Crook would have to make alternate plans for the Chiricahuas in Mexico.[21]

Meanwhile, after their victory over Mata Ortiz, Juh and Geronimo had led their followers back to the Sierra Madre, camping about twenty-five miles southwest of Carcay at Bugatseka (On Top Rocks White). This ranchería was situated at the top of a level pine forest. Juh, restless as always, stayed a few weeks and then took more than half the tribe, probably about 350 in all, fifty miles south toward the rugged country near the Aros River. Chatto, Naiche, Bonito, Jelikine, and Loco went with him.[22] Geronimo and Chihuahua remained at Bugatseka with the balance of the Chiricahuas, about 200 in all.

They would live in this area for the next six months, moving camp frequently between here and Madera. Peaches, who was with Geronimo and Chihuahua, said that the band would move "openly where they please. The country is so rugged that the Mexicans are afraid to come."[23]

The followers of Geronimo and Chihuahua needed supplies, for food was becoming scarce, and the mescal harvest was months away. According to Peaches, they had plenty of meat but little else.[24] By late December 1882, the two chiefs told their men to prepare for a raid into Sonora. Again, thanks to Betzinez, we have a good idea of the route they followed and the scope of the raid.[25]

About December 30, 1882, the raiding party set out for the Sonoran settlements. Betzinez went along, accompanying his cousin Beneactinay, as they crossed the Bavispe River below Oputo and moved southwesterly at a brisk trot across the rectangular north-south valley between Moctezuma and Tepache. Early morning, January 3, 1883, Geronimo took the lead of the forty-man war party, jogging until noon on a southerly route toward the Sierra de Huerta foothills. Chihuahua and his men were behind. Betzinez, an excellent runner, was among the first Apaches to wade the Moctezuma River and reach the designated rendezvous. Geronimo arrived later that night. Chihuahua, however, was delayed until the next morning. The previous afternoon (January 3, 1883), his warriors, "in considerable numbers" (probably about ten or fifteen men), had ambushed a mule train near Tepache, slaying Felicito Moreno, Mariano Zacanuri, and José Reyes Maldoñado, a fourteen-year-old boy. Three men escaped as the Apaches took everything. Captain Emilio Kosterlitzky's command from Moctezuma found the victims' remains the next day.[26]

After Chihuahua's arrival, the band headed to a favorite ambush site along the road connecting Ures with settlements along the Moctezuma River. Betzinez' narrative is clear on their objective. Either that day (January 4, 1883) or the next, the band lay "in wait for pack trains." They allowed several parties of travelers to pass unmolested for they needed supplies for the village. Finally, their scouts signaled the emergence of "two heavily laden burros [which] appeared to be the head of a column." Betzinez emerged from his hiding place when he heard the shots. The Indians quickly captured the train and its valuable stores. He placed the ambush about fifteen miles west of the Moctezuma River, which accords precisely with a Sonoran report of an Apache attack near the Pastoria ranch on Mexicans going to Cumpas from Ures. Francisco Figueroa owned the train, and he fought briefly until he saw five of his party killed, two men, including his brother, and three women, including his aunt and niece. He and the other survivors fled to the nearby Pastoria ranch. The raiders took the booty to the hills.[27]

But other raiding parties left their mark on unsuspecting Mexicans while Betzinez and others remained in the hills guarding the stock and loot. After resting a few days, the Indians, traveling by night, passed east of Baviacora, where on January 9, 1883, five Indians boldly entered a corral and stole horses. The next day twenty-five Chiricahuas attacked the Tobacachi mine fifteen miles west of Cumpas. They took everything, killing a teenage boy named David Duarte, and making off with two repeating rifles, five hundred rounds of badly needed cartridges, and twenty horses and mules. Finally, four days later, on January 14, 1883, a large band of Apaches assaulted eleven Mexicans at Cuesta del Durasno on the Sonora River between Huepac and Banámichi. They killed one man and took his arms and ammunition.[28]

In mid-January the successful raiders began their march back to the Sierra Madre. "Just before sunset we started east down the mountainside," recalled Betzinez. They were hoping to drive their stock across a wide valley northeast of Moctezuma in "pitch darkness." The young Chiricahua was responsible for driving eight to ten horses. By early morning the band had forded the Moctezuma River and now stopped to rest. Geronimo and Chihuahua conferred, and they decided to head northeast toward the summit of a high ridge, which they reached about daybreak. Again, they rested all day, as each man did sentry duty. Still, they saw no pursuers. Early the next morning they forded the Bavispe River south of Oputo and felt more comfortable as they neared their refuge in the Sierra Madre. As they closed in on camp, Chihuahua and another warrior went ahead to the base camp. They could report good news, for the raid had been successful, no men had been lost, and they had captured large amounts of stock and supplies (Betzinez had driven two mules with fifty-pound cakes of sugar). The women began preparations for a large "welcoming feast" for Geronimo's warriors, who reached the village about January 19, 1883. They had been absent for about three weeks.

These were prosperous times for Geronimo's followers, who were enjoying "excellent health, quiet [times], and good feeling among the various families." But, shortly after their arrival, destitute relatives from Juh's camp brought sobering news. Mexican "peasant warriors" from Chihuahua had attacked Juh's winter camp, inflicting significant casualties and taking many captives. Juh's warriors had been active in raiding Sonora since splitting from Geronimo in late November and were now paying the price.[29]

About December 10, 1882, citizens discovered the trail of a large band of Apaches, with women and children, in the mining country southeast of Trinidad. Later that month on December 29, 1882, a war party, generously estimated at one hundred warriors, killed three men and captured a train loaded with tobacco a few miles northwest of Sahuaripa. The next day they fired at Antonio Apodoca as he conducted four burros loaded with mescal. He abandoned his cargo to the Apaches, escaping to Sahuaripa. The war party with their spoils retreated to the winter camp that Juh had located in Sonora about five miles from the Chihuahua border. This mescal may have played a role in the events to come.[30]

Juh surely felt safe here because Mexican forces usually avoided the Sierra Madre in the winter months. And, by design, his men had not recently raided Chihuahua, whose volunteer soldiers he feared more than the forces from Sonora. To provide even more security, he had decided not to return to Guaynopa, which he knew would be the first objective of Chihuahuan troops if they mounted a campaign. Thus, he located the large village in a secluded arroyo between two forks of a tributary of the Sátachi River, about twenty-five miles due west of Guaynopa.

Yet, despite these precautions, at dawn on the frigid winter morning of January 24, 1883, two detachments of Chihuahua volunteer troops, most Tarahumara Indians from the small villages near Temosachic, were poised to strike the Chiricahua camp. Operating under orders from the governor of Chihuahua to relieve the "suffering" of the frontier towns, they had left Temosachic on January 6, 1883. Vigilant, determined, and resourceful, the Tarahumaras had earned the respect of the Chiricahuas, who admired their running abilities and feared their tenacity, especially once they cut a trail. Years later one Chiricahua described their perseverance: "If they get on your trail, even though you are on horseback, they will run all day and catch up to you."[31]

Miguel Dominguez superbly led the Chihuahuans. Marching toward Guaynopa, he ordered his men to make dry camps. He prohibited any fires for cooking or for relief from the freezing nights. After thoroughly scouting Guaynopa and finding no Indians, he opted to continue the campaign into Sonora. It is not clear from his report whether he had struck a trail or just got lucky from his bulldog determination. His scouts apparently discovered the village late on January 23. He had just divided his command, sending a detachment to search in a different direction. Dominguez immediately recalled them. He made plans to attack the camp at sunrise, January 24, 1883, with his immediate command. Having waited as long as he could for the rest of his men, at 5:30 A.M., he led his volunteer army of one hundred men in an assault of Juh's sleepy Apache camp from two directions.

Daklugie, who was there, declared that the Mexicans "dashed through our camp, firing as they came." Bullets whistled by his ears in both directions. Those Apaches not slain in the first assault abandoned their wickiups, carrying their weapons with them but leaving their possessions and, in some cases, families behind. For a while, the two sides battled fiercely, but the Apaches were unable to drive the Mexicans from their village. Many Tarahumaras showed mercy to the women and children who surrendered. After taking anything of value, the Mexicans burned the village. When the two absent companies arrived and reinforced Dominguez's command, the firing stopped. Dominguez's report is short on details. He simply said that the fight lasted three and a half hours, during which his command had killed and scalped twelve Indians, captured thirty-three women and children, and rescued a captive girl named Clemente García. They had also confiscated thirty-eight horses and two mules.

It was a catastrophic blow to the Chiricahuas. Among the captives were the wife and two children of Chatto, two wives and two children of Geronimo, and several close relatives of Naiche. And, though the Mexican report fails to mention the killing of any women and children, clearly not all the dead were warriors. The Nednhis lost the most; Juh lost his wife, a son-in-law, and at least one grandchild. Only four warriors from his band remained alive. Bonito's wife and child were among the dead. According to contemporary Apache accounts, the Mexicans had slain two men and ten women and children. Mexican authorities were not concerned whether a scalp was that of a male or female. The Chiricahuas had killed three and wounded four Mexicans in the ranchería fight.[32]

At about 3:00 P.M., Miguel Dominguez reassembled his force, now numbering about two hundred men, and retired from the village. They had gone about one-third of a mile when the Chiricahuas launched a blistering counterattack against the advance guard, killing four persons (two had already been wounded in the morning encounter) and wounding four more. The Apaches also recaptured ten horses and one mule. Yet Dominguez's men held steady and repulsed the assault, killing and wounding several more Chiricahuas. Betzinez heard from Apache participants that Juh lost two of his "best warriors" attempting to rescue their people. All told, Dominguez believed that he had killed, wounded, and captured eighty Apaches; Chiricahua accounts put their losses at fourteen dead, thirty-three captured, and an unknown number wounded. Moreover, the Mexican soldiers had pillaged their camp, leaving them with few possessions and little stock in the dead of winter, the season they called Ghost Face, which forced them to rely on stored foods until the blossoms of spring. With the loss of their camp and supplies, the survivors faced desperate times.[33]

It was a watershed moment for Chihuahua troops—a rare victory over Juh in warfare. Chihuahua's official newspaper was euphoric, hailing the accomplishment, praising its fighters for their "steadiness under fire and bravery. This time, the savages, led by the famous Juh, have gotten the worst of it."[34] For once, the Chiricahuas would have concurred with that blunt assessment. Juh's personal loss left him demoralized, perhaps draining his will to live and driving him into a melancholic state from which he never recovered. And, of course, he lost much prestige in the eyes of those Chiricahuas who had elected to follow his lead. He never again wielded any influence in tribal affairs.

Clearly, part of the blame for the calamity rested squarely on Juh's shoulders. Four months later, a Chiricahua told a reporter with Crook's expedition that a mescal binge had left Juh incapacitated at the time of the attack, which was a distinct possibility given his fondness for that drink and the capture of the mescal pack train three weeks before the fight.[35] The actions of his tribesmen in the days following the disaster suggest a general falling out with Juh. Betzinez said the defeat led to much dissatisfaction among the Indians, who began to quarrel among themselves. The destitute people moved north to Geronimo's camp.[36]

Whether Juh was with those who sought refuge in Geronimo's camp is not clear. Some reports say that Geronimo became angry with Juh, perhaps after learning of the capture of two of his wives and two children.[37] One Chiricahua, perhaps referring to this event, told Opler: "If the group is dissatisfied with the leader, . . . they may just move away and camp elsewhere and recognize another leader. Then the former leader is left alone with his family."[38] This was precisely the situation that Juh faced. He left the tribe, taking one warrior, his three teenage sons, and four women and children "into the recesses of the Sierra Madre," near the territory of the Yaqui Indians.[39] Daklugie, in an uncharacteristic moment of honest introspection, told Eve Ball, "It took a long time for my father to recover from that attack. In fact, I am not sure that he ever did."[40]

Now the tribe (except Juh's immediate family and Loco's Chihennes) looked to Geronimo for leadership. The tribe had lost 30 percent of its people since the outbreak on September 30, 1881. Outside of Nana, Geronimo was the oldest leader and the one who had the Power to avoid Mexican troops in the

Sierra Madre. Some undoubtedly believed that if he had been with Juh, he would have seen the enemies coming. He also had the support of the bravest men in the tribe, Chihuahua, Jelikine, and the promising young Chihenne chief Kaetenae. Tribal members, except Loco and his people, forgot his role in the disaster at Alisos Creek and Bosque San Diego. For now, they needed someone to keep them safe in the Sierra Madre, and his record of accomplishment since García's fight was good. Perhaps referring to these times, the Chokonen Kayitah put it best: "Geronimo was never really a chief but he became one because of all the trouble."[41]

Meanwhile, for the next month the Chiricahuas remained in the mountains near the headwaters of the Bavispe River. Throughout February and early March, Colonel Lorenzo García worked to marshal supplies and troops for a powerful strike against the Chiricahuas at Guaynopa. It was an impressive undertaking—a four-prong operation of 600 men (each division containing 150 soldiers) that converged on Guaynopa in mid-March. His army penetrated the Sierra Madre from several directions: one from the south near Tarachi; the second from the southwest at Chipajora (north of Sahuaripa); the third from the west near Nácori Chico; and the fourth from the northeast at Bavispe. If García could surprise the Apaches and execute his plan, the Apaches' only outlet for escape would be east into Chihuahua, where Terrazas was patrolling. He undoubtedly hoped to seal off that avenue once his army came together at Guaynopa.

Stocked with a two-week supply of rations, García left Nácori Chico on March 10. He took several precautions en route, forbidding fires and sending out scouts, hoping to locate and surprise the enemy. Recent snowfall hindered the command and made for uncomfortable nights in the mountains. His command reached Guaynopa first. The other units of his operation arrived soon after. But he encountered no Chiricahuas. When his army made the perilous climb to the brink of the canyon, it found only four empty rancherías and the trails of Indians steering to the north. Ironically, on its second-day march from Bavispe, this detachment, commanded by Emilio Kosterlitzky, which had also left on March 10, 1883, must have just missed crossing the trail of a one-hundred-man Chiricahua war party bound for Sonora and Arizona.[42]

Betzinez was wrong in his explanation that the chiefs organized the war party simply because they "were not satisfied to live in peace."[43] Actually, the leaders had several motives, some pragmatic, some ideological, and some survival based. The same morning that Kosterlitzky left Bavispe, the war party, which had spent the previous night south of Huachinera, separated into two groups. Their food supplies low, Geronimo and Chihuahua led one party of seventy-five to eighty warriors that planned to raid Ures and other towns along the Sonora River. Chatto and Bonito led the second group of twenty-six of the hardiest young men. They planned a lightning-quick invasion of Arizona to obtain ammunition, weapons, and the latest news about San Carlos.[44]

Chatto's raiders spared few in their path. Most of these men had fought the Mexicans in the January battle. Though they had plenty of sixteen-shot Winchesters, they were dangerously short of cartridges after the two battles at Sátachi Falls and the Mata Ortiz fight at Chocolate Pass. Other prominent warriors on this raid were Naiche, Cathla, Shoie, Dutchy, Beneactinay, Atelnietze, and Mangas. In addition, two teenage boys, Gooday and Haozous, volunteered as dikohes, or novices, probably to assist their uncle Mangas. Last, but not least, Peaches, a Cibecue Apache who had lost his family in the García fight, went along. His objective differed from those of the others. He hoped the raiding party would get close enough to the reservation for him to return to his people. The dependents of these two groups remained at Bugatseka with Loco and fourteen male survivors from Victorio's band.

Chatto's raiders crossed the mountains south of Huachinera and made a beeline northeast. After resting several days, on March 18, 1883, they ambushed three men near Cananea, killing two Mexicans and one American and taking nine horses. They also raided Hohstadt's ranch at Janaverachi and took more horses. The next day they waylaid a party of five men south of the customs house, killing two Americans and making off with two horses, two mules, and two pistols. Their killing spree in Sonora over, Chatto and Bonito led their now mounted men across the border on March 20, 1883.[45]

Once in Arizona, they struck a charcoal camp at sunset, March 21, quickly murdering four unarmed men who were cutting trees and burning charcoal. A few men, including P. R. Childs, fled to nearby tents, gathered their arms, and wisely took positions behind trees and bushes. The Chiricahuas tried to coax them out of the tents but without success. Then they opened fire, sending a hail of bullets into the tent. Still no response from the Americans. Two brave warriors, Beneactinay and Peaches, decided to charge the tent. Childs took aim at the first man and killed him. Seeing his friend fall, Peaches fled out of range. Dan Thrapp points out that Childs had unwittingly picked the right man on whom to display his marksmanship, at least as far as southwesterners were concerned, for if Childs had slain Peaches, he would have altered the course of Arizona's history.[46]

Childs hastened to Fort Huachuca with the news. Captain Daniel Madden, with a company of cavalry, returned to the camp with Childs. He recognized the corpse of Beneactinay as did several of his men. Madden messaged Crook: "He was well known as a Chiricahua Indian and a good scout."[47] Citizens arrived from Tombstone and Charleston. Enraged over the murders of unarmed men, they decapitated the corpse and carried the head in a sack back to Charleston, where they mounted it on a pole for public viewing.[48] They brought the scalp to a hotel in Tombstone with its "ears and eyebrows."[49]

Meanwhile, the next day (March 22, 1883), the raiders headed toward the Whetstone Mountains. They took at least seven more innocent lives on their way north. En route, in two separate attacks, they ambushed a Mexican and two Americans, killing the three men. They also cut the telegraph line before their scouts reported that a heavily loaded fourteen-mule pack train was coming along the road. The ambush was quick and fatal to the four men, three Mexicans and a Frenchman named Stephen Barthand. They took what they could carry, mainly arms and ammunition, destroyed everything else, and took the mules. After a short rest in the Whetstone Mountains, they crossed the San Pedro Valley on a northeasterly course, probably reaching the northeastern tip of Little Dragoon Mountains by early morning of March 23, when they again went into camp.[50]

By noon, March 23, they were on the trail toward the Winchester Mountains. Midafternoon they approached a ranch about two miles southwest of Point of Mountain. Here, Jack Howard, a prospector and a blacksmith, was shoeing horses in his corral with M. C. James. Absorbed in their work, the two Americans, hearing a sound, looked up to see seven Chiricahuas only a few yards away. Why the Apaches had approached without firing remains a mystery; Howard responded instinctively by grabbing his rifle and shooting one man off his horse. The other Indians picked him up and fled behind some large boulders in the nearby hills. Then the Americans saw twenty Apaches driving a herd of 100 to 125 horses and mules within range of the corral. Howard snapped several rounds at them without effect.[51]

Apache accounts mention Beneactinay's death but nothing about a wounded warrior. It therefore seems likely that Howard's shot had grazed the man, perhaps on the side of the head, knocking him unconscious from his horse. This warrior may have been Chatto himself, for years later he revealed that he had been wounded three times in battle. At some time between 1881 and 1883, he was with Naiche when an enemy's bullet knocked him out for twenty minutes before Naiche "brought him to." Though we will never know for sure whether Howard had wounded Chatto, the facts suggest this possibility.[52]

In any event, a few hours later they emerged from the high country at Point of Mountain and charged two mounted men riding on the road near Willcox. As in the case of the earlier victims, the presence of hostile Apaches startled them. Chatto's raiders dispatched them quickly and took cover in the hills, probably the Peloncillo range north of Steins. That night they continued toward Whitlock Cienega and the Peloncillo Mountains.[53] As the party went into camp, Cathla and Dutchy left to see Merejildo Grijalva, the Chiricahuas' former captive (one of the few whites whom they trusted), "to find out all [they could] about the agency" in case they had to surrender. This was the first indication that their tragic defeats in Mexico had aroused yearnings of peace in most of the tribe.[54]

It was about this time that Crook began to receive reports from the south about Chatto's raid. From Cloverdale, in southwestern New Mexico, Captain Crawford's Apache scouts were patrolling a narrow sector above and below the border. They thought the Chiricahuas would take advantage of the Peloncillo Mountain corridor if they crossed the line. But Chatto's raiders had penetrated the line over one hundred miles west of Cloverdale. The military command also appeared dumbfounded. No one seemed sure whether the raiders were from Mexico or were absent marauders from San Carlos. Crook was at Prescott, and only one commander of the forts south of the Gila had the proper information to recognize the significance of this raid. That officer was Captain Madden, who had four companies of cavalry at Huachuca, but he dropped the ball by not pursuing the hostiles. Likewise, garrisons at Bowie and Grant, if informed about these hostilities, could have had patrols in the field following the Indians.

The army's paralysis must have perplexed Chatto and Bonito. Their surprise attack and the speed of their incursion had added to the confusion and logistical breakdown. Information filtering north to Crook left him a few days behind the movements of the raiders. In fact, it was not until Agent Wilcox counted the Apaches at San Carlos on March 25 and verified that all were present that Crook realized the raiders were Chiricahuas from Mexico. The next day he responded to the secretary of the interior that the Chiricahuas "were the worst band of Indians in this country." As far as he was concerned, he would be "glad to hear [when] the last of the Chiricahuas were underground."[55]

At this crucial stage, Crook finally received some good fortune. Chatto's raiders had rested in the Peloncillo Mountains all day on March 24. At sunset they had gathered their herd and raced north on an all-night trip, planning to meet Dutchy and Cathla north of today's Duncan. By the morning of March 25, which was Easter Sunday, they stopped at Ash Springs in the upper San Simon Valley. Later that day they moved east into the hills, where most of the band slept, exhausted after an arduous eighteen-hour trip. Chatto and a few men left camp to "watch for anyone in pursuit." The next morning Peaches decided to return home to his relatives at San Carlos.

He gave two versions of his departure. In his first interview with Americans fewer than ten days later, he claimed to have made a daring nighttime escape when the warriors were sleeping: "[I] took off [my] moccasins, and crept up into the rocks and walked on them so they could not find my trail." At least that was what he told Lieutenant Davis, undoubtedly because he feared reprisals if he had told the truth—especially because he had admitted freely that he had been an active participant in the raid until Beneactinay's death.[56] His second version, given fifty years later to anthropologist Grenville Goodwin, seems closer to the truth. With his family and best friend (Beneactinay) dead, he told the Chiricahuas that he wanted to return to his people on the reservation. According to him, some Chiricahuas opposed it, but one chief said, "Let him go if he wants to see his people again." Family ties were important to Apaches, and every man could relate to Peaches' desire to rejoin his kinfolk. Who was the understanding leader who approved of Peaches' decision? This man was undoubtedly Bonito, the leader of the fighters at Chocolate Pass. Like Peaches he was by birth a Western Apache. Bonito commanded the respect of all the warriors. Even if there was dissent, no one dared to argue with him. So they gave Peaches "a gun, horse and saddle and he went back to San Carlos."[57] This version agrees with what Betzinez heard, that Peaches said, "Now I have lost my best friend [Beneactinay] I cannot go on. I am going to leave you and return to my old home country." The Chiricahuas gave him supplies and let him go.[58]

Meanwhile, Lieutenant Britton Davis had stationed "scouts and secret police all over the reservation. If hostiles come here [my] Indians will attack them at once and will kill all hostiles coming in. None have been on the reservation as of yet."[59] Soon after Davis penned this dispatch to headquarters, Peaches sneaked into the camp of Nadiskay, a White Mountain leader. Davis's Apache police soon heard of his presence (though they were unsure of the number). Early morning, March 31, 1883, Davis and some one hundred scouts and police marched twelve miles to Nadiskay's camp. By 3:00 A.M. April 1, 1883, Davis had his men in place. At daybreak, the scouts arrested Peaches and

Nadiskay (for harboring a hostile) without a struggle.[60] The next day Peaches revealed valuable information about the raid, even informing Davis by which route the raiders planned to return to Mexico. Yet Peaches was likely aware that this information was useless, for by then the raiders had already crossed the border.[61]

After Peaches left, Chatto and Bonito split up and struck at separate targets on Monday, March 26. One band looted a mining camp northwest of York's ranch, riddling three men with bullets; the second band picked up stock along the road between Clifton and Lordsburg. Incredibly, though the raiders had been in Arizona for almost one week, Colonel Mackenzie initially believed the hostiles "were a small force of renegade Apaches from San Carlos." In response, he ordered out four companies of cavalry, two from Fort Bayard and two from Fort Cummings, to intercept the Apaches if they headed south.

That evening Cathla and Dutchy rejoined their associates after their visit with Merejildo Grijalva, who apparently agreed to act as a go-between if they decided to surrender. But the raiders still had a long distance to travel until they reached the border. And, in their minds, they were still at war. The next morning, one band slew five more men at a stage station seven miles south of York's ranch. Then they rode into New Mexico, where later that day, near today's Virden, seven more persons fell victim to their Winchesters.[62] By the evening of Tuesday, March 27, Chatto's raiders found sanctity in the Burro Mountains, a familiar area that Chatto called Neb-kei-ya-den-de, meaning "Home Place" or "Land of Many Indians," referring to where Chatto had lived as a boy with Mangas Coloradas in the 1840s and 1850s.[63]

To this point, Chatto and Bonito's raid had created unrest and indignation among the citizens, uproar in the local press, and a general feeling that the military was powerless to do anything. Their victims were tough frontiersmen—miners, ranchers, and merchants who accepted the risk of operating in Apacheria. Public perception would dramatically change the next day after an Apache ambush resulted in the brutal killing of a wife and a husband, and the captivity of their small son. The reverberations were felt throughout the country.

Judge Hamilton C. McComas, his beautiful wife, Juniata, and their six-year-old son, Charley, were traveling along the road from Silver City to Lordsburg on March 28, 1883. Though the judge had heard the news about Apache raids in Arizona, he was not much worried. As historian Marc Simmons notes, he was a "fearless" man who had made several trips between the two towns, which "undoubtedly lulled [him] into a false sense of security."

Juniata had never accompanied her husband on these journeys, but reports of the panoramic scenery in the Burro Mountains intrigued her. And the spring-time weather made it an attractive time to go with her husband. At noon Wednesday, March 28, 1883, the judge brought his buckboard to a halt in Thompson Canyon, where he had seen a large walnut tree that offered perfect shelter for a picnic lunch. Minutes after beginning to eat lunch, the judge saw a few Apaches, the advance scouts of Chatto's raiders. At once, he and his family headed for the buckboard. He frantically turned it around, hoping that the Apaches would not pursue. But there was no mercy in their hearts; the raid's objectives were ammunition and plunder, and a man and a woman traveling alone in this isolated country were easy pickings.

The advance party, which probably included Atelnietze, a relative of Na-iche, shot the judge before he could gain any speed. He then jumped from the buckboard, taking his Winchester and a box of cartridges, imploring his wife to take the reins and flee with Charley. By this time, Chatto had ridden up with more men, and McComas fell mortally wounded near some bushes along the road. Juniata drove the buckboard about three hundred yards before an Apache bullet cut down the lead horse. Gamely, she jumped from the wagon, intending to grab Charley and flee. But one Chiricahua rode up behind her and with the butt of his rifle crushed her skull above the right ear. Then he finished her off with two more blows, probably with a pistol, to the head. Charley witnessed these frightful events, which probably left him "mute with shock."[64] He never recovered from the trauma. Six months later, Naiche ad-mitted that Charley had "taken a great fancy with my wife and stayed with her. . . . He could talk very little. We thought he had very little sense."[65]

Two warriors argued over who would take Charley McComas. As the dis-agreement heated up, Bonito and Naiche rode up with the rest of their men. Bonito, decisive as always, settled the affair by taking Charley onto his horse and securing him with a lariat to his body. While this was going on, the other men ransacked the buckboard and stripped the bodies, taking jewelry and cash.[66] By Chiricahua custom, the slayer of Judge McComas took his Win-chester rifle, colt revolver, and cartridges.[67] The raiders were on their way in ten to twelve minutes.

News of the massacre shocked residents of southwestern New Mexico, especially citizens of Lordsburg and Silver City. The two companies of the Fourth Cavalry under Captain William A. Thompson and a militia group from Shakespeare, a mining settlement in the Pyramid range two miles south-west of Lordsburg, had gone toward Steins Peak in the Peloncillo Mountains.

They hoped to ambush the Chiricahuas before they entered Mexico. The two cavalry companies under Lieutenant Colonel George Forsyth had marched west but missed the raiders. Chatto and Bonito had selected a route that provided less cover but would allow them to travel faster with their stolen herd. By mid-morning, March 29, they were close to the Animas Mountains. Here the main body went into camp. They were about twenty-five miles north of the border.

One chief, probably Chatto, took four men and doubled back to see whether troops followed. They were pleasantly surprised when they scanned the horizon with their binoculars and saw no pursuit. But they did see two men in a mule-drawn wagon beginning to ascend the gradual incline that led across a cluster of hills from Playas Valley into the Animas Valley. Bob Anderson and John Devine were conducting supplies and ammunition to a ranch in the Animas Mountains. The Chiricahuas fired a volley, striking both men, inflicting serious but not fatal wounds. The mules with the wagon stampeded toward the Apaches. The Americans watched helplessly as the Indians cut the harnesses and packed a large stock of ammunition, provisions, and eleven bottles of whiskey on the backs of the mules. The five Indians returned to their camp, literally in good spirits.[68]

The next day, as the Apaches rested their stock and drank some whiskey, either Chatto or Bonito must have examined San Luis Pass, their normal passageway into Mexico from the Animas Mountains. It was a fortunate move, for Captain Emmet Crawford, with a company of Apache scouts, had bivouacked in this remote area, cut off from communications. And because Lieutenant Davis had not then captured Peaches, Crawford had no idea that Chatto planned to return by San Luis Pass. With this knowledge, the chiefs altered their route, deciding to make a beeline toward Antelope Springs. The downside was they faced a thirty-mile stretch over mostly flat, open ground until they reached shelter in the Enmedio Mountains.[69] En route, on March 31, 1883, they claimed the last victim of their raid, a freighter named L. G. Raymond. Six days later they reached their base camp. They had acquired what they wanted and needed: guns, ammunition, provisions, and stock. All had come at a price, of course, the loss of Beneactinay and the defection of Peaches. For now, the men were relieved to be home with their families.[70]

Chatto had sent two men ahead to alert the camp that they were coming. Arriving shortly before the return of Geronimo and Chihuahua's war party, they also brought the sad news of Beneactinay's death. Betzinez was naturally distraught over the loss of his cousin, who had been with his family for much of the previous year. Beneactinay was also the son-in-law of Chihuahua, who, on seeing Betzinez' sorrow, tried to console him: "Young man, don't grieve too much over the loss of this beloved relative of ours. He was a very brave warrior."[71]

His cousin's death dampened what should have been a joyous celebration for Betzinez, for Geronimo's war party in Sonora had enjoyed tremendous success with a loss of only a few men. After splitting from Chatto on March 10, Geronimo's band of eighty men, all on foot, crossed the Bavispe River below Oputo and followed the old Apache trail that ran southwest across the valley between Moctezuma and Tepache. North of Batuc, they waded the Moctezuma River. By March 14, they had passed Pastoria, where they had ambushed a pack train in January. Betzinez mentioned that Mexicans near Baviacora took cover in the mountains as they saw the Apaches crossing the Sonora River. Sonoran reports from Baviacora verify his account, establishing this date at March 18, 1883. When Mexicans came upon Apaches butchering five steers, the Indians headed "into the high country."[72] Mexican National Guard troops saw them, but the presence of eighty Chiricahuas made the soldiers' decision easy. They abandoned pursuit. Two men returning north to Sinoquipe estimated the Apaches at one hundred warriors.[73]

To this point, they had carried out few raids. Geronimo and Chihuahua now decided to steal horses to mount the band, then attack every ranch and village they came upon.[74] On March 21 they assaulted a ranch owned by Al Felows, northeast of Ures, killing seven people, including two women. That same day they assaulted Carbo, a railroad station, killing several, perhaps as many as a dozen in all. Sidney De Long, former post sutler at Fort Bowie, described the reaction from Hermosillo as "panic stricken. No one will leave town or get off the railroad."[75]

Having encountered feeble resistance, the chiefs embarked on an ambitious plan to carry their raid southwest of Ures. According to Sonoran reports, the Chiricahuas divided into two groups. Betzinez, however, claims they stayed together in one powerful force, searching for pack trains but having to settle for attacking ranches and the suburbs of towns. At one city, Betzinez thought Álamos, Geronimo, and Chihuahua decided to put on a show of force. In a dramatic scene right out of a Hollywood movie, the warriors lined up in a row, shoulder to shoulder, as if they were going to charge the town. They could see the inhabitants climbing onto the roofs of their flat homes. But that is where the similarity in the scripts ends. Apaches rarely launched frontal assaults that could cost needless lives. Instead, they simply rode away.

By early April they decided to depart for the long trek home. They had accumulated an immense herd, which they drove east, across the Moctezuma River north of Batuc. Along the way, on April 4, 1883, fifteen warriors, probably the rearguard, battled two Americans southwest of Moctezuma. Joseph Frisby and his partner stood their ground, killing and scalping a "heavy-set Apache," wounding one or two others, and putting the rest to flight. On April 7, 1883, Geronimo and Chihuahua ambushed a pack train between Oputo and Bavispe, killing a man from Huásabas and taking loads of dry goods, blankets, and whiskey. That night, as the younger warriors did sentry duty, Betzinez watched in amazement as the older men got drunk. The next morning, despite their hangovers, Geronimo and Chihuahua gave orders to move out.[76]

Geronimo and Chihuahua's war party had brutally slain everyone in their path. Estimates vary as to the number of their victims. One report in Tucson, citing a dispatch from Hermosillo, claimed that Apaches had slain 93 persons, 27 of whom were Americans.[77] Another unconfirmed report put the dead at 115 men, women, and children.[78] Whatever the numbers, the Chiricahua war party had inflicted great loss of life and property on Sonora, leaving embattled state officials embarrassed. The ease of the band's movements from the Sierra Madre to Sonora's largest cities and the abject horror and devastation they left in their wake had allowed the press, on both sides of the border, to spew caustic criticism on military and civil officials.

The Chiricahuas judged their two forays as successes; they had met the goals of their raids—new guns, ammunition, provisions, and stock. In addition, they had opened the window to negotiations at San Carlos with their trusted friend Merejildo Grijalva. And, to top it all off, they had a blue-eyed, blond, angelic-looking six year-old-boy who could be used as a bargaining chip if they decided to surrender. Yet, in their myopic view from their sheltered seclusion in the Sierra Madre, they failed to realize the uproar their raids had evoked in both the United States and Mexico. And they probably had no idea that General Crook was planning to invade their strongholds in the Sierra Madre.

14

COOL HAND CROOK

We will catch those Chiricahuas inside forty days. And we did.
General Crook to Apache scouts

On December 23, 1882, Crawford enlisted 125 Apache scouts at San Carlos. The original plan called for him to leave for the border in ten days, but unclear circumstances forced a delay until early February. His force consisted of one hundred scouts (he assigned the other twenty-five to remain with Lieutenant Britton Davis at San Carlos) and two Chiricahua women who, with Eskebenti, had escaped from the hostiles the previous summer. Among the scouts was Bylas (the nephew of the man Victorio had slain in 1880); John Rope, a White Mountain Apache who left behind an account; and Na-nod-di, a Western Apache who had also escaped from the Chiricahuas the previous summer. Crawford's command remained nearly invisible to the surrounding communities, carefully avoiding settlements and public roads, until the captain bivouacked at Guadalupe Canyon about February 18, 1883. They had seen only one white man during their journey south.[1]

Crawford explained Crook's goals in a private letter to his friend Captain Charles Morton: "The object is to get what Chiricahuas we can to come in first and then to go for the balance." If necessary, however, the general was prepared to lead troops into Mexico to resolve the problem.[2] Along the way, Crawford received a message from General Crook informing him that Mexican troops had defeated the Chiricahuas (the attack on Juh's camp), which might force some Chiricahuas to move north. "Keep a sharp lookout and deal them a death blow, if possible," advised Crook.[3] Crawford immediately sent out twenty scouts to examine the Animas Mountains, but they found nothing. In March he dispatched small reconnoitering parties into Mexico. They also had no luck. Finally, in early April, he dispatched a group of six scouts that included John Rope, Na-nod-di, and the two Chiricahua women. One was called Nah-je-ke (Nosey), because her husband had cut off the tip of her nose, a punishment for infidelity. They went south from Guadalupe Canyon and camped near the Tupper battleground at the Enmedio Mountains.

Na-nod-di was skittish, justifiably concerned for his life, for his father-in-law had sent out a party to kill him after he and his wife had sneaked away from the Sierra Madre. Rope and the other scouts distrusted him, believing he would turn tail rather than fight. They vowed to shoot him if he tried to desert. The two women went out on their own near Carretas. The sergeant of scouts told them, "If you see [Chiricahuas] tell them to go to the captain [Crawford] at Guadalupe Canyon as he wants to meet them and make peace." After an absence of eight days, they returned empty-handed.[4]

Crawford had clearly grown weary of this assignment, pessimistic about finding the hostiles because "his scouts are afraid of both the Chiricahuas and the Mexican troops." He lamented, in an unofficial letter to Captain Morton, "I suppose George [Crook] will keep me down here for some time yet." Isolated along the border, cut off from communications, Crawford had no idea that Crook was then preparing for an unprecedented strike at the Chiricahuas below the border. And little did he know that he, as Crook's most trusted field officer, would be in the middle of it all.[5]

The success enjoyed by the two Chiricahua war parties in March 1883 provided Crook with a mandate for action. With the Chiricahuas living securely in the Sierra Madre Mountains, the decisive commander understood that a strong show of force in their strongholds was the only way either to defeat the hostiles or to convince them to return to San Carlos. Historian Dan Thrapp concluded that four requirements must be in place before the general could consider a foray into Mexico. He needed, first, a reason to launch military action, and Chatto's war party provided it; second, specific information about the Chiricahuas' location, and a trustworthy guide to take him there (Peaches filled that bill); third, permission from his superiors to launch operations in another country (after Chatto's deadly raid, that was a given); and, finally, cooperation from Mexican authorities, or at least an agreement not to interfere with his campaign.[6]

The last condition remained the sole obstacle to the plan, and this Crook hoped to resolve with a personal visit to Mexico. Mexican officials in Sonora and Chihuahua, who had been trying to wipe out the Chiricahuas for the previous eighteen months, were receptive to his message. These frontier authorities, charged with protecting the northern settlements from Apache raids, were less suspicious of Americans than were federal officials in Mexico. The previous year Mexico and the United States had signed a reciprocal rights treaty on July 29, 1882, that allowed troops in either country to cross the border in "hot pursuit." Crook knew that his plan failed to meet the definition of "hot pursuit" and he needed both permission and cooperation from Sonora and Chihuahua to carry it out.[7]

Thus, on March 30, 1883, the day before Chatto's raiders returned to Mexico, General George Crook informed his superiors of his plans to consult with Colonel Mackenzie in New Mexico and Mexican military leaders in Sonora and Chihuahua. The next day, General Sherman ordered Crook to pursue the Chiricahuas "regardless of department or national lines." No one could have conceived of the type of operation Crook had in mind.[8]

Crook's first stop would be Sonora. Sonora had always been the most remote and independent of Mexico's states. Recognizing this, Mexico's president Porfirio Díaz ensured that his followers ruled the state. Though apprehensive about American designs and influence, Sonora's rulers saw the financial stimulus to be derived from Americans' capital and investment.[9]

On April 9, 1883, Crook, his aide, Lieutenant John G. Bourke, and First Lieutenant Gustav J. Fiebeger arrived at Guaymas via the Sonora Railway Company line. Crook explained his plan to General José Carbo, who gave tacit approval to the operation. Officially, he lacked the authority to grant Crook what he wanted (pursuing the Apaches into Mexico) "without regard to trails." But he assured the American general that he shared his views on the Apache problem and "would do all in his power to aid in their subjugation." This was a remarkable concession to Crook, for he had clearly disclosed that a central part of his strategy was to employ Apache scouts to catch the Chiricahuas in the Sierra Madre. Crook had sold Sonoran military leaders on the scouts' vital role. Sonora's chief concern was how to distinguish Crook's Apache scouts from the hostiles. So Crook agreed to have them wear red headbands, a custom he continued for the duration of the Apache Wars. Next, he went to Chihuahua, met with Governor Mariano Samaniego, former governor Luis Terrazas, and General Ramon Raguero, and reached a similar understanding. Crook was ready for action.[10]

The Chiricahuas were oblivious to Crook's intentions. It never dawned on them that the general might lead American troops and Apache scouts on an expedition into their strongholds. While war plans dominated Crook's thoughts, the Chiricahuas went about their business of staying alive in the Sierra Madre. In mid-April, after the two war parties had returned to their base camp at

Bugatseka, fifteen warriors left on a stock raid at Oputo. They returned to camp with one hundred head of cattle, which they butchered the same day. A few days later, about April 20, 1882, a grass fire ignited. Before the villagers could contain it, a "great cloud was billowing high above the Sierra Madre." Fearing this would attract enemies, they immediately broke camp, moving northwest some twenty miles to another mountain southeast of Huachinera, though Betzinez in his account mistakenly placed the camp west of that town.[11]

Cracks in the coalition were beginning to show. The peace bloc, without Juh's domineering presence, was gaining more influence. Once settled in their new camp, the chiefs decided to send peace emissaries to San Carlos. They dispatched Dutchy and Gooday to see Merejildo Grijalva, who would act as their go-between with officials on the reservation. Both were members of Chatto and Bonito's raiding party. Their selection suggests that the peace bloc was now led by Bonito, Loco, and Mangas, each favoring a return to San Carlos, for Dutchy was a member of Bonito's group and Gooday a grandson of Loco and a nephew of Mangas. They left on April 22, 1883.[12]

Careful to avoid the Apache scouts patrolling the border, Dutchy and Gooday arrived at the ranch of Merejildo Grijalva about April 29, 1883. The next day Grijalva escorted them to Fort Thomas, where they met Lieutenant Colonel Andrew W. Evans, who failed to grasp the significance of this event. With Crook absent along the border, he shuffled them off, with a brief note, to Lieutenant Parker West at San Carlos: "They profess to be [from] the hostile camp in Chihuahua and to have been sent to see Agent Wilcox, with a view to returning to the reservation. You can listen to their story."[13] Britton Davis, who would eventually come to like and trust Dutchy, interviewed them. With Crook already in Mexico, and out of communication range, Davis had no choice but to place them under guard in the agency's calaboose. Dutchy, however, provided valuable insight into the Chiricahuas' state of mind and news about Charley McComas. The Apaches, except Juh, were eager to surrender. And Charley McComas was alive and well in Bonito's camp.[14]

As it turned out, Dutchy and Gooday had just avoided running into a strong force of 136 Mexican troops under Colonel Lorenzo García. His command had left Moctezuma on April 20, 1883, and easily cut the trail left by the Oputo raiders returning to the Sierra Madre. According to Betzinez, after the fire at Bugatseka, the chiefs had sent out scouts because they feared that the billows of smoke would draw attention to their location. On April 24, the scouts returned with news that Mexican troops would reach the canyon floor below the village by noon the next day. The whole tribe (except Juh) was together, thus putting their strength at one hundred warriors. The chiefs concealed their best fighters in outcrops "astride the trail." They deployed other warriors along the ridge with orders to ambush the Mexicans as they neared the top. Expecting the fusillade to force a chaotic retreat, the warriors concealed in lower positions would launch their attack as the Mexicans scrambled down the hillside. Meanwhile, a third group of fighters took positions at a "steep slope at the head of the canyon nearby with orders to prepare and roll rocks down on the enemy."

One detachment of eighty-six men wound its way, single file, in a methodical climb along the switchbacks, unaware of the impending danger. García sent the second force, some fifty men under Colonel Torres, on a flanking maneuver to the left. The warriors allowed García's men to approach within twenty feet of the mesa. Then they blasted them from their breastworks. The Mexicans retreated in a panic, leaving them vulnerable to Apache fighters on their right flank below them. Then the warriors at the crest began to roll rocks down on troops in the lower positions. Betzinez recalled that the noise from the canyon was "tremendous, what with the shooting, the yelling, and the crashing of large boulders." He credited the Mexicans for a courageous fight but thought the ambush had worked perfectly. After the initial retreat, García regrouped his men, and a sniping duel lasted for another two hours, when dusk arrived and the Mexicans retired from the bloody canyon. He had lost four killed and seven wounded; his men had fired 2,876 rounds, killing, he believed, eleven warriors and wounding many more. To this point, García's account generally agrees with Betzinez's recollections in terms of the time and duration of the battle, the Chiricahuas' division of forces, and the ferocity of the fight. The reliable Betzinez, however, did not admit to any Apache fatalities, a detail that was corroborated by what Chiricahuas later told Bourke and Crook.[15]

In the aftermath of the battle, a group of twenty-one Chihennes, mainly close relatives of Loco, including his wife, son, and grandson-in-law Tsedikizen, the former scout who had left San Carlos with Dutchy the previous summer, had become separated from the main band.[16] They decided to head north for the reservation. Tsedikizen tried to persuade Loco to accompany them, but he declined, telling them "he was too old to travel." He urged them to go on without him. Tsedikizen, reputed to have Power over guns, for in battle he could dodge enemy bullets, called on all his skills and Power to lead the group north to San Carlos, which they reached a month after leaving the Sierra

Madre.[17] After surrendering, he told Lieutenant West that they had followed the Peloncillo Mountain corridor from the border to the Gila, which meant they had entered New Mexico about twenty-five miles east of where Crook had crossed the border. They knew nothing of the general's operations. They also declared that Geronimo was the overall leader of the hostiles, confirming other reports that he had replaced Juh.[18]

In an ominous sign that caught Lieutenant Davis by surprise, Agent Wilcox inexplicably refused to take responsibility for the Chihennes. Instead, he suggested that they be kept by the military and be punished, a recommendation designed to undermine Crook and sabotage his plans. Of course Wilcox had no explanation for why the military should punish Loco's family, whom the hostiles had abducted from the reservation. His unexpected defiance perplexed Arizona's assistant adjutant general, James P. Martin, who ordered West to hold Loco's relatives and issue rations to them until the general returned from Mexico.[19]

While the chiefs in Mexico waited to hear news of Dutchy's mission, they held another caucus and decided to dispatch two parties on raids against Sonora and Chihuahua. The first group's objective (about twenty warriors under Chihuahua and his brother Ulzana) was stock; the second band's objective (thirty-six warriors led by Geronimo, Chatto, Bonito, Naiche, Kaetenae, Zele, and Jelikine) was captives, which they hoped to exchange for their people held by Chihuahua. The Sonoran raiders left three or four days before Geronimo, whose men left camp about May 6, 1883. Neither band was aware that General George Crook had by then penetrated the northern foothills of the Sierra Madre. Guided by their old friend Peaches, his command was moving stealthily and steadfastly toward what the Chiricahuas believed was their impregnable stronghold at Bugatseka.[20]

Crook had organized a formidable force of 193 Apache scouts under Chief of Scouts Al Sieber, Captain Emmet Crawford, and Lieutenant Charles Gatewood, supported by one company of 42 cavalrymen under Captain Adna Chaffee, and a pack train of 266 mules handled by 76 civilian packers.[21] Among the Indian scouts, Crook had Peaches, a man familiar with the Sierra Madre. A half-century later, Peaches recalled his first meeting with General Crook:

> General Crook telegraphed me to come right down to Willcox where
> he was. Al-chi-se had gone to General Crook and told him that he
> wanted me to go with him and his scouts on this campaign against the

Hai-a [Chiricahuas] because I had already been all over that country in Mexico and knew it [well]. So I went down to Willcox and reported to General Crook. He said he wanted me to guide his party down into Mexico and asked me if I knew where the Hai-a would be now. I told them that they ought to be in a certain place and if they were not there, I would know where else to look for them.[22]

The general also had two White Mountain men who had been with the hostiles, Na-nod-di and probably Eskebenti, both familiar with the incredibly rugged country south and east of Huachinera. And Toclanny, the only Chiricahua man to remain on the reservation, also joined up.[23]

By late April, Crook had assembled the entire force along the border at John Slaughter's San Bernardino ranch, formerly a famous Spanish hacienda until the Chiricahuas had driven the occupants away in the late 1830s. Here Crook held a meeting with the Apache scouts, seeking not only their opinion about capturing the Chiricahuas, but also expressing his intense determination and supreme confidence in the outcome. Peaches, who sat beside Crook, recalled that some scouts were pessimistic because they believed the task "was too hard a job." Another scout, a sergeant named Tu-is-ba, declared that the "Chiricahuas could hide like coyotes and could smell danger a long way like wild animals." Crook, after patiently listening, simply said, "All right. You will see. We will catch these Hai-a inside forty days." Crook then sent Peaches with a small squad of scouts into Mexico.[24]

On May 1, 1883, Crook's detachment entered Mexico. The first three days, they traveled over open ground as they headed for the bend of the Bavispe River southeast of today's Colonia Morelos. The only signs of life were a few turkeys and deer; that part of Sonora had been uninhabited since the mid-1830s. Peaches led them along the Bavispe River, passing by Bavispe, Bacerac, Huachinera, and then pausing at Teserobabi, another deserted ranch. They were now going to leave the river and begin a climb to the southeast, the region where Peaches expected to find the Chiricahuas.[25]

On May 11, 1883, Peaches told Crook that they were closing in on the favorite camping sites of the Chiricahuas. That day, the general met with his officers and scouts. They knew the trail was hot, for fresh signs were everywhere. The scouts were ready to fight, vowing to wipe out those Chiricahuas who resisted. Moreover, they were in no mood to show mercy to the incorrigible chiefs, like Juh and Geronimo, who they believed "ought to be put to death anyhow, as they would be all the time raising trouble." Crook reiterated his wish that the scouts spare the lives of the women, children, and any man who surrendered. Captain Crawford, lieutenants Gatewood and James O. Mackay, Chief of Scouts Al Sieber, Archie McIntosh, three interpreters (Mickey Free, Sam Bowman, and Severiano), with 143 Apache scouts, separated from Crook and the pack train to patrol ahead. John Rope went with Crawford, and on the morning of May 13, the command entered a pine forest that skirted occasional mountain pastures. Here "on top of a divide" they found the place where the Chiricahuas had had their camp (Crawford counted ninety-eight wickiups) at the time of García's attack. Toclanny pointed out to Rope an area where the warriors had held a war dance. From here, the Chiricahuas had split into three or four bands, one of which was Geronimo's war party, which had gone east to raid Chihuahua.[26]

Finally on May 15, Crawford's scouts (no troops were present) captured a Chokonen camp at Bugatseka.[27] Sherman Curley described the area: "The top is very rough and rocky, cut up with canyons, with lot of pine trees growing up."[28] The ranchería housed the followers of Chatto, Bonito, Naiche, and Chihuahua, who was the only chief near. He had just returned from a raid that very morning, and the rest of the men had left with Geronimo. The scouts killed several Chiricahuas, between four and nine according to various accounts, and captured five others, including a daughter of Bonito and a son of Naiche.[29] The attackers burned the camp, thirty wickiups in two clusters, and captured the herd of forty-seven horses and mules, which they packed with plunder to divide among themselves. A few Chokonens, looking on from rocky ridges, vowed to retaliate against the scouts: "All right, you are doing this way with us now, but some time we will do the same way with you." Crawford's scouts had achieved an astonishing victory. As we shall see, Crook's presence in their mountain sanctuary stunned the Chiricahuas, convincing even the most recalcitrant that they were no longer safe. Now to most of them, even San Carlos looked attractive. At least there, they might survive.[30]

But the victory came at a tragic cost. San Carlos Western Apache scouts had murdered in cold blood a Chiricahua woman (an aunt of Chihuahua) while she was trying to surrender. This act rankled in the breast of Chihuahua, who three days later told Crook, "If I was trying to make friends with someone, I would not go and raid their camp and shoot their relatives."[31] This brutal slaying led to an impetuous act of revenge by the son of the slain woman, Espida, also known as Spitty or Speedy, a hero of the García fight at Alisos Creek. "Using rocks, [he] brutally killed the small white captive Charley McComas."

The Indians never admitted the truth to Americans until years later, though enough rumors swirled around to leave some doubt as to his fate. They told Crook that the boy had run off during the attack and that they never found him, a yarn they told repeatedly in the years to come.[32]

Crook was still in a tenuous spot. After the attack, the Indians had scattered, and he had no idea what they would do next. He knew that a climactic fight to settle the matter was now impossible. Though he still had enough rations to remain in the mountains for another month, he did not relish the thought of dogging them through a country that was more difficult than he could have imagined. And now that the Chiricahuas were on guard, he was not confident of further success. Crook would have to be content with the destruction of the ranchería at Bugatseka. He understood that this was his one shot, and he decided to capitalize and exploit the cards dealt to him.

Therefore, as Thrapp concludes, Crook "now had to depend upon persuasion, diplomacy, and to some degree sheer bluff" to achieve his ultimate goal of convincing the Chiricahuas that he had come solely to take them back to San Carlos. His spirits undoubtedly improved when the oldest captive, a beautiful sixteen-year-old daughter of Bonito, with the enchanting name of Dja-na-il-tci (Antelopes Approach Her), thought that most of the chiefs would agree to return to the reservation, especially when they realized that Peaches and the Apache scouts were helping Crook. The next day, May 16, the general sent her and a companion to tell Chihuahua that he wanted to discuss peace. The day after, two women came into Crook's camp. One was a sister of Chihuahua, who told Crook her brother would come in but only if the general returned a particular white horse that the Apache scouts had captured during the attack on his camp.[33]

Crook sent the horse to Chihuahua, who made a bold and memorable entrance the morning of May 18. Wearing two revolvers on his belt and carrying a lance in his free hand, he galloped along the canyon floor through soldiers and scouts before bringing his horse to an abrupt halt in front of Crook's tent. Yet, this display of bravado masked a deep concern over the invasion of their stronghold. In truth, the attack was a devastating psychological blow to the morale of the Chiricahuas. Chihuahua thought the situation was "no good, all these scouts and soldiers here." Before leaving to gather up his people, he agreed to go to San Carlos.[34]

Small groups of Chiricahuas, at Chihuahua's urging, appeared at Crook's camp to surrender and get food. By May 19, 1883, about one hundred Indians were in. The majority identified themselves as Chokonens, which was predictable given that the scouts had captured a Chokonen ranchería.[35] Among the men was Fatty. He talked openly about his disdain for Mexicans and why he had decided to surrender. From him, the commander learned more about the loathing many Chiricahuas had for Mexicans. He told Crook that he hated Mexicans because they had killed his parents in the early 1860s. For that, "they must be repaid," he vowed. A month later, he said to Crawford that he intended to "kill Mexicans every time I see them, and chop them up into little pieces." He was pleased that they "now have guns to destroy them." Fatty explained why he came down from the mountains: "In Mexico, at the foot of the mountains, I heard footsteps. Before I went to bed, I heard footsteps. . . . I am getting tired of living in the mountains like a beast. So I want to live on the reservation. I want my wife and children to live in peace."[36]

That same day, Alchesay announced to those Chiricahuas who had surrendered that the scouts would return their horses and mules, for the women and children would need them to ride to San Carlos. This pleased the Chiricahuas, but they remained skittish because they were uncertain how Geronimo and Chatto's war party into Chihuahua would respond. "When the men get back, they may start shooting," the women warned the scouts. Hoping to prevent fighting, the women displayed white scraps of cloth around camp. There was little agreement on how the absent warriors would react.[37]

Then one of those events occurred that seemed normal to Apaches because of their relationship with their guardian spirits, and it involved Geronimo's war party in Chihuahua. On the evening of May 15, the very day the scouts had assaulted the Chiricahua ranchería, Geronimo's Power brought him a disturbing message. Jason Betzinez, who was with the raiders, recalled this remarkable story of Geronimo's clairvoyance. They were at least 120 miles from base camp (and knew nothing about Crook's presence) when they assembled to eat their evening meal. Suddenly, Geronimo proclaimed: "Men, our people whom we left at our base camp are now in the hands of U.S. troops. What shall we do?" Betzinez, close to one hundred years old when he told this story, could offer no explanation except that "I was there and saw it." Yahnozha, who was likely present, later told anthropologist Helge Ingstad that Geronimo "saw the enemy in a vision even when far away." Many of Eve Ball's and Morris Opler's informants also referred to Geronimo's ceremonial Power.[38]

The men with Geronimo unanimously decided to return to camp immediately. The only impediments to a quick return were five Mexican women, whom the Chiricahuas had captured on May 9 south of Carmen. Hoping to trade them for their families then held at Chihuahua City, Chatto and

Geronimo left on the trail a note declaring that they would bring their prisoners to Casas Grandes in fifteen days.[39]

Shortly before 9:00 A.M. on May 20, 1883, an excitement swept through Crook's camp. Geronimo's warriors had returned and were taking positions in the outcrops about one thousand feet above Crook's camp. The Western Apache scouts had seized their weapons and sought shelter behind trees. A few Chiricahua women went out toward the warriors, calling out to Kaetenae and Geronimo, assuring them that Crook only wanted peace. Finally, the chiefs asked four scouts to come up and parley. Peaches, Na-ni-lsoage, Dastine (related to Jelikine), and a Cibecue scout, Hac-ke-ha-gos-lid (a brother-in-law of Chatto), went to the Chiricahua positions and explained the situation. But the chiefs remained on edge, debating what to do. Once the scouts returned to camp, one warrior, perhaps Ahnandia, who had served as a scout with Toclanny, "raced into camp and threw his gun and belt on the ground." Then he embraced Toclanny, calling him brother, and shook hands with George Wrattan, a civilian scout with Sieber. That afternoon other Chiricahuas came in, and finally early that evening, Geronimo and other leaders came in to meet Crook. The commander was brusque, his message clear and blunt: he wanted to take them back to San Carlos, where they could live in peace.[40]

That night, the Chiricahuas held a dance in which a few of the Western Apaches participated.[41] The next morning Crook shared breakfast with Geronimo, Naiche, Jelikine, and Chatto. Geronimo later admitted that he "was much astonished to see General Crook there." He was deferential to Crook, believing him to be an omnipotent man blessed with supernatural powers, for no mere mortal, especially an American, could have invaded their sanctuary. He thought the general "was so powerful that he could command the sun, the moon, and everything."[42] Crook explained his reasons for his presence: "We had just come to look for them, and take them back with us, and not to fight with them, but to join with them like friends." Scout Curley closely watched the reaction of the Chiricahuas and noted that some of them "said all right, and others didn't say anything." Crook told Geronimo to surrender and return to the reservation or fight it out. The general continued with an astounding concession: "I am not going to take your arms from you because I am not afraid of you." At this point, according to Crook, Geronimo begged to return to the reservation.[43]

Yet Curley could sense uneasiness, and his intuition was right. Most of the chiefs, including Geronimo, were fuming and wanted vengeance. Later that day, Kaetenae and 78 others rode into camp, driving cattle stolen in

Chihuahua. By the end of the day, 229 Chiricahuas had surrendered. The next day, as Kaetenae was visiting the White Mountain scouts, a messenger summoned him to the Chiricahua camp. The chiefs planned to hold a dance that evening with the Western Apache scouts. The Chiricahuas' young women would participate by luring the scouts into their web. Then, at a prearranged signal, the warriors would rush in and kill the scouts. When Kaetenae agreed, they asked Jelikine to join the powwow.

Though not a chief, he was indisputably one of the bravest fighters in the tribe. But he was incredulous if not indignant at the treachery. He wanted nothing to do with their plan because the Cibecue band had raised him. "[These] White Mountain people are like relatives to me," he said, before leaving the council. His reluctance likely gave others second thoughts. Naiche, Chatto, and Bonito each had friends or kin with the White Mountain scouts. So Geronimo sent for Jelikine again. The shaman tried to persuade Jelikine to participate:

> My father-in-law tonight we mean to do as we told you. Whenever we
> have gone to war before, you have gone with us. But now you won't
> make up your mind to say yes or no. Jelikine answered: "I told you
> already that I would not help you do this." He was mad and started to
> walk away. In a little bit he turned back and came to the council again.
> He said, "You chiefs don't mean anything to me. I have been with you
> many times and helped you kill many Mexicans and Whites . . . and
> that is the way you got the clothes you are wearing now. I am the one
> who has killed these people for you and you have just followed behind
> me. I don't want to hear you talking this way to me again."

They held the dance that night, but Al Sieber cut it short because of the death of a scout. The Chiricahuas, if they had intended to carry out their plan, never got a chance to execute it.[44]

That same day the five Mexican women, one with a nursing baby, whom the Chiricahuas had left behind on the trail, arrived in camp. Chatto's brother Gon-altsis guided them to Crook's camp. They were a pitiful-looking group—frightened, starving, and thankful that the Virgin Mary had answered their prayers. Lieutenant Bourke assured them that the Americans would protect them. Even so, one Nednhi, a man named Washington, tried several times to bully them into moving to the Chiricahuas' camp. Finally, Bourke and several packers vowed to kill him if he touched the captives. Over the next few days, as more Chiricahuas came in (Loco and Nana brought their Chihennes in), Geronimo, Kaetenae, and Chatto left to search for Chihuahua and Juh.[45]

Chatto returned on May 26 and joined Loco and Crook for breakfast. Geronimo had sent him to ask Crook to wait four more days because the Indians were "very scattered." The chiefs did not want to leave for San Carlos until they accounted for every Chiricahua in the Sierra Madre. They still had not found Chihuahua, Juh, or a band of warriors who were "in charge of ponies and mules near the Aros River." Crook told Chatto he had to move because his supplies were running low. Two days later, Geronimo, Chatto, Chihuahua, and Kaetenae arrived with 116 Chiricahuas, augmenting the total to 384. On May 30, Geronimo and Bonito had breakfast with Crook. That morning they began their move to San Carlos. Geronimo returned on June 1 but left later that day. A White Mountain scout brought in the last group of Chiricahuas, headed by two Chokonens named Tu-n-tc-ile-sa-an (Red Water Resting), also known as Tuzzone, and Be-lin-te. With them were a few White Mountain people captured from Eagle Creek at the time of the massacre at Stevens's sheep camp. Tuzzone, a member of Chatto's band, would act as guide once they exited the Sierra Madre.[46]

On June 10, 1883, Crook reached the border with 300 Chiricahuas, including 45 men; two older band chiefs, Loco and Nana; and three fighting leaders—Bonito, Mangas, and Cathla. Crawford, when he made it to San Carlos, added the 22 members of Loco's band held at Thomas. When Dutchy and Gooday (released to Crawford's custody June 25) plus one more Apache showed up, the total reached 325 Chiricahuas.[47] Not all who had surrendered came in. Crook had rationed 384 Indians in late May, so 83 Chiricahuas had broken away. No one had heard from Juh. The other principal chiefs, Geronimo, Naiche, Chatto, Chihuahua, Kaetenae, and Zele (60 men in all) had promised to return at some unspecified date. But many members of their bands had blood relatives who had already eagerly moved to the reservation, which gave Crook some satisfaction. Though his critics would have a field day criticizing him for leaving about two hundred Chiricahuas in Mexico, the chiefs eventually kept their promises, albeit not on the timetable Crook had expected.[48]

The chiefs had assured the general that they would try to join him near San Bernardino.[49] Upon reaching Silver Creek on June 10, Crawford believed that the rest of the Chiricahuas would be "here inside three or four days."[50] John Rope said that Crook had given permission to several Chiricahuas to steal more stock in Mexico before joining Crook near San Bernardino! They had promised to come in as soon as possible.[51] While it was true that many prominent warriors remained in Mexico, Crook never gave them permission to increase their horse herd at Mexico's expense. Geronimo and the other chiefs did have every intention to come in. But they had two concerns. First, they were unable to find over one hundred of their people, in particular Juh, and they wanted to bring in every tribal member. Second, every chief had relatives in Mexican captivity, and they wanted to make one last attempt to recover them.

The evidence, however, is equivocal whether they had made these plans before leaving Crook. Naiche later revealed that he planned to accompany the general to San Carlos until several warriors persuaded him "to wait and see what could be done about the prisoners" in Mexico. Chatto concurred with Naiche, but Zele claimed that the Chiricahuas first considered this idea when Juh rejoined them about twenty days after Crook's departure. The Nednhi chief convinced the others that this was their last chance to recover their people before they went to the reservation. Likely both statements were true, for Juh was always ready to deal with the Mexicans at Casas Grandes, where he could obtain liquor. Regardless, they had clearly kept Crook in the dark about their intentions although Lieutenant Britton Davis later heard that they had promised Crook to return within "two moons." Crook, as usual, played his cards close to the vest and never officially admitted that the chiefs had given him that commitment.[52]

The general soon faced another unexpected obstacle. As he marched north from the border toward San Carlos, he learned that Agent Wilcox had refused to take charge of Loco's family a month before. One can easily imagine the reaction of the taciturn and unpretentious commander. The news astonished him. Now he telegraphed Wilcox that he had several hundred Chiricahuas who would need rations and a place to stay on the reservation. Again, in a decision that seems to defy explanation, the agent refused to accept them. Wilcox claimed that although the reservation Apaches were "happy for your success," they feared the bellicose Chiricahuas would disrupt the utopian existence that he had worked so hard to cultivate. According to him, these Apaches wanted the government to punish the Chiricahua leaders for their criminal acts and to relocate the warriors somewhere else. Yet Wilcox, the humanitarian, magnanimously consented to accept the women and children. He wired a copy of his refusal to his friend, Secretary of the Interior Teller.[53]

Despite the agent's misgivings, Crook decided to take them to San Carlos, which he expected to reach by June 20. He tried to reason with Wilcox that "it was much better to have the Chiricahuas on the reservation [than] on the warpath."⁵⁴ Though he justifiably felt betrayed by the agent, he exercised restraint in his public correspondence. Privately, however, he fumed, sarcastically describing Wilcox's deceit on the heels of his risky sortie into Mexico as a "fire in his rear."⁵⁵

What prompted Wilcox to pick a fight with the commanding general? He had probably become frustrated over Crook's unparalleled interference in Indian affairs. So a turf battle loomed, and the agent's opposition caught the military commander by surprise. However, surviving evidence is silent regarding any breach in their relationship. In fact, just three months before, Crook had defended Wilcox's performance as agent, urging Secretary Teller to support the agent or he would "most certainly regret it." Hoping it might deflect criticism directed at Wilcox, Crook consented to allow Teller to publish the letter. In late March the general again wrote Teller, praising the efficiency that had resulted from the dual control: "Our organization at San Carlos is so perfect that scarcely a pin can drop among the Indians without the fact being brought at once to our notice." The agent, he noted, "is not resting on a bed of roses. His every action is watched with malignant eyes not of Apaches but of people who have been making comfortable livings out of them."⁵⁶

John Bret Harte believes that Wilcox became emboldened to take on Crook after he prevented an invasion of San Carlos by a mob of vigilantes from Tombstone, known as the Rangers. Organized after Chatto's bloody raid, on April 23, 1883, they entered the agency seeking blood, at least until Agent Wilcox met with them and said they were free to find out for themselves whether any of his Apaches sympathized with the Chiricahuas. Wilcox had diffused the crisis, convincing the posse members that he had control of the reservation. This appeased the Rangers, and they returned to Tombstone, their honor intact. One small group did fire on an Apache of Eskiminzin's band, but fortunately without effect. The successful resolution of this situation without military assistance imbued Wilcox with confidence. It was a watershed moment, a "turning point in his administration" at San Carlos.⁵⁷

Riding high on this success, Wilcox decided to talk to the Apaches at San Carlos when he received Crook's message that the Chiricahuas were coming. They needed little encouragement to support him since Crook was then in Mexico. Wilcox's friend and superior Secretary Teller unequivocally supported Wilcox without consideration for either the terms Crook had granted the Chiricahuas or for the impact the agent's decision might have on the two hundred Apaches who remained in Mexico. He wrote to the secretary of war, Robert Todd Lincoln (the son of the former president), that the government should hold the warriors responsible for any criminal behavior. In addition, he advocated an elitist argument that he knew would be popular and compelling from a humanitarian point of view: take the children from their parents and send them to Carlisle Indian School in Pennsylvania. Lincoln wisely responded that he would not make a decision until he heard from Crook.[58]

Wilcox was far from done. Once he realized that his first salvo had only galvanized Crook, on June 16 he reiterated his position. Just in case the opposition of the Western Apaches was not reason enough, the agent cited budgetary problems and the responsibility he owed to his fellow southwesterners. Just the thought of placing the Chiricahuas at San Carlos was a "dangerous experiment," he wrote, one that will lead to a "new list of murders, rapes, child stealing, and robbery." Naturally, he offered no legitimate alternative, and none of his hyperbolic rhetoric strengthened his case. For example, there was never any record that the Chiricahuas raped their victims or their captives, as happened with some Indian tribes. Teller repeated his position to Lincoln; the Interior Department wanted no part of the Chiricahuas. Lincoln again prudently postponed a decision until he heard from Crook.[59]

The war of words was getting to Crook. In mid-June he had written that if he managed the Chiricahuas, he was confident of a "permanent peace." Two days later at Benson, after learning of Teller's position, Crook's frustration with the situation bubbled to the surface in a dispatch to his division commander, Major General John M. Schofield. The government must ration the Chiricahuas or they will "starve or go back on the warpath." Those still in Mexico will not surrender if their brethren are not "sustained" and treated well at San Carlos. And unless they come in, the fate of Charley McComas would remain unresolved. Finally, Crook called the Interior Department's bluff. (After all, they, not the War Department, were responsible for the management of American Indians.) He suggested that he would be "glad to get rid of the hard work and the responsibility their management will entail." Let the Interior Department accept its rightful responsibility. Schofield could sense Crook's frustration. He cited a letter in which Crook had boasted that his Apache policy had "always been successful, has never yet met with a failure and if allowed . . . will make the Chiricahuas' business a complete success." Schofield recommended to Washington that they "let him [Crook] work out the problem in his own way."[60]

Meanwhile, south of Willcox, Crook, Bourke, and a few aides had hitched a ride on two coaches to Tucson. The general also took the five Mexican women, whom he delivered to Mexican authorities there. Then he hastened to his headquarters at Prescott, where on his arrival on June 23, he found a telegram waiting from the Secretary Lincoln, who wanted to consult with him in person about the Chiricahuas. The general made plans for a cross-country trip.[61]

On the same day that Crook reached headquarters, Captain Crawford also arrived at San Carlos. Not surprisingly, Wilcox was in Denver (the summer's temperature at San Carlos typically recorded temperatures of well over one hundred degrees), though he had instructed his assistant to stop Crawford at the subagency. Wilcox's new attitude astonished Crawford, for when he had left to take his post at Cloverdale, the agent had come to his quarters to say that he was sorry to see Crawford leaving. Moreover, Wilcox had sent along his best wishes, hoping that Crawford would "pound thunder out of them [Chiricahuas]."[62] The night before reaching the agency, Crawford held a council with the Chiricahuas at Hawk Canyon, about twelve miles south of San Carlos. Sensing they were getting "a little uneasy," he urged them "not to believe anything they might hear upon their arrival at the agency relative to themselves either from white men or Indians." Al Sieber and one hundred scouts led the cavalcade as it crossed the Gila, followed by three hundred Chiricahuas, one hundred more scouts, four troops of cavalry, and the pack train. Scout John Rope observed that the Chiricahuas had marched through a gauntlet of Western Apaches lined up along both sides of the road to witness this historic event.[63]

An exhausted Crawford wanted only "to get something good to eat and some [new] clothes to wear." Crook had initially dismissed Wilcox's assertion that the Western Apaches did not want the Chiricahuas at San Carlos, labeling it as "bosh." Crawford decided to hear this for himself. He notified the chiefs that he would talk with them the next day.[64]

Crawford held the council in the former school, built during Tiffany's regime. Over the next two days, enduring oppressive heat that saw the thermometer climb to 115 degrees, he took testimony from twelve Western Apache chiefs (several had served as scouts in the campaign) from the White Mountain, Cibecue, San Carlos, and Tontos. One headman offering his opinion was, of all people, George, whom the Chiricahua chiefs, without exception, blamed for their September 30, 1881, outbreak. Each Western Apache leader expressed confidence and affection for General Crook. Symptomatic of their perspective were comments made by a San Carlos chief that Crook "does everything for our good." Few thought that the hostiles left in Mexico would return. The exception was a San Carlos leader named Knock-knee, who though he had no "confidence in men who step on rocks to hide their tracks" said that Kaetenae "had assured [him] that he would come in." He also believed that Naiche and Zele would return because members of their families had come in with Crawford.

The chiefs' comments showed that the tragic Camp Grant Massacre twelve years earlier remained indelibly etched in their thoughts. They held the Chiricahuas accountable for the invasion of the Tombstone Rangers. Eskinetal, a White Mountain chief, fretted that now "the citizens are mad at us [and] we are very uneasy about them." The Western Apache groups that had the least contact with the Chiricahuas, particularly the Southern and Northern Tontos, harbored the most animosity toward them. One Tonto headman, Kay-ca-say, thought they would kill anyone for an article of clothing and "always from ambuscade, for they are very treacherous." Another Tonto chief, a man named Snookes, echoed what most of the headmen had told Crawford: "If the Chiricahuas don't behave themselves and if the general says clean them out, we will do it. If they stay and behave themselves it is all right, if they have sense enough."

Their sentiments were much different from what Wilcox reported, though it was unclear which chiefs, if any, the agent had interviewed. Yet their reverence for Crook trumped whatever goodwill the agent had earned from turning back the Tombstone Rangers, especially because his frequent absences from the reservation prevented him from developing a rapport with his wards. And, of course, they had known the general much longer. Crook had risked his life to go after the Chiricahuas in Mexico, an action that won him much capital and respect from nearly every Apache on the reservation.

During the meeting, the Chiricahua chiefs and warriors had sat impassively, listening to every word. After hearing the concerns of the Western Apache leaders, Loco, Nana, Bonito, and Mangas spoke, assuring everyone present "that what they had promised to General Crook would be faithfully lived up to; that they had come back to the reservation to stay and would behave themselves. They were weary of running around the country and had no peace since they left the reservation."[65] Cathla and Fatty were also present. Years later Fatty recalled that Archie McIntosh urged him to speak up and tell the truth. He admitted that he had killed many Mexicans because they had killed most of his family. He spoke because his small band had no one to represent him with Naiche and Zele still in Mexico. Now he told Crawford he was tired of fighting and was eager to live in peace on the reservation. If asked, he would be willing to take messages to those in Mexico. The captain filed the offer away for future use.[66]

Wilcox was livid when he heard that Crawford had brought the Chiricahuas to San Carlos. On June 24 he wired Teller that the troops had forced the Chiricahuas onto the agency. He also refused to provide rations, but Crook had anticipated this and authorized Lieutenant Davis to draw stores from Fort Thomas. Crook, thin skinned when critics questioned his judgment or motives (both always beyond reproach), countered Wilcox's dispatch with a terse response: Wilcox's "report is incorrect." The commander explained that the cavalry and scouts simply served as escorts to ensure the safety of the Chiricahuas until they settled on the reservation. Even the secretary of war seemed to tire of the unnecessary controversy, writing that the Chiricahuas "were not forced on the reservation but were taken there under guard." With Crook scheduled to arrive in Washington the first week of July, Lincoln probably hoped that the crisis would be over by then.[67]

Although Crook might have felt that this controversy over turf at San Carlos had overshadowed the success of his campaign, praise for his operation poured in from all parts of the country.[68] General Sherman was pleased, admiring Crook's "boldness" and calling the operation a "complete success." Moreover, he believed it would have beneficial consequences for long-term Indian affairs in Arizona.[69] Even Mexico had kind words. Two dispatches from Hermosillo applauded Crook's operation. "Everything in the country looks brighter," wrote one observer. The United States Consul described the operation as a "brilliant achievement" that had evoked "great satisfaction" in Sonora, whose newspapers published several articles "to eulogize" the general.[70] Even the state of Chihuahua acknowledged the "gallant" work of the general, though it believed that the United States would rue the day that it allowed guilty Apaches to escape the justice due them. This staccato philosophy was precisely why the Chiricahuas would never surrender to Mexicans.[71]

On June 20, 1883, Crook issued General Orders Number 10, in which he awarded the lion's share of the credit to Captain Emmet Crawford and the officers, civilian scouts, and Apache scouts. Crawford, "sustained simply by a sense of duty and a determination to subdue a band of desperados so long a scourge to two nations," had earned the plaudits. Crook publicly acknowledged the captain's "courage, ability, and devotion to duty."[72] After the two-day meeting with the Western Apache chiefs, Crawford had felt "pretty used up," the result of crowding so many Apaches inside the agency headquarters under stifling heat. The official commendation touched the humble captain, who stoically declared that he "had done nothing more than we were ordered to do and were paid for."[73]

But the captain soon realized that his bold strike was only the first in a series of challenges that he would face over the coming months. Nothing had ever come easy at San Carlos. Crawford's assignment promised to be a thankless task, one we can assume his Spartan military training had never prepared him for. He must have looked forward to an amicable relationship with Agent Wilcox, but this was not to be. Several minor conflicts threatened to explode into major ones if not handled with care and thought. And with the continued controversy over the hostiles left in Mexico dominating Crook's thoughts, he must have given thanks daily that he had an officer with integrity and honor carrying out his policies at San Carlos.

15

CROOK AND CRAWFORD PLAY THE WAITING GAME

We began to find them [Chiricahuas] decidedly human. Much to my surprise I found that they had a keen sense of humor and were not averse to telling jokes on themselves as well as on others.

Lieutenant Britton Davis

With the wind at his back, on July 7, 1883, General Crook arrived in Washington, D.C., to meet with Secretary of War Robert Lincoln, Secretary of the Interior Henry Teller, and Commissioner of Indian Affairs Hiram Price. They discussed the military's role at the San Carlos Apache Indian Agency. Though details of the meeting are sparse, a self-assured Crook probably told Teller and Price that he would gladly relinquish all control of the Apaches to the Bureau of Indian Affairs. After all, Indian affairs properly fell under its jurisdiction, and the Apaches were lawfully Agent Philip Wilcox's responsibility. But Teller knew that Wilcox wanted nothing to do with the Chiricahuas. And Crook had already pointed out that the Chiricahuas in Mexico would remain there if the Americans mistreated, arrested, or removed their relatives to another location. Thus, when confronted with these options, Teller and Price backed down; Crook's reputation as an Apache authority, combined with his forceful arguments, had carried the day—as he had expected they would. Before this meeting, he and Agent Wilcox had operated under an informal agreement that had effectively resulted in dual control at the reservation. After the conference, the two cabinet members formalized this unique arrangement.[1]

The result was an official memorandum, dated July 7, 1883, signed by Lincoln and Teller, which sanctioned the arrangement in effect since Wilcox and

Crook had met in the fall of 1882. Regarding the Chiricahuas, the military would assume all responsibility, including feeding them. In addition, Captain Crawford would oversee and ration the Apache scouts and the Apache police force that guarded the reservation and protected Agent Wilcox (when he was there!) in the discharge of his duties. When Crook returned to headquarters in Prescott, he issued General Orders Number 13, which summarized the agreement reached in Washington. Wilcox's main duty was to ration the Western Apaches. In theory, the lines of authority were clear. But the sharing of responsibility, no matter how clearly defined on paper, required a cooperative attitude from both sides. The well-meaning Washington officials thought this would clear the air. Instead, Wilcox fumed because Crook had won the battle for control.[2]

Meanwhile, at San Carlos, the first winds of change were beginning to blow across the inhospitable country. Captain Crawford and his staff of four officers, which included two capable assistants, lieutenants Britton Davis and Charles Gatewood (whom Crook assigned to Fort Apache to oversee the White Mountain and Cibecue groups), a quartermaster, and a surgeon, took over a two-story adobe building that had housed the schoolteachers hired by Tiffany. The captain at once asked Crook to transfer his Company G, Third Cavalry, then at Fort Thomas under Lieutenant Parker West, to Crawford's command at San Carlos. Accordingly, they set up tents near the agency. Some ten of these troopers acted as clerks, storekeepers, and hospital stewards. It was not a coveted assignment. One officer recalled that the agency's only "good point [was] its winter climate." They unanimously referred to San Carlos as Hell's Forty Acres. Camped near the agency along both sides of the Gila and San Carlos rivers were the Apache scouts (with Al Sieber, chief of scouts, aided by Archie McIntosh and Sam Bowman), the government pack trains, and various Apache rancherías. The Chiricahuas settled east of the agency at the former site of Loco's village. They were completely dependent on rations, for the agency supported no game to hunt (except rabbits) and no agave to gather.[3]

The unsung military man and the true American hero of the Apache conflicts of the 1880s, Crawford was then thirty-eight years old and a veteran of the Civil War and the Sioux campaigns in the northern plains. Esteemed and implicitly trusted by his superiors, beloved and unabashedly revered by his subordinates and peers, and universally respected for his fairness by Apaches, Crawford epitomized the qualities and traits of the ideal officer. In many ways his personality and character were like that of Cochise. He was serious and selfless, honest and courageous, a man whose demeanor reflected a sense of melancholy. Lieutenant Davis thought he had a "keen sense of humor but something had saddened him in early life and I never knew him to laugh aloud." According to Davis, the altruistic captain's "wish was that he might die in the act of saving others."

Lieutenant Charles Elliott considered him the perfect mentor to younger officers. A bachelor, he was very popular with the children and spouses of his fellow officers. Mrs. Corbusier, wife of army surgeon William T. Corbusier, described him as "gentle, kind, and chivalrous, ever ready to undertake any perilous journey for which he might be detailed." Crawford left positive impressions on most civilians. Charles Connell thought him a "gentleman" but a strict disciplinarian. And packer Henry W. Daly described him as the "finest soldier and noblest gentleman I ever saw." One man whom he did not get along with was the Indian agent, Philip Wilcox.[4] Perhaps Crawford's closest friend was Captain Charles Morton, who described his friend in hagiographical terms:

> He was one of the nation's heroes. He had devoted all the days of his manhood to his country. . . . No man ever entertained higher ideals as a soldier; no man was ever more devoted to his duties; no man deserved more consideration from the people and the government; and no one had higher claims to have his example cherished and extolled. Though an exceedingly modest man, no one of his rank was better known in the army, more highly respected as a man and soldier. . . . No braver officer ever lived.[5]

With his position and responsibilities broadly defined by General Crook, Captain Crawford, called Tall Captain by the Apaches, set about to improve life for the Indians on the reservation. Like Crook, he believed that the Indian agents at San Carlos had historically contributed to the problems instead of providing solutions. And Wilcox, one of Arizona's earliest snowbirds, was in Denver for much of the summer. Even on duty he was, at best, indifferent to his wards.

Accordingly, Crawford responded to two of the Apaches' main complaints. First, he tackled the monopoly held by the Indian trader John A. Showalter, who just happened to be Wilcox's son-in-law. Since reservation policy prohibited the Apaches from leaving without a pass, they had to purchase goods from the agency trader. And he maintained a "take it or leave it" policy with respect to prices. After hearing the Apaches' justifiable complaints, Crawford intervened and persuaded him to cut his prices in half. Presumably, Showalter and his father-in-law still reaped a healthy profit.[6]

Next, Crawford addressed the beef ration and found out that the supplier was also systematically cheating the Indians. The beef contractor weighed the cattle after he delivered them to the agency. Someone had fixed the scales to overpay the supplier an additional fifteen hundred pounds of imaginary beef per week. Even worse, the contractor's practice was to water the stock before weighing it. Davis observed, "The government was paying a pretty stiff price for half a barrel of Gila River Water delivered with each beef." Crawford fired the contractor and changed the delivery practice. "With just rationing and fair prices in the trader's store . . . the rancor of the Indians quickly faded away," wrote Davis.[7]

The Chiricahuas were a concern but not a problem. Every day several men visited the agency seeking reassurance that the Americans would not betray them.[8] They had historical reasons to feel this way, and they probably knew that most Arizona citizens, the Mexican government, and the territorial press were demanding Chiricahua blood. The *Clifton Clarion*, whose readers had been the targets of several Apache raiding parties, wanted the Chiricahuas removed to Oklahoma. Crook expected the controversy. He articulated his views in an interview with the editors of the *Arizona Citizen* in Tucson shortly before he returned to headquarters in Prescott:

> As it stands now their spirit is broken, and they are mightily hum-
> bled. . . . No one likes to see these red-handed murderers, as nearly all
> of them are, go back to the reservation . . . . But what are we going
> to do? To kill them will not bring back the dead and to punish them
> will only lead to them leaving the reservation. They will take to the
> mountains only to be exterminated after a long period of time, and
> then only after they have killed thousands of white people. Now they
> are willing to go back to the reservation and settle down. They are
> tired of war and anxious for peace.[9]

But Agent Wilcox continued to undermine Crook, demanding that he punish the Indians for their atrocities when at war. Mexican leaders also joined in the chorus, insisting that Crook hold the savages responsible for their ac-tions. Terrazas issued a formal demand asking the United States to punish the "guilty" Chiricahuas for the sake of Chihuahua's safety and security.[10]

The War Department asked Crook to respond. On August 7, 1883, he con-ceded that he was "in full sympathy" with Terrazas's objective. Though the

Chiricahuas had committed many depredations in both countries, he realized "it would be impossible to exterminate them in their [Sierra Madre] mountain homes." The pragmatic choice was to accept their surrender under the condition that "their past misdeeds would not be punished provided that they behaved themselves in the future." To renege on this agreement would not only "be an act of perfidy and bad faith" but would also "prevent the return of the Chiricahuas left in the Sierra Madre" and lead to renewed hostilities. A little over a month later, Terrazas (whose soldiers were then trying to lure the hostiles into Casas Grandes to massacre them) agreed that Crook must honor his agreements. Yet, he had a new complaint—one that had no merit—charging that several Chiricahuas had escaped from San Carlos and rejoined Juh. As we shall see, he was referring to three Chiricahuas sent by Crawford to bring in the remainder of their people.[11]

Crawford faced two delicate challenges with the Chiricahuas: his first concern was to ensure that he had adequate food on hand to feed them. The secretary of war, Robert Lincoln, settled that issue in late July when he informed Crook that he had allocated funds from the Indian prisoners' account. Crook ordered that the ration be identical to what Wilcox was furnishing the Western Apaches. Accordingly, every two days Crawford's men dispensed the rations. The Chiricahuas might have actually benefited from being under control of the War Department, for the army did feed them regularly. Crawford's second concern was to prevent disturbances that could give the hostiles a reason not to come in; he had to manage the agency and gain the confidence of the Apaches. He relied on his personal integrity, experiences, and training to make decisions based on consistency, fairness, and common sense. His actions in settling two grievances went a long way to gain the trust and respect of the Chiricahuas.[12]

The first involved José María Madrid's arrival at the agency with a note from Lieutenant Gatewood at Fort Apache. Madrid, a citizen of Quemado, New Mexico, was seeking his son (Militon), whom Nana had captured two years before. That morning, August 4, 1883, Crawford invited him to witness the formal count of the Chiricahuas. From Crawford's headquarters, they anxiously watched as Nana came in with a Mexican boy, but his wife concealed the youth under her shawl, making it impossible for Madrid to make an identification. But the father saw something familiar and "begged to be allowed to see the boy's face as he said by his size and appearance he believed it was his boy." Crawford asked Nana to bring the boy to his office. Nana did so without hesitation. Crawford described the scene: "As soon as the father discovered him he jumped upon him and cried aloud that it was his child. The boy cried and denied that Nana was his father. Quite a scene ensued." At first

Nana dissembled, saying that he had captured the boy in Mexico. Crawford, however, knew otherwise. That night he sent an escort with Madrid and his son to Fort Apache.

A few hours later, Ramon, a prominent shaman from Loco's band, came into Crawford's office. With him was his sister, and, like Madrid, the Indians had a story to tell. They probably wondered whether the Tall Captain would grant them equal justice. After the Chiricahua outbreak of September 30, 1881, Captain Reuben Bernard's cavalry had captured Ramon's niece in the Dragoon Mountains and had given her to Merejildo Grijalva, who spoke Apache. Dutchy had seen her during his visit to Grijalva. The scout and his wife were rearing the girl (their only child had died in infancy), and a parental bond had developed among all concerned. Ramon and his sister wanted Crawford to return the girl to her natural mother. Crawford telegraphed Crook, who responded within two hours: "If Ramon proves the child to be his, she should be returned to him."

Crawford at once sent Lieutenant Britton Davis with the two Apaches to Grijalva's ranch near Solomonville. They found the ten-year-old girl. The mother "cried when she saw her child [but] the child said the squaw was not her mother, that Merejildo's wife was her mother. Merejildo cried, his wife cried, and they all cried." But in the end, the Grijalvas gave up the girl. Davis admitted that he "was glad to get away with the child." Justice was done, though Crawford believed the "child would have been better off with Merejildo." Most southwesterners would have agreed with his ethnocentric comments. His judicious decision, however, had earned him political capital. In typical fashion, the unpretentious captain said that the "Indians feel better satisfied than before."[13]

With these minor emergencies dissipated, Crook turned to the agency Chiricahuas for help. He had become increasingly concerned about their kinfolk in Mexico. In early July, rumors placing the hostiles near the border prompted him to send Captain William A. Rafferty, from Bowie, to investigate. Rafferty patrolled the line but found nothing.[14] On July 20, 1883, Crook requested that Crawford ask the Chiricahuas whether they had heard anything. They were no better informed than Crook.[15] On August 7, Crook sent an interesting note to Rafferty, then in southeastern Arizona. In it he tends to confirm Davis's "two moons" theory as the time frame that Geronimo and other chiefs had given to Crook but that he was loathe to admit publicly. The assistant adjutant general, Major James P. Martin, advised Rafferty: "The commanding general thinks we can expect the Chiricahuas' coming. He desires that you keep out a lookout for them and assist them all you can."[16]

On August 14, Crawford talked with several Chiricahuas about their people in Mexico. They had assured Archie McIntosh that they "are looking for them [to return] every day." Loco believed they would come to the reservation via the Mogollon and Burro mountains in New Mexico. Three days later, Crawford wired Crook requesting authority to send a few Chiricahuas "to hunt up their people" in Mexico. The Chiricahuas' representative was undoubtedly Bonito (close to Naiche and Chatto), who volunteered for the assignment, with Frijole (a Chihenne from Nana's group who was a friend of Kaetenae) and Fatty, one of the few Nednhis on the reservation. Crook heartily endorsed this proposal.[17]

Bonito estimated that his party would be absent about fifty days. They left on August 25, 1883, heading south along the Aravaipa Valley toward the Dragoon Mountains, where they crossed Sulphur Springs Valley for San Bernardino. From here, the three men headed south for the Sierra Madre Mountains.[18]

Meanwhile, Crook was feeling the heat. Grim reports of Chiricahuas' raiding and killing in Sonora showed up in Arizona newspapers. One editor opined that Crook deserved "the censure of our people from one end of the land to the other." When three months passed without word from the Chiricahuas, "the tension was growing greater and the General's anxiety increasing as the newspapers became more virulent in their attacks upon him and his policy." But it is difficult to imagine what else the general could do besides wait. He could organize another expedition, but that would be admitting failure.[19]

At this crucial stage, General Crook had to address another unpleasant subject, Charley McComas. Eugene F. Ware, a prominent state senator from Kansas, was Charley's uncle, and he was fighting mad because of the lack of information about his nephew. Writing to the secretary of state, Ware made it clear that he wasn't impugning Crook's integrity, but he couldn't resist taking a shot at the general while patting him on the back. Ware acknowledged that the public was demanding that Crook pull off a "feat almost impossible of performance, namely the capture of a boy alive and the punishment of the Indians." He also conceded "perhaps no other officer in the Army could have come as near accomplishing the purpose as General Crook." Then he got to his grievance: "Since General Crook's campaign [three months ago] nothing has been done to obtain the boy. It seems to me that if that boy was a British subject, the government would get him if it cost about half the island to do it." Then, to turn the screw tighter, he closed with a statement that he knew would infuriate Crook: "It may be true that our officers are too busy playing poker and the men in drinking whiskey, and having amateurish theatricals at their barracks to render much assistance." Teller forwarded the letter to the Secretary Lincoln, who sent it along to General Schofield, Crook's commanding officer in the Division of the Pacific.[20]

Crook understood that Ware was simply an uncle increasingly frustrated with the lack of information about his nephew. Thus, his initial response was understandably restrained. Not only were these allegations unfair, but they also seemed highly personal to Crook, who disdained the very vices charged by Ware. Crook admitted that he was "greatly embarrassed" about the uncertain status of little Charley McComas. But he hoped for "definite information" after the return of Bonito's party.[21] According to photographer Frank Randall, in a letter to Judge John A. Wright, the former law partner of Hamilton McComas, the prevailing thought of those closest to the Chiricahuas, which included Crawford and Al Sieber, was that the boy was dead. Crook, however, still held out hope.[22]

Although he had to exercise restraint in the official reply to Ware, he felt no such obligation in response to a letter from Judge Wright. Apparently the thin-skinned general remembered Ware's accusations and had grown weary of hearing about Charley McComas. The judge had written him that two citizens from Deming had talked about ransoming Charley from the Chiricahuas near Casas Grandes. Instead of encouraging their efforts, Crook had a bout of tone deafness, upbraiding them for undermining his attempts to recover the boy. From his response, we get a glimpse into the combative and sometimes arrogant heart of a man who had little tolerance for those who dared interfere in his business.

His letter was condescending, his arguments specious and impertinent: "I am rather sorry that those gentlemen who went after Charley McComas let the Indians know that we are anxious to have the boy, as in all my dealings with them I was careful to impress on them the fact that we cared very little for the boy but showed them the great advantage it would be to them to have him returned to his people." In retrospect, whatever Crook said about Charley McComas would have had no effect on his fate because he was not alive when the general made these statements. But Crook's incredible words "*that we cared very little for the boy*" must have dismayed the family and friends of the McComas family, who still prayed for his safe return. That he so cavalierly admitted this reveals how imperious and self-important he had become.[23]

About ten days before writing this letter, Crook had heard from Crawford, who had passed along important intelligence from Archie McIntosh and the Chiricahuas. McIntosh thought that the Chiricahuas had been "tampered with in some way," although he had his own agenda along with an unreliable record of predictions. In any case, Crawford concurred, noting, "Something is awry somewhere." The scout still thought that the Chiricahuas, except Juh and Geronimo, would come in. On September 23, 1883, Crawford met with Mangas and Loco at San Carlos. They said their people would be in within sixty days. It was unclear who gave them this information, or whether it was just a guess or a hunch. Therefore, Crawford decided to send his trusted assistant, Lieutenant Britton Davis, ten Apache scouts, and Chiricahua volunteers ("three of their best men," Kaydahzinne, Tah-ni-toe, and Nahn-tee-nesn) to help Davis. Each man was a member of Naiche's band, and Kaydahzinne and Nahn-tee-nesn were related to Chihuahua. On October 3, 1883, they left San Carlos to join Rafferty's command, which had been patrolling the line between the Animas Mountains and the San Bernardino ranch.[24]

Rafferty had also passed along news about Chiricahua activities in northeastern Chihuahua. He had talked to individuals who had been at Casas Grandes, and they claimed that the Chiricahuas were negotiating there. As we shall see, their appearance was a pragmatic move—one that many could have predicted under the circumstances. The *Arizona Weekly Citizen* proclaimed that the Chiricahuas had "shrewdly outwitted" the general. The editors' hyperbole only revealed how misinformed they were.[25]

The Chokonens, after Crook had left them in the Sierra Madre, needed to replenish their horse herd because Crawford's scouts had destroyed their camp. Thus, Chatto led a raiding party that harassed the Sierra Madre villages of Bavispe, Nácori Chico, and Bacadéhuachi. They stole stock from Bavispe three times between June 6 and June 18 and raided Nácori Chico on June 9. Though their objective was stock, in the late afternoon on June 17, 1883, the raiders "in considerable numbers," perhaps as many as twenty, assailed vaqueros at the Teraverachi ranch, a few miles southeast of Bacadéhuachi. They shot down José Téran while he worked his crops, captured Pedro Morales's wife (whom they killed soon after), and wounded two other men.[26] About June 22, 1883, Chatto's raiders rejoined the main body at Bugatseka. Soon after, they broke camp and moved several miles south, but not as far as the "Big River," their designation for the Aros River. They bivouacked in a canyon in the same mountains along the Sonora-Chihuahua border. Here, about June 25, Juh rode into camp with his family and another man. The Chiricahuas were together, 190 in all, including 60 fighting men.[27]

Then the summer rains appeared, forcing the band to remain in camp and consider their next move. Though the chiefs, including Juh, unanimously decided to return to San Carlos, they also concluded to make one last attempt to recover their people imprisoned in Chihuahua. Before they could do that, however, they needed supplies and stock. Thus, before moving toward Casas Grandes, they opted for a series of raids into Sonora. Their strategy was to focus on the districts of Moctezuma and Arispe, staying clear of Sahuaripa, believing troops from there were the only threat to their village.

Geronimo, Chatto, Chihuahua, and Naiche apparently crossed the Bavispe River south of Oputo. Here they divided. Geronimo probably led one division southeast toward Batuc; the second party headed northwest toward Cumpas. Within one week, they killed fourteen persons near Batuc, Moctezuma, and Fronteras, where they also stole 150 head of stock. By July 21, 1883, they had rejoined and taken positions to attack Nácori Chico, the last settlement before they reached their ranchería.

This vulnerable village featured a town plaza enclosed in a square with rows of adobe homes. Nácori Chico had weathered Chiricahua assaults for the last four decades. Cochise himself had made several assaults against this isolated village, but even he had never driven them away. Despite reports estimating Apaches at 150 warriors, there were, at most, only sixty Indian men and boys in Mexico able to bear arms. Most of them were lying in wait for first light to ambush the unsuspecting townspeople. One farmer, an early riser, had spotted them. That morning twenty-five men tried to dislodge the Apaches, whom the townspeople could see butchering cattle. Accounts suggest that National Guard troops under Lieutenant José Moreno charged the Apaches, who shot his horse from under him and wounded another man. Several more volleys forced his soldiers to take cover. Then four brave men emerged from the town and charged the Apaches. The Apaches, mistaking them for reinforcements, hastily retreated. In the confusion, one Mexican marksman, seeing Jelikine climbing a rock to higher ground, shot him through the head "from long range."[28]

His loss left the Apaches demoralized. Most of them returned to base camp after the fight. Others mourned the death of Jelikine, and the surviving evidence suggests that some fifteen men decided to turn around and avenge his death. Normally the slain man's relatives would agitate for vengeance. But despite Jelikine's Mexican blood, he was culturally an Apache and a much admired and venerated warrior. The indications we do have—the route of the raid, the blood left in its wake, and Geronimo's relationship to Jelikine—point to Geronimo's involvement.

Five days later, the raiders appeared without warning at the Rincoñada hacienda, nestled in the eastern foothills of the Huerta Mountains, about forty-five miles due east of Nácori Chico and a dozen miles south of Moctezuma.

Here, on the morning of July 26, 1883, they took some stock. Mexicans followed the trail of twelve to fifteen Apaches as they hastened north to Moctezuma, where at sundown they made off with twenty-five horses, mules, and burros from American Tom Smith (his guard was unarmed for some inexplicable reason). The Chiricahuas fired two shots and the herd stampeded.

Three days later (July 29), the Chiricahuas rounded the northern tip of the Huerta Mountains and took positions along the road that led northeast to Moctezuma, six miles away. That morning José Alday and José Montano had left their ranch for Moctezuma; the Chiricahuas riddled them with bullets. Then they swept by the Bacachi ranch, killing Mariano Moreno and adding twenty head of horses and mules to their growing herd. Here, they apparently split up. The smaller group remained with the stock while the second party of some ten men headed for the settlements south of Arispe along the Sonora River. On August 2 the group of ten killed José Mange near Baviacora (always a favorite target of Geronimo) and took his rifle and horse. Their raid a success, they reversed directions, returned to their rendezvous site, gathered their stolen herd, and returned to the Sierra Madre, reaching their base camp by August 9.[29]

About this time, a wife of Geronimo, who called herself Mañanita, walked into camp after a remarkable forty-four-day odyssey from Chihuahua City. Mexicans had captured her during the January attack on Juh's camp. Once outside Chihuahua City, she had followed her instincts and made for the high country. She had no moccasins, her feet and legs had become swollen from the journey, and she had lived on what she could forage ("herbs, roots, and berries"). Eventually she found Geronimo's camp near Tres Rios. From her they learned that thirty-five Chiricahuas were alive in captivity in Chihuahua City. These included Chatto's wife and two children, two other wives of Geronimo, and Chihuahua's brother.[30] This information helped to overcome whatever reservations they had about dealing with the Mexicans. Shortly after, the band broke camp and moved east to Piedras Verde (Green Stones), about a dozen miles southeast of Casas Grandes, where they hoped to make a treaty to get back their kinfolk held in captivity. Zele, however, led a raid for horses against Yepómera and Temosachic, where his party ravaged several ranches and killed one child. They needed stock for their trip to San Carlos.[31]

On August 30, 1883, two Chiricahua women approached a Mexican military camp about two miles east of Casas Grandes. They said Geronimo, Naiche, Chatto, and Juh were eager to make a treaty. Major Oñate rounded up twenty-five soldiers and, guided by the two women, set out for the ranchería fifteen miles away. He and four soldiers left their lines to meet with the chiefs. Juh requested that Chihuahua set aside for the Indians a section of twenty square miles between Piedras Verde and the Casas Grandes River. His people would require seeds and training for one year, when they would become self-sufficient, having completed the peaceful transformation to farmers. Oñate forwarded the request to Brigadier General Ramon Raguero in Chihuahua City. Either he or General Carlos Fuero authorized the diplomacy, offering the carrot to entice them in so their troops could trap and slaughter as many as possible. Fuero especially wanted to capture Geronimo and execute him for his role in the Mata Ortiz fight.[32]

A few days after this meeting, several adventurous Chiricahuas did enter Casas Grandes to trade with citizens under protection of a white flag. The intrepid Chihuahua was the first to go in, followed soon after by Juh, who sent word to Avencio Escudero, former jefe politico for the Galeana district. Juh wanted a formal pass to trade at Casas Grandes and told Escudero that he had a boy he was willing to exchange. They had stock, booty, and excess arms (but lacked ammunition) and were willing to trade them for cartridges and mescal, an often-lethal mixture. Mexicans did purchase two bracelets that belonged to the McComas family. Chief Chihuahua seemed wise to the Mexican's strategy. If they were planning a double-cross, it would not happen during the first visit but when the whole band was together. So he never returned after his one visit. Juh, who had many Mexican friends, was not so reluctant. The Mexicans sent mescal to the temporary Chiricahua camp and gave it to Juh when he was in Casas Grandes. According to Zele, who returned from his raid around September 6, Juh was "all the time drunk" from mescal provided by his Mexican friends.[33]

On September 12, 1883, a large group of Chiricahuas met Lieutenant Colonel Miguel González a few miles from Casas Grandes. Geronimo did most of the talking. He inquired about their captives in Chihuahua City, and González replied that he would pass along Geronimo's request to his superiors. Chatto, desperate to get back his wife and two children, told González that he would not go to San Carlos because he wanted "to make them [Mexicans] believe that he was on their side." González invited the Chiricahuas to move their village to a site near his encampment. Naiche refused the offer, saying, "You people have always talked nice to us poor people. . . . We don't believe you anymore."[34]

A second conference between the Chiricahuas and González occurred about September 20. Juh, Naiche, Geronimo, Chatto, Kaetenae, and Zele, with other warriors, again met outside Casas Grandes. González was play-ing for time. He knew that General Raguero was assembling a force of two hundred cavalry to place at his disposal. But he would not have them under his command for at least another week. He therefore had to gain the confidence of the Indians while stalling for time. According to Naiche, the Mexican of-ficer pledged to restore their captive people if the Chiricahuas came in, made a treaty, and went to work as farmers. As proof of his good faith, he promised to produce three of the prisoners in Chihuahua City, perhaps because Juh had three children he was willing to exchange. Despite Juh's presence, Geronimo again dominated the conversation. This day, however, Juh was so intoxicated that he had trouble even mounting his horse. Finally, after several attempts, he was successful. They began their journey toward Piedras Verde and went into camp several miles from Casas Grandes.[35]

The once powerful Nednhi chief, former contemporary and ally of Coch-ise, was now a leader without followers. Many believed that he was no longer fit to lead—particularly when mescal was available. He was drinking when-ever he could, and that desire for alcohol had clouded his judgment and forced him to take unnecessary risks. He was despondent and probably had no inten-tion of going to San Carlos. He had been born in Mexico, and that was where he wanted to stay. But something happened that morning of September 21, 1883, as he rode along the trail of a high bluff overlooking the Casas Grandes River. It was a trip he had probably made hundreds of times in his life. And, seemingly by choice, it would be his last voyage.

Several Mexicans had ridden with him along the trail the previous day. They had departed for Casas Grandes that evening of September 20, leaving several bottles of mescal for their Chiricahua friends. Juh had continued his binge, joined by others, including Chatto, who revealed that the mescal trad-ers had given him four bottles.[36] The next morning, an intoxicated Juh fell off his horse while riding along a high bank overlooking the Casas Grandes River and either perished from the fall or drowned after the impact left him uncon-scious. At least that is the historically accepted version.

In recent years, Daklugie, Juh's youngest son, has done his best to dispel the reports that his father died in such an unceremonious way. He allowed to Eve Ball that his father did drink to excess, but he insisted that Juh was sober the day of his death. It seems that he and his "segundo" Ponce took turns getting drunk at Casas Grandes while the other stayed sober, much like today's designated driver. Juh "scrupulously denied himself even one drink." While the chief was riding back to camp, the bank gave way and Juh fell into the Aros River. He either died of the impact from the fall or suffered a heart attack. This is Daklugie's version. But either his memory failed him (he told his version about seventy years later) or he used his imagination to create this story.[37]

If we appraise his account according to the facts as we know them, we find his story has many holes. First, Daklugie, no more than twelve years old, was not present, for only warriors were at the council near Casas Grandes the day before. Ponce, the affable guide for General Howard during his historic 1872 visit to Cochise, was definitely not there, for he had died in the late 1870s. Finally, all accounts say that Juh fell into the Casas Grandes River and not the Aros River, which was a two or three days' trip from Casas Grandes.

What did the Chiricahuas who were there say in the weeks following Juh's death? A few months later, Naiche, Kaetenae, and Zele, who were eyewitnesses, gave interviews to Crawford, who took down their statements verbatim. Of the three chiefs, Naiche furnished the most complete account: "He [Juh] got drunk one day in camp and got on a wild horse. The horse jumped on a high bank with him and threw him head forward into the river. I don't think there was enough water to drown him. I think in falling he hit his head and was killed. We found him lying with his head in the water dead." Kaetenae and Zele had the same observation: both said that Juh was drunk and "ran his horse over a high bank and was killed."[38]

Another man present was Perico, second cousin of Geronimo. He gave his version to Sol Tax, one of several anthropologists (along with Morris Opler) who interviewed elderly Chiricahuas on the Mescalero Reservation in 1931. Perico, one of many informants who talked about Juh's Power, related what he saw and heard that day on the bank of the Casas Grandes River. In addition to confirming Zele's and Kaetenae's insistence that Juh "ran his horse over a high bank," he adds other fascinating details.

> This chief [Juh] ran his horse real fast (with himself mounted) and made his horse jump a huge cliff, maybe a block high. Both man and horse died. He had told the people he was going to do this, and he told them that if they would come quickly and put him together again, he would come to life. But the people were all drunk and forgot, and came half-a-day later, and he remained dead. Maybe the man was drunk to do this, or maybe the spirit he was working for made him do it.
>
> About two or three nights later some people heard his voice, but couldn't see him. The spirit came back in the nighttime, and every-

body was scared, trembling, because he was a ghost. The ghost told them 'just because you people didn't do as I said, I will stay away from you forever.' Maybe the spirit who was working for him gave him Power to come back as a spirit.[39]

Years later the Chiricahuas told the story about a man who claimed to receive Power from a tanager bird. It seemed as if half of his predictions came true. This prophet had told Juh "that the time will come . . . when he will become the best rider living." Perhaps Juh had this in mind before he galloped off the cliff. Years later they discounted this prophesy because Juh "was killed on horseback. He ran over some rocks."[40]

The chiefs sent runners to the village with the news of Juh's death. His family and friends began to mourn. Loaded with mescal, some men continued their spree. Washington, one of the last of the Nednhis, shot and killed his wife and then fled from camp. He came back the next morning, surly and morose. Naiche and Chihuahua, acting as the village's police, tried to calm him, with the latter finally demanding that he "stop his threats." But Washington would not listen. Instead, he opened fire with his gun, perhaps wounding Chihuahua, at which point the no-nonsense chief picked up his rifle and "shot him in the head." He later recalled, "Washington was a good man but [I] had to kill him."[41]

News of Juh's death had reached Casas Grandes by September 23, when two Americans from Deming, D. C. Leroy and Charles Wilson, rode into town seeking to meet the Chiricahuas to find out the fate of Charley McComas. A week before, they had talked with Avencio Escudero, who told them that Juh was at Casas Grandes and had a "captive boy that he would sell if he could." They were eager to speak with the Chiricahuas, but the treaty negotiations had come to a halt after Juh's death. Three days later, the Chiricahuas had returned to the area. They met Perico, who was friendly with a family at Casas Grandes, on September 26.[42] Though Perico's Spanish was limited, the Americans learned that Juh's widow was holding an American boy. That evening Perico sent in a warrior who spoke better Spanish. He said that they could talk with Geronimo the next day.[43]

They met Geronimo, whom they described as well proportioned, carrying 190 pounds on a five-foot-ten-inch, broad-shouldered frame, five miles outside of Casas Grandes. They estimated his age at thirty-seven (he was actually about sixty). He had several battle scars: "A bullet wound across his forehead, a bullet still in his left thigh, and the third finger of his right hand is bent backward, also from a bullet wound." Before discussing the captive boy, Geronimo said, "I want to ask you a question and I don't want you to lie." What did they know about Crook's movements? He explained that his warriors (probably Zele's raiding party earlier that month) had reported cutting tracks of two men wearing moccasins. The Americans said they knew nothing of Crook or his movements. In fact, Zele had probably discovered the tracks of Bonito's party looking for their relatives at Tres Rios near Bugatseka. Geronimo clearly feared Crook and his Apache scouts, especially now that his men were low on cartridges. He would trade captives for cartridges, but he had to ask Juh's wife before making the exchange. Under no circumstances would he bring the boy to Casas Grandes, for he feared treachery. Instead, he told the Americans to return the next morning to make the exchange.

They kept their end of the bargain, but Geronimo became alarmed when a Mexican from Casas Grandes rode into camp mounted on a horse that he believed belonged to Joaquin Terrazas. He was concerned, for "if Terrazas is here then the treaty is no good." Wilson offered to go to the Apache camp, but supposing that the Mexicans might compel him to tell the exact location, Geronimo objected. That ended the negotiations, and the two Americans returned to Deming thinking that the boy might be alive.[44]

As it turned out, the Chiricahuas were talking to Mexicans about Charley McComas. Washington diplomats had asked federal officials in Mexico City for information about the boy. The request was forwarded to Joaquin Terrazas, who in turn, "requested several persons who reside in that neighborhood to speak" to the Apaches about the boy. The Chiricahuas were not going to admit anything to the military, but they spoke freely to several Mexican civilians whom they trusted. From the Indians, the Mexicans heard three versions of what had happened to Charley:

> Some of the Indians have said that Charley McComas was alive but that he was far away. Others said that, having been pursued in the mountains of Sonora by the forces of that state and that having been obliged to flee precipitously, the captive Charley McComas strayed off in said mountains and that he is supposed to have died in them. And, lastly, other Indians say that when General Crook in May last was in the Sierra Madre, and took several Indian prisoners . . . they, in their retreat, killed him.[45]

In August 1884, the *Rio Grande Republican* published an article titled "The Mystery Solved: How Poor Little Charlie McComas Was Murdered." The author claimed to have obtained the story from a Chiricahua woman at San Carlos. And though parts of her account were wrong (she claimed that they killed the boy in the Carcay Mountains after a skirmish with Mexican troops), the manner in which Charley died agrees with what Jason Betzinez revealed in 1959. According to her, "Charley being sick, was crying and unable to ride, [so] they beat his brains out with stones and threw his body into a gully." But the chiefs never deviated from their tale that Charley ran off during the Crawford fight and perished from the elements.[46]

Meanwhile, about a week after Juh's death, the Indians had returned to the neighborhood of Casas Grandes. Juh's two widows, their hair cut short after the death of their husband, told the news to Colonel Emilio Gallardo, who was skeptical of their story. Gallardo sent an officer to ask José Varela to investigate. Juh had called Varela his "foster brother," and they had remained lifelong friends. Varela spoke with Juh's two wives, who assured him that they were now widows. Varela also mentioned that they had cut their hair, a sign of mourning for a dead friend or relative. He believed that his Apache friend was indeed dead.[47]

While Juh's death was center stage during this time, the military authorities at Casas Grandes tried to restart the stalled negotiations. As a gesture of good faith, the Mexicans had sent three Chiricahua captives under a strong military escort to Casas Grandes. They were the bait to induce Geronimo back to the bargaining table. In early October, the warriors, led by Geronimo, Naiche, Chatto, Kaetenae, and Zele (an injured Chihuahua had remained at the base camp), met the military for the third time outside Casas Grandes. As it had been ten days since Juh's death, the Apaches had had ample time to regain their sobriety, much to the dismay of the Mexicans. Though both sides were poised to consummate a treaty, neither party intended to honor its terms. The Chiricahuas' finely honed senses were now keen—their antennas raised, prepared to scatter at the first sign of treachery. They would negotiate this treaty and play out this charade as long as they did not place their lives in danger. They only wanted their people returned.

On this occasion, they had brought three Mexican captives to exchange for their people. Colonel Gallardo offered clothes and rations if the Chiricahuas would make the treaty. Even some Mexican citizens who had been trading with the Chiricahuas had warned them to be wary of treachery.[48] Naiche immediately knew something was awry: "We found there about sixty soldiers had changed their uniforms and put on old citizens' clothes and had their guns hidden under their clothes. [They] had started out to our right and left to get around us." Geronimo suspected treachery and said to Kaetenae, "We might as well go back. There are too many soldiers." Naiche and Geronimo gave the order to withdraw before the soldiers surrounded them. Chatto summed up the experience: "The way the Mexicans make a treaty is to get [us] all together and then kill [us]." Before leaving, Geronimo cited some made-up excuse, promising to return in ten days with his entire band to consummate the treaty. This pledge forced Colonel Gallardo to cancel the operation in the hopes of exterminating the whole band when they returned.[49]

When they returned to base camp, they found an unexpected yet most welcome surprise: Bonito's party was there. It had taken them five weeks to track down their brethren. They described San Carlos in positive terms (at least they were safe and fed). Bonito explained that Crawford had sent him "to find out what was keeping the Chiricahuas." Bonito spoke privately to Naiche, urging him to go to San Carlos. They had come at an opportune moment, for the chiefs now realized that further talks with Mexicans would only get more of them killed or captured. Their only hope was that Crook might be successful in his diplomatic efforts with Mexico. Naiche, whose family was at San Carlos, quickly consented, as did Chihuahua, Kaetenae, and about a dozen of Loco's band, about one hundred in all. The balance, led by Geronimo, Chatto, and Zele, decided against returning for the time being. An ever-suspicious Geronimo wanted reassurance about the situation at San Carlos. Accordingly, he sent his eighteen-year-old son, Chappo, with Naiche's party. Those staying in Mexico also wanted to augment their horse herd, for they had traded a good deal of stock at Casas Grandes for cartridges and mescal.[50]

On October 6, 1883, the dozen Chihennes of Loco's band left for San Carlos. The next morning, about ninety Chiricahuas (including Bonito and Frijole) under Naiche, Kaetenae, and Chihuahua left for Arizona. Avoiding settlements and keeping to the high country, Naiche's party moved northwest at a slow but methodical pace. They crossed to the eastern side of the Sierra Madre and rode north, skirting the Teras Mountains to the Pitacaiche Mountains, which they called Big Mountain. Here the chiefs held a council. The main body would rest here for eight or nine days before continuing their trek north toward the border. Kaetenae and Ulzana would take eight men and one woman to retrieve items that they had cached and to make a horse raid against settlements on the Sonora River. On October 14, they left, agreeing to meet Naiche in southeastern Arizona in twenty days.[51]

About one week later, Naiche and Chihuahua moved their camp a few miles to the northeast, stopping at Embudos Canyon, a picturesque area Chiricahuas had favored for the previous two centuries. They planned to rest for a few days. This was their last stop before entering Arizona. Naiche and Bonito decided to send ahead Frijole with a young Chokonen to try to find Captain Rafferty's command near San Bernardino. But Rafferty was then about thirty miles east at Guadalupe Canyon. So Frijole headed north to Fort Bowie, which he reached the evening of October 22, 1883. Fortunately, he had his ration tag with him, and the commanding officer, Captain Leopold O. Parker, wired Crook, "Is he the one who went out with Bonito?" Though they had trouble communicating, Frijole was able to report that a party of ninety Chiricahuas was coming up from Mexico and would need rations and an escort to San Carlos.

The next morning Parker dispatched Lieutenant George K. Hunter, Lieutenant Thomas B. Dugan, and forty-two troopers with rations of "flour, coffee, sugar, and salt" for the Chiricahuas. In addition, Parker authorized Dugan to purchase fresh beef in open market. Frijole led them to the rendezvous point at Silver Creek, a few miles southeast of the Pedregosa Mountains and some ten miles north of the border. Seeing the Chiricahuas in camp, Hunter sent a courier to Cloverdale to get Rafferty and his command, which included Lieutenant Davis, his ten Western Apache scouts, and three Chiricahua volunteers, Kaydahzinne, Tah-ni-toe, and Nahn-tee-nesn.[52] They had been probing the country below the border looking for Naiche's people. Kaydahzinne had gone alone into Sonora and was overdue to return. Fortunately, Nahn-tee-nesn was a shaman, and he conducted a ceremony to locate him. In his vision, he saw Kaydahzinne in a mountain along the border and knew that he was safe.[53]

Naiche and Chihuahua had just got in from an all-night dash from Embudos Canyon. With a stretch of twenty-five miles of open country between them and the Arizona border, they led their people on the most dangerous part of their journey. They did not expect to run into Mexican soldiers as there were only a few abandoned ranches along the way, but they were on open ground, were short of ammunition, and had only eleven men to protect sixty-six women and children. Naturally, they wanted to avoid an encounter with Mexicans. They likely left Embudos Canyon late in the evening of October 23. Traveling all night in three groups of twenty-five, the advance party was near the border by sunrise the next morning. Naiche said that he and three men were in the rear guard driving the stock when between seven and nine Mexican soldiers at the deserted Cuchuverachi hacienda, "tried to cut [them] off." His party had only "one gun, two lances . . . and eleven rounds of ammunition." They escaped without harm. The Mexican report was remarkably similar. Eight soldiers had seen four Apaches with stock near Cuchuverachi. They pursued the Indians, who abandoned eleven head of stock during their flight. That was the only difference between the two accounts; Naiche failed to mention that he had lost some animals.[54]

On October 26, 1883, Captain Rafferty, Lieutenant Davis, and Mickey Free arrived at Silver Creek and relieved the detachment from Fort Bowie. Crawford had given Davis explicit orders: "Protect the Indians coming into [your] camp along the border; allow no one to interfere with them or have anything to say to them; and conduct them safely to the reservation."[55] Both men filed reports. Rafferty sent his to Crook, and Davis sent his to Crawford. The Chiricahuas were suspicious and refused to allow anyone to enter their camp or to examine their stock. Their reasons seem obvious, for they had three captive children taken in New Mexico during Nana's famous raid, and their stock consisted of animals recently stolen in Mexico. The chiefs revealed that Geronimo and Chatto would return in the coming months. Memories of losing his freedom when Clum had shackled him still haunted the Bedonkohe shaman. As proof of their goodwill, Chatto had sent relatives, and Geronimo had sent his son Chappo, who was to stay at San Carlos before returning to his father with information about conditions at San Carlos. Finally, Naiche said they would wait for eight days, when Kaetenae and Ulzana would be in with their group of men after they had retrieved some supplies they had cached. Though he was telling the truth, he neglected to add that they had left on one last raid for horses.[56]

Naturally, the fate of Charley McComas was ever present in the minds of Davis and Rafferty. They asked Mickey Free to find out what he could. Over the next two days, the scout mingled with the Chiricahuas, claiming that he had had a conversation with Naiche about the boy. Somehow, Mickey Free got the impression from Naiche that Charley was alive and well with Geronimo, who intended to use him as a bargaining chip on his return to the reservation. But Naiche was referring to another boy, not Charley McComas. Mickey Free probably misunderstood him. Perhaps it was an honest mistake by the scout. Even Lieutenant Davis remarked that the Chiricahuas "suspected him of coloring things to suit the whites; Sieber's opinion of him could not be printed in polite words."[57]

That same day Naiche and another man left for the reservation after learning from Tah-ni-toe that his wife had been ill. En route, he spent a night at Clay Beauford's ranch, where he told one American that his band would come in but that he was unsure about Geronimo's plans. The evening of November

1, 1883, he set foot on San Carlos, where Captain Crawford interviewed him four days later.[58]

Forty-eight hours after Naiche reached San Carlos, Kaetenae, on schedule, came riding into camp at Silver Creek. His party had ridden hard, wearing out his stock and men. It was the beginning of an irreconcilable relationship between Lieutenant Davis and the incorrigible Chihenne chief, who claimed he had never been on a reservation. Kaetenae and Ulzana had raided towns along the Sonora River. Ulzana, having accompanied his brother and Geronimo on several raids against Sonoran settlements since 1882, knew the country well. The initial part of their raid featured quick hit-and-run assaults. Their sole objective was horses and mules. On October 22, 1883, ten warriors killed several head of cattle and took seven horses and mules from the El Sauz ranch near Banámichi. The next day found them thirty miles north, where they picked up more horses, before sweeping by El Bandepa ranch near Arispe, where they added seven more mounts to their herd. They lay low for a few days before hitting a favorite target: Ignacio Pesqueira's Bacanuchi ranch, where they took twelve more horses and headed east toward Cumpas.[59]

Again, they regrouped in the hills for a few days, preparing for the last leg of their raid. At 5:00 a.m. on November 2, 1883, they slaughtered four men at the San Nicholas mine near Cumpas, taking their supplies and augmenting the band's herd by several more mounts. Troops picked up their trail, which led to the Pinito Mountains in the eastern part of the Sierra Madre. But they were unable to overtake the fast-moving raiders.[60] One hundred miles below the border, driving fifty to one hundred horses and mules, Kaetenae and Ulzana began their flight north. With no settlements between Oputo and the border, they had an unimpeded stretch of ninety miles. Sonora's only hope was to dispatch troops from Fronteras or Bavispe to cut off the raiders before they reached the border, but Kaetenae obviated this strategy by outdistancing them.

They probably drove their stock hard toward the bend of Bavispe River, and then turned north. Halting periodically to care for their stock, the next morning they found themselves near Pitaicache, just north of where the Bavispe River curves to the east. Here they stopped for a few hours before resuming their dash north to the border and Silver Creek, arriving there the evening of November 3, 1883. In all, they had covered one hundred miles in forty hours. Naiche's and Kaetenae's followers brought 109 horses and mules to the reservation. Kaetenae and Ulzana's raiders accounted for most of the herd. According to Captain Rafferty, the Chiricahuas were now "well mounted."

Kaetenae met with Rafferty and Davis the next morning. Rafferty, who was low on rations, told Kaetenae they must move that day. Given the events of the previous forty hours, the chief wanted to wait one day to rest his stock and to repair moccasins. But Rafferty would not back down, and they began a slow march toward White's ranch, opposite Turkey Creek on the west side of the Chiricahuas. They reached it on November 6, when Rafferty agreed to stay for one day, which satisfied Kaetenae, who Rafferty thought was head chief because the Indians showed him "great respect." Rafferty noticed that Kaetenae was skittish and made the entire group of ninety, including twenty-three warriors, quite nervous. They were all concerned, of course, about how the Americans and Western Apaches would treat them at San Carlos.

Luckily for all concerned, Bonito, whose bravery was matched only by Chihuahua's, succeeded in allaying their anxieties. Though the Chiricahuas continued to discourage any American visits to their camps, it soon became clear that they had three young captives. Davis and Mickey Free continued to believe that one might be the McComas boy, but these were just idle hopes. Finally, on November 15, 1883, the cavalcade reached San Carlos.[61]

With the first group now at the agency, Crook wasted no time in claiming victory. He had proved to his legion of critics (a misinformed and biased press and the apathetic and corrupt employees of the Indian Bureau) that his policies were right. He knew, however, that he could claim credit only when Geronimo and Chatto, the symbols of Chiricahua resistance now that Juh had died, came to San Carlos. Then it would be up to Crawford to use his judgment prudently and judiciously. He was Crook's man, and the Chiricahuas knew that. Few military men would have handled the daily problems with as much grace, fairness, consistency, and, when necessary, decisiveness. Knowing he had Crook's implicit support, he would stand up to the Chiricahuas when necessary. What he failed to anticipate was that Agent Philip Wilcox was sharpening his knives to prepare for a battle over control of the reservation.

16

NO CHIRICAHUAS ARE LEFT
IN MEXICO

If you were placed in our position with your relatives in captivity I think you would have done the same—try and get them out.

Chatto to Captain Emmet Crawford, March 3, 1884

With more than half the Chiricahuas who had remained in Mexico after Crook's expedition now at San Carlos, and the prognosis favorable for the return of the holdouts under Geronimo and Chatto, General George Crook felt vindicated. So what did he do? In a preview of the issues that would dominate affairs at San Carlos, he rebuked his critics, particularly a misguided and partisan press, which had dared question his judgment and actions. Included in his criticism, though unnamed, was Agent Philip Wilcox, who Crook believed was undermining Crawford's efforts at every turn. One wonders why the general declared victory when almost ninety Chiricahuas under Zele, Chatto, and Geronimo still lurked in the Sierra Madre.

In October 1883 Crook had embarked on a month-long tour to visit the Apaches at San Carlos and Fort Apache. He had several positive developments to crow about, not the least of which was his decision to allow the White Mountain groups, who numbered about nine hundred individuals, to relocate to Fort Apache the previous fall. Back at their historical homes and farming areas, they had seized this opportunity to raise bountiful "crops of corn, vegetables, and melons." Now self-sufficient, they no longer needed rations. To Crook, this was a "most gratifying improvement. They are thoroughly contented and satisfied." And the Chiricahuas, friendlier to the White Mountain groups than to the San Carlos or Tontos, had taken note. The White Mountain people had offered to "teach them what they have learned about taking care of their stock and farming."[1]

Crook happened to be at San Carlos on October 22 when news reached him that Naiche's party was about to cross the border into Arizona. About that time, three Indians from Loco's band had just reached the agency from the Sierra Madre. They were the advance party of a group of ten or eleven Chihennes, the balance of whom arrived at San Carlos in early November. Mid-November saw Captain Rafferty and Lieutenant Davis reach San Carlos with ninety Chiricahuas under Kaetenae and Chihuahua. With them were the two emissaries, Bonito and Frijole. On November 24, 1883, Crook announced the good news in a dispatch to Washington. He could not resist the temptation to rebuke his main critics, namely the territorial press, which had "worked up bitter feelings" to undermine his efforts.[2]

An analysis of what he wrote to his superiors reveals that he was equally adept at hurling his own "falsehoods" at his skeptics, for he spun a few yarns of his own. First, he unfairly blamed the press for the Chiricahuas' delay in coming in. He claimed that in "July and early part of August several small parties of Chiricahuas were seen this side of the border going north." These Indians were conversed with by several persons, who testify that the Chiricahuas "told them they were going to San Carlos." For some inexplicable reason, however, these Chiricahuas returned to Mexico. An omniscient Crook thought he knew why. During these chance meetings, these unnamed Americans had inadvertently sabotaged his operations by passing along deleterious rumors (which they had read in the newspapers) that Crook had become a lame duck commander. Thus, the skittish Chiricahuas had had second thoughts about their future at San Carlos and had immediately returned to the Sierra Madre. A nice tale, but it never happened.[3]

Hoping that Chiricahua testimony would corroborate what he imagined had taken place, Crook asked Captain Crawford to interview the Chiricahua chiefs upon returning to San Carlos. Their statements flatly contradicted his assertion. Crook had no reliable evidence that any Chiricahuas had crossed the border between June 10 and October 20, 1883. If they had entered Arizona or New Mexico, they would have avoided settlements of Americans at all cost. And he knew this. For over two weeks, he had Naiche's statement that "none of us even started north. If any Indians were seen near the border they were not Chiricahuas, for I would know for we always stayed together." His superiors in Washington had no reason to question the veracity of his report, so he spun this yarn to mute any criticism for the Chiricahuas' tardiness in returning from Mexico.[4]

Their return brought a set of new issues and old challenges. Naiche and Chihuahua adjusted quickly to reservation life. Kaetenae, however, was another matter. The youngest of the Chiricahua chiefs, at twenty-five, he claimed that he was a "Mexican Indian" who had never been on a reservation before. Perhaps he meant that he had never drawn rations at San Carlos. We know that about 150 Chiricahuas had fled Ojo Caliente rather than relocate to San Carlos when Clum removed Victorio and Loco in May 1877. It was probable that he was a part of those who refused to move.

Crawford met Kaetenae on November 17, 1883, two days after Kaetenae had reached San Carlos. From the onset, Crawford knew that the Chihenne chief would require a mixture of patience, firmness, and diplomacy. He described Kaetenae as the "worst of the outfit, very independent and surly." He initially mistook Kaetenae's militancy for influence because he thought that the Indians considered him "their principal chief." It was obvious at once that the chief, who had brought a herd of forty horses stolen in Sonora, thought that the sedentary life at San Carlos was not befitting a fighting Chiricahua leader. Of course he was right; the problem was that a war chief needed followers, and the high mortality rate in the Sierra Madre had left most of the Chiricahuas disillusioned.

Crawford warned Crook that Kaetenae was a "shrewd Indian who will need watching." He hoped that he could defer any confrontation until the rest of the Chiricahuas came in. Unless forced to take action, Crawford would choose the time, place, and appropriate issue to set the recalcitrant chief straight. Yet he wished to avoid controversy, knowing that Kaetenae was flexing his muscles, trying to figure out just how far he could push the captain. With Charley McComas's fate on Americans' minds, Crawford's priority was to persuade Kaetenae to turn over three boys (one Anglo and two Mexicans) whom his men had captured in New Mexico. Kaetenae "positively refused" until Mexico restored his captives to them.[5]

Crook wired Crawford that if the boy was Charley McComas, the Apaches must immediately turn him over.[6] Unfortunately, it was clear that he was not Charley. Instead of demanding the boys, which could have sent Kaetenae and his followers back to the Sierra Madre and given Geronimo a reason not to come in, Crawford opted for diplomacy. He paid particular attention to a white boy, about seven years old, held by Bacutla, a brother of Kaetenae.

Though he was unable to get a sufficiently "good look at his features" to identify him, his light-colored hair gave him away. Crawford guessed that the oldest boy, who was kept "herding their stock," might be Sylvester Sisneros from Valverde. He was mistaken, however, for it turned out that Sisneros was still with Geronimo. Crawford countered Kaetenae's refusal by invoking Crook's name: "I told him [Kaetenae] that you were endeavoring to get his people back for him and this would be a great help to [Crook] if he would give up these children, especially the white boy." Kaetenae agreed to talk it over with the other chiefs.[7]

Meanwhile, the captain was working privately through Archie McIntosh and his Apache wife, a relative of Chihuahua. Kaetenae promised to respond the next day, November 18. That morning he agreed to consider releasing them if the friends or relatives of the boys came to the agency. But he deferred a final decision until he met with the Chiricahua chiefs later that day. Crawford thought that Naiche, Bonito, and Chihuahua had told Kaetenae that they would not support his position. He was not sanguine, however, about the prospects for the captive's immediate release. If they refused to give up their captives, he advised Crook that any "attempt to take them had better be given up until Geronimo comes in." After all, Geronimo had sent his son Chappo "expressly to see how his people are being treated and to return and report to him. His son is a boy about eighteen years of age. I will hurry him back [to Geronimo] as soon as possible." Chappo was to return to his father in "three moons," meaning he would meet his father in January 1884.[8]

Crawford was prepared to act the moment he heard Kaetenae's decision. If he released the boys, the captain had an escort ready to transfer them to the safety of Fort Thomas. But Kaetenae was unyielding.[9] Crawford telegraphed the news to Crook, who replied, "Be firm. Don't allow Kaetenae to bluff you." Then, exhibiting the perspicacity for Apaches that he was famous for, he advised, "Use the other Chiricahuas [Bonito and Chihuahua] as far as possible to effect the purpose. Avoid using white soldiers under any circumstances, if possible."[10] The next day Judge Wright arrived on the stage from Silver City. Though pessimistic about finding Charley McComas, he had to see for himself. Crawford gave him the stark news that the Indians claimed that the boy had run off after the attack of May 15. Still, he vowed to keep hope alive until Chatto came because he had heard "an undercurrent of testimony" that Charley was with Chatto.[11]

Crawford ordered Kaetenae to bring in the seven-year-old white boy to Crawford's headquarters. Wright confirmed he was not McComas. No one knew the boy's identity. The child's face was painted, his right forearm had a tattoo of a "cross and arrowhead connected," and he spoke only Apache. Kaetenae revealed that several years before, they had captured him near a salt lick in Navajo country. Wright speculated that he might have been a Mormon boy whose parents the Apaches had killed when they captured him. He offered to find a home for the boy, but for now Crawford suggested that he stay with the Chiricahuas until the rest of the tribe came in.[12]

This minor crisis over, in early December Crawford reported, "Everything is peaceful." But Kaetenae still worried him. After observing his attitude and that of his followers, Crawford decided to keep the Chiricahuas at San Carlos for the winter, where he and his staff could keep an eye on Kaetenae. He informed the leaders, who accepted the decision without complaint. Davis recalled that Kaetenae had "made no effort to get on friendly terms with us." Crawford also talked with the chiefs about learning to farm in the spring. Mangas and Bonito wanted to plant near Fort Apache, and even Kaetenae seemed anxious to relocate there, though Crawford distrusted his motives. In a show of goodwill, he granted him permission to take eight men to examine the region's suitability to farm. He sent Archie McIntosh along to keep them out of trouble.[13]

A week after this cautiously optimistic report, the Chiricahua chiefs asked Crawford for a meeting. Bonito, who had just returned from examining Turkey Creek, acted as their spokesman. His people, especially the widows and orphans, needed clothing for the winter.[14] But that was far from his primary concern. Wilcox had just returned from Washington, where, according to rumors swirling around the agency, he had asked for permission to punish twelve of their prominent chiefs and warriors. Wilcox must have been aware of the potential harm his suggestion might engender—even if his superiors dismissed it out of hand. The chiefs and the headman were the sons and followers of Cochise and Mangas Coloradas. They remembered how the military had betrayed them.

Crawford realized their emotions were fragile. Brick by brick, he had tried to restore their confidence and gain their trust. Now, as Bonito said, they felt isolated and insecure, believing that Crook and Crawford were their only advocates. They appreciated the general's efforts on their behalf and "begged that he not leave them or give up control over them." Crawford reported that the Chiricahuas "are thoroughly posted on everything that takes place around here [as] a number of them understand both Spanish and English." They felt that "all the white people living on the outside of the reservation were down on them, and that the agent here, and all of his employees were down on them."

Crawford bristled at Wilcox's suggestion to seize the prominent men, which would have been an act of treachery and a clear violation of Crook's terms:

> If Agent Wilcox is agitating such a movement, and it should be ordered by superior authority, I hope an effort will be made before hand to turn all of them now here over to him in order that he may carry out this order.
>
> I know he is very anxious to have them punished as long as he has the military force here to do the punishing for him, but I think it would be advisable to turn them over to his charge so when the time comes to make the arrest of the twelve men he proposes, he can do it with agency police.

This was the first indication that Crawford was fed up with Wilcox. Unfortunately, the concept of dual control, a tenuous idea at best, had proven unworkable in practice for Wilcox. This bitter duel for control of the agency would become deeply personal and escalate in the weeks to come.[15]

By mid-December Kaetenae had returned from his inspection of the country at Fort Apache. As with Bonito and Mangas, he especially liked Turkey Creek, a wilderness area seventeen miles south of Fort Apache. It offered much to the Chiricahuas: good water, plenty of wood, adequate grazing, and excellent hunting. Moreover, the prospect of having their own homes remote from the San Carlos Apaches and Agent Wilcox at San Carlos appealed to them. Another benefit was its proximity to their only friends on the reservation, the Eastern White Mountain people. Although not the ideal place to plant, those interested in doing so would find plots of land on the east fork of the White River near Fort Apache, some fifteen miles from Turkey Creek. On December 15, 1883, Crawford informed Crook that the chiefs (almost certainly prompted by Kaetenae's return from Fort Apache) "want to talk over the matter with me tonight. Shall I let them go before spring?"[16]

Crook already had Crawford's view ("you know my reason for thinking so") that they should keep them at San Carlos until Geronimo and Chatto came in. He distrusted Kaetenae and wanted him kept close to the agency. Lieutenant Gatewood, in charge of the White Mountain Apaches at Fort Apache, was vehemently opposed to having the Chiricahuas in his neighborhood, particularly if he was to be responsible for them. He happened to be at

San Carlos when the Chiricahuas made their request. After returning to Fort Apache, Peaches alerted Gatewood that he had recently spoken to some Chiricahuas, probably Kaetenae's party inspecting Turkey Creek and vicinity, and that the "talk among themselves was bad." Gatewood warned Crawford that they would rue the day they allowed the Chiricahuas to relocate to Turkey Creek.[17]

In October Gatewood had conferred with Crook about this subject. If Crook decided to allow their relocation, the lieutenant had suggested that they break up the Chiricahua tribal structure, dividing them by family groups and assigning them to live with the various White Mountain and Cibecue clusters at "Cibecue, Carrizo Creek, Cedar Creek, Forestdale, and other places." Then Gatewood made a prophetic statement:

> But if they all settle in one place, the Lord only knows how long we shall be able to hold them there. When General Crook was here I mentioned this [idea] to him and he agreed that it would be a good plan. If the Chiricahuas buck against the idea of being scattered, perhaps the General may change his mind and allow them all to go the same place. But if I am to be held responsible for them, I most urgently request that they be scattered as proposed. Otherwise, I shall ask to be relieved.

Gatewood added another compelling reason for declining "to be responsible for their conduct." With court-martial duty and his obligations as judge of the Indian police court, "I have more than I can give my personal attention to now." Gatewood implored Crawford: "If you ask to be relieved, please arrange it, if you can, that I may not have to go to San Carlos."[18]

Meanwhile, Crawford had made plans to bring Geronimo and Chatto to the reservation. On December 11, 1883, Chihuahua, Chappo, and two other Chiricahuas left San Carlos to bring in Geronimo. One man was a former scout who spoke some English, which points to either Ahnandia or Dutchy, likely the former because he was a second cousin of Geronimo, and the second scout was probably Tuzzone. Chihuahua's involvement reveals how much Geronimo trusted him. Before leaving, Chappo told Crawford that his father feared troops and the possibility of "being put in the calaboose." He did not want soldiers to meet them at the border. Instead, Geronimo planned to make his way to Eagle Creek, where he hoped to live. The captain demurred: "After much persuasion and talk they finally agreed to come in at Guadalupe

Canyon." The next move surprised Crawford. Chappo, who had never "said anything to me or recognized me shook his hand and said it was all right." It was the first signal that he would be bringing his father a favorable report. They left for Fort Bowie, where they planned to leave their horses and go on foot into Sonora.[19]

With instructions from Captain Crawford, in mid-December Chihuahua's party rode into Fort Bowie. On December 18 they departed with a four-man escort. Chihuahua planned to show the soldiers where in Guadalupe Canyon they would enter the United States with Geronimo. The next day they stopped at Milton Joyce's Magnolia ranch, soon to be renamed Leslie's ranch, situated at the northeastern part of the Swisshelm Mountains some twenty-five miles north of the line.[20] Here they unexpectedly met thirteen Chiricahuas (eight men) under Zele, who had left Chatto in the Teras Mountains a month before. Chihuahua's party talked with Zele. Armed with the latest information, they told the corporal of their escort that Geronimo would not come up through Guadalupe Canyon but would enter near San Bernardino.

The next morning the two groups of Apaches headed off in opposite directions. Zele, with a small escort, went north to White's ranch, where they waited for Captain Rafferty. Chihuahua's men, with two soldiers as escort, went south to San Bernardino, where they planned to spend the night. They entered Sonora before dawn on December 21. They told the escort that they would return in twelve days. This, however, appears to have been a translation error. They were referring to Chatto's party, who, according to Zele, was to reach the border in about twelve days.[21]

Zele's arrival had caught everyone by surprise. He reached White's ranch on December 20 and waited until Captain Rafferty and his escort arrived from Fort Bowie. Rafferty also requested that Crawford dispatch Mickey Free from San Carlos to serve as interpreter. Because no one could speak Apache, the initial information was confusing. Once the controversial scout arrived, clear information began to emerge. Chatto's small party of twelve to fifteen people, apparently at either the Teras or Pitaicache Mountains, would be in within a few weeks; Geronimo and fifty to sixty people would not come until he increased his horse herd and heard from his son. He had moved camp south of Bugatseka and would be in no sooner than "thirty or forty days." Zele also said that six more Chiricahuas, four men and two women, were just south of San Bernardino and would be in shortly. They evidently had decided to come in later with Chatto.[22]

Rafferty sent Lieutenant John (Bo) Blake to White's ranch to escort Zele's group to San Carlos. En route to the reservation, Zele and his escort stopped at

Hooker's Sierra Bonita ranch. In an ironic twist, that night white horse thieves cut the fences and stole Zele's herd of thirty-four horses. Zele reached the reservation a day or two after Christmas. Fatty, who had gone out with Bonito the previous August, was with Zele.[23]

Zele's arrival with news of Chatto and Geronimo undoubtedly pleased Crawford, but he had another pressing matter that was threatening to affect the stability at San Carlos. Wilcox had never forgiven Crawford for calling a council with the Western Apache chiefs upon returning to the agency in June. The sharing of responsibilities had driven a wedge between them, forcing the agent to display his bottled-up frustration. In early August, a month after the July 7 agreement, he gave an interview to a Denver newspaper in which he took complete responsibility for the improvements at San Carlos. In particular, he noted that several bands had enjoyed bountiful crops because of the new policies to encourage planting and self-sufficiency. His remarks stung Crawford, normally an unflappable man, because he had seen that Wilcox, when he was at the agency, did as little as possible. Crawford could not resist adding, "The agent, I think, should give us some of the credit for the Apaches' industriousness."[24]

Crook noted that the do-nothing agent had frustrated Crawford. The general cautioned his trusted subordinate to remain focused on his duties and not to worry about who received or claimed credit for positive results. Crawford understood Crook's point, sheepishly replying, "I have always tried since I have been here to avoid a rumpus with the agent. I don't think I have ever given him cause to complain." But by then, Wilcox was seething over the joint control. In mid-September he wrote Teller requesting that the secretary revoke the July 7 agreement because Crawford had "too much discretion and authority." He was quick to point out that he "opposed the measures [of the agreement] and not the man." He was not prepared then to take on both Crawford and Crook.[25]

If the relationship was teetering then, it was about to hit rock bottom. This smoldering animosity burst forth in early November, when Crawford made a series of decisions that met with Wilcox's disapproval. On the surface, it would appear that Wilcox had justification to take the captain to task. But looking back with the benefit of Crawford's and Wilcox's sworn testimony, one concludes that Wilcox never let the facts get in the way of a bruised ego. So he told half-truths or lied. Incredibly, both Wilcox and Samuel B. Beaumont, acting agent during Wilcox's many absences, denied writing a letter dated February 9, 1884 (the catalyst for Crawford's request for a military court of inquiry), which concluded that if the dual control continued, "it would only be productive of unprofitable results to the Indians." While it is true that the assistant clerk, a man named A. B. Simmons penned the letter, he certainly did so under Wilcox's direction, for both Wilcox and Beaumont signed the letter.[26]

The fundamental problem at San Carlos was Wilcox's inability to wield any influence over his wards. They brought their problems to the captain, not Wilcox. Crawford had no systematic plan to grab more and more power; yet, it was an inevitable development as he handled more and more of the agency's business, often with the approval of the agent. At times, he probably should have referred some grievances to Wilcox. But the agent had never worked to gain their trust and had allied himself with the Indian trader, a government monopoly that the Apaches viewed with disdain. Wilcox hardly helped his cause when he was present, for he seemed happiest at the end of the day counting the daily cash receipts in the trader's store.[27]

Though Wilcox's resentment of Crawford clearly began the day the captain returned to San Carlos with the Chiricahuas from Mexico, the agent claimed that the tipping point had occurred when Crawford overreached his authority in the selection of Apache children to attend Carlisle Indian School. The idea originated with Crawford, who first proposed it on November 1, 1883. What offended Wilcox was not clear. Perhaps it was simply that Crawford had not run the matter by him, thus denying Wilcox the credit. A more likely scenario was that, as agent, Wilcox had to convince the Apaches of the benefits of sending their children away. But they spurned his overtures, which revealed just how little influence he had with the Indians. After weeks of trying, he had recruited only one child. He knew that his superior, Secretary of the Interior Teller, was expecting at least thirty children.

He needed Crawford's help, but the two were not on speaking terms. So on December 23, 1883, when Crawford had left his office to attend to business, Wilcox asked Lieutenant Parker West to "select thirty children" for the Carlisle Indian School. Explaining that he needed Crawford's authorization, West politely declined. Wilcox pleaded with him to get Crawford "to take charge of the matter. Tell Crawford for God's sake to go ahead and get them [children]. Get as many as he can. That Secretary Teller will be much obliged. I am tired of this whole God-Damned business having these Indians talking to me all day. They won't do anything I tell them."[28]

Crawford was up to the assignment. By early January he had used his influence to recruit thirty-six Apaches, bringing the combined total to thirty-seven. By the time the children left on January 23, he had augmented that figure to fifty-two children, forty-seven boys and five girls. Among them were six Chiricahua boys: Cis-dot-te-hey, the thirteen-year-old son of Bonito; Na-Tuzin (Lot Eyelash), a fifteen-year-old nephew of Bonito; Dar-dis-pe-nay (Stands in that Place), the seventeen-year-old son of Loco, who later became known as Dexter Loco; Cul-hol-chee, the thirteen-year-old son of Chief Gordo (who had died in Mexico); How-o-zin (Standing), the twelve-year-old brother of Kaetenae; and Is-kis or Sekis, a sixteen year-old son of Nash-slo-zey, a Chihenne from Loco's band. Crawford detailed Lieutenant Parker West to escort the children.[29] The Chiricahuas sent As-ka-do-del-ges, an "influential" scout known as Charley, as the chaperone.

Why was Wilcox upset at Crawford when the agent, under oath, admitted that he had enlisted his help? Wilcox had informed Secretary Teller that Crawford's interference "had greatly embarrassed him in their efforts to secure children." Yet he gave no specifics. In his own testimony, he admitted that he had turned over the matter to Crawford. His main grievance was that Crawford had failed to prepare the itemized list of the children in the format required by the Interior Department. This was a frivolous protest, given that the proposal had originated with Crawford, and he was responsible for its success. Wilcox could not bear the thought that Crawford would receive the credit for convincing the Apaches to send their children to school.[30]

The second breach in the relationship occurred about a month after Crawford's proposal for the children to attend school at Carlisle. The facts are straightforward. On December 2, 1883, Jesús Munguia arrived at San Carlos with a herd of horses and a letter of recommendation from Colonel Eugene Carr at Fort Lowell. Crawford permitted Munguia to place the horses in the quartermaster's corral. The Indian trader, Showalter, offered to buy the herd from Munguia. Showalter felt he had an advantage. After all, in his capacity he had a monopoly on business conducted with the reservation Apaches. So he low-balled Munguia, who flatly rejected his proposal and sold his horses directly to Crawford's Indian scouts. This enraged Wilcox, who lodged an official protest to Crawford. Beaumont, as acting agent (Wilcox was apparently then in Washington), signed the charge: "As such sales are in open violation of the law it becomes my duty to stop the sale and report the facts to the Honorable Commissioner of Indian Affairs. . . . You are requested to prevent further sales and detain the balance of Munguia's stock." Wilcox dutifully informed the commissioner, implying that Crawford had allowed Munguia to sell horses to any Indian on the reservation.

Wilcox had conveniently omitted one important fact, leaving the door wide open for Crawford to set the record straight, which closed the matter. He explained that he had allowed Munguia to sell horses only to "Indian scouts in the Military Service of the United States and to any others connected with the military service. . . . If I find that he is trading horses to any of the Indians under your charge, I will prevent it." Of course, Wilcox never mentioned that the only Indians buying horses were enlisted scouts under Crawford's command. Instead, in his misleading report, he made it appear that Crawford had violated the law, looking the other way while Munguia peddled horses to any Apache on the reservation. The real burr in Wilcox's saddle was that his son-in-law Showalter had wanted to buy the herd from Jesús Munguia at a wholesale price and sell to the Apaches at retail, thus realizing a healthy profit for him and the agent. Crawford saw no reason why the Apaches could not buy directly from the seller, thus eliminating the middleman's wholesale markup.[31]

With that hatchet not even buried, a third disagreement, which was probably the most acrimonious, erupted about the time of Munguia's visit. In this case, Crawford brandished the axe, flexing his muscles after his officers and Apaches complained to him about the quality of breeding stock of cows and bulls supplied under a November 11, 1883, contract with cattle baron Henry Hooker, the owner of the celebrated Sierra Bonita ranch. Hooker was to furnish nine hundred cows and thirty-five bulls at thirty-four dollars a head. Crawford discovered that neither Wilcox nor his subordinates had inspected the herd. At the request of Lieutenant West, Crawford appraised ten cows delivered to a Western Apache chief. He concluded that the government was paying thirty-four dollars a head for a "miserable lot of scrawny cows" that were worth no more than ten dollars each. Furthermore, many cows were too old to breed. Crawford smelled a fraud but was careful not to make that charge then.[32]

By throwing his hat into the ring, Crawford provided Wilcox with a legitimate reason to complain that he had overstepped his bounds. The responsibility for issuing rations and distributing breeding stock, and ensuring that the quality met standards, fell solely with Wilcox. But when Crawford received these complaints, he felt duty bound to investigate. He immediately incurred the wrath of Wilcox and Hooker. The agent tersely admitted that he was "angry at Crawford's interference in something that did not belong to him."[33] Wilcox defended Hooker in a letter written to the *Arizona Livestock Journal*. He painted a rosy picture during the festive Yuletide season at San Carlos: "A large portion of these [Hooker's] cows have been issued to the Indians, who are well pleased, and in most cases taking good care of their valuable Christmas presents. The cows are all from Mr. Hooker's Sierra Bonita Ranch, are superior graded stock, and lend a domestic appearance to the villages along the Gila and San Carlos Rivers, [one] full of promise and peace for the future."[34]

Hooker asked Crawford to send an officer to his ranch to help pick out stock, but the captain refused, explaining that he had no jurisdiction to do so. Hooker responded that it was unfair to reject stock after receipt. They were at an impasse, and Hooker eventually wanted out of the contract. But he was not going to go quietly. In February he came out with both barrels blazing in a letter to the commissioner of Indian affairs, Hiram Price. A long-standing critic of the military, Hooker thought Crook a "shiftless coward who had no ability to devise or execute a policy." He blamed the army for "every Apache outbreak in the last ten years."[35] He questioned Crawford's integrity and the role of the military. His hate-filled diatribe had metastasized into a bitterness and revulsion that seemed to defy explanation:

> Certain military officers prejudice the Indians against the Agent by suggesting to the Indians that the agent is defrauding them. . . . It will be to the benefit of the public and the interests of Indians on the reservation that the United States Army not be allowed within one hundred miles of the reservation. . . . I believe that Captain Crawford in command of San Carlos is incompetent for the position he holds and through malice and prejudice will abuse his official duties to accomplish a malicious end. I and every Agent in Arizona under the Interior Department for the last ten years will certify to the same.
>
> [He further claimed] that women are debauched by the troops, that drunkenness and gambling are prevalent [wherever] our troops are. . . . Military is only interested in promotions. Owing to my outspokenness in this matter, I believe it is the intent by many on command to deprive me of my rights in any and all contracts.[36]

By this time, Teller must have wished he had never heard of the July 7 agreement for dual control. On February 2, 1884, he asked Lincoln to consider relieving Crawford from duty because he was undermining Wilcox's authority.[37] One week later, Wilcox sent a long letter to Commissioner Price in which he said that to continue the agreement of July 7, 1883, would produce "unprofitable results for the Indians." Wilcox cited a pattern of interference that had begun when Crawford had returned with the Chiricahuas—meddling in farming operations, illegally protecting Chiricahua murderers such as Dutchy and those responsible for the death of the McComas family, and allowing the execution of a Yuma Indian (who had murdered his wife) after a jury of his peers had convicted him of murder. Surprisingly, he made no charges about Jesús Munguia, or Crawford's alleged obstruction during the selection of the children for Indian school at Carlisle, or Crawford's interference with Hooker's cow contract. When Crawford heard about these allegations, he called for a court of inquiry.[38]

With these series of disagreements, which had left Crawford unscathed, Wilcox retaliated when he got the chance. The Chiricahuas would need seeds and tools to begin planting at Turkey Creek in the spring of 1884. Crawford had assumed that the War Department would have to furnish these necessities, for "it would be impossible for me to get anything from the Agent here in the way of farming implements and seed." He was so desperate that he asked permission to use a fund of 187 dollars, generated from the sale of scouts' rations and hides, to purchase what he could in Tucson. But he realized that would not go far.

Crook was a step ahead of Crawford. Two weeks earlier he had written Secretary of War Lincoln that he expected the new Chiricahua arrivals to swell their ranks to more than five hundred individuals. They were "anxious to begin farming." Crook, however, suggested that the Interior Department furnish the funding for seeds and farming tools. He requested twenty plows, 140 shovels and spades, thirty hoes, forty single sets of harness, and ten two-horse wagons. He also needed $2,000 placed at Crawford's disposal to purchase seeds. Lincoln concurred, sending the request along to Teller, who instructed Wilcox to cooperate with Crawford "to the extent of funds on hand." Crawford sent the agent a list of the seeds he needed: 2,400 pounds of corn, 1,200 pounds of beans, 1,200 pounds of potatoes, 1,400 pounds of wheat, ten pounds of pumpkin, five pounds of water melon, four pounds of red pepper, three pounds of cantaloupe, and two pounds of onions. Wilcox agreed to order the material. Teller authorized the purchase in mid-January. Crook and Crawford requested that Wilcox deliver the seeds and tools by the end of February 1884, but Wilcox dropped the ball and failed to notify Crawford of any problems.[39]

With concerns about tools and seeds put on the back burner, Crawford again focused his attention on Chatto and Geronimo. In early January, Crook ordered Rafferty, Davis, and one troop of cavalry to return to San Bernardino.[40] Zele had thought Chatto would come in with Geronimo, perhaps reaching the border by mid-January. But in mid-December, after Zele had left Chatto, Mexican troops had surprised his camp, likely near the Teras Mountains, and confiscated much of his stock. Chatto admitted that this "delayed him till matters had quieted down a little, when he stole back again pretty much the identical stock that the Mexicans had taken." Driving a herd of eighty-nine mules and horses with Mexican brands ("legitimate" spoils of war, according to Chatto), Chatto's small party of ten men and ten women and children reached San Bernardino on February 7, 1884. With the men was likely Tuz-zone, one of the four Chiricahuas who had left with Chihuahua and Chappo. Also with Chatto was José First, a one-time Mexican captive. Chatto was in good spirits.[41]

Captain Rafferty and Chatto had concerns. The captain had seen a consistent pattern with every group of Chiricahuas returning from Sonora. Each had reached the border with large herds of stock with Mexican brands, a potential diplomatic nightmare. This was a problem for "the Mexican government and the San Carlos authorities" to iron out. But he recommended that American officials make it plain to them that they "cannot do so any more." The plight of the Chiricahuas held prisoner in Chihuahua City, which included Chatto's wife and two children, was Chatto's paramount worry. Rafferty told him to inform Crawford, who would pass along the information to Crook. Hoping that Geronimo would soon be in, Rafferty decided to remain at San Bernardino for the present.[42]

After waiting for some twelve days, Rafferty departed for San Carlos with Chatto's group; Davis took his scouts to Cloverdale, where he expected Geronimo to surface. Rafferty reached San Carlos on February 28. Four days later Crawford met with Chatto, who explained the reasons for the delay in coming to the reservations. As a husband and father whose wife and two children were captives in Chihuahua, he had done all he could to get them back. He spoke candidly about his feelings. After Mexicans had captured his family, "he cried—his heart was sick." He longed for their former country, hoping that the government would "give him back his land," which he said had extended "from Bowie to Huachuca and [over] to Hot Springs." He formerly had "been on a crooked trail" but now wanted the treaty to "last as long as the sun." Chatto said, "all the chiefs are friends but we fight sometimes." He also recognized that they had some "bad men who will quarrel, but we will straighten them out." Crawford would come to trust Chatto's sincere words.[43]

Meanwhile, on February 25, 1884, three days before Chatto's arrival at the reservation, Geronimo had crossed the line and gone into camp at Skeleton Canyon. With him were seven men and twenty-two women and children. Geronimo expected two more men, who were rounding up horses, to come in the next day. He had left his ranchería southeast of Bugatseka on January

26, 1884. His party traveled slowly to the border, for they had a large herd of horses and mules along with 135 head of cattle recently stolen from Casa de Janos. That day Geronimo divided the cattle among the members of his group. He asked Lieutenant Davis to "tell General Crook we have left the mountains and are going to San Carlos as we told him we would when we surrendered to him last summer." But this likely failed to gain the confidence of Crook, for Geronimo was coming in almost seven months later than promised if we accept the "two moons" theory. The only Chiricahuas left in the Sierra Madre were a small group of twenty-five, which included six men, two of whom were sons of Juh and one a brother of Kaetenae. Geronimo was unsure whether they had started for the reservation. He believed that they would come in, for they could not remain alone in the mountains.[44]

While Davis was in camp at San Bernardino Springs, a United States customs agent in Tombstone noticed Geronimo's herd of stolen stock. He hastened to Tombstone and reported this information to the customs officer, John E. Clark, and his assistant, William Howland. From their perspective, Geronimo was smuggling stock into Arizona without paying the tariff. They decided to intercept Davis's party and confiscate Geronimo's stock at Sulphur Springs ranch. They arrived before Davis and the Chiricahuas because Geronimo wanted to travel slowly to fatten up his stock on the nourishing grasslands of Sulphur Springs Valley. They assumed Davis would help them confiscate Geronimo's stock. Davis pointed out that Geronimo's party, armed with Winchesters and Remington rifles, "would not give up without a fight." The chief had left three men as herders to guard their stock, which they kept several hundred yards away from the ranch's herd. Accordingly, he dispatched a courier to Wilcox to telegraph Crook for instructions. He convinced Clark not to act until the next day, when he expected to hear from the general.

Meanwhile, Davis believed that if Clark attempted to take Geronimo's stock, a fight would result, with him in the cross fire. He needed to devise a plan to avoid this catastrophe, which would result in Geronimo returning to Mexico. Fortunately for him, Lieutenant Bo Blake, who had escorted Zele's group to San Carlos, had ridden in from Bowie with fifteen troopers to help escort Geronimo's party to San Carlos. Since Blake was his superior officer, Davis asked him "to take command and order him [Davis] to remain at the Springs, subject to the Marshal's orders, while he [Blake] with the pack train, the Indians, and their livestock lit out for the reservation as soon as the Marshal and the cowboys were asleep." To accomplish this, Blake produced a quart of Scotch whiskey. The officers played the part of gracious public servants, watching while Clark and Howland drank the "lion's share." Once they turned in for the night, Davis and Blake put their plan in motion.

But first they would have to persuade Geronimo. Davis sent for his head scout, a Western Apache sergeant who "hated Geronimo from the depths of his soul." He told the scout that he "was going to move camp at once and wanted his assistance in persuading Geronimo to listen to reason." Then he sent for Geronimo. It was a dramatic confrontation. The chief and the lieutenant were in the center of a circle surrounded by scouts and Chiricahuas, each side armed to the teeth. Bo Blake, "with his pistol drawn but concealed under his coat," backed up Davis, who explained the predicament to Geronimo. Davis outlined a plan in which he wanted Geronimo to sneak away with his people and stock while the customs men were sleeping. Lieutenant Blake would take them to the reservation. Geronimo's reply, an "emphatic No," came as no surprise to Davis. He dared the customs officers to take action. "If these men thought that they could take his cattle away from him, let them try it tomorrow. He was going back to bed."

Before Davis could react, the resolute sergeant of the Apache scouts seized control of the situation. Davis recalled that "words shot from him like the rattle of a machine gun in action as he faced Geronimo," who tried to respond but wisely went silent when he saw the determination of the scout sergeant. Then Davis, sensing that Geronimo had capitulated, wisely gave him a chance to save face. Perhaps "his people were not smart enough to get away without the men at the ranch knowing it?" Davis noted "what a joke it would be on the officers in the ranch" when they woke up and discovered that the Chiricahuas had slipped away. That struck a chord with Geronimo and his men. They quietly broke camp and left with Lieutenant Blake. Davis stayed at the ranch, waiting for the customs agents to wake up. They were astonished when they realized what had happened: "The wickiups stood as they had left them, the fresh meat they had jerked was lying on the bushes, the camp fires smoldering and not an Indian in sight." They decided to return to Tombstone. Before departing, Clark paid tribute to Davis's and Geronimo's ingenuity: they had pulled off a "mighty slick trick . . . I would never have believed it possible if I had not seen it."[45]

On March 10, 1884, Crawford wrote to Crook that Davis had telegraphed him saying that he and Geronimo would not reach the agency until March 20. The recent rains had left the Gila too swollen to cross.[46] On March 14, however, Crawford advised Crook that Geronimo's party would be in sooner, and he planned to see the chief before he reached the agency: "I think it best to talk with Geronimo before his arrival here among the other Indians for I think I can accomplish more." Kaetenae was giving Crawford more trouble, and he wanted to establish his authority and the ground rules before Geronimo set foot on the reservation.

Accordingly, the next day he took Archie McIntosh and Bonito to meet Geronimo. Crawford told the chief that he had to relinquish his stolen stock. He knew Geronimo would "strongly object." He listened patiently as Geronimo insisted that the stock was his property taken from his enemy. The shaman promised to give the captain an answer the next evening. Crawford had a trump card in Bonito, now a scout and a fearless fighter who never backed down from a challenge. Crawford correctly believed that Bonito "would have some influence with him [Geronimo]." The leader reached San Carlos the next day and went into camp with the rest of the Chiricahuas. Bonito must have persuaded Geronimo to part with his stock, for it now seemed to Crawford that Geronimo would deliver it up without much trouble. Crook had modified the original demand, instructing Crawford to inform Geronimo that he could keep his horses and mules but had to turn over the cattle.[47] Crawford's men took custody of eighty-eight head of cattle, which he sold at public auction on June 26, 1884, for $1,762.50 cents. Crook sent the proceeds to Mexico.[48]

A few days later Geronimo tried to explain to Crawford the reasons for his delay in Mexico. First, he had to "get some horses and cattle to bring here. He was poor and did not think that he had friends here to give him these things." On one hand, he said that he had come in to fulfill his promise to Crook. On the other hand, it was apparent that if his son had given him an unfavorable report, he would have remained in Mexico. Chappo and Chihuahua had told him that San Carlos was "not unhealthy like it had been before. All the Indians go to bed early and get up late and have nothing to fear."[49] He still had concerns, however, especially about their captives in Mexico, and he hoped that General Crook would help to restore them. Finally, he declared that he had "come here with the understanding that everything he has asked for will be granted. He remembers everything that the general told him in the Sierra Madre." Crawford listened patiently without referring to the obvious inconsistencies in the shaman's logic, for Geronimo, judging by the mendacious statements he uttered so casually, had obviously become very comfortable with deceit and falsehoods.[50]

The captain had also asked about Charley McComas. He wrote Judge Wright the sad news that Geronimo, who had a Mexican boy with him, had corroborated the statements made by the other chiefs that they had not seen Charley McComas after the attack in the Sierra Madre. Crawford had come to the sad conclusion that the boy was dead. "This is what they all say and I am satisfied it is so." Of course, neither he nor Crook had any idea that the Indians were dissembling about the manner of the boy's death. Crook sent his condolences to Judge Wright, expressing "the sad disappointment this gives me, for I could not have felt a deeper interest in his recovery had he been my own child."[51]

The ennui of everyday life at San Carlos had given way to excitement with the news of the much-anticipated return of Geronimo. Crawford was relieved that Chatto's and Geronimo's returns to San Carlos had gone without incident. The last thing he needed was more turmoil. He had recently dealt with a series of especially exasperating issues and problems including his ongoing difficulties with Wilcox, the still undelivered promised farming tools and seeds for the Chiricahuas, and the logistics of relocating the Chiricahuas to Turkey Creek. But perhaps his most potentially explosive problem appeared on March 10, when he was told by his "secret scouts" that Kaetenae, who had just lost all of his horses but two gambling while playing the hoop and pole game, had decided to leave the reservation for Mexico. Maybe he only wanted to raid for horses to replace those lost. Or maybe he had no intention of returning. Whatever his motives, we can say that measured by inflexible opposition to whites, no Chiricahua could then match Kaetenae, who was trying to hold on to the vestiges of his former way of life and his prominence as a successful raider and war chief.

He began to stir up trouble in early March, when Chihuahua returned to San Carlos with the news of Geronimo's impending arrival. Eager to return to his family after an absence of one hundred days, Chihuahua had left Davis at Skeleton Canyon, picked up his horse at Bowie, and returned to the reservation. The excitement generated by Geronimo's arrival seemed to galvanize Kaetenae, who bragged that "he had never been whipped" by troops. He tried to restore his influence with talk about leaving for Mexico once the "grass was up and the rains were out of the mountains." Archie McIntosh guessed that of the thirteen men in his band, only half would follow him, and that must have included his two brothers, Bacutla and Kinzhuna. Crawford's first impulse was to arrest Kaetenae, but he and McIntosh were concerned about the effect it might have on Geronimo. They decided to defer the decision until Geronimo came in. But the captain concurred with McIntosh's prediction that "sooner or later [Kaetenae] will have to be killed or sent away."

Crawford vowed to take the consequences if he tried anything before Geronimo's arrival. "I don't propose to let him get away," he assured Crook. Furthermore, he had the support of the Chiricahuas (Chokonens) who are "all friendly and I believe are well satisfied." In the event of a confrontation, McIntosh predicted that they (referring to Chihuahua and Bonito) would "kill him [Kaetenae] before they would allow him to get the rest of them in trouble." Though the affair had caused Crawford a "great deal of uneasiness," he assured Crook that they had the situation under control.[52]

Four days later, on March 14, 1884, the day before Crawford was to meet Geronimo, he provided more information to Crook. The lines of demarcation were clear:

> I have no fears of any of the other Indians except Kaetenae and his few followers. Naiche, Bonito, Loco, Mangas, and Zele live together while Kaetenae and Nana live apart from them. Chatto has joined them [Naiche's party] lately. The former are all very friendly. I can depend on them. Bonito and Naiche are both scouts. I intend to make Mangas [a scout] also. Bonito told me openly the other day that when he promised you [Crook] he came here to stay, he meant what he said. [He warned] that there is a party of dissatisfied men living together (meaning Kaetenae and his outfit) whom I would hear from sooner or later. [Bonito] said he was a soldier and would do whatever he was told. . . . Naiche came to me on his own accord after Bonito's talk and I made him a soldier.

He also had enlisted the services of Chihuahua to keep an eye on Kaetenae.[53]

Three days later, irony as well as destiny made its appearance at Crawford's headquarters as he nearly pulled the trigger on Kaetenae. A young man from the latter's band had "terribly abused a squaw." Crawford sent for the perpetrator, but he refused to come. He sent for him a second time, ordering the chiefs to bring him in. Kaetenae and the boy's father, probably a man named Chobegoza, came in with the accused boy. It was clear they were spoiling for a confrontation. They quickly learned that intimidation would get them nowhere with Crawford. He "sentenced him to thirty days in the calaboose." The warrior defied Crawford, declaring he would not go. Then Chobegoza stepped between his son and Crawford, brandishing a knife at the officer. Next Kaetenae weighed in, challenging Crawford to "put us all in." Crawford responded decisively to defuse the crisis. He told them that Crook had chosen him for this job. Chobegoza's son would either go to the calaboose for thirty days or Crawford "would pack up and leave and they could run it to suit themselves."

Crawford had called their bluff. They knew that Wilcox had refused to take them in, and that no one—not even Kaetenae—wanted to face the possibility that Crook and Crawford, their only friends on the reservation, would abandon them.

An unlikely hero emerged. Dutchy, the former scout under indictment for the murder of Jacob Ferrin in July 1882, stepped forward in support of the captain. Grabbing Crawford's arm, he declared that the "man would go to the calaboose." Dutchy's bold actions had saved the day and possibly Kaetenae's life. Crawford had calculated that his threat to leave them to fend for themselves would force a decision by the Chiricahuas, who he knew felt isolated and unwelcome at San Carlos. But he could not have foreseen what would happen that evening. A contrite Kaetenae came to his office and asked "to be made a scout." Crawford, dumbfounded at the turn of events, agreed, on the condition that Kaetenae and his followers "behave" in the future. Relieved, he wrote Crook that things "look brighter now."[54]

Two days later Crawford received a letter from Crook approving his actions. He was especially pleased that Crawford had employed the Chiricahuas to "enforce the punishment." He also thought it was proper to enlist Kaetenae as scout "provided you keep a proper watch over him." On March 19, Crawford informed Crook that he was "better pleased with affairs of the last two days." Hoping that Kaetenae had come to his senses, Crawford enlisted him as a scout the next day.[55]

Though he still had concerns and issues with Wilcox, Crawford hoped that he had turned a corner regarding the enormous responsibilities on his plate. In mid-March he had dispatched Fatty and two warriors to bring in the last group of Chiricahuas. On April 20 they returned empty handed, followed shortly after by two warriors who said they had left twenty of their people in Guadalupe Canyon. They wanted an escort to the reservation, which Crawford sent in the form of Kaetenae. They came in on May 14, 1884, with twenty Indians, four of whom were warriors, including a brother of Kaetenae, Nezulkide, and two of Juh's sons.[56]

For a teasing moment, the future seemed filled with optimism and hope. But nothing ever came easy at San Carlos. Reality soon set in. Crawford still faced many hurdles in the way of progress and stability. Yet, he could resolve these issues, for none were insurmountable. With a little luck, a lot of patience, fair treatment, and pragmatic decisions, he hoped to begin the Chiricahuas' transformation from warriors and raiders to farmers and stock raisers.

17

NEW HOME, NEW AGENT, NEW HOPE

Kaetenae is the promoter and ring leader of all disturbances.
He is now in the calaboose at [San Carlos]. He won't give you
further trouble.
                    Crawford to Davis, June 25, 1884

Soon after the confrontation with Kaetenae, Crawford began preparations
to relocate the Chiricahuas to Turkey Creek, seventeen miles south of Fort
Apache, where he hoped they would learn to plant and eventually raise stock.
That Crook and Crawford had come to this decision suggests how confident
they were in their abilities to manage the Chiricahuas and how strongly they
believed that hostilities were over for good. Crawford had governed with a
balance of equitable treatment and impartial decisions. The Chiricahuas had
responded in kind, which may have given Crook and Crawford a false sense of
security. They were supremely confident in their ability to oversee the Chiricahuas—even if the band was isolated at Turkey Creek. After all, Lieutenant
Charles Gatewood had served with success as the White Mountain agent from
Fort Apache. The military hierarchy expected nothing less from Lieutenant
Britton Davis (whom Crook named to be their agent at Turkey Creek) and the
Chiricahuas. But, of course, only time would tell whether Davis could get the
same results.

Some Americans and a few Chiricahuas were apprehensive about the move.
Perhaps the latter had grown so comfortable with Captain Crawford and his
staff of interpreters and assistants that they wanted to remain near him and the
main agency. Perhaps some were apprehensive of what Kaetenae would do
when he was free from Crawford's control. Given Chiricahuas' experiences

with Americans, they were usually slow to accept change, for in every transition, they had lost territory, and each experiment had left them fewer in numbers.

Crook also wrestled with a final decision. In February 1884, Gatewood wrote a second letter trying to sway Crawford and Crook from moving the Chiricahuas to Eagle Creek. He warned them not to expect help from the White Mountain people, whose fear of the Chiricahuas made them reluctant neighbors. Gatewood predicted that if Crook relocated the Chiricahuas to Turkey Creek, they "will not stay for one year."[1]

Crawford thought Gatewood was overreacting because the Chiricahuas, except Kaetenae, had behaved well at San Carlos. In fact, he had disciplined only two Chiricahuas during their first eight months there. "I can't say as much for the White Mountain [Apaches]," observed Crawford.[2] The *Arizona Silver Belt*, out of Globe, offered a popular solution to the Chiricahua presence. Expressing a view favored by most Arizonans, it suggested that officials arrest Chatto and Geronimo and put them on trial for murder. Once the jury fulfilled its responsibility and inevitably found them guilty, the justice system could execute them. Then, the Indian Bureau must remove the tribe to Indian Territory.[3]

Geronimo claimed that during their talks in the Sierra Madre, General Crook had promised him Eagle Creek as his home. In an outrageous display of arrogance, he proclaimed that he had made peace, and he expected "to get the land he wanted." Crawford explained that Eagle Creek was on private property. Geronimo offered a practical solution: "Can't the land be bought from those Americans and be given to the Indians?" He explained his thinking to Crawford:

> Here in San Carlos it does not seem to him that it is very well, because there is no grass, no good water, and there is some sickness here, too. He would like to live where there is lots of water, lots of land, and lots of wild animals. He knows where there is such a place [Eagle Creek]. He wants to know where they are to live [and] whether they will have enough land to live together. . . . He does not think that his people should be prevented from going to Eagle Creek. There is plenty of land, plenty of grass, and all his people could live there. . . . He begs Captain Crawford to help get this land.
>
> Camp Apache is not good as there is no game around there and he has heard that the Indians have to come here [San Carlos] to get their rations. Also, the ground is not sufficient to live on. Not enough land

to plant melons, corn, etc. . . . He is astonished that this is being refused. If we can't go to Eagle Creek then we want to go to Ash Creek
and see how that country is.[4]

Accordingly, after talking with Geronimo, Crawford granted permission
to Kaetenae, Loco, and Mangas to examine Ash Creek and Nantanes Plateau.
They left on March 23, 1884, with Archie McIntosh.[5] It would appear that the
Chokonens led by Naiche, Bonito, and Chatto, who had closer ties to the Eastern White Mountain group, were willing to move to Turkey Creek, which
was only twenty miles north of Ash Creek. The Chihenne chiefs had open
minds. Geronimo remained adamantly opposed to Turkey Creek. As far as he
was concerned, the region had another drawback, which he pointed out while
trying to dissuade Crawford from sending them there: "There is no mescal to
bake around Fort Apache. We will starve to death there."[6] In spite of that, no
matter their band affiliation, it appeared that most wanted to remain together.
Geronimo said "we want to be alone and have no Indians but Chiricahuas with
us." Chatto shared this view, hoping they would "live together and make a
tribe once more."[7]

But Geronimo was missing the big picture. Hoping the Chiricahuas would
become self-sufficient like the White Mountain people, Crook wanted to turn
them into farmers and stock raisers. Until then, however, the army would
continue to issue regular rations. The new location should have pleased the
Chiricahuas, for it contained good water, grazing, and hunting. The winter
months, however, promised dramatic changes from conditions at San Carlos,
for the elevation at Turkey Creek was five thousand feet higher, which meant
heavy snows and frigid weather. To well-meaning Americans, Turkey Creek
afforded the Indians the same benefits as their former homes in the Black
Range, San Mateo, and Chiricahua Mountains. One American officer compared Turkey Creek to the Chiricahuas' former homes in the Sierra Madre.[8]

After weeks of procrastination, by early April the Chiricahuas consented
to move to Turkey Creek.[9] Crook agreed, but before Crawford could relocate them, he urgently needed the seeds and farming tools that Wilcox had
promised to deliver by the end of February. In early March, Crawford asked
the agent when he planned to turn over the promised supplies. Wilcox ignored him. On March 2 Crawford sent Al Sieber to Tucson to buy what he
could from a fund of 187 dollars. A few weeks later, Crook asked Crawford
whether the "seeds and implements for the Chiricahuas have arrived." Finally, on April 5, Wilcox informed Crawford that he required authorization

from the commissioner of Indian affairs before he could furnish the supplies. Crook was livid over the obstruction and bureaucratic nonsense, for Secretary Teller, who was responsible for the Bureau of Indian Affairs, had previously approved a three-thousand-dollar expenditure earmarked for seeds and tools for the Chiricahuas.[10]

It took Washington over a week to address something that Teller had ordered Wilcox to take care of three months before. Again, the two cabinet members, Secretary of War Lincoln and Secretary of the Interior Teller, became involved. When Lincoln reiterated his determination to support Crawford and Crook, Teller seemed almost desperate to rid himself of the thorny issue. But he would do so on his terms. Assuming this would allow Wilcox, who had been railing against Crawford's interference, to save face, Teller ordered the agent to bypass Crawford and turn over the farming supplies directly to the Chiricahuas. After all, he reasoned, Crawford was responsible for the "police control" at San Carlos and not farming operations.[11]

Meanwhile, as Teller and Lincoln tried to reach a solution in Washington, Crawford was getting nervous waiting for an answer. On April 17 he advised Crook that the Chiricahuas were ready to move to Turkey Creek, but they needed seeds and tools. Finally, a week after Teller issued the order, Wilcox turned over the precious supplies. A relieved Crawford did not bother saying who received the distribution. The Indians were "ready to start," but the Black River, which flowed between the agency and Turkey Creek, "was impassable."[12]

In the midst of this minor emergency, Crawford and Crook faced another unwelcome bump in the road—one that threatened to turn into a crisis. Al Sieber had brought evidence to Crawford that the Scotch-Chippewa scout Archie McIntosh, Crook's most trusted guide, who had come to Arizona with the general in 1871, had embezzled rations meant for the Chiricahuas. Despite Archie's affinity for the bottle and tall tales, he had the supreme confidence of Crook. Yet the man who had once saved Crook's life was beginning to think he was indispensable. He was in the inner circle of those who counted. Yet, for rations that cost the government the paltry sum of $254.68, he had sold out his reputation and pocketed the money, perhaps receiving $500.00.[13] Outside the inner circle, he was a man who rubbed others the wrong way (most of all, Al Sieber). In Bourke's words, he had "been spoiled by too much consideration and attention."[14]

After receiving these charges, Crawford sent Lieutenant Parker West, recently back from escorting the Apache children to Carlisle, to investigate.

Crook advised Crawford that if the allegations proved to be true, he was to "discharge him and explain the reasons to the Indians."[15] On April 6, 1884, West returned, telling Crawford that the charges were true. Crawford called a meeting with the Chiricahua leaders. Their reaction stunned the captain: "They all said they wanted Archie kept. They said it made no difference if he took half of their rations [for] he was a good man & could have them." Crawford sent for McIntosh, who admitted guilt, rationalizing his conduct by saying, "it was done at every Military Post in the Department." This sealed Archie's fate with the scrupulously honest Crawford. The chiefs asked Crawford to notify Crook that they "wanted him kept but if you said discharge him all right." After the council adjourned, Geronimo, Mangas, and Chatto remained behind to talk with Crawford. They supported the decision to fire McIntosh, telling him it "was right, that their women and children ought to have [the] rations."

Crawford told McIntosh he could appeal the decision to Crook. McIntosh probably thought he had some chips to call in from his old friend and commander. He met with the chiefs and prepared a telegram to Crook, signed by every Chiricahua chief except Nana. They wanted McIntosh to remain with them, but their support was tepid and ephemeral. The telegraph operator refused to send it without Crawford's approval. Crawford exploded, ordering McIntosh off the reservation for "breeding discontent." When the chiefs understood just how angry Crawford was with McIntosh, they folded their tents and lined up behind Crawford. Even Chihuahua, a relative of McIntosh's wife, realized that Crawford was right and that McIntosh deserved his punishment.[16]

Crawford also faced another situation that demanded his attention. On April 21, 1884, Crook had issued orders to convene the court of inquiry to address Wilcox's charges of misconduct by Crawford. The court scheduled the trial to begin on April 29, 1884, at San Carlos. Crawford enlisted the services of his close friend Captain Charles Morton as counsel.[17]

About the time the hearing was to begin, Crawford had one burden removed when Lieutenant Davis, with a troop of cavalry, a pack train, and several wagonloads of rations and Chiricahua possessions, led the entire tribe of 512 persons away from the agency to their new homes. Betzinez described the journey that led to Fort Thomas and then turned abruptly north to the Gila Mountains, the same trail they had taken when Geronimo had "scattered" the Chihennes two years before. The morning of the third day, they bivouacked south of the Black River, which was still too high to ford. After waiting for two days, Davis used his ingenuity. Remembering that in his "duck hunting" days as a boy he had used a "canvas boat," he converted the wagons into pontoon crafts. He wrapped canvas sheets around the wagons and ordered his men to tie ropes to trees on both sides of the river's banks. It was a crude pulley system, but the Apaches, eager to get to their new homes, embraced the operation. Suddenly the atmosphere turned into a carnival-like atmosphere. The soldiers and Indians packed supplies and the women and children on the boats. Four or five Apaches swam alongside and, taking advantage of a swift current and the rope pulleys, guided the boats to safety. The younger men took the three hundred horses and mules downstream and found a place where they could safely cross. By the second day, everyone was across the river without any serious mishaps.[18]

Shortly after crossing the Black River, the Indians became more euphoric when a party of soldiers under General George Crook overtook them a few miles south of Turkey Creek. The presence of their "beloved" general had a comforting and reassuring effect on the Chiricahuas, who had not seen him in almost a year. At 3:00 the next afternoon, he called a council, attended by the chiefs (except Kaetenae, who had gone to the border to escort the last party of Chiricahuas) and by the leading men. José First and Mangas's wife Huera (also known as Francesca) served as the Spanish to Apache interpreters.

The Indians were clearly aware of the power struggle between Crawford and Wilcox. Crook was their "government," the man they looked to for guidance and protection. Betzinez remembered that Crook gave "them some good fatherly advice, mainly to settle down and go to work." Most of the chiefs spoke, with Naiche's comments "that we are all happy and contented" representative of the general theme. Bonito and Chatto made the most poignant comments. The former talked about the deadly attack on Juh's camp by Mexican Indians "who wear sandals on their feet." Bourke thought these were the Opata Indians of Sonora, but Bonito was referring to the Tarahumaras of Chihuahua, who had "killed or captured [many] women and children." Now Bonito revealed that he was "alone in this world; I have no brothers, no relatives."[19] Chatto urged the general to use his influence to restore their relatives held by Mexico. Chatto furnished the names of his wife, son, daughter, niece, and two other kinfolk, while Geronimo mentioned his wife and daughter. Crook promised to do what he could. Chatto never forgot Crook's words, for they had given him hope of seeing his loved ones. Showing his gratitude for Crook's efforts, he would become fiercely loyal to Davis and Crook. Toward the end of the meeting, four chiefs, Chatto, Bonito, Loco, and Mangas, agreed to go to Washington on behalf of their people.[20]

The Indians reached Turkey Creek on May 9, 1884. They immediately appreciated the change of scenery. Betzinez gave thanks because they were away from the "unfriendly" San Carlos Apaches. At an altitude of almost eight thousand feet, Turkey Creek was a much healthier location, with its "pine covered mountains and upland meadows traversed by clear, cold streams." Kaywaykla told Eve Ball that the "country was much to our liking—mountains with streams, timber, game, and privacy." Besides hunting wild game, they supplemented their diet by gathering wild vegetables, berries, and nuts. It was an auspicious beginning for the Chiricahuas as the entire tribe was together on a reservation for the first time in their history. Almost a half-century later, Kinzhuna remembered how grateful he was for the seed and goats that the government issued to them.[21]

Their new agent, Lieutenant Davis, had to return immediately to San Carlos to testify at Crawford's court of inquiry. During his absence, Crawford asked Lieutenant Gatewood to supervise matters from Fort Apache. In turn, he designated Lieutenant Hampton M. Roach to look after the Indians. Crawford had also detailed nine troopers of Company G, Third Cavalry, who had grown up on farms, to instruct the Chiricahuas on how to plow and plant. Though the harnesses were too big for the Indians' ponies, with the help of soldiers and civilians, the Chiricahuas improvised and began to plant. Roach was a rarity among officers, having risen through the ranks after winning a medal of honor in a three-day fight with the Utes in 1879.[22] Though unfamiliar with the Chiricahuas, he did his best to impress on them the urgent need to begin planting, for it was late in the season. Though unavoidable because of Crawford's court of inquiry, a new officer at this time was bound to run into problems with the Indians.

Fortunately, Lieutenant Parker West, his testimony in the Crawford inquiry completed, relieved Roach about May 20. He sympathized with his predecessor, knowing that the army had placed him in an untenable position: "Roach did not know these people [and] consequently did not know how to handle them." Details are sparse, but some minor flare-ups took place. In truth, any stranger would have had problems gaining the Indians' trust and confidence. West had a chance. The Chiricahuas knew him because of his duty at San Carlos and his role in escorting their children to Carlisle four months before.[23]

Despite the controversy, Roach and Gatewood, with the cooperation of the chiefs, had succeeded in getting seeds in the ground. Later estimates suggest that between sixty and seventy-five acres were under cultivation, with corn the main crop and a smaller amount of barley and potatoes. The Indians knew that a month later the corn sprouts would be suitable for making tiswin, which was perhaps one reason why the Chiricahuas embraced the project with such enthusiasm. They also planted, on a small scale, watermelons, pumpkins, and onions. West's first order of business was to inspect their farming areas on the east fork of the White River. He happily reported that every chief, except Kaetenae, was at work. They asked West to tell General Crook that "they are at work and doing just what he told them." West found 132 Chiricahuas working under Chatto, Mangas, Geronimo, and Naiche, and members of Zele's, Loco's, and Kaetenae's bands were tilling the earth. After finishing the planting, the Apaches planned to leave twenty men and women there to maintain the fields. The balance of the Chiricahuas, some four hundred, were busy at Turkey Creek establishing their homes and beginning to plant in a few isolated areas. West, impressed with the early efforts, thought life at Turkey Creek was "taking hold very well."[24]

West at once proved that he was cut from the same cloth as Crawford and Davis when he handled an incident, seemingly minor in nature, in an efficient and pragmatic manner. On May 30 a battered woman came to him, complaining that her husband, Zele, had beaten her "several times for no cause." Men typically administered these punishments, sometimes ferocious beatings, with logs of firewood, or as Davis preferred to call them, "stout sticks."[25] West investigated, concluded she was telling the truth, and separated them. Zele not only ignored his efforts as a marriage counselor but told him he would repeat the act (and surely he would have) if he felt she deserved it. West asked Crawford for orders, telling Zele that he "would have to abide by [Crawford's] decision." He found out that the "cause of trouble [was] two wives, I think."[26]

Zele's defiance signaled an important dichotomy: on matters of administration, the Chiricahuas would follow orders, but they would brook no interference from anyone on cultural issues. In fact, some old-time leaders were prepared to ignore the agent's advice. What happened in their camps was their business. But what was West to do when the young woman came to him, battered and bruised, complaining about the beatings? He had intervened only when asked to. This would prove to be a difficult issue over the next year.

Though no one could have then realized the ramifications, the incident foreshadowed the controversy ahead when Americans tried to enforce their mores to eliminate Chiricahua practices they found abhorrent. The barbarous customs that Crook wanted to stop included a man's right to beat his wife and to punish her for adultery by cutting off the tip of her nose. And he definitely wanted to end the practice of making tiswin. At San Carlos, without shelled corn and camped within two miles of Crawford, they were under his thumb.

They could do nothing without his knowledge. To well-meaning Americans, no rational Chiricahua could object to these common sense issues. But to Apaches, these were cultural traditions that the government—even Crook—had no right to legislate.

These were serious matters to the Indians. Not one Chiricahua chief—not even moderates such as Loco, Zele, Bonito, and Mangas—would have supported Crook's edict to abolish the practice of making and drinking tiswin, which they viewed as a social beverage. The Americans had their whiskey and beer. The Apaches had their tiswin. Moreover, many scouts whom Davis would come to depend on drank tiswin, or "grey water," during social dances and sacred ceremonies. Consequently, prohibition found no popular support. Their newfound privacy and freedoms at Turkey Creek, where their camps were dispersed and, in some cases, several miles away from Davis, gave them a chance to reinstate this practice. And with corn the dominant crop in Chiricahua fields, Americans had to wonder what would happen after corn sprouts emerged from the earth after the spring 1884 planting.[27]

On June 2, 1884, Lieutenant Davis left San Carlos for Turkey Creek. Three days later, he relieved West, taking charge of 527 Chiricahuas, including 23 scouts. So who were these scouts who would prove so valuable to Davis, whom the Apaches called Fat Boy? Nine were Chokonens, including Naiche, Chihuahua, Bonito, and Cathla; seven were Chihennes, including Charley, Kaetenae, Ramon, and Tsedikizen; three were Bedonkohes including Bonito, Geronimo's son Chappo (who served as Davis's orderly) and his second cousin Perico, a mighty warrior and dream shaman. And three were Davis's secret scouts—Dasendy, a sister of Charley; Na-nod-di (He trots), the Western Apache married to a Chihenne; and Das-e-klest (also called Frank), apparently a Chihenne who was the brother of Mrs. McIntosh. They were to report any suspicious activities to Davis. Years later, Davis recalled that Chatto was his first sergeant, but he would not enlist him until July 1, 1884.[28]

Not since Crawford's return to San Carlos ten months earlier had spirits seemed so high. Davis pitched his eight-foot A-frame tent on a "little glade" on the banks of Turkey Creek in the foothills of the White Mountains. Next to his new home he set up a large hospital tent, in which he stored a month's worth of rations. Sam Bowman was with him as cook and camp helper; the controversial Mickey Free served as Apache-to-Spanish interpreter; and José Montoya as Spanish-to-English interpreter. Compared to the barren San Carlos, the country was a paradise, rich with vegetation and wildlife. The summer climate was ideal. Davis thought it a delightful place. He particularly took note of the streams in his vicinity, filled with so many trout he wondered how the fish "found food enough to eat."[29]

Mangas, Geronimo, and Chihuahua had selected village sites several miles east from his camp on Bonito Creek. After the scrutiny at San Carlos, they undoubtedly appreciated the seclusion, privacy, and freedom. But the most incorrigible of the chiefs, Kaetenae, had made his camp on top of a ridge that overlooked Davis's headquarters.[30]

Davis's first official act was to inspect the farms on the east fork of the White River. In mid-June, he informed Crawford that despite the lateness in planting, they were doing well.[31] After returning to Turkey Creek, he met the chiefs to lay out the ground rules. He emphasized two important points: they must not make tiswin, and they must stop mistreating their women. His pleas fell flat. Kaetenae, recognizing the opposition, seized the opportunity and urged them to disregard the rules altogether. Surprisingly, Davis found that the chiefs were "nearly" unanimously opposed to Crook's rules. They countered Davis's order by saying that the only agreement they had made with the general was to live in peace. There was no discussion concerning "their family affairs, and they were free to conduct them as they saw fit." As for tiswin, they had "always made [it] and it had done them no harm. They did not want any of their people put in jail for making it." Chihuahua, still an enlisted scout, was the most vocal in his denunciation of Crook's policy. Davis ominously noted that the meeting "broke up with no agreement by the chiefs to accept the General's orders." Despite their opposition, Davis made it clear that he would enforce Crook's rules.[32]

A few days later, Kaetenae tested him. Lieutenant Parker West was to visit Davis for dinner Saturday, June 21, 1884. Davis had boasted of the fine turkey dinners that he had enjoyed, so he invited West to join him for a few days. That morning Davis followed the creek and began to ascend toward the ridge where Kaetenae and his band had camped. About halfway up, he heard a gobble. After thinking for a moment, he reversed directions, went along the creek, and shot the turkey. He and West enjoyed their "turkey dinner, and after the usual smoke and talk, turned in. Hardly had we put out the candle when a pebble hit the top of my tent and rolled down the side—the signal from a secret service scout."

Davis crawled out the back of his tent and twenty yards north found Mickey Free and one of his secret scouts, Dasendy. Her first words were a question: Why had Davis turned around halfway up the trail that led to Kaetenae's camp? He explained that he had heard a turkey gobble. She declared that turkey must have been "the good spirit of one of your ancestors," for it almost certainly saved Davis's life and prevented a likely outbreak. That morning Kaetenae's band had been enjoying a tiswin binge when they saw the lieutenant, his rifle in hands, approaching the mesa. Assuming that someone had informed Davis about the tiswin, Kaetenae and his men had taken positions at the crest of the ridge, ready to ambush him. Years later, Davis sardonically recalled, "Had I shown my head above the ridge of that bluff it would have received more lead than it could well have accommodated."[33]

Since shelled corn was not part of the Indians' rations, one might ask where Kaetenae's women got the sprouts to grind and make into tiswin. It clearly came from the fields along the east fork or at Turkey Creek, likely the former. The drinking party had continued throughout the day and evening. Dasendy said that Kaetenae "says he is going to make trouble here. There is a dance going on and he is talking to some of the men. He sent an Indian up the creek to warn the other chiefs." Davis later heard that Kaetenae's problems were "caused by his having two squaws," but he failed to elaborate further. Perhaps he talked of leaving the reservation to suit one wife or to leave the other. Regardless, in the time it took Davis to return to his tent, he had made a decision. He would arrest Kaetenae the next morning. He decided to send West to Fort Apache for troops and Gatewood's White Mountain and Cibecue scouts. At 11:00 p.m., he scribbled a quick note for West to telegraph to Crawford once he got to Fort Apache: "I think that matters had better not be delayed. As far as I can learn very few, if any, other men have joined him yet, and I doubt if more than a few more will. Delay may make matters worse. If trouble does not start tonight, I will arrest Kaetenae at sunrise."[34]

West reached Apache about 2:30 a.m. on June 22. Three hours later Captain Allen Smith, who had just arrived for duty at the fort three days earlier, was in the saddle with two troops of the Fourth Cavalry and six of Gatewood's White Mountain scouts. If everything went as expected, their presence would serve as a show of force and nothing more. Davis planned to call on his Chiricahua scouts and the chiefs for support. But no one could predict the outcome. He knew of the disaster at Cibecue, and the grisly death of Albert Sterling. He thought that Chatto, Bonito, Loco, Mangas, and Zele would support him. He believed that Naiche and Geronimo would remain neutral. He knew that Kaetenae had a core of followers from the young men of the tribe, but his band numbered but seventeen men, survivors of Victorio's and Juh's groups. Of these, perhaps a handful might join him and fight, but no one knew for sure. Davis trusted one member of Kaetenae's band, Charley, a loyal scout.[35]

In the gathering dawn over Turkey Creek, Davis dispatched his scouts to bring the chiefs to his tent for a talk. Shortly after sunrise, West rode into camp with two troops of cavalry and six White Mountain scouts. Davis had West deploy his troopers two hundred yards behind the hospital tent, where he planned to meet the chiefs and leading men. With Mickey Free and José Montoya by his side, Davis met the chiefs and prominent men, who were all armed because of the presence of soldiers. But because Kaetenae had not showed, Davis sent another message to him. He finally appeared with his men, stopping at a "pine tree a hundred yards in front of the tent." Thinking he might be the reason for the gathering, Kaetenae spoke a few words to his men and came on alone. He boldly quickened his gait and "strode up to within three feet of [Davis] before he stopped and demanded angrily why I had sent for him." Davis, calling Kaetenae's bluff, pulled no punches: "I told him that he had never been satisfied since coming on to the reservation and was causing trouble and dissatisfaction among the other Indians." Crawford had warned him to behave, but Kaetenae had continued his defiance. Besides Dasendy's warning, two other secret scouts, Na-nod-di and Das-e-klest, had confirmed that Kaetenae was talking about leaving the reservation.[36] Davis told him that he was under arrest and would have to plead his case to Captain Crawford at San Carlos.[37]

These words seemed to sober up Kaetenae, who demanded to know his accusers. Davis refused to give them up, saying only that Crawford would tell him at San Carlos. Kaetenae, seemingly stunned by Davis's threats, "wheeled in his tracks and started for his men [who] spread out, leveled their guns, and started toward the tent to meet him, their breech locks clicking as they came on." Then two scouts sprang into action, ready to enforce Davis's order. Charley and Dutchy, as he had in the March showdown with Chobegoza and Kaetenae, followed the defiant chief "with their rifles cocked and loaded."

For Davis, it was a dramatic and dangerous confrontation, one that easily could have exploded into a blood bath. Forty-five years later he remembered the scene: it had seemed like a "three cornered bet as to who would get me—Kaetenae's band, the Indians around me, or the troops in the rear." Fortunately, there were no itchy trigger fingers that day. And Kaetenae, who had gathered up his men, returned for a second time to confront Davis. The group stopped ten feet from him, and Kaetenae stepped forward. He was "trembling with rage so that he could hardly speak." Again, he demanded to know who had made these charges against him. Davis repeated that Crawford would tell him. The lieutenant's next move was risky but undeniably brazen:

he disarmed the chief. Davis unbuckled "his cartridge belt with the revolver and threw it over [his] arm."[38] Kaetenae had wilted, "his bravado falling from him like a discarded cloak."

The crisis was over. Bonito offered to take Kaetenae to San Carlos if Davis returned his weapon to him. Davis consented, and Charley and Chihuahua rounded out the escort party. Later that day an army surgeon set Chihuahua's broken arm, so José First took his place. In a telegram to Crawford the day after the arrest, Davis proudly pointed out that he had avoided using soldiers and Gatewood's scouts in making the arrest. "I used the [Chiricahua] chiefs entirely."[39]

This account is not in accord with that of Eve Ball, whose informants were quick to blame Kaetenae's problems on Chatto because of the latter's friendship with Davis. This revisionist history put forth by Ball's informants finds its way into many of her accounts dealing with events of the 1880s, when the tribe became polarized into war and peace factions. Many of her informants were associated with the "hostile" camp. Their vitriolic hatred and maligning of Chatto bordered on paranoia; to them he was the devil incarnate. Her version of Kaetenae's arrest, published in the book *In the Days of Victorio*, is loaded with errors and faulty memories. For example, she writes that Chatto, Peaches, and Mickey Free were involved in the arrest. Well, Peaches was not present, and the only Apaches directly involved in the arrest were Chiricahuas. Chatto, though present, was not then a scout (he would enlist ten days later). He had no reported role though he surely supported Davis as did many other Chiricahua leaders. According to her informants, Chihuahua defied Davis and quit as scout. Yet, until he got treatment for a broken arm the very day that Davis arrested Kaetenae, Chihuahua was going to serve as one of Kaetenae's escorts to San Carlos. Ball also wrote that the White Mountain Apaches helped in the arrest. We have seen, from Davis's telegram the day after the arrest, that no Western Apaches participated. Then she claimed that American soldiers took Kaetenae to San Carlos, but Bonito, Charley, and José First carried out that task. Finally, she wrote that Kaetenae never had a trial. As we shall see, he did have a trial, though whether it was a fair one is another issue. We can conclude that Ball's informants were usually very wrong and obviously biased in their scathing denunciation of Chatto.[40]

That evening Davis reported that the excitement had "quieted down." The next morning (June 23, 1884), José Montoya and the three Chiricahua scouts set out for San Carlos with Kaetenae. That same day, Crawford began building a case against him. He informed Crook that Kaetenae was "the promoter and ringleader in all disturbances." He pledged to give "him a trial and let him stand the consequences." Two days later, Montoya's party turned the trouble-maker over to Crawford, who immediately led Kaetenae to the guardhouse, where he was "ironed and confined." Kaetenae then fully realized the gravity of his situation. He promised Crawford that in the future he "will be the best Indian on the reservation." But Crawford now held all the cards. He had heard the same pledge three months before. In his mind, because this was Kaetenae's third violation, he had earned, in today's terms, the "three strikes and you are out" penalty. Even before the trial, Crawford had assured Davis that "he won't give you any more trouble." The captain had decided, in the best interest of all concerned, to make an example of Kaetenae and remove his disruptive influ-ence from the reservation.[41]

That night he revealed his plans for Kaetenae in a private letter to his friend Captain Charles Morton, stationed at Fort Thomas. Kaetenae "had trouble with his squaw & talked of leaving." But Crawford was sure that the chief "could not scam up a corporal's guard if he had attempted to leave." He as-sured his friend that the punishment he had in mind would "have a good effect on the rest." He had confined Kaetenae to "the calaboose, heavily ironed." If the Indian jury convicted him, Crawford had in mind to recommend a three-year sentence in Alcatraz.[42]

Two days later, on June 27, 1884, the trial began. From a jury pool of three hundred men, he selected twelve Western Apache chiefs (eleven San Carlos and Tonto and one White Mountain). Their objective surely was to please Crawford, who served as the "impartial" judge. Clearly, the fix was in, for the captain had already decided the outcome and sentence before the trial began. Crawford appointed Eskiminzin the jury foreman. Antonio Díaz translated from Apache to Spanish, and José Montoya translated from Spanish to English. At 10:45 A.M., Kaetenae came in to hear the three counts made by Crawford:

> First, Kaetenae on or about March 17, 1884, at San Carlos, A.T. tried to induce a number of Chiricahua and Warm Spring Apache Indians to go on the war path; second, Kaetenae did premeditatedly violate certain promises made to Captain Emmet Crawford, Third Cavalry, Commanding, consequent upon the acceptance of which he was in-stalled as scout; third, Kaetenae did on or about June 21, 1884, on Turkey Creek, A. T. attempt to create a disturbance among Chir-icahua and Warm Springs Indians living there, encouraging them to make an outbreak against the authority that controlled them.

Crawford added two more informal charges: Kaetenae had broken his promise to "behave" that he had made to General Crook in the Sierra Madre; and while an enlisted scout, he had disobeyed a direct order from his commanding officer, Lieutenant Britton Davis, when he had refused to appear when first summoned the morning of June 22, 1884.

Crawford acted as both prosecutor and judge. He refused to reveal the identity of Kaetenae's accusers. His evidence was his firsthand experiences, the remarks of Archie McIntosh, and a letter that Britton Davis had written about the events of June 21, 1884. Then Crawford played the "removal card," as we might describe it today. Designed to evoke fear in the minds of the Apache jurors, he claimed that if Kaetenae had broken out, "it would have turned everything here upside down." Americans would have held "every Apache at San Carlos responsible, demanding that they be taken out of Arizona."

Kaetenae tried to defend himself. First, he said that he did not know any of the Western Apache jurors and adamantly denied any wrongdoing. His enemies had fabricated these charges. He pointed out that he had left the reservation only once, and that was to escort his brother to the reservation the previous month. He had not stolen anything and had done nothing wrong. Crawford rested the case, remarking, "I don't care what Kaetenae says in his statement; I know that everything I say is the truth." Crawford represented the Truth, the Whole Truth, and Nothing but the Truth. He knew fully the effect his words would have on the twelve Western Apache chiefs, who wanted to please him. The arguments heard, he sent the jury to another room to deliberate. Forty minutes later they returned with a unanimous verdict—guilty, and a recommendation that Kaetenae "be punished severely."

Before sentencing, Crawford allowed Kaetenae to speak:

> I am not guilty of these charges. The proof of the truth of what I say
> is that I have sent my brother to school which I would not have done
> had I intended going on the warpath. You know now what I think
> about all this. Since I cannot get away, I must undergo any punishment
> you wish to give me. Everything that has been told you against me is
> false and reported by enemies only. Perhaps you will not believe what
> I say but I have always wanted to live peaceably on the reservation. I
> intended turning over to you the Mexican boy captives with my band
> in order that you might return them to their parents. But now I do
> not know what to do about them. I told General Crook in the Sierra
> Madre that I would return and remain quiet on the reservation. I have

not deceived him; I want to stay here. . . . Whenever you want you
can send to my camp for the Mexican captives living there. . . . In the
future, I will not think of doing anything wrong nor have I done so
up to this time. You may watch me but you will find that I will not
break my word. I never do so. All I want is that you release me.

Kaetenae clearly realized that Crawford had decided to make an example
of him. He pleaded for another chance, but his words changed nothing. He
was a victim of his past behavior and defiant attitude. Now Crawford's heart
was stone. He knew that Davis needed his unconditional support, and he was
the one ready to lower the ax. Without any sentimentality, he sentenced the
chief to "three years' confinement in irons." Eskiminzin affirmed Crawford's
decision, remembering "at one time I was one of the worst Indians on the reservation until they punished me, putting irons on my legs. All this was good
medicine for me and it will be good for him."[43]

That afternoon Crawford telegraphed the verdict to Crook and Davis. Of
the former, he requested permission to send Kaetenae to Fort Grant, which
was south of the reservation. He filed his official report to Crook's headquarters the next day, June 28, 1884. Crawford recommended that Kaetenae receive a three-year sentence to Alcatraz, where "he be kept in irons . . . dressed
in white man's clothing, and be compelled to do manual labor."[44] He conceded that his few friends might "be indignant," but the three Chiricahuas
then at San Carlos—Bonito, Charley, and José First—thought that punishing
Kaetenae "was all right." Yet he cautioned Davis "to keep a strong lookout."
Betzinez recalled that a few of the chiefs, including Naiche and Geronimo,
were "alarmed and angered by the sentence." Perhaps this was their private
reaction in words uttered in council. But they never gave Davis any indication
that they were upset. And, as we shall see, the verdict proved to be a humbling
lesson to Geronimo.[45]

After reviewing the file, Crook had second thoughts about whether the
punishment fit the crime. Able to look at the case more dispassionately than
Crawford, he concluded there might be "some doubt" about Kaetenae's intentions—especially with the evidence and testimony relating to the incident of
June 21, 1884. He questioned whether Crawford still believed "it was best that
he should be sent beyond the limits of the department." Crawford answered
affirmatively. The next day, on July 12, 1884, Crook wired division headquarters that it was not safe to keep Kaetenae in confinement at Fort Grant. He
requested permission to send him in exile to Alcatraz "with the next detach-

ment of couriers from this department." Five days later, the War Department authorized the transfer. On August 2, 1884, Crook softened the conditions of Kaetenae's sentence. He recommended that the chief "be kept in irons at hard labor for one month and then his confinement relaxed [and] he be permitted to go on the island and then to San Francisco."[46]

If closure on Kaetenae had left Crawford relieved and satisfied, he must have been elated when he received the findings of the court of inquiry in mid-July. It concluded

> that Captain Crawford's administration of affairs at San Carlos has been wise, just, and in the best interests of the Indians. . . . The position held by Captain Crawford is a difficult and thankless one to fill, and the Court believes it would be difficult to find a man as suitable for it as he is. There is not the slightest proof of any act on the part of Captain Crawford that could in any way unfit him to remain [as agent]. . . . On the contrary, it is apparent that every act of his administration has had its inspiration in his firm desire to advance the condition of the tribes in industry and morals.[47]

Charles Connell, a civilian at San Carlos, thought, "any attempt to besmirch the character and efficiency of Captain Crawford was a decided failure." Wilcox's testimony revealed that his charges were spurious and personal. He had fought Crawford tooth and nail, and now he had too much baggage to remain. He resigned at the end of August.[48]

Meanwhile, concerns that the Chiricahuas would respond militantly to Kaetenae's arrest would prove to be unfounded. Instead, Davis recalled, "peace reigned in camp." The tribe had settled into a carefree life at Turkey Creek. Davis issued them weekly rations of coffee, sugar, beans, and flour. By design, he issued no corn. They received their beef rations at Fort Apache. While the women did the work, the men settled into a life occupied by hunting, "loafing, and gambling."[49]

The summer of 1884 at Turkey Creek passed without significant trouble. Davis and the Chiricahuas became better acquainted with each other, and the relationship grew stronger. He was surprised to discover that the Indians were more than just savages. After hearing their stories of enforced removals, he began to understand why they had resisted. He recognized that most had no fight left in them; and he wondered, as the Chiricahuas would in the twentieth century, why the Indians "showed no resentment of the way they had been treated in the past."[50] They asked him why the government had removed them from their ancestral homelands to the "malarial river bottoms of the Gila." Ever present in their thoughts was a fear of the future, given their experiences of the previous two decades. "Above all, they wondered if they would be now allowed to live in peace," noted Davis.[51]

On July 1, 1884, Davis took the first step in formalizing his relationship with Chatto, enlisting him as scout and appointing him sergeant. Crook had authorized him to bring Company B, Indian Scouts, to a strength of thirty scouts. Besides Chatto, Davis enlisted six other scouts, including Cooney (a close friend of Chatto), Noche, and Geronimo's second cousin, Fun, the revered young warrior who was the hero of the García fight.[52] Davis relied on Chatto to provide daily reports. And Chatto, buoyed by Crook's promise to see what he could do about his family held prisoner in Chihuahua, instantly gained the trust of Davis. Four decades later, when in the twilight of his life, the lieutenant described Chatto as "one of the finest men, red or white, I have ever known."[53]

Davis, fostering concerns in the aftermath of Kaetenae's arrest, showed that he was flexible to legitimate Chiricahua requests. That summer, responding to a request from several chiefs, he decided to allow half the tribe to go to Ash Creek to gather acorns, probably those of the Emory oak. They ate the nuts or pounded them into a fine powder, which they mixed with jerked meat and fat into a form of meatballs, then stored them for later use.[54] Yet, whatever simmering unrest felt by Kaetenae's handful of followers, it soon became clear to Davis and Crawford that the Chiricahua chiefs had taken note of his punishment.[55]

As Crook began efforts to get Mexico to release their Chiricahua captives, Davis decided to confront the delicate issue of the four New Mexican boys held by the Chiricahuas. Crawford had been corresponding with relatives of the boys captured during Victorio's and Nana's raids. The captain realized they were more likely to turn over these boys, who had lived with them between three and five years, to their blood relatives. The first week of August, family members began to arrive from New Mexico, anxious to liberate the boys. On August 2, 1884, two men from Quemado, José María Madrid and Jesús Padilla, were the first of three parties to arrive at Fort Apache from New Mexico. With the help of Gatewood and Crawford, Madrid had retrieved one son at San Carlos from Nana exactly one year before. Now they were back to get their sons, Clemente Madrid and Pablo Padilla. Davis, pessimistic about the outcome, telegraphed Crawford with an amazing assertion: "To get these children will be a doubtful undertaking. If they are identified do you wish me to turn them over to the Mexicans, whether Indians are willing or not?"

Despite Davis's misgivings, that day Geronimo stepped in and turned the boy over to his relatives. Crawford gloated to Crook: "The success was due to the absence of Kaetenae." That day the happy fathers returned to Fort Apache with their sons. Captain Will W. Daugherty, noticing the destitute position of the men, generously provided them four days of rations to tide them over on their return trip to New Mexico.[56] Davis conceded that all had gone much better than he had anticipated and that he was expecting no "trouble to grow out of this matter."[57]

The second group from New Mexico reached Turkey Creek on September 21, 1884. José María Sanches and Fernandez Padilla had come from Las Padillas near Isleta. They were seeking Louis Padilla, the largest and oldest of the captives, whom the Chihennes had held for some five years. He had adapted well to Apache life, learning their language and gaining the trust of Kaetenae, becoming a member of his extended family. The Apaches called him He Who Steals Love because of his winning personality.[58] Padilla initially wanted to remain with the Apaches. When he saw his grandfather and uncle, however, he changed his mind. Kaetenae's wife, a strong-willed woman named Guyan, "did not want to give him up." Davis dismissed her defiance and said he would "take him whether or not they liked it." She finally acquiesced and released the boy to Davis, who hurried him off to Fort Apache that day.[59]

Sylvester Sisneros, who was with Geronimo harvesting crops at the east fork of the White River, was their last captive. On October 6, 1884, the Bedonkohe chief released him when the boy recognized his uncle.[60] Their bargaining chips gone, the Chiricahuas were anxious to hear news about their family members held captive in Mexico. And Loco wanted news about a group of twenty Chihennes who had fled to Fort Wingate when Geronimo's warriors forced Loco's band to leave San Carlos in April 1882. Crook was coming for a visit, and they planned to talk to him about their people.

Meanwhile, as the summer temperatures began to cool, Davis and the Chiricahuas came to the logical decision to move their camps to the country near Fort Apache (2,800 hundred feet lower than Turkey Creek) before the first snow. Crawford seconded Davis's request, thinking (erroneously) that many Chiricahuas would remain at Turkey Creek and that Davis could "manage them as well [from] Fort Apache." Before the movement, which apparently took place in early November, the Chiricahuas planned to hold a "heap big dance [the] first snappy day of fall."

Although Davis is silent on the subject of tiswin, it was apparent that the Chiricahua women were having a field day making the liquor, which was available in copious amounts. A few weeks before the dance, Davis and Bowman inspected the Indian farms at East Fork. Davis was disappointed in the harvest, although he explained that the planting "was done too late in the season." They estimated the harvest would produce 45,000 pounds of corn, 1,800 pounds of barley, 200 watermelons, 150 cantaloupes, 300 pumpkins, and a few pounds of peppers and onions. Another report cited these same numbers and added 3,000 pounds of potatoes. Davis estimated that the Indians had sixty acres under cultivation; another observer thought seventy-five.[61]

The corn yield was a double-edged sword. Though it supplemented their weekly rations of beef, flour, sugar, coffee, and salt, the Apaches also set aside some of the crop to make tiswin. They may have added the potatoes to the brew for extra punch.[62] And at this dance, the Chiricahuas enjoyed their favorite social drink. Even the scouts, including Chatto, the sergeant of scouts, continued to drink tiswin, a practice Davis would be unable to control.

One Chiricahua related to Morris Opler an anecdote about Chatto, reciting the story of an event that occurred during the celebration mentioned by Davis in the fall of 1884. Chatto was training his sixteen-year-old nephew to be a warrior. That summer he had paid special attention to the teenager, teaching him as his father had to ride, shoot, and hunt. This boy was fearless and "would do what Chatto told him whether it was dangerous or not." The chief decided to show off his nephew's abilities. He walked over to a "big crowd where they were drinking tiswin." He announced that his nephew "can ride any horse bareback with no rope on it." One man replied, "We all like to see things like that. We will bet you two five-gallon cans of tiswin. You get that boy, let him ride down that hill bareback, down that steep hill." Chatto accepted the wager, for "in those days [a] five gallon [tiswin] can was worth a horse [or] a belt of cartridges or a gun and belt." They gave his nephew a "bronco" horse with a "rope around his nose, nothing else." Then the boy "rode the horse down the hill just like nothing. The horse pitched all around with him. The horse could not shake him off."[63]

A few weeks after the dance, the Chiricahuas had another reason to celebrate. General Crook had arrived at Fort Apache on his third annual fall tour of the reservation. The principal chiefs showed up, with Chatto and Geronimo especially eager to show off their farms. Robert Frazer, a member of the Indian Rights Association based in Philadelphia, said the chiefs told Crook "they wanted to turn their faces the same way as the whites, to work, and raise money." Crook, concerned that they might harbor some resentment over Kaetenae, was thinking about commuting his sentence at Alcatraz. He discovered, surprisingly, that the chiefs, particularly Geronimo, had appreciated the tranquillity in Kaetenae's absence. They did not want him back, fearing that he would revert to his old ways of creating "excitement and restlessness." He decided to postpone the decision until next spring. But the one thing they wanted from Crook was justice. After all, they had released their captives taken in legitimate warfare. In return, they wanted their captives in Mexico and New Mexico restored to them. Crook explained what he was trying to do.[64]

Three months earlier, on July 11, 1884, he had asked the War Department to investigate the status of the Indian prisoners in Mexico. Crook recognized this as the most important subject to the Indians, who "are constantly urging that steps be taken to secure their return." He pointed out that as long as Mexico held their people, "these remained an inducement" for their relatives to return to Mexico and resume raiding for their "own captives to exchange." And in late September this issue bubbled to the surface when Loco returned from a visit to the Navajo reservation with his wife. About ten members of his band remained at Fort Union, and he was anxious for them to rejoin his people. Unfortunately for the concerned parties, the wheels of American bureaucracy moved slowly. It would take five months for authorities in Washington to allow the Chihennes at Fort Union to rejoin Loco.[65]

Robert Frazer's main concern for the Chiricahuas was their need for clothing, They had not received any cloth from the Interior Department because it had refused to accept responsibility for their care; this standing also left them ineligible to receive any of the annual annuities, a stupid policy that Crook and Crawford were then trying to amend. But to Frazer the travesty was evident. The men "came to the conference wearing the same clothing, I am told, that they had when they were out on the warpath." Their children "were running around in rags or naked . . . and the widows, with no one to care for them, have nothing to wear." Lieutenant Davis told him they do not "average more than one blanket per family." Frazer urged his organization to allocate $1,800 for blankets and clothing to make the Chiricahuas "self-supporting."[66]

But generally, the state of affairs at Turkey Creek in fall 1884 was one of hope and promise. The Chiricahuas had enjoyed the fruits of their first harvest and knew they had the potential to increase significantly their yields the next spring. The chiefs seemed content, for they had plenty to eat from the rations issued by the War Department, which they supplemented by hunting and gathering. They were confident that the military hierarchy of Crook,

Crawford, and Davis had their best interests at heart. To be sure, the bureaucratic battles between Crawford and Wilcox had caused unnecessary problems, but Crook and Crawford had exposed the pettiness of the former agent. So, as the Chiricahuas prepared to move to their winter homes near Fort Apache, everyone thought that the Apache Wars were over. But an insidious foe lurked, just waiting to sprout and seize their minds and spirits. Davis could not have realized it then, but the rowdy tiswin parties at Turkey Creek (which had done no serious damage up to that point) would produce big trouble in the months to come. The honeymoon was over. Years later Britton Davis, with the clear vision of hindsight, wondered why he had not seen it coming.[67]

18

PRELUDE TO DISASTER

Geronimo and the others [who left the reservation] never said anything to anyone unless they knew they would fall in with their plan.

Ramon (a Chihenne in Loco's band) to Captain Francis
Edwin Pierce

In mid-November, soon after the first snowfall, Davis led the Chiricahuas to their winter camps in the lower country near Fort Apache. He selected a site along the White River three miles above the fort; the Chiricahuas made camp a few miles east along the river and in secluded canyons in the foothills of the White Mountains. The quartermaster at Fort Apache, trying to make Davis as comfortable as possible, furnished him with a "twelve-foot wall tent, floored, [with] the sides boarded up to the eaves of the roof." Davis came to appreciate his new quarters, for the coming winter of 1884–85 would be brutally cold and unusually snowy.[1]

Once settled in their new homes, the Chiricahuas looked forward to a quiet winter. They had plenty to eat because the army continued to provide sufficient food: one pound of beef and flour to each of them daily regardless of age and smaller quantities of coffee, sugar, beans, and salt.[2] The one staple they had in abundance was shelled corn, and they apparently had no need to use it to augment their food supply. Consequently, they had plenty on hand to make tiswin, in defiance of Davis's orders. Davis later recalled that winter as one in which the Chiricahuas "drew their rations, gambled, loafed, and quarreled."[3]

Davis, remaining close to quarters because of the harsh winter conditions, had to rely on his scouts and interpreters for information. And evidence suggests that many scouts enjoyed their tiswin. On December 8, 1884, an informant reported to Davis that "there was another tiswin drunk last night,"

implying that this activity had become a frequent occurrence. That day, however, a severe blizzard had kept Davis confined to quarters. Unfortunately,
these were not isolated incidents. In mid-December he arrested several Chiricahuas for tiswin-related activities. On Christmas Eve he telegraphed Crawford, conceding he was unable to stop this activity: "We are having a great deal
of trouble this winter with tiswin parties. The Apache calaboose has quite a
number of Chiricahua and White Mountain Apaches in it under that charge."
They were serving sentences ranging from ten days to two weeks, but his dis-
ciplinary actions had no effect on the tiswin problem. Davis admitted that he
could not arrest everyone involved with tiswin. Instead he went after the most
"aggravated cases."[4]

Though this disturbing trend troubled him, Davis was more concerned
about the attitude of the Chiricahua chiefs, especially when Chihuahua and
Mangas complained about scouts arresting their friends or relatives for making the drink, consuming it, or causing a disturbance. Chihuahua's response
came as no surprise, for the independent chief always protested "on all matters
of discipline." But Mangas's attitude puzzled Davis. The lieutenant never expected trouble from Mangas, who often joined Loco to support Davis. Mangas
had been one of the "most tractable of the Indians." That he chose tiswin as
the issue on which to make a stand clearly perplexed the lieutenant. He soon
learned why. Because one of Mangas's wives, Huera, was a "skillful tiswin
maker," her product was regularly in "great demand." Davis did not completely realize it then, but the Chiricahuas' defiance of the edict against tiswin
was a serious subject. They were simply not going to give it up.[5]

Crook had heard rumblings that the Chiricahuas believed that he had
reneged on his promises. They were referring to their captives and annuity
goods. Crook was doing everything possible about the former, but the responsibility for the latter lay with the new agent, Charles D. Ford, who had refused
to turn over the annuities to Crawford and Davis. This time, as Crook liked
to say, there were two sides to the story. And this time an impartial arbitrator
would have laid the blame for the delay in annuities at the feet of one man,
Captain Crawford.

Named by the secretary of the interior to replace Wilcox, Ford, a thirty-
six-year-old Colorado pioneer, was yet one more agent who knew nothing
about Apaches. The beneficiary of friendship with two important Colorado
Republican senators, Ford's appointment, like his predecessor's, was political.
That was where the similarity ended. Optimistic, ambitious, and resourceful,
he arrived at San Carlos with an open mind and a determination to carry out
his duties. He combined sincere convictions and a strong work ethic with a

pleasant personality and relaxed demeanor. Ford reached San Carlos in mid-November. He hoped that his actions and conscientiousness would be the tonic to win over the Indians and Crawford. The Apaches at San Carlos, who had seen their share of uninterested and corrupt officials, gave him a chance. Unfortunately for Ford, Crawford did not intend to reach out to the new civil agent, no matter what he said or did.

For the first two weeks that Ford was at San Carlos, Crawford snubbed him. Ford had little time to dwell on this juvenile behavior. Wilcox had left the agency buildings in a dilapidated condition, and most of the employees were inefficient and corrupt. Ford discharged six of the nine holdovers from Wilcox's regime. But not Samuel Beaumont, whom Crawford detested. Beaumont had denied responsibility (when actually he was involved) for the misleading letter written on February 9, 1884, that had prompted Crawford to call for a court of inquiry. Ford needed Beaumont's services until he could find a competent replacement.[6]

The first interaction between Crawford and Ford came on December 5, 1884. That day, Ford issued the annuity goods to the Indians at San Carlos. He set aside a portion for the White Mountains and Chiricahuas at Fort Apache. Crawford, without checking with Ford, ordered Davis and Gatewood to bring a pack train to San Carlos for their annuities. The captain reasoned that Ford should have no contact with them because they were under the jurisdiction of the War Department. Ford explained to Crawford that the Bureau of Indian Affairs' regulations required him or one of his employees to witness the distribution. Crawford had heard a rumor that Ford intended to send his archenemy, Samuel Beaumont, to Apache to oversee the transaction. Regardless, Crawford conveniently overlooked the fact that the Interior Department was responsible for issuing the annuities, and that Ford, as its agent, had a fiduciary responsibility for the proper accounting and distribution of the goods.

A stalemate resulted, with Ford the one standing on principle. The agent offered to compromise. He would go to Fort Apache with Davis and Gatewood to observe the doling out of annuities. This way, he was complying with regulations. Crawford, however, was obstinate and inflexible. After several weeks of waiting for Ford to turn over the annuities, on January 4, 1885, he ordered Davis and Gatewood to return to Fort Apache with empty pack trains. Their return without the vital supplies was a major disappointment to the Chiricahuas, who urgently needed blankets and clothing. Some took this opportunity to besmirch Crook's character, saying that he had reneged on his promises. They knew only that ten thousand pounds of annuities designated for them were still in the storehouse at San Carlos.

The real losers were the White Mountain and Chiricahua Apaches, who bore the brunt of Crawford's irrational behavior. Even a January 21, 1885, plea from Davis that the stalemate had "caused considerable dissatisfaction" with the Chiricahuas failed to move Crawford from his irrational position. Once again, the Chiricahuas and White Mountain Apaches had become the pawns in the struggle for dual control.[7]

Meanwhile, Agent Ford turned his attention to farming operations for his wards. He overruled Crawford's decisions about allocating farming lands along the San Carlos River. In truth, one could ask why Crawford, who was in charge of the police control of the agency, had bothered getting involved with farming operations, which fell into the bailiwick of the civil agent. On January 19, 1885, Ford, who had just finished his second month on the job, stood up to Crawford. To the commissioner of Indian affairs he registered a protest against Crawford's interference:

> The right to direct the farming operations of my Indians has been as-sumed and is now being exercised by Captain Crawford. Against my written protest on Saturday [January 17, 1885], he obliged a band of Indians to perform work [that] I had forbidden. He deprived them of a portion of their tools, which he carried to Military Headquarters.
>
> The same Indians while proceeding to work this morning under my personal supervision were taken from me by Crawford's orders and sent to engage in work I had forbidden . . . [and] are now doing under direction of white soldiers. Unless the rights of my office are promptly sustained, I ask for the immediate appointment of my successor.

The commissioner of Indian affairs, Hiram Price, forwarded the letter to the secretary of the interior, remarking that "immediate action" was necessary because Crawford had overstepped his authority. The secretary of the interior agreed, adding in a note to Secretary of War Lincoln that he had hoped that "greater harmony would prevail" with the appointment of Ford. Lincoln con-curred, admonishing Sheridan to inform Crook that Crawford's jurisdiction was "police control" and not farming operations. He ruled that Crawford had clearly "gone beyond his proper authority and this he should carefully refrain from doing."[8]

When Crook first heard of the controversy, he realized that Crawford was wrong, but he loathed admitting such officially. So he stated the bare facts and ignored the real issue of whether Crawford had abused his power. He deftly framed the argument as a difference of opinion between Ford and Crawford. In conclusion, he adopted a strategy that he unveiled anytime someone dared to question his motives or results: "In the event that the views of the Indian Agent are approved, I respectfully request that matters referred to in the agreement July 7, 1883, be relegated to the control of the Interior Department, and that I be relieved from all responsibilities herein imposed."[9]

His immediate superior General John Pope, commanding the Division of the Pacific, went one step further: "General Crook's management of these Indians has been marked by unusual and surprising success, and if matters are left in his charge even a few years longer all fears of Indian trouble in Arizona may be dismissed." Sweeping Crawford's misuse of power aside, he explained that the idea of joint control was inherently flawed and would always cause conflict between the military and civil branches. After all, he rationalized, "It is not human nature that such an anomalous relation should escape such troubles, but in view of General Crook's superior ability and experience, and the great success he has met with, I must emphatically recommend that, instead of relieving him as he suggests, the entire control of the Indians be turned over to him."[10]

Nevertheless, even Crook had become weary of the turmoil at San Carlos. Moreover, he knew that the Interior Department did not covet the job of assuming control of San Carlos because they had everything to lose and nothing to gain. In 1884, not one Apache raid occurred in Arizona—the first such year since 1874, and perhaps since 1830. The political fallout could be immense if the department knuckled under to Crook's threats, took back control of San Carlos, and an outbreak followed. Crook realized two things: Crawford was wrong, undoubtedly suffering burnout from the stress of two years of laborious duty without interruption; and the Interior Department would not take him up on his offer.

Accordingly, when he received Sheridan's advice, which had not demanded Crawford's head, he knew that he had preserved the status quo. Yet, almost as an afterthought, he pointed out that there was "another side of the question." On February 14, 1885, the War Department informed Crook that he was too important to be relieved from "Indian duty . . . [for] the public interest [must] be held in abeyance for the present." Of course, the general already knew that. The ruling ended the controversy for now, but it did nothing to improve Crawford's broken relationship with Ford.[11]

By late February Crawford had had enough. The War Department had ordered his regiment, the Third Cavalry, to Texas, and he wanted to go with his men. According to Crook, Crawford "was so much interfered with [by Agent Ford] and annoyed by constant disputes that I could not refuse his request to be relieved from this thankless task."[12] By this time, Crook realized that the transfer was in everyone's best interest, particularly that of his devoted subordinate, who had done yeoman's work at the agency but had now become ineffective. Crook needed a new face at San Carlos, and on February 27, 1885, he issued General Orders Number 7:

> Captain Emmet Crawford . . . is relieved from the police control of the San Carlos reservation and will be succeeded by Capstan F. E. Pierce, First Infantry, who will be governed in the performance of his duties by General Orders No. 13 of 1883 from these Headquarters.
>
> The Department Commander wishes to express his appreciation of the valuable assistance rendered by him in engaging the recently hostile Apaches in the pursuit of peace and industry upon their reservation and to recognize that the satisfactory results attained in this direction are chiefly due to the able manner in which he and those associated with him administered the duties of their official and thankless task.[13]

Crawford was not the only one ecstatic with his change in scenery. The editors of the *Arizona Silver Belt*, who were erstwhile critics of Crook's policies, celebrated Crawford's departure, labeling him a "disturbing influence."[14]

Lieutenant Charles Gatewood, in charge of the White Mountain Apaches at Fort Apache, offered another view. Like Davis and Crawford, he had grown weary of the job and frustrated by the stalemate over annuities. He obviously hoped that Crawford's transfer signaled a change in his future. He fired off a telegram to Crawford: "I congratulate you on being relieved. What is to become of Davis and myself?" Unfortunately, Davis stood a better chance of being relieved from duty than Gatewood because he was in the Third Cavalry while his friend's Sixth Cavalry was transferred to New Mexico in 1884. Crook, however, felt that he could not part with either of his "Indian men." He asked Major General Pope to allow Davis to remain on duty with the Chiricahuas: "He has shown such a marked adaptability for this work. I deem his services and experience in this direction so valuable as to justify this special request." Whether they liked it or not (and certainly Gatewood wanted out), they would have to remain at their posts for now. Gatewood's relationship with Crook continued to deteriorate that spring. In fact, he even submitted a letter of resignation. But of course, Crook refused to accept it.[15]

After Crawford's recent bizarre behavior and authoritarian rule, Captain Francis Edwin Pierce was just what San Carlos needed. Born in New York City in 1833, he joined the 108th New York Infantry in 1862, and by the end of the Civil War had displayed repeatedly his courage in several bloody battles. He had suffered three serious wounds, one of which cost him the sight in one eye. During his time in the service, he had earned a reputation as a fine officer who made common sense decisions. He arrived at San Carlos on March 4, 1885, and promptly took command of the "police control" on March 28, 1884, when Crawford left for Texas. Pierce at once set out to establish cordial relations with Agent Ford. Within days, the tensions of the previous two years dissipated as Pierce and Ford cooperated with each other to improve the plight of their wards.[16] Pierce would become, in the words of one contemporary officer, one of the best "Indian men" that we ever had.[17]

In the midst of this turnover, Davis and the Chiricahuas continued to get along despite a ripple of discontent over the fate of their captives and the absence of annuities. They could count their blessings, for they continued to receive weekly rations, which they supplemented with "fruits and berries gathered in the woods." Many leaders made regular visits to the post. Years later Lieutenant James Parker, stationed at Fort Apache that winter, had some interesting anecdotes about the Chiricahuas. He recalled that the winter "was extremely cold, with deep snows." The men spent their time loafing, while the women worked in camp. They were content and so well fed that "one rarely saw an Indian hunting." He thought Geronimo, whom he saw frequently at Fort Apache, was "friendly and good natured."

He remembered a time that Geronimo showed a sense of humor. Parker and the post surgeon, N. N. Fisher, were out hunting one day with Geronimo, who had become friendly with the doctor after receiving treatment for an illness. Taking a break during the hunt, Fisher decided to have a smoke. He "picked up two pieces of wood and asked Geronimo to produce a light by rubbing the sticks together." When Geronimo understood what the doctor was asking, he "fell into paroxysms of laughter at the thought that a white man could hope to produce fire with two damp twigs."[18]

By early February the first signs of warmer weather had arrived. Davis reported that the Chiricahuas were ready to plant barley. These Indians included Jason Betzinez and his uncle, Geronimo, who asked Davis to visit his farm.

The old warrior proudly displayed a "small blister" which had developed from his long hours working his crops. But he was really a dilettante at work, as Davis soon discovered. When he visited Geronimo at his field, Davis saw him "sitting on a rail in the shade of a tree with one of his wives fanning him. His other two wives were busy tending to their crops." On February 19, 1885, Crook reported that the farming prospects were favorable "to lead them out from a life of vagabonds to one of peace and self-maintenance."[19]

Late that month the chiefs announced they would be returning to Turkey Creek. Before doing so, they scheduled a dance for the night of February 27, 1885.[20] Naturally, they invited their neighbors, the White Mountain people, to attend. Also present were lieutenants Gatewood and Roach, who had come from Fort Apache hoping that a White Mountain outlaw named Gar would dare to show up. Some months before, he had escaped from Fort Apache's jail. Betzinez described Gar as a "good-looking young man, strong and quick in his actions, but with a jealous disposition and a violent temper."

Gatewood felt that Gar would be unable to "resist the lure of the dance and feast, especially as he was related to some of the Chiricahuas." Even the Chiricahuas predicted he might show up, for he had been living as a renegade in the coniferous White Mountains. About midnight, two Chiricahua scouts (one was probably Chatto) came to Davis with the news that Gar was dancing with a group of Indians "in the obscurity of shadows cast by the pines." Davis sprang into action. With the two scouts, he circled behind Gar. Then, suddenly, one Chiricahua "grabbed [Gar] and threw him to the ground." Davis said that Gar, who spoke some English, begged for his life, pledging to be a good Indian. Gatewood took him to the Fort Apache calaboose, where a few weeks later an Apache guard helped him escape. Gar returned to his outlaw life until his own people set a trap "with a pretty woman" and killed him.[21]

Davis later thought that the participation of the Chiricahua scouts in the arrest of Gar might have caused bitter feelings with some White Mountain Apaches. And Chatto's role, if that is what it was, may have permanently ruptured his shaky relationship with Geronimo, a rupture that, according to the reliable Charles Connell, took place in early 1885.[22] The ever-suspicious shaman no doubt felt some empathy for any Apache arrested and put in confinement. Still, there was no outward sign of unrest with the Chiricahuas that spring, despite a rumor spread by an employee at San Carlos of an imminent uprising. In early April, Crook pointed out that the Chiricahuas were "all quiet and contented and seemed in earnest in their intentions to become self-supporting."[23]

Meanwhile, in April 1885 Davis could finally report favorable news to the Chiricahuas about their captives. After months of procrastination, the commissioner of Indian affairs and General Phil Sheridan decided to allow the Chihennes held at Fort Union, who belonged to Loco's band, to rejoin their kinfolk at San Carlos. He asked the War Department to transfer them from Fort Union to Fort Apache.[24]

Fed up with Mexico's denials that they were holding Chiricahua captives, in mid-March the State Department asked Crook to furnish specific information. Accordingly, he asked Captain Pierce to "procure through Davis and Gatewood as complete lists as possible of the Indians held as captives in Mexico." He wanted all the pertinent information—names, sexes, ages, dates, and details of each capture. By early April, Davis had completed the challenging task. He provided an itemized list of ninety-five Chiricahuas, almost all victims of Tres Castillos, Alisos Creek, Casas Grandes, and Sátachi Falls.[25] On April 7, 1885, Crook forwarded the comprehensive list to the adjutant general's office in Washington.[26]

Crook was a sincere advocate of the Indians' cause and a humanitarian by nature. He was concerned that they had lost faith in him over his promises about captives and annuities. What would become clear, however, was that the adult males on this list, as Crook had thought, were dead. Colonel Lorenzo García had given sixteen children captured at Alisos Creek to local families at Bavispe, Bacerac, Granados, Huásabas, Arispe, and Hermosillo. Of these, six had died, nine were living, and the fate of one was unknown. If Mexico was holding Chiricahuas, Crook hoped that his arguments might persuade the officials to let them go. In any event, it gave a glimmer of hope to their relatives at Turkey Creek.[27]

In late April, Crook received good news about captives and annuities. First, on April 29, 1885, he wrote the governor of Chihuahua. Although his information was a month old, it turned out to be reliable. Mexico had released thirteen Chiricahuas, all women, and recent reports placed them some one hundred miles south of Chihuahua City. Three days later the governor confirmed the report but offered no details. Unfortunately, Mexico's generosity ended the moment they released them from bondage. Traveling on foot, the women would take several months to reach the border. Still, the positive news gave Crook something to crow about. Those waiting for information on their kinfolk were euphoric.[28]

On the heels of this happy outcome came another positive development. Again, Crook could claim some credit for pushing Pierce to resolve the matter.

On April 17, 1885, Pierce had informed him that 10,000 pounds of goods remained in the warehouse for distribution to the Chiricahua and White Mountain Apaches. He asked Crook to provide transportation.[29]

Captain Pierce and Agent Ford had found a solution to the unresolved annuity controversy. Ford, who was making tremendous progress on farming operations without Crawford's interference, explained the situation to Pierce: "To file my papers, I have to issue the goods in person." He assured Pierce that he would refrain from interacting with the Chiricahuas. And seeing how hard Ford was working to improve the situation for the Apaches, Pierce had come to like and respect the agent. The trip to Apache would also afford Captain Pierce the chance to meet the Chiricahuas.

In late April, Lieutenant Davis arrived at San Carlos with the pack train from Fort Apache. Davis met with Pierce, assuring him that the Chiricahuas were "quiet and seemed thoroughly satisfied."[30] On May 6, Pierce, Davis, and Ford left San Carlos with the pack train full of annuities. They reached Apache a few days later and announced they would issue the goods on May 10.[31]

That day the Chiricahuas came to Fort Apache to receive the long-awaited annuities, which Davis and Gatewood also provided to the White Mountain Apaches. The operation went smoothly, though Geronimo was surly because he had wanted Davis to dispense their presents at Turkey Creek. He was also suspicious about Crawford's transfer, believing that Crook would never have let his trusted subordinate leave. Geronimo logically concluded that if Crawford had gone, then Crook must also have left and taken the captain with him. And that worried him, despite Davis's assurances that Crook remained in charge.[32]

Pierce and Davis deliberately kept Ford away from the Indian villages. Ford, as promised, remained as unobtrusive as possible. He later explained that Pierce and Davis preferred "to keep them [Chiricahuas] isolated from the representatives of the Interior Department." Yet, his eyes and ears were open, and he remarked on what he had seen and what he had heard. He was astonished when the Chiricahua men arrived carrying their Winchester rifles (only scouts and police could carry arms at San Carlos). Ford mentioned that the War Department was issuing more than enough food to them (which concurs with Apache accounts). His sources told him that they actually had an "abundance to eat and a small surplus which they have been in the habit of selling or gambling away to the White Mountain Indians." He seemed contrite, if not remorseful, that he and Crawford had been unable to agree over the issue of clothing and blankets, which could have alleviated their suffering during the previous winter. Ford thought they were "well clothed," though he conceded that the "blankets I issued them would have been acceptable during the winter months and added to their comfort."

Based on what he heard, Ford was unimpressed by their efforts at farming. The women did most of the work on the forty-fifty acres of crops, mainly corn and melons, according to him, though the Chiricahuas had planted some barley, a better cash crop than melons. It was also obvious that Davis's Indians had traded many of their farming tools to the White Mountain Apaches, who probably put them to better use. In recent months the government had purchased 1,500 sheep for them, which was the only stock they had besides horses. Though his report was accurate, Ford had no point of reference by which to compare these results, meager as they may have been.[33]

The evening of May 10, 1885, the Chiricahuas held a dance at their camps near their farms on the White River, three miles above the post.[34] Several army officers from Fort Apache, including Captain Allen Smith and his son Allen, attended the dance as spectators. The young boy never forgot the experience. It was dark when they reached the camp. The moon and a large bonfire provided the only light for the onlookers. From the boy's description, he was witnessing a crown dance. A medicine man named Chino, a Chihenne in Loco's band, directed one set of masked dancers; two other shamans assisted him.[35] One warrior dancing was Ulzana, who—only seven months later—would return to this very spot with vengeance on his mind. Young Allen Smith described a poignant scene that was the highlight of the evening. It involved Naiche and his son, a small boy of three or four years of age, who, emulating the older warriors, danced "vigorously" with them. The audience, Apaches and whites, enjoyed watching the youth, who eagerly began dancing "as soon as his feet hit the ground." They appreciated the entertainment, greeting him with "whoops and howls of applause."[36]

The next week proved to be one of the most significant moments in the history of the Chiricahuas, with Sunday, May 17, 1885, a watershed if not a catastrophic day, setting the stage for disastrous consequences for the tribe. The days immediately preceding featured the usual suspects: the use of the intoxicating and forbidden drink tiswin and its effects (one American said one drink of it "would make a jack rabbit slap a wildcat in the face"), which turned reasonable men like Naiche, Mangas, and Chihuahua into willing followers of the inveterately suspicious Geronimo.[37] Not even the most sagacious medicine man could have foreseen the emotional upheaval within the tribe in the wake of May 17, 1885. The events of those days split the tribe and led, in some cases, to heartfelt animosities for decades between those who left the reservation and those who remained and cooperated with the American military to quell the outbreak.

A day-by-day summary might be helpful to examine the circumstances leading up to the breakout and to understand the motivations of those who left the reservation.

Monday, May 11, 1885

The morning after issuing annuities, Captain Pierce and Lieutenant Davis visited the Chiricahua farms on East Fork. Pierce came across an unexpected site—Chiricahuas herding sheep in a pasture. Next, the two officers inspected the Chiricahuas' crops, which Pierce estimated at twenty acres of barley and twenty acres of corn. Though the chiefs were proud of their results, Pierce observed that the fields were not "well cultivated or well fenced and it is easy to distinguish them from the fields of the White Mountain Indians when they are planted side by side." In concluding his report, Pierce remarked, "If they would apply their energy, and make use of their great natural ability for good purposes, they would develop more rapidly than any other Indians." Pierce recognized that two indulgences preventing the Chiricahuas from turning away from their "wild and fierce" ways were drunkenness and gambling. Yet, despite these concerns, he thought "they were no worse today than many other Indians on the reservation have been."[38]

Tuesday, May 12, 1885

Early in the morning Pierce, Davis, and the Chiricahuas moved to Turkey Creek. The two officers "inspected" the camps, talked with the "chiefs, influential men, and queried the women." That afternoon the Indians celebrated Pierce's presence with a feast. After eating, he addressed the Indians, complimenting them on their progress, which praise he promised to pass along to Crook in his report. Naiche looked dapper "in a long-tailed, senatorial 'jim-swinger' coat" and from a wagon made a speech about the "blessings of peace." Then Geronimo chimed in, echoing the sentiments of Naiche. Pierce summed up his impressions of the Chiricahuas' state of mind on May 12, 1885, as "cheerful and contented. All indications [are] that they will remain quiet."[39]

WEDNESDAY, MAY 13, 1885

Pierce left Turkey Creek for San Carlos. He forded the Black River and encamped south of it, probably at Fort Thomas.[40] Davis returned to his tent at East Fork. From here he could oversee the Chiricahua's farming operations. Meanwhile, at Turkey Creek, the Chiricahuas begin preparations for a dance and celebration the next day. Tiswin would of course flow freely. The women had gathered the rich corn sprouts from the twenty acres under cultivation at East Fork.

THURSDAY, MAY 14, 1885

Pierce returned to the agency at San Carlos, satisfied with the visit.[41] The last thing he expected was to receive word of trouble with the Chiricahuas. Meanwhile, this day at the camps along Bonito Creek, the chiefs and prominent men had decided to take a stand against Crook's edict banning them from drinking tiswin and from punishing their wives if they misbehaved. It started with Mangas and Geronimo, both of whom were upset that Davis had recently arrested members of their bands for tiswin violations. The master tiswin brewers in the Chiricahua camps were busy making their product, including the skillful Huera. Captured by Mexicans as a girl, she had lived several years with the prominent Samaniego family of Bavispe, Sonora. Here she had learned to speak Spanish and to perfect the practice of making corn beer. Davis remarked that her "wares were in great demand."

This day every Chiricahua chief except Chatto and most of the men, except the scouts on duty at East Fork, drank tiswin in Mangas's and Geronimo's camp on Bonito Creek. Mangas had invited his nephew Naiche and Chihuahua to partake. Then he sent an invitation to Loco and Zele. Though one account suggests that Geronimo and Mangas coerced Loco and Zele to drink, the allure of excellent tiswin made by Huera was simply too enticing to pass up. Of the 120 men in the tribe, some 80 to 90 imbibed the potent social drink. It was a scheduled drunk, with Mangas and Chihuahua most agitated over the prohibition policy. They planned to confront Davis the next morning. After all, the calaboose was incapable of holding all of them.

Why they chose this moment to defy authorities is unclear. But with Crawford gone, they may have hoped to capitalize on his absence to test Captain Pierce, who had not yet earned their respect. They clearly thought that their strength in numbers would carry the day. And they certainly could not have foreseen how quickly the situation could spiral out of control. They wanted only to enjoy the same privileges as whites, who clearly enjoyed their own alcoholic beverages.

FRIDAY MAY 15, 1885

When Davis rolled out of bed and opened the flap door to his tent that sunny spring morning, he discovered thirty Chiricahua leaders and prominent men waiting outside his tent. No women or children were present. Fearing that the lieutenant had heard about their tiswin party and called in troops, the leaders had posted a couple of warriors on a high knoll to watch the trail from Fort Apache, only three miles from East Fork. Despite their concerns, Davis had not heard one word about their binge. And neither had those scouts with him.

The chiefs, armed with knives and a few revolvers, wanted to talk to Davis, who promptly invited them inside his tent. Present were Loco, Nana, Zele, Bonito, Mangas, Naiche, Chihuahua, and Geronimo. They were hung over, and the last four mentioned were drunk, with Chihuahua the most intoxicated. Once in the tent, they squatted in a semicircle in front of Davis. Outside the tent, Chatto and the scouts stood guard, armed with their Springfield rifles. The atmosphere of this meeting was in stark contrast to Davis's confrontation with Kaetenae. Davis, though startled by their presence, did not feel threatened.

The group had selected Loco, who had a good rapport with Davis, to open the discussion. He "began a slow and halting harangue," which was too much for an impatient Chihuahua ("palpably drunk and in an ugly humor") to bear. He angrily interrupted the Chihenne chief: "What I have to say can be said in a few words. Then Loco can take the rest of the day to talk if he wishes to do so." Chihuahua reiterated his position that the government had no right to tell them what they could drink or how they should treat their women if they misbehaved. After all, Chihuahua reasoned, "The white man drank wine and whiskey, even the soldiers of the posts." The chiefs felt they had kept to the letter of their agreement with General Crook in the Sierra Madre.

Davis explained that Crook had forbidden them from making tiswin to protect themselves from arguments that often led to altercations and violent deaths. He pointed out that within the past month, a man had stabbed his wife during a tiswin party. If others had not interfered, he would have killed her. The Indians had "hushed this up, doctoring the woman themselves, and thought I did not know about it." The chiefs sat passively listening until Davis began to address the subject of wife beating. Old Nana could not stomach another word. Standing up, he told the interpreter, Mickey Free, to inform Davis to mind his own business: "He can't advise me how to treat my woman. He is only a boy. I killed men before he was born." With that, Nana stormed out of the tent.

Chihuahua resumed his monologue, defiantly challenging Davis: "We all drank tiswin last night, all of us in the tent and those outside, except the scouts, and many more. What are you going to do about it? Are you going to put us all in jail? You have no jail big enough even if you could put us all in jail." Davis calmly told the chiefs that this was an issue for Crook to decide. He would telegraph the general and let them know his response. Then Bonito and Zele, probably realizing they were in this far deeper than they had expected, tried to say something to Davis. But a belligerent Chihuahua interrupted them.

Davis wrote to Pierce:

> There was an extensive tiswin drunk last night and this morning the following chiefs and headman came up to say they and their bands were all engaged in it: Geronimo, Chihuahua, Mangas, Natchez [Naiche], Zele, and Loco. The whole business is a put up job to save those who were drunk. I have found out the women who have made the tiswin, and will confine them as well as a scout who was also engaged in the drunk. . . . The guardhouse here is not large enough to hold all of them and the arrest of so many prominent men will probably cause trouble. Have told the Indians I would lay the matter before the General, requesting at the same time that their captives in Mexico be withheld. I think they are trying to screen Natchez and Chihuahua.[42]

When Captain Pierce received the telegram later that morning, he failed to grasp the seriousness of the event. He later conceded to Crook that he had misread the situation because of his pleasant talks with the Chiricahuas a few days before. He never thought that a tiswin drunk would lead to an outbreak. Neither did the Indians. After all, he had just heard Naiche and Geronimo preaching to the tribe about the benefits of peace. To get a second opinion, he brought Davis's telegram to his adviser, Al Sieber. Pierce woke up Sieber, whose mind was as lucid as Chihuahua's after an all-night bender. Without giving any thought to the issue, he told Pierce, "It's nothing more than a tiswin drunk. Don't pay any attention to it. Davis will handle it."

Sieber's judgment, when sober, was dependable. When hung over, of course, he could be dead wrong. To Pierce's credit, when later asked by Crook why he had pigeonholed the note, he never mentioned Sieber's advice. He took responsibility for the egregious mistake. "I did not consider it a serious matter at the time and did not connect it any way with an intention on the part of the Chiricahuas to leave the reservation."[43]

Unfortunately, his lack of experience with the Chiricahuas led to this misjudgment, which was compounded many times over by his decision to keep Crook out of the loop and Davis in the dark as he waited for a response from headquarters. Crawford would have sent it to Crook with suggestions on how to diffuse the crisis. And Crook would have ordered that his subordinates take decisive yet measured steps to punish those involved in the drunk—especially Chihuahua, Mangas, and Huera. Furthermore, if we use Kaetenae's case as precedent, Crawford would have handed out a two-week sentence in the calaboose. The other leaders involved would have received warnings or lighter penalties. Not one chief was in danger of receiving the punishment that Kaetenae had earned because he was a three-time loser who had tried to incite hostilities. At this point, no one—not Davis and not the Chiricahuas—was thinking about anyone leaving the reservation after the meeting in Davis's tent.

In any event, Davis told the chiefs that it might be some time before he heard from Crook. By mid-morning they had returned to their camps, "satisfied with this arrangement." Or so he thought. As the alcohol wore off, Geronimo and Mangas suddenly realized that their display of bravado might have ramifications. One of Davis's early reports, before he had a chance to weigh all his information, suggested that they considered leaving for Mexico that night but had decided against it only because they did not have enough followers. He would later amend this. They had not yet come to that conclusion, but with the passing of every hour, a skittish Geronimo, who according to one Chiricahua who knew him, was always "very serious and scared," became more frightened.[44] Lurking in the recesses of his mind were John Clum, Kaetenae, Mangas Coloradas, and Cochise. And Mangas, nominally a "quiet, peace-loving man," who had never been particularly close to Geronimo, was hearing it from his wife, Huera, who disliked Americans and feared that Davis would arrest her. Moreover, Mangas had his own horrifying memories and dread of American troops, who had seized his father and executed him in 1863.

As Davis waited near Fort Apache for Crook's instructions, he saw "some of the malcontents each day and had frequent reports from the scouts." He naturally believed that Crook had received the message and was making the necessary behind-the-scenes arrangements to handle the situation. Until that time, all he could do was wait. Unfortunately, the need to wait for Crook's response kept him bottled up at Apache, away from the activities going on in Geronimo and Mangas's camp on Bonito Creek.

Neither he nor his scouts had any idea that the situation there was growing more critical with each passing hour. The lack of information only served as fodder for their lively imaginations, which, by then, were beginning to run wild in anticipation of what Crook was planning. In their minds, they would have to confront two possible scenarios: Crook and Davis were planning some bold and devious move that would result in punitive and arbitrarily harsh punishment. Or a new officer had replaced Crook, just as Pierce had replaced Crawford, and this fear of the unknown was probably greater than dealing with Crook, who was usually fair. During the day, Geronimo convinced himself that his embittered relationship with Chatto, the duplicity of interpreter Mickey Free, and the disregard shown him by Lieutenant Davis (who clearly disliked him) could only lead to one indisputable result: they were out to get him. He had forgotten the mutual goodwill expressed five days before when Captain Pierce visited. It had vanished, replaced by paranoia. As Chatto had once observed, "Talk of troops made Geronimo like a wild animal."[45]

The comments of two other Apaches only stirred up the hornet's nest, adding fuel to Geronimo's fears. Nadiskay (Nde-tce-le, Shore Man), an Eastern White Mountain man married to a Chiricahua, came to their camp from Fort Apache.[46] He had heard all the rumors, one of which was that Crook had ordered Davis and the scouts to arrest Geronimo and Mangas. Furthermore, he had heard that authorities had authorized Davis to kill the two chiefs if they resisted. Huera, Mangas's wife, agreed with Nadiskay, telling her husband and Geronimo that Crook would order Davis to confine them in the guardhouse. According to Perico, who was in the camp, the Chiricahuas feared that Crook would punish them as he had Kaetenae, and then remove their families out of Arizona.[47]

Though the rumors were untrue, Geronimo and Mangas believed them. When threatened, Geronimo, a survivalist, always consulted with his guardian spirit, which inevitably told him to run. And for the fourth time in his life, he decided to flee from American control. That day he sent a boy from his band to Fort Apache to call in two scouts, his second cousins Fun and Tisna. Later that day they showed up.

In analyzing this pivotal moment in Chiricahua history, we should not underestimate the influence of Huera, whose Apache name was Tze-gu-juni (Pretty Mouth). Always reclusive when near Americans (except for John Bourke, whom she liked), she was openly contemptuous of Davis on the rare occasion that he saw her. She never showed up for rations, instead sending in a younger woman to receive her share. Besides her expertise with making tiswin, her contemporaries considered her a medicine woman.[48] Knowing that Davis would punish her for brewing the tiswin, she gave a rousing speech urging the men to defy the authorities and go to Sonora. According to one account, which sounds apocryphal but probably was true, she challenged the Apaches' manhood. Why should they submit like women to the arrest and punishment that was sure to come? She issued a call to arms: "If you are warriors you will take to the warpath and then the Gray Fox [Crook] must catch you before you are punished."[49]

By that afternoon, Mangas and Geronimo had persuaded between fifteen and twenty men to leave. They had two problems. They needed more men; most especially they needed the influential Chihuahua and the respected Naiche. Both had listened to the talk about leaving but had not committed to going. And they had to round up their stock for their flight. Geronimo had to think of something to persuade Chihuahua and Naiche to leave.

MAY 17, 1885

At dawn, a man from Naiche's band left camp on Bonito Creek and, as on any other day, headed to his crops at East Fork. He knew that Geronimo and Mangas planned to bolt from the reservation later that day. Meanwhile, that afternoon, Geronimo ordered Fun and Tisna to return to their normal duties with Lieutenant Davis. They would rejoin him after they had carried out an important assignment—the assassination of Davis and Chatto. Sometime that afternoon, as the followers of Geronimo and Mangas began packing their belongings and gathering in their stock, Geronimo announced to Naiche and Chihuahua that his cousins had by now killed Davis and Chatto. Once they saw that accomplished, the scouts would desert and join Mangas and him. This report stunned Chihuahua and Naiche, who felt guilty by association, believing that "wholesale arrests" would follow.[50] Chihuahua, a devoted family man, thought Crook would send him to join Kaetenae at Alcatraz.[51] But once the charismatic Chihuahua and the respected son of Cochise threw their hats in the ring, they drew additional men to their cause. They would leave at dusk.

Davis continued to wait for Crook's orders. By noon, he had developed second thoughts about what was going on at Bonito Creek. He sent Na-nod-di and another man (his secret scouts) to Geronimo's camp. Neither Davis nor Chatto had any idea that trouble was imminent. And on this score, Davis had underestimated Geronimo's resourcefulness and determination. He had had no contact with the Chiricahuas at Bonito Creek since the fateful Friday morning meeting. He probably knew Geronimo better than any American. Davis described him as a "thoroughly vicious, intractable, and treacherous man. His only redeeming qualities were courage and determination. His word, no matter how earnestly pledged, was worthless. His history [was] a series of broken pledges and incitements to outbreaks."[52]

While Davis was at Fort Apache, Sam Bowman had remained at East Fork. About 2:30 P.M. he saw a Chokonen from Naiche's band walking toward his tent. He had been "working the field all day in plain sight" of Bowman. The young man dropped a bombshell. A party of Chiricahuas was going to leave the reservation that night. He wanted Bowman to know that he would not go "with the crowd, for he was a good man."[53] After the man left, Bowman went to Chatto, and the two rushed to Fort Apache with the news. They arrived about 4:00 P.M. and found Davis umpiring a baseball game at the post. They had few particulars and really had no idea how many Chiricahuas planned to leave, but they knew that Geronimo and Mangas were the ringleaders. At once the post became a bevy of activity. Sometime after 7:00 P.M., Captain Allen Smith, two companies of cavalry, Gatewood, and eleven White Mountain scouts took the trail toward Turkey Creek, where they expected to join Davis and his Chiricahua scouts. Smith's orders were simple: "Arrest Geronimo and other disaffected Indians."[54]

Davis had returned to East Fork to muster his Chiricahua scouts. He had no idea that Geronimo had sent men to kill him and Chatto. Yet he was suspicious, for he felt that as many as one-half of the scouts might desert. He had complete faith in three of them, Chatto, Charley, and Dutchy.[55] But of the thirty scouts currently enlisted, ten came from bands whose chiefs would leave the reservation. Over forty years later, he described this tense moment in which he prepared for the worst. He stationed two scouts, Chatto and Charley, on each side of the door to his tent and Dutchy on one flank.[56] Chatto had rounded up eleven other scouts. He ordered them to "ground arms," which meant to stand at attention "with their rifle butts on the ground."

Davis ordered the three scouts to shoot the first "man who raised his gun from the ground." What he did not know was that of the eleven scouts in line, three were planning treachery. Cathla had joined Fun and Tisna. But once they saw the precautions taken by Chatto and Davis, they realized their plans were too risky.[57] After Davis went into his tent, they "slipped out of the ranks and disappeared," running off to join the hostiles. A fourth scout, Atelnietze, who was not present during the roll call, also deserted. As it turned out, that night 34 men (including the four scouts who deserted), 8 teenage boys, and 92 women and children left the reservation. The chiefs were Geronimo, Naiche, Mangas, Chihuahua, and old Nana. Ten days later, a group of 10 women and children of Naiche's band left, putting the total of Chiricahuas off the reservation at 144. About 400 remained under Chatto, Zele, Bonito, Bacutla, and Loco. Bonito and Chatto were "very bitter" against those who left. Crook always believed that if the telegram had reached him, the strife would never have occurred.[58]

Hoping to keep their plans quiet, they wasted no efforts trying to convince the chiefs at Turkey Creek to go along. They would have rebuffed any overtures, though members from each band (except Chatto's and Loco's) did join in the exodus mainly because of kinship ties. No evidence has surfaced to support Crook's later claim that Geronimo tried to coerce Chatto, while plotting to kill him when he refused.[59] The Bedonkohe leader knew Chatto would remain loyal to Davis.

The uprising was a direct result of the events of May 14–15 and the escalating anxiety during the next two days. And when coupled with a dreadful fear of punishment and frightening rumors of possible exile and removal of their families out of Arizona, Davis had a recipe for disaster. These factors explain why the chiefs left, but not why so many of their followers joined them. Certainly, kinship and loyalty played important roles, especially with Geronimo's followers and to a lesser extent with those of Chihuahua and Naiche.[60] And some left because they were restless at Fort Apache and just preferred the old way of life in the Sierra Madre. This would apply to several men of Kaetenae's old band who had joined the exodus. Many were survivors of the Victorio War, and some were relatives of Juh. Captain Pierce saw it that way, but he oversimplified his assessment in noting that the malcontents left because they would "rather live the life" of a hostile.[61]

The *Arizona Silver Belt*, the newspaper closest to the scene, reported the inevitable rumor that the uprising had been brewing for months. Even the levelheaded Captain Pierce opined that they "were planning the move for a long time." He admitted, however, that he had no proof. He later interviewed several chiefs and prominent men on the reservation who gave a clear picture of what they thought had happened. The leading spirits of the rebellion, Geronimo and Mangas, had never uttered one word about leaving the reservation before their tiswin party. So there was no premeditation. Most of those Chiricahuas who remained on the reservation were in the dark almost as much as Davis. Zele said that he "had no idea they were leaving until shortly before their departure." Bacutla and Bish-to-yey (a member of Naiche's band), claimed that they heard about the turmoil only after it had happened. Loco said that a few members of his band gave him the news that night, hours after the outbreak. Perhaps Ramon, a Chihenne medicine man from Loco's band, made the most telling observation. He declared that Geronimo and his followers "never said anything to anyone unless they knew they would fall in with their plans." According to him, only those who went out knew of the "secret plans."[62]

Were there other peripheral factors that might have encouraged the events of May 17, 1885? Captain Crawford believed that Wilcox and Ford withheld annuities as part of a planned strategy to undermine him and foster discontent with the Chiricahuas.[63] Samuel Beaumont, Wilcox's and Ford's assistant, said Geronimo left because Crook had reneged on his promises.[64] Six months later, Agent Ford uncharitably blamed the uprising on Captain Pierce for failing to distribute the annuity goods in a timely fashion.[65] The *Arizona Silver Belt* predictably vilified Crawford and Crook, placing the blame squarely on the divided authority.[66] And Lieutenant Charles Gatewood, in a recently published book on his writings, hypothesizes that a new law passed by Congress inspired the rebellion. Recent legislation had transferred jurisdiction of certain crimes committed on reservations from Indian courts to civil courts, which alarmed the skittish Chiricahuas. Pierce told Gatewood and Davis to advise their Apaches of the new law. Gatewood believed that Davis had discussed the ramifications with the Chiricahuas. Though Davis never mentioned this as an issue in the outbreak, Gatewood insisted that it was a leading factor.[67]

Whether Crook and Davis could have taken steps to prevent the trouble is debatable. To begin with, Crook should have provided Davis with sufficient soldiers to keep the same close rein on the Indians as Crawford had had at San Carlos. Crook should have treated them like every other Indian at San Carlos. First, the military should have disarmed them and insisted that every chief, once at Turkey Creek, apply his efforts to this new way of life. The incarceration of Kaetenae had proved to be a good lesson, at least temporarily, but in the long term, it fostered an irrational fear among the leaders that they could be next. Davis should have also made examples of those men and leaders who continued to disregard his edict about drinking tiswin. In retrospect, Crook had allowed them too much freedom at Turkey Creek, for they still had old-time leaders unwilling to obey all of Crook's rules.

Using Lieutenant Davis' census list as a guide, I have pieced together, from several sources of information, a compilation by band of those men who left the reservation and those who remained, most of whom served as scouts for Crook in the upcoming campaigns. The table tells us that 42 of the 118 men and teenage boys left the reservation. Of the 76 who remained, at least 57 served as scouts against the hostiles in the campaign to follow. The 19 not enlisting as scouts were too old or too young or were enrolled at the Carlisle Indian School. A deep chasm emerged between these factions. After all, the actions of the hostiles affected the lives of everyone who stayed on the reservation for both the short and the long term.

Summary of Chiricahua men and teenage boys tagged by Lieutenant Britton Davis

	Chief	Total men	Left reservation, May 1885	Served as scout, 1885–86	Neither
Chiricahua					
Band A	Naiche	21	13	7	1
Band B	Geronimo	10	8	2	0
Band C	Bonito	12	2	7	3
Band D	Zele	11	3	5	3
Band E	Chatto	9	0	8	1
Total		63	26	29	8
Warm Springs					
Band A	Nana	4	3	1	0
Band B	Loco	29	0	20	9
Band C	Bacutla	16	8	6	2
Band D	Mangas	6	5	1	0
Total		55	16	28	11
Grand total		118	42	57	19

Not everyone serving under Crook believed in his methods, especially his philosophy with the Chiricahuas. The *Arizona Silver Belt*, a relentless critic of Crook and Crawford, said that of the territory's total population of 100,000, Crook would be lucky to muster a dozen supporters for his Apache policy. Although this estimate is hyperbolic, most Arizona citizens, because of what they read or experienced, would have disapproved of Crook's decisions concerning Apaches.

Ironically, a letter written from Fort Apache on May 7, 1885, ten days before the eruption, was not only critical of Crook's policies but remarkably prescient in its predictions: "The [Chiricahuas] are peaceable for the present but the peculiar policy followed here by General Crook is only calculated to defer the final settlement of the great question. The whole thing [will] ultimately have an unhappy ending, and probably the responsibility will be on someone who will succeed General Crook."[68] Crook would have condemned this statement, though there is no evidence to suggest that he was aware of it. Not that it would have mattered. He placed no importance on the comments of anonymous sources. Because he was supremely confident in his methods, introspection was not a characteristic that he relied on. We will never know whether this prediction was a lucky guess, or a clairvoyant prophecy based on observation and sound intelligence. Yet, this critic would ultimately have the last laugh, and at Crook's expense.

19

CROOK EMPOWERS CHATTO

I have known Geronimo all my life and have never known anything good about him. General Crook called on me personally
and asked me to organize a detachment of scouts [whom] I directed in Mexico.

Chatto

"The people pine for dead Indians," declared one American in a letter to the
Arizona Weekly Miner soon after the outbreak. That this summed up the feelings of most, if not all, southwesterners, there can be little doubt. But to put
an end to the Indian threat would be no easy matter.[1]

The fleeing Chiricahuas knew that soldiers and scouts were on their trail.
About 7:00 P.M. on May 17, an hour or two after the Indians had slipped away,
Captain Allen Smith, with three lieutenants and two companies of troops (one
hundred men of the Fourth Cavalry), a pack train, and twenty-one Apache
scouts under Davis and Gatewood, had left Fort Apache. After marching six
miles toward Turkey Creek, Chatto met a Chiricahua who gave him ominous
news. Naiche and Chihuahua had left with Mangas and Geronimo, which
more than doubled the estimated force involved in the outbreak. Davis sent a
rider to Fort Apache to deliver this information. Chatto with ten Chiricahua
scouts took the lead toward the camps on Bonito Creek, which they found
empty. One group of warriors, after leaving their camp on the creek, had cut
the telegraph wires to Fort Apache. To delay the repair crew, the Apaches had
reattached the spliced sections with buckskin.[2]

Chatto's scouts ferreted out the trail, which, by design, led over difficult
terrain, through canyons and creek beds, over mesas and ridges, thus making
the journey a difficult one for beast and man. After several mishaps related to
the night travel, injuries to several horses and a broken leg for one trooper,

they finally reached the Black River about 3:00 A.M. on May 18. Heeding the advice of Davis and Gatewood, Smith decided to rest and delay the crossing until daybreak. Two hours later, they began to ford the river. With binoculars, they could see the Chiricahuas about six miles ahead. They had altered course, going east toward Eagle Creek. Chatto was now certain that the rumors he had heard from Chiricahuas who had remained behind were true. Mangas was in command, and he was leading the hostiles for the Black Range in New Mexico. The direction of the trail confirmed his suspicions. If Geronimo had been calling the shots, they would have moved southeast toward the Gila and Peloncillo Mountains, whose corridor they would follow south into Mexico as quickly as possible.[3]

But the other leaders, Naiche, Chihuahua, and to some extent Mangas, had haunting memories of their perilous existence in the Sierra Madre before Crook's 1883 expedition. Not only were they concerned about Sonoran troops, but the Tarahumara Indians from Chihuahua worried them even more. They expected Crook and his Western Apache scouts to sniff out their trail. But whether they thought that Chatto and Loco would succeed in galvanizing their own people to hunt them is unclear. After all, kinship played an important role in Chiricahua society; however, many of the band and family structures had fractured during the past thirty-five years, when conflicts and disease had reduced their population by a staggering 73 percent.[4]

Meanwhile, Chatto and his scouts had become excited after spotting the hostiles about six miles ahead. Chatto implored the troops to "hurry, hurry." Lieutenant James Parker concurred, itching to push his men and scouts forward to overtake the Indians. But Captain Smith, a greenhorn in Indian fighting, overruled both men, which frustrated Parker, who thought his superior too cautious. The Chiricahuas clearly felt the presence of the troops, for they abandoned several horses in their haste to keep ahead of their pursuers. By 2:00 P.M. the weary troopers had reached Eagle Creek; here they bivouacked at Stevens's ranch. The pack train was several hours behind. The men and, more important, the horses were spent and hungry. Smith's command waited for their pack train, which arrived seven hours later. They had marched sixty-five miles in nineteen hours. The break, however, turned into a sixteen-hour stopover. During this time, the Apaches put another sixty miles between themselves and Smith's command.[5]

The next day, May 19, 1885, their trail continued to the northeast as they hoped to make their rendezvous site in the Mogollon Mountains north of Alma, New Mexico. The chiefs sent out raiding parties to steal, plunder, and kill. Smith's troopers came across the mutilated remains of their victims. The Indians had slaughtered five unsuspecting ranchers and travelers and one prospector, three at Blue Creek and three at Little Blue Creek. They ambushed each man at close range, taking his stock, weapons, and ammunition. After killing the two Luther brothers on Blue Creek, they ransacked their house. By mid-afternoon the band had reached camp in the Mogollon Mountains, Chihuahua and Naiche's group in one cluster; Geronimo and Mangas's followers in another.[6]

It was here that Chihuahua and Naiche learned about Geronimo's duplicity in the proposed killing of Davis and Chatto. Atelnietze, a Chokonen related to Naiche and one of the four scouts who had deserted, had just come in with one of the raiding parties. He told Chihuahua and Ulzana that Davis and Chatto were alive. Chihuahua was furious, realizing that he and Naiche had joined the outbreak under false pretenses. He immediately vowed to kill Geronimo. Taking Ulzana and Atelnietze, with rifles in hand, he headed to Geronimo's camp.[7]

But Geronimo was one step ahead of Chihuahua. One of his men had warned him, thus changing the course of Chiricahua history. False bravado and idle threats were not part of Chihuahua's makeup. He would have shot down Geronimo, and the outbreak may have been over. The disastrous post-1886 consequences may well have been averted. Geronimo feared Chihuahua. He had seen him kill the troublesome Nednhi Washington in their camp in Mexico during summer 1883. He knew that Chihuahua was coming loaded for bear; he knew that he could not reason with him, or lie his way out. So he and Mangas broke camp and fled east. Naiche, who happened to be with Mangas, went with them.

Hoping to lie low before returning to the agency, Chihuahua went farther north in the Mogollons. Another group of a half-dozen men and their families, probably Nednhis under Nat-cul-baye, known as José María Elías, set out for Sonora.[8] The fragile Chiricahua unity was broken. It would soon become apparent that there was no dominant leader in the flight. But could Crook and Davis take advantage of this fissure?

Meanwhile, Davis and Chatto had left Smith's detachment to return to Fort Apache. Both men thought that they "were in for a long campaign." To this point Davis knew that Crook was operating blindly, shifting troops to positions along the anticipated routes of the Chiricahuas. He had to apprise the general of the situation. Chatto also wanted to return so that he could "organize a sufficient number of scouts to hunt the hostiles down." Davis and his Chiricahua scouts left Gatewood and Smith either the afternoon of May 18 or early the next morning. They reached Fort Apache early evening, May 19, 1885.[9]

To this point, Crook had shown remarkable yet characteristic patience. He was not a leader who overreacted, threw temper tantrums, or second-guessed his officers. He trusted their judgment, and he knew that Davis would report to him at the first opportunity. Once the soldiers had repaired the telegraph line, Davis's first dispatch from Apache reached Crook. Details were necessarily sparse. All Davis could say was that Mangas and Geronimo were leaving the reservation that evening with between twenty and twenty-five men. A second dispatch noted the involvement of Chihuahua and Naiche, thus doubling the estimated size of the hostile group.[10]

Though in the dark about every aspect of the outbreak, Crook had made a series of logical moves. First, he fired off telegrams to the governors of Chihuahua and Sonora, to local newspapers, to Colonel Luther P. Bradley (commander of the District of New Mexico), and to his superiors in the chain of command: General John Pope and the War Department in Washington. He could report only cursory details. Next, he ordered his commanders at posts between the hostiles and the border to station cavalry units guarding the routes that he anticipated the Chiricahuas would follow. His subordinates responded quickly: Fort Grant's troopers guarded San Simon, Fort Bowie's cavalrymen watched over Doubtful Canyon and Steins Pass, Fort Huachuca's horsemen patrolled near Skeleton and Guadalupe canyons.[11]

Davis sent a dispatch from Fort Apache on the evening of May 19. Because he had just got in from Smith's command, details were again necessarily sparse. The communication, however, furnished Crook with the most important piece of information. Chatto felt sure that Mangas was going into the Black Range. The lieutenant also added that Chatto and Bonito were "very bitter" and were then organizing a company of scouts "to hunt hostiles down." This concise communication was just what Crook needed to direct his commanders in the field. He immediately telegraphed Davis, asking him for a full report of the outbreak: "All the information you have in the entire matter." He also approved Davis's plan to organize more scouts, and he authorized the use of the pack train to support their efforts: "Follow it until some results are obtained." Sanguine about squashing the uprising, he authorized Davis to extend an olive branch to any hostile who wanted to return. He suggested that Davis send the scouts as emissaries to open negotiations with the hostiles and convince them to return to the reservation or, at worst, isolate any Chiricahuas who might have second thoughts about leaving the reservation.[12]

Davis had also briefed Lieutenant Colonel Wade at Fort Apache, who at once wired Bradley with fresh information. Bradley responded quickly, hurrying off in person to Fort Bayard to direct the campaign. He also ordered out four companies of the Sixth Cavalry in three detachments toward the Gila and Mogollon mountains from Bayard. Furthermore, if the Indians remained in the mountains along the Gila, he would call in two companies of cavalry from Fort Wingate. And Crook, who planned to make his field headquarters at Bayard, agreed to place any Arizona troops operating in New Mexico under Bradley's command except the Apache scouts of Davis and Gatewood, to whom Crook had given separate instructions to try to end the campaign by diplomacy.[13]

Meanwhile, at Fort Apache, Davis had a busy day on Wednesday, May 20. Early that morning, he summoned the Chiricahuas in for a count to find out who had left the reservation. He informed Crook that four scouts, thirty men, eight large boys, and ninety-two women and children were absent. Later that day he wrote a long dispatch, giving full details about the causes and circumstances surrounding the outbreak. He stated that Geronimo and Mangas had attempted to convince the entire tribe to leave, but Bonito, Zele, and Loco "refused though threatened with death." Moreover, Geronimo and Mangas had forced Nana, Naiche, and Chihuahua to join them.[14]

Neither statement was completely correct. And the claim that they "forced" the three chiefs to leave (which implies coercion) is impossible to accept given that the ringleaders had no influence over them. Mangas was Naiche's uncle, and Geronimo was Nana's brother-in-law. Although Chihuahua and Geronimo had been close during the Sierra Madre years, the independent Chihuahua was the bravest warrior, toughest fighter, and most decisive chief. Geronimo and Mangas would not have dared to threaten him. Davis undoubtedly heard this yarn, spun to make the two Chokonen chiefs look like victims. Chihuahua and Naiche left because they feared the consequences engendered by Geronimo's false scenario. So, from a logical point of view, we can say that without Geronimo's deceit, Chihuahua and Naiche would not have left. Chihuahua later lamented his gullibility in acting on Geronimo's words.[15]

Crook, as only he could, processed this intelligence and sprang into action. Accepting Davis's report as fact, he thought an opportunity existed to divide and conquer the hostiles. To accomplish this, he believed that the loyal Chiricahua scouts were his best bet to end the uprising. Put in today's terms, Crook wanted them to take ownership of the problem. He made it clear that he would hold them accountable for their actions. Hours after receiving Davis's comprehensive report, he outlined his strategy in a telegram to his trusted lieutenant:

> Explain to the Indians that for more than a year I have been trying to get their captives who were in Mexico and New Mexico, and now just as they are beginning to return this trouble has occurred, and unless it is satisfactorily settled up and peaceful times restored, all the business of returning the captives will have to be stopped.
>
> It is all-important to impress on the Indians that success in procuring the return of their captive people depends on the successful outcome of this matter. To this end as many of the Indians outside of the scouts as desire to go in pursuit should be encouraged and permitted to do so.
>
> [Encourage Chihuahua and Naiche] and others [who] were forced to go out, to disintegrate the refugees, and induce a return of those who are [the] least guilty and the destruction of the ringleaders if possible. If that cannot be done, [then] capture them and bring them in for further disposition.[16]

Crook sent similar instructions to Captain Pierce, whom he had ordered to scout the Black Range with the San Carlos Apache scouts.[17]

On the evening of May 21, 1885, Chatto and Bonito, with most of the four hundred Chiricahuas on the reservation, held a war dance at their camps on East Fork. To the Chiricahua scouts, these new duties, tracking down their own people, many of them friends and relatives, were distasteful, not what they had anticipated when they first enlisted. But those who had relatives incarcerated in Mexico, and those who disliked Geronimo, had incentive to go after him. The latter group included most of the Chihennes, who held Geronimo responsible for the tragedy at Alisos Creek. They understood that their enemy was now their own people, whose actions had threatened the future of those remaining on the reservation and had undermined Crook's efforts at getting their people released from bondage in Mexico. Those reservation Chiricahuas directed their anger at the symbolic leader of the hostiles,

Geronimo. And with good cause. He had put the scouts in a horrible position, as one Chiricahua remarked years later: "In this way he caused Apache to fight Apache, and all sorts of trouble to break out among our people."[18]

Their leader was Chatto, who many Chiricahuas believed had "great medicine." In later years, he revealed that his source of power came from dreams, which foretold the future, and from muscular tremors that proved to be reliable warnings of imminent danger. These guided his actions. This night, as the tribe assembled on open ground for a war dance, he showed the scouts what they must do, no matter how distasteful to some. A war shaman led the singing, exhorting the men to demonstrate bravery to the tribe. It was customary for the shaman to call out the names of the men who would participate in the war party. Here were twenty-six scouts, brave men who had pledged their loyalty to Davis. Ten-year-old Sam Kenoi was present. Forty-five years later, he described the scene to anthropologist Morris Opler: "Then the singer called [Chatto] by name. He said: 'Chatto you are a man. You are known to be a great warrior. You have fought your enemies in close battle. We are calling on you to dance.' As soon as he heard this Chatto had his gun ready. He sprang out there, shooting into the air. Then they kept singing and calling another name and another until four or five were out there dancing."[19]

Though Mangas and Chatto had grown up together (frequently in the same village) and were first cousins, their paths had diverged after the deaths of their fathers. A few years later, Mangas married a daughter of Victorio and joined the chief's Chihenne group. His ties, by custom, bound him to Victorio. In the late 1860s Chatto, after the death of his father, probably José Mangas, had married a Chokonen woman. He therefore joined the chief whom he held great reverence for, Cochise. During the years of the Chiricahua Reservation, he had come to know Naiche. At San Carlos in the late 1870s, they began a close friendship that would last for more than forty years. Dos-teh-seh, Naiche's mother, who had stayed at San Carlos with her daughter, was Chatto's first cousin.[20]

Clearly one overriding factor dictated why Chatto had assumed the vital role as leader of the scouts and trusted advisor of Crook, Crawford, and Davis. He loved his wife and two children. It was one thing to grieve for a fallen child or spouse. It was another thing to grieve, knowing they were living in a Mexican household in Chihuahua City. This melancholic thought consumed him. And he believed the general was the only man who could restore his family. He trusted Crook, and he wanted the general to trust him. As Crook

explained to one skeptical officer at Fort Bayard: "It was in Chatto's interest to keep faith with us, for the Mexicans held his [family] and his prospect
of recovering them depended on his good behavior." Naturally, it seemed to
Chatto that the fate of his family might rest on whether he captured or killed
Geronimo.[21]

Davis had elected to leave four scouts to oversee the daily activities at Fort
Apache: Bonito, Noche, Ramon (the Chihenne shaman), and Kinzhuna, one
of the youngest scouts, who was in his early twenties. Said by some to have
been a brother of Kaetenae, he had enlisted exactly one month before the
outbreak. Except for one week between enlistments, he would be on duty for
the next year. His situation was unique: one brother, Kaetenae, was in prison
at Alcatraz; a second brother, Bacutla, had stayed on the reservation; a third
brother, Nezulkide, had left with the hostiles. In later years, he remarked that
he "was like a policeman." He had to see that all was well in order, and he assisted Bowman "in the issuing of rations."[22]

Among the Chiricahua scouts with Chatto were his good friend Cooney,
Charley, Tuzzone, and Feliz, all sergeants, and other notables such as Dutchy,
Kayitah, Martine, José First, and Gon-altsis, Chatto's brother. Fifteen of the
twenty-two scouts were Chokonens, and seven were Chihennes. Seven were
under the age of twenty-five.

The scouts took nothing to slow them down. The army had issued them
the Springfield rifle, two cartridge belts of twenty-five rounds each, blue shirt
and pants (usually not worn), blanket, a small tent, and a butcher knife. This
was "all the outfit we needed," recalled one scout.[23] They received the regular
army ration less the daily ration for soap, candles, and vinegar, which Crook
agreed to substitute for a half pound of tobacco per month.[24] Their commanding officer furnished them with strips of red cloth to wear as headbands to
distinguish them from the hostiles. Each scout carried his own tweezers, an
awl for repairing moccasins, and the always handy bag of pollen.[25]

Jason Betzinez, who never served as a scout, said that those who enlisted
"were as happy as bird dogs turned loose in a field full of quail."[26] Yet, those
who served thought differently, for their work was dangerous and demanding, physically and emotionally. Betzinez's romanticized comments would
have amused Chatto, who recalled the rigors of fieldwork:

> Any general, or officer, or soldier of that time knows what hardship it
> was to campaign after hostiles at that time. In summer time the heat

is fearful. In winter the cold is severe. . . . I carried a double cartridge belt with forty-five to fifty rounds of ammunition. The belt was as rough as cowhide. It rubbed the skin from my back as I led men over the small ridges and in different parts of the country. My gun was loaded and my hand was on the trigger, following fresh trails of the hostiles, not knowing what moment a bullet might go through my forehead or breast if we were ambushed.[27]

On May 22, 1885, Davis left Fort Apache with fifty-eight scouts: thirty-two White Mountains, twenty-two Chiricahuas, and four San Carlos Apaches whom Pierce had sent from the agency. They headed for Mogollon country, where, that very day, Captain Allen Smith's command walked into a Chiricahua ambush at Devils Canyon, some twenty miles northeast of Alma.[28]

Smith's troopers and Gatewood's White Mountain scouts had followed the trail of Mangas and Geronimo's group from the San Francisco River east along Devils Creek into a "wooded and broken country." The White Mountain scouts, unfamiliar with the area, were understandably cautious, "remaining close to the head of the column, fearful of an ambush." About midday they entered Devils Canyon, a deep ravine no more than fifty yards wide and surrounded by two hills some five hundred feet above the floor. Captain Smith decided to march single file along the creek into the narrow canyon. Here he stopped for lunch and to take a bath. This order astonished Lieutenant Parker, who thought the "situation invited attack."

Despite the presence of Gatewood's scouts, the detachment had no idea that the Chiricahuas were waiting. And, having exposed the command by camping in such a precarious position, Smith further compounded this misjudgment by committing a cardinal sin when he failed to post pickets on the rim of the canyon. As the weary troopers bivouacked, Geronimo, Mangas, and Naiche placed their men in four positions along the ridge. Their warriors nearly encircled the command. Though outnumbered six to one, they were not intimidated. The band of twenty warriors was composed of both young and veteran fighters, with a few newcomers learning the ropes. With Geronimo was his son Chappo; his second cousins, the three Bedonkohe brothers, Perico, Fun, and Tisna; another cousin Ahnandia; and his brother-in-law Yahnozha, who probably had his orderly, a fourteen year-old youth named Kanseah. Several Nednhis rounded out the attacking group: Geronimo's son-in-law Dah-Ke-Ya; Nezegochin; Askildega (Kilth-de-gai); two sons of Juh, Delzhinne (Elgede) and Daklegon (their mother was also Geronimo's first cousin); and Zachia, probably a nephew of Juh. Also concealed along the heights of the canyon that day were two dependable fighters: Frijole, a former scout and respected warrior who had ridden with Victorio and Nana, and Chinche, a brother of Ponce. Two young Chihennes from Mangas's band who had survived Tres Castillos, Len-see and Seeltoe, were also probably present. Rounding out the warriors were Naiche; his father-in-law, Beshe; and a young man named Hunlona. Finally, left in camp to care for the women and children were two grandfathers, Nana (Geronimo's brother-in-law) and the aged Eskinolteze, Nana's cousin.[29]

After the White Mountain scouts ate a quick lunch, Smith ordered them to scale the ridge on the east side of the canyon. They were to look for signs and perform sentry duty. As they neared the rim, Geronimo triggered the ambush, firing the first shot and severely wounding one scout. That was the signal for the rest of the warriors to unleash a "thunderous volley" so loud that a rancher ten miles away heard the opening salvos reverberate along the sides of the canyon. Lieutenant Parker, sensing they were "encircled" ordered his troopers, many instinctively trying to get their horses to safety, to "damn the horses. Get your carbines and come with me."

Because the heaviest volleys were coming from rifle pits on the eastern rim, Parker and Lieutenant Leighton Finley began to dash up the rocky slopes with seventeen troopers following. As they climbed, they ran into panic-stricken White Mountain scouts retreating from the crest and troopers trying to gather their mounts, which were grazing along the hill. Moreover, Parker's men had to contend with volleys coming from troopers below them in the canyon. A few months before, Parker had been hunting with the very Apache, Geronimo, who was now trying to cut him down. The troopers followed Parker's path, luckily dodging the bullets that "were pouring down." The Apaches overshot their targets below them. Parker led his men to cover behind rocky ledges, where they rested and caught their breath. It had taken the soldiers a half-hour to reach the summit. Parker's steadfast leadership and audacious counterattack had carried the day. The Chiricahuas had wounded two troopers and one scout before they withdrew. Gatewood arrived a few minutes later with his scouts, followed soon after by Captain Smith, dressed in his drawers and boots. For this, the *Silver City Enterprise* sarcastically dubbed the fight, "The Battle of the Shirt Tail."

The scouts and cavalrymen followed one trail that led to a deserted camp about five hundred yards away. The Apaches had left chunks of beef roasting over the campfires, which numbered either seventeen or nineteen, depending on who did the counting. The scouts and soldiers also recovered three horses, supplies, and the torn-up discharge papers for Naiche, whose term as scout had expired on September 12, 1884. After a half-hearted march, Captain Smith decided to turn back, vowing to continue pursuit the next morning.[30]

Though his decision irked Lieutenant Parker, they could not have overtaken the band, which traveled rapidly all day and night through incredibly rough country. After the fight, Naiche and one man left to rejoin his people who were with Chihuahua. Geronimo and Mangas decided to put as much distance between themselves and Smith's command as they possibly could. So, they wanted to get into Victorio's former country in the east part of the Black Range. Thirty hours after the Devils Canyon fight, they had dropped down from the lofty heights of the Mogollons to the east fork of the Gila. Here raiders killed two men near "old Camp Vincent" on Diamond Creek.[31]

With Victorio's old range dotted with new settlements, Mangas, Geronimo, and Nana pondered their next move. They had four options: remain in the Black Range, head northeast to Ojo Caliente and the San Mateo Mountains, cross the Rio Grande into Mescalero country, or heed Geronimo's advice and head for Mexico. By the morning of May 24, 1885, the chiefs had ruled out the first two options. They decided that Geronimo would take six men and two women to the northeast. He would escort the women across the Rio Grande, and they would go to Mescalero and explore what options, if any, that reservation might offer. Mangas would take the balance, about forty, which included about a dozen men, and head southeast toward Kingston, where they would wait for Geronimo.

Geronimo's party crossed the continental divide sixteen miles northwest of today's Chloride. What he saw must have stunned him. Mining towns seemed to have sprouted from the ground. Just seven miles away from Geronimo lay Grafton, a silver mining town that boasted a school and three hundred settlers.[32] Even larger settlements lay to the south and east: Chloride, Fairview, Hermosa, and Kingston. Hillsboro's population had increased significantly. Along the five creeks that flowed into the Rio Grande, Hispanics and Americans had established new ranches and farms. Clearly, the Chiricahuas' former country was not safe.

Geronimo first went to Antelope Springs, nine miles north of Grafton, where he and two men discovered three Americans, Charles Stevenson, Harvey Moreland, and Frank Adams. They ambushed them from short range. The Americans never had a chance. The remainder of Geronimo's party joined him after the attack and shared in the looting of their victims' possessions and stock. Then Geronimo split up his group. He sent four men on a horse raid to the south. He took his wife She-gha, another woman, and two men (one was probably Yahnozha, She-gha's brother) and went southeast, following an Indian trail between Chloride and Fairview (today called Winston). As Betzinez had once noted, Geronimo preferred a fast trot when out on a "scout." His trail was distinct because one of his moccasins had an unusually large boot heel, leaving a distinct heel print. Geronimo escorted the two women to the Rio Grande. They traveled all night along Palomas Creek to the Caballo Mountains; then the women embarked on their mission to Mescalero.

Geronimo and his two warriors remained in seclusion until dark, when they moved south to Seco Creek, which they traversed into the Black Range to its South Fork. Here, on the morning of May 26, 1885, they met up with the four men who had left them two days before at Antelope Springs. The four had stolen six horses at Hermosa the night before. Geronimo led them off to the southeast toward Emory Pass in the Black Range. Meanwhile, Mangas and the main band were a few miles east of Kingston, where a citizen saw them in the late afternoon of May 26, 1885. He hastened to Kingston with the news. Immediately townspeople sent a runner to Major James Biddle, who had bivouacked two miles east of there with two companies of the Sixth Cavalry.[33]

Colonel Bradley had ordered Biddle with his eighty-three troopers from Fort Wingate to go by rail to Lake Valley. Arriving there about 3:00 P.M. on May 23, Biddle went to Hillsboro. Three days later he was near Kingston. He had gained Captain Rafferty's M Troop, Sixth Cavalry, from Fort Bayard, but had lost Captain Chaffee's I Troop, which had gone north to examine the creeks along the eastern side of the Black Range. When he received the report that Apaches were near, he sent out Lieutenant Hanna, with ten men and one Navajo scout, to appraise the report. Hanna confirmed it was a Chiricahua trail and sent a dispatch rider to bring up Biddle's force. It was too late to follow.

An hour before dawn May 27, 1885, Biddle and Hanna began their march. At daybreak they found the Mangas's camp, recently deserted. The trail scattered, with one under Mangas going east, perhaps along Tierra Blanca Creek. Mangas was happy that Biddle's scout had taken the bait, for he was leading the soldiers away from the main body of women and children, likely under Nana, which was going southwest toward the Mimbres Mountains. At noon on May 27, 1885, Mangas's fighters took positions on a "high, precipitous, rocky hill." Hanna and his advance party thought the Indians wanted "to make a stand here." Biddle sent Captain Henry M. Kendall with Troop A on a flanking maneuver to their right, while he took the rest of the command and marched toward the hill. But he had misjudged Mangas's intentions. "As soon as they saw Kendall's command begin their ascent," thus blocking Mangas from going east, the chief happily "doubled back to the west." That night, when the soldiers bivouacked near the eastern face of the Mimbres Mountains, Mangas's rearguard fired three shots to alert the main body that Biddle had made camp for the night.

The next morning, Mangas's group crossed the Mimbres range and followed the trail to Mule Springs, about ten miles northeast of Fort Cummings. At noon, a group of five Chiricahuas joined the main body. This was Geronimo, who had left two men behind to await the return of his envoys to Mescalero. He knew they were in the clear. Biddle had stopped at Cummings to rest and refit, and the next morning he again sent Lieutenant Hanna with a small detachment, which cut the trail of some forty-fifty Apaches, including nineteen men. Again, Biddle reported that five warriors occasionally trotted along the trail, one of whom had left a "remarkable-sized" moccasin print, which he learned afterwards was Geronimo's. On May 29, 1885, Geronimo and Mangas skirted Tres Hermanas, crossed the border, and stopped at Palomas Lake, a few miles into Chihuahua.[34] They were the second group of Chiricahuas to enter Mexico. One small band had crossed about a week before them. On May 27, 1885, this group had killed three American miners near Nacozari.[35] From here Geronimo's trail led west along the Corralitos River, where they waited to hear from their messengers to Mescalero.[36]

Meanwhile, the Mescaleros did not lay out the welcome mat for She-gha and her companion, who arrived at the Mescalero agency on May 26, 1885. They found that the chaos of the early 1880s had given way to stability and peace, primarily because of the diligence and even-handed judgment of Agent William Llewellyn.[37] One of his most successful innovations was the establishment of a thirty-man police force, drawn from the Jicarillas and Mescaleros, whom he had charged with stamping out the making of tiswin. Llewellyn had personally designed the uniforms of "blue cloth edged with red and brass buttons on which was pictured an Indian shaking hands with a white man at a plow." Inscribed on the shirt was an inscription that read, "God helps those who help themselves." Just three days before the arrival of Geronimo's messengers, Llewellyn, Albert Fountain, and another American had met with several Mescalero chiefs, among them San Juan and Roman Chiquita. They had heard of the outbreak and vowed to "fight Geronimo" if he tried to disrupt the tranquillity at Mescalero.[38]

The Chiricahua women never had a chance. The Mescaleros' prior association with Victorio and Nana in the early 1880s had taught them a lesson.

This alliance had resulted only in unnecessary deaths and tighter government control. Therefore, as soon as the two envoys set foot on the agency, the reservation police seized them and turned them over to Agent Llewellyn and Major James J. Van Horn, who held them in jail at Fort Stanton. According to them, Geronimo was prepared to meet any disaffected Mescaleros in the San Andres Mountains, where they would join forces to raid the settlements east of the Rio Grande. The next day a patrol left Fort Stanton for the San Andres Mountains, but they found nothing. Their presence, however, prompted the army and Llewellyn to enlist twenty Mescalero scouts to protect mining communities in the Black Range and the Mogollons. The army stationed four squads of five scouts at Alma, Malone, Hillsboro, and Fairview. They were paid fifteen dollars per month, forage for their ponies when available, and arms and ammunition to those who needed it. Among the scouts at Hillsboro was Choneska, the Chihenne who had married into the Mescaleros after coming to their reservation in summer 1882.[39]

Meanwhile, because Geronimo and Mangas had attracted the attention of the military, the second group, mostly Chokonens under Chihuahua and Naiche, remained in the upper Mogollon Mountains near old Fort Tularosa. After splitting from Geronimo, Chihuahua had hoped to return to San Carlos. But his scouts had seen Davis's patrol heading his way, and that frightened him. Crook had left the door wide open and would have accepted their return with an insignificant punishment. Yet they had no way of knowing this, and their fears of stern punishment and separation from their family had left them to conclude that Mexico was their only option.

About May 24, 1885, they led their seventy followers south.[40] With soldiers carpeting the country between them and the border, they needed fresh horses for their flight into Mexico. Since Naiche had left family members on the reservation, he likely sent a few warriors to Fort Apache to bring them out. On May 26 raiding parties struck Walworth's and Caldwell's ranches along Mogollon Creek, stealing horses and wounding a Mexican cowboy. Early the next morning, Chihuahua and the main body crossed the Gila and then struck Bear Creek, which he, with the women and children, followed east to Juniper Springs, about ten miles northwest of Silver City. Here they encamped, waiting for the warriors to come in with fresh stock. That morning (May 27) Naiche and Ulzana had fanned out with most of the men and scoured the countryside for horses. Ranchers saw one group of eight Apaches in the Mangas Valley at 8:00 A.M. By mid-afternoon Naiche's party had followed Chihuahua into the mountains along Bear Creek, east of Pinos Altos.

They were not looking for a fight, but as they came across empty homesteads, they ransacked the dwellings and took anything of value. Early that afternoon, a rancher named Wes Welty reported seeing twenty-five Indians near his ranch on Bear Creek. He dispatched a messenger to Silver City for help. A relief party of forty men rushed to the scene. Later that night, they found Chihuahua's abandoned camp at Juniper Springs. He had gone north toward the Pinos Altos Mountains, leaving along the trail seven ponies the group had shot after they gave out. The relief party returned to Silver City.[41]

Meanwhile, Naiche's raiders had met Chihuahua at Juniper Springs and dropped off their stolen stock. Then, as Chihuahua moved north with the women and children, Naiche took most of the warriors, between fifteen and twenty, on a diversionary raid, hoping to steal horses and attract the attention of the troops and Apache scouts.[42] They planned to meet in five days on the Gila north of Mangas Springs. The posse from Silver City had followed Chihuahua's party, which included a few men with the women and children. He had hoped to hole up for several days in the rugged country north of the junction of Sapillo Creek and the Gila.

Late that afternoon, May 27, more reports reached Silver City about the Chiricahuas' presence. A panic-stricken Mexican raced into town, claiming he had seen thirty Apaches about five miles north of town. In gathering up his family, he had left his three-year-old daughter behind with another family. A party of thirteen men went to the wood camp. What they found horrified them: the mutilated bodies of the Marques family, one man, one women, and two children, as well as the three-year-old girl already mentioned by the name of Pas Rascon. "It was a pitiful site to witness, one that drew tears from strong men." They found the wife with several chest wounds while holding in her hands pictures of the virgin and a saint to whom she was praying to save her children. It was a brutal, savage deed that was uncharacteristic of a Naiche-led raid, which seems to suggest that a few warriors seeking vengeance on Mexicans had done it. The innocent Marques family was in the wrong place at the wrong time. But, as the chief later told Crook, it was war, and war meant killing on both sides.[43]

The early morning of May 28, 1885, Naiche led his raiders east toward Pinos Altos, which his father and grandfather had attacked twenty-four years before. They rested at Twin Sisters Peak, two miles northeast of the town. Two days later, hoping to draw troops away from Chihuahua, they raided a ranch two miles from Fort Bayard and then went east into the Black Range. By that time, as we shall see, Chihuahua was occupied with Davis and Chatto.[44]

The outbreak, the Marques massacre, and the military's inability to catch the Chiricahuas aroused acrimonious feelings among citizens and the press, who began to call for vigilante justice—the oft-heard battle cry stemming from frustration with military operations. The *Silver City Black Range* expressed hopes that the present outbreak would "cause another movement to be considered." During these highly emotional times, no one considered that the outbreak involved fewer than three percent of the 5,000 Indians at San Carlos.[45]

While Naiche tried to lead soldiers away from the main body, Lieutenant Davis and Chatto's scouts picked up Chihuahua's trail on May 28, 1885, and followed it to the Gila River. Early the next morning they spotted his ranchería a few miles north of the confluence of Sapillo Creek and the Gila. From Davis's description, it appears that Chatto led the command north along Sheep Spring Canyon, a two-mile-long defile that runs north to south. Along the way the scouts found the bodies of two babies who had just been born. Chatto's scouts and Chihuahua's sentinels seem to have spotted each other and opened fire about the same time. Chihuahua abandoned the camp for the higher ground, perhaps Granny Mountain. Davis thought both sides had exchanged one hundred rounds in all before his scouts captured the camp plus seventeen horses, two mules, six saddles, and, most satisfying to Davis, "the breakfast of a fat cow they were preparing."[46]

After the skirmish, Chatto took several scouts who were members of Naiche's band and tried to open talks with the hostiles. These were Kayitah, his cousin Astoye, Notah, and Yahlo. The last three men were in their early twenties and apparently had no influence or close ties with Chihuahua. Kayitah, however, had grown up with Naiche. Unfortunately, Naiche was leading the raiders near Bayard.[47] If he had been present, Chatto might have succeeded in opening up talks, given their former friendship and kinfolk. Davis apparently was not too sympathetic with this tactic, but he followed Crook's instructions to try to convince any "disaffected" Chiricahuas to surrender.[48]

The mission, however, failed, and that night Chihuahua broke camp and moved north to a "very high hill," probably Brushy Mountain. Early the next morning he rounded the mountain to the north and then rapidly moved west until he came to Turkey Creek, which he followed to the western foothills of the Pinos Altos Mountains. The night of May 31, 1885, he crossed Mangas Valley and followed the Gila by today's Cliff, where, according to plan, he rendezvoused with Naiche's raiders early the morning of June 1, 1885. The band intact, it now lit out for the mountains west of there. About twenty miles northeast, they unexpectedly found a sawmill, which they attacked, killing Ned Ford and stealing eight horses. Frank Bennett, the former scout who was now at the Carlisle Mining Camp, reported that the raiders numbered twenty-two men and were heading south to Duncan. He telegraphed Bowie to warn them that the Apaches were heading toward Steins Peak.

The next day the Chiricahuas struck the Gila near Duncan, where they stole more horses. Instead of continuing south into the Peloncillos, they moved west to Whitlock Mountain via Ash Peak. Here they probably picked up a dozen Chokonens, ten women and children from Naiche's band who had left the reservation on May 28 with two warriors sent by Naiche. This party also stole horses near Fort Thomas two days later. Resting in the Whitlock Mountain for a few hours, they resumed their flight to the southeast and the Peloncillo Mountain corridor to Mexico. Davis, Chatto, and the scouts were more than one day behind them.[49]

Yet a determined group of citizens, the Duncan militia, was on their trail. On June 4, 1885, twenty-four men under W. J. Parks and Lane Fisher left Duncan about 2:00 P.M. and picked up the trail leading to Ash Peak and the foothills of the Whitlock Mountains. From here the Chiricahuas had angled off to the southeast for the Peloncillos. The next morning, June 5, they resumed the pursuit along the western Peloncillos before it turned abruptly into the range and over to the east side just north of Horseshoe Canyon. Dusk was approaching when the militia spotted the Chiricahuas, who at once reversed directions, galloping back into the Peloncillos at the mouth of Doubtful Canyon. Inexplicably, the troops picketed there had withdrawn to Fort Bowie, thus leaving the Apaches an unimpeded run to the western mouth of the canyon.[50]

The militia had closed the gap to two hundred yards when a running fight began. Both sides got off shots—perhaps one hundred rounds altogether—with little effect to either side. During the confusion, one woman, a Chiricahua named Cah-gah-ahshy, a wife of Chinche, who had left the agency without her, mounted her horse with a cradleboard on her back. The strap became loose, and the cradle with her nine-month-old son fell to the ground in Doubtful Canyon. The militia picked up the boy and brought him and a large herd of horses and mules (twenty-two to thirty-seven, depending on the accounts) to Lordsburg. Naiche and Chihuahua exited Doubtful Canyon on the west side and traveled all night through the San Simon Valley to a familiar camping place in the Chiricahua mountains southeast of Fort Bowie. All except Cah-gah-ahshy. She returned to look for her baby. Not finding him, she eventually returned to Fort Apache.[51]

Most of the band, except a rearguard of six men who were several miles behind the main body, had crossed within a few miles of San Simon, where the picket force had withdrawn to its home base at Fort Grant. Naiche and Chihuahua led their followers into Wood Canyon in the Chiricahua Mountains. By the evening of June 6, the band had taken cover in Wood Canyon, near its junction with Cottonwood Creek. En route, they had butchered some cattle and stolen horses from a ranch. The next morning (June 7), Naiche and Chihuahua crossed over to the west side, emerging into the Sulphur Springs Valley by way of the confluence of Pinery Canyon and Bonita Canyon. At the mouth of the latter place, they passed the Prue ranch, only a dozen miles from Fort Bowie. Mrs. Prue watched in astonishment as the entire group, which she estimated at 125 (they numbered half that), disappeared south toward Turkey Creek, where a few hours later the warriors stole horses from White's El Dorado ranch.[52]

The next morning Naiche and Chihuahua split, having made plans to rejoin in the Sierra Madre Mountains. About 4:00 A.M. on June 8, Naiche took about thirty-five followers southwest into the Mule Mountains, where he would await the arrival of the rearguard. Chihuahua took the balance, about thirty, and crossed the Pedregosas to the San Bernardino Valley, then to Guadalupe Canyon, where he expected to find soldiers. He quietly led his followers to a high hill south of the canyon, from where he could examine the military activity in the canyon.

What he saw must have delighted him. Only a small picket force of one sergeant and seven privates was on hand to guard three army tents and wagons loaded with forty days of rations and between 7,000 and 10,000 rounds of ammunition. They were all that remained of three companies of the Fourth Cavalry that Crook had ordered to Guadalupe Canyon. Shortly after their arrival, Captain Henry W. Lawton had relocated two companies to Langs ranch at the eastern entrance of the canyon, leaving Captain Hatfield and one troop at the western side. The day before (June 7), a rancher had arrived to report that the Apaches were in the Chiricahua Mountains. Hatfield decided to take his troop and investigate, leaving behind seven men on sick duty and Private William B. Jett, who was driving a supply wagon between Huachuca and Guadalupe Canyon. It was, as one officer later noted, a foolish decision by Hatfield to leave such a small force "behind in a death trap." Hatfield later rationalized his decision by saying that the men were vulnerable because the sergeant had disregarded his orders. If Hatfield had left another ten men, Chihuahua would have probably continued his flight into Mexico.

Taking his twelve fighters, eight men and four older boys, Chihuahua moved into position to waylay the camp. They tied their horses in a canyon a few hundred yards away. We will never know for sure which warriors were with him, but we can make a good guess. They were brave and tested fighters: his brother Ulzana, Cathla, and Nazee (Nah-do-Zhinne)—all had fought with Cochise. Also likely present were Shoie, José Second, and Tissnolthos, a relative of Chihuahua by marriage. Among the boys were surely Ulzana's teenage son and Dodostenay, a relative of Chihuahua. Chihuahua led his fighters along a spur of the mountain, which obscured their movements from the sentry. Moreover, the lookout, Private Deza Vislavki, a new recruit, had abandoned his post fifteen minutes before he was to be relieved, thus leaving the detail without a sentinel. Chihuahua took this opportunity to move his men even closer.

At noon, June 8, 1885, just as the soldiers began to eat lunch, Chihuahua crept up behind rooks to a bluff twenty-five yards from camp. Then, suddenly, he fired the first shot into the forehead of Private John H. Neihouse, killing him instantly. The ambush so startled the soldiers that a few men actually thought that Neihouse had shot himself. A "thunderous volley" at close range followed Chihuahua's opening salvo. None of the soldiers had their rifles by their side. As was customary, they had stacked them near the wagons while they ate lunch. Private Vislavki had a pistol, but one warrior shot him while he tried to escape to the hill on the north side of the canyon. Of the six remaining men, two escaped early in the fighting.

The remaining four troopers retrieved their rifles and ammunition and sought cover behind the wagons. For an hour, they sniped at the Apache positions on the bluff above their camp. Crook had once said that in an Apache fight, one never sees an Indian, only the puffs of smoke rising from their rifles. Private Jett would have concurred: he remembered that they returned fire but saw only the "smoke from the guns of Indians." The soldiers saw only one Apache during the hour-long combat. When the canvas from the ammunition wagons caught fire, the four men knew they had to make a run for the hill behind them. With cartridges exploding, the diversion helped them during their dash for the hill. Private John Schnitzer carried Sergeant Peter Mennich, already wounded three times, to the crest of the hill where one of Chihuahua's men sent a bullet through the sergeant's head, finally killing him. The other three men escaped. Chihuahua's raiders made off with five cavalry mounts and two mules before heading toward Mexico. Years later, the chief proudly admitted to an American officer that he had led the raid; his only regret was that five of the eight men had escaped.[53]

With Chihuahua now in Mexico, only Naiche remained north of the border. He had taken his followers into the Mule Mountains and established a temporary camp in Dixie Canyon. The afternoon of June 9, Milt Gillman and William A. Daniels, customs house inspector, followed a fresh trail from the eastern side of the Mule Mountains into Dixie Canyon. Here they saw smoke and with binoculars could see the Chiricahuas. Immediately, seven or eight warriors began a gallop toward the two Americans, intent on blocking their retreat from the mouth of the canyon. Daniels turned his horse around, saying to Gillman, "let's get out of here." He snapped off a few rounds from his revolver, and Gillman fired four shots from his Winchester, without effect. One warrior dismounted from his horse and aimed at Daniels, shooting him in the leg through the rifle scabbard. His horse fell, broke its neck, and threw Daniels to the ground, where he lay still, either pinned under his mount or stunned by the fall. Gillman had continued to ride for the mouth of the canyon, outdistancing his pursuers. He watched in horror as an Apache rode up to Daniels and pumped several rounds into the head of his fallen friend. He went to Bisbee with the news. When Tombstone's residents heard of the Daniels murder, they organized a militia force to avenge his death. But Naiche had led his followers into Mexico, going into the San Jose Mountains in northern Sonora.[54]

That same day, Crook received authorization to enlist another two hundred Apache scouts.[55] He had by then accepted the distressing truth that the cavalry had failed in its efforts to stop the Indians from crossing the border into Mexico. The ineffectiveness of his troops neither surprised nor disappointed him. He had made the correct moves, but he knew from experience that his commanders in the field had faced a stacked deck. In some cases, officers who preferred garrison life to field duty had hamstrung their command. Every commander was hampered by having to rest his horse while the Indians simply rode theirs to death and replaced them with fresh mounts from nearby ranches. The Apaches' other major advantage was that they owned the night. While the troops encamped, the Chiricahuas, with their familiarity of the terrain, put considerable distance between them and their pursuers.

It was a classic mismatch. During the twenty-five days it took the last group of Chiricahuas to enter Mexico, the troops, usually with the aid of Apache scouts, had come close to the Indians four times. Each time was on the Chiricahuas' terms: twice they had ambushed detachments camped in canyons; twice they had employed diversionary tactics, carried out to perfection by Mangas and Naiche.

By early June, Crook knew that he would have to send troops into Mexico. Central to his strategy were, of course, Apache scouts to guide his field officers. Unlike the 1883 campaign, which had only one Chiricahua scout, this time he wanted to feature as many as possible. Crook, Davis, and Lummis believed that the Chiricahua scouts were far superior to Western Apache scouts.[56] He rested his hopes and reputation on the efforts of his tested subordinates—Davis and Crawford, whom he had called back from Texas. He remained confident that Chatto's scouts would hunt down the hostiles and either kill them or force them to surrender. Though sensitive to criticism, a self-confident Crook, for the most part, took it in stride. The *Silver City Enterprise* asserted that Crook be held "criminally responsible" for every citizen killed by the Chiricahuas.[57]

This myopic view of Crook's culpability was the consensus of most southwesterners, who never considered that the country they were mining, ranching, and occupying had been, only a quarter century before, the unchallenged domain and home of the Chiricahua Apaches. The government had never bought their land; the Chiricahuas had never ceded their country.

Few whites understood that this latest breakout had not occurred in a vacuum. No one cared, as we would say today, to connect the dots that would have revealed that this outbreak was the culmination of a quarter century of distrust, suspicion, and intermittent warfare that had begun with the Bascom Affair and the wanton execution of Mangas Coloradas. It was no coincidence that the leaders of the final outbreak had firsthand recollections of these seminal events, which had become seared in their memories.

20

CROOK SENDS HIS "INDIAN MEN" INTO MEXICO

I will go to Mexico and capture Geronimo's band. That is why
I enlisted.
> Sergeant of Scouts Bylas, White Mountain chief

We went to Mexico not to fight them but to make peace with
them and bring them back as friends.
> Mithlo, Chiricahua Apache scout with
> Captain Wirt Davis's command

With the Chiricahuas now safely in Mexico, Crook focused his thoughts on the next phase of the campaign. His enemy would not make it easy for him. They had separated into four groups, initially living in northwestern Chihuahua and northeastern Sonora. This development troubled Crook, for it undermined his strategy to put a quick end to the war. In his mind, they had made a calculated decision to divide because they had learned a lesson from his 1883 campaign, when he had found the entire tribe camped near Bugatseka.[1] Yet Crook had misconstrued the reason for this development. It was not based on pragmatism or strategy. Instead, it was simply a result of tribal politics and personal animosities between the chiefs. He had no way of knowing that the entire group of hostiles, after splitting up on May 19, 1885, would never come together again in one band during the duration of the war.

Rumors of course were rampant during these confusing times, some wildly improbable. Two were especially noteworthy. Crook responded to one and probably heard the other. The Mexican consul in Tombstone had wired Washington saying that he "had proof" that the Chiricahuas had left San Carlos so that they could go to Sonora "to aid the Yaquis." The Yaquis, mortal enemies of the Apaches, were then at war with Sonora. Crook immediately discredited the rumor with a terse response: "It is impossible that the information . . . is correct."[2] An even more irrational conjecture came from Winslow, Arizona. This one claimed that a well-armed war party of 160 Navajos, Utes, and Paiutes was "on [its] way to join Geronimo's band." Now, the Chiricahuas would have appreciated help, but they hardly knew these Indians. Like writers of Hollywood Westerns, these uninformed whites had no idea of the historical relationships between tribes and often imagined these fictional alliances between Indians who, historically, were enemies.[3]

On May 28, 1885, Crook left Prescott to establish his field headquarters at Fort Bayard, which was then the hub of the action. Three days later he reached Bayard. The hostiles, however, were not behaving in tune with the current theory that they would stay in the mountains north and east of the Gila. And, as he would soon find out, they had already left the Mogollon and Black Range. Geronimo and Mangas were then in Mexico; Naiche and Chihuahua were en route to Sonora. Crook's first dispatch to Sheridan in Washington painted a grim picture, with gloomy prospects for a quick solution. He conceded that "the country is very much alarmed and the most radical measures must be taken to suppress the trouble which, however, will be a matter of great difficulty."[4]

When the secretary of war asked whether "anything more can be done to protect the settlers," Crook launched into a tirade blaming the outbreak on the Interior Department and on the scapegoat of the day, "dual control." Before offering particular steps to alleviate the crisis, he digressed and seized the opportunity to attack the issue that had been a problem between the civil Indian agents and Crawford. Although still unaware of Davis's telegram of May 15, 1885, Crook had analyzed Davis's lengthy report of May 21, which covered in detail the events leading to the breakout. Therefore, he understood completely what had led to the uprising. He reminded Sheridan that he had asked to be relieved from all responsibilities at San Carlos. After reciting the systemic problems inherent with dual control, he unequivocally recommended that the War Department relinquish accountability of the reservation to its rightful supervisor, the Interior Department. Nor did he want his officers on the reservation in a role subordinate to that of the civil Indian agent. Yet he magnanimously agreed to stay—reluctantly of course—if he were "given entire control of the reservation. The same hand that feeds should punish. Dual control or anything approaching it must be carefully avoided."

Crook had anticipated that his power play would work. After clarifying his position, he addressed the concerns of the secretary of war. He needed two hundred more Apache scouts, additional pack mules, and the "authority to hunt the Apaches in Mexico." He wanted assurance from Mexico that its forces would cooperate with his troops and Apache scouts. Sheridan approved his requests, authorizing the expedition into Mexico according to the reciprocal crossing treaty then in effect. He was confident that Mexican forces would welcome Crook's troops. The War Department and the Interior Department agreed to consider Crook's suggestions.[5]

Crook realized he faced a long war, with hard campaigning in Mexico. On June 4, 1885, he had transferred Captain Crawford from Texas back to his staff. Crawford had arrived in Deming on June 6, 1885, and conferred with Crook, who had given him marching orders to take a command into Mexico. Chatto, who had a good idea where the hostiles would go, was Crawford's principal advisor. After Crook's trusted subordinate left for the border, Crook moved to Fort Bowie, only ten miles from the Southern Pacific Railroad, where he established his field headquarters, and, in accordance with Sheridan's wishes, he immediately began preparations for a second column to follow Crawford into Sonora.[6]

The Chiricahuas' four groups were scattered in the Sierra Madre. Furthest east was the group led by Geronimo and Mangas, who, like clockwork, had stopped to trade at Casas Grandes, where they lingered for a few days, until they became uneasy and vacated the area about June 10. They went to their old strongholds at Bugatseka, where they joined the first group to enter Mexico, probably under Nat-cul-baye.[7]

As for Chihuahua's bunch, Captain Henry Lawton with three troops of the Fourth Cavalry had barreled their way south from Guadalupe Canyon, through the rugged terrain of the western Espuelas Mountains, before striking the Bavispe River near Batepito, north of the Teras Mountains in the Sierra Madre. Lawton estimated Chihuahua's group at twelve fighters and at least twenty women and children. The Indians had killed thirteen horses along the way, but not the larger and more valuable cavalry mounts from Guadalupe Canyon. Their shod prints allowed Lawton's scouts to follow the trail to the Bavispe River near Batepito. Here, on June 13, 1885, Lawton abandoned the trail and returned to Arizona, his men and horses played out.[8]

Chihuahua continued south, across the Bavispe River, until he reached Teras Mountains, known to the Chiricahuas as Djic-lic, "Big Juniper Berries."[9] This place was an important area in which to gather the juniper berries, which have a "reddish tinge when they are ripe and fall to the ground." The Indians often ate the berries raw, added water to soften them up, or mixed them with mescal cakes to provide flavor. Unfortunately for them, the fruit would not be ripe for another month or so.[10]

Naiche joined Chihuahua soon after. A small force from Huachuca under Lieutenant Richards (former commander of Apache scouts who had argued against releasing his Chiricahua scouts after Loco's forced removal in April 1882), reinforced by thirty volunteers from Tombstone, had followed Naiche's trail from the San Jose Mountains to Bacoachi, Sonora, where the Chiricahua group divided into smaller parties. On June 12, the Americans, lacking "pack mules," decided to return to Arizona. Sonoran officials reported that the Indians had gone into the Teras Mountains.[11]

They were right. Naiche crossed the Fronteras River near Turicachi before joining Chihuahua in the Teras Mountains about June 14. After a few days' rest, Naiche headed south into the heart of the Sierra Madre to join Geronimo and Mangas at Bugatseka. Chihuahua sent some of his men on a raid toward Moctezuma, where on June 17 and June 18 they stole stock. The prefect of Moctezuma, Francisco Arvizu, implored the governor to send help. Instead, Governor Luis Torres, who had petitioned the Díaz administration in Mexico City for help only four days after the outbreak, told Arvizu to fend for himself. Federal and local National Guard soldiers were then busy fighting the Yaquis and Mayos in the south part of Sonora. Until that conflict subsided, Arvizu "would have to rely on the patriotism of his own people." Magnanimously, he encouraged Arvizu to present a bill to the state for expenses incurred during the campaign.[12]

Chihuahua went southeast and stopped on a rocky ledge about fifteen miles northeast of Oputo on the night of June 22, 1885. He was unaware that American troops, guided by Chatto and twenty-one of his kinfolk, were then in camp north of Oputo.

Early morning, June 8, 1885, Crawford, one troop of Sixth Cavalry from Wingate under Captain Henry M. Kendall, twelve Mescalero scouts (probably under their chief, San Juan), Lieutenant Charles Elliott from San Carlos, and Chief Packer Henry W. Daly, with his pack train, boarded a special train at Deming and headed west. At Separ, they unpacked their stock and supplies and rode south toward Skeleton Canyon. The next day they met Lieutenant Davis and his fifty-eight scouts, just in from Bowie. Crawford took command of Davis and his scouts. It was a happy reunion for the two men, especially for Davis, who held Crawford in the highest esteem. Soon after, Al Sieber arrived with a second pack train of fifty mules. Crawford sent the Mescaleros, who were unfamiliar with the Sierra Madre, back to their reservation. He had ninety-two scouts (including Chatto's twenty-two Chiricahuas), A Troop, Sixth Cavalry, and two pack trains. He also had the latest intelligence, and the perspicacity of Chatto, who would perform yeoman's duty during the weeks to come.

From here forward, Crawford relied on Chatto's advice. Confident that Naiche and Chihuahua planned to meet in the Teras Mountains northeast of Oputo, Chatto decided to march directly to the Bavispe River below Oputo, thereby getting south of the assembly point. To achieve this without alerting the hostiles, he recommended that they enter the Sierra Madre from the Chihuahua side. Before the command left, Crook had second thoughts about Kendall's cavalry troop, giving Crawford the option to leave it at the border if he thought it might slow him down. Crawford and Davis, however, believed they needed the cavalry to protect the pack train, so they brought them along.[13] Accordingly, on June 11, 1885, they set out for Langs ranch and then through San Luis Pass into Chihuahua. That night they camped at the En-medio Mountains. For Chatto and Davis, this was the beginning of the most grueling and demanding three months of their lives.[14]

Chatto said that once in Mexico, Crawford had placed him "in charge of the whole outfit."[15] The next day they began a series of sixteen-hour marches, with one break, enduring temperatures that reached over 120 degrees. Chatto led the command into the Sierra Madre from the Carretas plains. One night they bivouacked near a mescal camp east of Bavispe. The entire group of ninety-two Apaches, including Chatto, got drunk. Early next morning they struck the Bavispe River and for a few days followed the same trail used by Crook in 1883. Mexican officials at several towns recognized Chatto, asking him about his former associate, Geronimo. The command followed the eastern bend of the Bavispe River as it threaded south to Huachinera. Below there, they angled southwest (Crook had gone southeast into the heart of the range in 1883), where they took a fork that crossed the mountain for Huásabas. During the trip, one White Mountain shaman, U-clen-ay, received good news from his Power: They would have a fight with the hostiles and catch several Chiricahuas. The trail now became "exceedingly rough, through interminable canyons" that were "all but impracticable for animals." Finally they reached Huásabas before moving north along the Bavispe River, where Chatto expected to find the hostiles in the Teras Mountains.

On June 19, the command scouted the country north along the Bavispe River. Dusk found them twelve miles north of Oputo, where they decided to encamp. Soon after, the Americans heard a commotion among the scouts. One scout raced into camp with the news that Mexicans had shot two scouts along the trail. One was dead; the second, Jahs-te-shu-ee, was wounded.[16] Hung over, the three scouts had been unable to keep up with the main body. The scout camp, across the Bavispe River from the troopers, was in an uproar. Davis described the scene: "Hell or at least the threat of it, broke loose in the scout camp. Thirty or forty scouts immediately stripped for battle and started for Oputo, about twelve miles away, determined to kill any Mexicans they could find." Nearly every Western Apache scout favored leaving immediately for Arizona. The Chiricahuas, used to unexpected encounters and crises, took it all in stride. Finally, Chatto and a few White Mountain scouts helped Crawford's officers to quiet the ringleaders. The next day Davis and Chatto took a small group of scouts to the site of the ambush and buried the scout.[17]

Chatto's hunch about the rendezvous site paid dividends a few days later. On June 22, 1885, the scouts found a trail of eight to ten warriors who had stolen some stock at Oputo. These were Chihuahua's men, and the scouts tracked them for a short distance before returning to camp. Chatto took control. With Crawford's blessings, he selected thirty scouts to accompany him and Big Dave, the White Mountain sergeant. Though Davis and Sieber wanted to go along, Crawford vetoed their proposal, believing that they would only slow Chatto's group. Crawford told Chatto to find the camp, and, if possible, to hold their positions until the arrival of the rest of the command. "Just as the moon rose over the distant peaks," Chatto's command, leading three pack mules loaded with two days' rations and one hundred rounds per man, "silently stole out of camp." They picked up the trail and followed it until 9:00 P.M., when it began to rain, which obliterated the tracks. Chatto ordered a halt to make camp.

The next morning Chatto and Big Dave resumed the hunt. Rain and mist obscured visibility. But anticipating where Chihuahua had camped, Chatto led them doggedly toward the mountain. En route, they found eight butchered cattle, which confirmed his suspicions. About 9:00 A.M. the rain stopped, and when the sun broke through the clouds, the spirits of the scouts soared. Seconds later, Chatto, looking through binoculars, espied Chihuahua's camp about five hundred yards away at El Tigre, a rocky spur that connected to the main range. According to one Tonto scout, Oskay-be-no-tah (The Flying Fighter), a veteran of twelve enlistments dating back to the 1870s, Chatto took control. He took five scouts and flanked the camp; the balance, under Big Dave, moved closer to the camp, waiting for Chatto to open the attack. He hoped to drive the Chiricahuas toward Big Dave's scouts.

The Chokonen chief fired the first volley into the camp, followed by the five men with him. The attack threw the camp into bedlam. Then the scouts from below the camp unleashed a volley. During these opening salvos, the attackers mortally wounded the Chiricahua sentry, the sixteen-year-old son of Ulzana. Another volley killed an old woman, probably a mother-in-law of Chihuahua, whose men tried to protect the women and children. One warrior, José Second, led them to shelter in a cave. While evacuating their camp, one scout put a bullet into the thigh of Cathla, a warrior known for his courage and marksmanship. Two men carried him from the village. Chihuahua's men knew better than to slug it out with the scouts. Once away from camp, they fled, leaving their women and children safely in the cave. Though the warriors tried to lure the scouts away from the village, Chatto refused to take the bait. Consequently, they soon found the fifteen women and children and took them into custody.

The victors captured the entire camp—five horses taken from Guadalupe Canyon, one mule, two revolvers, cartridge belts, three saddles, and other supplies. Chihuahua, seven men, four boys, and three women and children had escaped. The scouts' only casualty was Big Dave, shot through the elbow. Among the captives were Chihuahua's entire family and Ulzana's wife and two children. Thinking that Chihuahua would feel dispirited by the loss of his family, Chatto released one woman to go to the chief with an offer either to kill Geronimo or surrender. The chief might have taken the first option if Geronimo had been with him. But the assault on their camp had the opposite effect on Chihuahua and Ulzana. The former had become enraged, blaming his problems on Geronimo and Chatto. Now, without his family, it seemed as though demons had a stranglehold on his mind, as he later told Crook. The brothers would remember the role that Chatto played in the death of Ulzana's son and the capture of their families. Eschewing any thoughts of surrender, they vowed vengeance on Chatto.[18]

The scouts returned in two groups to Crawford's camp. One party arrived late the same day (June 23) with the details. The second group, with the prisoners, returned triumphantly the morning of June 24. Lieutenant Elliott, with a Mexican guide from Oputo, mounted on mules, left the next morning bearing dispatches to Crook at Bowie, arriving at 8:00 A.M. on June 28, after "the hardest and most trying ride of my life." He had traveled almost two hundred miles in three days. Crook sent Elliott to Langs ranch, to await the arrival of fresh supplies and Company G, Fourth Cavalry, under Lieutenant Guy E. Huse. They set out for their plunge into the Sierra Madre to join Crawford and relieve Captain Kendall's troop.[19]

On June 26, a day after Elliott's departure, Crawford sent Lieutenant Hanna with an escort of ten troopers, Daly's empty pack train, and some ten Apache scouts to take twelve Chiricahua prisoners to Fort Bowie. Of the original fifteen captives, Ulzana's son had died. Chatto had sent one woman to Chihuahua, and one woman was too ill or injured to travel. She was left at Moctezuma, her fate unknown.[20] Among the scouts returning were the clairvoyant medicine man U-clen-ay, Goody, and two Chokonens, Kayitah and Dutchy, both of whom had probably been mainstays in the attack on Chihuahua's camp. Drinking mescal the night before they left, Dutchy had become roaring drunk, completely disrupting the camp. Crawford had had his fill of intoxicated scouts. Although he remembered Dutchy's courageous support during the Kaetenae confrontations, he had to make an example of him. Thus he sent him to Bowie, where Crook could decide his punishment. Hanna, after meeting with the prisoners, observed that their five weeks away from the reservation "had been no pleasure excursion for them." Crawford had warned him to keep an eye out for hostiles, who might try to free their relatives.

Hanna had no wagon in which to transport the wounded. Ulzana's wife, Nah-zis-eh, in extreme pain with gunshot wounds in both thighs, had to ride a horse. He did everything possible to keep her comfortable. The second day out, they crossed the trail of a large band of Chiricahuas going east across the mountains. This was a raiding party under Geronimo, who may have had Naiche, Nana, and Mangas with him. This discovery concerned the scouts, who told Hanna to make camp in a defensive position. Believing that if an attack came, it would be at dawn, Hanna woke everyone at 3:00 A.M. The assault never came, and on July 2, 1885, Hanna arrived at Bowie and turned over three scouts under arrest (including Dutchy) and eleven Chiricahua prisoners. Scout Goody, married to a sister of Chihuahua named Nah-yah-di-nith, had taken custody of a son of Chihuahua.

Soon after the prisoners' arrival, Crook, recognizing that the Apaches would have difficulties adapting to confinement in the guardhouse, had the soldiers construct a pen using telegraph poles as posts. He hoped that Chihuahua would surrender once he discovered his family was safe at Bowie. The general ordered the three scouts shackled and confined in the guardhouse. Crook, meanwhile, asked that Lieutenant Roach at Fort Apache send horses to Fort Thomas for seven scouts, including U-clen-ay, Goody, and Kayitah. They returned to the reservation with Lieutenant Charles Gatewood, just in from a fruitless scout into New Mexico.[21]

Crook had sent Gatewood back to Fort Apache the first week of June. On June 9, 1885, after receiving authorization from the War Department to enlist two hundred more Apache scouts, Crook instructed Captain Pierce at San

Carlos to "select the best Indians on the reservation [including] as many Chiricahuas as possible." Accordingly, Gatewood enlisted seventy-five scouts, of
whom sixteen were Chiricahuas and the balance White Mountains. By then
Crook had told him to return with his scouts to the Gila country, where he
believed that Mangas and a small band were hiding out. Either "destroy them
or run them out of the country" was his decree to Gatewood. By this time,
however, the few warriors whom Geronimo had left behind to await the messengers to Mescalero had followed him into Mexico.[22]

On June 16, Gatewood swung out of Fort Apache with a pack train and the
scouts. Gatewood wanted Chihennes who knew the Gila River country and
the Black Range north and east of Silver City. Loco had obliged his wishes,
furnishing him with several reliable men from his band, among them Massai, Tsedikizen, and Stalosh. Others who joined were the Chokonen brothers, Espida (Speedy or Spitty) and Kaydahzinne, both nephews of Chihuahua;
Nahn-tee-nesn, a Chokonen shaman related to Chihuahua; and Mithlo. Finally, Toosigah, the only man from Geronimo's band then on the reservation, also signed on. A Chihenne who had grown up in the Black Range, he
had married the daughter of Beshe, Naiche's father-in-law and a member of
Geronimo's group.[23] The Chihenne scouts were bitter toward the hostiles; but
the Chokonens, especially the three kinfolk of Chihuahua, had joined hoping to save the lives of their relatives who had left the reservation. Gatewood
found no hostiles in New Mexico because there were none to find. Much to
his chagrin, his two-week scout did nothing but wear out men and mounts.
He characterized the ordeal in a letter to his wife: "Our trip has been without
interest. Up one hill and down another would sum up the whole thing."

Fortunately for Gatewood, Crook ordered him to bring the scouts to Fort
Bowie. Captain Wirt Davis, then ready to open a second front in the Sierra
Madre, needed the Chiricahuas, for they were the only ones who knew that
range. On July 5, Gatewood arrived and turned over his scouts. He was re-
lieved when Crook returned him to duty at Fort Apache. With Davis and
Gatewood absent, Lieutenant Roach was doing double duty. He relied on Sam
Bowman, who was ill equipped to manage the Indians. Crook realized that
he was only buying time until Gatewood could reestablish stability at Fort
Apache. Gatewood left Bowie for Apache with Kayitah and the other scouts
from Crawford's campaign.[24]

Gatewood was en route to Apache when the Chiricahuas had another tiswin
drunk. And this was not the first such offense since the outbreak. Without
any supervision, the Indians found the availability of corn sprouts and shelled

corn just too much a temptation. The two most important chiefs left at Fort Apache, Bonito and Loco, led by example: they got drunk. It was obvious that the lure of tiswin had drowned out the lessons of May 17, 1885. They certainly wanted to keep this activity quiet. On July 9, 1885, Roach gave Crook the disturbing facts:

> Bonito's squaw killed another woman last night in a tiswin drunk. The drunk was general throughout camp. Loco, who was also drunk, came in and reported that Bonito's band was about to leave. He afterwards modified this to the statement that Bonito and his squaw had left. Chatto's wife warned Bowman to leave camp, which he did. I had White Mountain Scouts [in] ambush near the camp watching all night and sent Bowman in at daylight. They report that no one has left and Bowman confirms it. Bowman now acknowledged to me that the drunks are of frequent occurrences. He has lied to me systematically since my return in his daily reports to me. I have Bonito's squaw just confined in the guardhouse. Bonito is now near and denied his squaw's guilt, saying it was done after repeated provocation. He and the balance take the drunkenness as a matter of course and in a what are you going to do about it sort of a way. I very much fear trouble and believe that unless a display of force is made here, the outbreak of the balance of these Indians is only a question of time.[25]

Crook told Roach to warn the Chiricahuas that they "must behave themselves. If they don't, it will only be a matter of time until they all come to grief." He wanted no display of force, which "might precipitate matters by frightening them off." Recognizing that the Chiricahua chiefs had failed him, he suggested that Roach use the influence of the White Mountain chief Alchesay to control them: "Tell Al-chi-se he must straighten this out. If they break out now, it will injure all the Indians very seriously." If Alchesay thought diplomacy would fail, Crook encouraged him to "take extreme measures" to control the agency Chiricahuas. He clearly trusted Alchesay. But he was also implying that the White Mountain people had as much to lose as the Chiricahuas, proving that he was not above telling a little white lie to get results. He immediately wired Gatewood "to take charge of this matter" once he reached Fort Apache.[26]

The one thing Crook hoped to prevent were civilian casualties in Arizona and New Mexico. The press was crucifying him at every turn, and petitions and letters from citizens were depicting a state of unbridled emergency. Farmers, ranchers, miners, and businessmen were complaining to Washington, even to President Grover Cleveland. In mid-June, Sam Carusi penned one such letter from Lochiel, a few miles north of the border in the Patagonia Mountains, the contents of which were symptomatic of the hysteria that gripped the border settlements:

> We are surrounded by Apaches. We have many women and small children with us. We are poorly armed; there is not a soldier in hundreds of miles of us. Must we, who build up Republics and pave the way for civilization, be shot down, butchered, tortured, and robbed by the marauding red devils, who are now devastating our beautiful land? . . . The Indians are within ten miles of this place with not a soldier in pursuit.

Carusi wanted white troopers, specifically the Third Cavalry, "Indian fighters to a man," whom Sheridan had transferred to Texas and replaced with a "horde of cowardly Negroes, the Tenth U.S. Cavalry."

However, Lochiel was not "surrounded" by the Chiricahuas. Admittedly, communications were sparse, rumors rampant, and paranoia the order of the day when it came to Apaches, so we can accept Carusi's embellishment because of the chaos of those times. Yet, he made several misstatements. First, he certainly knew that Fort Huachuca was within fifty miles of his house. He may not have known that soldiers from that post were then returning from their pursuit of Chiricahuas into Sonora. Moreover, the hostiles had not come within forty miles of his house. His concerns were real, and, as a father, he did fear for his family's safety (he had eight children in his home). But his letter reflected the disrespectful attitude held by most frontier residents toward the military. And it displayed clearly the overt bigotry—the absolute contempt—that many southwesterners felt toward the black troopers, who had performed just as well as white cavalry units when given the chance to prove their mettle in the Victorio campaigns.[27]

Crook was then organizing a second offensive under Captain Wirt Davis to launch simultaneous operations against the hostiles from both sides of the Sierra Madre. And if they tried to cross the border, as he expected they would, he had placed a line of troops—eleven companies of cavalry and two companies of infantry—to cover the usual entry points and waterholes. In case they penetrated that cordon of troops, Crook had stationed companies of the Tenth

Cavalry between the border and the railroad, thus providing a second line of protection. These two divisions comprised about one thousand men and one hundred Apache scouts. Furthermore, backing up them was still a third line, "soldiers along the railroad," available for rapid deployment to "any desired point along the whole front." Finally, Crook could call on garrisons between the railroad and the reservation, in the unlikely event that the Chiricahuas broke through the soldiers' lines.[28] In reality, the hostiles planned to remain in Mexico. They could get plenty of ammunition for their Winchesters there, and they believed that the lofty uplifts of the Sierra Madre Mountains offered their best bet to survive.

Meanwhile, Captain Wirt Davis was preparing to cross the border into Mexico. He had two pack trains and the following personnel: lieutenants Robert D. Walsh and James B. Erwin and thirty-eight troopers of the Fourth Cavalry; Charlie Roberts and Buckskin Frank Leslie as chiefs of scouts; Assistant Surgeon Henry P. Birmingham; and Lieutenant Mathias W. Day (winner of the medal of honor in the Victorio War for rescuing a trooper under hot fire), who commanded the 102 Apache scouts. The Apache scouts included San Carlos, White Mountain, and sixteen Chiricahuas whom Gatewood had enlisted the previous month. As they were leaving Fort Bowie, the scouts, who wore white headbands to distinguish themselves from Crawford's scouts, who wore red headbands, stopped in front of Crook's house. Here the general addressed them. Years later, Walter Hooke, a rookie scout, remembered what he said: "Geronimo is killing white women and children. If you capture these wild Chiricahuas then all these American people will help you at San Carlos and the ones who live far off will help you also." Bylas, one of eight sergeants of scouts, told Crook, "If I see any of them I will not let them get away."[29] Bylas, whose father Djs-lata-ha (Ear Tips) was chief among the Eastern White Mountain Apaches, still wanted to get even with the Chiricahuas, especially Geronimo, whom he despised, for their massacre at Stevens's sheep camp and Victorio's slaying of Bylas's uncle.[30]

Overshadowed by Crook's Apache-wise officers—Crawford, Gatewood, and Britton Davis—Captain Wirt Davis was the unsung officer of the Geronimo War. He was not your typical army captain. To begin with, shortly before the Civil War he had run away from the University of Virginia to St. Louis, where he had enlisted as a private in the cavalry. Though he was from Richmond, he fought for the Union, working his way up the ranks, and in 1863 the army commissioned him a lieutenant. During his Civil War service, he earned two brevets for outstanding service. After the war, he saw significant action against the Indians of the northern plains and in the fight at Horseshoe Canyon in 1882. Thought by some to be the best cavalry commander in the Fourth Cavalry, he was also a hard drinker, but he abstained when on field duty. An expert shooter with a carbine and pistol, he was viewed by many of his peers and troopers as the best pistol shot they had seen. One man recalled that Davis "could keep a tin can jumping in front of him with a revolver." The captain was a quiet, unpretentious man devoted to the army. At five feet ten inches, with a handlebar mustache and hair now more gray than blond, he looked more like a gentle-hearted grandfather than a veteran Indian fighter. Yet, he had the "weather-beaten face of most of the cavalry officers who have spent their lives in the frontier." When asked about the reliability of Apache scouts, he calmly replied that he "had no apprehension whatsoever. If he had [had] any, he would not [have gone] out with them."[31]

Davis's command followed Crawford's trail into the Sierra Madre. By July 20, 1885, his force had reached Huépari Creek, about midway between Huachinera and Oputo. To this point they had met neither hostiles nor Crawford, who, after the attack on Chihuahua's camp, had gone south to the Aros River.[32]

The last week of June, the Chiricahuas, except Chihuahua's group of fifteen, had left the Sierra Madre to raid the towns along the Sonora River below Arispe. This time they had taken their women and children. They could not risk leaving them unprotected in any of their mountain strongholds because of the presence of the Chiricahua scouts. Geronimo, Mangas, and Naiche led this group of one hundred Chiricahuas, which included about thirty warriors and teenage boys. The first week of July, raiders stole stock near Sinoquipe and killed a man from Huepac. On July 10, 1885, Captain Leonardo Gómez and 150 nationals picked up the Indians' trail, which led northeast. The next morning, he discovered three butchered horses. That day he followed the trail to the summit of the Carmen Mountains, where the Chiricahuas had located their base camp. He estimated their numbers at between eighty and one hundred. On July 12, as Gómez pushed on relentlessly, Geronimo and Mangas felt the pressure.

The chiefs decided to split up into three groups. Geronimo, with most of the women and children, continued to the northeast. Mangas led a second group east; Naiche with his group of about thirty-five went north, hooking up with Chihuahua about a week later. Gómez decided to follow Geronimo's trail, which crossed the road between Bacoachi and Cumpas, heading straight for the Purica Mountains, twelve miles southwest of Turicachi. On July 16,

Gómez's command detected Apaches fleeing from their camp. Their trail led east to the Pinito Mountain, just west of the Bavispe River. Here Mangas's party had joined the other Apaches with horses and cattle. Gómez's scout ended here. Before retiring to refit and rest at Cuchuta, he sent word to the prefect of Moctezuma, who warned the settlements along the western part of the Bavispe River.[33]

At dusk on July 20, a mail rider from Moctezuma rode into Wirt Davis's camp on Huépari Creek and told him that the hostiles had gone to the Teras Mountains. After consulting with the Chiricahua scouts, Davis decided to leave the next morning at dawn. Hoping to surprise the Chiricahuas from the south, his command traversed the Oputo and Madera mountains. Eleven hours later, they stopped to camp on the Bavispe River, six miles north of Oputo.[34]

That evening a group of Mexicans from Oputo came into camp with news. They had cut a trail that went toward La Jolla (or La Joya) Mountains before turning back. This rugged area, tucked inside the east and west branches of the Bavispe, was evidently in the southern part of the El Tigre Mountains, which the Chiricahuas called Zisl-bi-tu-ba-da-nes-line (Mountain, River Encircles It), referring to the course of the Bavispe River.[35] It had long been a favorite camping area of the Chokonens and Nednhis, offering protection from enemies, abundant game, and bountiful mescal on the eastern slopes. One Mexican offered to show Davis the trail. Captain Davis sent Bylas, Cooley, and four scouts (one, possibly Binday, was part Chiricahua) with the Mexican. Davis told Bylas that if he found the ranchería he was to send two scouts back to Davis, who would bring the rest of the scouts and soldiers to surround the area.

In retrospect, Davis should have sent a larger force with Bylas. Walter Hooke, who was part of this group, recounted the details of this patrol to Grenville Goodwin forty-five years later. It is remarkable how much he remembered of their pursuit. His account provides us with a rare vignette that we can use with Captain Davis's report of his daily operations. Hooke recalled that the Mexican took them into the canyon as far as his men had dared to venture. Then he stopped abruptly, shook hands with the six scouts, and told Bylas: "If the Chiricahuas see you scouts, they will kill all of you because they are bad fighters who have killed lots of Mexicans."

Bylas and the Chiricahua scout easily followed the tracks. The latter seemed to know where the trail would lead, and he showed his companions how to descend into the canyon "on his back, using his hands and feet, while resting his rifle on his stomach and chest." Here they found a few butchered horses and saw two women on horseback riding toward them. The women dismounted to gather the fruit of the prickly pear cactus, which was then becoming ripe. Soon after, they hollered out that their men had seen the scouts "so don't try to hide." They said, "we don't like it here and want to go back to San Carlos." The Chiricahua scout knew this was a common strategy of the hostiles who "wanted only for us to show ourselves so [they] could kill us." He was right. Finally, about noon, with the aid of binoculars, Hooke spotted several warriors on a ridge of the highest mountain. Bylas knew that the main camp had to be there, so he dispatched two scouts to summon Captain Davis.[36]

They did not reach Wirt Davis until about 8:00 that night (July 22). For some reason, the captain had moved his command closer to Oputo. At once the camp bustled with activity, and the command left at midnight, following the Bavispe north for ten miles, where they bivouacked at daybreak. The hostiles were still about ten miles northeast of them. Resting his main force, that afternoon Davis sent his scouts (about ninety-six) with at least fifteen Chiricahuas to rendezvous with Bylas. At 7:00 P.M. on July 23, Davis led the cavalry on foot to join the scouts. Early the next morning, Bylas and the seven scout sergeants divided their men and stealthily surrounded Geronimo's camp. Bylas took the most dangerous position, slowly ascending the mountain to the place where they had seen the hostiles. As dawn approached, Hooke recalled the suspenseful moment: "The birds started to sing, and we raised our heads from where we were lying and looked." The camp was still. As visibility improved, "we saw that only the camp was there. There was no one in it. . . . That would have been a good place to fight and kill all the Chiricahuas but instead we had surrounded [them] for nothing." The Chiricahua scouts announced that this had been Geronimo's camp.[37]

Hooke later learned the reason for Geronimo's sudden departure the night before. The Chiricahuas had not detected Bylas's scouts, but an old, crippled Apache woman had warned Geronimo that "if [we] stay here one more night there will be trouble coming." Geronimo discounted her warning, but his followers took her seriously, which suggests she was a reliable medicine woman with Power. By the evening of July 22, as Wirt Davis began his march to join Bylas, the band "had gone to the top of the mountain there and looked down as they were afraid. So finally Geronimo believed this crippled woman and they moved camp so we missed them."[38]

Though disappointed that Geronimo and Mangas had slipped away, Captain Davis and his officers regrouped. A few days later, they met with the scouts. Davis requested that a medicine man conduct a ceremony to figure out where Geronimo had gone. Only one Apache, Gush-i-guu, consented to use his Power. His specialty was healing the sick, but he told Captain Davis that his Power was omnipotent: "I can tell all things," he confidently proclaimed. The Apaches "tied up" four drums (four buckets provided by the soldiers) for the ceremony. That night the officers attended the service. All the scouts helped the medicine man sing. Around midnight his Power began to talk to him. He went into a detailed litany of the daily movements of the hostiles and what the scouts would find. He said that Geronimo's followers had camped at the crest of El Tigre Mountains, "on a long narrow bed." Then they had moved down toward the Bavispe River, where the women had gathered acorns. From here, they went to a mountain opposite Bugatseka, where they had cooked mescal. The hostiles had left one large piece of mescal behind. Gush-i-guu said that if the scouts found this piece of mescal, then "all will be good." At Geronimo's camp, he said, they would see a yellow mule. Then the scouts would attack the village at Bugatseka, killing a few and capturing many women and children.

On August 2, 1885, Lieutenant Day, Chief of Scouts Roberts, and eighty-six scouts cut the trail. The morning of August 7, 1885, Day ordered Bylas to take six scouts to reconnoiter the country. Bylas, however, wanted twenty-five, or at least fifteen, because the last time he had only six scouts, the Chiricahuas had eluded his grasp while he waited for the main body to arrive. He wanted a sufficient force to fight in case he encountered Geronimo. Day refused, and a stalemate followed until the lieutenant acquiesced and gave Bylas fifteen men.

Bylas again took the lead. Later that morning he found Geronimo's camp at the southern tip of Bugatseka, near the spot where Crawford's scouts had attacked Chatto and Bonito's ranchería in 1883. Day and the main body joined Bylas's force. The scouts were stoic and loyal. When Day began to tire, Bylas urged him on. In the early afternoon of August 7, 1885, as Day and the scouts took positions to surround the village, a mule tied to a bush began to bray and run around, which alerted the Chiricahuas. Bylas thus had to open the assault before his men had completed the maneuver.

Details about the assault are sparse, and reports vary as to the casualties. The first accounts claimed that the scouts killed Nana, Geronimo's son (Chappo), another man, one woman, and one thirteen year-old boy. Subsequent information amended the dead to two women and one boy, who died after a stray bullet struck a rock that ricocheted into the boy's eye, killing him instantly. There can be no disagreement about the prisoners—fifteen women and children captured, among whom were Geronimo's three wives and five children, and the wives of Perico, Beshe, Dah-Ke-Ya, and Mangas, who turned out to be Huera, a ringleader in the outbreak. The scouts wounded three of the prisoners, including Geronimo's daughter Dohn-say.

At the first salvos, the scouts saw Geronimo pick up his young son and run from the camp through a gauntlet of firepower. Both Chiricahuas and Western Apaches tried to bring him down. Some scouts believed they had wounded him, for he eventually dropped the boy before escaping. But the evidence was at best equivocal. Scout Sherman Curley, then with Britton Davis, heard from scouts that they had "shot [at] Geronimo but he got away." Several men were absent from the village, either raiding or hunting. Those who escaped had to leap from a "steep bluff" to safety. Hooke recalled that "every single thing that the medicine man had told us [had] come true." Lieutenant Day was the only white man in the fight.[39]

The assault scattered Geronimo's group. Mangas and his small party headed for Juh's old stronghold at Guaynopa. He never rejoined Geronimo or the other chiefs until after the surrender.[40] Geronimo and Nana, with about forty followers, headed southeast toward Chihuahua. Meanwhile, Lieutenant Day's command returned to the pack train, where they unexpectedly found Captain Crawford and Chatto.

They had returned from south of Nácori after a month of fruitless scouting. Thinking that Chihuahua had gone to the eastern part of the range, Crawford had dispatched Britton Davis to scout to the Aros River, but to his surprise, he had not found any tracks.[41] Eager for information, Crawford took custody of Wirt Davis's prisoners. He and Chatto interrogated two of Geronimo's wives, but they knew nothing of Geronimo's immediate plans. They did say that Naiche was in the mountains west of the Sierra Madre. They knew nothing of Chihuahua because they had not seen him since May 19. Then, according to Chatto, "Crawford took [the] women down to his tent and questioned them all about Geronimo." They reiterated what they had told Chatto. Crawford then made a move that seemed uncharacteristic of him. He pulled out his revolver and threatened the women. They "were on the verge of tears, but they claimed they did not know [anything]." Crawford backed down. This was a sign that the two months of exacting duty in Sonora were beginning to wear on Crawford. He knew that Crook needed results, and he was prepared to straddle the line to achieve them.[42]

The commanders of each detachment sent dispatches to Crook. First, Wirt Davis sent Frank Leslie to take dispatches to the general, giving him the details of Day's victory over Geronimo. Because Crawford had seen that cavalry were useless in the mountains, he sent Lieutenant Huse and his Troop C, Fourth Cavalry (thirty-one troopers), and five Apache scouts to escort the captives to Fort Bowie.[43] Slowed considerably by daily torrents of thunderstorms that swelled the banks of the Bavispe River, they arrived at Bowie on September 2, 1885, seventeen days later. Meanwhile, Crawford had decided to take his command and follow Geronimo's trail to wherever it might lead. Wirt Davis, his pack train just in from the border with supplies to last until the end of September, headed for the western side of the Sierra Madre, where his scouts believed they would find Chihuahua and Naiche.[44]

Captain Wirt Davis had heard from the prefect of Moctezuma on August 23, 1885, that Chiricahuas were in the mountains northeast of Tepache. He at once left his camp some six miles east of Bacadéhuachi and marched through the towns of Granados and Huásabas, reaching the Hacienda de Tonibabi, eight miles east of Moctezuma, on August 26. By then Leslie had returned from Fort Bowie with two scouts, one of whom was Dutchy. Crook had released him from the guardhouse, describing him as "one of our staunch friends," who would be "useful" to Wirt Davis. That same day, a vaquero from Granados came in with the news that they had found the hostiles' trail. The captain planned to leave at dark and travel all night, hoping to surprise the Apaches the next morning. His plans changed, however, after Mexican general Diego Guerra, then at Moctezuma, sent a courier with a message that he would come to his camp the next morning to discuss strategy.[45]

Mexico's secretary of war, Pedro Hinojosa, had dispatched Guerra from Hidalgo del Parral to Chihuahua City, from where he had marched to the Apache frontier with a large force of 366 men of the Eleventh Regiment. Hinojosa wanted nothing less than the destruction of every Apache, regardless of age or sex. Guerra's force had followed the route used by Crawford and Davis. From Bavispe, he followed the river south to Huachinera and then moved southwest to the other side of the Sierra Madre Mountains to Moctezuma.[46]

General Guerra and a dozen of his staff rode into Captain Davis's camp the morning of August 27, 1885. Forty-five years later, Hooke recalled the general's ostentatious uniform and outfit: "He was all dressed up. He had silver buttons on both sides of his coat, and silver eagles on each side of his hat. His saddle was all silver mounted with big conchos and eagles. His horse had silver eagles on both sides of his bridle also." Guerra informed Captain Davis that one of his squads had fought the Chiricahuas just two days earlier, on August

25. This was Chihuahua's mobile group of twelve men (which included four teenage boys). They had routed the Mexican force, killing two men. Hooke believed that General Guerra had stormed off after ordering Davis to leave the country; yet, Captain Davis reported no such disagreement. He said the general had asked for Apache scouts, but that Bylas, acting as the leader, refused to go with the Mexicans. It would appear that Bylas's refusal upset Guerra, and that Hooke mistook this for anger toward the Americans.[47]

Regardless, not long after, Davis broke camp and picked up Chihuahua's trail. The next day his force came to a canyon between two rocky hills, where Chihuahua had ambushed and slain two Mexican soldiers. In the Mexicans' haste to leave the battlefield, they must have left their corpses on the ground, for Hooke remembered that the area "smelled bad [so] there must have been a lot of dead bodies there." Captain Davis hurried the command along. Soon after, they found the "Chiricahua tracks and started to follow them." That night Wirt Davis's force camped at the foot of a mountain southeast of Tepache.[48]

Chihuahua had not been idle during this period. In fact, we can state unequivocally that his small band of fifteen committed nearly all the depredations in Sonora during the summer of 1885. Unencumbered by dependents and angry at the world, Chihuahua was a dangerous man, fighting to survive against overwhelming odds. Indifferent to his own fate, he felt that he had nothing more to lose. By the third week of July, he had joined forces with Naiche, who was in the mountains northwest of Bacoachi. They had to raid to survive. But it would appear as though Chihuahua and Naiche's sole strategy was to avoid the heart of the Sierra Madre, where American and Mexican forces were then operating.

On July 20, 1885, Chiricahuas lay in ambush at Jaralito Springs, reported to be fifteen miles north of Cananea. At 10:00 A.M. four American miners rode up to fill their canteens. As they dismounted, the Indians opened fire, killing James Gillum and wounding Sydney Markham. The other two Americans, Ed Garland and Charles Henley, took cover. They helplessly watched the Apaches take everything, their stock, baggage, and money. That same day, the Indians assaulted two Mexicans driving sheep south to the Bacanuchi ranch, killing one herder and wounding the other. Commander Florencio Ruiz, with soldiers from Santa Cruz, followed, but Chihuahua's rear guard surprised him, killing two of his men. The next day, July 21, they ambushed and killed two more Mexicans who were out rounding up horses and cattle. Then they split up: Naiche led the largest party, probably thirty-five in all, including women and children, into the Pinito Mountains twenty miles southwest of Santa Cruz.[49]

Chihuahua's group of fifteen entered Arizona a few miles northeast of Santa Cruz on July 23. That day, three of his men killed a mail carrier, Frank Patterson. Chihuahua took the main group and traveled all night, stealing stock along the way, before finding shelter in the Whetstone Mountains after killing a Mexican. Chihuahua was testing Crook's defenses to determine the feasibility of moving north to Fort Apache, where he assumed Crook had sent his family. But he saw that the country was full of soldiers. Two troops of cavalry under captains Hatfield and Wood, from their outposts along the border, had cut his trail. They followed it to the San Pedro River and from here southeast toward the San Jose Mountains in Sonora. As usual, they were several hours behind Chihuahua, who, feeling the pressure, abandoned some forty head of recently stolen horses. The Americans followed the trail into the Azul Mountains and then on to Cananea, where they turned back on July 28.[50]

In early August, the two Chokonen chiefs rejoined in the Azul Mountains (fifteen miles southwest of Cananea), where Mexican soldiers found a recently abandoned village on August 5. The Chiricahuas had moved east toward Cumpas, where on August 3, 1885, a party estimated at fifty Apaches (but probably no more than half that number) raided that town and returned to their ranchería in the Azul Mountains, where they holed up for about a week before striking again. August 14, 1885, was perhaps their bloodiest day of the war as they added another seven or eight victims. That day they assaulted the Basachuca ranch, killing as many as seven people, including two women and two children. A few days later, they cleaned out a ranch of John Hohstadt, probably at Janaverachi, looting his house and "carrying off provisions, guns and ammunition." Finally, on August 18 Naiche and Chihuahua led their men against the Cananea mine, wounding two men, stealing stock, and slaughtering several head of stock.

Again, they divided. Naiche went south to the mountains between the Moctezuma and Sonora River, probably camping in either the Huerta Mountains or the Batuco Mountains, north of Batuc. Chihuahua took his fifteen followers and made a beeline east through the Ajos Mountains. The next day his party crossed the Fronteras River between Cuchuta and Turicachi, en route for the Bavispe River. A week later they had worked their way south, passing Oputo and Huásabas, to the junction of the Yaqui River, where Chihuahua had hoped to regroup.[51]

The presence of Captain Wirt Davis and his Chiricahua and Western Apache scouts allowed Chihuahua no rest. On August 30, 1885, they found Chihuahua's deserted camp on the summit of Mount Salitral, directly west of the junction of the Bavispe and Yaqui rivers. The scouts found a few saddles and the carcasses of twenty-four horses, which the Chiricahuas had slaughtered rather than allow them to fall into the hands of the scouts.

Neither Wirt Davis nor Hooke had any doubts about the identity of the hostiles. Hooke recalled that it was not Geronimo but the Chokonens of Chihuahua and Naiche. According to Wirt Davis, his scouts said that they were following Chihuahua's group of "twelve bucks, one squaw and one or two boys." Among the Chiricahua scouts were two nephews and another relative of Chihuahua. They predicted that Chihuahua would eventually try to reach the Chihuahua side of the mountains through the Teras range. As for Naiche, they thought he was "somewhere to the west." They suggested that Davis return to their former base along the Bavispe River, twelve miles north of Oputo.[52]

Chihuahua now realized that two American forces with their Chiricahua allies were operating in the Sierra Madre. After leaving Mount Salitral, he had few options: he could move east into the more inaccessible part of the range, toward Juh's former strongholds at Guaynopa. But if he considered this option, he scrapped it, for he knew that Crawford and Chatto had moved their base camp on the Aros River. With this in mind, he moved west along the old Chiricahua raiding route to the Sonora River. This meant fording the Moctezuma River north of Batuc to unite with Naiche, before moving northwest to the settlements along the Sonora.

This area afforded Chihuahua the means to get what he needed. Pack trains and haciendas remained inviting targets. On September 4, 1885, the war party raided the Terahuacachi and Tres Alamos ranches north of Baviacora. Eyewitnesses placed the Chiricahua numbers at forty, which, if true, meant that Naiche had brought his dependents. At Terahuacachi they killed Roque Yanes and wounded another man. Afterwards they moved north along the Sonora River, stealing stock. Eight days later, they wounded two men near Arispe. From here they turned east, hoping to make it safely into the Sierra Madre.[53]

Naiche and Chihuahua again divided, agreeing to meet near the Teras Mountains. The evening of September 14, Chihuahua took fourteen horses and mules from the American ranch between Nacozari and Cumpas. The next day, vaqueros from the Meza ranch, five miles northeast of Cumpas, saw fifteen Chiricahuas, ten mounted and five on foot, driving stock. This was Chihuahua's group, and three days later, on the afternoon of September 18, 1885, his scouts spotted a party of five Americans who had left Nacozari en route to a mining claim in the Juriquipa Mountains. They had originally outfitted at Tombstone and were traveling with several burros packed with mining supplies and provisions, "everything that a miner uses in his outfit." Chihuahua was waiting. Though his opening salvo did no apparent damage, it frightened off two men, who abandoned their three friends and fled for their lives. That left two men and one woman to fend off the Chiricahuas. One brave man fired several shots from his Winchester and a few charges from a shotgun before a Chiricahua volley cut him down. Then the woman, Belle Davis, ran over to her companion, unbuckled his cartridge belt, grabbed his Winchester and shotgun, and fired four "loads of buckshot at the hostiles." She and her husband crawled into shelter behind rocks. Unwilling to approach the two entrenched Americans and anticipating that the two who had escaped would bring help, Chihuahua abandoned the fight.

But on the morning after the attack, September 19, Captain Davis had left camp with his troop of cavalry, 102 scouts, and two pack trains. He had just received a letter from P. G. Hatcher informing him of the raid at the American ranch five days earlier. He hoped that his guides would cut the trail of the Chiricahuas. After going about five miles, they saw two people "lying under the shade of a tree." Mistaking the Apache scouts for hostiles, the Americans began to run. Captain Davis yelled at them to stop. A relieved Belle Davis, wearing a cartridge belt and carrying a shotgun in one hand, recounted the harrowing events of the day before. At once Davis went into action. Guided by the two Americans, he took the cavalry troop, eighty-four scouts, and one pack train to the scene of the ambush. Here they buried the dead American and gathered up what remained of the mining supplies—several burros, pack saddles, gunpowder, caps, and other equipment. The Chiricahuas had taken Mr. Davis's five-hundred-dollar horse but were in too much of a hurry to destroy the rest.[54]

Determined to overtake the hostiles, Davis's scouts picked up the trail and followed it day and night. Bylas, Cooley, and a few Chiricahuas led the advance scouts. The second night found the command at the base of the ridge in El Tigre Mountains, where they had surrounded Geronimo's vacant camp two months earlier. This time, however, the trail led north, as the scouts had predicted, toward the Teras Mountains.

Late in the afternoon of September 22, Chihuahua and Naiche opened fire on Cooley's advance party of scouts. Captain Davis, mounted on a mule, was a few miles behind when he heard the gunshots. Immediately he exhorted the other scouts to follow him and get into the fight. Hooke recalled, "Some of the scouts got scared and pretended to give out." Naiche and Chihuahua had left part of their herd behind, knowing the scouts would stop to secure these valuable prizes. Then the two chiefs had taken cover "in the brush on the side of the mountain" below a ridge. For the second and final time in the campaign, the Chiricahuas made a stand on ground of their choosing. But five scouts, including two Cibecue sergeants, one a brother of Cooley, had gone to the right toward a "little cliff." They were unaware that a few Chiricahuas had concealed themselves behind rocks on the cliff. One scout never knew what hit him. A Chiricahua fighter, from ten feet away, killed him at the "foot of the cliff." Then the warrior, seeing Cooley's brother, who was a short man, jumped from the cliff. He pointed and waved his gun several times, hesitating to shoot because he thought the man was too small to be a scout. Finally, the scout ran away behind some bushes, when the Chiricahua, realizing he was a scout, unsheathed his butcher knife and challenged the Western Apache to come out and fight like a man. As this was going on, the other three scouts just watched, afraid of getting too close to their battle-tested foes. Cooley's brother remained hidden.

Meanwhile, the Chiricahuas had pinned down Cooley and several of his scouts. Hooke later recalled running toward Cooley, "the bullets going by me, but I didn't care. It was as if I was crazy." Cooley cautioned him, "My cousin, get down in a wash and out of sight. These Chiricahuas are good shots and will hit you." For the next few hours, the fight became a long-range affair. Hooke recalled there "were lots of Chiricahua men there, with a few of their women." In reality, there were no more than twenty-five warriors contending with a party four times their size. But the Chiricahuas "never showed themselves" and suffered no casualties.

As darkness enveloped the battlefield, the customary lull in the fighting occurred. Naiche and Chihuahua had succeeded in protecting their women and children, who had climbed over the crest behind them to the other side. Then Davis's force heard a solitary Chiricahua voice from across the canyon: "We have killed one *Bi-ni-e-dine* [Western Apache] all ready." The voice was likely that of Chihuahua, defiant as ever. It was ironic that the only other casualty was a Chiricahua scout, Espida, or Speedy, whom the hostiles had wounded in the leg. Speedy, a nephew of Chihuahua, was the young man who had brutally killed Charley McComas after Western Apache scouts had shot down his mother at Bugatseka.[55]

One Chiricahua scout, Nahn-tee-nesn (Long Loins), a relative of Chihua-hua, recognized the latter's voice. A tall medicine man, about forty years old, he emerged from cover and shouted across the canyon to Chihuahua: "We are looking for you, and want to be friends, not to fight."[56] Chihuahua responded, "All right, then. We will go on that bluff there and talk it over." Nahn-tee-nesn asked Davis for a horse to ride over to meet with Chihuahua, but the captain refused to allow it, declaring that the hostiles "would kill" him. The scout reassured the captain: "No they would not kill me; they are my relatives." Captain Davis missed an excellent opportunity to perhaps bring in more than half the remaining hostiles.

Davis's decision was unfortunate though understandable. If Crook had been there, he would have extended an olive branch to Chihuahua. Unfortunately, Davis did not have a personal relationship with any of the Chiricahuas or enough trust in his scouts. His most experienced scouts were two Chihennes—Massai and Tsedikizen—and the Chokonen Dutchy, and they had little sway with either him or the hostiles. When Nahn-tee-nesn failed to appear, it confirmed in the minds of Naiche and Chihuahua that the Americans wanted only war. Later that evening, with the moon illuminating the battleground, the scouts heard the Chiricahua leaders holler "Whoo" from four directions. This was the signal for the warriors to break off the engagement and head for the ridge behind them.[57]

Davis and the scouts held a council. Ish-lsin-na-gosl, the brother of the dead Cibecue scout, met with Cooley, whose brother was missing and presumed dead. Ish-lsin-na-gosl pointed out, "We came here to fight. For this reason I want you to go with me no matter if the Chiricahuas are still there, and start to fight them right now." Cooley urged him to wait, for "we don't want you to get killed." Ish-lsin-na-gosl chided Cooley: "You always talked like a man when you were back at Cibecue; you were always ready to point your gun at somebody." Undaunted, he vowed to go alone to find the body of his brother.

Ish-lsin-na-gosl and eleven scouts set out toward the cliff. Walter Hooke was the youngest; the rest were men "who understood about war." They found the corpse, and Ish-lsin-na-gosl went over to his brother. Hooke described the poignant scene: the scout embraced his brother's body and "talked to him, just as if he were alive. All right, you are killed now; you are traveling by yourself now. This is what we joined up as scouts for, and I am still here. I intended to go with you also, but I missed out." The scout untied a blanket from his waist and covered his brother. Then he thanked the eleven brave men, especially the San Carlos scouts, who had courageously accompanied him: "When I go back to Cibecue again at the tulipai [tiswin] parties I will talk of you, and that is the way I will remember you." Cooley's brother, the diminutive sergeant, emerged unscathed from his hiding place.

The next morning the entire command returned to the site. They were appalled at what they saw. The Chiricahuas had mutilated the body of Ish-lsin-na-gosl's brother, severing his nose and sticking a butcher knife through the face where the nose had been. The scouts tried to dislodge it but were unable. Then Captain Davis dismounted from his mule and "managed to pull the knife out." The scouts and many soldiers cried at what the Chiricahuas had done. Davis addressed the scouts: "What the Chiricahuas have done here is wrong. . . . The other Chiricahuas are all up at San Carlos and Fort Apache. But these Chiricahuas down here, still on the warpath, will never go back to San Carlos or Fort Apache because they have done wrong on this body."[58]

Captain Wirt Davis would never be more right.

21

"MOCCASIN TRACKS LEFT IN THE SAND"

The General [Crook] will give $100 for each head of a hostile
Chiricahua buck brought in by an Indian scout or volunteer.
Cyrus Roberts to Lieutenant Charles Gatewood,
September 30, 1885

On August 13, 1885, six days after Lieutenant Mathias W. Day surprised
Geronimo's camp at Bugatseka, Captain Emmet Crawford's scouts picked up
the trail, which led east, of twenty-five or thirty Chiricahuas (about ten men).
Led by Geronimo and Nana, they were thirty-six hours ahead of their pursuers. Crawford estimated that Geronimo had spent two days rounding up his
followers. No one knew where he was going. At some point during his flight
across the mountains, he had made a decision: he would return to Fort Apache
and attempt to recover his family captured in Day's attack.[1]

His plan, resourceful and resolute, revealed how desperate the sixty-three-
year-old shaman was to reunite with his loved ones. Angie Debo, Geronimo's
biographer, notes that he based his decision on "economic necessity as well as
sentiment." After all, she explains, "Apaches were devoted to their families.
Also, in their well-structured division of labor a man without a wife to prepare food and clothing was as seriously handicapped economically as was a
woman without a male provider."[2]

After Geronimo's party left Bugatseka, they headed southeast and passed
through the canyon at the junction of Tres Rios, where Crook had pitched
his tent in May 1883. Crawford decided to send Lieutenant Britton Davis, Al
Sieber, Mickey Free, and Chatto, with forty-two handpicked scouts to follow the trail. Three packers who handled seven mules carrying three days'
rations and extra ammunition rounded out the party.[3] They left camp under

a steady rain, one that continued over the next five days, which slowed their hunt for the hostiles. The Chiricahuas may have believed that Geronimo had summoned the rain, for he had such a ceremony. Perico described how the chief would sit down and sing, invariably bringing rain with an hour's time.[4]

Geronimo had made pursuit easier because the hostiles had one shod mule, which served as a beacon imprinted along the trail. Unshod ponies rounded out the balance of Geronimo's stock, which the Chiricahuas killed for food as they gave out. Geronimo probably underestimated the resolve of Davis, Sieber, and Chatto—each of whom had ample reasons to end the shaman's raiding life or, even better, his natural life. Geronimo knew that the march would be an ordeal for any party that dared to follow him. He likely thought that the rough country would force Crawford to turn back and abandon the trail. But Crawford and Davis matched Geronimo's determination.[5]

Geronimo's trail was predictable; it led east to the most rugged part of the Sierra Madre. Several peaks soared to elevations of 8,500 to 9,000 feet. Thus began a grueling chase, one long remembered by those men and scouts who had endured enormous hardships and difficulties because of the terrain and rainy weather. Packer Henry Daly thought the mules were perfect for the terrain and elements. He noted they were as "sure footed as a chamois, and as careful with a load on its back as a mother with a child in her arms. Every mule was a pet with the packers, and each knew its name when spoken to in a voice of caution or word of encouragement as well as a human being in a similar position would understand it."[6]

The sun rose bright and clear on August 18, 1885. With it came a commensurate rise in the spirits of Crawford's command. But Lieutenant Davis's silence worried the captain, for he had not heard a word from him. Accordingly, he decided to send Lieutenant Elliott forward with eight scouts, two packers, and six mules to carry rations for Davis's command.[7] With Elliott was Sherman Curley, the San Carlos scout who had married a daughter of Cochise. The scouts had little trouble following Davis's trail. After leaving the Sierra Madre range, Elliott could see a valley ahead dotted by grazing cattle feeding on lush green grass. He had to cross the foothills of the San Miguel range, which lay fifteen miles southeast of San Buenaventura. Elliott was relieved when two Chiricahua scouts, one of whom was Toclanny, an exceptional tracker, came into his camp. Davis had sent them back for rations. Elliott pushed ahead, with the two scouts at the front.[8]

Toclanny led the way across the San Miguel range. In the late afternoon of August 22, Elliott's command camped in the foothills. The lieutenant knew that Davis was near, but he was unaware that Mexican soldiers were then looking for Davis's party. Following Crawford's instructions, Davis had killed a few cattle belonging to the San Miguel hacienda. He had seen a Mexican herder, who had also seen the Apaches, which sent him racing off to the hacienda to spread the alarm. A Mexican force, mainly Tarahumara Indians from the ranch, went out in pursuit. But they struck Elliott's trail first. By noon the next day, they had taken positions in a canyon ahead of Elliott, ready to spring their trap. Fortunately for the lieutenant, early that afternoon (August 23), the sky turned ominously dark. To protect his supplies from the imminent storm, he made camp about six or seven hundred yards from the Mexican force. If he and his group had continued into the canyon, Elliott thought the Mexicans would "have murdered us beyond doubt."

While Elliott and the packers were unpacking the rations and supplies under a cottonwood tree, a scout spotted a Mexican on the ridge ahead. Elliott assumed that he was a vaquero looking for strays. Unperturbed, the lieutenant continued securing the camp until a thunderous volley scattered leaves from the cottonwood tree above him. A second salvo forced Elliott and his scouts to take cover in nearby rocks. Toclanny and the other Chiricahua scout, who were returning from hunting, immediately began shooting back. Then the Mexicans began to "advance slowly, keeping under cover" to within five hundred yards. Sherman Curley remembered that the Mexicans "kept on firing . . . with all the bullets striking around us." The scouts began to shoot back until Elliott ordered them to stop.

What followed next showed that the reflexive response by Mexicans to anything Apache was treachery. Lieutenant Elliott bravely stepped out from the cottonwood trees, unarmed, and waved a white handkerchief. He called out that he was a "friend, an American officer with tame Apaches."[9] One Mexican yelled out "esta bueno [all right]," which was immediately followed by a command from an officer to unleash another barrage on the lieutenant. Fortunately, they were not good shots. Elliott was incredulous, chalking it up as a "noble sample of Mexican chivalry." After cursing them out, he moved closer to the Mexicans' positions. This time, three Mexicans came forward to talk; the rest moved into a posture closer to the camp. Elliott, believing that the skirmish was over, called for Babcock, a packer who spoke Spanish, to come forward and interpret. As luck would have it, Toclanny and the other Chiricahua scout, whose Apache name was Di-bu-do, had fled when they had heard Elliott give the cease-fire command. They went off to find Davis, whose camp was near.[10]

The conversation began amiably as the Mexicans shook hands "most cordially" and engaged in small talk with Elliott. He was just beginning to accept the affair as an honest mistake when the Mexicans suddenly "leveled their half-cocked rifles" and asked Elliott why he had killed three head of cattle belonging to the San Miguel hacienda. Elliott did some quick thinking. He explained that his men had killed two head of cattle for food; the command that killed the three cattle was camped "just over the hill with fifty Apache scouts." His resourcefulness might have saved the lives of his men. The Mexican leader told him to order "these Indians out from the rocks or we will kill you where you stand." Elliott initially refused, explaining that he did not speak Apache. But the Mexican officer countered, "You claim to be friendly, [so] do it at once." The Apache sergeant, a Yavapai known as Rowdy to the Americans, convinced the scouts to come out from the rocks. Elliott would be forever grateful: "I owe my life and the ultimate safety of my small command to [him]."[11]

But they obeyed Rowdy's order only reluctantly. At least one scout was much disgusted with the outcome. Sherman Curley recalled the scene:

> We came out of the rocks to an open, level place, holding our rifles in our hands. Our lieutenant [Elliott] told us to drop our rifles and cartridge belts to the ground. We did so. Then the Mexican soldiers came up and surrounded us. They had some kind of liquor they had been drinking. I do not know what it was. They looked like pretty mean kind of Mexicans, all right. They were little, short, black-skinned men and on their feet they wore sandals. There were about fifty of them. . . . They told us to stand close in line, as they wanted to tie our hands. Some of us did not want this, and tried to stop it. Then they punched us with the butts of their guns. They tied our hands tight behind our backs. Our lieutenant just stood there, and looked at us. I guess he must have wanted things that way.[12]

Curley's criticism of Elliott was unfair. Sure, he was young, only two years removed from West Point. Yet, he had shown initiative and unquestionable courage during the campaign. He had traveled with one assistant from the Sierra Madre to deliver a message to Crook at Fort Bowie, and a review of his military career suggests that he showed nerve and determination under fire. In the end, he had saved his command and property and had avoided an international incident, the two things that mattered the most.

Three miles south of San Buenaventura, they came across a force of one hundred troops of the Eleventh Cavalry ("many [were] ex-convicts") under Lieutenant Colonel Mesilla.[13] He heard Elliott's explanation but was dubious.

He kept Elliott's command under arrest. Curley became even more concerned because Mesilla "just sat there, playing with his revolver in his hand. These Mexican soldiers were mean, it seems to me. They kill their prisoners and do not give any quarter."[14]

Mesilla took the prisoners to San Buenaventura and paraded them along the main street. Elliott recalled that they heard the "hoots and yells of a howling mob, which heaped upon [them] the most vile and disgusting epithets." Mesilla turned over the scouts and Americans to another officer, who locked them up in a cell. The scouts were particularly concerned. Curley remembered that they "were afraid to sleep." So, they sat up the entire night, hoping that To-clanny and Di-bu-do had caught up with Davis.[15]

Indeed, they had found Davis and Chatto a few hours after leaving Elliott. Perched on a small knoll a quarter-mile from camp, they breathlessly informed their friends that Mexican troops had wiped out Elliott's command. Naturally, this evoked an immediate reaction from Davis's scouts. Before Davis knew what was going on, the scouts "shedding their clothing and loading their guns" bolted from camp. Sieber jumped on his mule, followed by Davis on his. They finally overtook the scouts about a half mile from camp and got the details from Toclanny and Di-bu-do. The scouts unanimously wanted "to pursue the Mexicans, kill as many as possible, and then start for the United States." Davis and Sieber finally persuaded them to move to the scene of Elliott's skirmish before taking any action.[16]

They reached Elliott's abandoned camp just before dark and found nothing but the property left behind. This scenario convinced Davis that the Mexicans had captured Elliott's command, for if a massacre had occurred, the Mexicans would have left the corpses on the ground where they fell. Davis returned to his camp and decided to go alone to San Buenaventura to explain the situation. He told Sieber to keep the scouts with him. If he failed to return by the next morning, Sieber was to turn back with the scouts and find Crawford.

The lieutenant faced miserable conditions for his journey. Rain dogged him most of the night, and it was as "dark as the proverbial stack of black cats." Midway to town, he saw four riders approaching. They were two Mexican officers and two soldiers. Davis explained the purpose of his trip, and they assured him that Elliott's party was safe. After a lightning flash, Davis saw one Mexican suddenly become agitated. He turned around and "in the dim afterglow of the flash" saw about ten scouts, including Chatto, the Chihenne Guydelkon, and a Western Apache named Nosey, whose brother was with Elliott. Thinking that Davis might need their help, they had stolen away from camp without Sieber's knowledge. The four Mexicans were so frightened that they could not move. After Davis explained the situation to Chatto, they decided to send back two scouts to bring Sieber and the rest of the scouts to San Buenaventura the next morning.[17]

The Mexicans escorted Davis and his scouts to the quarters of the commander in town. Lieutenant Colonel Mesilla joined them. Davis's fluency in Spanish cleared up the matter within minutes. After a courteous exchange of compliments, a few cursory toasts, Davis and Elliott were on their way to the jail. From his cell, Sherman Curley saw Nosey, Chatto, and a "short, fat man" he called Nantan da-yosla-ha (Britton Davis). Despite two guards "pacing in front of the door," Chatto and Nosey boldly "came to the jail and told us to come out."[18]

Davis took the affair in stride. He had cleared up the misunderstanding with Mesilla. Elliott, however, was seething at the treachery carried out by the Tarahumara Indians, who were volunteer soldiers and avowed enemies of the Chiricahuas. After telling Davis that the Tarahumaras had fired about one hundred shots at him, he said that he hoped to return to Mexico "with a saber in my hand and a troop of cavalry at my back."[19]

Mid-morning (August 24, 1885), Davis, Sieber, and Chatto resumed their pursuit of Geronimo, minus ten scouts whom Davis had left with Elliott because they had become "footsore."[20] Elliott marched his men south toward his campsite. Near here they met Captain Crawford, who, after hearing the details of Elliott's adventure, "complimented" him for "getting out of the scrape as well as he did." But Crawford was also doing a slow burn, thinking that the Mexicans should be grateful for the efforts of his men and scouts. Instead of bypassing San Buenaventura, he decided to make a show of force to protest their treatment of Elliott's party. He marched his force into San Buenaventura.

Two Mexican officials asked Crawford for a meeting. He left fifty scouts and a dozen or so packers out in the street. They could see through the windows that a conversation was going on. The skittish scouts, rifles in hand and ready for action, were growing nervous by the second, for they distrusted Mexicans. The Apache sergeants decided to go into the office and demand that the officers leave immediately. The Mexicans were looking for payment, perhaps for the stock that Davis and Elliott had killed. The scouts said, "We would not pay anything" and took the officers out of the office. They immediately marched straight through town before stopping for the night at a ranch. That evening another Mexican officer rode up with a detachment, and he told Crawford to "leave Mexico right away." By this time, Crawford's patience had worn thin. He challenged the order, declaring that if the Mexicans wanted to fight, they should come ahead and "we will fight right now." That night the scouts slept with their rifles by their side. Crawford eventually led his men past Casas Grandes to the Carretas hacienda, where he stopped to rest and refit.[21]

Meanwhile, Davis, after leaving Elliott on August 24, had returned to the area where they had last seen Geronimo's trail. Though he had not realized it then, Geronimo's scouts had heard the shots when Davis's Apaches had slaughtered the three head of cattle on August 20 or 21. The hostiles had scattered, going south.[22] Davis would never get close to Geronimo. The Chiricahuas had stolen fresh horses from Terrazas's Santa Clara ranch east of Namiquipa. Then they reversed directions, heading north, putting distance between themselves and their pursuers. On August 28, 1885, Davis's detachment climbed to the crest of a mountain, from which the scouts saw in the distance "small dots on the plain." These were the members of Geronimo's group. Davis's only hope now was to keep the pressure on them.[23]

At this point, Davis was still uncertain about Geronimo's destination. His scouts, believing that Nana was in charge, thought the hostiles were going to the Mescalero Reservation.[24] Three days later, after Davis's party had traveled 125 miles north, it ran into Mesilla's force, which was also on Geronimo's trail. Mesilla told him that his troops had the situation in hand. Under the terms of the treaty, Davis had no choice but to abandon pursuit and return to the United States. He was far from disappointed, "for we were practically at the end of our rope." In fact, he was still one hundred miles southwest of El Paso, and the remaining trip across the desert would prove to be far more demanding than either he or his scouts could have imagined. Their stock gave out, they ran out of rations, and the arduous march had shredded their moccasins to the flesh. Toclanny never forgot the hardship: "We were hungry lots of time, thirsty, and my legs ached from being tired. But [we] went on just the same."[25] It was a credit to the leadership of Davis and Chatto that they brought the command into Fort Bliss (El Paso) on September 5, 1885. Indeed, no one believed they had crossed the Sierra Madre from the Sonora side and survived the trek across the Chihuahuan desert.[26]

Davis immediately wired General Crook at Fort Bowie with the news that Geronimo was moving north into New Mexico. He reported that the Chiricahua scouts thought he might head to the San Mateo Mountains. Crook relayed this intelligence to Colonel Luther Bradley, who ordered a detachment stationed at Fairview, the closest settlement to the San Mateo Mountains, to send patrols east and west of there.[27] Unfortunately, because Bradley had returned the Mescalero scouts to their reservation in August, his troopers lacked the indispensable guides to track down Geronimo.[28] Crook was unsure of the size of Geronimo's party. As it turned out, Nana had separated from Geronimo, taking about fifteen followers (five of whom were men) into the mountains northwest of Janos. Geronimo took the balance, five men and four or five women, and crossed the line undetected at a point several miles east of Palomas Lake, easily avoiding the army's patrols.[29]

Those men with Geronimo were mostly relatives or men who had lost wives during Day's attack at Bugatseka. Accompanying Geronimo was Chinche, a thirty-five-year-old Chihenne or Bedonkohe whose wife had lost her baby at Doubtful Canyon and then returned to the reservation; Chappo, Geronimo's son; two twenty-year-old Nednhi men, Dah-Ke-Ya, who had married Geronimo's daughter Dohn-say, and Hunlona; and a sixth man who was probably Beshe, who had lost one wife, captured by Day's scouts.[30]

In his autobiography years later, Geronimo suggested that they went north to elude American troops and scouts operating in Mexico.[31] If true, then Nana and the rest of his band would have accompanied him. His objective was clear. Assuming that Crook had sent Geronimo's people captured by Day's command to the reservation at Fort Apache, Geronimo had decided to launch a surprise raid to recover them. With Crook's cordon of troops and scouts blocking his favorite passageway to the reservation, the Peloncillo Mountain corridor, he had decided to swing east and take a circuitous approach to the reservation from that direction.

He crossed the line some ten miles east of Palomas Lake. Instead of taking the usual route north via the Florida Mountains, he led his small group east before striking the West Potrillo Mountains. By September 7, he was resting comfortably in the northern part of this range. The evening of September 8, he moved silently across the desert to the Good Sight Mountains, a narrow, north-to-south broken range, about thirty miles northeast of Deming. Here, on the ninth, they rested all day. About midnight, Geronimo led his followers on a trot along an old Apache trail toward Mule Springs. To this point, his party had been invisible.[32]

The next morning, four Mexicans (two men and two women) were traveling along the road to Lake Valley from Fort Cummings when they saw eight Apaches east of Mule Springs. Neither party wanted anything to do with the other. The Mexicans turned back to Cummings and reported the news. The incident marked the first time that whites in New Mexico had seen Geronimo's party.[33]

So far the first leg of Geronimo's strategy had worked. He was in his home country and near the mountains in which he could easily outrun his enemy. Neither troops nor citizens were then in pursuit. Though the Chiricahua scouts thought he was heading for the San Mateo Mountains, no one really knew what he was up to. Crook thought he would seek refuge at either the Mescalero Reservation, where Nana had friends, or the Navajo Reservation, where Mangas had relatives. But neither Nana nor Mangas was with Geronimo. Colonel Bradley, acting on the same assumption as Crook, had asked his commanding officers at Fort Wingate and Fort Stanton to inform the agents that the military would pay one hundred dollars for the head of any hostile Chiricahua. But Geronimo had no plans to visit either reservation.[34]

Crook had initially misread the motivation behind the resourceful shaman's incursion. Geronimo would have been surprised, perhaps amused, to learn that Americans thought the objective of his foray was either to plunder or to gain recruits at reservations whose inhabitants were unsympathetic to him. After the Mexican party spotted him on September 10, he knew that he had to launch the second part of his plan—a diversionary raid to obscure his actual purpose.

That afternoon Brady Pollock left his ranch on Macho Creek in search of stray horses. When he stopped near a clump of trees, Geronimo ambushed him, sending two bullets into his body. Then the warriors smashed in his head, took his horse, and rode several miles north to McKnight's ranch on Berrenda Creek, which they sacked, taking sixteen horses. After resting that night in the foothills of the Mimbres Mountains, at daybreak they moved west through Gavilan Canyon. No troops or citizens were following. But Geronimo knew it was only a matter of time. He had one day left before he could get into the lofty uplifts of the Black Range.[35]

September 11, 1885, would be a violent day for Geronimo's small group of fighters. They would slaughter every man in their path from ambush; they would loot homes and take whatever supplies and ammunition they could carry. By mid-morning they had claimed their first victim. Avaristo Abeyta was cutting poles three miles east of San Lorenzo, perhaps in Quien Sabe Canyon. He tried to flee when he saw the Indians, but they shot his horse out from under him and then finished him off. An hour later, in Gallinas Canyon, they ambushed George Horn, slaying him.

Soon after, they spotted two boys herding cattle. It was about 11:00 A.M. The lads were seventeen-year-old Martin McKinn and his brother, eleven-year-old

Santiago. That morning, their father, John McKinn, had left his ranch with a few neighbors to buy their winter's supply of fruit at Las Cruces. He had sent his sons to herd cattle in Gallinas Canyon, two miles north of the ranch. Like Pollock, they never had a chance. The two brothers had just stopped to eat lunch. Martin was reading a book while his younger brother played along the rocks of the creek. Then a shot rang out, and Santiago McKinn watched as an Indian, whom he later identified as Geronimo, ran over to the lifeless body of his brother and smashed his head in. Santiago ran into some brush, but the Indians captured him. In shock, he watched Geronimo don his brother's shirt and coat. Taking Santiago McKinn with them, they headed for the Mimbres River, a few miles above San Lorenzo.[36]

It was almost impossible to avoid meeting whites in this part of the country. Mining camps were everywhere, and ranches lay scattered on both sides of the Mimbres. Before reaching the river, they descended into Noonday Canyon, where a group of miners had built cabins to take advantage of its reliable spring. It was 11:30 A.M., and the camp was empty. The warriors sent volleys into the houses, a procedure they followed whenever they were unsure about whether a dwelling contained occupants. Next, they looted the cabins, took a few things of value, six head of stock, and, as McKinn watched, torched the cabins. Four men had been observing some three hundred yards away. When the Apaches saw them, they sent a few shots their way. One bullet creased the ear of Peter Kinney. Then the Indians disappeared across the Mimbres. Geronimo and his five warriors rode in front while the women, with Santiago McKinn, followed in the rear. They spent the night in a canyon somewhere north of Georgetown.[37]

Early the next morning, they came across two woodchoppers and killed one (either George Burns or a man named Aubra). The other man escaped. Then they struck the Mimbres, following it north to the Allen ranch, located on the Upper Mimbres. By then word had spread that Apaches were in the vicinity. Mrs. Allen was alone with her three children when they spotted Geronimo's party coming toward the ranch. She and her children escaped into the brush, but not before she had an encounter with a "burly big buck," a term which fits the popular description of Geronimo, though Chinche was also above average in size. Her dog lunged at the Indian, which provided Mrs. Allen enough time to escape. Geronimo could easily have tracked down and butchered the family. He probably realized that they were no threat to his small band, and slaying them would have evoked a rage and given his pursuers more incentive for revenge. Again, the Apaches took what they wanted. Mrs. Allen and her children walked eight miles to a sawmill operated by soldiers from Fort Bayard.[38]

By this time, troops were on the trail. Cavalry from Bayard, state militia from Hillsboro, and a small party of ranchers, which included the father of Santiago McKinn, were in pursuit. After leaving Allen's ranch, Geronimo's party spent part of the night near the confluence of Sapillo Creek and the Mimbres. Early the next morning, September 13, Geronimo decided it was time to put distance between him and his pursuers. He began a rapid movement to the northwest, traveling all day toward the Gila wilderness. The party's only food was what they had stolen, and some fresh horsemeat, which was "good when [one is] hungry," Santiago McKinn would later remark. According to McKinn, they stopped for the night in Black Canyon, about eight miles southeast of the famous Gila Hot Springs.

At dawn on Monday, September 14, the mobile raiders left for the Gila River. Passing Hot Springs, they continued to the west fork of the Gila River. Here, near the junction of Little Creek, they had the good luck to find the empty cabin of William Grudging. The day before, he and his brothers had returned from Silver City with a fresh store of supplies. Geronimo's party took flour, sugar, molasses, bacon, and other articles. Though the soldiers and militia were but a few hours behind, they decided at that point to give up the pursuit. Even John McKinn turned back, believing that if they pursued too closely, the Apaches would kill his boy.[39]

By the afternoon of September 15, 1885, the raiders had reached their destination—a hidden canyon, called Teepee Canyon, just northeast of Mogollon Peak. This was a remote area away from settlements in a most inaccessible part of the range. The surrounding peaks soared to elevations over ten thousand feet. One New Mexico pioneer described the place as a "natural fortress." It was so secluded that the Indians "could build all the fires they wanted and the blaze could not be seen over the rim of the bluffs that surrounded them." Even better, a mountain spring provided clear, cold water to the ranchería.[40]

From this secluded retreat, the shaman must have assumed that Crook had positioned troops and scouts around the reservation. But, in his provincial world, he had no conception that his raid from Mexico had generated a flurry of activity—correspondence between federal and state military officials to the War Department in Washington, which ultimately led to executive decisions that would profoundly affect the fate of every Chiricahua Apache tribe member, whether or not he or she was hostile.

Crook had been busy that summer. He had recently returned from a meeting in Benson with Sonora's governor Luis Torres, at which they had discussed the need for both countries to cooperate against the hostiles. Torres assured Crook that Sonora would not interfere with his operations below the border even if the two federal governments failed to extend the reciprocal crossing treaty. After he returned to Sonora, Torres sent out a directive to the prefects of the frontier districts to assist American forces in pursuit of the Chiricahuas.[41]

Convinced that the "Interior Department has been a hindrance rather than a help," George Crook had finally persuaded Washington officials to cancel the "dual control" at San Carlos and place the reservation under his responsibility.[42] Though he relished the victory, the speed with which the bureaucracy in Washington had succumbed to his wishes probably surprised even him. Crook had first broached this subject three weeks after the breakout. He had admonished his superior, General Pope, that "dual control . . . must be carefully avoided." And he had threatened to withdraw from the shared responsibility at San Carlos unless the Interior Department gave him unfettered control. Otherwise, he would refuse to "assume the responsibility [for] these Indians' good behavior."[43]

Crook's rant was noted; his not so subtle threat to take his ball and go home was heard, but nothing came of it then. For several weeks, the status quo prevailed until General Pope took action after Lieutenant John McDonald tried to arrest an Indian serving on Agent Charles Ford's police force. Ford thought the charge bogus and refused to acknowledge McDonald's authority. Although Ford's denial was based on principle and law, Crook and Pope framed the argument to suit their objective. On July 27, 1885, Pope staked out his ground: either give Crook full authority or the military would leave San Carlos in control of Agent Ford. Secretary of the Interior Lucius Q. C. Lamar ran up the white flag. Ford had done a good job at San Carlos, but Lamar agreed to "temporarily turn over control" of San Carlos to the military. On August 1, 1885, Pope designated Captain Pierce as the temporary agent. Two weeks later, President Cleveland signed the order suspending Ford and appointing Pierce. It was astonishing how quickly Crook's wishes had prevailed.[44]

One could have predicted Crook's next move. He suggested that Bradley "go in person" to the Navajo Reservation to find out whether the hostiles had reached out to friends there. Bradley's response did not come soon enough for Crook, who had become frustrated with the colonel's inattention to detail and his management style. As a commander, Crook wanted every piece of information. After feeling left in the dark about Geronimo's movements in New Mexico, he asked Bradley to ensure that all dispatches from the field be complete so that he would "be able to act intelligently."[45]

Crook resented Bradley's superior, General Nelson Miles, commander of the Department of the Missouri, and felt hamstrung because he had only nominal control over all military operations in the Southwest. Buoyed by his victory in squeezing out Agent Charles Ford, in mid-September he embarked on a more challenging mission. He wanted absolute control over the military District of New Mexico, which had been part of the Department of the Missouri for the previous twenty years. He could kill two birds with one stone. It made sense logistically, for the Chiricahuas were a threat to both Arizona and New Mexico, and it would remove that territory from the command of General Nelson Miles, who had been privately gloating over the constant drumbeat of criticism that Crook was getting from both the southwestern press and some military personnel in Washington.[46]

Miles had championed the popular stance in Washington (positions taken by President Cleveland and General Sheridan) that Crook relied too much on Apache scouts instead of soldiers. Miles, who had never felt much empathy for Indians—especially Apaches—made no bones about his view that Crook had formulated an ill-advised policy. Crook's critics naturally shared a jaundiced view of the Indian scouts, whose loyalties, they assumed, lay with their own people—even if they were hostile. Miles was also Crook's rival for a promotion that was imminent because of General Pope's scheduled retirement in March 1886. Miles had powerful military and political connections, but his abrasive personality and unbridled ambitions rubbed many in the military hierarchy the wrong way. Crook had his backers, but even Sheridan was tiring of the Chiricahua story.

On September 19, 1885, a clearly exasperated Crook blasted Miles, who, he said, believed "that by moving troops to certain points he could satisfy public opinion and by catering to individual interests he could make capital at my expense." Naturally, Miles bristled at the suggestion, for Crook had pointed out the baseness of Miles's argument. And with Miles stationed comfortably at Leavenworth, Crook, as long as he enjoyed the confidence of his superiors, had the upper hand in this debate. Yet New Mexico governor Edmond Ross had just written President Cleveland to insist that this "conflict in authority" between Miles and Crook was not helping matters. Ross backed Miles, whose policies, the governor thought, would keep his state safer.[47]

Crook mulled over a third important issue. He knew that the war would end only when the Chiricahuas decided to surrender. He realized that the warriors, especially the leaders, would not capitulate without specific terms. They would fight to the last man rather than give up unconditionally. The government had to settle on a policy. And with Geronimo in U.S. territory, Crook had to know what conditions Washington would authorize him to offer. His current orders to field commanders were simple: if the hostiles resisted, then the troops must kill them, but if they offered to surrender, the officers should accept the offer and confine them securely in the guardhouse. Then, following the law, Crook planned to turn them over to civil officials if they had warrants for their arrests. Of course, he realized the probability of the hostiles capitulating without terms was near zero.[48]

While waiting for news of Geronimo's activities in New Mexico, however, he had second thoughts. He settled on a pragmatic solution that he knew would ignite a firestorm of criticism in the Southwest.

> It has been my intention to turn over to the civil authorities any hostile bucks captured for trial under provisions of Section 9 of the Act of Congress approved March 3, 1885, with reference to jurisdiction of the Courts over certain offences committed by the Indians. But after consulting with several prominent lawyers, I have become convinced there would never be enough evidence to convict them. Unless aided by some stroke of good fortune, it will take years to kill all of these hostiles situated as they are. It is desirable to have them surrender and this they will not do if they think they will be killed or even worse, turned over to civil authorities. It is believed they could be induced to surrender after a little more hammering, if they are assured their lives will not be forfeited and they would simply be transported [removed from Arizona].[49]

Crook sent this proposal through proper channels. He knew that General Pope, commander of the Division of the Pacific, would forward it to the War Department. Pope asked for a speedy decision while pointing out that Geronimo's outbreak was a result of "causes not within the power of General Crook."[50]

General Sheridan had to make a decision. Just a few days before, he had passed along to General Miles a recommendation by Indian Inspector Frank Armstrong (endorsed by Secretary of the Interior Lamar) to remove the Chiricahuas at Fort Apache to Fort Leavenworth, Kansas. Armstrong, after inspecting San Carlos that summer, was now a self-professed expert on the state of mind of the reservation Chiricahuas. Ignoring the inconvenient fact that half the men were scouting for Crawford and Wirt Davis, and that their dependents were at Fort Apache, he foolishly passed along the popular but groundless opinion that if Geronimo could "communicate with them, they [reservation Chiricahuas] would take to the warpath." This inane assessment was either disingenuous or a product of Armstrong's reading of the south-western newspapers.[51]

While Sheridan waited to hear from Miles and Schofield, he settled on a policy that would govern the status of any hostiles who surrendered:

> The hostile Chiricahuas have forfeited their lives by their outbreak and savage acts of butchery and deserve no consideration whatsoever. As a matter of policy, however, and to terminate an already prolonged and wearing struggle which if pursued to the end may involve a sac-rifice of many innocent lives and much property, I recommend that General Crook be authorized to secure their surrender as prisoners-of-war to be transported to some distant point [as were] the criminal Comanches and Cheyennes from the Indian Territory in 1875. They should never be allowed to return to Arizona and New Mexico.

Secretary of War William Endicott accepted Sheridan's plan with two ad-ditions. He added the clause that the surrender must include all the hostile Chiricahuas. Furthermore, he designated Fort Marion, Florida, as their future homes, the location alluded to by Sheridan.[52]

With one stroke of the pen, Sheridan had established the government's pol-icy toward the hostile Chiricahuas. It was now out of Crook's hands. Geron-imo's incursion into the United States had forced him and officials in the na-tion's capital to settle on a course, which, on the surface, seemed just—if it had not gone any further. As we shall see, however, that would not be the case.

A few weeks later, Sheridan received Miles's endorsement of Armstrong's recommendation ("a wise suggestion," thought Miles) to transfer the peaceful Chiricahuas at Fort Apache to Fort Leavenworth. But Miles's superior, Gen-eral Schofield, prudently ignored Armstrong's proposal and refused to intrude in Crook's jurisdiction. And he especially opposed moving the Apaches to Fort Leavenworth. Sheridan would have the final word: "I disapprove the recom-mendation of Indian Inspector Armstrong and General Miles in so far as they recommend sending the Chiricahuas to Fort Leavenworth." Unfortunately for the Chiricahuas on the reservation, the longer hostilities continued, the more irrational and extreme the government's position would become toward them.[53]

Meanwhile, Geronimo's and Crook's paths inched closer to a clash that the latter would have relished. Crook saw the chief as his problem, the symbolic icon of the outbreak, and he was frustrated that the shaman had exploited the weakness of his defense. Crook's mind was racing as he tried to counter Geronimo's next move. After reading a report that his scouts had wounded Geronimo during the attack at Bugatseka, he now thought (wishful thinking) that the warrior "might be dead." But in case the shaman was still breathing, he formulated a strategy. He told Captain Pierce at San Carlos to brace for a visit from Geronimo. He suggested that Pierce "notify the White Mountain Indians that they must keep a secret watch over the Chiricahua camps," particularly at points "where they are likely to come on to the reservation." If the hostiles offered to surrender, Pierce should accept it and secure them. If they entered the reservation with hostile intent, he should kill them.[54]

On September 18, 1885, Geronimo left his camp in the Mogollons and headed west. His first stop was at Pleasenton, three miles south of Glenwood on the San Francisco River. That evening they stole three horses from two ranches. The next morning, they were in Arizona along the upper Blue River in Graham County, about sixty-five miles northwest of Clifton. Here they shot William Rasberry through the mouth, killing him instantly. His neighbor, Frank Manning, was with him but escaped to the ranch. He counted five or six warriors with two women.[55] Later that day, September 19, they traveled due west, passing Mount Ord two days later. Leaving one warrior and a woman behind with their horses, at dusk on September 21, 1885, they struck out for the east fork of the White River. Here they expected to find the Chiricahua camps. Gatewood had scouts patrolling the area, but with the pall of night obscuring Geronimo's movements, he had no problems slipping past them.[56]

They reached East Fork shortly before 1:00 A.M. on September 22, 1885, but found only a White Mountain woman guarding her farm. She told Geronimo that Gatewood had moved the Chiricahua camps closer to Fort Apache. She also informed him that the only members of his family in the Chiricahua camp were his wife She-gha and his child. She-gha was the wife captured at Mescalero nine days after the outbreak. The prisoner took Geronimo to the Chiricahua camp and pointed out his wife's wickiup. Without alarming the camp, Geronimo entered the dwelling and took She-gha, their three-year-old child, and the other woman captured at Mescalero. It is unclear in which Chiricahua camp she was living for only two men from Geronimo's group had remained on the reservation, and they were serving as scouts. It seems probable that she had joined Bacutla's band because one of his followers was Chobegoza, whose son was with Mangas. Chobegoza, one of Geronimo's few friends left at the agency, either spoke to Geronimo or knew of his presence without alerting authorities.

After stealing horses from the White Mountain Apaches, Geronimo's group left as quietly as they had arrived. The chief wanted to put as much distance as he could between himself and the pursuit that would follow. But the news of the raid alarmed everyone. By daybreak the White Mountain camps had taken on the appearance of an armed fortress. Alchesay gathered men to go after Geronimo. At 9:00 A.M. on September 22, a patrol under Severiano returned empty handed. Gatewood felt sure that some Chiricahuas expected a visit from Geronimo, but his assumption was wrong, and he corrected it later that day. Less than an hour later, Gatewood reported that there were five in all, including Geronimo. They had raced south in two parties, the smaller numbering two men, toward the Black River and, Gatewood thought, Stevens's Ranch.[57]

Crook's first response, predictably, was to demand that the White Mountain and Chiricahua Apaches assume responsibility for Geronimo. He told Gatewood not to call on troops from Apache. Rely on Alchesay and his White Mountain Apaches, he insisted, and assure them that they will be compensated for their efforts. He also asked Gatewood to enlist the help of any Chiricahuas who were "enemies of Geronimo." The general wanted Geronimo's party captured or killed. Gatewood telegraphed Crook the prediction that "they [White Mountain Apaches] will either kill Geronimo or run him off the reservation. [They] cannot be trusted to take him prisoner." That was all right with the general: "Kill Geronimo and his entire party." Soon after, he modified that order, advising Gatewood to tell the scouts that capturing Geronimo was preferable to allowing him to escape to Mexico.[58]

Just by coincidence, Lieutenant Britton Davis was at this very time en route to Fort Apache from Fort Bowie. Like Crawford and Gatewood, the stress of the past two years of Indian duty had worn him out. He was tired of the responsibilities of agent. When in El Paso with Chatto and his scouts, he had met an old friend of his father, who happened to be the president of a conglomeration that owned the Corralitos hacienda in northwestern Chihuahua. He had offered Davis the job as manager of the ranch, and Davis had accepted and resigned from the army. At Fort Bowie, General Crook asked him to reconsider. But Davis had had enough. It was a deep blow to Crook. The anti-Crook newspapers, which included the *Arizona Weekly Citizen*, claimed that Davis had resigned because of Crook. The army, it reported, had lost "one of the brightest, bravest, and most useful officers in the service." The *Silver City Enterprise* made up a tale that Davis had become disillusioned with Crook, who, in turn, had forced Davis out, but never explained how they arrived at this curious and erroneous conclusion.[59]

Davis was at Fort Thomas when he heard the news of Geronimo's raid at Apache. He immediately went to Apache to help his friend Lieutenant Gatewood. On September 23, he conducted his own investigation. He concluded that Geronimo's sole purpose was to "find out what had become of his captive people." Until Geronimo knew their location, Davis believed that he would remain in the area. He also conjectured that Mangas had gone to the Navajo Reservation to induce his relatives there to join him.[60]

This time Davis was wrong on both scores. At the time he made this guess, Geronimo was probably east of Eagle Creek, some seventy-five miles away. But Davis's opinion went a long way with Crook. Colonel Bradley corroborated Davis's opinion when he sent a telegram to notify Crook that on September 23, citizens had discovered a trail of a dozen Chiricahuas near today's Winston. Bradley questioned whether this might be Chihuahua and asked the logical question: "Have any of Chihuahua's party ever lived on the Warm Springs [Ojo Caliente] Reservation?" Because of Davis's thoughts, Crook believed that this was Mangas going north to the Navajo Reservation. But this assumption was wrong, for he was in hiding south of Guaynopa, Juh's former stronghold.[61]

In fact, Nana likely led this party. He had come north by the Florida Mountains after crossing the border about the time that Geronimo was carrying out his raid near Fort Apache. Nana led his people through the Black Range, a little north of the route Geronimo had taken. He committed no depredations. Two days later, on September 25, Bradley reported that citizens had spotted Apaches near Horse Springs. Whether this was Nana's or Geronimo's group returning from Fort Apache was unclear. But Nana knew where Geronimo planned to camp and probably reached the secluded site before Geronimo.[62]

Meanwhile, despite Crook's counter moves, Geronimo had returned to New Mexico undetected by troops or scouts. The evening of September 27, 1885, at Cactus Flat, about five miles northwest of Buckhorn, he ambushed A. L. Sabourne, who was driving a wagon loaded with merchandise to Cooney City. He died instantly from a bullet into his chest fired from the hills. The Indians plundered the wagon, which contained a large lot of candy that they ate in one sitting. Santiago McKinn remembered that the Apaches felt ill the next day from the overdose of sweets. They remained in camp for another week as they feasted on their captured stock and food taken from Sabourne's wagon. Little Santiago McKinn believed that his captors actually decided his fate by gambling. Happily for him, the side that favored sparing his life won. Geronimo's party left for Mexico about October 6, 1885.[63]

Right on the heels of Geronimo's distinct moccasin prints, Crook faced another band of raiders racing up from Mexico under Naiche and Chihuahua. The timing of their foray coincidentally diverted attention from Geronimo to them—though the two chiefs were unaware of Geronimo's movements above the border. There was no coordination between the two groups.

The last news of them was of their fight with Captain Wirt Davis's command in the Teras Mountains on September 22, 1885. His scouts had ferreted out the trail of twenty-five Chiricahuas who had crossed the Bavispe River and dropped into the Carretas plains just inside the Chihuahua border. The scouts assumed they were attempting to return to Fort Apache to find out about Chihuahua's family.

On the morning of September 26, 1885, Crawford's and Wirt Davis's commands joined on Carretas Creek. Crawford, after receiving a message from Davis the night before, had already sent Lieutenant Charles Elliott with fifty scouts to follow the trail. Now the united command broke camp and marched north. At 3:00 that afternoon, Captain Davis sent a courier to Langs ranch, just north of the border in New Mexico, with the information that the Chiricahuas were going north. He thought they would cross the border through Guadalupe Canyon, or perhaps at San Bernardino. His first guess was right.[64]

The commanding officer at Langs ranch sent a dispatch to Captain John William Martin at Guadalupe Canyon. Martin had received the note late on the 27th or early on the 28th but had failed to act immediately on the information. The Chiricahuas had passed through Guadalupe Canyon some four or five miles above, probably meaning east, of Martin's two cavalry companies and Apache scouts.

Elliott's scouts were the first to reach Guadalupe Canyon. The lieutenant sent to Captain Davis the information that the hostiles had bypassed the soldiers at Guadalupe Canyon. Wirt Davis, who had been in the Sierra Madre Mountains chasing the Chiricahuas for almost three months, was hardly in a forgiving mood. Caustically he advised Captain Martin, "I can send you information, but I cannot furnish you with brains." The next morning Davis sent out Martin with one company of cavalry and scouts. No one expected any results. Martin was a day behind the Indians. Lieutenant Elliott summed up the situation: "Nothing yet invented has ever caught a Chiricahua in the mountains, certainly not from the rear."[65]

Crook received word of the border crossing about twenty-four hours after it happened.[66] He gave explicit orders to Lieutenant Gatewood and Lieutenant Colonel James Wade at Fort Apache. Clearly unimpressed by the White

Mountain Apaches' efforts to subdue Geronimo the week before, he told Gatewood to ask for help on his behalf. If they failed to take action, he ordered Gatewood to warn them it "will interfere very seriously with their future welfare." He had decided to move the Chiricahuas closer to Fort Apache under "the pretense that it is necessary to prevent the families of the scouts who are away from being injured by the hostiles." Once Gatewood implemented the plan, he wanted the White Mountain Apaches to guard their camp and to kill any hostile who showed his face. Crook told Gatewood to let them know that "whoever succeeds in killing a Chiricahua will be well paid." The general also wrote Wade at Fort Apache, cautioning him to "hold troops in readiness to support Gatewood." He warned both officers not to reveal the "facts" to the Chiricahuas. All they needed to know was that the hostiles might be coming.[67]

The next morning, Crook, revealing signs of desperation, turned the screws even tighter. His exasperation (though unfounded) with the White Mountain Apaches was apparent. They had no chance at capturing Geronimo, but he thought their failure suggested apathy and disinterest. And he felt they were acting ungratefully to him—that they were forgetful of his diligent efforts on their behalf. Naturally, the thin-skinned commander took this as a personal affront. Ignoring the inconvenient fact that some fifty White Mountain and Cibecue Apaches had spent the summer trailing the hostiles in Mexico, he decided to prey on their fears:

> The general will give $100 for each head of a hostile Chiricahua buck brought in by an Indian scout or volunteer. Tell the White Mountain Indians that the general . . . is getting tired of doing all of their work for them and that he will ask to go away from here and they will probably then get another big-bellied agent who will move them all to San Carlos and that he won't come back again to help them out of any more scrapes.[68]

It was obvious to anyone hearing these words what he meant. He had saved them from the regime of Agent Tiffany, and he wanted to collect on that debt with Chiricahua blood.

Meanwhile, Chatto's Chiricahua scouts, who had returned to Fort Bowie with Lieutenant Davis, were concerned that the raiders, if they slipped through the lines, would seek vengeance on the scouts' families at Fort Apache. Chatto feared that Chihuahua would particularly target his family. After all, he had led the raid on Chihuahua's camp. The fearless Chokonen leader, consumed by rage and vengeance, would have relished the chance to get even. Crook agreed to send three scouts selected by their peers to return to Fort Apache to look after their families. He sent them to Willcox by train. Here they were to take either a stage or other transportation to the fort. The Chiricahuas chose Toosigah. Crook had ordered Gatewood to pay close attention to Naiche's family, for his mother and sister had not left the reservation.[69]

Soon after making these arrangements, Crook finally received some good news. Naiche and Chihuahua had divided once they reached the Chiricahua Mountains. One party of twelve men under Chihuahua went north along the eastern face; Naiche led the other group north and skirted the western side. Captain Martin, Crawford, and Elliott stayed on the trail of Chihuahua's group, which, for some reason, did not cross the San Simon Valley into the Peloncillo Mountains. The presence of troops in the San Simon and Sulphur Springs valleys coupled with the threat posed by two hundred Apache scouts, which included Chatto and some thirty-five Chiricahuas, had deterred Chihuahua. A foray to their former homes at Fort Apache was too risky.[70]

With scouts and soldiers in front of him, Chihuahua decided to return west through the heart of the Chiricahuas to rendezvous with Naiche's party. But first he needed fresh mounts. On September 29, his men killed an unidentified American prospector in Cave Creek Canyon. The next morning they began rounding up horses belonging to the Keating ranch about eight miles north of Galeyville. Mistaking the Indians for cowboys, Michael Keating rode out to meet them. One Chiricahua shot Keating in the head, killing him instantly. Timothy Shanahan, a ranch employee, took refuge in the ranch house and watched as the Indians, working in a businesslike manner, picked out the best dozen horses and took them away. From here, they went a mile to the southwest and looted the empty Sullivan cabin, where they butchered Keating's mule. Afterwards, they rode southwest to a ranch on Whitetail Creek, where late that night they loosened the hobbles of forty horses and took them away while cowboys who had assembled for the fall roundup slept soundly.[71]

By the next morning, October 1, Chihuahua had crossed to the western side and traversed Pinery Canyon to Pine Canyon via Downey Pass. After continuing south, later that day they halted at Morse Canyon, just south of Turkey Creek, where they shot John McGowan in the abdomen before continuing to the prearranged assembly point with Naiche.[72]

Naiche had been busy in the Sulphur Springs Valley. At 3:00 A.M. on October 1, 1885, his warriors had run off fifty horses and mules from the Sulphur Springs ranch, the very same place where Britton Davis and Geronimo had experienced their dramatic confrontation twenty months before. At this time, Silas Bryant, a rancher in the Dragoons, was hauling supplies from Willcox to his ranch. Arriving there in the late evening of September 30, he quartered his six mules in the corral. About 3:00 the next morning, sounds of horses' hoof-beats from the corral awakened him. Five feet from him was a "big" Chiricahua man with a rifle aimed at him. This was undoubtedly Naiche, for only two of the hostiles stood taller than five feet eight inches. Bryant, though blessed with a strong, athletic physique, knew well enough to keep quiet.[73]

Despite a guard and a watchdog, a few Apaches had "cut the binding and raised three or four pickets of the stockade corral. Then they frightened the animals by shaking a blanket and stampeded fifty or more horses and mules." With that, Naiche faded into the darkness, sparing Bryant's life. Moments later, Bryant sounded the alarm, but it was dark, and the thieves had run off most of the stock, including Bryant's six mules. That morning a few warriors left the main body and killed Mike Noonan, a much-respected rancher, in the doorway of his cabin in the Dragoons. The next day, October 2, they joined Chihuahua in the lower Chiricahuas.[74]

Crook sent out a patrol under Crawford and Chatto to the west side of the Chiricahuas. Mid-afternoon on October 2, 1885, they found a trail that headed south toward Mud Springs. By 3:00 the next morning, they had con-ceded pursuit was fruitless. Crawford sent a courier to Fort Bowie: "Scouts say they [Naiche and Chihuahua] are going back to Sonora." Crawford tersely accepted that "the only thing to be done is to make another campaign against them in Sonora."[75]

General Crook agreed. On October 3, he met Arizona governor Frederick A. Tritle and Colonel Bradley in Deming, New Mexico, to discuss the next phase of operations. On October 10, 1885, Crawford and his scouts held a long meeting with Crook. The scouts were pleased with the decision to dis-charge them so that they could return to their families and their farms.

The commanding general appreciated Chatto's efforts, pointing out that the sergeant of scouts had done "everything in his power to overtake and pun-ish the renegades." Crook had learned from former captives in Mexico that "Chatto's wife and children were in the city of Chihuahua in the custody of a Mexican." He implored the War Department to take the necessary steps to get the Chiricahua captives, especially Chatto's family, released from bondage in Mexico: "There is nothing he would appreciate more."[76]

On October 11, 1885, Crook outlined phase two of his strategy to Gen-eral John Pope. The four months of duty in the Sierra Madre had worn out his officers, scouts, and mules. They needed "rest and recuperation." He had decided to discharge the current scouts and enlist replacements in November. He would send Crawford and Wirt Davis to resume operations in the Sierra Madre. One thing Crook hoped might occur was that the hostiles would come together in one band in their "winter quarters."[77]

Pope passed along his subordinate's proposal to Washington, only adding that the "outlook promises no speedy results." In the five months of relentless pursuit, his troops and scouts had captured or killed about thirty women and children but had not put a dent in the ranks of the forty-two fighting men, who were still divided into four groups: Chihuahua, Naiche, Geronimo and Nana, and Mangas. Crook hoped that they would make a winter camp together in the lower canyons or valleys of the Sierra Madre, where Crawford or Wirt Davis might get a shot at them. Pope continued to encourage Washington to allow Crook "to work out this problem according to his own judgment." Though there was increasing frustration in Washington, General Sheridan remained steadfast behind Crook, endorsing his plans for the next phase.[78]

22

THE TRAIL TO ESPINOSA
DEL DIABLO

[It is time] after nearly a five-month campaign . . . [that] we ar-
raign General Crook at the bar of public opinion and state the
charges and substantiating facts against him.
Wilcox Stockman, October 23, 1885

As Crook, Crawford, and Wirt Davis began to regroup and formulate plans
for their next operations into Mexico, the two Chiricahua raiding parties in
Arizona and New Mexico slipped past the troops guarding the border and
headed for familiar ground in Mexico. They executed this maneuver with
ease, for they knew soldiers and scouts were guarding water holes and passes
along the border. Naiche and Chihuahua entered Mexico first, traversing the
Hatchet Mountains in the New Mexico panhandle through the Alamo Hueco
range on October 6, 1885. A few days later, some warriors pilfered stock at
Bavispe, but the citizens, lacking serviceable weapons, were unable to pursue.
The raiders eventually returned to their base camp, hidden high in the Carcay
Mountains, at a place they called Plentiful Pines.[1]

The same day that Naiche and Chihuahua entered Mexico, Geronimo and
Nana left the Mogollons bound for Mexico. They had Santiago McKinn with
them. On October 8, a small raiding party began rounding up stock from
ranches along the Gila, Mangas Valley, and the Burro Mountains. Major Samuel Sumner pursued with cavalry but lost the trail that led north toward Blue
Creek before the raiders pivoted and headed south. They were a diversionary party to allow the main group under Geronimo to put some distance between themselves and pursuers. Geronimo's party traveled by night until they

reached the Animas Valley, where they stole thirty horses from a ranch before crossing the border late on October 9, 1885.

The smaller raiding party was a day or two behind him. On October 10, they ambushed two troopers at Cowboy Pass in the lower Peloncillo Mountains, about fifteen miles north of Cloverdale. Their first salvo killed Private Hickman and wounded Private Sylvester Grover, both of the Fourth Cavalry. Grover's mount ran for five hundred yards before it collapsed and died. Grover fought off his attackers until the Indians broke off the fight, taking Hickman's horse, cartridge belt, and weapons. Grover thought he would die before anyone found him. Fortunately for him, a group of seven discharged scouts and packers came along in time to save his life.[2]

Meanwhile, Geronimo had headed toward Casas Grandes. On October 11, 1885, his men fired on a pack train going to Bavispe, but no one was hurt. Later that day, near Casa de Janos, they clashed with vaqueros from the Ramos hacienda, killing one man before reversing directions toward Carretas. From here, he went south to their pine-studded base camp at Bent-ci-iye, where he met Naiche and Chihuahua for the first time since their split May 19.

When news of the vaquero's death reached Casas Grandes, officials dispatched a party to overtake an Apache woman who had left town that morning. The Mexicans took her into custody. She belonged to Mangas's group and denied his involvement in the killing, which she pinned on Geronimo. Since splitting from Geronimo after Bylas's attack on their camp at Bugatseka, Mangas and his small band of about twenty had stayed at Guaynopa and in the region south of the Aros River. Mangas had his wife, Dilth-cley-ih, a daughter of Victorio, and six men, four Chihennes and two Nednhis. The Chihennes were Eskinolteze, Frijole, Ni-Losh, and the seventeen-year-old Goso. The two Nednhis were Delzhinne (Talline to Mexicans, Elgede to Americans) and his fifteen-year-old brother, Daklegon. Since mid-September, only the elderly Eskinolteze and a few older women had ventured into Casas Grandes to trade "jewelry, watches, and buckskins for food and other articles."[3]

When the woman from his group failed to return, Mangas immediately broke camp and set out for the mountains. Daklegon, Juh's middle son, was then away from the village. On returning, he found the ranchería abandoned. Looking for his family, he went to Casas Grandes, where Juh had many friends. Here, federal troops, thinking he might be useful, took him in. By late October Crook received a report that the teenage boy was living in the soldiers' quarters and wearing a uniform. The officers planned to use him to lure in other Chiricahuas.[4]

Fifty miles east of Casas Grandes, Naiche, Chihuahua, and Geronimo settled on a new plan. Despite the overwhelming odds, surrender was not even
on their radar screen. They remembered Crawford's harsh sentence levied on
Kaetenae (upheld by Crook) for only talking about going to Mexico. They
could only speculate on what was in store for those who had left the reservation and committed depredations. Crook's punishment would be far more
punitive—probably death by hanging—like that of the three scouts who had
deserted at Cibecue. Or maybe he might turn them over to civil authorities
for trial. Neither option looked good. They remained in the dark about where
Crook was holding their families. Knowing for sure that they were not at Fort
Apache, the chiefs thought that San Carlos was one possibility. The chiefs decided to attempt a daring rescue. The intrepid Chihuahua would lead a diversionary foray into New Mexico; Ulzana would take a second group of twelve
men on a raid to Fort Apache.

Ulzana's party consisted of men who wanted to recover their wives and
children, whom the scouts had captured the previous summer, and other men
who had left their families at Turkey Creek. Ulzana and Perico fell into the
first category; Cathla, Moh-tsos, Tah-ni-toe, Len-see, and Shoie fell into the
second. The other known members of Ulzana's party were Atelnietze, Fun,
Kanseah, Yahnozha, and a nineteen-year-old Nednhi, Zachia (Azariquelch).[5]
Six of the twelve men had served as scouts during their time on the reservation. Three had deserted (Atelnietze, Cathla, and Fun) on May 17, 1885. A
mobile and lethal fighting force, they had powerful motives beyond just the
recovery of their kinfolk. They also longed for vengeance against the scouts,
and to take prisoners, whom, according to Geronimo's instructions, they were
to carry back to Mexico. If they failed to find out where their families were,
they thought at least the men who had left their families behind could retrieve
their loved ones.[6]

In mid-October, Chihuahua, Ulzana, and some twenty warriors and teenage boys left the Carcay Mountains.[7] At the same time, Geronimo, Nana, and
Naiche, with about a dozen warriors and teenage boys and some sixty women
and children, left on a raid toward Yepómera, Chihuahua.

Chihuahua and Ulzana first went into camp at Corral de Piedra, in the
southeast part of the Fresnal Mountains, some thirty miles east of Janos. Before striking north on their famous foray, they decided to raid the Sabinal
mines, where John Baker had discovered a silver vein the previous summer.
Sabinal was eight miles south of Corral de Piedra, a known stronghold of
the Chiricahuas. On October 17, 1885, Chihuahua raided the settlement. A

"sharp clash" followed, but no one was hurt. The Indians stole eleven horses. Eight or nine days later. Chihuahua and Ulzana crossed the railroad tracks south of Lake Guzman and forged north for the border.[8]

East of the Boca Grande Mountains, the brothers split up. Ulzana took eleven men, rounded this range to the south, and entered New Mexico's bootheel from the east. He hoped to move north through the Animas Mountains, a forty-mile north-south range that overlooked two basins, the Playas on the east and the Animas on the west. He probably spent one day lodged in the Alamo Hueco range before using the night's cover to enter the Animas range. For several days his small band holed up at the base of Animas Peak. Scouts fanned out, probing the country north, looking for an opportunity to dash toward the reservation. While Ulzana conducted his surveillance, Chihuahua crossed the border on a quick-moving diversionary raid designed to divert the military's attention to him, thus opening a gap in Crook's defenses for Ulzana.

Chihuahua had led his group of about eight men and two women across the border east of Palomas, near Geronimo's entrance two months earlier. Unlike Geronimo, who took a circuitous route to get to the Black Range, Chihuahua made a beeline north, skirting the Floridas and heading for the target-rich country around Lake Valley. On November 2, 1885, his men rounded up horses from ranches and then surprised Jewitt's wood camp, slaying Charles Martin as he cooked supper. They looted the camp, packed provisions, rifles, and ammunition on a mule, and continued north to the Mimbres Mountains and Percha Creek. Over the next few days, they wounded a man and stole more stock. The raiders "appear perfectly unconcerned as to their pursuers, either military, militia, or citizens," remarked one observer. Finally, Chihuahua went south, crossing the railroad tracks east of Cambray, a water depot for the railroad, about 5:30 P.M. on November 6, 1885. He was moving fast toward the West Potrillo Mountains.

Captain Adna Chaffee, the former San Carlos agent between the regimes of Hart and Tiffany, pursued with thirty-five men and a few Navajo scouts. It was a grueling trip across the parched country to the Mexican border. His men and stock played out, Chaffee detoured east to the Rio Grande for water. Chihuahua had crossed the border on November 7, heading south toward the Candelaria range. From here the chief eventually moved east to the Escondida Mountains and to Casas Grandes, where he opened negotiations to trade in late November.[9]

Meanwhile, Ulzana, having concluded that his Peloncillo corridor route north was too dangerous, left the Animas Mountains on November 3. He retraced his route into Chihuahua, and followed his brother's trail into New Mexico.[10] About 8:30 A.M. on November 7, 1885, Ulzana's party committed its first hostile act on American soil, in the southeast corner of the Florida Mountains. Five warriors on foot ambushed two military couriers returning to Captain Kendall's command. They killed Antonio, a Navajo scout, and wounded Private Abbott, shot through the chest. The raiders took their carbines and horses. Two couriers from Captain Kendall's command reached the scene shortly after the fight. They took the seriously wounded Abbott to the depot at Cambray, where they put him on a train for treatment at Fort Bliss.[11]

Three hours later, Ulzana's party had moved seven miles north to two ranches of the Missouri Cattle Company, occupied by John Shy and Andrew Yeater. The evidence is unclear whether the five men who had slain Antonio were with Ulzana. Early reports said that seven Indians attacked Shy; in later years, he suggested that they numbered at least thirteen, perhaps more.[12] Yeater and his wife were absent in Deming; Shy had just sat down for his noon meal with his wife and eleven-year-old son when he heard a sound outside the window. When he investigated, he saw an Apache aim his rifle at him. Hoping that Shy might be persuaded to come out and talk, the warrior said he was a "good Indian." But Shy's instincts told him otherwise. He "hollered to his wife to look out" and ran to get his Winchester rifle. Then a burst of gunfire peppered the windows. Shy refused to panic. He sent his wife and boy upstairs and kept the Indians at bay with his Winchester. The Chiricahuas fled to positions behind rocks at two places. They were not prepared to rush the house and suffer needless casualties. After what Shy thought was an hour of skirmishing, the Apaches, concerned that a relief party might arrive at any moment, tried to entice Shy to come out. One Apache said they were scouts for the army. Who was this Chiricahua? Perhaps Cathla, since scouts had noticed tracks of a "disabled man." Cathla, wounded in the leg a few months earlier, had also been to Washington, D.C., in 1876 with Taza and undoubtedly knew some English. Shy wisely ignored their disingenuous offer.

Ulzana was getting nervous. The country was full of troops, and there was no telling when they might hear a cavalry bugle. He sent his men to Yeater's ranch, only eight feet from Shy's. They looted the place and then set it ablaze. Unfortunately for Shy, "a gust of wind" roared up the canyon and the fire spread to his ranch. Shy gathered up his wife and child, stuffed his pockets with cartridges, and dashed out the front door, his wife and son behind him. Shy could hear bullets slamming into the house and door as they made a forty-yard dash through the smoke to a gulch that led to a nearby hill. Leading his family to cover behind a large boulder, Shy found five Apaches there. He emptied his Winchester, driving them off. He believed that he had wounded a Chiricahua. If so, it was probably Cathla whom he had hit, for the Apache's friends left him behind in the mountains when Ulzana moved into Arizona.[13]

Finally, the raiders left to the north. Shy had lost everything in the fire, which had engulfed his home so quickly that the raiders got nothing. With smoke visible for miles, Ulzana had to withdraw his men. Shy's house incinerated, his possessions destroyed, his son wounded through the hip, and his wife, in the confusion, missing in the brush (she was later found), his heroic stand earned him legendary status in the Southwest. One brave and desperate man had battled a dozen Chiricahuas to a stalemate. Shy epitomized the courage and character of southwestern pioneers.

After attacking Shy, the Indians ambushed Andrew J. Yeater and his wife, who were returning from Deming with supplies. According to one account, Yeater fired thirteen rounds from his Winchester before the Apaches cut him down. The Apaches stripped his wife, which led to initial reports that they had also raped her. But this heinous act was not a practice of the Chiricahuas. A subsequent report set the record straight: "The only mark on her was a blow to the head from a hatchet."[14]

Shortly after a relief party from Deming made the ghastly discovery, a dog led them to a mesquite bush, where they found Mrs. Shy hiding. She related the events of that day to Captain Henry W. Sprole, who pushed on to Shy's ranch. They found Shy and his son that evening. By then, Ulzana had sliced through the lines to the north, crossed the railroad tracks, and gained the Mimbres Mountains northwest of Berrenda Creek. Captain Kendall's Navajo guide stated that the party now consisted of ten Apaches. On the evening of November 8, the mobile Apaches killed two more men, wounded another, and stole more horses before disappearing into the lofty country west of Kingston. Then it seemed as though they went underground for two weeks. They were careful not to call attention to themselves as they methodically worked their way west toward Arizona and the object of their raid, Fort Apache.[15]

The raid generated an uproar in the territorial press. The rhetoric became heated in southwestern New Mexico, especially with the killing of Mrs. Yeater and the understandable frustration over the raiders marauding with impunity despite the presence of militia and army forces. Increasingly, Crook was becoming the target, and his Apache scouts the scapegoats. Representative of the hyperbolic criticism was an editorial published in the *Silver City Enterprise*. The editors launched a scurrilous, personal attack on the general, disparaging him as a "liar, coward, [and] murderer. . . . The blood of all those victims cries vengeance against you." One Silver City man advocated the organization of a vigilante posse to "KKK" the Apaches at San Carlos.[16]

To this man and to many politicians and military leaders in Washington, who had grown weary of the decade-long Chiricahua hostilities, every Apache at San Carlos was a potential hostile. This unfounded sentiment ignored these indisputable facts: (1) Only 144 Chiricahuas of the 5,000 Apaches at San Carlos and Fort Apache had left the reservation; (2) the reservation Apaches had provided neither aid nor recruits to the hostiles; (3) the men on the reservation had enlisted as scouts to track down the hostiles; (4) Geronimo had few friends among the 400 Chiricahuas on the reservation and even fewer among the Western Apache groups at San Carlos and Fort Apache.

Those who wanted to punish or remove every Chiricahua Apache from Arizona would not have believed these facts. Instead, they assumed that as Apaches, their sympathies lay inherently with the hostiles. The press, some military officers, territorial politicians, and federal officials repeated this so often that it became accepted as gospel. Even worse, this misconceived and fallacious belief became the guiding precept for the new policy adopted by the federal government toward the Chiricahua Apaches. And it came about as a direct result of Ulzana's foray—just as Geronimo's foray was the embryo for the policy to remove all hostiles who had surrendered to Fort Marion in Florida.

News of the raid reverberated through the halls of the War Department. Though the raiders had killed fewer than ten people, the reaction was the same as if the victims had numbered in the hundreds. The first to discredit Crook was his rival, General Miles, whose responsibility included the military District of New Mexico. He capitalized on the opportunity to impugn Crook's policies by characterizing the situation in New Mexico as "not satisfactory." He now favored consolidating the two departments under one command, but incredibly, not under Crook. Since the "Apaches pass back and forth between the camps of troops," Miles thought that one "active and experienced officer [should] direct the movement of the troops and require them to act in concert." To accomplish this, he requested the services of Colonel Eugene Carr, then on recruiting duty in St. Louis.

It was a cheap shot aimed at Crook's backside by an officer resting comfortably at Fort Leavenworth, five hundred miles from the scene of hostilities. Miles's superior, General John Schofield, forwarded the letter to Sheridan. A former classmate at West Point of Crook and Sheridan, Schofield noted the contradictions in Miles's arguments, pointing out that "there is [no] divided responsibility. . . . General Crook has been given full responsibility, and I don't know what better can be done under present circumstances." He refused the request for Colonel Carr. Instead, Schofield suggested that Sheridan call Miles's bluff. If he "is so anxious to try his skill upon the Apaches, perhaps it might be best to give him the opportunity. But this is, of course, for [you] to judge." Sheridan, who had served as best man in Miles's wedding, recognized Miles's well-known penchant for second-guessing a fellow officer who might be a competitor for a promotion that he was seeking.[17]

General Phil Sheridan was then thinking about Crook and the Chiricahuas. Unlike Miles, he was searching for solutions, not pointing fingers. Boyhood friends and roommates at West Point, Crook and Sheridan had seen their relationship deteriorate since the Civil War. Crook never forgave Sheridan for lying to him and taking credit for a military maneuver suggested by Crook that had led to a Union victory. Moreover, profound philosophical differences in Indian policy left each, especially Crook, intolerant of the other's views. In reality, the two men had little in common. Sheridan was impulsive and decisive; Crook was cautious and decisive. Sheridan's biographer, Paul Hutton, wrote that Sheridan saw things in "black and white" while Crook saw "shades of gray."[18] The post–Civil War years had seen Sheridan's star rise as Sherman's hand-picked man to succeed him as commander of the army. Once Sherman retired in early 1884, Sheridan replaced his friend. He was a good manager, delegating responsibility to his subordinates along with the discretion and flexibility to carry out their assignments.

Just before the latest round of raids, Sheridan had cautioned southwesterners to be patient with Crook's policies, but after hearing the news of the raids in early November, he threw his hands up in frustration. Like many officials in Washington, D.C., he was tiring of the Chiricahua story. On November 19, 1885, he telegraphed Crook to advise him that "complaints are constantly reaching the President from Arizona and New Mexico. Can you give me any assurances of the speedy termination of the Apache troubles?" Crook was not about to make any promises: "All is being done that in my judgment can be done for the suppression of these Indian troubles. I have no means of knowing how long this trouble may last yet." Sheridan finally decided that the only solution was to remove the Chiricahuas, both peaceful and hostile, out of the Southwest. He made this proposal to the secretary of war, William C. Endicott, who while concurring suggested that Sheridan go to Arizona to gauge Crook's feelings.[19]

Ulzana's incursion did nothing to alter Crook's plans for a second offensive into the Sierra Madre. The second week of October, he had gone to the Navajo Reservation to check out rumors that Mangas was near. At Fort Wingate, Crook had met with Mariana, "the only [Navajo] who might have anything to do with the hostiles." But he knew nothing. After the fruitless journey, Crook returned to headquarters at Bowie, where he and Crawford discharged his scouts.[20]

Soon after, the loyal captain left for Fort Apache to enlist new scouts to replace those whose terms had expired. Meanwhile, Captain Wirt Davis had gone to San Carlos to sign up new scouts for his second campaign into Mexico. Crawford wanted to raise four companies of twenty-five scouts with as many Chiricahuas as possible. But many men, including Chatto, did not reenlist, for the four-month campaign had worn them out. To make matters worse, Lieutenant Roach had arrested Bonito and Zele and sent them to the guardhouse. Bonito was mixed up in a tiswin drunk that had led to a woman's death. Zele had been absent when Lieutenant Roach made a count, probably because he feared arrest after beating his wife again, despite warnings of the ramifications. To escape Zele's wrath, she had fled to San Carlos. Because Crook wanted at least one prominent chief to act as overall commander of the scouts, he authorized Crawford to pardon the two chiefs if he needed them for the campaign. But neither man wanted to serve as scout for what promised to be a grueling winter campaign into Sonora. Zele was getting up in age, and Bonito, who had recently married a White Mountain woman, was beginning to distance himself from the Chiricahuas.[21]

Crawford had no trouble enlisting Chiricahuas, but the White Mountain Apaches were not as eager.[22] He had talked to Loco, whose band members resented Geronimo for the tragedy at Alisos Creek that had claimed so many Chihenne lives. On November 7, 1885, Lieutenant Marion P. Maus, a thirty-five-year-old graduate of West Point who would serve as second in command to Crawford, enlisted two companies of twenty-five scouts each. Company A included nearly every adult male from Loco's band; Company B consisted of White Mountain and Cibecue Apaches. The scouts in Company A were Chihennes and a few Chokonens, including Chatto's younger brother Gon-altsis. Their sergeants were Charley, Guydelkon, Tsedekizen, and Ruby, who, in his early fifties, was probably the oldest scout. The last two were Loco's sons-in-law; clearly, he had assigned them the special task of protecting the officers. Other notables such as Massai, Juan Segotset, and Balatchu rounded out the ranks.[23]

Lieutenant William Ewen Shipp, a twenty-four-year-old West Point graduate, recruited eight White Mountains and seventeen Chiricahuas to serve in Company D. Noche, Cooney, Cuso (probably Fatty), and Tuzzone served as sergeants, and Dutchy, Kaydahzinne, Espida, Nahn-tee-nesn, and Astoye were among the privates. Noche, Fatty, and Tuzzone knew the Sierra Madre Mountains because they had lived there with Juh and Cochise. Noche assumed Chatto's position as leader of the Chiricahua scouts. To round out the detail, Shipp signed up twenty-five White Mountain and Cibecue scouts for Company C. Crawford purposely excluded troops because he felt that during the summer campaign, the soldiers "were a burden." The one hundred scouts formed the Second Battalion of Indian Scouts.[24]

Crook was also covering his bases. And on November 11, 1885, he told Crawford "you may have to go to New Mexico to run [Ulzana's party] out of the country." This time he had the option of calling on the Chiricahua scouts, for when Geronimo made his foray, they were in Mexico. Three days later, Crook made another astute decision to thwart the raiders if they showed up at Fort Apache. Having learned a lesson from Geronimo's raid at Fort Apache, at Crawford's urging Crook ordered Lieutenant Roach to send the families of the hostiles to San Carlos. Noting that the transfer was for their safety and not a punishment, Crook told Captain Pierce to treat them as guests. Moreover, he advised Pierce to use the agency scouts to "keep general supervision over them."[25]

The two refitted scout battalions were ready for action. On November 16, 1885, Captain Wirt Davis reached Fort Bowie with one hundred scouts from San Carlos. Davis also had three pack trains, four officers, and George Wrattan as chief of scouts. On November 21, 1885, Crook ordered Davis back to Mexico. While he was en route, Captain Joseph H. Dorst, with thirty-six horse soldiers of the Fourth Cavalry, joined him at Guadalupe Canyon. They eventually went into a base camp at Carretas, near the Sonora–Chihuahua border. Crawford was ready to depart Fort Apache on November 18. Crook had heard nothing of the hostiles in New Mexico. It was as if the earth had swallowed up Ulzana's party. Thus, he ordered Crawford's command, which consisted of five officers, two chiefs of scouts (Tom Horn and William Harrison), one hospital steward, one interpreter (Concepcion), one hundred Apache scouts, and three pack trains, each with forty-five mules and a dozen civilian packers, about 142 men in all, to come to Fort Bowie.[26]

The day before Crawford's departure, Ulzana's raiders had crossed the New Mexico line into Arizona. On November 17, 1885, they stole every head of stock from the ranch of the "Blucher boys" on the San Francisco River, some sixty miles north of Clifton. Then, instead of following Geronimo's route, they dipped southwest to Eagle Creek, where they killed eight horses.[27] From here, they went north to the Black River and moved on toward Turkey Creek, which they found empty of Chiricahuas. Knowing that Chiricahua camps and farms were at the east fork of the White River, they swung east to Bonito Creek, where they left horses to pick up after their raid. From here, Ulzana took his men to East Fork, where they knew Chatto had his farm. To Ulzana's delight, from a distance they could see two persons, Chatto and his wife, working their crops. Ulzana had vowed to kill Chatto. It was early afternoon, November 23, 1885.

Chatto was on guard. He was always disinclined to speak about his Power, but he was a deeply religious man who prayed every morning. As Ulzana contemplated his next step, he suddenly saw Chatto and his wife drop everything, jump on a horse, and head downriver to Fort Apache. The hostiles became alarmed, thinking someone had warned Chatto. Many years later, one of Ulzana's party asked Chatto why he had fled: "Oh, yes! I remember that time. I was working and all of a sudden I got a muscular tremor sign, which I knew from experience, meant something bad is going to happen. Drop everything. So I did."[28] Chatto brought his family to Fort Apache, where his wife and children remained until Ulzana left the area. Later that day, Ulzana captured four Chiricahuas, one boy and three women. The boy escaped that evening and told Lieutenant James Lockett everything that the raiders had revealed to him. Lockett, who had just succeeded Gatewood nine days earlier, moved the rest of the Chiricahuas to a camp near the fort.[29]

Later that evening or early the next morning (November 24), the raiders killed two men, William Waldo and William (Billy) Harrison, who were watching the government's beef herd at Turkey Creek. That morning they ran off Bonito's horses and killed several head of Chiricahua stock. From the Chiricahua women, Ulzana learned that the military had recently moved many of their relatives to San Carlos for safekeeping. Ulzana reportedly vowed to remain until they had slain Chatto. That morning he released two women, telling them his party was going to Eagle Creek. The third woman, Ta-tay-gy, also known as Tse-Dha-Dilth-Theilth Bi-yah-neta, stayed with Perico, eventually becoming his second wife.

They started south toward the Black River but after several miles doubled back toward Fort Apache. At dusk, they encamped on a plateau about eight miles southwest of the fort. Meanwhile, at noon that day, Chatto and seventeen scouts (seven Chiricahuas and ten White Mountains) joined Lieutenant Charles E. Nordstrom, Tenth Cavalry, and ten men in pursuit of Ulzana. They followed the trail until dark, when it became too late to do anything.[30]

But Ulzana was west of Turkey Creek. While his men stopped to eat, he assigned sentry duty to the youngest warrior, Jaspar Kanseah, the teenager who had served as Yahnozha's orderly.

> Jaspar [was] on a ridge to watch and stand guard. Finally, Jaspar was relieved by another boy, a good-looking young Chiricahua [Azariquelch, or Zachia]. A few minutes later, as he was sitting there on the ridge with his gun across his knees, looking in the opposite direction, a San Carlos [Cibecue] Indian crept up behind him and shot him. As soon as he shot, he was on this boy with his knife and cut his head off.[31]

The killer was a Carrizo chief named Sánchez, also known as Iron or Metal Tooth, who had married a White Mountain woman. His motive was Crook's one-hundred-dollar reward for the head of any hostile. He grabbed the trophy, placed it in a buckskin sack, and fled to his camp. Hearing that Ulzana was after him, he fled to Fort Apache and dropped the grisly bounty, the head of Azariquelch, on the table of the commanding officer.[32]

Sánchez might as well have attacked a hornet's nest. His beheading of the young warrior enraged the Chiricahuas:

> The rest of the Chiricahuas came up to see what [Sánchez] had done. They were as angry as could be. They found out who had done this and went to his camp to get him. But he had been warned and got away. His wife and several children were there, though, and they killed them and left them lying right there. They went out and began shooting into other [White Mountain] camps. They were so angry they didn't care what they did. Then they made for the hills.[33]

That evening and in the early morning of November 25, near the junction of the Black and White rivers, they attacked several rancherías, including Sánchez's, and slaughtered twenty-one White Mountain Apaches, four men, eleven women, and six children. They also captured a woman named Na-dis-ough and her younger brother. She had seen the raiders kill her father, brother, and cousin. One old man, returning from hunting, watched from a ridge as Ulzana's frenzied party turned their wrath on his grandson. They smashed his brains in with a rock and threw him into a fire to roast. The incensed grandfather aimed his Sharps rifle and thought he wounded one hostile. As the Chiricahuas left with their two prisoners, they threatened to behead them if they tried to escape. Na-dis-ough remembered that she was sobbing, but Atelnietze forced her to go with him.[34]

Crook, furious at this turn of events, had two concerns. First, he knew that the White Mountain Apaches remained his best hope of subduing Ulzana. They had the capability and incentive to bring him to justice. With this on his mind, he ordered Lieutenant Lockett to "get the White Mountains to hunt the country for the hostiles and kill them all. Furnish them with arms and ammunition." In a second telegram he told Lockett to "impress on the White Mountain Indians that they must kill all the hostiles otherwise they will be in constant danger. Tell them that the hostiles should not have it all their own way amongst so many Indians." He lamented that the raiders could easily bypass the water holes guarded by his troops. Ulzana's men carried their water "in the entrails of cattle or horses killed along the way."[35] Once a raiding party slipped past the cordon of troops between the railroad and the border, Crook thought that the terrain, combined with their ability to move great distances after dark, rendered "any pursuit almost a farce."[36]

Then he addressed a situation that was beginning to gain momentum. Some White Mountain leaders, especially Sánchez, wanted to exact vengeance on the Chiricahuas. And since Ulzana was moving rapidly, it would have been an exercise in futility to track him down. Thus, Sánchez decided to settle his score with the reservation Chiricahuas. Lockett had moved them near Fort Apache after Geronimo's raid. Sánchez's overt hostility concerned Loco and other Chiricahuas. After, all, nearly every man of his band was serving with Crawford. Fortunately, Crook got wind of Sánchez's bellicosity. He ordered Lockett "to watch carefully that no harm comes to the Chiricahuas camped close to the post." To stress further his position, Crook telegraphed the same order to the commanding officer at Fort Apache.[37]

It took the unassailable presence of Chatto to defuse the situation. On returning from his patrol on November 26, he assured the White Mountain chiefs that the Chiricahuas were just as "outraged" as they were. Lieutenant Lockett reported that he was trying to broker "a better feeling on the part of the White Mountain Apaches toward the [reservation] Chiricahuas." The last thing Crook needed was a war between the Chiricahuas and the Cibecue and White Mountain groups at Fort Apache. They had furnished one hundred scouts for Crawford's expedition, of whom forty-two were Chiricahuas. Crawford reached Fort Bowie on Thanksgiving Day, November 26.[38]

That same day, Crook sent several telegrams to Captain Pierce at San Carlos, warning him to prepare for a visit from the hostiles. And since the hostiles probably assumed that the two wives of Ulzana and a "wife of Geronimo's brother" (Perico) were at San Carlos (they were still at Fort Bowie), Crook ordered Pierce to "arm all the Indians you can and scatter them among the camps . . . . Have all the Indians warned and prepared to defend themselves." He also ordered Pierce to send out Al Sieber with scouts to kill or capture Ulzana's party.[39]

Ulzana no longer had the advantage of stealth and surprise. As usual with a Chiricahua raiding party, he moved fast through the mountains by day and the valleys by night. His warriors sliced telegraph wires at several places. On November 28, 1885, he crossed the Gila about twenty miles east of San Carlos. Na-dis-ough saw the hostiles slay a teenage White Mountain boy "with rocks" while stealing horses from Bylas's camp along the Gila. Bylas had been Captain Wirt Davis's most determined scout in his first expedition. Bylas's people reported that the hostiles, who numbered ten men, had killed three Americans before going into the mountains near Black Rock on November 29. If they kept that course, they would drop into the Arivaipa Valley and angle off toward the Dragoon Mountains and Sonora.[40]

On November 28, 1885, Crook met with Crawford's scouts. The conversation was probably direct and to the point. According to the diary of Charles Roberts, whose father, Cyrus, was an aide to General Crook, they had decided not to tell the scouts of Ulzana's slaughter of the White Mountain Apaches for they would "want to go back to Fort Apache." Perhaps Crook's staff debated this, but deception was never the general's trademark. He decided to inform the scouts. According to Harvey Nashkin, a White Mountain scout, Crawford did convey what happened. Chatto gave the Chiricahua scouts a pep talk. The telegraph operator wired his words to Fort Bowie. He urged the scouts "to exterminate the hostile band."[41]

The next day Lieutenant General Philip Sheridan arrived at Fort Bowie to a seventeen-gun salute. With him were his staff and Colonel Luther Bradley, commander of the District of New Mexico. Sheridan had already decided to endorse a policy that would remove every Chiricahua, reservation or hostile, from the Southwest. The only thing left to determine was when and how the government would implement its imperious decision. As expected, Crook strongly disagreed. To support his position, Crook called in Crawford, an officer universally respected by his peers and superiors. Crawford, too, was incredulous at the thought. How could the army expect his Chiricahua scouts to help the military when the same government was ready to betray them and remove them and their families to another region? To Crawford such a decision was unethical and unworthy of the military's code of honor. He presented such a well-reasoned argument that it persuaded Sheridan to postpone the removal. Before leaving the next day, Sheridan agreed officially to turn over the District of New Mexico to Crook's Department of Arizona.[42] Miles predictably took the news as a personal affront, assuming that some underhanded agreement had taken place between Sheridan and Crook to make him look bad.[43]

Meanwhile, Crook had one last meeting with Crawford's team of officers and scouts. They were ready to hunt down the hostiles "as long as we could find one track to follow," wrote Tom Horn.[44] But before they entered Mexico, Crook dispatched the command to cut off Ulzana's raiders in case they tried to get to Mexico via the Dragoon Mountains. They wasted nearly ten days searching for signs but found nothing. Ulzana had returned east to the Mogollon Mountains in New Mexico, killing at least three more men along the way, including Seth and Lorenzo Wright from Safford, whom they ambushed from close range.[45]

During this time, Crook was getting regular reports about the Chiricahuas from his scout below the border, Andrew Ames at Casas Grandes. And with Britton Davis having relocated to the Corralitos hacienda, he provided the general with information and acted as a liaison for Ames.

Mangas and Chihuahua had been in the neighborhood of Casas Grandes. On November 24, 1885, Davis reported to Crook that officials at Casas Grandes had written him that the entire group of hostiles was negotiating there. But only Chihuahua and seven men had come in to trade on November 23, 1885, two weeks after leaving Captain Chaffee eating their trail dust. The fearless but cautious chief had made sure that Terrazas was not near. He had learned not to trust the Mexican military. He listened to the local officials talk treaty and agreed to bring in the other chiefs, but he refused to enter the town. He wanted only to exchange his stolen stock for mescal, food, and other articles before rejoining Naiche in Sonora. Chihuahua mentioned nothing about the other chiefs.[46] In fact, at that time Naiche and Geronimo's raiding parties killed five people in the district of Ures and Sahuaripa in Sonora.[47]

More Chiricahuas came in on December 2, 1885. Unaware of Chihuahua's visit, they had come to check on Daklegon and to talk peace. Their timing could not have been worse. Expecting Chihuahua to bring in the entire band, the military was on hand to seize his party. Instead, Delzhinne, Frijole, Nachol, and two women approached Casas Grandes and solicited peace for Mangas, who had tried to keep his distance from the other chiefs. Years later he characterized his activities after splitting from Geronimo: "No one was chasing me." And he had "no intention to do any harm to anybody." Delzhinne, mounted on his father's horse, made a striking appearance. Terrazas was absent, but federal troops from Mexico's Eleventh Battalion were there, waiting for Chihuahua and other chiefs to fall into their trap.[48]

At Casas Grandes, the small party met with Colonel Gallerdo and Lieutenant Francisco Castro, who claimed that they were anxious to talk terms. Delzhinne made the fatal mistake of trusting him. When the Apaches came near, Castro's soldiers surrounded them. After taking them into custody, Castro had them shackled. One woman agreed to take a message to Mangas, whose camp was near. That night Castro deployed seventy men to an arroyo near town, where they waited in ambush all night. But Mangas never showed.[49]

Little did they know that Mangas now had two warriors, the feeble Eskinolteze and the sixteen-year-old Goso. Knowing that he would share the same fate, Mangas had broken camp and headed south to the Aros River. He would have no contact with the other chiefs until he joined them in Florida in late 1886. Soon after, Lieutenant Joseph Pettit, stationed at Langs ranch, sent three Americans, two civilians and one soldier, disguised as prospectors, to Casas Grandes. They were to find out the latest news of the Chiricahuas. They saw Delzhinne's party secured in leg irons. Joseph Felmer, who had married an Apache in the 1860s and provided good service to Crook in the early 1870s, spoke to Delzhinne. The young Nednhi related the circumstances of his capture. Felmer asked whether he would reveal the location of his band in exchange for liberty. Delzhinne's one-word answer would have made his father proud, "No." On December 19, 1885, the federal soldiers sent them under heavy guard to San Buenaventura. From here, officials transferred them to Chihuahua City and then, on January 6, 1886, to Mexico City, where they eventually died in prison, apparently from smallpox.[50]

About this time, Captain Wirt Davis had reached Carretas. In early December, he sent George Wrattan with a guide to Ramos, where he was to meet Andrew Ames. Ames heard that the Chiricahuas were in the Carcay range, where Chihuahua had headed after his visit to Casas Grandes. Not finding Naiche, he had left toward the Aros River. Over the next seven weeks, Captain Wirt Davis spent time with Britton Davis at Corralitos and met with Joaquin Terrazas, but he never saw a hostile. As Mexicans reported various Apache signs—moccasin tracks (made by Tarahumara sandals) or smoke from mountains (from a hot spring), Captain Wirt Davis dutifully followed up every report of imaginary Apaches. He thought many Mexicans were afflicted with a mental disorder that he termed "Chiricahuas on the brain." On January 2, 1886, he wrote Crook to advise him that the hostiles had left the Casas Grandes area and moved 125 miles south on the Chihuahua side of the Sierra Madre.[51]

Captain Davis's sources were right in one respect. Mangas had retired to the Chihuahua side of the Sierra Madre, north of Dolores. The main body, however, under Chihuahua, Naiche, Geronimo, and Nana had joined for the first time since splitting on May 19, 1885. In mid-October, Naiche and Geronimo had raided near Temosachic, killing three men. And on October 27, they attacked the small mining town of Dolores, below the Aros River, slaying three men and occupying part of the village. After the raids, they moved to the unchartered fastness between the Sátachi River and the Aros River, incredibly rough country that Sonoran troops rarely penetrated.[52] In late January, just as he was preparing to cross the Sierra Madre to the Sonora side, Wirt Davis heard that Crawford had attacked the Chiricahua camp near the Aros River.[53]

We have no idea what was going though the mind of Captain Emmet Crawford on December 11, 1885, when he led his command into Sonora. We do know, however, that seventeen days earlier, while en route to Fort Bowie, he had spent the night at Fort Grant. Here, he renewed acquaintances with an old friend, Captain Charles Cooper. After dinner, they reminisced about their shared experiences. Crawford gave Cooper's family a crash course on Apaches and talked about the upcoming campaign. Though conceding that General Crook's request for his services flattered him, he also revealed that he dreaded another trip into the Sierra Madre Mountains. This time, he had a premonition "that when I go down into Mexico I will not return."[54]

His first stop was at a site about twenty miles north of Fronteras. The next day, he sent Lieutenant Maus ahead to notify authorities there that his command would continue south to Nacozari. Maus heard nothing new of the hostiles. Five days later, on December 17, 1885, they encamped near Nacozari. From here, Noche and Cooney led the command east, crossing the Bavispe

River to the Teras and El Tigre ranges, where they expected to find fresh signs. But Naiche and Geronimo had left the region about a month earlier. Crawford's chief of scouts, Tom Horn, took a detachment of scouts and followed tracks from the Carcay Mountains that led south toward the Aros River. He thought that he had cut the trail of Ulzana's raiders, but they were still in the United States. Instead, his scouts had discovered Chihuahua's party, which was moving south to unite with Naiche. Horn claimed that his scouts doggedly stayed on the trail.[55]

On December 22, 1885, Crawford camped at the ranch of an American named George Woodward, a mile north of Huásabas. Woodward, the same man who had inadvertently killed a scout the previous June, provided him with the latest news on the hostiles, who, he said, were southeast between Nácori Chico and Sahuaripa. Crawford discussed the matter with Noche and other principal scouts. They assured him that they would "find the hostiles if [they are] living in Sonora."[56]

On Christmas Day, Crawford led his command south toward Nácori Chico. Horn left with ten scouts, including Noche, whose knowledge of the Sierra Madre rivaled Geronimo's.[57] Other Chiricahuas with Horn were Tsedekizen, Fatty, Cooney, and Juan Segotset. They would not see Crawford for the next two weeks. Years later Horn recalled his impressions of the captain.

> I did not know Crawford, but he had a great reputation as a "go-to-em" kind of fellow, and no man would look at him and call him afraid or negligent. He looked good to me; he had a regular wolf snap to his jaw. Really, the only thing that I was afraid of was that the country would be too rough [for him]. When I was leaving him fifteen days before he said: "Now Chief, you show me the way and I will be there in Hank Monk time."[58]

Meanwhile, Crawford camped on a plateau two miles south of Nácori Chico. Shortly after his arrival, a courier arrived from Sahuaripa with the news that a week earlier he had seen twelve hostiles driving horses and mules about forty miles south of Nácori. Then another man reported that he had seen two hostiles, one who was lame, between Nácori Chico and Sahuaripa. The scouts assumed this man was Nana. Instead, this was probably Cathla, the wounded warrior from Ulzana's party, who had found his people after his journey from New Mexico. With this intelligence, Crawford recognized an opportunity "to strike a trail." That day, he sent Lieutenant Samson L. Faison and two pack trains to Langs ranch to replenish supplies.

The last day of 1885 Crawford led Daly's pack train, three officers (surgeon Thomas B. Davis, Maus, and Shipp), and the scouts in a march fifteen miles south along Nácori Creek to their base camp of the previous summer. That evening, Deputy Marshal C. B. Kelton arrived from Tombstone with a warrant for the arrest of Dutchy for killing Jacob Ferrin in 1882. Crawford convinced Kelton, a noted guide and frontiersman in his own right, that any attempt to arrest Dutchy would "cause dissatisfaction" among the scouts. Maus said that the scouts became "intensely excited" until Kelton agreed to postpone the arrest and return to Tombstone. Perhaps to divert attention from this delicate situation, Crawford made two announcements: first, he promised a reward of one hundred dollars to the scout who found the hostile camp; second, the command would leave the morning of January 3, 1886. He would take three or four of the toughest pack mules, three packers, and some seventy-five scouts, all on foot, to follow the advance scouts under Horn and Noche toward the Aros River, where Mexicans had reported that Geronimo had made camp. He left Daly in charge of the pack train and a few of the sick scouts.[59]

The night before leaving, the White Mountain shaman named Nah-waz-she-tah (Nosey), "unrolled his sacred buckskin" and held a solemn ceremony, which impressed the American officers. The warriors danced and sang before kneeling and kissing the sacred object. Then, they held a council to proclaim, "They meant to do their duty." Some forty-five years later, the Chiricahua scout Kinzhuna recalled the medicine man's purpose and prophecy: "He went to protect them. What happened next was his secret. If anything was going to happen, he knew it. He sang. That night he told the scouts that . . . we will see Geronimo. And it happened."[60]

Meanwhile, Tom Horn and Noche's scouts were several miles in advance. After fording the Aros River, they cut a trail of five hostiles (probably the same group seen near Huachinera on Christmas Day by Joe Felmer), which merged into a larger one with stolen stock and horses.[61] On January 7, 1886, Horn sent the Bedonkohe corporal Juan Segotset and another scout with dispatches to Crawford. Now that they had struck a trail, the captain sent Segotset to their base camp with orders for Daly to follow with the pack train. Then Crawford led his force across the Aros River into the rugged region between the Sátachi River and the Aros River. Noche, Fatty, and Horn, traveling mostly at night, led the advance team over a difficult trail that led toward Espinosa del Diablo—Devils Backbone—just west of the Chihuahua line.

Crawford's force hiked through what seemed like a maze of canyons and ascended waves of steep ridges and perilous precipices. Along the trail, they came across the carcasses of butchered cattle, clear indications that they were getting closer to the hostiles. From the signs, the scouts announced that Naiche was with Geronimo. Perhaps Naiche, like his father Cochise, preferred to use buckskin horseshoes to protect the feet of his mounts. Lieutenant Shipp thought the "country was so rough that it seemed that nature must have made a special effort in that direction."[62]

Maus appreciated that his Chihenne guides took their responsibilities seriously—especially when it came to his well-being. At some point along the trail, he had left the command to hunt. He had not ventured far from camp when he saw Sergeant Ruby, who was Loco's son-in-law. Ruby had taken his father-in-law's instructions to heart. Because the scouts had discovered signs of the hostiles in the vicinity, Ruby ordered Maus to return to camp. Maus also realized that, despite lacking formal military training, they needed no instructions. The scouts were natural guides and trackers when on the march. Maus marveled at their skill and instincts: "Nothing escaped their watchful eyes as they marched silently in their moccasined feet. . . . Their system of advance guards and flankers was perfect."[63]

Shipp, who had fifteen Chokonens, one Bedonkohe (Binday), and one Nednhi (Fatty) in his Company D, was equally amazed—especially with Noche and his two assistants, Cooney and Fatty. He described the pair as "short, big-chested men with an almost unlimited power of endurance; in their savage way they were as honest and loyal as men could be, and were splendid scouts." If Shipp had any misgivings regarding Crawford's decision to leave the troops behind, they quickly evaporated after he observed the scouts' movements in the Sierra Madre. He explained: "Watching the scouts one could not help thinking how hopeless was the attempt to catch the hostile Chiricahuas with men trained and equipped in the manner of our own soldiers." He also recognized the vast advantages the self-reliant Chiricahua scouts had over their Western Apache counterparts: "The Chiricahuas were a never-ending source of wonder. Their knowledge of country; their powers of observation and deduction; their watchfulness, endurance, and ability to take care of themselves under all circumstances made them seem at times like superior beings from another world." Shipp closed his remarks by observing, "If our little army of 25,000 was composed of such men, and animated by the proper spirit, it would be unconquerable by the best army now existing in Europe." Clearly, the Chiricahua scouts had Shipp's stamp of approval.[64]

About noon on January 9, 1886, Crawford's command resumed its march.[65] At sunset, two scouts from Noche's advance group came into camp with exciting news. They had found the hostiles' camp on a high ridge in the remote region of Espinosa del Diablo, about ten or twelve miles to the southeast. Without hesitation, Crawford decided to make an all-night march, hoping to get into position to attack the camp by dawn. Leaving behind his surgeon (Davis), interpreter (Concepcion), three packers, a few "played out" scouts, and eleven pack miles, he embarked on the fateful trip. With him were Maus, Shipp, Chief of Scouts William H. Harrison, hospital steward Private Frank J. Nemick (G Troop, Fourth Cavalry), and about seventy-seven scouts, half of them Chiricahuas.

The Americans donned moccasins to "avoid making noise." Having already marched for six hours, they faced a grueling twelve-hour trek during a "dark and moonless night over a solid rock mountain, [and] down dark canyons that seemed bottomless." To the Chiricahua scouts, it was just another all-night trip, one they had made repeatedly when they were on the opposing side trying to elude Mexican pursuit. But to the half-dozen Americans—officers and packers—it was a night they never forgot. Lieutenant Shipp, by then unabashedly respectful of the Chiricahua scouts, thought "it was a wonder how the scouts could follow the trail." Lieutenant Maus watched over Crawford like a younger brother. The captain's resolve inspired him. The oldest officer at forty-one, he frequently used his rifle as a walking stick. He survived the ordeal, Maus thought, because of his "unconquerable will."[66]

Shortly before sunrise, January 10, 1886, Crawford's command met up with Noche, Fatty, and Tom Horn. They were northeast of the Chiricahua camp. Sensing an opportunity to bring this campaign to a close, Crawford, after conferring with Noche and Horn, decided to surround the camp. He and Harrison stayed on the north side, while Horn, Maus, and Shipp took a detail of scouts and worked their way to the east, south, and west respectively. To this point, the hostiles had no idea that an American force guided by their own people was within two hundred miles of them. They felt so secure that they posted no sentinels. But they had another form of an early warning system— their mules and burros, "watchdogs of an Indian camp." As the command moved into position, it inevitably displaced a few rocks, which slid down the hill and alerted the burros to danger. They began braying, which alarmed the early risers in camp.[67]

Dawn had not yet broken when three warriors went to the herd to investigate. Then, just as Maus had almost succeeded in getting behind the camp on the south side, he saw "flames bursting from the rifles" in the camp above him. He thought that the hostiles had opened the fight. Scout Harvey Nashkin said the hostiles had fired at a White Mountain scout, Jin-ni-lsa-ke (Jin-ni-ke), a sergeant of scouts under Shipp. But Shipp, who was in position on the west side, believed that the scouts had fired first at a few hostiles who had gone to check on the mules after hearing their cries. Horn agreed with Shipp, saying that the scouts had opened fire prematurely on two warriors because the hostiles were inviting targets for White Mountain scouts bent on avenging kinfolk killed by Ulzana near Fort Apache.[68]

Nevertheless, once the attack began, the chiefs took charge. Because the ranchería was about four hundred yards from the herd, the women and children enjoyed a good head start as they evacuated the camp. The chiefs rallied their men to fight off the scouts. Horn could clearly hear Geronimo's voice ordering the women and children to abandon the village and run southwest toward the Aros River, thus splitting Maus's and Shipp's positions. Poor visibility contributed to the confusion that characterized the moment as each side fired at the other without any casualties.

The scouts launched a haphazard pursuit for a few hours. They were disorganized, however, and most were too wary of the hostiles to get close. Some Chiricahua scouts did succeed in talking with the hostiles. Naiche said he wanted to come in and talk with Crawford. The hostiles, who numbered about eighty in all, with twenty-three or twenty-four men, had abandoned everything—their food, blankets, and stock, thirty head of horses and mules, nearly their entire herd. It was going to be difficult for them to survive in the high mountains without these necessities. Crawford's men occupied the village. Then he waited for Naiche's next move.[69]

The hostiles had two choices: surrender or run. To be sure, they could put distance between themselves and Crawford's detail, but the scouts had already surprised them in what Geronimo considered their safest stronghold. Moreover, Chihuahua and Naiche were concerned because they had not heard a word from Ulzana's party. What happened next must have satisfied the fatigued Crawford. That afternoon Naiche sent a woman into the scout's camp.[70] From her comments, and what Naiche had told the scouts earlier that day, the hostiles were clearly ready to surrender and return (they hoped) to the reservation. Crawford had already sent two scouts to bring up Dr. Davis's party, for the captain needed the services of Concepcion, his Apache-to-Spanish interpreter, who was with Davis. After giving the emissary some food, Crawford agreed to meet the chiefs the next day on a plateau about one mile from camp.

First Lieutenant William Shipp had some misgivings about the fight. He regretted that the early morning conditions had made it difficult "to tell friend from foe." He and Maus had fired only two shots. Had the scouts charged the camp at first fire, he believed that they would have captured the women and children, though he conceded that his company would have paid dearly in blood to accomplish this. Both Maus and Shipp concurred on two telling observations. The White Mountain Apaches feared the hostiles. And the Chiricahua scouts "had little desire to kill their brethren," a sentiment shared by twentieth-century Chiricahuas. The sole exception was Geronimo, for some Chihennes would have shot him down if given the opportunity. Horn's recollections specifically mentioned the good work that the Chihenne Tsedekizen, a sergeant with Maus, did in pursuing the hostiles.[71]

Crawford, expecting no trouble from the hostiles, bivouacked about one hundred yards above the abandoned ranchería. That afternoon, the scouts gathered up the useless material and burned it. Recognizing that everyone was dead tired from twenty-four hours of marching and fighting, Crawford allowed the command to catch up on their sleep around "big fires" that were lit to provide some comfort in the bitter cold nights. One Chiricahua scout, on sentry duty with five others on a hill east of camp, became concerned when most of the sentinels fell asleep. He attributed this unusual phenomenon to the supernatural. And with Geronimo nearby, he was convinced that the shaman had shot a "sleeping spell on the whole outfit." So the scout, who may have been the Chihenne Eskin-zion (later known as Jim Miller), employed his own ceremony to counteract Geronimo's Power. So he "sang and sang, and finally all woke up." When Geronimo saw that the scout's ceremony had compromised his Power, he began "yelling at the medicine man."[72]

Although Crawford was exhausted, he must have gone to sleep satisfied that he had accomplished the major part of his objective. He knew that he yet faced a difficult march to the border. But he and Crook had carried out a march in 1883 with four times the number of hostiles. For now, he needed a good night's sleep. He would plan his next move after he spoke to the hostile chiefs the next morning.

23

THE ROAD TO EMBUDOS CANYON

It has been so sad about poor Crawford—murdered like a dog.
First Lieutenant Marion P. Maus to Cyrus Roberts,
January 23, 1886

All the momentum bought by the capture of the hostiles' camp evaporated suddenly and irrevocably before Crawford's command had its first cup of coffee the morning of January 11, 1886, the darkest hour of the campaign. Western Apache scout Harvey Nashkin, a veteran of campaigns dating from the Victorio War, rose before dawn that morning. A sergeant in Company B under Maus, he immediately started a fire. It was about 6:00 A.M., still dark, misty, and foggy. No one knew that a Chihuahuan force of 128 men, Tarahumara Indians from the villages south of Yepómera, were near. With only a few burros to carry supplies and ammunition for their Remington rifles, the Tarahumaras had marched for seventeen days from the eastern side of the Sierra Madre.

Ninety minutes later, a few of Crawford's Apache scouts cried out that Mexicans were coming; moments later, the scouts, assuming they were Captain Wirt Davis's command, began shouting out in Apache, expecting a response from his Apache scouts. Instead, the Tarahumaras, who had taken positions "in white rocks in the hills" some two hundred yards above the scouts, responded with a volley from their .44-caliber Remington rifles. Nashkin was incredulous. It seemed to him that the shooters had targeted his position, for the gunfire had scattered the embers of his campfire and wounded three scouts, one of whom was sleeping. The dazed scouts fled to cover behind rocks.[1]

Believing the attack was the product of a simple misunderstanding, most scouts did not return fire. Yet, the few who did shoot, a half-dozen or so Chiricahua scouts on a high ridge east of camp, responded vigorously. Meanwhile, the three American officers, who had been sleeping together near a campfire, responded at once. Crawford ordered Maus and Shipp, with Tom Horn, to "go ahead and see about it." The two lieutenants and Horn raced to the scene. Crawford borrowed a white handkerchief from the hospital steward, Private Nemick, and followed them. The Americans called out to the Mexicans, repeatedly identifying themselves as American soldiers. Finally, fifteen minutes after the first shot, the firing ceased. Only a few scouts had returned fire, which led the Mexican officers to conclude erroneously that Crawford's command was small and lacked ammunition. It was a fatal assumption.

With this lull in the action, Maus, Crawford, and Horn (each unarmed) emerged from the rocks to meet ten Mexicans (all armed), under their commander Major Mauricio Corredor. A tall, powerfully built man from Arisiachic, Chihuahua, he had earned statewide fame as the slayer of Victorio. Fifteen of his soldiers moved around in front and to the right of the American peace party. Unknown to the Americans, Corredor's force had no peaceful intentions. Treachery was their plan. Once the unarmed Americans emerged from cover, they planned to overpower them and take as many Apache scalps as possible. Had Corredor realized that the Apaches were scouts hunting down the hostiles it probably would not have mattered. After all, their hair brought the same bounty as that of a hostile.[2]

Horn was about one hundred feet in advance of Maus and Crawford, who was waving a white handkerchief as a sign of peace. They watched as Major Corredor and three or four men walked briskly past Horn toward them, ignoring his greetings. Crawford and Maus approached to within six feet of Corredor (who looked nervous and frightened) when the lieutenant said, in Spanish: "Don't you see we are American soldiers. Look at my uniform and the captain's." Corredor now seemed to have second thoughts about carrying out his double cross. He seemed genuinely sorry, explaining that they assumed the scouts were hostiles.

Behind each group of officers were Indians who were mortal enemies of each other. Though the Western Apache scouts had had no contact with the Tarahumaras on the Chihuahua side of the Sierra Madre, the Chiricahuas and the Tarahumaras were bitter foes. The latter had helped Terrazas defeat Victorio at Tres Castillos and had single-handedly struck the devastating blow to Juh at Sátachi Falls. Supremely confident of a surefire victory that promised valuable spoils and cash for hair, they were not about to back down from a fight. After all, the Chihuahua treasury had reportedly paid Corredor two thousand pesos for Victorio's scalp.[3]

Harvey Nashkin could hear one Mexican telling his men that the "scouts' hair was good and long and that this was the best thing to make hair ropes of, so kill all of them, and we will get their hair."[4] The rhetoric between the two tribes grew more heated. With their leaders insulting each other, neither side had anyone to control the boiling rage of their men. Chiricahua oral history agrees that both sides were challenging the other's manhood. It would appear that the taunts gained momentum as their officers talked. The Chiricahuas said: "Don't run [away] if you are men [for] you are going to meet up with men today." They were surely referring to the large number of women and children killed or captured at Tres Castillos and Sátachi Falls. The Tarahumaras defended their bravery: "We are the troops that cleaned out Victorio's bunch. . . . We killed Victorio and we can kill every one of you."[5] The Tarahumara machismo rankled in the breasts of the Chiricahua scout leaders. Each had lost kinfolk at either Tres Castillos or Sátachi Falls. Tsedekizen, the audacious Chihenne leader of Maus's Company A, was ready to lead his men into battle.

During this back and forth banter, the scouts had brought up a pack mule and begun to replenish their cartridge belts. Then one Chiricahua, probably Fatty, declared, "All right, get ready. We are going to fire on you right now."[6] The American and Mexican officers were unaware of the critical moment until they heard the "sharp snap of the breechloaders" as the scouts inserted their cartridges. However, Major Corredor, who had seen the heads and rifles of fifty to sixty scouts concealed in rocks thirty yards in front of him, became noticeably nervous. He began to back away from open ground toward Horn. While the parley was going on, which lasted less than ten minutes, other Mexicans moved around to their left, toward the highest hill on Crawford's right flank. Crawford, sensing the explosive situation, said to Maus, "For God's sake, don't let them fire." Corredor and another officer, realizing that they had based their treachery on faulty assumptions, said, "No tiros, No tiros" (Don't shoot, don't shoot), imploring Crawford to restrain his scouts. Now, Maus pivoted and walked briskly toward the scouts, ordering them not to shoot. Crawford "climbed on a five-foot high rock, conspicuous above every other object," waving his flag of truce. About twenty-five yards from the captain, one member of Corredor's peace party had taken cover near a "little tree." Evidently the one designated to open the double cross, he fired the first shot, sending a bullet into Crawford's forehead, mortally wounding the stoic captain.[7]

Immediately the firing became general as the Mexicans deliberately took aim at every American. Corredor turned to Horn and smiled as he snapped off a round at the unarmed scout, wounding him in the arm; another Tarahumara took two shots at Private Nemick (just missing him), and others targeted Shipp and Maus, but they missed their marks. Both escaped to cover, with one Chiricahua scout grabbing Shipp and pulling him to safety. Once the fight erupted, "no Power could stop the firing," observed Lieutenant Maus. Within seconds, the scouts pummeled Corredor's party, unleashing a hail of bullets on the architects of the duplicity. Meanwhile, Maus turned to see Major Corredor seeking safety near the foot of the high hill on their right flank. However, three scouts were "lying very close and could not be seen." One was the Bedonkohe warrior Binday, likely the son of She-neah, the clairvoyant shaman killed in the Mata Ortiz fight. He took deliberate aim and shot Corredor through the heart. Dutchy, who was Crawford's orderly, slew the man who had shot Crawford. Thirteen Apache bullets pierced the body of Corredor's second in command, Lieutenant Juan de la Cruz, whose brother watched in horror. In less than a minute, the loyal scouts had killed or wounded nine of the ten-man "peace party." Twenty-five years later, Mithlo boasted to Major Hugh L. Scott that the faithful scouts "had held [their] ground and did not run away."[8]

Shipp stated that most of the fighting was done by one company of Chiricahua scouts. This concurs with Chiricahua oral history, which singled out Sergeant Tsedekizen, who was reckless with his life, for he possessed Power over guns. Several times he demonstrated bravery in the teeth of the combat. At the opening of the battle, he led a handful of like-minded followers and emerged from cover to get better angles from which to shoot at Corredor's peace party. Said one Chiricahua eyewitness, "All the soldiers shot at him but couldn't hit him. One who might want to shoot him would fall down or drop his gun. Then Tsedekizen would kill him instead." His inspired followers, fueled by adrenaline and guided by instincts sharpened since their dikohe training, fought to avenge their loved ones captured or killed at Tres Castillos and Sátachi Falls.

Maus sent Tsedekizen with a company of Chiricahua scouts, to thwart a Tarahumara attempt to flank them and take the high ground. The Chiricahuas showed their mettle, holding the point and driving away the aggressors. Finally, realizing their situation was hopeless for assault, the Tarahumaras withdrew to a series of hills between three and five hundred yards west of the American force. During this second fight, "not one of the scouts got so much as a scratch." According to Shipp, the Americans did not fire a round during the second sortie.[9] After the firing subsided, Tsedekizen asked Horn for permission to launch an offensive against the Tarahumaras, but Horn held him back.[10]

Years later, Tsedekizen, Cooney, Tuzzone, Astoye, Kinzhuna, and Guydel-kon would laugh in amusement as they remembered how Corredor's party fell "over each other trying to get out of the way."[11] The commanding officers of both armies were either dead or mortally wounded. The Tarahumaras were demoralized, indecisive, and desperate. Their two officers were dead. Without the steadying hand of Corredor, a beloved figure in Chihuahua, they seemed lost. In contrast, the American and Apache force, led by Maus, Shipp, Noche, and Tsedekizen had risen to the occasion.

Despite a wound in his arm, Tom Horn opened up a dialogue with the Mexicans, now led by Sergeant Santa Ana Perez. They were afraid to come to Maus's camp, so Horn courageously went out alone to theirs, some three hundred yards away. An intrepid Maus joined him, and together they brokered yet another cease-fire.

As expected, the mortal wounds suffered by their beloved captain had, as one officer described it, "cast a gloom that we could not shake off." They found Crawford lying below the boulder that he had mounted. He had a "ghastly wound" in his head, with his brains splattered over his face. His orderly, Dutchy, bound his head with a red cloth. Though Crawford was still breathing, it was only a matter of time. About that moment, the two scouts dispatched by Crawford the day before came in with Concepcion, Davis, a few packers, and ten pack mules. They brought needed food and ammunition. Davis could do nothing for Crawford. Maus magnanimously allowed Davis to treat five Mexicans wounded in the fight.[12]

The hostiles had watched the battle from the bluffs across the river. They still wanted to discuss terms, but not until the Tarahumaras left the area. Of the remaining Americans, the man they were most familiar with was the second chief of scouts, William Harrison, whom they knew from their days at Ojo Caliente in the early 1870s.[13] They knew nothing of Maus or Shipp and were barely acquainted with Horn, despite his published tales to the contrary. They had faith in Crawford, understood that he was Crook's righthand man, and remembered his fair decisions as agent. If Crawford had lived, they would have surrendered to him and accompanied him north.[14]

The day after the battle, January 12, 1886, Lieutenant Maus and Concepcion brought six horses (the hostiles' confiscated stock) to the Tarahumaras' camp. The Tarahumaras rejected the horses and claimed that Maus was in Mexico illegally. Detaining Maus, they allowed Concepcion to return to camp for documents from Crawford's belongings to prove that they were legally in Mexico. When Concepcion explained the situation, the Apache scouts "began stripping for a fight, taking positions in the rocks, [and] shouting defiantly" at their hated foes. According to at least one account, the hostiles joined in the fun, sending word that they would join the scouts "to thrash" their common enemies.[15] These threats took the starch from the Tarahumaras, who had no appetite for another clash. Maus settled the dispute, agreeing to send six mules to the Mexicans so they could transport their wounded back to Chihuahua.[16]

The next day Maus decided to break camp and return to Nácori Chico. They had nearly depleted their rations, their cartridge belts were almost empty, and their pack train under Daly was somewhere in the hinterlands to the northwest. They hoped that the hostiles would honor their promises to Crawford. The important matter at hand was to separate from the Tarahumaras, for the hostiles would not come in until Maus accomplished that. Under a steady rain the first day, the command trudged west four miles before bivouacking near a creek. Everyone had taken turns carrying the two seriously wounded men, Crawford and one scout. That night Geronimo sent a messenger to Maus, asking for a meeting the next morning. He insisted that Maus and his escort come to the conference unarmed.[17]

Early the morning of January 14, Maus, Horn, Noche, and four scouts met with two Chiricahuas, one of whom was Nat-cul-baye. They promised that the chiefs would be in the next day. Geronimo, Naiche, Chihuahua, and Nana appeared the next morning, January 15. Although Naiche was the nominal chief (according to Santiago McKinn, the others in the band addressed him as *nantan*, meaning leader), Geronimo opened the conversation by asking Maus the purpose of his mission. Maus never wavered: "I came to capture or destroy you and your band." After this direct response, the chiefs agreed to meet General Crook "near the line in one month." In a later report, Maus was more specific, placing the location "near San Bernardino." As a show of good faith, the next day, January 16, they turned over Nana, one other warrior, and seven women and children, which included one wife (Ih-tedda) and daughter of Geronimo and one wife and a son of Naiche. Geronimo promised Noche that he would send word to him if something happened to prevent them from keeping their commitment.[18]

506 FROM COCHISE TO GERONIMO

Then they went their separate ways. Maus's command met Daly's pack train and continued to Nácori Chico; en route, on January 17, 1886, Captain Crawford miraculously opened his eyes and put his arm around Lieutenant Maus, who assured him that he would "arrange his affairs." Crawford could only shake his head in response before he lost consciousness five minutes later. He took his last breath the next day. Both lieutenants labeled his death an assassination.[19]

The man most affected by Crawford's death was naturally Lieutenant Marion Maus. The weight of command had fallen on his shoulders, and he had responded to the challenge. He finally reached Nácori Chico on January 22, 1885, where he secured four boards, nailed them together, and buried Crawford.

After sending a courier to Crook, Maus was anxious to put distance between his command and the "infernal Mexicans," as he called them. On January 22, 1886, he began his "homeward march." He passed by Bacadéhuachi on January 24 and Huachinera three days later. On January 28, the detail went by Bacerac and Bavispe. At both places, the Mexicans "made unfriendly demonstrations." At Bavispe, 140 Mexican troops were there, and their commander insisted on escorting Maus's command "out of the country." Maus knew his scouts would not tolerate the presence of Mexican troops. He warned the commander that if they came, "it would mean war." Fortunately, Major Emilio Kosterlitzky interceded and the troops kept their distance. That evening Maus's command camped at Cañada de Janos, about seven miles from Bavispe.[20]

With one crisis averted, Maus soon faced another unexpected situation. That evening the merchants of Bavispe smuggled a "large quantity" of mescal into the scouts' camp. The Apaches had cash confiscated from the Chiricahuas' ranchería; the sellers had mescal. Both sides were happy with the arrangement. But not Maus. Despite his precautions, the Mexicans sold the mescal and "got half of my command drunk." Either that evening, or early the next morning, he faced a volatile situation. For some reason, bad blood was simmering between one company of White Mountain scouts and one company of Chiricahua scouts. Mescal was the fuse that nearly touched off a bloody confrontation. What we do know is this: the Chiricahuas and White Mountains loaded their rifles and squared off at each other, ready to fire. Between their lines was a brawl between the first sergeants of each company (either Noche or Tsedikizen for the Chiricahuas). Maus's intervention prevented a pitched battle from occurring. He finally crossed the border and reached Langs ranch on February 1, 1886.[21]

The loss of Crawford was a bitter pill for Crook and officers who had served with him. His men had lost an inspirational leader, a highly principled man who was always calm and reassuring. Lieutenant Shipp had served with him for two months. He succinctly described the traits personified by Crawford: "It would be well if all of us could keep in our minds the memory of this devoted and chivalrous soldier, whose whole life was one long sacrifice, and whose death was the direct result of his efforts to save others. . . . Let us try to remember this one as our ideal of what a true man should be."[22]

Crawford's death devastated Crook. Normally not an impetuous man, in a private moment he lashed out at Mexicans, saying that if he had been there, "his troops would have whipped those Mexicans well." He issued General Field Orders Number 2, paying homage to his friend and subordinate.

> Fort Bowie, January 30, 1886
> With feelings of the deepest sorrow, The Brigadier General Commanding announces the death of Captain Emmet Crawford, 3rd Cavalry . . . . His loss is irrepressing. . . . Brave as a lion, tender and gentle as a woman, always averse to alluding to his own achievements, temperate, noble, and wise, who was during his life, an honor to his profession and in death is an example to his comrades.[23]

Meanwhile, as Maus and the scouts were working their way north, Chihuahua also had gone north with five or six men to search for Ulzana, who was long overdue.

In early December, Ulzana had decided to return to the Mogollon Mountains in New Mexico. On December 5, he and his party had ransacked the Mule Springs ranch, a dozen miles west of Cactus Flats, and taken ten horses. The next morning, December 6, 1885, six Indians surprised George Kinney and Charles Clarke, who were repairing a wagon, and riddled them with bullets. The hostiles also took Kinney's 45-60 Sharps rifle and forty rounds of ammunition. After receiving this dispatch, Crook predicted that Ulzana would attempt to return to Mexico through the Good Sight and Florida mountains. Ulzana continued to be anything but predictable.[24]

Three days later, they burned Lillie's ranch near Clear Creek, not far from the head of the middle fork of the Gila River, killing two more men, Lillie and Prior. The sun had just disappeared over the horizon when the raiders leisurely left the burning cabin and began to pack their horses with the stolen loot. Much to their astonishment, they saw eleven Americans (three citizens, Lieutenant Samuel W. Fountain, and seven troopers) on foot, sprinting across the valley toward them, shooting as they ran. Ulzana abandoned everything except two horses as his band fled up the hill behind Lillie's cabin. From the ridge, Ulzana's party opened a firefight, which featured the deafening volley from Kinney's 45-60 Sharps rifle, but no one was hurt. Fountain, in his initial report written two days after the fight, placed Ulzana's party at sixteen, including two women, but we know that the raiders numbered ten men and the two women and one boy taken near Fort Apache. Fountain's brave men captured everything—fourteen horses (seven from the Mule Springs ranch raid), one mule, twenty-six blankets, and one Winchester rifle with ammunition. In his report to headquarters, he admitted, "I have no idea if this is the last of the struggle in the Mogollons."[25]

Fountain and Ulzana would meet again. Needing horses, Ulzana set his sight on the Siggins ranch at Dry Creek, not far from the main road to Alma. This time he turned the tables on the brave Fountain, with far more tragic results. In mid-December, C. P. Elliott from Siggins ranch had seen signs of Apaches along Dry Creek, two miles from the ranch. The morning of December 19, 1885, had dawned stormy and overcast, a gloomy precursor to a tragedy that no one, except perhaps Ulzana, had seen coming.

Fountain's command consisted of one officer, a surgeon, nineteen cavalrymen, ten Navajo scouts, and two civilian scouts (including J. McKinney, who had been so valuable in the earlier patrol). Fountain had labored behind the main body, suffering from the debilitating effect of dysentery and trying to hurry the Navajo scouts' exit from camp. Once he had accomplished that, he galloped forward and joined the rear of the column. Suddenly, he heard one shot, followed by a volley of fire, directed at the vanguard of his men.

Scout McKinney, who had been riding side by side with a courier going to Silver City, was in front of the column. Before they reached Soldiers Hill, the messenger took another trail, leading off to the east. Behind McKinney were Assistant Surgeon Thomas J. C. Maddox, Lieutenant De Rosey Cabell, and a half-dozen troopers. Oblivious to danger, several cavalrymen had begun to sing a song, "Good-By, My Lover, Good By." For some, it would be their last words. Halfway up the hill, the trail turned sharply right. Ulzana allowed McKinney to ascend two-thirds the way along the narrow trail leading toward a saddle at the crest; then he sprung the trap from the ridge about forty yards away. It was 8:30 in the morning.

Two men lay concealed with Ulzana on the ridge; he had placed seven more warriors in two groups hidden in the brush and rocks below on his flanks. In an ambush of this type, the chief usually fired the first shot as a signal for the others to open fire. McKinney said that one Apache on the ridge smiled at him before firing a shot. He had likely seen Ulzana, opening the battle. But McKinney's horse had seen a reflection from the barrel of Ulzana's rifle and instinctively jerked its head, saving the life of the scout. The bullet smashed into the forehead of his steed, killing it instantly, and pinning McKinney's Winchester rifle in the scabbard under the horse. McKinney finally extricated his rifle and responded, picking off one Apache, he thought, but there was no Apache blood spilled that day. The second cross-fire volley from nine rifles in three positions killed Private Frank Hutton and wounded Maddox and Corporal Wallace McFarland. At the base of the hill, Fountain and Lieutenant Cabell dismounted and rushed to the aid of their fallen comrades. As they crossed the road, the Apache fire killed two more privates. At least four men tried to rescue Maddox, who warned them not to try, for he thought his wound was fatal. Regardless, Private Daniel Collins, a blacksmith, tried to aid him before the Apaches mortally wounded him and then killed Maddox. They also wounded Lieutenant Cabell in the hand.

Fountain and several men made their way up the ridge from the right flank as "the firing was continued at close range." He joined the Navajo scouts who had climbed the ridge shortly before him. The brief but deadly clash ended when Ulzana abandoned the ridge. According to Fountain, his soldiers thought they had wounded a few Apaches before they slipped from view into the "rough country where horses can not go." In all, Fountain had lost five men killed and three wounded. In the aftermath, he was utterly devastated, in "severe shock," thought one man who met him that evening.[26]

Fountain remarked later that the Indians were "so close that I am sure that I recognized one of the hostiles and spoke to him at San Antonio [September 1886] when Geronimo and his band were turned over to me by Captain Lawton." Fountain told him, "You and I exchanged shots in the fight at Dry Creek and missed each other." The Apache, who was either Perico or Yahnozha, both renowned marksmen, did not deny his involvement. His defense was, "No, it was not I. I never miss my man." Naiche simply smiled when he heard the explanation.[27]

By then, Ulzana had decided to leave New Mexico. On December 24, 1885, he found his ticket to Mexico—forty horses at Steeple Rock, north of Carlisle, near which they killed three men and wounded two or three others. On Christmas Day, they crossed the Gila near Duncan, Arizona, and continued their dash south at a furious speed. Lieutenant John McDonald arrived with thirty-four Navajo scouts, who promptly refused to follow the trail below the Gila River. From Duncan, a company of Arizona Rangers pursued and pressured them to abandon "eleven horses and mules, one gun, one butcher knife, a sack of beef, and an old fashioned shot pouch with powder horn." After following for two days, the rangers' horses gave out. In the early hours of December 26, Ulzana crossed the San Simon Valley to the Chiricahua Mountains, only a dozen miles from Crook's headquarters. That morning they set upon two men near Galeyville, Deputy Sheriff Casper Albert and Bill Reese, killing both before traversing the Chiricahua Mountains in heavy snowfall.[28]

After holing up in the Chiricahuas for two days, in the early evening on December 29, 1885, Ulzana led his raiders into the Sulphur Springs Valley. He rounded the Swisshelm Mountains, took four old horses from Whitley's ranch, and continued southwest toward the Mule Mountains. The next day, his men waylaid two men driving a buggy from Crouch's ranch to Tombstone. The two men saw twelve Apaches emerge from cover forty yards away to fire a volley at them. One bullet creased the nose of one man. The skittish horses ran away, overturning the buggy, and throwing the men clear. They ran back to Crouch's ranch, where, later that day, about dusk, the raiders committed their last depredation on United States soil. According to eyewitness Charles Crouch, thirteen Apaches stole thirteen horses from his father's pasture. As mentioned before, this was the correct number for Ulzana' party—ten men and their captives from Fort Apache, two women and one boy.[29]

That evening one of the prisoners, the White Mountain woman named Nadis-ough, found herself at the rear of the band, which, she said, was riding "as rapidly as possible." Throughout the thirty-five days that she was a prisoner of Ulzana, the men had kept a close eye on her. The Chiricahuas had warned the three captives that they would kill anyone who tried to escape. Moreover, to frighten them further, they had vowed to "cut their heads off" as Sánchez had done to Azariquelch. When the horse in front of her disappeared into the night, she turned her mount off the trail and went west. After she was sure that her captors were not following her, she rested in the mountains until daybreak. The next morning, several cowboys from Crouch's ranch saw her riding one of the stolen horses and took her into custody. They brought her to Tombstone, where the sheriff arrested her for horse stealing. Fortunately, John Clum happened to be living there and served as her interpreter at the hearing held on January 6, 1885. She explained that she had escaped from her captors, the Chiricahuas. Clum telegraphed Captain Pierce at San Carlos, and he verified her story, writing that it "is undoubtedly true."[30]

Meanwhile, on December 31, 1885, Ulzana finally crossed into Sonora a few miles southeast of the San Pedro River, far to the west of the canyons that they usually traversed to enter Mexico. His raiders had been in the United States for nearly two months. Deadly ambushes were his calling card. In the public's eyes, he had completely embarrassed the military, which was powerless either to find him or to impede his operations. He had paralyzed activities and disrupted travel and commerce in southwestern New Mexico and southeastern Arizona. His men had killed without quarter, intimidated settlements, and had, unwittingly, set the wheels in motion for a tougher federal Indian policy toward all Chiricahuas, peaceful or hostile.

Had the raid accomplished its objectives? No, for they had not recovered their families, thanks to Crook's quick transfer of their families to San Carlos, and they had not taken vengeance on Chatto or any other scouts for their role in the attack on Chihuahua's ranchería. Ulzana's raid had sown hostility and distrust between the reservation White Mountain people and the reservation Chiricahuas. According to Crook's tally, while Ulzana was in New Mexico and Arizona, his raiders had killed thirty-eight persons and stolen over 250 horses and mules. He had lost one man, the promising young Azariquelch, slain by Sánchez. If anything, the general had understated the fatalities. Considering everything, Ulzana's raid with his small band ranked with Nana's raid as the most remarkable Chiricahua foray from Mexico during the 1880s.[31]

Safely in Sonora, Ulzana's party put four bullets into a vaquero drinking at a spring south of the custom house. They took his pistol and horse and headed for the heart of the San Jose Mountains, bivouacking below the summit of a peak that soared to 8,356 feet. With no troops dogging them for the first time in six weeks, the raiders rested here for several days before heading south on January 6.[32]

On the evening of January 7, 1886, three travelers reached Bacoachi with news that they had seen a trail of fifteen mounted Apaches coming south from the San Jose Mountains. Another party reached Bacoachi to report that they had discovered tracks of ten Apaches driving ten cattle in the Purica Mountains, east of Nacozari. The trail was at least a day old, for we know that at 11:00 A.M. on January 8, 1886, Ulzana's party fired two volleys at three men at Pozo Hediondo, the site of the celebrated January 1851 fight between one hundred Sonoran troops under future governor Ignacio Pesqueira and three hundred Chiricahuas under Mangas Coloradas.[33] Only Ulzana may have participated in that fight; the others had undoubtedly heard the stories from their elders, especially Geronimo, who had enhanced his reputation in the battle.

Francisco García and his two companions left behind two burros, hoping that would satisfy Ulzana. He took them and led his men to the mountains, probably returning to the Teras or El Tigre Mountains, where Chihuahua met him about January 22.[34]

Meanwhile, General Crook could only wait until he heard from the hostiles. Patience, however, was not a virtue in our nation's capital. Two days before year's end, Sheridan, upon hearing from President Cleveland, asked Crook for information, preferably positive, or at least something to hang his hat on. Silver City officials had sent two telegrams in nine days to the president, itemizing the murders carried out by Ulzana's party and condemning the military's ineffectiveness. Although somewhat exaggerated (for example, they claimed that "all outlying ranchers are deserted [and] every industry is prostrated"), it drew attention to their plight. In response to Sheridan, Crook recited the current state of operations but refused to predict the immediate rosy outcome that Sheridan longed to hear.[35]

Crook believed in keeping them his superiors on a need-to-know basis. Isolated at Bowie, he remained oblivious to the inner workings of Washington. He had no idea that the political landscape beneath him was shifting, and that his superiors were approaching the intersection of change, one that the commander-in-chief, President Cleveland, was contemplating because he had lost confidence in Crook. Sheridan still supported his West Point roommate, believing that Crook remained the preeminent military man when it came to the Chiricahuas.

Both Miles and Crook had their supporters in Congress. Miles had influential advocates from civilian and business interests in the Southwest, which was beginning to tip the scales in his favor. Even more telling, Crook enjoyed support from only two newspapers in Arizona, the *Star* in Tucson, and the *Courier* in Prescott. Both continued to carry his water. But the remainder, particularly the *Arizona Silver Belt* and the *Tombstone Epitaph* were censorious of Crook's methods, especially his reliance on the Chiricahua scouts.[36]

Crook's supporters in Congress met with Cleveland "to protest against Crook's removal" but the president disingenuously denied the rumor that he was even considering this action. Cleveland told one southwesterner, the former Mescalero agent William Llewellyn, that he "had great confidence" in Crook, but "the killing of settlers must stop." Even Llewellyn, once a staunch admirer of Crook, thought he had made two mistakes: he relied too much on the Chiricahua scouts and failed to "fill the mountains of southern New Mexico and Arizona with soldiers." These two opinions, repeated frequently by the press, had become indisputable facts in the minds of Crook's critics. One officer, Lieutenant John Bigelow, stationed at the Mowry mines in the Patagonia Mountains, opined in his diary that the officers had mixed opinions on the question of Crook's policies. If Crook was concerned about rumors and the rumblings Washington, he failed to show it.[37]

All was quiet at Fort Bowie until the utterly melancholic news of Crawford's death reached Crook. Maus, who had arrived at Langs ranch in southwestern New Mexico on February 1, 1886, had little time to reflect on what had occurred. After the taxing events of the previous month, he must have assumed that Crook, normally a sponge for information and details, would want to be briefed on what had happened. Maus needed to meet Crook, explain the reasons behind his decisions, and perhaps get a pat on the back for "bringing the command out safely." He feared that uninformed officers might second-guess his actions: "I don't want any reflections cast upon me and won't have it." Under extraordinarily trying circumstances, he had acted decisively at critical moments. It is difficult to imagine anyone handling the situation any better.[38]

While Maus recuperated at Langs ranch (he had hardly slept on the return march, watching his Apache prisoners), Crook left Bowie for two days to hunt snipe and ducks at San Simon. As each day went by without word from the commander, Maus became more desperate to talk to someone. He longed to speak to the general before he headed south to meet the hostiles. He found a friendly ear with Captain Cyrus Swan Roberts, Crook's aide, who was living with his boss at Fort Bowie. Recognizing Maus's fragile state of mind, Roberts had written to him a few personal letters that had provided comfort. In Maus's letter of February 6, he thanked Roberts for his "kind letters." He lamented, "I wish I could see you and talk to you."[39]

The events of the past month, combined with Crook's inexplicable silence, which Maus must have interpreted as disapproval, tormented the brave lieutenant. Yet, for some reason, Crook had no plans to meet with Maus. Whether the general had deliberately snubbed Maus is unclear. He clearly had no empathy for what Maus had been through and seemed unwilling to recognize what he had accomplished under tremendously trying circumstances. It was possible that Crawford's death had so afflicted Crook that it impaired his judgment. Or maybe it was just part of Crook's peculiar personality and leadership style. Unlike Miles, who cultivated feelings of loyalty from his subordinates and "made friends who swore by him," Crook, according to one officer who had served under him, "expected the greatest sacrifices from his subordinates while doing nothing for them."[40]

Four days after Maus reached Langs ranch, Crook ordered him to return to Mexico to set up a base camp below San Bernardino to await the hostiles. Crook gave him no authority to discuss terms. Maus's assignment was to open communications and keep them in camp until Crook arrived to negotiate. Although the order disappointed many scouts, who were hoping to return to their families at Fort Apache, at least they would not face the daily grind of dealing with Mexicans and campaigning in the Sierra Madre.[41]

The next day, February 6, 1886, he left Langs ranch and stopped at Guadalupe Canyon. That evening, he wrote a note to Crook's aide, Captain Cyrus Roberts. Maus, clearly troubled, was reaching out for help and understanding. He had heard rumors that armchair quarterbacks were suggesting that he should have responded more forcefully after the Mexicans had slain Crawford. And he may have heard about Crook's first reaction, that "he would have turned in and whipped these Mexicans well," which seemed to be the popular sentiment of many army officers, each unfamiliar with the enormous challenges confronted by Maus along the Aros River.[42]

Despite Crook's silence, Maus felt duty bound to complete the mission to ensure that Crawford's death was not in vain. Although hopeful that the hostiles would fulfill their promises, he cautioned Roberts to make sure that Dorst's command remained in place at Carretas. He felt that Naiche and his band would surrender. He thought the others were prepared to "sacrifice Geronimo," if necessary, in exchange for favorable terms. He assured Crook, "I can get [his] head." Because Crook had given him no orders about terms, Maus wanted to know what he could offer to close the deal. On February 7, 1886, Maus led his men to a camp along San Bernardino Creek. The first report had his location five miles south of the line; later reports placed the distance between eight and ten miles. Maus waited to hear from the Chiricahuas.[43]

Meanwhile, at Bowie, Crook made plans for the conference. On February 1, 1886, Sheridan had sent a telegram to remind him to adhere to the policy set on September 30, 1885, which stated that the hostiles must surrender as prisoners of war and agree to go to Florida. The government would never allow them to return to the Southwest. Sheridan gave Crook a little wiggle room, however, instructing him "not to make any promises to the hostiles unless it is necessary to secure their surrender." On February 10, 1886, Crook telegraphed his superior, General Pope, that he was waiting to hear exactly "where the renegades want to talk to me," thereby confirming that the eventual place of the meeting, Embudos Canyon, was not prearranged.[44]

In mid-February, Maus, concerned that the hostiles might raid the reservation, allowed a small party of scouts to investigate affairs at Fort Apache. The scouts were unaware that the Chiricahuas were then raiding in two bands the districts of Sahuaripa and Moctezuma. Noche and Charley selected Dutchy and Gon-altsis (Chatto's brother) to go to Fort Apache. They expected to be gone for twenty days. En route, they stopped at Bowie, met with Crook, and told him that the Chiricahuas would surrender, but that they would not be in until mid-March. After the interview, Crook concluded that the hostiles "are very cautious and suspicious and may not be willing to surrender unconditionally."[45]

To increase the odds of success, he enlisted the help of his trusted friend, the White Mountain chief Alchesay, then at Fort Apache, and the mother of Naiche, Cochise's widow Dos-teh-seh, who, he assumed, was at Fort Apache. She, however, had moved to San Carlos with her daughter, Naithlotonz, who had married Gokliz, a San Carlos Apache. Crook ordered Lieutenant Lockett at Apache to furnish Alchesay with transportation to San Carlos, where he was to pick up Dos-teh-seh. On February 10, 1886, with a sergeant as escort, they boarded a stage at Fort Thomas for Fort Bowie. Alchesay set up camp near the Chiricahua captives at Bowie. Crook planned to take the two Apaches to the meeting with the hostiles.[46]

He also decided to bring the White Mountain woman, Na-dis-ough, still at Tombstone, to Bowie "so that she can be present when I have my expected interview with the Chiricahuas." Her presence might have evoked suspicions and fears among members of Ulzana's party, who after all had killed at least thirty-eight people and would hardly have relished her appearance as a potential eyewitness. On February 21, 1886, she arrived at Fort Bowie.[47]

Meanwhile, Maus waited patiently in camp. He kept a party of scouts out to the south, probably at Pitaicache Peak, north of the bend of the Bavispe River. Every few days, he sent a terse message to Crook: "Nothing of importance to report." About the only excitement during the first month at Maus's camp was a situation four hundred yards south of John Slaughter's San Bernardino ranch. The Tribolet brothers, Siegfried and Robert, with assistance from their other brothers Godfrey and Charley, had established a mescal camp, selling the beverage to several scouts.[48] Maus sent two officers, Lieutenants Shipp and Faison, to persuade them to stop selling mescal to the scouts. One brother met them defiantly, saying that the military could not touch them, for they "had moved below the line on purpose to get away from the law." Although he promised to stop selling to the scouts, he "kept it right up." In light of what would happen a month later, Shipp should have destroyed the operation.[49]

Though nothing of significance occurred for Maus during the last three weeks in February, the hostiles had been replenishing the stock and supplies lost during Crawford's attack on their camp. At this time, they expected Crook to allow them to return to the reservation with their stock under their former status. This, naturally, meant more raiding and killing in Sonora.

On January 31, 1886, a party of twelve to fifteen Apaches, probably under Geronimo, waylaid two men about six miles north of Sahuaripa. They mortally wounded Lieutenant Francisco Hurtado and shot his horse. The raiders continued east toward the settlements along the Sonora River, historically a favorite target of Geronimo.

Meanwhile, to the north, on February 9, 1886, Chihuahua and Ulzana ambushed a mule train between Oputo and Huásabas, slaying four men, Cipriano Velarde, Jesús María Durazo, Jesús Valencia, and Francisco Laborin, all from Oputo. Two days later, they assaulted the Capadeguachi ranch, some ten miles southwest of Oputo. National troops from Huásabas and Granados rode to the rescue and drove off the Apaches. From Moctezuma, General Diego Guerra conceded that he had no clue where the Indians were living.[50]

In mid-February, Chihuahua and Ulzana's raiders moved west toward Cumpas. Their party, apparently reduced when several men left to join Naiche and Geronimo, numbered between eight and ten men. Their first victim was an American named Resse, whom they ambushed near Cumpas, killing him and wounding his associate, a man named Quirk.[51] On February 17, they raided a ranch near Cumpas and killed two men, Luis Peralta and an American. Peralta's wife and child remained hidden until Major Kosterlitzky's relief party found them. Later that night, the raiders stole stock and an ox cart from a corral at Salvador Hoyas's ranch. (The ox cart would later be seen in possession of the scouts, either bought or won from the hostiles in gambling.)

As they went north, several inviting targets lay in their path. The morning of February 18, they raided three ranches between Cumpas and Nacozari. The first target was the Noria ranch, where they stole stock and wounded a man, who told Kosterlitzky that he had heard gunfire from the Ventura ranch. The major raced to the scene and found Francisco Martinez unconscious from two gunshot wounds. The trail led northeast toward the Alisos ranch, where the raiders stole more cattle. Loaded with one hundred horses, mules, and cattle, they headed north. En route, they killed two Americans, William Brown and

James Moses, at the Grand Republic mine. From here, they changed directions toward the Bavispe River and the Pilares Mountains.

Meanwhile, Geronimo's raiders struck at Banámichi and Motepori, killing two men at the former place and taking a great deal of stock. At Banámichi, authorities had no resources to mount a pursuit, explaining that their soldiers, with most of the town's firearms, were south fighting the Yaquis. The raiders followed the Sonora River north to the Ajos Mountains, where in early March they decided to make one more raid against Sonora before heading north toward the border.[52]

Shortly before sunrise, March 8, 1886, twenty-two Chiricahuas, all on foot, emerged from a canyon near the Mababi ranch of John Hohstadt, located on the eastern face of the Ajos Mountains, midway between Bacoachi and Fronteras. An early rising vaquero saw them and hastened back to the ranch, alerting Hohstadt, his brother, and two other Americans. They left the ranch and took cover, waiting for the Apaches to fall into their trap. As expected, the Indians stealthily worked their way toward the corral. John Hohstadt raised his Winchester, drawing a bead on a warrior about to open the gate. His bullet slammed into the forehead of Chinche, killing him instantly. Hohstadt's friends also began shooting, wounding (they thought) two more Apaches before they scattered, making off with two horses. They left Chinche's body where it fell. It seems ironic, given the unprecedented efforts employed by Crook and Terrazas, that an American rancher in Mexico could claim credit for the only Chiricahua man killed in battle by whites during the sixteen-month campaign. That day, Hohstadt or one of his men took Chinche's scalp, cut off his ears, stripped his clothing (finding $38.50) and cremated his corpse in a "log heap" bonfire.

Chinche's death incensed the Apaches. As with the death of Azariquelch, they had to avenge it, meaning they would take out their rage on innocent people. That afternoon, scouts brought word that they had spotted a party of Mexicans coming along the road from Bacoachi. It consisted of seven people—four men, one woman, and two children. They halted at Capulin, a spring about one-half mile from Mababi. Then the Apaches unveiled their trap, quickly killing three men and capturing a pregnant woman, Felipa Andrada, and her two children, ages one and three. After brutally killing them, they cut open Andrada's stomach, took the unborn child from her womb, and placed it in her arms. One man, Jesús Anselmo, escaped the carnage, eventually returning on foot to Bacoachi. A few hours later, about 5:00 P.M., Refugio Frederico rode by the horrible scene en route to Fronteras. The Apaches opened fire on him, wounding him and his horse.[53]

Meanwhile, Chihuahua and Ulzana raided the Cuchuta ranch, twelve miles east of Mababi, wounding one man and stealing twenty-five horses and mules. Like that of Geronimo and Naiche, their trail led to the southeast, toward Pilares and the Teras Mountains. Both raiding parties were now ready to meet Crook.[54]

Crook patiently awaited word from Maus about the hostiles. He passed the days at Fort Bowie by hunting quail, playing whist at night, and watching a baseball game between a team stationed at Bonita Canyon and a squad from Fort Bowie. However, President Cleveland and General Sheridan in Washington, the White Mountain scouts with Maus, and the southwestern press were growing more impatient by the day. On March 12, 1886, Sheridan, who had heard nothing from Crook in a month, requested information. Crook repeated what Dutchy and Gon-altsis had told him a month before. The hostiles were collecting their scattered stock and cached plunder (a euphemism for new booty acquired by raiding), and he thought they would arrive by the end of the month.[55]

The day before Sheridan's telegram, Lieutenant Maus finally had some news to report. It hardly stopped the presses. The four scouts sent to Fort Apache in February were overdue, which left the other scouts, especially the White Mountain contingent, very much concerned that something had gone awry. From their comments, Maus concluded that the hostiles might send a party to ascertain "the feeling on the reservation." Yet Noche, the leader of the Chiricahua scouts, discounted that possibility, believing the hostiles would come in by the end of the month.[56]

Even the *Tombstone Epitaph*, which had published a steady stream of rumors about Crook and Geronimo, finally threw up the white flag and surrendered. In February and early March, it reported phantom Mexican-Apache battles, the desertion and treachery of the Chiricahua scouts, and several invented conferences between Crook and Geronimo. The editors conceded that according to their various reports, Geronimo had been killed off three times and had surrendered to Crook five times. Finally, on March 9, it admitted that its sources were incredibly unreliable. One informant, a recently retired soldier, turned out to be an Associated Press source who happened to be drunk when he was interviewed. One would think that admission alone would have sobered up their reporting. Yet, they ended their apology by claiming that Crook and Geronimo were supposed to have met on March 6, 1885, when, in reality, Maus had not then heard from Geronimo. Finally, on March 25, the *Epitaph* conceded that the "public has been surfeited with rumors," and until the newspaper had indisputable facts, it would "give them [rumors] a rest."[57]

On March 14, 1886, either Maus's picket force at Pitaicache or the hostiles sent a smoke signal from a high point about eighteen miles south of Maus. The lieutenant took four scouts, including Noche, and rode toward Pitaicache, where he met four Indians (a man, woman, and two boys) sent by Geronimo and Naiche. The man had a fresh wound in the foot, probably received six days earlier in the fight at Mababi ranch. They admitted that they had lost one man, obviously Chinche, in the fight. The balance of the hostiles, except Mangas, was in the mountains on the other side of the Bavispe. All signs suggested that they had gone to the Pilares and Teras mountains after the brutal murders near Hohstadt's ranch and the raid at Cuchuta. Considering what Maus had recently been through, he was concerned that he would face a repeat encounter if Mexican troops followed the hostiles' into his camp. Accordingly, he suggested that Crook order troops from Silver Creek or Guadalupe Canyon to reinforce his small command, which consisted of only Apache scouts and civilian packers. He also recommended that the general, with Naiche's mother, "lose no time in coming to my camp."[58]

Crook ignored Maus. He never wanted to appear too desperate or too eager for them to surrender. He refused to reward the hostiles with anything until he arrived to negotiate. Furthermore, he had one more chip to use, and he would remain at Bowie until he could use it. The day he received Maus's dispatch, on March 16, he sent a telegram to General Pope in San Francisco. He asked him to release Kaetenae from Alcatraz and send him by train, with an escort, to Bowie. Once Kaetenae arrived, he would begin the trip with Dos-teh-seh, Alchesay, Na-dis-ough, and Crook for northern Sonora. Crook planned to leave on March 21, 1886. Of course, he never bothered to inform Maus.[59]

Naiche, Geronimo, and twenty-two warriors with a large herd of stolen stock reached Maus's camp at Pitaicache on March 19. They vowed to fight any Mexican troops who dared to follow them. They refused to go any farther north until Crook arrived. As far as they were concerned, Crook could meet them here, which contradicts the oft-stated theory that Embudos Canyon was the prearranged council site. They told Maus that only Crook "can decide what they will do."[60]

Three days later, on March 22, 1886, Maus convinced the hostiles that they would be safer from Mexicans if they moved camp toward the border. Geronimo and Naiche selected Embudos Canyon, twelve miles north. They would go no farther until they talked with Crook. In this picturesque gorge, eighteen miles below the border, which the Indians knew as Green Water Running, they enjoyed the benefits of good grass, a creek of cold, clear water, and security offered by the presence of high country south and east of camp. Henry Daly described their arrival. Seventy-five Chiricahuas "swept around the base of the foot hills on the opposite side of the stream, like a whirlwind, dashing by us as in review, and rode on by our camp until lost from view in the timber." The packers could hear Geronimo "giving orders to his warriors as he carefully selected the site."[61] They joined the nine Chiricahuas who had already surrendered. Only Chihuahua and seven warriors were absent.[62]

With no news about Crook, a pervasive tension dominated the atmosphere in camp. Maus and the Chiricahuas were growing concerned about Crook's absence. Maus, probably biting his tongue, warned the general, "I would not be surprised if they left before long. They continuously ask when you will be down, and the scouts also [ask]." The hostiles were hungry, but the best Maus could do was to issue some flour and sugar. He urged Crook to send "some word in regard to his movements."[63]

After observing the hostiles for four days, Maus thought they were tired of running. The majority, he thought, would surrender unconditionally, for they "believe in [Crook] sincerely." Chihuahua and his seven warriors had not yet come in. With him, he declared, was "the entire party" that had killed the White Mountain people. Left unsaid was the sticky issue of whether the White Mountain scouts might seek vengeance against them. Only half of Chihuahua's party had ridden with Ulzana, six of them already in camp with Geronimo and Naiche.[64]

The very same day that Maus reached Embudos Canyon, Kaetenae arrived by train at Bowie Station. Crook had originally planned to head south on March 21, but he had to postpone the departure date because the train that Kaetenae had boarded was "wrecked or delayed between San Francisco and Los Angeles." As usual, he cloaked his plans in secrecy. Twenty months at Alcatraz had transformed Kaetenae into an "apostle of peace," according to Captain John G. Bourke.[65]

The administrative structure that Kaetenae had left had also changed. His adversaries, Captain Crawford and Lieutenant Davis, were either dead or out of the army. Kaetenae, grateful for his freedom, met the general at Fort Bowie, where Crook explained the role that the former war chief would play in the negotiations. Undoubtedly, Crook promised to reunite him with his family at Fort Apache. That afternoon, Kaetenae, Alchesay, Dos-teh-seh, and

Na-dis-ough left the fort with Thomas Moore (the celebrated packer just in from Wyoming), two interpreters, Charles M. Straus (ex-mayor of Tucson), and a fifty-six-mule pack train. They spent the night at White's ranch, opposite Turkey Creek.[66]

At 7:09 A.M. on March 23, 1886, Crook, his two aides, John Bourke and Cyrus Roberts, and the latter's precocious twelve-year-old son, Charles, left Fort Bowie by buckboard. They pulled into Mud Springs, fifty-five miles from the fort, at 5:30 P.M., where they passed the night comfortably in three large Sibley tents. Their first stop the next morning, at 8:00, was Silver Creek. They found two companies of Fourth Cavalry under Captain Allen Smith, the same officer whom Geronimo and Mangas had ambushed in Devils Canyon five days after the outbreak. They also met Camillus Sidney Fly, a photographer from Tombstone. He had learned of Crook's meeting and asked him whether he and his assistant, a man named Chase, could tag along. Crook agreed, and for that historians are in his debt. They bivouacked that evening, March 24, 1886, a few miles below the border at Contraband Springs.[67]

By then Lieutenant Maus had received word that General Crook would arrive the next day. He must have felt relieved, for Geronimo had asked about Crook daily. Maus could offer nothing specific, which intensified Geronimo's fear of treachery. The other problem was Charles Tribolet, the beef contractor, who had continued to sell whiskey and mescal, but this time to the hostiles. According to Henry Daly, Crook's inexplicable delay and Tribolet's mescal had left the hostiles in an unpleasant way. It was far from certain that they would surrender, thought Daly.[68]

Crook rode into Embudos Canyon an hour before noon on March 25. Before meeting the Chiricahuas, he halted at the packer's camp for lunch. The outspoken Daly told Crook that he was glad to see him, but he questioned his delay, for it had left the hostiles in an "ugly mood as a result of their debauch." Soon after lunch, Naiche, Geronimo, and several followers came in. The general wasted no time in convening the long-awaited council. Crook selected the location "under the shade of a cottonwood and a sycamore tree [and] seated himself on a little ledge at the base of a knoll." Crook's party attended the conference, along with lieutenants Maus, Shipp, and Faison and several scouts, including Noche. Even the beef contractor and mescal merchant, Charles Tribolet, wandered in, but Maus ordered him away. As they walked to the meeting ground, Captain Bourke invited Henry Daly to come and "hear the old man give Geronimo h—l." Daly thought Crook could have adopted this hard-line policy a week earlier. Now, with the hostiles sulky, morose, and many suffering from hangovers, he suggested it might be wise to proceed with caution.

Bourke has the best description of the historic meeting. He counted twenty-four warriors either at the conference or within earshot. Every man and boy carried a Winchester or Springfield rifle with two cartridge belts full of ammunition. Their clothing and blankets were new, indicating that they had "refitted themselves" since Crawford's attack on their camp. Crook thought they looked defiant, as "fierce as so many tigers." Despite this, he had no inclination to deviate from his plans and orders.

It was obvious from the beginning that Crook had assumed a businesslike, unsympathetic demeanor, clearly indignant with Geronimo. Before beginning, the shaman had a brief conversation with Naiche. Then he launched into an explanation of why he had left the reservation. He blamed Lieutenant Britton Davis, Chatto, and Mickey Free—in short, everyone but himself. He pointed out that he had left the reservation only after Nadiskay and Huera had warned him that his enemies planned to seize and then kill him. As he talked and talked, clutching a small buckskin pouch, beads of perspiration rolled down his cheeks. Crook just stared impassively at the ground, apparently not at all interested in the shaman's words, which he supposed were lies. Finally, when Geronimo finished talking, the general's response was particularly humiliating: "Your mouth talks too many ways." Here, or at some point, Geronimo became exasperated with Crook's comportment and said, "I want no more of this." This remark evoked some stirring among the hostiles until Naiche "waved his hand to keep quiet."

Toward the end of the council, the scouts shouted out that riders were coming. Although the sentry initially supposed they were Mexicans, they turned out to be Chihuahua, Ulzana, and six warriors driving a herd of stolen horses. Maus thought that their presence might disrupt negotiations, given the well-earned belligerent reputation of the two brothers. This was the first time the White Mountain scouts had laid eyes on the man who had engineered the slaughter of twenty-one of their people. Arriving without a care, Ulzana defiantly rode his horse through the packer's camp, disturbing the dinner of several men. All of Chihuahua's rage vanished, however, once he laid eyes on Crook. He walked over and shook his hand. All of a sudden, in his own words, he "began to think well . . . his heart had quieted down." The warrior brothers stood on the perimeter for the last part of the council and were included in the celebrated C. S. Fly photo that featured the eyewitnesses to history, to the verbal showdown between Crook and Geronimo.

Crook ended the council by stating his terms: "You must make up your own mind whether you will stay out on the warpath or surrender unconditionally. If you stay out, I'll keep after you and kill the last one, even if it takes fifty years." He told the chiefs to return to their camp and "reflect on what they were to do before giving me their answer." They were not dealing from a position of strength. They wanted to surrender and return to Fort Apache under their former status. Yet, Crook had offered them nothing, which gave him room to move toward the U.S. policy adopted on September 30, 1885. "The result of the interview indicated nothing," wrote Crook in his diary. That evening he sent Alchesay and Kaetenae to their camp "to talk them into going away until this thing was forgotten and the excitement was allayed." This was the first indication that he was prepared to modify his terms of unconditional surrender. Even these two influential leaders had trouble getting the hostiles to listen.[69]

The next morning, March 26, Fly, Bourke, and Straus visited the hostiles' camp. Fly found Geronimo very cooperative. That morning he took most of his celebrated photos. It was then that the visitors saw Santiago McKinn, the boy captured by Geronimo on the Mimbres six months before. That afternoon Crook held private meetings with "Naiche, Geronimo, Chihuahua, and others with reference to their leaving this country for the east to remain until they change their ideas and the feeling against them here dies out." Kaetenae had continued to preach as Crook's disciple of peace. Finally, to close the deal, Crook agreed to limit their exile in the East to two years before allowing them to return to Arizona. He believed that Sheridan's letter of February 1, 1886, had given him the appropriate authority to deviate from the September 30, 1886, policy "if necessary to secure their surrender." That evening Kaetenae quietly informed Crook that Chihuahua, who desperately wanted to see his family, would surrender the next morning. Crook sent a courier to Bowie with a curt message for Sheridan: "Today things look more favorable."[70]

At high noon the next day, March 27, 1886, Chihuahaua, Naiche, Geronimo, Cathla, and Nana came in to formally surrender. Chihuahua offered his hand to Crook, saying, "I surrender myself to you, because I believe in you and you do not deceive us." Relieved that the war was over, the general took Chihuahua's hand and said one word in Apache, "En-juh," meaning "it is well." Naiche was next, and he parroted Chihuahua's thoughts: "When I was free, I gave orders, but now I surrender to you." Geronimo was the last to speak: "Once I moved about like the wind. Now I surrender to you and that is all. . . . My heart is yours, and I hope that yours will be mine."[71]

Geronimo, Chihuahua, Cathla, and Tah-ni-toe asked Crook to send their wives and children from San Carlos and Fort Bowie to meet them. Geronimo's wife was Eschichilla (probably Zi-yeh). Captain Roberts asked Pierce to forward her. Geronimo also had a wife and daughter at Fort Bowie, and Crook, believing that the "surrender was bona fide," issued orders for them to meet him along the trail.[72]

That night, Charles Tribolet, who had set up a camp about three miles away, sold the Chiricahuas three "five gallon demijohns of whiskey" for three hundred dollars. They took the booze to their camp. Later that evening, Daly recalled that "pandemonium reigned in the camp . . . and the Apache yell could be frequently heard and an occasional shot fired." Later that night, several inebriated hostiles fired shots toward the packers' camp; a few of the rowdiest even targeted the soldiers' tents, although the rounds landed harmlessly beyond. Early the next morning, Kaetenae and Alchesay told Crook that Naiche had passed out in a drunken stupor.[73]

Despite this backdrop of chaos, Crook, as planned, left Embudos Canyon at 6:45 the next morning, March 28. A few miles north they ran into Geronimo, Cathla, and three warriors, "drunk as lords," riding two mules. Geronimo embraced Bourke, assuring him that he would follow "with his people in a little while." Their condition disgusted Bourke, who sensed, in the words of his biographer, "impending disaster." He warned Crook to "have Tribolet killed as a foe to human society. If you don't, it will be the biggest mistake of your life."[74]

The omniscient Crook stuck to his plans and continued triumphantly for Fort Bowie, leaving three officers (Maus, Shipp, and Faison), Alchesay, Kaetenae, the scouts, and the pack train to escort the hostiles to Bowie. Packer Henry Daly was incredulous. For a moment he thought about questioning the general's decision, but he felt such conduct would show disrespect to a man he very much admired. Crook explained that his official duties required him to be in telegraphic correspondence with Sheridan. Perhaps he felt that he had to get to Bowie to explain his reasons for deviating from the terms of unconditional surrender.[75]

That morning, Maus had hoped to move the hostiles early but found that impracticable because of their inebriated condition. Nevertheless, he decided to break camp with Chihuahua's followers, who represented more than half the band. Sending the pack train forward to his former base camp ten miles below the border, the battle-tested lieutenant stayed behind with an interpreter, Kaetenae, Alchesay, and the scouts. The hostiles finally broke camp about noon. Maus met Geronimo midafternoon, but the shaman cautioned him to keep his distance, for many of his people were still drunk. The hostiles camped a half mile from the pack train. That evening Naiche, still under the influence, shot his wife in the leg. His judgment impaired, he thought she was flirting with another man.[76]

Maus was more optimistic in his first dispatch the next morning, when he advised Crook that he was sending Lieutenant Shipp "with sufficient support" to destroy Tribolet's supply of alcohol. He had issued a liberal supply of beef to the Indians, and it was apparent to Kaetenae and Alchesay that the "good spree" had ended. Maus expected to cross the border and reach Silver Creek that evening. He predicted a "quiet march in good order."[77]

Geronimo and Naiche had different plans. Although the Chiricahuas took the lead and broke camp "bright and early," they did not intend to cross the border. After proceeding about seven or eight miles, Maus and Daly became incredulous when they saw that the "head of the column had halted and gone into camp," two miles south of the line. They told Maus that the recent ordeal had left their stock played out, and that their people were recovering from the aftereffects of their recent binge.

Another telltale sign, which should have raised Maus's antennae, occurred when Chihuahua, with about fifty-one of the ninety-two hostiles, established his own camp apart from Naiche and Geronimo. Maus bivouacked just north of Geronimo, and east of Chihuahua. Daly immediately became suspicious, telling Maus that this sudden stop, after such a brief march, meant one thing: "The Chiricahuas had gone as far toward Fort Bowie as they intended on going." Although Maus was concerned, he had seen positive signs that had assuaged his feelings. The Indians were behaving better and seemed to be less surly. Besides, Shipp had destroyed Tribolet's mescal camp, and Maus had even seen an unarmed Geronimo away from camp, searching for stray horses.[78]

Daly still thought something was in the air. Shortly after dark, a warrior from Geronimo's camp fired a shot over the heads of the men in Maus's camp. Soon after, two Chiricahuas, "one very drunk and the other seemingly sober, came by our fire and made wild gesticulations, at the same time cursing us in a mixture of Spanish and Apache." Daly was certain the hostiles were warning them to turn in so they could begin preparations for flight. Everyone except Lieutenant Maus and Daly went to bed. Soon after, a man fired another shot from Geronimo's camp. Daly told Maus that in the morning, "there would not be a Chiricahua in camp." The lieutenant disagreed "and went off to bed." Daly soon followed him.

Geronimo and Naiche partially fulfilled Daly's prophecy when, at 3:00 A.M. on March 30, Daly heard the "faint tinkle" of the bell horse trotting to camp. If the hostiles did sneak away, they would pass by the herd and scare the bell horse into returning to camp. Those with Chihuahua were still sleeping, but Geronimo and Naiche, eighteen other warriors, and twenty-two women and children had left about 2:30 A.M.[79]

Inexplicably, no one—not Alchesay, not Kaetenae, and not Noche—claimed to know the intent of Geronimo and Naiche. Four years later, Naiche told Crook that he thought the others knew "about it but did not want to go out." By "others," he meant Chihuahua's group, who, having heard of their plans, set up a separate camp from Naiche and Geronimo. During the previous two days, as they had suffered through the resulting hangover, Naiche and Geronimo had had time to reflect on Crook's behavior toward them. Eschewing any pretense at diplomacy, the general had, by his brusque manner, puzzled and frightened them. From their perspective, he "had talked bad to them." They were unsure whether they could trust him. They wondered if Crook's early exit from camp meant that he had some pernicious plan to betray them. As Naiche admitted four years later, "we were drunk" and afraid of the uncertainty of life in Florida.[80]

One other misconceived notion began to consume their alcohol-induced, irrational thoughts, especially those of Geronimo. They believed that Crook had decided to designate Chatto as chief of the tribe, effectively placing him in charge of them. By then, Chatto and Geronimo detested each other, engaged as they were in strong feelings that each man would take to the grave.[81]

The combination of liquor, Crook's indifference, and fears for their lives under Chatto's rule was enough to persuade them to renege on their promises to Crook, whom they left standing on the sidelines at Fort Bowie, looking like a foreman of a hopelessly deadlocked jury. Their flight would prolong the war by five months and cause Crook, already upset because President Cleveland had overruled the terms that he had negotiated (insisting on unconditional surrender), to request to be relieved from duty in Arizona. In the end, this change would have profound ramifications for the Chiricahua tribe. They had lost their one advocate, an influential man who would have continued to work on their behalf.

All these disparate events since the breakout had now come together to shape federal Indian policy toward the Chiricahua tribe. It was like a wave that would not stop cresting. First, after Geronimo's raid at Fort Apache on September 22, 1885, Washington officials had established a policy to deport every hostile Chiricahua from the Southwest. This policy would forbid a return to their ancestral grounds. Second, after Ulzana's foray in November 1885, Secretary of War Endicott and General Sheridan, with the blessing of President Cleveland, expanded federal policy to remove all Chiricahuas, reservation and hostile, from the Southwest. The tribe would pay a tremendous toll in the wake of their flight, one that no Apaches in their wildest nightmares could have foreseen.

We will never know what the fate of the hostiles would have been if the entire group had capitulated with Maus. Perhaps public pressure would have forced the president to honor the terms under which they had surrendered. But the escape changed everything for Chihuahua and his followers. They had no idea that Cleveland and Sheridan had already disavowed the terms under which they had capitulated.

For the Chiricahuas, a twenty-seven-year nightmare was about to begin.

24

GENERAL MILES TO THE RESCUE

Geronimo will never come in now.
Chihuahua

After a nine-hour ride through a sandstorm, General Crook reached Fort Bowie at 3:00 P.M. on March 29, 1886. He must have felt satisfied, if not vindicated, for as far as he was concerned, the war was over. Not batting an eye, that day he telegraphed Sheridan to explain why he was unable to get the unconditional surrender that his superiors in Washington, including the president, had demanded. But, he reasoned, "I had to act at once," so he accepted the Chiricahuas' proposal. And, given the circumstances at Embudos Canyon, he felt that he had used the discretion accorded him by orders from Washington. After all, Sheridan had authorized him, if necessary, to deviate from the unconditional surrender terms.[1]

One day later, Crook's euphoria turned to despair.

On March 30, 1886, he received two messages, each deeply troubling. The first communication was a telegram from General Sheridan informing him that President Cleveland had overruled Crook's agreement with the Chiricahuas. Accordingly, Sheridan instructed Crook to go back to the table and tell the hostiles that the government would spare their lives, but nothing else. If the hostiles refused these terms, Sheridan ordered Crook to deploy his troops and "complete the destruction of the hostiles." In essence, Cleveland and Sheridan had authorized Crook to slaughter any Indian refusing to surrender unconditionally even though the two sides were negotiating in good faith. The order dripped with irony. President Cleveland and General Sheridan's final solution demonstrated a mutual disdain for the Chiricahuas—the same disdain exhibited by Lieutenant George N. Bascom toward Cochise a quarter century before. The imperious edict stunned Crook, who felt betrayed by both President Cleveland and Sheridan. They had compromised his integrity, a trait he valued above all. Nevertheless, even if it were practicable to follow through with Sheridan's wishes, Crook's strong sense of honor would have prevented him from doing so.[2]

The second communication, a dispatch from Guadalupe Canyon, arrived late afternoon or early evening by courier. His message from Lieutenant Maus announced the escape of Geronimo and Naiche's party. Crook immediately wired the news to Sheridan, who became dumbfounded, and then furious. He saw a conspiracy between the Apache scouts and the hostiles. The treacherous scouts must have deceived Crook, who was blind to their cunning ways. On March 31, 1886, Sheridan responded tersely that the "escape has occasioned great disappointment. It seems strange that Geronimo and party could have escaped without the knowledge of the scouts." The comments spoke volumes about Sheridan's ideology and state of mind. Crook shot back that his scouts were "thoroughly loyal [and] would have prevented the hostiles leaving had it been possible."[3]

In a second dispatch, Crook advised Sheridan that to tell the Indians "the terms on which they surrendered are disapproved would, in my judgment, not only make it impossible for me to negotiate with them, but result in them scattering to the mountains." Because Sheridan could not debate that issue, he responded by suggesting that Crook adopt a new "defensive" philosophy in which he would rely on the forty-six companies of infantry and the forty companies of cavalry to guard the frontier from Apache incursions. Sheridan was telling Crook to cease offensive campaigns into Mexico and to rely on the regular troops instead of the Apache scouts. It was a slap in Crook's face, and both men knew it. The generals had lost faith in each other. And Sheridan, knowing that Crook's first instinct when backed into a corner was to threaten resignation, got what he wanted. After a thoughtful response, which included an honest summary of the campaign and a vigorous defense of his policies, an exhausted Crook conceded that he might be "too much wedded to my own views. [Therefore] I respectfully request that I may now be relieved from this command." This time Crook meant what he said. He had had enough of Geronimo, the citizens and newspapers of Arizona, and Washington's arm-chair quarterbacks, who thought they knew more than the commanders on the ground.[4]

The psychological end for Crook's command in Arizona came on April 2, 1886, a day replete with poignant moments and noteworthy events, some emotionally satisfying and others profoundly sad.

Sheridan informed Crook that he accepted his request to be relieved from duty and transferred him to command the Department of the Platte. He named General Nelson Miles to replace him. Crook must have felt relief and then closure from the arduous responsibilities.[5]

About noon, Lieutenant Samson Faison, with some twenty scouts (Lieutenant Maus and the balance had gone after Geronimo and Naiche), brought in Chihuahua with fifty followers. They approached the fort from Bear Canyon, riding single-file by Crook's headquarters before disappearing down the arroyo toward Siphon Canyon. The scouts wore blue coats to distinguish them from the former hostiles. Chihuahua's group and the scouts went into camp less than a mile west of the fort, where twenty-three women and children (including Chihuahua's family) joined them.[6]

Their arrival delayed a solemn moment in the history of Fort Bowie. Ten days earlier, the remains of Crook's most trusted field commander, Captain Emmet Crawford, had been brought to the fort from Nácori Chico, Sonora. The entire garrison had turned out to pay homage to his memory. Captain John Bourke led a solemn procession of troops, who ushered the corpse of their beloved captain to Bowie Station. From here, Bourke accompanied the coffin to Kearney, Nebraska. The soldier-ethnologist was leaving Apacheria for an assignment in Washington. He remained a concerned advocate for the plight of the Chiricahuas in the post-1886 years. In the span of a few hours, Crook had resigned his command, witnessed the symbolic departure of his best field commander, and dispatched his devoted aide and staunchest defender to a desk job in Washington. Indeed, it must have been a day to reflect on what he had lost.[7]

That afternoon Crook had other pressing matters. On the heels of Lieutenant Faison's party arrived Sheriff Robert Hatch of Tombstone with a warrant for the arrest of Nana, Chihuahua, and other hostiles. Crook refused to comply with the order unless directed to do so by the secretary of war. Chihuahua, with Alchesay and Kaetenae, held a one-hour meeting at his headquarters at the fort. Chihuahua, ecstatic after reuniting with his family, openly conceded that he had committed many depredations. But he blamed Geronimo for having "dragged him off the reservation with lies." Naiche, he thought, would eventually come in, but Geronimo "would never come in now." Crook, however, did not disclose to the chief that President Cleveland had rejected the terms. He urged Sheridan to arrange to transfer them "immediately."[8]

The next day, April 3, Sheridan ordered Crook to send Chihuahua's party, "as soon as practicable," to Fort Marion, Florida. Early that afternoon, Lieutenant Maus returned from his fruitless pursuit of the forty-two hostiles under Geronimo and Naiche. He had tracked them toward Fronteras, where their trail had scattered. By then, the Apaches were on foot. Neither Maus nor his scouts held out any hopes of catching them. So he abandoned pursuit and headed for Bowie. Near Riggs ranch in Bonita Canyon, two warriors, one a brother of Kaetenae and the second a brother of Chipuesa (Chepuede), walked into camp and surrendered. The first man was Nezulkide, and the second was probably Shoie. They said that they were sleeping when they heard the others leaving, so they thought something was wrong and left. When satisfied that this was not the case, they decided to take leave of Geronimo and Naiche. Likely, they simply had second thoughts and, in Shoie's case, wanted to see their families. They probably left after Geronimo and Naiche decided to abandon their stock, for they claimed to have left two horses and a mule near the San Bernardino ranch. These defections reduced the hostiles to forty in all, eighteen of whom were men.[9]

Meanwhile, Crook worked diligently to tie up loose ends. On April 4, he informed Sheridan that he would not tell his prisoners about the president's ruling because if Geronimo and Naiche were to find out, they would never surrender. The very next day, Sheridan sent two telegrams to Crook, the first approving his decision, and the second justifying its deceitful ploy because "Geronimo [broke] every condition of the surrender" and thus nullified the terms under which Chihuahua's party had surrendered. Crook's diary entry reveals his disgust: Sheridan was "trying to say something without saying it." As Martin Schmitt notes, "This would be the legal basis for holding the Apaches in exile indefinitely."[10]

On April 6, Crook had another busy day. That morning, Chihuahua turned over to him the young New Mexican boy, Santiago McKinn. Although a captive for only six months, the boy had become "absolutely Indianized." Santiago refused to leave the Indian camp with any American, so Chihuahua had to bring him personally to the fort. When Chihuahua left him with Crook and his staff, Santiago "acted like a wild animal in a trap." He was defiant, refusing to speak in any language but Apache, and insisting that he wanted to stay with the Apaches. Finally, the soldiers got him on a wagon that took him to Bowie Station. Two days later, he had a happy reunion with his father in Deming, New Mexico.[11]

Later that day, April 6, Crook met with the Apache scouts and Chihuahua. First, he gave the scouts a six-word message that sent shock waves throughout the room: "I am going to leave you." He thanked them for their loyalty and accomplishments. And he addressed the two most pressing issues as he saw them: tiswin binges ("you get it in your stomach and there is no sense left") and raising stock. He advised them to stop the first practice and to work hard at raising sheep instead of cattle. The scouts were naturally concerned about his replacement. He assured them that the new commander would be a "good and honest man." Then he turned to Chihuahua and informed him to have his people ready to leave before noon the next day. And he probably gave him the good news that he had asked Captain Pierce at San Carlos to send the chief's three-year-old son, who was with Goody in Cassadore's band, to Bowie Station that evening.[12]

The Chiricahua cavalcade, mounted on horses and mules, departed Bowie at 11:30 A.M., April 7, 1886. In all, they numbered seventy-six—Chihuahua's original fifty-one, the two men brought in by Maus, and the twenty-three captives taken the previous year. Crook accompanied them in a buckboard. At Bowie Station, amidst a blinding windstorm, Chihuahua had a joyful reunion with his son, thus bringing the final count to seventy-seven: fifteen men, twenty-nine women, and thirty-three children. He also met two officers. The first was Lieutenant James Richards, who had commanded an Apache scout company in the early 1880s. He would be their temporary agent in Florida. The quartermaster at Bowie had furnished him with enough rations for the trip, and Crook had authorized an advance of $125 so that Richards could purchase coffee en route. The second officer was Captain Egbert Barnum Savage, whose Company G, Eighth Infantry, would be the escort to Florida. Savage's detail had spent the last three months at Bowie Station. He and his men were delighted to receive the "lucky assignment."

Before boarding the train, the scouts disarmed the band. This was a potentially explosive situation, for in all the years on reservations under American control, the men had never given up their weapons. According to Crook, this exercise produced "considerable nervousness among the men." But Chihuahua's strong leadership defused the situation. Once arrangements were completed, the prisoners climbed aboard the special train of four emigrant sleepers, three for the Indians and one for the troop escort, which would take them to Fort Marion, Florida.

Among the fifteen men were some of the "bravest and ablest" warriors. They were: Chihuahua, Ulzana, Nana, Cathla, Shoie, Nezulkide, Nahdozin, Eskinye, José Second, Seeltoe, Len-see, Ni-losh, Nezegochin, Tisna, and Dah-Ke-Ya. Two men were suffering from recent gunshot wounds. Cathla still limped from a wound suffered the previous summer. Only one Indian spoke some English. Five of the men were in their late teens or early twenties. With Chihuahua were two wives and three children of Geronimo, two wives and two children of Naiche (his mother had returned to Fort Apache), and Huera, the expert tiswin brewer and wife of Mangas. They believed they would serve a two-year sentence in the East. At least that was their agreement with Crook. Only two men, José Second and Nahdozin, would ever return to the Southwest. They reached Fort Marion on April 13, 1886. Back at Bowie that night, Crook confided his private thoughts to his diary: "It is a big relief to get rid of them."[13]

Crook waited patiently for Miles's arrival. Miles had left Fort Leavenworth on April 7 and reached the fort the afternoon of April 11. The loud charges from the fort's six-pound cannon announced his arrival. His coach, drawn by six mules, came to a stop in front of the house of Major Eugene B. Beaumont, the post commander. As General Miles emerged from the ambulance, Crook walked over to greet him. The two men had a businesslike handshake. After dinner with Beaumont, Miles walked over to Crook's office, and Crook gave him the lay of the land before formally relinquishing command of the military Department of Arizona. The next day, April 12, 1886, he held a final meeting with Maus's and Shipp's Chiricahua and White Mountain scouts. Lummis described the moving scene as many of the prominent scouts, such as Noche, Charley, and Dutchy, embraced the Gray Fox. General Miles said a few words to the scouts, but it was clear to all that he did not intend to stake his reputation on their efforts. Lieutenant Maus and the scouts left for Fort Apache about noon; an hour later, General Crook departed Fort Bowie for his headquarters in Prescott.[14]

With few exceptions, the Arizona press celebrated Crook's departure. The *Tombstone Epitaph* chose to make its point with satire: "The citizens of Cochise County bid you an affectionate farewell and trust that your declining years may be as quiet and peaceful as has been your military career in Arizona."[15] Miles was honest when he claimed that he "did not welcome the order with any degree of satisfaction." He looked at the assignment as an opportunity to succeed in a situation where Crook had failed, at least in the views of Sheridan and Cleveland. One day after accepting Crook's resignation, Sheridan told Miles that he wanted "vigorous operations [by] making active and prominent use of the regular troops." Miles understood the message. Take care of the remaining hostiles by eschewing Crook's over-reliance on Apache scouts and diplomacy. Yet, once he surveyed the scene and talked to other officers, it was clear that he faced a daunting challenge. Charles Lummis pressed him on what he would do with the scouts. From a private conversation with Miles, he inferred that the general would like to employ them, but "there are indications" that the president wants to run the campaign from Washington.

Miles's success hinged on what the hostiles did rather than on what he did. Washington was anxious for a quick resolution. Nonetheless, even if he ran a perfect campaign, Geronimo and Naiche controlled the agenda. They could prolong the war for months and even years if they decided to remain in the Sierra Madre Mountains. Only a handful of experienced officers would have bet that regular troops operating in Mexico could strike a crippling blow against them in the Sierra Madres. Whether he liked it or not, Miles was staking his reputation on regular soldiers and a few Apache scouts (none from Fort Apache, which had eliminated most of the White Mountain and all the Chiricahuas) who were unfamiliar with the terrain in Mexico. They were supposed to track them down and force them to capitulate. He did not like his chances.[16]

In the days after Crook left, Miles began to draw up plans. Because he had brought only a few staff members with him, he apparently wrote most of the blueprint that would become his policy statement of April 20, 1886. But he knew that even if he adopted Sheridan's plan, it was hardly an ironclad guarantee to success, for Sheridan's instructions were replete with inherent fallacies not evident to Washington officials. After thoughtful consideration, he adopted an idea first suggested to him by Crook's Chiricahua scouts. They had proposed sending two prominent Chiricahuas, Ulzana and Shoie, as emissaries to the hostiles. They had to be men the hostiles trusted. But Miles had a problem, for these two men were then in Florida. On April 18, 1886, he telegraphed Sheridan to ask him to send them "to me with as little delay as possible." It was a request that Crook would have made, and Sheridan, knowing that Ulzana had led the bloody raid six months before, was in no humor to grant it. His response was terse: "The Lieutenant General disapproves." Sheridan clearly wanted the regular army to run down the hostiles. Yet Miles's thought of sending emissaries to the hostiles remained an option if the offensive bogged down.[17]

On April 20, 1886, Miles released General Orders Number 7, which provided the framework of a policy written to satisfy Sheridan. Regular soldiers would take over the responsibility. He designated cavalry for pursuit and scouting and infantry for occupying strategic mountain passes, guarding known waterholes, escorting supply trains, and protecting storage depots.[18] He organized an elite strike force, under Captain Henry W. Lawton, a powerful and athletic commander who packed 225 pounds on a six-foot five-inch muscular frame. Miles's handpicked medical officer was Assistant Surgeon Leonard Wood, an athletic Harvard graduate who exuded self-confidence. His boundless energy and competitive nature were perfect fits for the campaign that Miles had in mind. Both officers, especially Wood, believed that the "right sort of white man" could prove to be more than a match for the Apaches in their mountain homes.[19] The troops would do the fighting, not Indian scouts. Miles's regime would employ only "reliable" scouts (a euphemism for no Chiricahuas from Fort Apache), who would accompany the troops as "trailers," not as combat soldiers. Retired Lieutenant Britton Davis thought that the Miles policy was "midway" between Crook's and the one stipulated by Sheridan.[20]

Miles had to formulate a new wrinkle to distinguish his command from Crook's regime. Twelve-year-old Charlie Roberts, in his diary entry of April 15, wrote, "General Miles is going to establish signal stations on top of the high peaks about the border. The signal stations will be supplied with telescopes and heliographs and will give notice when the hostiles are approaching." Indeed, these stations would become an integral part of the general's strategy to protect settlers north of the border. In theory, they might provide an early warning system for commanders to deploy troops to ambush unsuspecting Apaches. He brought in signal corps officers, who established twenty-seven "districts of observation" with heliograph stations located on the summits of the mountains in southeastern Arizona and southwestern New Mexico. Between April 27 and July 24, Lieutenant Edward E. Dravo and Lieutenant Alvarado M. Fuller established thirty stations.

These stations could have made significant contributions to operations if the Chiricahuas were living and operating in United States territory. During the period they were functional, however, only one band under Naiche raided in Arizona, and they were in the territory for only about twenty days. Furthermore, his party, when in U.S. territory, usually traveled at night, when the heliograph crews were sleeping because they could not see anything. Miles deserves credit for ingenuity, but in reality, his innovation did nothing to end the campaign and was not a factor in the final surrender, despite Miles's claims to the contrary, which appear in his book *Personal Recollections,* published in 1896. [21]

Meanwhile, expecting that Crook would send the Chiricahua scouts after them in the Sierra Madre, Geronimo and Naiche decided to head west. In the early afternoon on April 3, six warriors raided the ranch of their old adversary Cayetano Silvas, five miles east of Fronteras. Here they butchered five animals, took a dozen more (oxen and horses), before moving east to Cuquiárachi, where they took four more horses. Another band raided Janaverachi ranch, taking twenty-five horses. As the raiders rejoined the main body, they all headed toward John Hohstadt's Mababi ranch, the site of Chinche's death the month before. After cutting the trail, Silvas estimated the Apache numbers at forty, clearly the entire group of hostiles. After resting in the Ajos Mountains for a short time, on April 11, the entire band ("thirty to forty mounted Apaches") raided Duron's ranch near Bacoachi, butchering several head and stealing more stock. Anticipating pursuit, the band turned west, crossed the Sonora River, and continued to the lofty Azul Mountains southwest of Cananea. Here, on the summit, which topped out at 8,040 feet, they established a camp that featured a good spring. "No one could approach within twenty-five miles without being seen," according to trooper Lawrence Vinton, who inspected the site shortly after the Chiricahuas had left.[22]

By April 19, 1886, Geronimo and Naiche had left the Azul Mountains. The next day, they killed two men and three women, then continued south toward Imuris, where they ran off some stock from the Aribabi ranch. At 9:00 A.M. on April 23, they suddenly appeared in force at the Casita ranch. Several men were doing their morning chores when the Apaches opened fire, cutting down the owner and wounding his son. According to one account, the Indians could have slain the man's wife and small child, but they allowed them to take refuge at their hacienda. Some vaqueros galloped to Imuris with the news, spreading the rumors that the Apaches had slain everyone on the ranch, some fifteen people. Immediately a relief force of ten nationals under Joaquin Quiroga rushed to the scene, where they found the bodies of three men. The Apaches waylaid them, killing two soldiers, Francisco Grijalva and Estarislio Bonilla. A larger force of soldiers from Magdalena and Imuris ferreted out the trail, but by then the fast-moving Chiricahuas had put a great distance between them and their pursuers.

The next day the Indians moved north along the eastern face of the Pinito Mountains, about twenty miles southeast of Nogales. Six warriors stole six head of stock from the Cibuta ranch. Then they disappeared into the Pinito Mountains, crossing the summit to its east side. Leaving a few men with the women and children at deserted ruins, which featured a large stone corral, on April 26, 1886, Geronimo and Naiche took the rest of the men north to the Buena Vista ranch, on the border ten miles east of Nogales. Here they surprised four men making mescal or wine. In a brisk fight, the Indians killed three Mexicans and one American. Before leaving, the Apaches smashed in their heads, leaving them like jelly. After entering Arizona, they ambushed two Mexicans near Calabasas, killing one man and chasing the second man into town.[23]

Calabasas was then a small development, featuring a hotel and about a "dozen poor looking houses and shanties." Early the next morning, its occupants were stunned to see six or eight warriors enter the town and take six horses before stampeding away. George Atkinson led six men into a canyon about a mile northwest of town, where he unexpectedly met the Apaches, who commenced firing, wounding one man in the arm and chasing Atkinson's group back to town. The Chiricahuas' businesslike approach during the skirmish surprised Atkinson.[24]

By 9:00 A.M., they had moved west to the cattle ranch of Artisan L. Peck, six miles west of the Santa Cruz River and eight miles northwest of Nogales. Earlier that morning, Peck and a neighbor, Charlie Owens, had left to search for stray stock. One young warrior caught the attention of the family dogs as he climbed into the corral. Hearing the barking, Peck's pregnant wife, Petra, sent her young niece, Trinidad Verdin, to investigate. She told her aunt that an Apache was sitting in the corner of the corral near the chicken coop. Petra rushed outside with her baby in her arms. The Apache shot her, picked up the fallen baby by the legs, and slammed his head into an adobe wall. According to at least one account, the Apache was a young man who spoke some English. Meanwhile, after witnessing these horrible atrocities, Trinidad ran into the house and hid under a bed. Soon after, fifteen Indians came in and ransacked the house. One man found Trinidad under a bed, dragged her out feet first, and was ready to kill her. Fortunately for her, Geronimo walked in and saved her life. He put her on a horse behind his son, Chappo. Before leaving, the men burned the blacksmith shop and took about a dozen head of horses, some cattle, a Winchester rifle, and two revolvers.

Next, they rode about two miles west to a ridge, where they spotted Peck and Charlie Owens. Both men were unarmed. They were "lassoing a bull" when they heard gunshots and the sound of bullets going over their heads. Both men mounted their horses to escape. The Indians shot Owens through the neck, killing him, and then a bullet smashed into Peck's horse, sending both the rider and horse down. A few warriors struck Peck with rifle butts, and he began to stir. The Apaches then took him to a knoll and formed a circle around him. One young Apache, "who spoke good English," introduced him to Geronimo. The chief addressed him as Mangas Coloradas (Red Sleeves), for he was wearing red flannel underwear under his shirt, which he had rolled up above his elbow. Peck saw his niece, who was sobbing hysterically, mounted behind an Apache. The English-speaking Apache warned him, under penalty of death, not to speak to his niece. Regardless, she related what had happened before the warrior intervened.

Geronimo told Peck that he "was a good man" so he spared his life. They stripped him to his underwear and took his boots. Only Geronimo knows why he let him go—perhaps because he was unarmed, perhaps because he knew what it was like to lose a family, or perhaps because Peck's red sleeves reminded him, nostalgically, of times with Mangas Coloradas. Other accounts have suggested that Geronimo released him because Peck knew a renegade Mexican with the Apaches or because he pretended to be insane, a version that Lieutenant Leonard Wood apparently heard and repeated. Neither was the case. No renegade Mexicans were riding with the hostiles, and Peck never feigned insanity. The warrior said that if he went to his ranch, they would kill him. Peck disregarded that advice and returned to find the bodies of his wife and child.[25]

According to Trinidad Verdin, the raiders went southwest into the Pajarito Mountains, a narrow ten-mile range that runs east to west along the border. But before doing so, the next day (April 28), one small group of men, under Geronimo, killed one man and wounded another near Oro Blanco, about ten miles west of Peck's ranch, and stole fifty horses.[26] On April 29 the chief swung south through the Oro Blanco Mountains and entered Sonora via the Pajarito Mountains, crossing the railroad tracks south of Nogales on early May 1. Geronimo was returning to the Pinito Mountains to pick up his women and children. He reached the range on May 2, 1886. By then, he and Naiche were aware that a company of American soldiers was a day behind them.

Captain Thomas C. Lebo with K Troop, Tenth Cavalry, led the resolute troopers who had followed the hostiles' trail from Calabasas. Veterans of the Victorio campaign, they had heard about the senseless killings at Peck's ranch, and they wanted Apache blood. Once Geronimo reversed direction and headed for the mountains, they frequently had to walk their mounts. The Apaches unwittingly helped their pursuers (who had no Indian guides) by littering the trail with the carcasses of some thirty horses. On May 2, the troopers endured a gruesome twenty-seven-mile march over "an awful trail" that led them to the east face of the Pinitos. Next morning, May 3, they broke camp at 6:00 A.M. and entered the canyon known today as Cajon de los Negros, named in honor of the black troopers of the Tenth Cavalry.

Here they found evidence of a "large camp" and followed the trail until midafternoon, when they came across the Chiricahuas about two hundred yards away on a "tongue of broken lava-like rock [on the] saddle of a very high mountain." Lebo designated every fourth trooper to hold the horses, formed a skirmish line, and set out on a deliberate pace toward the Apaches, who had taken "impregnable positions on a semi-circular cliff." Geronimo and Naiche must have admired the courage of the troopers, who occupied positions a few hundred yards below their concealed positions. Corporal Edward Scott fired the first shot, which drew an immediate volley that shattered his kneecap and killed Private Joseph Hollis.

Seeing Scott incapacitated, Lieutenant Powhatan K. Clarke rushed in to rescue the corporal, eventually pulling him to safety as he "heard bullets whiz and strike within six inches of his head." For this inspiring act of courage, he not only received a medal of honor but also became the subject of a drawing by Frederick Remington that memorialized his fearlessness under withering fire. Captain Lebo was just as brave. (One historian thought he "embodied the best qualities of the frontier cavalry officer.") After mounting a boulder, he coolly called out orders and advice to his men, who responded in kind. The fight lasted about an hour, during which each side fired from cover without any more casualties. At one point, several warriors tried to outflank the soldiers to run off their horses, but Lebo thwarted that effort by ordering the sergeant to remove the horses to a site farther down the canyon. Officers and troopers thought they had battled between eighty and one hundred warriors, slaying two Apaches and wounding one. But perception rarely equaled reality in an Apache fight. Geronimo and Naiche, with only sixteen men and two teenage boys, and suffering no casualties, had stopped Lebo's pursuit in its tracks.[27]

In keeping with his policy to allow the hostiles no rest, Miles had sent another command to relieve Lebo and follow the trail. Lieutenant Harry C. Benson, one company of Fourth Cavalry, and five Apache scouts marched to Lebo's campsite. On May 5, his scouts found the trail, which led south to the "worst possible country to travel over." That day three mules fell over the cliffs into canyons. To compound matters, his scouts were nervous about lurking hostiles, his lead scout deserted, and the Chiricahuas had set fires to further impede his command. On May 10, Captain Henry Lawton and his command took over and two days later found the bodies of three Mexicans and two Americans. At one Apache camp, they found a woman's hat, thought to be the one worn by Trinidad Verdin. Lawton supposed the Indians would continue south along the Magdalena River, but Geronimo and Naiche had reversed direction and slipped away.[28]

While the American troops were chasing shadows in the Pinito Mountains, the Chiricahuas had turned to the northwest, crossed the railroad tracks, and gone into the Cibuta Mountains. On May 10, vaqueros reported the entire band with seventy horses in the Huscomes Mountains, twenty-five miles south of Nogales. That evening an advance party of six warriors waylaid two Americans about three miles southeast of Barnett's Arizona ranch, killing Charles Murray and Thomas Shaw.[29]

The next day two Mexican forces battled the Chiricahuas at a place called Pinalta, just north of the Huscomes Mountains. National Guard troops from Magdalena walked into an ambush before noon. Within minutes, the Apaches had slain two Mexicans and wounded another three men, one mortally. They retired to the east side of Moritas Canyon. That afternoon a force of 150 men from Altar, many of them Papago Indians, reached the battlefield. The Chiricahua fighters (estimated generously at sixty or seventy strong) again opened fire from the ridges above; this time the Papagos and Mexicans simply ran, leaving behind thirty-three horses and much of their supplies. The next day the commander justified his departure on a shortage of "ammunition and provisions." Actually, the Mexicans suffered from a shortage of leadership and courage. During the rout, the Apaches openly displayed Peck's niece, inviting the Mexicans and their Indian allies to come and rescue her.[30]

Judging by what happened next, it appears that Naiche and Geronimo had two goals. Their first, naturally, was survival; the second was to find out what options were on the table with Americans. This clearly was Naiche's decision, and most of the men supported him. He would lead the party north. They knew that troops were patrolling the border from today's Columbus, New Mexico, to Nogales. They had to find a vulnerable point at which to enter Arizona and decided to move east. Three days after the fight at Pinalta, they were thirty-five miles east, where vaqueros at the Milpillas ranch, just east of the Cocóspera Mountains, spotted them. A vaquero rode to the camp of Captain Charles Hatfield on the San Pedro River three miles south of the border. An hour later, Hatfield, whose men were recuperating after a two-week patrol to the Ajos Mountains in Sonora, had his famous White Horse troop in the saddle. By sundown, they were a few miles from the ranch when a vaquero rode in with the news that at 3:00 P.M. that day, ten Chiricahuas had run off thirty horses, driving them toward the Cuitaco Mountains, east of Santa Cruz.

At 4:30 A.M., May 15, Hatfield's command of thirty-four troopers, guided by two Mexicans, Ramon Moreno and Xavier Mendez, followed the plainly marked trail. By 9:00 A.M. Hatfield's men were approaching the summit of the range (almost 6,600 feet high) when the scout in advance climbed a ridge and spotted the Apaches' camp. Something caught the eye of an alert Indian. The

Apaches grabbed their rifles and ammunition and removed the women and children to the rear, out of sight. The warriors ambushed Hatfield's troopers from a distance of two or three hundred yards. But Hatfield owned the high ground, and the Apaches, after a brief exchange of fire, melted away before the soldiers' eyes.

The Mexican scouts watched two Indians, Naiche and Geronimo, use their field glasses to assess the situation. The skirmish was brief—no casualties on either side. But Hatfield had scored a victory, recovering twenty-one horses, fifteen saddles, blankets, and food. The two Mexican scouts counted twenty-one bedrolls left in camp. Hatfield thought the camp contained seventy Apaches, which was almost twice their actual numbers. He decided to continue to Santa Cruz, the closest settlement. At noon, about three miles from town, Geronimo and Naiche turned the tables on Hatfield, waylaying him at a spring in a narrow ravine, killing two men, wounding two more, and recovering their stock and supplies. In addition, they took four horses, one of which was Hatfield's personal mount.[31]

The next day about 11:00 in the morning, Lieutenant Robert A. Brown and I Troop, Fourth Cavalry, stunned the Chiricahuas, who had halted to rest in an arroyo in the western foothills of the Cananea Mountains. He recovered five horses (two of which belonged to Hatfield's troopers) seven Winchester rifles, ammunition, and a few saddles. The troopers saw Geronimo jump on a white mule and escape. It proved to be only a temporary setback. That night the Chiricahuas replaced their loss by taking twenty-five horses from Santa Cruz.[32]

It was after either this attack or the first engagement with Hatfield that one of Naiche's closest friends, Tah-ni-toe, was missing in action. During the confusion, he was cut off from his people, losing his horse and weapon. He could have rejoined his friends, but he was weary of running and homesick, for he had not seen his wife, E-dood-lah, for exactly one year. Anxious to see his family, at Embudos Canyon he had asked Crook to send her to meet him at Fort Bowie, but the escape had obviated those plans. He decided to return to Fort Apache, even if he had to walk the entire way.[33]

After Brown's skirmish, Naiche decided to attempt a risky maneuver. He sent five men east to the San Jose Mountains, where they planned to enter Arizona to draw the attention of troops along the border. He and Geronimo with most of their people would continue toward Nogales.

We do not know who led this small group of men, but we can make a case for Atelnietze, whom Naiche referred to as "brother." During the day, May

17, the five-man raiding party came across five Mexicans with a pack train of mules loaded with mescal. Two Mexicans had weapons, and the Apaches killed them. They captured the other three and tied them up. The chief, evidently feeling good after getting his fill of the drink, released them, saying, "You may go; you had no rifles [so] we will not harm you." Early in the morning of May 18, the Indians entered Arizona through the Mule Mountains and promptly ran off horses from Antelope Springs, twelve miles east of Tombstone. They drove the stock into the Dragoon Mountains, where on May 19 they wounded a man and killed Fred Latley at Granite Springs. After this, they lay low for a few days, waiting to meet Naiche north of the Dragoon Mountains.[34]

Meanwhile, Naiche and Geronimo drove their band toward the border. They spent the night of May 17 south of the Buena Vista ranch, the site of their crossing three weeks earlier. They pivoted to the southwest, with Trinidad Verdin still traveling with them. Captain Lawton's force was a day behind. That afternoon, as they were about to cross the railroad tracks and head west, they saw two vaqueros, the Andrade brothers, coming toward them. The chiefs dispatched a small party to ambush them. Their opening salvo cut down one brother; the second brother took cover behind a tree and put up a fierce fight before he fell victim. The next day the Apaches skirted the northern part of the Cibuta Mountains, swung to the northwest through Planchas Canyon, and halted for a brief time to kill two Americans (J. Sullivan and D. McCarty) and a Mexican courier sent from Barnett's Arizona ranch to warn the mining settlement. The Indians were in such a hurry that they left the slain men's saddled horses, which, covered with blood, made their way to the silver mining settlement without their riders. Late that day, Naiche and Geronimo entered Arizona through the Pajarito Mountains and descended into Bear Canyon. Captain Lawton easily followed their trail by the carcasses of butchered stock and corpses left in their wake.[35]

Miles had remained in the area to coordinate the campaign from his headquarters in a hotel at Calabasas, sometimes at Nogales, and occasionally at Fort Huachuca. His men had more than held their own during the twenty-three days the Chiricahuas had crisscrossed the country below Nogales. The cavalry, for the most part without Apache scouts, had proved their mettle by operating in this inhospitable desert and these jagged mountains. Miles could move troops and supplies to pick up fresh trails, and cooperative Sonoran ranchers provided water, forage, and supplies.

At this time, with the desertion of Tah-ni-toe and the five-man diversionary raiding party in the Dragoons, the Chiricahuas numbered thirty-four individuals. Geronimo did not intend to leave Mexico until he had acceptable terms with an officer whom he could trust. As we shall see, he had good reason to stay clear of Arizona. He returned to Sonora with two men, two women, one child, and Trinidad Verdin.[36]

Naiche took twenty-seven followers north (eight men and nineteen women and children). He planned to rendezvous with the party that had preceded him into Arizona before traveling north to Fort Apache. It was not clear what he wanted to accomplish. Perhaps he wanted to send out feelers to Crook, but he, of course, was gone. According to Tah-ni-toe, they were disheartened, and several men and most of the women were clearly in favor of surrendering. In any event, this trip could hardly be considered a mission of peace because the Chiricahuas would slay at least thirteen people during their eighteen days in Arizona. Years later Naiche explained to Crook, "We were afraid. It was war. Anybody who saw us would kill us, and we did the same thing."[37]

Naiche's party raced north and crossed the Santa Rita Mountains to the Whetstones, where they fell upon three Mexicans, killing them on May 20. Two days later, early May 22, they raided the Telles ranch in the southwestern foothills of the Rincon Mountains. They captured a boy, the seven-year-old son of Juan Gastelo, and threw stones at his mother, who escaped with a few bruises. A seventeen-man posse trailed the Chiricahuas for some ten miles, overtaking them as they were roasting beef. The Indians fled, leaving eight horses and the boy behind. That night Naiche and five warriors headed for the Winchester Mountains, where the next day they met the raiding party from the Dragoons. Naiche's party now numbered eleven men, and they moved rapidly north. Ten miles south of Fort Thomas, they assaulted a lime camp, killing Frank Thurston. At 7:00 P.M. May 23, eight warriors (Naiche sent three men back to the Rincons to escort the women and children back to the border) crossed the Gila River seven miles southeast of Fort Thomas. The next morning they killed a man and took eight horses near today's Eden. Their destination was hardly a mystery to anyone: Fort Apache.[38]

Meanwhile, General Miles, at Calabasas, braced for their appearance at Fort Apache. Misreading the situation, he predicted that the hostiles were looking for a place to drop off their wounded and to recruit new fighters. This baseless forecast parroted those uninformed editorials so prevalent in Arizona's press. Clearly, Miles had no idea that nearly every able-bodied Chiricahua man at Fort Apache had served as a scout against the hostiles. And he could not conceive that those with kinship ties to the hostiles had no desire to cast their lot with their misguided brethren.[39]

Although he had been in Arizona now some six weeks, Miles still had no idea when he might succeed. He made two moves: first, he extended the olive branch; second, he rattled the saber. On May 20, he asked Captain Pierce at San Carlos, "Do you have anyone who will go to Geronimo's camp?" Pierce knew the answer without checking with the chiefs at San Carlos. He immediately responded, "There is no one here who will venture into the hostile camp. Perhaps Kaetenae, who is at [Fort] Apache, will attempt it." Next, although he wanted to avoid using Chiricahuas, he reluctantly asked Lieutenant Colonel Wade to sound out the Chiricahuas about taking a message to Geronimo. Wade spoke to the Chiricahua chiefs but found no takers.[40]

Second, he authorized a bounty of two thousand dollars for Geronimo, "dead or alive [and] fifty dollars for each warrior." When Miles heard that Mexicans were fighting the Apaches near Tres Alamos, he told Captain Lebo to recruit more Mexicans. Lebo could offer "four dollars per day and two thousand dollars if they get Geronimo." Miles also authorized Captain Pierce at San Carlos to "offer them any reasonable reward for Geronimo's capture." Yet, not one Apache at San Carlos jumped at Miles's blood money.[41]

The War Department later condemned this policy, but the territorial delegate from Arizona, Curtis Bean, advocated that the government establish a bounty of twenty-five thousand dollars for Geronimo's scalp. And from the land of Dixie came another suggestion: Georgia bloodhounds. "These dogs make no mistakes and will stay on the trail day and night until they overtake their game."[42]

As usual, rumors swirled during these confusing times. On May 24 alone, one historian notes, the telegraph lines transmitted fourteen messages between Miles and his commanders in the field and at military posts. Miles assumed that the deep-rooted sympathies of the reservation Apaches, particularly the Chiricahuas at Fort Apache, must inherently lie with the hostiles. One report reached him that the hostiles were trying to "get near Eskiminzin," the Arivaipa chief. Miles telegraphed his concerns to Captain Pierce at San Carlos, who sent a man to keep an eye on him. He found the chief at work in his fields, "with his rifle fastened to his back." Then came the predictable if not timeworn report that Naiche was heading into Navajo country. Colonel Bradley reassured Miles that "if hostiles come, the Navajos will capture them." Geronimo and Naiche "had no friends in Navajo Country."[43] Indeed, authorities would have been hard pressed to find any Indian allies or sympathizers in Arizona or New Mexico.

After hearing that Naiche's party had crossed the Gila, Wade informed Miles, "It hardly seems possible that they will come in here but I am doing everything in my power to be ready for them, if they do come." He predicted that if they came, it would be at night. He thought there was "no danger of any [reservation Chiricahuas] joining the hostiles." And the White Mountain Apaches wanted a crack at avenging their relatives killed by Ulzana the previous November. They pledged to patrol the country between the Black River and Fort Apache. Yet, despite these precautions, Naiche with seven men crossed the Black River to Bonito Creek and camped in a secluded area northeast of its junction with the Little and Big Bonito. At dusk on May 25, they left their horses in a meadow and hid their saddles, bridles, blankets, and supplies in the trees and bushes beneath a ridge. They struck out on foot for the Chiricahua camps about seven miles away.

Three weeks earlier Cooney, the sergeant of scouts with Noche under Lieutenant Shipp, had gone to San Carlos and escorted the women and children related to the hostiles back to Apache. So when Naiche sneaked into the village, probably that of his old group headed by Bish-to-yey, he saw his mother, Dos-teh-seh and other relatives. Wade believed that only one man had entered the camp, but the sparse evidence is ambiguous. Naiche remained a short time, found out that Crook had sent his immediate family away, learned that the Chiricahua scouts were no longer on his trail, and then left, apparently in ill humor.[44]

Wade informed Miles of this development. Miles and his staff had left Calabasas and taken the train to Willcox. He telegraphed Wade that it was "important to take that buck in." He suggested that Wade send out an elderly Chiricahua to make contact with the hostiles. Unfortunately, after two nights of talking to the Chiricahua chiefs, he was unable to persuade any of them to undertake the mission. Even though Wade had made an effort to develop a rapport with the Indians, the chiefs were still apprehensive. They considered "the hostiles [their] enemies. If they went, the hostiles would not believe them, might kill them, or might force them to go along with them." Finally, the evening of May 26, two women agreed to go—Naiche's mother, Dos-teh-seh, and another unidentified woman, whose son was with Naiche. She may have been Et-tso-hnn (Bonita), the mother of Fun, who had come north with Naiche. The only message they carried was a vague promise that Naiche's party would be "treated justly." But if they were contemplating surrendering, of course, those terms were meaningless.[45]

On the afternoon of May 26, 1886, Captain John T. Morrison, with Troop A, Tenth Cavalry, and ten Apache scouts, discovered the saddles, horses, and supplies that Naiche had left behind. He was careful not to disturb any of the Indians' possessions, and his men carefully wiped clean any trace of their presence. They lay in ambush all night waiting for Naiche's return. By morning, his troopers' perseverance was wearing thin. Many of the men complained that the hostiles must have discovered their trap. Captain Morrison urged patience. Finally, about 7:00 A.M. on May 27, they spotted Naiche, who had appeared on the rim of the canyon directly opposite the soldiers. With binoculars, Naiche studied the area, looking for any presence of life, listening for any strange noise.

Satisfied that all was well, he motioned a man forward, followed by the other men. Single file, they began to descend along the trail to the canyon. Naiche was in front, cautiously examining signs, when suddenly he shouted a warning cry. Each Apache scrambled for cover to the ridge behind him. Morrison's men fired one ineffective volley, mounted their horses, and rode to the ridge, but the Chiricahuas were gone. What triggered Naiche's flight? The most likely version suggests he saw a single boot print that the soldiers had neglected to wipe away; another newspaper report states that despite Morrison's pleas for patience, "one very impatient buffalo soldier could restrain himself no longer. He raised his head for a peek at the Apaches, who saw him, scattered and fled." Regardless, Naiche was gone. His horses and supplies were in the hands of the troops, but that hardly fazed him. Later that day, several parties of scouts tried to follow the trail, which led north "through very rough country."[46]

This was the scenario when the two concerned Chiricahua mothers went out in search of their sons. In case they met soldiers, they carried with them a safe conduct pass signed by Wade. Two days later, on May 29, they returned, denying that they had spoken to their sons. Yet, Dos-teh-seh may have met Naiche, either up close or from a distance, because of what she said to Lieutenant Colonel Wade then and what she revealed to him later. On her return, she told Wade that the hostiles "had a bad scare [Morrison's ambush] and will be very cautious for a few days." She thought they would remain in the vicinity unless troops continued to harass them. Three months later, she confirmed to Wade that she had seen Naiche, whom she called an "ungrateful son [who] would have nothing to do with her."[47]

Naiche had come north with an open mind, possibly ready to surrender. When Miles received Wade's first report of Dos-teh-seh's efforts, he thought the hostiles might be looking to surrender. He therefore telegraphed Wade specific terms beyond his original promise of "just treatment." Wade acknowledged the new terms, saying that he wished that he had had "this authority when the two [women] went out before." They ventured out again, but by this time, Naiche had vacated the area. On May 30, Naiche's party raided Hampson's ranch on Eagle Creek, slaying two Americans, before moving west toward Fort Thomas. By early June, they had returned to the Rincon Mountains. Here they discovered that the main band of twenty-five had already departed toward the border. Troops and citizens had made it too dangerous to wait for Naiche's return.[48]

The first group took two American lives before crossing into Sonora via the Pajarito Mountains on June 1, 1886. Meanwhile, Naiche led his men south and on June 3 killed Clinton Davis four miles east of the Vail ranch. The next day, they added another victim, a man named Carr. Two days later raiders stole stock from Mathews ranch and Courtney's ranch in the Whetstones, stealing forty horses at the latter's place. On June 6, the last victim of Naiche's raid fell near Harshaw, a man named Thomas Hunt.

Naiche struck for the Patagonia Mountains. At dusk, Lieutenant Robert D. Walsh, with twenty-six men of B Troop, Fourth Cavalry, and thirteen Apache scouts intercepted his band near the Mowry mines in the Patagonia Mountains. The parties simultaneously spotted each other. The Chiricahuas jumped off their horses and abandoned everything, stock, flour, and cooking utensils, before escaping into the high country. According to Walsh, his detail recovered six horses and four mules, which he gave to his scouts to ride. His surprise failed to impede Naiche's progress south. By morning, June 7, the group was in Sonora. Although Miles's heliograph stations provided the intelligence leading to Walsh's success, because the Chiricahuas remained south of the border for the rest of the summer, the stations' contribution was minor during the rest of the campaign.[49]

Meanwhile, on May 30, 1886, General Miles submitted a report summarizing operations for the month. He termed the results "in the main, satisfactory." He conceded that his men had done "all that can be expected." Yet, he cautioned his superiors that difficult times lay ahead and "many more lives may be lost." He also boasted that the "Indians on the reservation have been restrained and the number of hostiles slightly reduced." With respect to the first point, no force—and certainly not Miles's soldiers—played any role in preventing the Indians at San Carlos and Fort Apache from joining the hostiles—they simply preferred life at the agency and had nothing but contempt for the hostiles. Furthermore, his statement that the hostiles were "slightly reduced" in numbers also was false, but one that he could make because his commanders had erroneously reported Chiricahua losses in Lebo's and Hatfield's fights.[50]

Eight days later, Miles reported that his men had driven Naiche into Sonora, but only after the chief's warriors had slain thirteen "unarmed persons
near remote places." Few of the victims were unarmed, of course, but a little
white lie never bothered Miles. Sheridan, however, was accustomed to the
commander's tendency to stretch the truth. In mid-June, Miles warned that
his present force was insufficient to restrain the forty thousand Indians in Arizona and New Mexico. Of course, this was yet another example of Miles's
propaganda packaged in a pleasing pouch, or in this case a deceptive telegram.
But even Sheridan could not swallow Miles's duplicitous statement, declaring that it was "calculated to mislead." After all, there may have been forty
thousand Indians in his department, but the hostiles numbered but forty in all,
eighteen of whom were men (excluding Mangas's small party).[51]

Miles, knowing that Sheridan would disapprove, intentionally failed to
disclose that he was continuing to explore diplomatic means (Dos-teh-seh's
efforts) to secure surrender. When her attempts proved fruitless, he decided to
turn to the Chiricahuas' former agent, Tom Jeffords, hoping that a partnership
with Cochise's wife might be the ticket into Naiche's camp. But it was too late.
By the time Jeffords got under way, Naiche had slipped into Sonora.[52]

After crossing the border on June 7, Naiche led his band southwest, skirting
the San Lazaro hacienda en route to the Pinito Mountains, which he reached
later that day. Two days later he returned to the Apache ranchería on the highest ridge of the Azul Mountains, where as planned he met Geronimo. The shaman had been quiet after separating from Naiche on May 19. Trini Verdin was
with him. She said that they had journeyed southwest into the uninhabited
desert country north of Altar, an unfamiliar region to them. A gray-haired
man acted as the advance scout. This man was probably Nat-cul-baye. With
them were two women (their wives), one young warrior (probably Hunlona),
and a young girl. Trini recalled that they treated her well. The only time the
men scolded her, she said, occurred when she left footprints instead of step-
ping on rocks. After several days of wandering, the small party turned back.
On May 27, 1886, vaqueros from San Lazaro cut Geronimo's trail, which led
from Santa Barbara into the Pinito Mountains, from where he had moved
southeast to the summit of the Azul Mountains to meet Naiche and the main
band.[53]

After a two-day stay, the beleaguered band of forty came to a pragmatic
decision. They left the Azul Mountains and went into the Madera Mountains.
Here, according to both Trini Verdin and official Sonoran reports, they split
into three parties. Trini recalled that on or about June 11, a "tall, slender,

sway-backed young Indian, who sometimes seemed to give orders [obviously Naiche], took six men and some women and children and went up a high mountain to the southwest." The mountain was surely a peak in the Cucurpe Mountains. Trini Verdin went east with Geronimo's party of six Indians. A third group of nine warriors, with a few women, went northeast. The parties planned to join near the junction of the Aros and Yaqui rivers north of Sahuaripa.[54]

General Miles was ready to send his command into the Sierra Madre, believing that the hostiles would certainly return there. Now he would find out whether his elite strike force, led by the energetic and resourceful Captain Lawton and Assistant Surgeon Wood, could handle the rigors of pursuing an enemy whose sole purpose was to stay alive.

Lawton's command had logged five hundred miles in its pursuit of the Chiricahuas in May. He needed fresh Indian scouts and soldiers for a campaign into Sonora. Confident in his strategy, he repeated, "We can yet come up with the hostiles & meet them successfully but I must have good strong men who believe in possibility of success & officers willing to sustain a few hardships and set cheerful example." This assignment required physically fit soldiers: "I want officers who can walk." Success would follow "hard and continued labor [by men] content with such hardship & self denial and only men of character and physical strength are fit for such work."[55]

The evening of June 7, Captain Lawton left Nogales to assume command of Lieutenant Walsh's company, which was following Naiche toward the Pinito Mountains. The next day his force struck the trail. With him were some forty troopers and twenty Apache scouts under lieutenants Finley and Walsh. Assistant Surgeon Wood, with the pack train, crossed the border on June 12, several days behind Lawton, who by then had found the abandoned base camp in the Azul Mountains. On June 18, the command entered a canyon and unexpectedly ran into a Mexican force that had had a deadly encounter with Geronimo the day before.[56]

The Mexican leader was Patricio Valenzuela, owner of the Agua Fria hacienda, eight miles east of Cucurpe. The evening of June 16, his vaqueros had found a butchered cow and ox at Tapacadepe. The tracks suggested the involvement of four Apaches. Valenzuela assembled a force of twenty-one men, which was augmented by nine mounted men with a pack mule carrying extra cartridges from Cucurpe. The entire force was mounted. After marching north about eight miles from Agua Fria, about midday, June 17, they reached El Gusano and stopped to water their horses. Soon after, they unexpectedly ran into Geronimo's party, which had also stopped to rest. Trini Verdin thought the Apaches saw the Mexicans first. Abandoning their supplies, Geronimo gave orders to flee. He mounted a horse and helped Trini to get up behind him. Valenzuela's force bravely charged the camp, firing on the fleeing Apaches, who retired up a box canyon. Meanwhile, Geronimo watched helplessly as a Mexican salvo wounded his wife. She dismounted and emptied a revolver at the enemy before Mexican volleys cut her down in a hail of bullets. At this time, Geronimo tried to escape, but his horse stumbled over a boulder, tripping him up. He and Trini were thrown from the horse. Calling for her to follow, he scampered to cover into the rocks. Instead, she escaped to the Mexicans, who had captured the camp and were already ogling saddles, clothing, coffee pots, and gunpowder.

Valenzuela faced a difficult choice. Geronimo had taken cover in the rocks in a box canyon. Perhaps slightly wounded, he had crawled into a cave with his 1873 Springfield rifle. Valenzuela admitted that he could not see him, even with his spyglass. He deployed his soldiers along the "two ridges encircling the canyon." He had cautioned his men not to "expose themselves to plain sight," but Francisco Valenzuela y Munguia got careless. Geronimo, known for his marksmanship, "brought him down with one shot and he rolled down the cliff." The lone marksman killed two more men and wounded a third as the Mexicans attempted to approach his concealed position. At dusk, Valenzuela called off the flanking movement. The three slain men had bullet holes in their heads, testimony to the remarkable sharp shooting of Geronimo.[57]

The next day Lawton's command met Valenzuela's force on the battlefield. The Sonorans, initially mistaking his Apache scouts for hostiles, were ready to open fire until the officers convinced them otherwise. Lawton's men saw the dead Mexicans and the corpse of Geronimo's wife, freshly scalped, for Sonora still paid bounties for Apache hair. And they interviewed Trini Verdin. Lawton wrote his wife that he "would have given anything to have gotten the girl myself." Lawton joined Valenzuela's command and returned to Agua Fria ranch to await the arrival of Benson's fresh troops and Indian scouts. Valenzuela, distressed at the loss of three of his men, termed the affair a "memorable tragedy."[58]

Yet there were more victims in Sonora that day. Seventy-five miles southeast of Geronimo's fight, Naiche's party of about twenty, which included seven men, had slain four Mexicans at Escondida, between Motepori and Banámichi. They went south into the Aconchi Mountains, where they apparently remained for a while before striking an old Apache trail toward Tepache and the

Sierra Madre. Meanwhile, the third party had appeared at John Hohstadt's Janaverachi ranch in the northern Ajos Mountains. Here they butchered several
head of cattle before crossing the Sonora River to the Manzinal Mountains.
Their appearances at three different places kept them ahead of Lawton's command and Mexican troops, but their pursuers knew they would seek refuge
in the Sierra Madre. The only question was where. Would it be the upper
Bavispe near Geronimo's favorite haunts in the Teras range, as many Sonoran
officials predicted? Or would they return to the uninhabited country along the
Aros River, where Crawford had found them?[59]

Lawton believed that the three parties would join to "make a permanent
camp." And once they did, "we may have some chance of finding them." Determination and effort, combined with a strong sense of duty, were Lawton's
trademarks. And, from a personal perspective, he viewed this as an opportunity to enhance his "reputation" in order to earn "good favor and all the
credit I can get" from Miles.[60] But Lawton had no idea of the challenges that
lay ahead.

25

ALL CHIRICAHUAS ARE CREATED EQUAL

> We have not slept for six months and are worn out.
> Geronimo, August 27, 1886

Four days after Geronimo's fight north of Cucurpe, Lawton wrote his wife that he was waiting at Valenzuela's Agua Fria ranch for Lieutenant Benson to return with fresh troops and supplies from Huachuca before resuming his march toward the Sierra Madre. "Somebody must do something and I am going to try and do it," he vowed.[1] On June 22, Tom Horn, one civilian scout, and three soldiers rode into camp with a message from Benson, whose command had camped near Cumpas. On June 23, Lawton's command finally left for the Sonora River. Lieutenant Brown with thirty Apache scouts and the infantry from Huachuca joined him at Sinoquipe. Lawton decided to send Assistant Surgeon Wood with Brown's company of scouts to the site of Naiche's attack on June 17. Lawton took the infantry and cavalry to Cumpas to refit.[2]

Here Lawton encamped, again waiting until Wood and Brown arrived with the Indian scouts. The snail's pace of the operation was threatening to overwhelm Lawton: the food was bad, insects made sleeping almost impossible, and 120-degree days were common. Moreover, the morale of the nineteen infantry from Huachuca, chosen because they were best suited to endure the physical challenges of desert and mountain campaigning, was nearly mutinous. And for some inexplicable reason, no officer was available at Huachuca to command the infantry. Wood formed his first impressions of the infantry's sergeant when he was "brought into camp with his hands tied behind him and his gun lashed across his back." Lawton was discouraged.

The inactivity in camp magnified his frustrations. He detested Sonora, which he termed "a godforsaken country with godforsaken people living in it." As far as he was concerned, "the Indians are better than the Mexicans." Assistant Surgeon Leonard Wood's arrival on July 2 was the tonic that lifted Lawton's spirits. The indefatigable New England doctor was a human dynamo, treating over one hundred sick people at Cumpas and then agreeing to take command of the demoralized infantry.[3]

Shortly after Wood's appearance, a courier from Moctezuma arrived with news. On July 1, the Chiricahuas had slain José Rodríguez at a mescal ranch near Tepache, twenty-five miles southeast. Late in the afternoon on July 6, Lawton left Moctezuma bound for Tepache, where he hoped his scouts would discover a trail. Realizing that cavalry in mountainous country was useless, Lawton took only a pack train, Lieutenant Brown, thirty Apache scouts, and nineteen infantrymen under Wood.[4]

They had marched several miles when a courier rode in with a dispatch from the prefect of Moctezuma. At Tonibabi, a ranch eight miles east of there, Chiricahuas had shot a man earlier that day. Assuming this was the party reported near Tepache, Lawton reversed directions and hurried to the ranch, where Wood cut the bullet from the man's shoulder. When the Apache scouts found the trail, which had unexpectedly come from the north, Lawton now realized that he had two parties of Indians. The next day, July 7, his scouts cut the trail of two horses and one mule going south.[5]

This was apparently Geronimo's party of five. On June 20, 1886, three days after the battle in the box canyon, Geronimo had swept by the ranch of Leonardo Gómez, north of Arispe. Gómez had picked up the trail of six Apaches going east. On June 25, another detachment had picked up the trail of six Apaches, two on foot, near Cumpas. Both commanders thought the Indians were bound for the Teras Mountains. If so, Geronimo's stay there was brief. He eventually headed south toward Tepache.[6]

Lawton's scouts had trouble following the trail. The rainy season had begun, and torrential storms washed out the tracks. On July 9, Lawton and Wood went to Tepache for the latest news. They learned that citizens had seen hostiles the day before. Although the Western Apache scouts could follow a trail, they were clearly unfamiliar with the area. Thus, when Mexican officials offered the services of two men who knew the country, Lawton wisely accepted.[7]

The Apaches went southeast toward the Yaqui River. Lieutenant Brown with his thirty Apache scouts took the lead, followed by Lawton, Wood, nineteen infantrymen, and the pack train. They were now penetrating "the worst mountains imaginable [with] the roughest kinds of canyons." Sizzling heat forced the men to march in their "drawers and undershirts." On July 11,

Lawton, frustrated though still resolute, lamented, "Everything seems to be going wrong." He was determined to carry out his assignment but felt that his superiors had left him hanging on a very thin branch. He observed, "I have been told by all my commanding officers that I can have anything I want but I have not been given anything. Yet . . . I have one good quality, I do not get discouraged and will never give up." One day later, on July 12, Lawton felt better when he reached the Yaqui River and his scouts found that the small trail of Apaches had merged into another trail of twenty animals that came from the west. This was Naiche's group. Lawton now thought that his initial instincts were correct: "The small parties were coming together [to form] the main camp."[8]

At noon the next day (July 13), two of Brown's scouts, "wet with perspiration" ran into camp with welcome news. They had found the Chiricahua village on a low saddle between two buttes overlooking the Yaqui River, about six miles below its junction with the Aros River. Lawton, then about eight miles from the hostile camp, left immediately with Wood's infantry and the two scouts, who led them to a summit on the northeast corner of the Pavos Mountains. From here, they could see the Chiricahua camp, "hemmed in on two sides by mountains." Wood saw "fires burning, Indian ponies picketed out, [and] a good many Indians, men, women, and children moving about in all directions." Hoping to gain positions "well above their camp," the twenty-seven-year-old Brown, who would lead a brigade against the Germans in World War I, had already launched a flanking movement to the left. He planned to assault the village and drive the Indians toward Lawton's infantry. Lawton's force had just begun to approach the ranchería when he heard gunfire. His men rushed to the village and found it occupied by Brown's scouts, who had fired at ghosts. The Chiricahuas had escaped through the canebrake upriver. Lawton was "so disappointed as to be sick, for here was the chance we had been looking for so long, and it slipped from me without being able to do anything to prevent it."[9]

Wood found out a few months later that one warrior who was out hunting had discovered their trail and immediately returned to camp and spread the alarm. Naiche remembered that the sudden appearance left him so discouraged that he felt like "giving up." He was not feeling well, and one young woman was seven months pregnant when "they had to scamper." A few months later, Geronimo expressed his admiration for Lawton's dogged determination.[10]

Lawton's only consolation was that the hostiles, whom the scouts estimated to be "at least thirty," had left everything behind, camp equipment, provisions, horses and mules, which numbered nineteen. The scouts took the spoils of war and for the next few days devoted their energy to their new prizes instead of following the hostiles. In reality, Lawton's men needed a rest. He had pushed himself to the point of exhaustion during the forced march. And his second in command, Assistant Surgeon Wood, had been suffering from a tarantula bite that he had to repeatedly lance. Indeed, he nearly lost his life, and in the coming weeks, Lawton almost perished from illness. For the next three weeks, Lawton lingered along the Aros River, hoping that Brown's scouts might pick up the trail. But the Chiricahuas had vacated the Sierra Madre and gone west.[11]

Meanwhile, on July 31, Lawton wrote his wife that he planned to stay in the mountains "until Geronimo is killed or surrenders." The next day, much to his dismay, he learned that Lieutenant Charles Gatewood was near with two Chiricahua scouts. General Miles had sent them to find Geronimo and to convince him to surrender.[12]

In late June, Miles had gone to Fort Apache to build a case for the recommendations made the previous summer by Indian Inspector Frank Armstrong, who had called for the removal of the reservation Chiricahuas to Fort Leavenworth, Kansas. The momentum for this initiative, which had reached a boiling point with Sheridan during Ulzana's raid the previous November, had since died down in Washington. Miles, who had supported Armstrong's plan, was determined to resurrect the issue. His words were ominous. He was examining the "serious question of the final disposition" of the Chiricahuas at Fort Apache.[13]

He had previously discussed the logistics of carrying out this operation with Captain Pierce at San Carlos and Lieutenant Colonel Wade at Fort Apache. He asked Wade to find out the feelings of the Chiricahuas about removal. On May 5, 1886, Wade temporarily shelved the matter until the paymaster paid the Chiricahua scouts for their time with Crawford's command. Sometime later that month, he talked to the chiefs about transferring to another unidentified location. His remarks naturally stirred up some of the Indians, especially Zele and Noche (Crawford's indispensable scout). Both considered fleeing with their followers (about 110 in all) to Fort Union. In response, Wade locked them in the guardhouse at San Carlos. Furthermore, Loco, who had relatives on the Navajo Reservation, would have taken his people there if permitted, especially in light of their problems with the White Mountain people after Ulzana's raid. A majority of the Chiricahuas at Fort Apache would have agreed to move to reservations in New Mexico.[14]

The general played every chip in his arsenal to ensure the success of his visit. With the hostiles now heading for the Sierra Madre, Miles realized that the odds on Lawton striking a telling blow had dropped considerably. He had hired Tom Jeffords to act as his adviser and liaison to the Chiricahuas. Next, probably acting on Jeffords's advice, he released Zele and his nephew, Noche, and sent them to Fort Apache. Finally, he invited Special Agent L. Q. C. Lamar, Jr., son of the secretary of the interior (and a supporter of Armstrong's proposal), to join him. According to Miles, he asked Lamar only to foster a spirit of cooperation between the War and Interior departments—a spirit absent during Crook's tenure. Perhaps he was telling the truth.[15]

Miles and Lamar arrived at Fort Apache on June 30. The next day, with Jeffords by their side, they met the Chiricahuas' principal men. The presence of their former agent undoubtedly helped Miles to gain their confidence. What Miles saw appalled him. The Chiricahuas had come to the meeting carrying their weapons. He also heard about the ongoing tiswin binges, for the Chiricahuas were planting corn, and this meant a bountiful supply of sprouts with which to brew their favorite beverage.[16]

Miles explained the purpose of his visit and the necessity (for their own welfare) of moving them to a new reservation. According to Noche, Cooney, and Toclanny, the general gave them two reasons: "People [Apaches and whites] don't seem to like you." Cooney and Toclanny were more specific, blaming the White Mountain Apaches, particularly Sánchez, the slayer of Azariquelch. Cooney added that Miles stated, "The Indians at Apache were getting drunk [on tiswin] all the time and killing each other." Miles noted that "the discharge of rifles and pistols in their savage orgies" often broke the stillness of the nights. He asked the leaders to form a delegation to visit Washington to discuss plans for their future. En route, they would examine two potential sites for their new homes. During a second meeting a few days later, ten of the principal men agreed to go. Among them were Chatto and Noche for the Chokonens, and Loco, Kaetenae, and Charley for the Chihennes. They left on July 13, 1886.[17]

Another development took place on July 1, 1886. Miles spoke to Tah-ni-toe, the warrior who had left Naiche in mid-May and surrendered to Wade on June 27. Tah-ni-toe reiterated what he had said to Wade. Many hostiles were disheartened and anxious to give up. Again, Miles's thoughts turned to diplomacy.[18] This admission had given Miles the welcome justification (in case Sheridan questioned his decision) to adopt new diplomatic measures to end the war. Accordingly, he asked the Chiricahuas for volunteers to take terms to

Geronimo and Naiche. He wanted men "who had been out with Geronimo." His initial plea fell flat.[19]

Tah-ni-toe, after a long journey on foot from Mexico, wanted no part of the mission. And the fearless Bonito wanted nothing to do with the hostiles. He had recently married a White Mountain woman from Alchesay's band. In the spring of 1886, he took his extended family, nine individuals, and joined his wife's people, who were also his people by birth. After hearing the talk of removal, he informed Wade that he was participating in the conference as a White Mountain Apache and not as a Chiricahua.[20] Loco's Chihennes, who had responded to Crawford's call for scouts, were also out of the question. His men disliked Geronimo, whom they blamed for the tragedy on Alisos Creek.

That left the Chokonens. Miles turned to Noche (whom he had met at Fort Bowie) and Chatto for help. With Chiva too old for leadership, Noche had replaced Bonito as head of his small band. The next day, July 2, 1886, Noche recommended Kayitah, and Chatto suggested Martine, who had married the widow of Chinche. Both men had relatives with the hostiles and were well acquainted with Geronimo.

On July 3, Miles briefly considered sending them to Fort Bowie, where Lieutenant Richards was about to embark with Apache scouts into Mexico.[21] He had second thoughts, however, and held them back until he could decide who would lead the peace party. Jeffords seemed like a logical choice, but Miles opted to overlook him. Perhaps the general wanted a military man to ensure that the credit for a successful result would accrue to him and his officers.

On July 7, Lieutenant Thaddeus W. Jones officially enlisted Kayitah and Martine as scouts. Two days later, Miles gave them a safe conduct pass. And, following the advice of Wade, he made a profoundly important decision to name Lieutenant Charles Gatewood to head up the peace party. Miles, predictably, had kept the news of his olive branch from Sheridan. Although he had no authority to offer terms to the hostiles, he sanctioned an offer of limited conditions (sparing their lives). In a letter to the *Army and Navy Journal*, one officer from Fort Apache concisely explained the rationale: "Miles was assuming all responsibility for the surrender feeling that the country will back him in winding up a tedious campaign."[22]

Miles had to persuade Gatewood, then stationed in New Mexico, to accept the job. On July 13, Miles met him in Albuquerque and explained the mission. According to Louis Kraft, in his seminal work *Gatewood and Geronimo*, the lieutenant thought the "mission sounded like a fool's errand." The assignment—finding Geronimo in the Sierra Madre with two Chiricahuas and a small escort—held no appeal to him. After Miles sweetened the pot, offering to hire him as aide-de-camp, Gatewood reluctantly accepted the task. In Albuquerque, he convinced George Wrattan, a twenty-year-old man who had worked at San Carlos for several years, to join the peace party.[23]

Three days later, Gatewood and Wrattan met Kayitah and Martine at Bowie. Here, Gatewood added Frank Huston, an experienced packer, to handle the three pack mules. Miles had directed Major Beaumont, the post commander, to provide Gatewood with a string of riding mules and supplies. Fearful the Chiricahuas might capture Gatewood and use him as a bargaining chip, he had ordered Gatewood to take a twenty-five man military escort for protection. Beaumont claimed he could not spare any troops, but he assured Gatewood that he could pick up an escort en route to Mexico. Gatewood stopped at Cloverdale, but one look at the garrison convinced him they were ill equipped to handle the rigors of field duty in Mexico. On July 21, 1886, his party reached Carretas, the base used by Captain Wirt Davis's command during his second campaign. By then, Gatewood had added a sixth man to his party, a rancher named Tex Whaley, who would serve as courier.[24]

At Carretas, he found Lieutenant James Parker, the same man whom Geronimo had known at Fort Apache. Gatewood had heard that Parker had seen an Apache trail, but it was three weeks old, and the summer rains had washed it away. Gatewood was ready to scuttle the mission, but Parker would have none of that talk. He vowed to put the lieutenant on a trail. After Gatewood rested for six days to recover from an illness, perhaps dysentery, his party, with Parker's command as escort, headed into the Sierra Madre. On August 3, they rode into Lawton's camp near the junction of the Nácori and Aros rivers.[25]

Gatewood told Wood that he had "no faith in the plan and [was] disgusted with it." Lawton reached an understanding that would permit Gatewood to present General Miles's terms to Geronimo and Naiche if circumstances allowed.[26] On August 8, 1886, Lawton decided to take the advice of Kayitah and Martine and embark on a "long scout" to the southeast, where Crawford had found the Chiricahuas. Yet Gatewood was not feeling well and asked Wood to place him on sick leave so that he could return to Fort Bowie. Wood refused to authorize it. Lawton, now recognizing that prospects were bleak for a military solution, began to view Gatewood's mission more positively. He wrote his wife: "Now that I have Gatewood with me, and he has authority to communicate with them and offer them a chance to surrender, I have great hopes of winding up the war soon. All I want now is to find the trail again."[27]

Lawton's "long scout" lasted all of eight miles. On August 8, 1886, two couriers returned from Sahuaripa with the first definite news of the Chiricahuas since July 21, 1886. They had ambushed a mule train near Ures. Lawton immediately pivoted the command in its tracks and headed for his former camp north of the Aros River. He expected to hear that the hostiles were either west or north of him. He thought they would avoid the country below the Aros as long as his command was there.[28]

While Lawton had seemed stuck in quicksand along the junctions of the Nácori and Aros rivers, the thirty-eight hostiles had left the Sierra Madre and raced toward Ures. On July 23, 1886, Naiche and Geronimo lay in ambush above a canyon in the Mazatan Mountains. A sixty-mule pack train was taking provisions to Ures. It had been three years since the Chiricahuas had raided near Sonora's one-time capital city. Their surprise was complete: five men were slain; one man and two women escaped. The Chiricahuas gained much-needed provisions and mounts. They packed what they wanted on fifteen mules and slit the throats of the remaining forty-five.

Over the next few days they mounted the entire band courtesy of horse ranches near Nácori Grande. They met no resistance, for the state had deployed local National Guard units in the south to fight the Yaquis. One week later, Naiche and Geronimo were fifty miles north in mountains east of Baviacora, where three Mexicans discovered a trail of men, women, and children. After resting a few days, the chiefs left the Sonora River and headed northeast toward a familiar destination—the rugged Teras Mountains just south of Batepito.[29]

Before reaching their destination, Geronimo and Naiche launched four attacks during a five-day period beginning August 8, 1886. For all but two of their men, these actions would be the last of their lives. On August 8, twenty mounted warriors killed Antonio Vázquez and Ramón Castillo at the San Luis mines near Cumpas. The next day, they ambushed Antonio Gonzáles, a courier taking dispatches to Lawton, a few miles north of Cumpas. The first fire killed Gonzáles' horse, but he escaped on foot to Cumpas. The third day, August 11, 1886, found the Chiricahuas twenty miles north of Cumpas. At 11:00 A.M., Naiche and Geronimo ambushed six Americans who had left Santa Rosa mines in pursuit of them. At the onset of the melee, one American faced off against Naiche. Both men fired at the same time. The American's bullet slammed into the rear sight of Naiche's rifle, grazing his arm and chest before striking his leg. Naiche's first shot missed, but a second volley killed the American. A few weeks later Naiche admitted to his role in the fight, telling one American that his opponent had been very brave. The battle, depending on accounts, lasted either four or seven hours and left three Americans dead (J. E. O'Brien, P. Hatcher, and John Thompson) and two wounded. One man,

James Kirk, escaped injury and rode to Bacoachi for help. The Apaches took the horses and weapons of the slain men. On the Indian side, besides Naiche's wounds, the American gunfire had wounded Geronimo. Their fourth raid occurred the next day, when they harassed Turicachi, taking some stock. Their trail led north to the Cuchuta hacienda.[30]

Here, from a ridge on a nearby hill, Geronimo spoke to three Mexicans and offered a truce. It was early in the evening of August 13, 1886. The three vaqueros backtracked to Cuchuta and passed along the proposal to the alcalde, José Rios. He went out with a small party and talked with Geronimo. Rios scheduled formal talks two days later with the prefect of Fronteras. The next day, Antonio Gonzáles, returning to Huachuca with dispatches from Lawton, met Geronimo (who had his arm in a sling), Naiche, Nat-cul-baye, and three vaqueros from Cuchuta. The following day, August 15, 1886, the prefect from Fronteras met the chiefs, who agreed to wait eight days for terms from Governor Torres. A few days later, two Apache women arrived at Fronteras to pick up supplies and mescal. Meanwhile, Geronimo moved east across the mountains and camped near Cuchuverachi.[31]

As we shall see, Geronimo had no plans to surrender to Mexicans.

The hostiles were tired of running, and many, especially Naiche and Geronimo, longed to see their families, then in Florida. They were ready to surrender to Americans. But the initial contact had to be with an American whom they could trust. For this to occur, this American must first find them.[32]

While Geronimo and Naiche remained in the area waiting for their two women to return from Fronteras with their coveted mescal, Governor Torres set the conditions for peace. He offered an armistice in return for a pledge that the Chiricahuas would turn in their weapons and move to a designated place, where Mexican officials would watch over them and provide necessities. He directed the prefect of Arispe, Jesús Aguirre, to proffer these terms to the Chiricahuas. Not surprisingly, the governor had treachery up his sleeve. The official Mexican policy for Apache captives, as demonstrated by their actions after capturing Juh's sons and others at Casas Grandes in late 1885, was a life sentence in prison at Mexico City. This was Torres's intent, though he did not reveal it to Aguirre, who was supposed to negotiate with Geronimo. If Geronimo rejected these terms, Torres's orders to Aguirre were to deploy more troops with the goal to wipe out the entire band.[33]

In case the current bounty of three hundred pesos was insufficient incentive, Torres increased it to five hundred pesos. He offered the same sum to the families of soldiers killed in action. Aguirre rushed to Fronteras and on

August 21 received a telegram with the governor's terms. If Geronimo accepted, Aguirre was to send the Chiricahuas with an escort of troops to Ures. With the cease-fire due to end in two days, Aguirre went to Cuchuta, but Geronimo had left the area.[34]

Early the morning of August 21, the two Chiricahua women, with two warriors sent by Geronimo to check on them, left Fronteras for their camp. The evening before, they had spoken to Lieutenant Wilber E. Wilder, who had passed along General Miles's terms (presumably that their lives would be spared). They offered to take Wilder and another man to Geronimo's camp, but Wilder demurred, telling them to return to Geronimo and get his guarantee for safe passage. The four Chiricahuas with three ponies loaded with food and mescal were en route to the Teras Mountains just south of the inverted horseshoe bend of the Bavispe.[35]

Who were the two Chiricahua women who bravely entered town to purchase mescal? According to a contemporary Mexican report, their Spanish names were Felicitas and Cruz.[36] But, according to Kayitah and Martine, their Apache names were Tah-das-te and Dejonah. The identity of the first woman has never been in doubt. She was then married to Ahnandia, a warrior with Geronimo, who had left his first wife on the reservation. Somehow, Eve Ball has transformed the identity of the second woman, clearly identified as Dejonah, to Lozen, a sister of Victorio. Eve Ball was the first writer to suggest this, and she did so apparently from information received from Apache sources. Writers have repeated this so often that it has become part of the historical record. But Dejonah was definitely not Lozen. She was probably the Spanish-speaking wife of Nat-cul-baye, also known as Elías. Since Dejonah disappears from the Chiricahua historical record, it seems probable that she was the wife of one of the two adult males (seven Apaches in all) who avoided deportation to Florida by escaping the night before they reached Fort Bowie. Lozen remained on the reservation during the final Geronimo War and went to Florida with Loco's band.[37]

The news of the Apache women at Fronteras eventually spurred Gatewood into action. At 2:00 A.M. on August 19, his small party, with six soldiers as escort, left Lawton's camp east of Nacozari and headed north. After a ride of fifty-five miles, they reached Cuchuta that evening. Gatewood rode to Fronteras the next day but apparently did not speak to the two women. Finally, late in the afternoon of August 22, Gatewood left with his party, Tom Horn, José Yeskes, and six or eight soldiers from Wilder's command. Kayitah and Martine ferreted out the trail of Apaches, which merged into a trail going toward Batepito. About noon on August 24, the two scouts advised Gatewood to bivouac on the Bavispe near its junction with the San Bernardino River. On the opposite bank of the river loomed the base of the Teras Mountains, historically a favorite camping spot of the Chiricahuas. It was a site well known to Martine and Kayitah, who were certain that the hostiles were camped about four miles away. George Wrattan said the hostiles' position was on "the steepest slopes on the steepest mountain in Mexico."[38]

Kayitah and Martine began the climb toward the Indian camp. One carried a white flag mounted on a century plant. They were unsure what kind of reception they would receive. For two days, the hostiles had been on a mescal binge. Fortunately, the men had sobered up, perhaps because of the news concerning the Americans' interest in discussing terms. Yet, Geronimo never appreciated the Chiricahua scouts working for the military. And the presence of Martine, a close friend of Chatto, bought him no goodwill. But Kayitah's cousin, the renowned runner and celebrated marksman Yahnozha, was one of several men on the ridge watching the two men below. After they explained the purpose of their visit, Yahnozha beckoned them to come up. Although Martine and Kayitah's account makes no mention of impending danger, some Apache testimony suggests that Geronimo wanted to kill the messengers. When Perico, Fun, and Yahnozha stood up to him, however, threatening to shoot the first person that followed his order, Geronimo backed down, or so the story goes.

Kayitah painted a grim picture for their survival. "You have no friends whatever in this world." He pointed out the dire consequences if they remained at war: "Their aim is to kill every one of you if it takes fifty years." Geronimo and Naiche listened to Kayitah's words. As proof of his good intentions, Geronimo sent Martine back to Gatewood with a piece of cooked mescal. And Naiche privately told Martine to assure Gatewood that his life was safe regardless of the outcome. Kayitah spent the night in the hostiles' camp.[39]

Martine reached Gatewood's camp about sundown and presented the mescal to the lieutenant, who took it as the good faith gesture that Geronimo intended. Martine said that Geronimo would meet him the next morning and discuss terms. All at once, the mood in camp turned bright. Gatewood cut the mescal into strips and gave each man a slice. For the first time, Gatewood's entourage went to sleep with realistic hopes that peace was near. The next morning, August 25, 1886, Martine led Gatewood's party, which included Lieutenant Brown and thirty scouts, toward Geronimo's camp.

Gatewood carried fifteen pounds of tobacco and rations. After following the river east for about two miles, the party began an ascent toward the ranchería. Here, an unarmed Apache appeared on a ridge above them and said that Geronimo wanted to talk peace. Shortly after, three armed warriors, including Perico, appeared. They told Gatewood to send Brown and the scouts back to camp. And they said that Naiche wanted to talk in a glade along the river, where they would find wood, water, and shade.

The warriors arrived one at a time from various directions. The two chiefs were among the last to come in. Geronimo laid his rifle down and walked briskly over to Gatewood, who was sitting on Yahnozha's saddle mounted over a log, and shook hands. Then Naiche, reticent and melancholy, entered camp, walked over, and shook Gatewood's hand. After some small talk, Gatewood passed around the tobacco, and all began to puff away. Then Geronimo asked the lieutenant for General Miles's terms. Gatewood did not hesitate: "Surrender and you will be sent to join the rest of your people in Florida, there to await the decision of the President as to your final disposition. Accept these terms or fight it out to the end." Geronimo replied that they would make peace if Miles allowed them to return to the reservation under their former status. But Gatewood said that his offer was final. The Chiricahuas retired to the canebrake and talked for about an hour. In their minds, the government had always allowed them to return to the reservation after an end to hostilities. If the Americans truly wanted peace, this condition should be the cornerstone of any agreement.

At noon, they broke for lunch and then resumed talking. Geronimo played the best card he had. With a resolute look of determination, he said to the lieutenant: "Take us to the reservation or fight." Gatewood was understandably concerned for his party's safety, and Naiche sensed it, assuring the lieutenant his party could depart in peace if talks broke down. Naiche's words were the tonic that Gatewood needed to hear. In response to Geronimo's ultimatum, in a matter of fact tone, the lieutenant said that the government had already sent the Chiricahuas at Fort Apache to Florida. His words resonated like a powerful punch to the stomach, knocking the wind out of the Apaches. Gatewood said the only Apaches left at San Carlos and Fort Apache were Western Apaches. Geronimo was incredulous, asking Gatewood whether he was telling the truth or saying this as a ploy to get them to surrender. One wonders how Kayitah and Martine felt when they heard this news.

The thunderbolt sent the hostiles into another brief council. When Geronimo returned, he curtly announced they would continue at war. But they wanted to roast a beef and talk throughout the night. A weary Gatewood had had enough. Toward sunset, he decided to return to his base camp. He knew the Indians might debate this decision all night, and he had nothing further to add. As he was about to leave, Geronimo made an impassioned appeal, one that reflected his faith in Gatewood and the desperation of his situation: "We want your advice. Consider yourself one of us and not a white man. Remember all that has been said today, and as an Apache, what would you advise us to do?" Gatewood responded, "I would trust General Miles and take him at his word." That evening Gatewood returned to camp with a cautious optimism. Naiche had been characteristically quiet, letting Geronimo do the talking. Yet, it was clear to the lieutenant that Naiche missed his family and was leaning toward surrendering.

The next morning, August 26, 1886, Geronimo came to Gatewood's camp and announced that they would surrender. They were tired of running, and many, including Geronimo, Naiche, Perico, Ahnandia, and Moh-tsos, had wives and children in Florida whom they yearned to see. They agreed to march north, with their weapons, which they would keep until the formal surrender to General Miles. Gatewood's party was to remain with them, while Lawton's command could ride near to protect them from Mexican troops.[40]

Although the news surely satisfied General Miles, at that moment he was dealing with the thorny issue of the Chiricahuas at Fort Apache. Contrary to Gatewood's assurance that they were in Florida, they had not left. Gatewood had assumed, based on what Miles had told him in Albuquerque, that the removal had taken place. By then, the die had been cast in Washington. Regarding Geronimo, President Cleveland's preference was to hang him. The day before Gatewood met Geronimo, Cleveland had decided to remove the reservation Chiricahuas to Fort Marion, Florida. Common perception has painted Miles as the villain for this callous double cross, yet he never suggested sending them to Florida. In fact, he called it a sickly place, believing that many of the mountain-bred Apaches would perish in the humid climate. Miles's role, unwitting as it was, had an ironic twist, for his words provided the fodder by which Sheridan recommended this unfortunate policy to the president.[41]

On July 3, 1886, Miles had renewed the idea for removal when he telegraphed General Howard that "there are the strongest military reasons these Indians should be removed outside of Arizona." After observing the Chiricahuas for four days, on July 7, he penned another report to division headquarters in San Francisco. In the first section, he built a formidable case for removal, explaining the military necessity for transferring the Chiricahuas to

Indian Territory, today's Oklahoma. Yet, he based his reasons on a dubious set of facts and a few half-truths. In contrast, the second section dealt with his choice for their new reservation. Here Miles revealed a common-sense, compassionate approach that, if adopted, would have altered the course of Chiricahua history for the better. Unfortunately for all concerned, Sheridan did not read the report until twenty-three days later. And by then, Cleveland's cabinet members had debated and rejected the idea of removal to the Indian Territory because it would require Congress to legislate a change to existing law.[42]

Meanwhile, on July 17, 1886, the Chiricahua delegation of ten men and three women, escorted by Captain Joseph H. Dorst, arrived in Washington. The delegation included their four principal leaders at Fort Apache, Chatto, Noche, Loco, and Kaetenae, with the important scouts Charley, Guydelkon, and Gon-altsis (Chatto's brother, whose Spanish name was Patricio). The women were two wives and one granddaughter of Loco. Once in Washington, they checked into the Beveridge Hotel, eight blocks from the White House, where many Indian delegations had stayed during visits to the president.[43]

On July 26, 1886, the Chiricahuas had their much-anticipated appointment with Secretary of War Endicott. Three men, Chatto, Kaetenae, and Charley, represented the Apaches, with Chatto serving as their spokesman. They preferred to live at Fort Apache, where they had good water, grass, and places to plant. Chatto asked the government to intercede with Mexico to restore his family to him. Endicott promised to investigate. The next day, they had a cursory meeting with President Cleveland, who presented Chatto with a silver peace medal, which the chief interpreted as an indication that the government would permit them to remain at Fort Apache. In neither meeting did Endicott or Cleveland discuss a new site for a reservation. Both parties looked forward to their return to Arizona.[44]

Three days later, the world of the Chiricahuas changed suddenly and irrevocably, when General Sheridan, who had not met the delegation, read Miles's July 7 missive outlining the reasons to move the Chiricahuas from Arizona. Miles had mailed the letter through proper channels to the Division of the Pacific, which forwarded it to the adjutant general's office on July 19. The War Department received it eight days later—the same day the Chiricahuas met President Cleveland. And Sheridan finally reviewed it on July 30, 1886.

Miles's justification for removal jolted the steel-fisted commander into making a knee-jerk decision to recommend removal of the Chiricahua adult males from Fort Apache to Fort Marion, Florida. Two statements deeply troubled him. Miles stated that the reservation Chiricahuas were "in better fighting condition today than ever before," a ridiculous assertion. The next declaration sealed the fate of the reservation Chiricahuas. The inevitable defeat of the hostiles was no guarantee that peace would prevail in Arizona. The sons of the reservation Chiricahuas at Fort Apache will become the "Geronimos of tomorrow," an ominous yet groundless warning that was utterly preposterous. This prediction, worthy of the yellow journalism in Arizona, echoed the dire tidings of irresponsible newspaper editors who had no clue about affairs at Fort Apache. This time, however, the military commander of the Department of Arizona, who may have believed what he wrote, had made the assertion.[45]

Naturally, Miles neglected to point out that (1) the peaceful Chiricahuas had remained on the reservation the last three years; (2) at least three-fourths of the eighty-one men had served as scouts against the hostiles; and (3) at no time did they furnish either recruits or supplies to the hostiles. One wonders if he was even aware of these facts, given that they ran contrary to his preconceived beliefs. Miles probably had no idea that everything in his report would be taken as gospel by Sheridan, who was usually wary of his pronouncements. This time, however, he swallowed Miles's contentions because they confirmed his suspicions that Crook had sugarcoated the truth about the reservation Chiricahuas and the loyalty of his scouts.

Sheridan could not fathom that a state of undeclared civil war existed between the peaceful and hostile factions of the Chiricahuas. This division was a matter of rights, not states' rights, but those of the four hundred Chiricahuas who had elected to remain on the reservation and move on to a new life of raising crops and managing livestock. He was unable to conceive that the tribe's dichotomy was founded on sincere ideological grounds, the result of an honest and pragmatic choice by those who rejected a war that had taken the lives of 57 percent of the tribe's members since the closing of their two reservations a decade before.

With Miles's characterizations fresh in his memory bank, Sheridan reached another unfounded conclusion—that many of the seventy-one men at Fort Apache would jump the reservation and join Geronimo once the Washington delegation returned to Fort Apache empty handed. To prevent this, he suggested sending them and the adult Chiricahua males at Fort Apache to Fort Marion, Florida, "to be held as prisoners of war until the final resolution of the Geronimo troubles."[46]

To be sure, Sheridan's options on location were limited. Unable to send the Apaches to Indian Territory, he was unwilling to shift Arizona's burden to any place west of the Mississippi. Thus, by default, he chose Fort Marion, where Chihuahua's group was living. As he was the commanding general of the army, his advice carried enormous weight with Secretary of War Endicott, who conveyed Sheridan's thoughts to President Cleveland. Both men trusted Sheridan's judgment. President Cleveland called an emergency meeting for the next day, July 31, at the White House.

He invited Secretary of War Endicott, Secretary of the Interior Lamar, Lamar's son, Captain Dorst, and Captain Bourke. Expanding on Sheridan's initial suggestion, President Cleveland outlined his proposal to remove all Chiricahuas at Fort Apache and the Washington delegation to Fort Marion. He asked each member to consider whether this action would be "proper and expedient." Bourke vigorously opposed the idea.

He cautioned against adopting a policy that treated all Chiricahuas the same, when most of the tribe had remained loyal and served honorably as scouts. He insisted it would be a gross violation of Crook's agreement made in the Sierra Madre Mountains three years before. And he argued that removing them from Arizona could unsettle other Apaches. Dorst argued to the contrary. He pointed out that the Chiricahuas had few Apache friends at either San Carlos or Fort Apache. And he could not resist passing along the time-worn bromide that Geronimo would try to gain recruits from Fort Apache. Bourke struggled to make sense of what was unfolding before his eyes. When Endicott asked Dorst about the logistics of removing the Chiricahuas from Fort Apache, the secretary of war's position confirmed Bourke's suspicions that President Cleveland had already made up his mind to relocate the Chiricahuas to Florida.[47]

Once the conference ended, Sheridan telegraphed Miles to report that his proposal to move the Chiricahuas to any location west of the "Missouri River . . . can not be entertained." The next sentence must have surprised Miles. Sheridan, on behalf of the president, asked his opinion about using force to arrest the reservation Chiricahuas and their Washington delegation in order to remove them to Fort Marion, Florida. The next day, August 1, 1886, Miles responded by admitting "there would be some advantage, but some serious objections occur to me." Meanwhile, he suggested that Captain Dorst take the delegation, which was planning to return to Arizona, to Carlisle Indian School, where Loco, Kaetenae, and Noche had relatives and band members (sent by Crawford in January 1884). This would buy time until President Cleveland came to a final decision.[48]

The following day, August 2, 1886, Miles outlined the pros and cons of removal. As to the pros, he conceded that the citizens of Arizona would be

grateful the moment the removal was completed. Second, with the Chiricahuas gone, the army could draw down its forces, transferring troops to other
trouble spots, including the Mexican border. The cons included several valid
points. The Chiricahuas would consider it a breach of faith, other Indians
might become reluctant to travel to Washington, and the eastern press and hu-
manitarians might object to consigning a mountain race to the tropical climate
of Florida. He also predicted that this policy would harden the resolve of the
hostiles because they would expect a harsher punishment than their relatives
on the reservation.

Miles continued to press his case for a common-sense approach: he pleaded,
"there must be some safe place where the Government can locate these wards
away from the canyons and mountains of Arizona that would be agreeable to
them." So he came up with another recommendation—land in Oklahoma's
panhandle, called No Man's Land, which he thought might be available.[49]

In Washington, the stars, in the form of Cleveland's administration, aligned
against the Chiricahuas. One by one, Secretary of the Interior Lamar on August 10, New Mexico's governor Edmund Ross (a friend of Miles), and Secretary of War Endicott endorsed Sheridan's plan, which President Cleveland had
expanded to include the entire tribe. By August 16, the adjutant general, R. C.
Drum, advised Captain Dorst, who was then at Fort Leavenworth, Kansas, to
continue to appease the Chiricahua delegation because their removal "is so
probable." On August 20, Miles assured Sheridan that Wade was prepared to
carry out the operation at Fort Apache.

Wade believed that some would favor the motion; others would oppose it.
But they would not voice an opinion until their leaders returned from Washington. And many continued to fear that a removal would lead to further punishment for "past offenses." Miles, evidently tired of the drama, ended his
telegram with his endorsement: "I pray that it may receive the approval of the
Government." Finally, on August 24, Cleveland issued his decision authorizing the removal of the Chiricahuas to Fort Marion. The next day, August 25,
Sheridan telegraphed Miles: "as a preliminary step, these Indians must go to
Fort Marion."[50]

Miles tried to inform Lieutenant Colonel Wade of the order, but the telegraph lines between Willcox and Fort Apache were down. Several newspapers
had published the decision about removal, which concerned Miles. He feared
the news could trigger a Chiricahua outbreak before his order to secure them
reached Wade. With their four leading chiefs in Washington, the reservation
Chiricahuas were in a state of paralysis until the delegation returned. Chiva,

now head of Bonito's small band; Bish-to-yey; and Zele were not about to leave. And the Chihennes did not intend to do anything until Kaetenae and Loco returned. Finally, Wade received the order and scheduled the double cross for Sunday, August 29, when the Chiricahuas came to the fort for their weekly rations. Miles sent four troops of cavalry from San Carlos, Fort Thomas, and Alma, New Mexico, in case Wade needed them.[51]

Even as Wade was making his plans, on August 28, Miles made one final attempt to dissuade Washington from sending the Chiricahuas to Fort Marion. He telegraphed the adjutant general in Washington and suggested that the government reconsider the location. Instead of Florida, he proposed sending them to Fort Union, where, at some future date, they could be transferred 1,200 miles east. One has to admire Miles's persistence, but it was too late.[52]

Sunday, August 29, Miles spent two hours with the telegraph operator in Willcox, asking the operator at Fort Apache to provide him a play-by-play account of the roundup of the unsuspecting Chiricahuas. The operator had a bird's eye view from an office overlooking the grounds. At noon, the Chiricahuas lined up to receive their weekly ration tickets. Cooney and four Chiricahua men served as scouts to maintain order. Toclanny was in line to receive his ticket when a troop of cavalry appeared "as if they were going somewhere." Instead of exiting the fort, they "turned out and joined the infantry and [White Mountain] scouts to surround the Chiricahuas." The Chiricahua men stood there holding their weapons, unsure of their next step. Neither side wanted a fight. At this critical juncture, Wade appeared to calm the potentially explosive scene. After assuring the Chiricahuas that no harm would come to anyone, he ordered them to sit down. They obeyed and helplessly watched as the troops disarmed the five Chiricahua scouts, taking their cartridge belts and rifles. One by one, the rest of the men faced the same humiliating experience, the first for some of them—especially the Chokonens. Wade had the women and children establish their village near the fort.[53]

Soon after, the troops herded the men into a horse barn, where Wade informed them that the government had decided to send them to a new place. He insisted that the soldiers wanted peace. A few hours later, scouts from San Carlos brought in Tuzzone, a former sergeant of scouts under Crawford, and his wife from San Carlos, who had run away from him. The Western Apache scouts escorted him to the horse barn with the rest of the men. For the next nine days, they remained there under heavy guard. The betrayal baffled them. After all, most of the prisoners had served honorably as scouts against the hostiles. According to Betzinez, Massai was the only warrior who tried to incite an uprising, but he found no support. Years later, one man, who had been a boy at this time, blamed their problems on Geronimo—a sentiment held by many of the peaceful Chiricahuas and their descendants into the twentieth century.[54]

Miles had waited for the description of events at Fort Apache with much anxiety. No matter how careful the preparations, no matter how competent the officer, the situation could have turned violent within the walls of Fort Apache. But Wade's experience, judgment, and calming influence prevailed, averting a potential massacre of Apaches who had done nothing wrong. He deserved enormous credit for defusing the crisis and securing 382 Chiricahuas without bloodshed.[55]

Miles was reluctant to focus on the Geronimo negotiations until Wade had carried out his assignment at Fort Apache. Yet, as he waited for Washington's decision, his mind was racing, leading him to conclusions based on irrational fears and sophomoric impatience. His belief that Geronimo and Naiche might make peace with Sonora and raid Arizona revealed a fundamental ignorance of the relationship between the two races. Furthermore, after receiving a report that Kayitah and Martine were reluctant to leave the command and find the trail, he again jumped to conclusions, warning Lawton not to "trust them." He told Lawton that if they refuse to go "into the hostile camp and demand their surrender," he was to dismiss them. By the time Lawton received this communication, the two scouts had completed their part of the bargain, and Gatewood was talking with Geronimo.[56]

On August 29, only hours after Wade had completed the roundup, Miles directed Forsyth to inform Lawton that he would not see the hostiles until they sent hostages as a show of good faith.[57] Miles was not going to repeat Crook's mistake. He was reluctant to place himself in any situation by which the hostiles could slip away and embarrass him. This fear seemed to govern every suggestion or order.

On August 27, Lawton's command and the hostiles, thirty-eight in all, began to move north from the Bavispe River. In accordance with Geronimo's wishes, Gatewood and his interpreters went with him. The two groups took parallel routes. The Apaches moved north along the western foothills and Lawton took a course on their left flank. At night, they made separate camps. The second day, at Rusballo, a few miles north of Pitaicache, 180 Mexican troops under Jesús Aguirre, the prefect of Arispe, approached the American lines. He wanted to see for himself whether Geronimo had actually surrendered.

After the American officers met with Aguirre's party, Geronimo walked in from the canebrakes, "dragging his Winchester rifle by the muzzle with his left hand, & his six-shooter handy in front of his left hip." Gatewood introduced the two men. What happened next astounded the Americans. After shaking hands, Aguirre "shoved his revolver around to his front & Geronimo grasped his and drew it half-way out of his holster." He had a "most fiendish expression" on his face. It appeared that the two old adversaries would shoot each other on the spot. But Aguirre finally "put his hands behind him," and Geronimo "dropped his right hand by his side." During a brief conversation, Geronimo explained that he would never surrender to Mexicans because he knew their plan was to kill them. In contrast, he said, "Whatever happens, they [the Americans] will not murder me or my people." Geronimo ordered Aguirre to take his army and go south, for he was going north with the Americans.[58]

This major crisis averted, a few days later another one appeared on the horizon. And it originated with the narcissistic Miles. His letters to Lawton suggested a reprehensible course of action. To begin with, Miles did not intend to meet Geronimo until the chief was either six feet under or secured in leg irons. Incredibly, he sent a series of messages to Lawton, authorizing him to use any means to "seize Geronimo and Naiche." In another communication, he assured Lawton that he would back up any tactic, underhanded or not, to achieve the desired results. And yet, another fiendish thought occurred to Miles: "Send for them and tell them that you have a message from me and the President. Then tell them to lay down their arms and remain in your camp."[59]

These suggestions almost led to another disaster. In camp at Guadalupe Canyon on August 31, Lieutenant Abiel L. Smith, perhaps aware of Miles's sentiments, openly talked about surrounding the Apaches if they tried to break away. It was an incredibly stupid remark, and his words and actions frightened the Indians into leaving camp. Gatewood could see the fruits of his efforts blowing away in the desert sand. The confrontation pitted Gatewood, the junior officer, against Smith, the senior lieutenant (Lawton was then absent from camp). According to some accounts, Gatewood threatened to shoot the first soldier who interfered in his business. Wood, who apparently initially sided with Smith, backed down. Then, he had the good sense to send a message to Lawton, imploring him to return to camp at once. Later that day (August 31, 1886), Gatewood restored order, aided by Lawton's return.[60]

The next morning, Gatewood and Geronimo sent George Wrattan and Kayitah, with Perico as a hostage, to Fort Bowie. By the time they arrived, probably on September 2, they discovered that General Miles had left that morning for the border. Miles, like Crook, had hoped to bring Naiche's mother to help with the negotiations. He had asked Wade to send her to Fort Bowie, but she refused to go. In fact, knowing that the removal of the Chiricahuas was imminent, she asked Wade to allow her to relocate to San Carlos to live with her daughter, Naithlotonz, who was married to Gokliz, a Western Apache. Naiche, she said, was an "ungrateful son"; in contrast, her daughter "has always been kind and will take care of her."

Miles's deportment disgusted Lawton, who wrote his wife on September 2, 1886: "I cannot get Miles to come out and the Indians are getting uneasy about it." That same day he wrote Miles, whose silence he interpreted as disapproval of his conduct. The stress of escorting the hostiles north, without any encouragement or approval by the general, left him second-guessing his involvement with Geronimo: "[I] regretted a thousand times that Lieutenant Gatewood found my command." And he dismissed Miles's lamebrain suggestions of treachery, pointing out the fallacy of such a proposal. He might "kill one or two of them, but it would only make everything much worse." Finally, on September 3, Miles informed Lawton from Camp Rucker in the Chiricahua Mountains that he would be over that day to meet the hostiles. At 3:00 P.M., the reluctant general finally arrived at Skeleton Canyon in the Peloncillo Mountains. Gatewood and Lawton must have heaved a big sigh of relief, for their long ordeal was finally ending. They knew that Geronimo and Naiche would surrender, which meant they could return to their families.[61]

Shortly after Miles arrived, Geronimo came down from his camp in the mountains to meet him. He walked up to Miles and shook his hand. After the interpreter introduced Miles as a friend, Geronimo responded, "I have been in need of friends. Why has he not been with me?" This moment of levity broke the ice, and the two men had a respectful conversation. Unlike Crook, whose attitude had been contentious, Miles was receptive, listening patiently and respectfully. The general's terms were simple: "Lay down your arms and come with me to Fort Bowie and in five days you will see your families now in Florida with Chihuahua and no harm will come to you."[62]

Naiche was back in the hills, waiting for his "brother" to appear with some horses they had left in Sonora. He was concerned for his safety because of the proximity of Mexican soldiers. Naiche had no living brothers. He was waiting for Atelnietze, a member of Naiche's band, who bore a striking resemblance to the chief in height and appearance. (He is pictured in the center of one of Fly's photos with Naiche's family.) About eight years older than Naiche, he was probably a first cousin, a son of one of Cochise's brothers or sisters. The morning of September 4, 1886, Gatewood and Geronimo rode to Naiche's camp to bring his band in to surrender to Miles. Naiche was waiting on a bluff for Atelnietze when Gatewood asked him to fulfill the promises that the chief had made to him. Naiche agreed, brought his band to Miles's camp, and formally surrendered. Miles thought the chief was suspicious and fearful of treachery because of the soldiers' treatment of Mangas Coloradas, his grandfather.[63]

Early the next morning, Miles, Geronimo, Naiche, three men, and one woman left in the general's ambulance for Fort Bowie, which they reached later that day. Miles continued to reassure the chiefs that their past activities would be forgotten or "wiped out." That night they were disarmed and placed in the calaboose.

Midafternoon of that same day, the balance of the hostiles started north with Lawton, Gatewood, and Wood. The evening of September 7, they bivouacked six miles south of Fort Bowie. That night Chappo's wife had a baby. Early in the morning of September 8, Lieutenant Robert F. Ames galloped into Lawton's camp, awakening Indians and soldiers alike, and scattering the former. Wood called Ames's actions "idiotic." When the Chiricahuas regrouped, the soldiers discovered that two men, one teenage boy, three women, and one child were missing. The two adult males were Atelnietze and Natcul-baye, also known as Elías. They had headed south into Sonora, where they were to enjoy another decade of freedom, occasionally raiding on both sides of the border.[64]

By this time, Miles desperately wanted the Chiricahuas out of his territory. He had made an agreement with Geronimo and Naiche, who had surrendered as "brave men to brave men."[65] He ignored a September 7 telegram from Sheridan to hold them at Fort Bowie until President Cleveland, who believed the surrender was unconditional, decided their fate. Sheridan and Cleveland favored turning the men over to the civil authorities for trial, which, if carried out, would have delighted the southwestern press and politicians. That evening, Miles telegraphed Sheridan that Fort Bowie did not have the facilities to hold them. He continued, "Everything is arranged to move them and I earnestly request permission to move them out of this mountain country, at least as far as Fort Bliss, Union, or Fort Marion."[66]

Lawton's command brought the balance of the Indians into Fort Bowie the morning of September 8. After disarming them on the parade ground, a few hours later the soldiers loaded the hostiles into wagons and escorted them to Bowie Station for the first leg of their trip to Florida. As they left the fort, the post's band played "Auld Land Syne," an appropriate climax to the quarter century warfare between the two races that had erupted four hundred yards below the post in 1861. At 2:55 P.M. on September 8, 1886, the train departed Bowie station with the Chiricahua hostiles and the two loyal scouts, Martine and Kayitah. Captain Lawton had command of the detail that provided security.[67]

Before the train left Bowie Station, a telegram arrived that spelled out President Cleveland's decision to retain the hostiles at Bowie. But Miles's aide, Captain William A. Thompson, kept the order from Miles until the train had pulled out from Bowie Station. Miles claimed that he was unaware of the order until six weeks later. Yet he was certainly aware of the telegram received the day before ordering him to keep the hostiles locked up at Fort Bowie.[68]

That very day, September 8, 1886, Lieutenant Colonel Wade and detachments of infantry, cavalry, and Western Apache scouts were moving 383 Chiricahuas from Fort Apache to Holbrook, ninety miles north. Miles had ordered Wade to take Dos-teh-seh, for "if you leave one, others will want to stay." Her daughter and Western Apache son-in-law, Gokliz, elected to accompany her. Wade had planned to embark by September 4, but transportation delays, logistical problems with rations, and bad weather forced him to suspend the trip until the morning of September 7. The infantry marched in the front and rear of the cavalcade, and the cavalry troopers on the flanks. To prevent escape, the soldiers bound the hands of the Chiricahua men and loaded them into army wagons. The women and children marched along with their personal possessions, 140 horses and mules, and hundreds of dogs.

Progress was slow because of muddy roads. The first day several wagons capsized while crossing the White River, but no one drowned. That night they camped at Cooley's ranch. Here the Western Apache scouts held a dance attended by the Chiricahua women. Their husbands could only watch, wondering what they had done to merit this humiliation.[69]

On September 12, 1886, they reached Holbrook. That night, the Western Apache scouts held another dance with the Chiricahua women. The next morning, Wade began the process of loading the entire band into the trains. Wade's command of ninety-two soldiers and officers occupied the first and last berths. Except for a few scouts, the Apaches had never been on a train. The women and children loaded as many of their possessions as possible into two of the cars. Naturally, they had no choice but to leave their wagons, horses, and dogs behind. Before boarding, the soldiers untied the hands of the Chiricahua men, who took this last opportunity to shake hands with the Western Apache scouts and Wade's soldiers.

The trip east was one never forgotten by those who made it. The cars could carry between fifty and sixty persons. Because the average car held forty-seven Apaches, they had comfortable seating and in the first part of the trip had beds to sleep in, according to Jason Betzinez. To prevent escape, the windows were nailed shut, preventing ventilation. The soldiers placed chamber pots in the small "salons" for the Apaches to relieve themselves in private. When the trains stopped every one hundred miles to take on water for the boilers, soldiers or railroad personnel emptied the waste containers. The stench, however, permeated the cars, which were already sweltering from the lack of fresh air. During the trip (some say in New Mexico, others in Missouri), Massai jumped from the train. He made his way to his ancestral home and lived as an outlaw for many years. The peaceful Chiricahuas finally reached Fort Marion in the early hours of September 20, 1886. Here they joined Chihuahua's group and Chatto and Loco's Washington delegation.[70]

Besides Atelnietze's small group, the only hostiles at large were Mangas's small band of eleven individuals (three men and eight women and children), which surrendered near Fort Apache on October 18.[71] They were also sent to Florida. En route, the aged Eskinolteze died. All Chiricahuas, except Atelnietze's party of seven and some fifteen who had intermarried with Western Apaches or joined relatives with San Carlos and White Mountain groups, were banished from Arizona. The two years of exile promised by Crook would turn into twenty-seven years as prisoners of war. The last phase of Chiricahua Apache warfare, with Geronimo as the symbolic leader, would cost the tribe dearly in blood and spirit. And the irony of it all was that the loyal Chiricahuas, who had so honorably served Crook and Miles, received the same sentence as the hostiles who had murdered and plundered throughout the last Apache War. Of course, this was just another in a litany of broken promises and treaties dating back to Puritanical times in colonial Massachusetts. It remains today a national betrayal and an egregious disgrace unworthy of a country founded on the democratic ideals of liberty, equality, and justice for all.

EPILOGUE

It had taken the Cleveland administration all of forty-five days to sort out Miles's explanations and to conclude that the hostiles had surrendered conditionally. Despite this, President Cleveland decided that sparing their lives was enough. He ordered the warriors sent to Fort Pickens at Santa Rosa Island in Pensacola, Florida, while their families joined Chihuahua's party and the reservation Chiricahuas at Fort Marion in St. Augustine. Separating the men from their families was clearly a violation of the terms of surrender. But it occurred. Geronimo and Naiche's men (Perico, Fun, Yahnozha, Ahnandia, Tissnolthtos, Chappo, Beshe, La-zi-yah, Nah-bay, Moh-tsos, Kilth-de-gai, Hunlona, and Zhonne) reached their destination on October 25, followed by Mangas and Goso on November 6.[1]

The conditions at Fort Pickens for the formerly hostile warriors were far superior to those of their relatives living at Fort Marion. Built in 1695 by the Spanish, Marion had deteriorated into a crumbling, run-down structure and tourist attraction able to accommodate perhaps 150 Apaches—not five hundred. They lived in 130 conical Sibley tents resting on raised wooden floors on the terreplein of Fort Marion's open area. A narrow passageway divided the tents. A few areas were designated for cooking. The congested area was unsanitary and unhealthy, and it afforded no privacy.[2]

During the first six weeks the Indians were at Fort Marion, a series of significant developments plagued the Apaches, threatening the physical and psychological well-being of a people whose morale was already shattered by the loss of their homes and their displacement to an alien land. To begin with, the War Department slashed the Apaches' rations in half. Moreover, pork was initially part of the allotment, and the Apaches had absolutely no use for it. This Spartan diet exacerbated an already pressing issue: sickness. During the seven months of confinement at Fort Marion, 367 of the 502 Chiricahuas sought medical attention for malaria, dysentery, bronchitis, and tuberculosis, diseases that would take a devastating toll on the Apaches. They had brought the infections from Arizona, but the oppressive conditions on the trains only accelerated the spread of these communicable diseases. The cramped quarters at Marion, with daily contact between healthy and infected Apaches, guaranteed future outbreaks of tuberculosis. By the end of the year, twenty-one Chiricahuas had perished, about half from tuberculosis.[3]

Notwithstanding this calamity, the major jolt to their emotional stability occurred in early November, when Washington ordered the post commander at Marion to select students for the Carlisle Indian School in Pennsylvania. The Chiricahuas, who had already lost everything but their children, had no say in the matter. The military selected forty-four students (thirty-two boys and twelve girls) between the ages of twelve and twenty-two. Even Lieutenant Stephen Mills, who carried out the assignment, found the affair distasteful. The Apaches remember the occasion as the "stealing of the children." Left unspoken by the parents and grandparents were even stronger words of despair. What more could they bear? Indeed, the emotional trauma would have been too much for them if they had known, as Angie Debo points out, that Carlisle "was a death trap" of infected students carrying the tuberculosis germ.[4]

The Chiricahuas felt alone and helpless, but their former advocates, Captain John Bourke and General George Crook, were watching from the periphery. Both were appalled at the treatment of those who had served as scouts and remained peaceful on the reservation. To be sure, each had to exercise caution because the Cleveland administration would construe criticism as an indictment of Miles and the administration. Bourke especially could not afford to antagonize Secretary of War Endicott, who had helped him gain his assignment in Washington. As early as October 1, 1886, Crook had written Bourke about getting the Indian Rights Association in Philadelphia to investigate the situation at Fort Marion.

Early in 1887, a discreet Bourke wrote to Herbert Welsh, secretary of the Indian Rights Association, providing him with all the pertinent information needed to address the issue with the Cleveland administration. Endicott procrastinated, hoping the issue would die quietly. But Welsh was persistent, and Endicott agreed to investigate. The Indian Rights Association called the attention of the public to the injustices. Eastern newspapers printed informed articles decrying the administration's betrayal of the reservation Chiricahuas and chastising it for not complying with the surrender terms. Finally, in early March, the government allowed Bourke and Welsh to inspect Fort Marion. The lack of food, inadequate clothing, and deplorable sanitation had left them "poor, soft and weak," according to Chatto, who had greeted Bourke as an old friend.[5]

Their findings convinced the administration to move the Indians. It first decided to send them to join Geronimo and Naiche at Fort Pickens. But when Bourke and Welsh got wind of that idea, they forced it to be withdrawn. Next, Endicott sent Bourke to inspect the Mount Vernon Barracks in Mobile, Alabama. The location was not ideal, but Bourke thought it an improvement over their current state. He recommended the removal of the Apaches to Mobile. The air was pure, and the climate, except for a few weeks in the summer, was warm in the day and cool at night. The downside was the lack of arable land, for a dense pine forest smothered the 2,162 acres.[6]

A few days before the scheduled transfer, Captain Richard H. Pratt showed up, with a prized Chiricahua student from Carlisle, to take more students for the school. Not one Apache volunteered. Then Pratt ordered the children to line up and selected sixty-two. The oldest was twenty-seven-year-old Jason Betzinez, who adapted as well as any Apache. Again, the stoic parents sat idly by, trying to credit the White Man's argument that their children's education in a distant land was more important than their right to love and raise their children as they saw fit.[7]

On April 27, 1887, the removal to Mount Vernon took place. Thanks to the efforts of Welsh and Bourke, the administration permitted thirty-one dependents and relatives of Geronimo and Naiche's group to join them at Fort Pickens. The balance of the 353 reached their new homes the next day. Little did they know how grim their stay would be.[8]

To begin with, although the chiefs with their followers spread out to recover the privacy they had lacked in Florida, they still faced a host of problems, all directly or indirectly affecting their health. There was little to do, and little land to farm. Torrential rains and mosquitoes were the norm, and the government continued to subsist them on half-rations, which aggravated their diseased condition. Tuberculosis continued to plague them. That fall, General Sheridan ordered the rations restored in full, which helped. Early in 1888, the healthy Apache men began constructing cabins to house each family unit. By June the project was complete.[9]

In May 1888 Geronimo and Naiche's group of forty-six at Fort Pickens were moved to Mount Vernon. Naiche spoke for his people: "We are tired of salt water and sand." He declared that they wanted farms so they could work and gain the fruits of their efforts. And the War Department shipped off to Carlisle five young men: Hunlona; his younger brother, Mike; Geronimo's son, Chappo; Zhonne; and Goso. Tuberculosis would claim the lives of all except Zhonne. The Chiricahua students at Carlisle were particularly hard hit. By the summer of 1889, 27 of the original 106 had died, 25 from tuberculosis. By the end of that year, Lieutenant Guy Howard reported that one-fourth of the tribe had perished since the fall of 1886.[10]

Though the Chiricahuas enjoyed more space and freedom at Mount Vernon, Captain John Bourke recognized quickly that Alabama was only a stop-gap measure, a move made until the government could find a place where they could farm. General Crook was also concerned. He continued to work on behalf of the Chiricahua scouts, who had sacrificed so much to help him. After inspecting a potential reservation site in North Carolina, in early 1890, the unpretentious Crook showed up unannounced at Mount Vernon. His arrival was probably the most exciting event for the Chiricahuas since their removal to Florida. Crook immediately expressed his contempt for Geronimo, refusing to allow him to speak, "for he is such a liar." But the reunion with his scouts, especially Chatto, was a poignant moment. He listened carefully to their compelling story of injustice and betrayal. Unfortunately, Crook passed away three months later.

The deaths continued to mount. One historian notes that the germ "with its roots in Arizona, took hold in Florida, and burst into an epidemic in Alabama." Tuberculosis at Mount Vernon continued to deplete their numbers: forty-three, between July 1, 1889, and June 30, 1890; fifty-three between July 1, 1890, and June 30, 1891; and forty-five between July 1, 1891, and June 30, 1892. From the time of their removal from Arizona through October 2, 1894, the Chiricahuas had lost 280 members, about half the tribe.[11]

Recognizing the travesty, General Nelson Miles sent Lieutenant Hugh L. Scott from Fort Sill with Captain Marion Maus, then a member of Miles's staff, to talk to the Chiricahuas at Mount Vernon. The meeting took place in late August 1894. Maus they could respect. The former hostiles and scouts remembered him for his courageous leadership under fire after Crawford's death near the Aros River. To him the chiefs and headmen addressed their concerns: the high mortality rate and the need for farms they could work. Because "most of the old people are dead," Chatto urged Maus to take quick action. The Indians also wanted their children (about forty-five) returned from Carlisle. Maus encapsulated their feelings with one statement: they pleaded for a place "where they could not only look up at the sun but see mountains." Finally, on October 4, 1894, the survivors of the eight-year nightmare in Florida and Alabama reached Fort Sill, Oklahoma.

When they met their new neighbors, the Kiowas and Comanches, they could not speak with either tribe. The Plains tribes tried to communicate in sign language, but the Apaches were unfamiliar with the universal language of the Plains Indians. Then the Comanches summoned some Kiowa-Apaches; perhaps the Chiricahuas understood half the conversation. Finally, after each tribe had produced a young Indian educated at Carlisle, the Indians, using English as the facilitator, were able to communicate.[12]

Although they remained prisoners of war under the jurisdiction of the War Department, the Apaches saw their lives improve dramatically at Fort Sill. The tuberculosis epidemic had finally run its course. The tribe adapted quickly to the life of the cowboy and farmer, raising stock and crops. Yet, as the years elapsed, many of the older Chiricahuas still yearned to return to the Southwest. And every few years, well-meaning Americans debated the idea of moving the Chiricahuas to New Mexico. All they wanted was their own land and liberation from the POW status. In 1911 Benedict Jozhe, frustrated at the lack of progress on this simple issue, asked Major Hugh Scott a series of moving questions that cried out for answers. "Don't we have any rights in the United States at all? What is the trouble? Are we human beings in the United States? What are we? We are not Canadians or Africans and we are not from Europe. But we are natives of the United States. Why can't the government fix us up right, be right for us, and give us what we ask for?"[13]

Finally, the government allowed the Chiricahuas to decide whether they wished to remain in Oklahoma or to relocate to the Mescalero Reservation in southeastern New Mexico. On April 4, 1913, 163 Chiricahuas (about 70 percent of the tribe), including Naiche, Chatto, and many of the prominent scouts, arrived at the Mescalero Reservation in New Mexico to begin a new life. Their twenty-seven years as prisoners of war under the jurisdiction of the War Department were over. The seventy-eight Chiricahuas who stayed in Oklahoma received land allotments. Today, their descendants live in Oklahoma and on the Mescalero Reservation in New Mexico.[14]

While the tribe was endeavoring to survive in an alien land amid epidemics and the government-sanctioned kidnapping of their children, the two men who had escaped from Lawton's command the night before deportation to Florida were continuing to live the precarious life of free Apaches. By necessity, they occasionally raided on both sides of the border. Atelnietze, whom Naiche called brother, lived until 1896, when American troops, guided by the incomparable Merejildo Grijalva, killed him in the Espuelas Mountains in northeastern Sonora.[15] Nat-cul-baye, whose father had ridden with Cochise and whose grandfather with Mangas Coloradas, passed from the scene about 1900. Massai, who had jumped off the train in September 1886, lived into the 1900s. It is possible that the descendants of Atelnietze and Nat-cul-baye lived as free Apaches in the Sierra Madre to the 1920s or 1930s.

The hardy chiefs and headmen survived tuberculosis and other diseases to live long lives. Chiva was the first to go, passing away at Mount Vernon Barracks, May 19, 1889. Other deaths occurring there were Fun (suicide) in 1892; Dutchy (drunken brawl with a soldier at Mount Vernon) in 1893; Cathla (drunken brawl with a Chiricahua) in 1894. At Fort Sill the following men died: Nana and Zele in 1896; Chihuahua and Mangas in 1901; Loco in 1905; and Ulzana and Geronimo in 1909. At Mescalero, the following men passed on: Noche in 1914; Kaetenae in 1918; Naiche in 1921; Chatto, Fatty, Kayitah, and Perico in 1934; and Martine in 1937.

ABBREVIATIONS
USED IN NOTES

AHS   Arizona Historical Society
CIA   Commissioner of Indian Affairs
DAZ   Department of Arizona
GC   Gatewood Collection
GP   Grenville Goodwin Papers
LC   Library of Congress
LR   Letters Received
LS   Letters Sent
NA   U.S. National Archives
OP   Morris Edward Opler Papers
PSC   Post at San Carlos
RG   Record Group
SA   Sonoran Archives
SED   Senate Executive Document
TP   Benjamin Thomas Papers
UO   University of Oregon
USMHI   United States Military History Institute

NOTES

CHAPTER 1. THE FIRST CHIRICAHUA RESERVATIONS

Epigraph: Library of Congress (hereafter LC), Hugh Scott Papers, box 70, Apache folder, "Proceedings of Conference with the Apache Prisoners of War at Fort Sill Reservation," September 21, 1911.

1. National Archives (hereafter NA), RG75, Reports of Inspections of the Field Jurisdictions of the Office of Indian Affairs, 1873–1900, M1070, R2, Watkins to CIA (Commissioner of Indian Affairs), April 13, 1878.

2. See Sweeney, *Cochise*, 352–86, and Sweeney, *Making Peace with Cochise*, 83–103, for details of Howard's trip and the treaty he made with Cochise.

3. Sweeney, *Cochise*, 368–70.

4. NA, RG75, T21, Records of the New Mexico Superintendency of Indian Affairs, 1849–1880, R17, Ayers to Pope, December 31, 1872. Ayers reported 844 Apaches at Tularosa; 429 Chihennes under Victorio, Loco, and Ponce; 125 Bedonkohes under Chiva and Gordo; and the balance, some 300, White Mountain Apaches visiting Chiva. For the Apaches at Chiricahua see, Sweeney, *Cochise*, 368–70.

5. Hodge, *Handbook of American Indians*, vol. 1, 63; Perry, *Western Apache Heritage*, 135–39.

6. Goodwin, *Social Organization*, 1.

7. Perry, *Western Apache Heritage*, 18–20, 49–53; Basso and Opler, *Apachean Culture History*, 4.

8. Anthropologist Morris Opler concluded that the Chiricahuas consisted of three bands: the Eastern Chiricahuas (Chihennes), the Central Chiricahuas (Chokonens), and the Southern Chiricahuas (Nednhis). The Chiricahuas recalled another band, the Bedonkohes. Geronimo was a Bedonkohe by birth. By 1883, conflicts with Mexican and American forces had so reduced the numbers of the Bedonkohes and Nednhis that their survivors assimilated into the Chokonens and Chihennes. Opler, *Life-Way*, 1–2; Barrett, *Geronimo's Story*, 12–14; Ball, *Indeh*, 22; Debo, *Geronimo*, 71; Betzinez, *I Fought with Geronimo*, 14–15.

9. Cornell University, Morris Edward Opler Papers, 14-25-3238 (hereafter OP), box 35, folder 5, Martine interview.

10. OP, box 35, folder 3, Kinzhuna interview; folder 5, Guydelkon interview, Chatto interview. In 1911, Chatto had told Major Hugh Scott that his father was a brother of Mangas Coloradas. "Proceedings of Conference with the Apache Prisoners of War."

11. OP, box 35, folder 5, Chatto interview.

12. Ibid.; Martine interview.

13. OP, box 35, folder 5, Martine interview.

14. OP, box 35, folder 4, Fatty interview.

15. Sweeney, *Cochise*, 4, 212; *Santa Fe New Mexican*, December 2, 1880.

16. University of Chicago, Special Collections, Sol Tax Papers, box 10, folder 17, Martine interview.

17. OP, box 35, folder 5, Martine interview, Sam Kenoi interview.

18. Sweeney, *Cochise*, 76, 90, 249; Sweeney, *Mangas Coloradas,* 179, 253.

19. OP, box 35, folder 5, Martine interview; Jason Betzinez also heard that Juh's father was a leader of the Nednhis. Betzinez, "My People," 62.

20. Goodwin, *Western Apache Raiding and Warfare*, 110.

21. Opler, *Life-Way*, 369.

22. Sweeney, *Cochise*, 377–79.

23. NA, RG75, Records of the Arizona Superintendency, M734, R7, Wilbur to CIA, March 31, 1873. I would like to thank Jeanne Marion of Tucson for bringing this to my attention.

24. *Estrella de Occidente*, January 9, 1874; Sweeney, *Cochise*, 372–85, for a discussion of this major controversy.

25. *Estrella de Occidente*, June 20, 1873; *Alta California*, May 13, 1873; Sweeney, *Cochise*, 380–81.

26. Griswold, "Fort Sill Apaches," 100.

27. *Arizona Citizen*, June 14, 1873; NA, RG75, Letters Received (LR), Office of Indian Affairs, Arizona Superintendency, M234, R8, Jeffords to Howard, February 11, 1873; Museum of New Mexico, Benjamin Thomas Papers (hereafter TP), Thomas to Dudley, May 31, 1873.

28. Arizona Historical Society (AHS), Fred Hughes Papers, *Arizona Daily Star*, 1886; Sweeney, *Cochise*, 383; *Weekly Arizona Miner*, September 27, 1873, October 25, 1873; *Las Cruces Borderer*, August 9, 1873.

29. NA, RG94, LR, Adjutant General's Office, M666, R123, Price to Willard, August 1, 1873; TP, Thomas to Dudley, August 7, 1873.

30. NA, RG94, LR, Adjutant General's Office, M666, R123, Price to Willard, August 1, 1873; TP, Thomas to Dudley, August 7, 1873. For a discussion of the controversy between Jeffords and Price, with statements made by Crook and Howard, see Sweeney, *Cochise*, 384–85.

31. TP, Thomas to Dudley, August 30, 1873, September 3, 1873.

32. NA, RG75, M234, R581, various census data.

33. NA, RG75, M1070, R1, Vandever to Smith, October 18, 1873.

34. NA, RG75, M234, R11, Jeffords to Smith, November 25, 1874.

CHAPTER 2. PRELUDE TO REMOVAL

Epigraph: Scott Papers, box 70, Record of Conference with Apache Indians, Prisoners of War on Fort Sill Military Reservation, October 16, 1911.

1. Sweeney, *Cochise*, 386–87.

2. Ball, *Indeh*, 31.

3. *Arizona Weekly Citizen*, December 27, 1873, February 21, 1874, May 16, 1874.

4. TP, Thomas to Dudley, October 7, 1873, December 3, 1873, January 12, 1874.

5. NA, RG75, M234, R563, Dudley to Smith, March 6, 1874, in which he enclosed a copy of the *Las Cruces Borderer*, February 21, 1874; Bowdoin College, Howard Papers, May to Howard, May 4, 1874; *Report of the Commissioner of Indian Affairs*, 1874, 300–302.

6. OP, box 35, folder 5, Sam Kenoi interview.

7. Sweeney, *Cochise*, 391–93; *Report of the Commissioner of Indian Affairs*, 1874, 300–302.

8. *Arizona Weekly Citizen*, May 16, 1874.

9. Griswold, "Fort Sill Apaches," 100. Nah-de-yole (1858–1896) would bear Naiche three children. NA, RG75, M234, R10, Jeffords to Smith, June 10, 1874; NA, RG393, LR, Department of Arizona (DAZ), Stacey to Arnold, July 13, 1879; Sweeney, *Cochise*, 393–95.

10. *Estrella de Occidente*, May 8, 1874, July 31, 1874, August 14, 1874, August 28, 1874; *Oficial Semanario*, October 18, 1874; Sweeney, *Cochise*, 392.

11. NA, RG393, Letters Sent (LS), Fort Tularosa, Shorkley to Price, July 11, 1874; *Estrella de Occidente*, July 27, 1874.

12. See Sweeney, *Cochise*, 52–53 and 86–87, for examples of Sonora's military pursuing Chiricahuas into Chihuahua.

13. AHS, Sonoran Archives (SA), roll 20, Ochoa to Governor of Sonora, August 26, 1874, September 11, 1874, and September 18, 1874; Governor of Sonora to Governor of Chihuahua, September 6, 1874; *Estrella de Occidente*, August 14, 1874, August 28, 1874, September 11, 1874; Hatfield, *Chasing Shadows*, 12–14; Miguel Tinker Salas, *In the Shadow of the Eagles*, 62–64.

14. *Estrella de Occidente*, November 13, 1874; *Oficial Semanario*, October 18, 1874.

15. NA, RG75, M1070, R1, Report of J. W. Daniels, September 20, 1874; *Estrella de Occidente*, November 13, 1874.

16. TP, Dudley to Thomas, June 20, 1874, October 7, 1874; Thomas to Smith, August 31, 1874.

17. OP, box 35, folder 4, Kinzhuna biography; *Arizona Citizen*, August 8, 1874; NA, RG75, M234, R562, Apaches rationed at Tularosa, June 13, 1874; *Annual Report of the Commissioner of Indian Affairs*, 1874, 59.

18. *Arizona Citizen*, April 15, 1876.

19. Ibid., May 22, 1875, July 10, 1875, November 29, 1873.

20. *Estrella de Occidente*, June 18, 1875.

21. Ibid., January 22, 1875, January 29, 1875, February 5, 1875.

22. Ibid., April 30, 1875, June 18, 1875; *Weekly Arizona Miner*, May 21, 1875; Jeffords's annual report, August 21, 1875.

23. *Estrella de Occidente*, June 25, 1875, July 9, 1875, July 16, 1875; Acuña, *Sonoran Strongman*, 122–24.

24. *Grant County Herald,* August 8, 1875, September 19, 1875.

25. *Estrella de Occidente*, October 8, 1875.

26. Lockwood, *The Apache Indians*, 126; Ball, *Indeh*, 47.

27. *Estrella de Occidente*, June 20, 1873.

28. *Estrella de Occidente*, November 26, 1875, December 24, 1875; *Arizona Weekly Citizen*, March 11, 1876.

29. *Report of the Commissioner of Indian Affairs*, 1875, 122–23; *Grant County Herald*, July 22, 1876.

30. NA, RG75, M234, R565. Shaw to Commissioner of Indian Affairs, November 18 [?], 1875. This letter contains a summary of the number of Apaches rationed between December 1874 and September 1875. Shaw's numbers are meaningless because of the formula he used to derive them.

31. See Thrapp, *Al Sieber*, 156–69, for a complete account of the closing of the Verde reservation and the removal of its occupants to San Carlos; Thrapp, *Encyclopedia*, 1, 427.

32. *Report of the Commissioner of Indian Affairs*, 1875, 122–23; *Grant County Herald*, April 25, 1875.

33. Carmony, *Apache Days and Tombstone Nights*, 2–4.

34. Ibid., 5–6; Thrapp, *Conquest of Apacheria*, 164–65; Lockwood, *The Apache Indians*, 209–10.

35. Thrapp, *Al Sieber*, 158.

36. Thrapp, *Conquest of Apacheria*, 166–67; Davisson, "Fort Apache," 74–75; Ogle, *Federal Control*, 150–52.

37. Thrapp, *Conquest of Apacheria*, 166–67; Davisson, "Fort Apache," 74–75; Ogle, *Federal Control*, 150–52; Lockwood, *The Apache Indians*, 211–14.

38. Goodwin, *Social Organization*, 609.

39. NA, RG75, Jeffords's annual report, August 21, 1875; *Arizona Weekly Citizen*, October 9, 1875; *Grant County Herald*, July 22, 1876; Arizona State Museum, Grenville Goodwin Papers (hereafter GP), Mrs. Andrew Stanley's account.

40. Fort Bowie Files, roll 3, Jeffords to Wallace, August 21, 1875; Wallace to AAG, DAZ, August 22, 1875; AAG, DAZ to Wallace, September 1, 1875.

41. This melee took place in the Chiricahua Mountains near Pinery Canyon. GP, Mrs. Andrew Stanley's account; NA, RG75, M234, R16, Jeffords to Smith, May 2, 1876; Jeffords final report, October 3, 1876.

42. NA, RG217, Records of the U. S. General Accounting Office, Smith to Jeffords, December 23, 1875.

43. The eight camps were probably Taza, Cathla, Chihuahua (Chokonens); Gordo, Chiva, Esquine (Bedonkohes); Juh and Nolgee (Nednhis).

44. Altshuler, *Cavalry Yellow and Infantry Blue*, 216–17.

45. NA, RG75, M1070, R1, Kemble to Smith, December 30, 1875.

CHAPTER 3. REMOVAL TO SAN CARLOS

Epigraph: *Arizona Weekly Citizen*, June 10, 1876.

1. Jones, *Forty Years*, 236–39.

2. NA, RG75, M234, R 14, Jeffords to E. P. Smith, December 6, 1875, January 19, 1876; NA, RG217, number 8469, Thomas Jeffords accounts, J. Q. Smith to Jeffords, December 23, 1875.

3. NA, RG75, M234, R14, Jeffords to Smith, January 19, 1876; R16, Jeffords to Smith, March 4, 1876; *Grant County Herald*, July 22, 1876.

4. See Sweeney, *Cochise*, 50–51, 190.

5. *Grant County Herald*, April 29, 1876.

6. *Arizona Weekly Citizen*, February 19, 1876, April 29, 1876.

7. NA, RG75, M234, R16, Jeffords to Smith, April 27, 1876; *Grant County Herald*, July 22, 1876; *Annual Report by the Commissioner of Indian Affairs*, 1876;Jeffords's final report, October 3, 1876, 3–4; Ogle, *Federal Control*, 165; Griswold, "Fort Sill Apaches," 124; Barrett, *Geronimo's Story*, 129.

8. *Grant County Herald*, April 29, 1876, July 22, 1876.

9. OP, box 36, folder 3, Sam Kenoi interview; *Arizona Miner*, June 9, 1876; *Annual Report by the Commissioner of Indian Affairs*, 1876, Jeffords's final report, October 3, 1876, 3–4; Farish, *History of Arizona*, 2:238. Four years earlier, Rogers had been accused of selling whiskey to the soldiers at Fort Bowie. He had followed the paymaster into Bowie and sold it to the soldiers "in the bush," or off the military reservation. NA, RG393, LS, Fort Bowie, Evans to AAG, DAZ, March 6, 1872.

10. Farish, *History of Arizona*, 2:238–39; NA, RG75, M234, R16, Jeffords to Smith, April 27, 1876.

11. Ibid,; *Arizona Weekly Citizen*, April 15, 1876; Spence won the Medal of Honor for his actions in the October 20, 1869, battle against Cochise in Rucker Canyon. See Sweeney, *Cochise*, 272–77.

12. *Arizona Weekly Citizen*, April 15, 1876.

13. NA, RG75, N234, R16, Jeffords to Smith, April 27, 1876; Farish, *History of Arizona*, 2:238–39.

14. Post Returns, Fort Bowie; *Arizona Weekly Citizen*, September 30, 1876; *Mesilla News*, April 22, 1876.

15. *Grant County Herald*, July 22, 1876.

16. *Annual Report by the Commissioner of Indian Affairs*, 1876. Jeffords's final report, October 3, 1876, 3–4.

17. Farish, *History of Arizona*, 2:238.

18. *Arizona Weekly Citizen*, September 30, 1876.

19. NA, RG75, M234, R16, Jeffords to Smith, April 27, 1876; *Arizona Weekly Citizen*, April 15, 1876, April 22, 1876.

20. NA, RG75, M234, R16, Jeffords to Smith, April 27, 1876; *Arizona Weekly Citizen*, April 15, 1876, April 22, 1876; *Arizona Weekly Citizen*, September 30, 1876.

21. NA, RG75, M234, R16, Jeffords to Smith, April 27, 1876; RG393, LS, Fort Bowie, McLellan to Ogilby, April 25, 1876; McLellan to AG, DAZ, April 11, 1876; *Arizona Weekly Citizen*, April 15, 1876.

22. *Arizona Weekly Citizen*, April 15, 1876, May 6, 1876; Jeffords, in his June 30, 1876, report, wrote that Esquine's band numbered 44 men and 126 women and children. *Grant County Herald*, July 22, 1876.

23. *Grant County Herald*, May 13, 1876.

24. *Mesilla News*, April 22, 1876.

25. *Santa Fe New Mexican*, May 2, 1876; *New York Times*, November 28, 1880; NA, RG75, M234, R568, Shaw to Smith, April 22, 1876. Agent John Shaw, in his census compiled during the summer of 1876, noted that Chisito "was killed by Apaches." NA, RG75, M234, R572, Shaw to Commissioner of Indian Affairs, September 3, 1877; R569, Hatch to AAAG, District of New Mexico, May 20, 1876; NA, RG393, LS, Fort Craig, Shorkley to Morrow, April 23, 1876; NA, RG393, LR, Fort Craig, Hatch to Shorkley, April 24, 1876; NA, RG75, M1070, R2, Kemble to Smith, May 17, 1876.

26. *Arizona Weekly Citizen*, April 15, 1876; NA, RG75, M234, R16, Clum to Safford, April 14, 1876; Safford to Clum, April 15, 1876; Clum to Commissioner of Indian Affairs, April 18, 1876, May 6, 1876; Safford to Smith, April 17, 1876; Ogle, *Federal Control*, 166; NA, RG94, M666, roll 265, Safford to Smith, May 6, 1876; Secretary of War to the Secretary of the Interior, May 16, 1876; Kautz to AGO, May 19, 1876. Biddle, *Reminiscences*, 164.

27. *Arizona Weekly Citizen*, April 15, 1876, May 20, 1876; NA, RG393, LR, Fort Bowie, AAG, DAZ to Commanding Officer, Fort Bowie, April 22, 1876.

28. *Arizona Weekly Citizen*, May 6, 1876; *Grant County Herald*, July 22, 1876.

29. NA, RG75, M234, R16, Jeffords to Smith, May 12, 1876; *Grant County Herald*, July 22, 1876; Farish, *History of Arizona*, 2:239.

30. *Boletin Oficial,* April 21, 1876, April 28, 1876, May 12, 1876, May 19, 1876.

31. *Grant County Herald*, July 22, 1876; NA, RG75, M234, R16, Jeffords to Smith, May 12, 1876.

32. *Grant County Herald.* July 22, 1876; *Arizona Weekly Citizen*, May 13, 1876; NA, RG94, M666, R265, Clum to CIA, May 13, 1876.

33. NA, RG94, M666, R265, Kautz to AG, Military Division of the Pacific, June 30, 1876; AHS, Fred Hughes Papers.

34. Grijalva, a captive of the Chiricahuas for more than a decade, escaped in 1859. From the 1860s through the early 1870s, he was Cochise's nemesis, leading many important scouts against the Chokonens. For a biography, see Sweeney, *Merejildo Grijalva.*

35. NA, RG75, M234, R16, Clum to CIA, May 23, 1876; *Arizona Weekly Citizen*, May 27, 1876.

36. *Grant County Herald*, July 22, 1876.

37. AHS, Hughes Papers, *Arizona Daily Star*, January 31, 1886; *Arizona Weekly Citizen*, June 3, 1876; NA, RG94, M666, R265, Kautz to AAG, Military Division of the Pacific, June 30, 1876.

38. NA, RG393, Telegrams Received, Fort Bowie, Martin to CO, Fort Bowie, May 31, 1876; NA, RG94, M666, R265, Kautz to AG, Military Division of the Pacific, June 3, 1876.

39. NA, RG94, M666, R265, Kautz to AAAG, Military Division of the Pacific, June 3, 1876, June 30, 1876.

40. *Arizona Weekly Citizen*, June 10, 1876; AHS, Hughes Papers, *Arizona Daily Star*, January 31, 1886. Geronimo recalled that tiswin was involved. Barrett, *Geronimo's Story*, 129.

41. NA, RG75, M234, R16, Jeffords to Smith, June 6, 1876.

42. *Arizona Weekly Citizen*, June 10, 1876; *Grant County Herald*, July 17, 1876; Lockwood, *The Apache Indians*, 216–17; *Annual Report of the Commissioner of Indian Affairs*, 1876, 10–11; Farish, *History of Arizona*, 2:238–39; NA, RG75, M234, R16, Clum to Commissioner of Indian Affairs, June 5, 1876.

43. *Arizona Weekly Citizen*, June 10, 1876; *Grant County Herald*, July 17, 1876.

44. *Grant County Herald*, July 17, 1876; NA, RG75, M234, R16, Clum to Commissioner, June 5, 1876; NA, RG94, M666, R265, Kautz to AAG, Division of the Pacific, June 30, 1876.

45. *Arizona Weekly Citizen*, June 10, 1876.

46. In fact, the Chokonens were not disarmed until September 1886.

47. *Arizona Weekly Citizen*, June 10, 1876; AHS, Hughes Papers, *Arizona Daily Star*, January 31, 1886.

48. *Grant County Herald*, July 12, 1876; NA, RG94, M666, R265, Kautz to AAG, Military Division of the Pacific, June 30, 1876; Clum to Kautz, June 8, 1876; Clum, *Apache Agent*, 181–82; Carmony, *Apache Days and Tombstone Nights*. 114; Fontana, *An Englishman's Arizona*, xx.

49. *Grant County Herald*, July 22, 1876; *Arizona Weekly Citizen*, July 22, 1876; Goodwin, *Western Apache Raiding and Warfare*, 102, Carmony, *Apache Days and Tombstone Nights*, 114–15; Clum, *Apache Agent*, 182–83; NA, RG75, M234, R16, Clum to Commissioner of Indian Affairs, June 10, 1876.

50. Clum, *Apache Agent*, 182–83; *Arizona Weekly Citizen*, June 17, 1876, March 29, 1884, April 12, 1876. *Grant County Herald*, July 22, 1876.

51. *Arizona Weekly Citizen*, July 1, 1876; NA, RG75, M234, R16, Clum to CIA, June 16, 1876, June 17, 1876; *Mesilla News*, July 1, 1876.

52. *Annual Report of the Commissioner of Indian Affairs*, 1876, 10–11; NA, RG94, M666, R265, Kautz to AAG, Military Division of the Pacific, June 30, 1876.

53. NA, RG75, M234, R568, Shaw to Smith, June 22, 1876, July 3, 1876, July 17, 1876, July 21, 1876; Davis to Smith, October 23, 1876.

54. *Grant County Herald*, July 22, 1876.

55. *Arizona Miner*, June 8, 1876.

56. NA, RG75, M1070, R1, Vandever to CIA, October 18, 1873; Daniels to CIA, September 29, 1874; Kemble to CIA, December 30, 1875.

57. NA, RG217, Jeffords's accounts, entry 8469.

58. *Arizona Weekly Citizen*, June 10, 1876.

59. *Arizona Miner*, June 9, 1876.

60. *Arizona Weekly Citizen*, June 10, 1876.

61. *Grant County Herald*, June 24, 1876.

62. *Arizona Weekly Citizen*, June 24, 1876.

CHAPTER 4. GERONIMO'S AND CLUM'S TRAVELS

Epigraph: OP, box 37, folder 36, Autobiography of Sam Haozous.

1. NA, RG75, M234, R16, Clum to Smith, June 19, 1876.

2. Hart, *Old Forts of the Far West*, 82.

3. R. W. Frazer, *Forts of the West*, 9.

4. *Weekly Arizona Miner*, October 4, 1873.

5. Sweeney, *Cochise*, 264.

6. Ball, *Indeh*, 49.

7. Clum, *Apache Agent*, 185; *Arizona Weekly Citizen*, July 1, 1876, July 22, 1876.

8. NA, RG75, M1070, R1, Clum to Kautz, July 26, 1876; Charles Lummis had heard from Sidney De Long that Nahilzay had originally gone with Geronimo and Juh and returned with them in late 1879. But this was wrong, for Nahilzay had surrendered in late 1877. In early 1878, he was reported on Eagle Creek, according to Palmer Valor. University of Arizona, Charles Lummis Papers; GP, Palmer Valor interview.

9. Altshuler, *Starting with Defiance*, 54–55.

10. Clum, *Apache Agent*, 185–89. The best account of Clum's journey east is Shapard, "A Federally Funded Wedding and Honeymoon."

11. Clum, *Apache Agent*, 185–95; Turner, *Red Men Calling on the Great White Father*, 137–44.

12. Turner, *Red Men Calling on the Great White Father*, 144.

13. The two men killed near Pinery Canyon were George Todenworth and Joseph L. Cadotte. A third man, David Burroughs, testified that there were fifteen Apaches, and that he thought he had killed two of them. *Arizona Weekly Citizen*, July 22, 1876; NA RG94, M666, R265, Kautz to AAG, Military Division of the Pacific, October 23, 1876. Fontana, *An Englishman's Arizona*, xix, 29–30.

14. *Arizona Weekly Citizen*, August 26, 1876.

15. *Arizona Weekly Citizen*, October 21, 1876, November 11, 1876; NA, RG393, LS, Camp Thomas, Bailey to AAG, DAZ, February 23, 1877.

16. Clum, *Apache Agent*, 199–201; Ball, *Indeh*, 61. Ball tells a story, probably apocryphal, that Naiche came to the agency but Clum refused to see him. So he "stood at the door" for three days before Clum explained the circumstances surrounding Taza's death. Ball, *In the Days of Victorio*, 51–52.

17. *Boletin Oficial*, August 11, 1876; Wasserman, *Capitalists, Caciques, and Revolution*, 31–35; *Arizona Weekly Citizen*, August 5, 1876; on July 20, 1876, Geronimo arrived at Ojo Caliente with Delgadito, a son of the famous 1850s chief by the same name. The latter's Apache name was Nonithian, the father of Jason Betzinez. NA, RG75, M234, R568, Shaw to Smith, July 21, 1876; Griswold, "Ft. Sill Apaches," 115–16.

18. Acuña, *Sonoran Strongman*, 125–131.

19. AHS, SA, R20, Vilelosola to governor, September 4, 1876.

20. Ibid., Vilelosola to governor, August 27, 1876.

21. Thrapp, *Encyclopedia*, 3:1378–79.

22. *Arizona Weekly Citizen*, November 4, 1876; *Grant County Herald*, November 11, 1876; *Boletin Oficial*, November 3, 1876.

23. *Boletin Oficial*, November 3, 1876; *Arizona Weekly Citizen*, November 11, 1876.

24. *Boletin Oficial*, December 15, 1876; *Las Cinco Vocales*, December 10, 1876; SA, R20, Cuen to governor, November 10, 1876.

25. *Grant County Herald*, September 9, 1876; Ungnade, *Guide to the New Mexico Mountains*, 163; Basehart, "Chiricahua Apache Subsistence," 78–79; Opler, "Mountain Spirits," 129–30.

26. More than 180,000 African Americans fought for the Union during the Civil War. On June 28, 1866, Congress authorized the establishment of six regiments, two cavalry and four infantry. The two cavalry regiments became the Ninth and Tenth Cavalry. Leckie, *The Buffalo Soldiers,* 5–6.

27. *Grant County Herald*, September 9, 1876. There is disagreement as to the Apaches' losses, though Carroll's official reports, which place the numbers at one dead and three wounded, are the most reliable. Thrapp, *Victorio*, 183; NA, RG393, LR, District of New Mexico, M1088, R27, CO, Fort Selden, to AAG, District of NM, September 18, 1876; *Santa Fe New Mexican*, September 18, 1876, put the Apache casualties at sixteen dead, while the *Arizona Weekly Citizen*, September 23, 1876, reported fourteen dead.

28. NA, RG75, M234, R568, Shaw to Smith, June 22, 1876, July 3, 1876.

29. Ibid., Shaw to Smith, July 21, 1876, September 30, 1876.

30. On April 3, 1876, the commissioner of Indian Affairs, John Q. Smith, had ordered Kemble to conduct a "special investigation of affairs at Ojo Caliente." His report confirmed the opinion of Indian officials in Washington: Shaw displayed no initiative and had reversed most of Thomas's successful policies, even allowing the Indians to decide how he should dispense rations. NA, RG75, M1070, R29, Kemble to Smith, May 17, 1876.

31. Thrapp, *Victorio*, 181–82.

32. Giese, *Forts of New Mexico*, 19.

33. OP, box 35, folder 4, Kinzhuna biography.

34. NA, RG75, M234, R569, Shaw to Smith, September 8, 1876; NA, RG393, LRDISTNM, M1088, R28, Wright to CO, Camp Vincent, September 25, 1876; *Grant County Herald*, September 9, 1876.

35. NA, RG75, M234, R569, Shaw to Smith, October 7, 1876; Thrapp, *Victorio*, 182.

36. NA, RG393, LRDISTNM, M1088, R27, Davis to Smith, November 20, 1876.

37. Ibid., Davis to Hatch, November 3, 1876.

38. Ibid., Steelhammer to AAAG, District of New Mexico, November 26, 1876.

39. NA, RG75, M234, R566, Davis to Commissioner of Indian Affairs, December 2, 1876.

40. NA, RG75, T21, R24, summary list of Apaches rationed at Ojo Caliente, January 1877–April 1877.

41. Thrapp, *Victorio*, 183.

42. Thrapp, "The Indian Scouts," 145.

43. Joyce Evelyn Mason, "Indian Scouts in the Apache Wars," 25–26, 122–23; Thrapp, "The Indian Scouts," 144–45.

44. *Arizona Weekly Citizen*, December 23, 1876, January 6, 1877; NA, RG75, M234, R19, Rucker to Post Adjutant, Camp Bowie, January 14, 1877.

45. *Arizona Weekly Citizen*, December 23, 1876, January 6, 1877; NA, RG75, M234, R19, Rucker to Post Adjutant, Camp Bowie, January 14, 1877; NA, RG94, M666, R265, Rucker to Post Adjutant, Fort Bowie, January 14, 1877; University of Chicago Library, Special Collections, Sol Tax Papers, box 19, folder 15, Perico interview.

46. Thrapp, *Victorio*, 185.

47. Barrett, *Geronimo's Story*, 124–27.

48. Sam Haozous, a Bedonkohe, was the son of Goonah-hleenah and Nah-ke-de-sah, a daughter of Mangas Coloradas. Born in the mid-1860s, Haozous was listed in Loco's band in the 1885 census. The noted twentieth-century artist and sculptor Allen Houser is one of his descendants. Griswold, "Fort Sill Apaches," 55.

49. OP, box 37, folder 36, Haozous autobiography.

50. OP, box 35, folder 4, Balatchu account.

51. *Arizona Weekly Citizen*, February 10, 1877. A few years later Hughes told Charles Connell that he believed Juh had led the raid. AHS, Connell manuscript, "Apaches Past and Present."

52. Fontana, *An Englishman's Arizona*, 53.

53. *Arizona Weekly Citizen*, February 10, 1877, February 17, 1877; *Weekly Arizona Miner*, April 13,1877. Andrew Wallace, "General August V. Kautz in Arizona ," 61; AHS, William Devers Hayden file.

54. Goff, *Arizona Territorial Officials*, 56–57; H. E. Dunlap, "Clay Beauford," 50–51; Ogle, *Federal Control*, 161–70.

55. *Weekly Arizona Miner*, April 13, 1877; *Arizona Weekly Citizen*, March 17, 1877, March 24, 1877; Wallace, "General August V. Kautz in Arizona," 61–62. Wallace has a good account of Kautz's verbal joust with Safford and Clum.

56. *Weekly Arizona Miner*, April 6, 1877.

57. Clay Beauford's real name was Welford C. Bridwell. For a biography, see Thrapp, *Encyclopedia*, 1:168–69.

58. *Arizona Weekly Citizen*, February 24, 1877; Dunlap, "Clay Beauford," 50–51.

59. NA, RG75, M234, R19, Whitney to Martin, February 28, 1877; Thrapp, *Victorio*, 185.

60. NA, RG75, M234, R18, Safford to Commissioner of Indian Affairs, March 18, 1877; *Arizona Weekly Citizen*, March 24, 1877.

61. NA, RG94, M666, R326, Smith to Clum, March 29, 1877.

62. Thrapp, *Victorio*, 186.

63. NA, RG75, T21, R24, Apaches rationed at Ojo Caliente, January 5, 1877–April 28, 1877.

64. Thrapp, *Victorio*, 186–88.

65. Ibid., 186–90; Carmony, *Apache Days and Tombstone Nights*, 121–24.

66. *Arizona Weekly Citizen*, April 24, 1877.

67. Barrett, *Geronimo's Story*, 131–32.

68. Carmony, *Apache Days and Tombstone Nights*, 124– 25.

69. *Arizona Weekly Citizen*, May 5, 1877.

70. Ibid., April 28, 1877, May 5, 1877; Thrapp, *Victorio*, 186–89.

71. Thrapp, *Victorio*, 188–89.

72. OP, box 37, folder 36, Haozous autobiography.

73. Clum identified Nulah in *Apache Agent*, 240–41. An informant of Morris Opler identified Jatu, Chatto, and Cunneh (Cooney), "Mountain Spirits," 125–29.

74. Carmony, *Apache Days and Tombstone Nights*, points out that a serious smallpox outbreak raged in southern Arizona during the spring of 1877. Over two hundred perished from the disease in the Tucson area (131); Clum, *Apache Agent*, 249.

75. *Arizona Weekly Citizen*, May 19, 1877.

CHAPTER 5. NEW TROUBLES AT SAN CARLOS

Epigraph: NA, RG393, M1088, R31, "Statement of Apache Indian Chiefs Held in Council," Fort Wingate, October 24, 1877.

1. Ogle, *Federal Control*, 177–78; Clum, *Apache Agent*, 250–54; Thrapp, *Victorio*, 192–93.

2. OP, box 37, folder 26, Perico interview.

3. See Opler, *Life-Way*, 105–106, for a discussion of the role of the clown as a "servant" to the mountain spirits.

4. Opler, "Mountain Spirits of the Chiricahua Apache," 126–29; OP, box 37, folder 26, Perico interview.

5. GP, Mrs. Andrew Stanley interview.

6. NA, RG75, M234, R572, Whitney to Smith, May 8, 1877; *Grant County Herald*, May 19, 1877.

7. *Grant County Herald*, May 19, 1877.

8. GP, Mrs. Andrew Stanley's interview; NA, RG393, Fort Bowie Records, Wallace to AAG, DAZ, May 30, 1877, June 4, 1877, June 6, 1877, June 11, 1877. *Arizona Weekly Citizen*, June 2, 1877, June 9, 1877, June 16, 1877.

9. Robles left a mother and two small children; Sanchez left a wife and three small children; *Arizona Weekly Citizen*, April 21, 1877; NA, RG75, M234, R19, Craig to CO, Camp in Huachuca Mountains, April 22, 1877.

10. *Arizona Weekly Citizen*, May 26, 1877; *Grant County Herald*, May 12, 1877, May 19, 1877. The *Herald* placed the women and children in Pionsenay's party at eleven, but a subsequent report revealed that twenty-seven Chiricahuas were confined in the guardhouse, which must have included the men arrested by Clum at Ojo Caliente. *Grant County Herald*, August 25, 1877.

11. NA, RG75, M234, R19, Vandever to CIA, June 8, 1877; Ogle, *Federal Control*, 181–82; *Arizona Weekly Citizen*, August 4, 1877.

12. NA, RG75, M1070, R2, Vandever to CIA, June 19, 1877; *Arizona Weekly Citizen*, August 4, 1877; NA, RG75, M234, R18, Sweeney to CIA, July 7, 1877.

13. NA, RG75, M1070, R2, Vandever to CIA, July 16, 1877.

14. Debo, *Geronimo*, 113–14. Sam Haozous recalled that Geronimo was released from his irons before Victorio's outbreak from San Carlos. OP, box 37, folder 36, Haozous autobiography.

15. *Grant County Herald*, August 25, 1877.

16. Betzinez, *I Fought with Geronimo*, 46.

17. NA, RG94, M666, R366, Kautz to AG, Division of the Pacific, September 28, 1877; Ogle, *Federal Control*, 182–83.

18. NA, RG94, M666, R366, Kautz to AG, Division of the Pacific, September 28, 1877; Ogle, *Federal Control*, 182–83; NA, RG75, M234, R19, Abbot to AAG, DAZ, September 22, 1877.

19. NA, RG393, E204, Miscellaneous Records, DAZ, "Brief of Indian Affairs at San Carlos, 1877–78"; NA, RG75, M1070, R2, Vandever to CIA, August 28, 1877.

20. NA, RG75, M1070, R2, Vandever to CIA, August 30, 1877; NA, RG94, M666, R366, Martin to McDowell, September 3, 1877; Hanna to Post Adjutant, Fort Huachuca, September 28, 1877; NA, RG393, E204, "Brief of Indian Affairs at San Carlos, 1877–78"; *Arizona Weekly Citizen*, September 8, 1877, September 15, 1877.

21. *Arizona Weekly Citizen*, September 15, 1877; NA, RG94, M666, R366, Hoag to Bailey, September 2, 1877.

22. *Arizona Weekly Citizen*, September 15, 1877, September 22, 1877; *Weekly Arizona Miner*, November 16, 1877; NA, RG75, M234, R19, Hart to CIA, September 18, 1877; McDowell to AGO, October 11, 1877; NA, RG94, M366, R366, Hoag to Bailey, September 2, 1877.

23. NA, RG75, M234, R19, Hart to CIA, September 18, 1877; NA, RG94, M666, R366, Kautz to AAG, Division of the Pacific, September 28, 1877, with enclosures; *Grant County Herald*, September 22, 1877; NA, RG393, E204, "Brief of Indian Affairs at San Carlos, 1877–78"; NA, RG75, M234, R19, Hart to CIA, September 18, 1877; Thrapp, *Victorio*, 196–98.

24. NA, RG75, M1070, R2, Vandever to CIA, October 23, 1877; NA, M234, R572, Whitney to CIA, November 30, 1877; *Arizona Weekly Citizen*, September 15, 1877; NA, RG393, M1088, R31, "Statement of Apache Indian Chiefs in Council, October 24, 1877."

25. NA, RG75, M1070, R2, Vandever to CIA, September 12, 1877, September 18, 1877, October 23, 1877. NA, RG75, M234, R19, Kautz to AG, Military Division of the Pacific, September 28, 1877; Abbot to AAG, DAZ, September 22, 1877.

26. OP, box 37, folder 36, Haozous biography.

27. *Grant County Herald*, September 22, 1877; NA, RG393, E204, "Brief of Indian Affairs at San Carlos, 1877–78"; NA, RG75, M234, R19, Hart to CIA, September 18, 1877; Thrapp, *Victorio*, 196–97.

28. GP, Palmer Valor interview.

29. NA, RG94, M666, R366, Kautz to AG, Division of the Pacific, October 4, 1877; Tupper to Post Adjutant, Camp Grant, September 18, 1877.

30. *Weekly Arizona Miner*, November 30, 1877.

31. NA, RG393, M1088, R31, "Statement of Apache Indian Chiefs in Council," Fort Wingate, October 24, 1877.

32. Sweeney, *Mangas Coloradas*, 214.

33. NA, RG393, M1088, R29, Jewett to AAG, District of New Mexico, September 17, 1877, September 24, 1877.

34. NA, RG393, M1088, R31, Jewett to AAAG, District of New Mexico, September 24, 1877, September 29, 1877, October 4, 1877; Keam to Jewett, October 8, 1877; Salzman, "Geronimo," 227–28.

35. Thrapp, *Victorio*, 201–203; Yale University, John Vance Lauderdale Papers, scrapbooks, September–October 1877, 214, 216–17.

36. NA, RG393, M1088, R31, "Statement of Apache Indian Chiefs held in Council," Fort Wingate, October 24, 1877.

37. Ibid., Swaine to AAG, District of New Mexico, November 1, 1877; R29, AAG, Dept. of the Missouri, to CO, District of New Mexico, October 18, 1877; D. A. Miller, *California Column*, 165.

38. NA, RG393, E204, "Brief of Indian Affairs at San Carlos, 1877–78"; NA, RG75, M1070, R2, Hart to Vandever, September 24, 1877.

39. *Arizona Weekly Citizen*, October 13, 1877, November 9, 1877.

40. NA, RG393, E204, "Brief of Indian Affairs at San Carlos, 1877–78"; NA, RG75, M234, R20, Hart to CIA, December 15, 1877.

41. A patrol from Bavispe had examined the site of Juh's camp at Guaynopa about May 22, 1877. The Apaches had recently left, though the camp showed signs of having been "lived in for some period of time." AHS, SA, R19, García Morales to Governor, June 23, 1877.

42. Nentvig, *Rudo Ensayo*, 93, 120.

43. Betzinez, *I Fought with Geronimo*, 81–82.

44. Alonso, *Thread of Blood*, 40–41, 101–103.

45. *Boletin Oficial*, July 27, 1877.

46. AHS, SA, R20, Cuen to Governor, June 1, 1877, Prefect of Moctezuma to Governor, July 11, 1877; SA, R19, García Morales to Governor, June 23, 1877.

47. Ibid., Cuen to Governor, June 25, 1877, June 29, 1877, and July 6, 1877.

48. Ibid., Cuen to Governor, July 6, 1877; Cuen to Secretary of State, August 3, 1877.

49. Ibid., Cuen to Governor, September 21, 1877; *Grant County Herald*, August 11, 1877; NA, RG393, M1088, R31, Ochoa to Rucker, August 20, 1877.

50. AHS, SA, R20, Cuen to Governor, September 21, 1877.

51. Ibid., Cuen to Governor, September 28, 1877; *Boletin Oficial*, October 26, 1877, November 2, 1877.

52. AHS, SA, R20, Secretary of State to Governor, no date, probably in November 1877.

53. Ibid., Serna to Prefects of Moctezuma and Sahuaripa, September 21, 1877.

54. On June 26, 1870, Maldoñado had battled Cochise in the lower Dragoons. See Sweeney, *Cochise*, 280–81.

55. *Boletin Oficial*, November 16, 1877, December 7, 1877.

56. Sweeney, *Cochise*, 344.

57. *Boletin Oficial*, December 7, 1877.

58. Ibid.

59. *Arizona Weekly Star*, December 20, 1877; *Weekly Arizona Miner*, December 14, 1877; NA, RG75, M234, R20, Hart to CIA, December 15, 1877; NA, RG393, E204, "Brief of Indian Affairs at San Carlos, 1877–78."

60. NA, RG75, M234, R20, Hart to CIA, December 15, 1877; *Arizona Weekly Star*, December 20, 1877; *Weekly Arizona Miner*, December 28, 1877; S. Robinson, *Apache Voices*, 101–104.

CHAPTER 6. THE COST OF FREEDOM

Epigraph: Betzinez, *I Fought with Geronimo*, 83.

1. NA, RG75, M234, R22, Kautz to AG, Dept. of the Pacific, December 13, 1877; Hart to CIA, December 15, 1877; *Arizona Weekly Star*, December 20, 1877.

2. Fort Bowie Files, CO, Camp Thomas, to CO, Camp Bowie, December 13, 1877; Compton to Wallace, December 13, 1877; NA, RG75, M234, R22, Rucker to AG, DAZ, December 31, 1877.

3. *La Era Nueva*, December 20, 1877.

4. Carter, *From Yorktown to Santiago*, 194–95; *Arizona Weekly Star*, December 27, 1877; *Arizona Weekly Citizen*, February 25, 1878; NA, RG75, M234, R22, Rucker to AG, Dept. of Arizona, December 31, 1877.

5. The Chiricahuas normally refrained from mentioning the names of the deceased because they feared that the spirit might hear them and return. In addition, it "would only remind them of the one who died and bring them sorrow." To get around this taboo, "a qualifying phrase must be mentioned." Thus, when the name of the dead was said, they added a phrase that meant "who used to be called." Opler, *Life-Way*, 472–78.

6. GP, Mrs. Stanley's interview.

7. *La Era Nueva*, January 5, 1878; *Boletin Oficial*, February 15, 1877; AHS, SA, R20, Elias to Governor, January 21, 1878.

8. *Boletin Oficial*, February 1, 1878, February 22, 1878; *La Era Nueva*, February 24, 1878; AHS, SA, R20, García Morales to Governor, February 8, 1878.

9. *La Era Nueva*, April 7, 1878; *Boletin Oficial*, April 5, 1878.

10. AHS, SA, R20, Prefect of Arispe to Governor, April 9, 1878.

11. *Boletin Oficial*, January 12, 1877; AHS, SA, R20, García Morales to Governor, May 20, 1878.

12. *Boletin Oficial*, April 26, 1878; *La Era Nueva*, April 21, 1878.

13. AHS, SA, R20, Morales to Governor, March 13, 1878; Corella to Governor, May 2, 1878.

14. *Boletin Oficial*, April 5, 1878; SA, R20, García Morales to Governor, May 20, 1878.

15. *Boletin Oficial,* May 3, 1878.

16. Ibid.

17. NA, RG75, M234, R22, Mariscal to Ochoa, April 12, 1878; Willcox to Ochoa April 27, 1878.

18. S. Hatfield, *Chasing Shadows,* 23–39.

19. AHS, SA, R20, Cuen to Governor, two letters dated June 7, 1878; García Morales to Governor, July 7, 1878.

20. Ibid., Morales to Governor, August 26, 1878; Cuen to Governor, undated, written in late July 1878.

21. NA, RG75, M574, R74, Special Files of the Office of Indian Affairs, 1807–1904, file 270, Hammond to Hayt, March 14, 1879, March 24, 1879, and April 18, 1879.

22. Ibid.; NA, RG75, M234, R20, French to CIA, April 15, 1878; E. F. Ferry to T. W. Ferry, April 15, 1878.

23. NA, RG393, "Brief of Indian Affairs at San Carlos, 1877–1878."

24. *Arizona Weekly Citizen,* March 8, 1878.

25. NA, RG75, M1070, R2, Watkins to CIA, April 13, 1878.

26. *Arizona Weekly Citizen,* April 5, 1878.

27. NA, RG393, "Brief of Indian Affairs at San Carlos, 1877–78." *Arizona Daily Miner,* July 30, 1878; Ogle, *Federal Control,* 192–93.

28. *Globe Silver Belt,* June 13, 1878.

29. Ball, *In the Days of Victorio,* 28, 52.

30. Ball, *Indeh,* 37.

31. NA, RG75, M234, R20, Hart to CIA, October 22, 1878.

32. *Arizona Weekly Citizen,* October 5, 1878. NA, RG75, M234, R20, Hart to CIA, November 5, 1878.

33. Debo speculates that the suicide victim was the son of Nana because first, Geronimo's sister had married Nana, and second, Betzinez stated that Nana and his family were then present at San Carlos. Debo, *Geronimo,* 117. But Betzinez had confused this with the September 30, 1881, outbreak. Nana was not at San Carlos in August 1878; he had left with Victorio in September 1877.

34. NA, RG393, "Brief of Indian Affairs at San Carlos, 1877–78."

35. NA, RG393, Miscellaneous Records, DAZ, 1875–1879, Smerdon to Abbot, August 7, 1878.

36. Ibid., Abbot to CO, Camp Thomas, August 7, 1878. Ogle has Geronimo leaving on April 4, 1878, with Ponce, Francisco, and others. But this was wrong. Francisco had left with Loco and Victorio in September 1877. Ponce probably also left then. Ogle, *Federal Control,* 198.

37. AHS, SA, R20, García Morales to Governor, August 26, 1878.

38. Wasserman, *Capitalists, Caciques, and Revolution,* 32–36.

39. See Sweeney, *Cochise* and *Mangas Coloradas,* for discussions of these treaties.

40. AHS, SA, R20, García Morales to Governor, September 30, 1878.

41. Ibid.

42. *Grant County Herald,* October 5, 1878; *Globe Silver Belt,* October 17, 1878.

43. NA, RG393, "Brief of Indian Affairs at San Carlos, 1877–1878"; NA, RG75, M234, R22, Abbot to AAG, DAZ, September 15, 1878.

44. NA, RG75, M234, R22, Compton to AAG, DAZ, September 18, 1878; Abbot to AAG, DAZ, September 15, 1878, September 18, 1878.

45. *Boletin Oficial*, November 8, 1878.

46. NA, RG393, LS, Fort Thomas, Abbot to AG, DAZ, December 4, 1878; Carter, *From Yorktown to Santiago*, 199; NA, RG75, M234, R22, Willcox to AAG, Division of the Pacific, September 24, 1878. Most officers who headed the Apache scout companies became close to the Indians. Lieutenant Perrine asked that the scouts' wages be sent to him so that he could deliver in person the funds to the scouts' wives at San Carlos. NA, RG75, M234, R20, Perrine to AG, DAZ, October 8, 1878.

47. NA, RG393, LS, Fort Thomas, Abbot to AAG, DAZ, December 4, 1878.

48. AHS, SA, R20, Antinnes to Governor, November 8, 1878, November 15, 1878; *Oficial Periodico*, November 29, 1878, January 3, 1879.

49. NA, RG393, LS, Fort Thomas, Abbot to AAG, DAZ, December 4, 1878; *Arizona Weekly Star*, December 12, 1878; OP, box 37, folder 36.

50. *Boletin Oficial*, January 3, 1879; Barrett, *Geronimo's Story*, 102.

51. OP, box 35, folder 4, Balatchu interview.

Chapter 7. Resistance, Survival, Misery

Epigraph: Opler, "The Geronimo Campaign of 1886," 363.

1. OP, box 37, folder 36, Haozous autobiography.

2. Quoted in Graves, *Thomas Varker Keam*, 88.

3. NA, RG92, Quartermaster Consolidated Files, "Expenditures Incidental to Indian Wars." From October 1877 through June 1878, the cost was $8,469.03, and from July 1878 through September 1878, $3,763.07.

4. NA, RG94, M666, R366, Watkins to Hayt, July 16, 1878; NA, RG75, M1070, R29, Watkins to CIA, June 10, 1878.

5. Thrapp, *Victorio*, 208.

6. See ibid., 208–211, for details of this removal.

7. OP, box 35, folder 3, Balatchu interview.

8. OP, box 35. folder 4, Kenoi interview.

9. Betzinez, *I Fought with Geronimo*, 54–55.

10. OP, box 37, folder 36, Haozous autobiography.

11. Kvasnicka and Viola, *The Commissioners of Indian Affairs*, 161–62.

12. Ogle, *Federal Control*, 188–96; NA, RG393, LR, DAZ, Hammond to CIA, April 18, 1879.

13. NA, RG393, LS, DAZ, Martin to Compton, February 27, 1879.

14. Ibid., Martin to CO, Camp McDowell, February 27, 1879; Martin to Compton, February 27, 1879.

15. NA, RG393, Field LR, DAZ, Compton to AAG, DAZ, March 6, 1879.

16. Ibid., Compton to AAG, DAZ, March 9, 1879.

17. NA, RG393, LS, DAZ, Willcox to AG, Division of the Pacific, April 2, 1879.

18. *Arizona Weekly Citizen*, March 14, 1879.

19. NA, RG393, LS, DAZ, Willcox to AG, Division of the Pacific, April 2, 1879.

20. *Arizona Weekly Star*, April 17, 1879; Bret Harte, "The San Carlos Indian Reservation," 496.

21. NA, RG393, LS, DAZ, Martin to CO, Camp Thomas, May 12, 1879.

22. Thrapp, *Victorio*, 212–13; *Thirty-Four*, December 18, 1879, December 25, 1879.

23. Thrapp, *Victorio*, 214–15.

24. NA, RG393, LS, Fort Thomas, Stacey to Willcox, May 18, 1879; NA, RG393, LS, DAZ, Willcox to AGO, Division of the Pacific, May 19, 1879; Willcox to Hatch, May 19, 1879.

25. *Grant County Herald*, February 21, 1880, February 28, 1880; NA, RG94, M1495, R14, Special Files of Headquarters, Division of the Missouri, Relating to Military Operations and Administration, Hatch to AAG, Headquarters of the Division of the Missouri, June 4, 1879; NA, M666, R366, Hatch to AG, Division of the Missouri, June 6, 1879; Rakocy, *Mogollon Diary*, 62–63; McKenna, *Black Range Tales*, 180.

26. Thrapp, *Victorio*, 216–17.

27. Ogle, *Federal Control*, 192–196; Kvasnicka and Viola, *The Commissioners of Indian Affairs,*, 161–62.

28. NA, RG393, LS, DAZ, Stacey to AAG, DAZ, June 12, 1879.

29. Ibid., Willcox to AG, Division of the Pacific, June 13, 1879; Ogle, *Federal Control*, 197.

30. NA, RG393, LS, DAZ, Willcox to AGO, Division of the Pacific, June 24, 1879, July 7, 1879; Willcox to Hammond, July 2, 1879; Carter, *The Life of Lieutenant General Chaffee*, 84–85.

31. NA, RG393, LR, DAZ, Stacey to AAG, DAZ, July 13, 1879.

32. Ibid., Hammond to CIA, April 18, 1879.

33. Ibid., Stacey to AAG, DAZ, July 13, 1879; RG393, Field LR, DAZ, Hart to Grant, July 13, 1879.

34. NA, RG393, Field LR, DAZ, Chaffee to CO, Camp Thomas, July 16, 1879; Howard to Compton, July 16, 1879.

35. Ibid,; Arnold to AAG, DAZ, July 16, 1879.

36. Cruse, *Apache Days and After*, 39.

37. Carter, *The Life of Lieutenant General Chaffee*, 85.

38. NA, RG393, Field LR, DAZ, Arnold to AAG, DAZ, July 16, 1879.

39. GP, Palmer Valor interview.

40. Santee, *Apache Land*, 181.

41. AHS, MS 707, San Carlos Records, Chaffee to CIA, July 26, 1879, August 11, 1879;; Thrapp, *Victorio,* 217–19. Since Victorio had taken no more than eighty-five followers, the balance of some sixty Chihennes were those who had settled at the Mescalero agency after separating from Victorio in fall 1877.

42. AHS, MS 707, San Carlos Letterbook, 1879–1880.

43. AHS, MS 707, San Carlos Records, Chaffee to Parker August 25, 1879; Chaffee to Saltin, August 28, 1879; GP, Palmer Valor interview.

44. NA, RG393, Field LS, DAZ, Compton to Hart, February 13, 1879.

45. NA, RG393, Field LR, DAZ, Compton to McClellan, March 24, 1879.

46. Ogle, *Federal Control*, 198, note 110, states that McDowell stopped the efforts in the fall of 1879.

47. *Periodico Oficial del Gobierno del Estado de Chihuahua*, April 13, 1879.

48. AHS, SA, R20, Antinnes to Governor, February 21, 1879.

49. Ibid., Arvizu to Governor, April 14, 1879, April 16, 1879, Prefect of Arispe to Governor, June 24, 1879.

50. Ibid., Prefect of Arispe to Governor, June 24, 1879.

51. S. Hatfield, *Chasing Shadows,* 33–35.

52. NA, RG94, M1495, R14, Scott to Second Assistant Secretary of State, November 29, 1879; Wasserman, *Capitalists, Caciques, and Revolution*, 36–37. Thrapp, *Juh*, 10–11.

53. NA, RG393, Field LS, DAZ, Arnold to Howard, August 26, 1879.

54. NA, RG393, LS, DAZ. Willcox to Hatch, September 2, 1879.

55. Ibid., Willcox to AG, Division of the Pacific, September 5, 1879.

56. S. Robinson, *Apache Voices*, 103; Opler, "The Geronimo Campaign of 1886," 363; Kenoi said it was his stepfather, Fatty, who brought in Juh, but I think he is confusing this with another mission carried out by Fatty, who had served as an important messenger in fall 1883 to bring in Geronimo and Chatto after General George Crook's celebrated campaign into the Sierra Madre Mountains in May 1883.

57. NA, RG393, LS, DAZ, Willcox to AG, Division of the Pacific, September 13, 1879; Martin to Haskell, September 13, 1879; NA, RG393, Field LR, DAZ, Elias to CO, Headquarters, Troops in the Field, August 25, 1879.

58. NA, RG393, LS, DAZ, Martin to Haskell, September 14, 1879.

59. NA, RG393, Post Records, Camp Rucker, Martin to CO, Fort Lowell, October 2, 1879; Howard Papers, Guy Howard to father, October 8, 1879.

60. NA, RG393, Field LR, DAZ, Arnold to AAG, DAZ, July 18, 1879. NA, RG75, M234, R25, Stacey to AAG, DAZ, August 9, 1879; R23, Chaffee to CIA, September 9, 1879.

61. *Arizona Weekly Star*, August 7, 1879, August 14, 1879; *Arizona Daily Star*, August 5, 1879, August 17, 1879; NA, RG75, M234, R23, Chaffee to CIA, September 9, 1879.

62. NA, RG393, Field LR, DAZ, Arnold to AAG, DAZ, August 26, 1879. NA, RG75, M234, R23, Chaffee to CIA, September 9, 1879. Sonnichsen, *The Mescalero Apaches*, 180–81; Thrapp, *Victorio*, 218–19.

63. NA, RG94, M1495, R14, Scott to Second Assistant Secretary of State, November 29, 1879.

64. Thrapp, *Victorio*, 220, 237; Billington, *New Mexico's Buffalo Soldiers*, 89; Schubert, *Black Valor*, 53; *Grant County Herald*, September 20, 1879.

65. NA, RG123, Claim 4082, *Chavez vs. the United States and Apache Indians*.

66. *Grant County Herald*, September 20, 1879; Connell, "Apaches Past and Present," chapter 16.

67. Ibid.; Thrapp, *Juh*, 11; NA, RG94, M666, R36, Scott to Sec. Evarts, November 7, 1879

68. See Thrapp, *Victorio*, 239–46, for details.

69. Ibid., 246–47; Thrapp, *Juh*, 12.

70. Aranda, "Apache Depredations in Doña Ana County," 3–8.

71. See Thrapp, *Victorio*, 252–61, and *Juh*, 12–17, for the details of Victorio's movements and the attacks in the Candelario Mountains.

72. NA, LR, AGO, 1879, 8294, McDowell to AGO, December 26, 1879, which contains two letters from Lieutenant Haskell, December 16, 1879, December 21, 1879 (hereafter Haskell correspondence).

73. OP, box 37, folder 35, Martine interview; S. Robinson, *Apache Voices*, 103; Ball, *Indeh*, 73.

74. Haskell correspondence. In 1883 George told Captain Emmet Crawford about his role: "The first time I went into the mountains to bring in the Chiricahuas they promised to settle here and live forever behaving themselves but they didn't keep their promise." NA, RG393, LR, DAZ, Crawford to AAG, DAZ, June 26, 1883.

75. Ball, *Indeh*, 73.

76. *Arizona Weekly Star*, December 25, 1879.

77. Haskell correspondence; *New York Times*, June 4, 1880.

78. Radbourne, "The Juh-Geronimo Surrender of 1879," 1–18.

79. *Grant County Herald*, December 13, 1879; NA, RG393, LS, DAZ. Willcox to Haskell, December 15, 1879.

80. Radbourne, "The Juh-Geronimo Surrender of 1879," 11; NA, RG393, LS, DAZ, Willcox to Haskell, December 16, 1879; Salzman, "Geronimo," 236.

81. Goodwin, "Experiences of an Indian Scout," 1, 50–55.

82. NA, RG75, M234, R26, Chaffee to CIA, January 9, 1880.

83. *Arizona Weekly Star*, January 8, 1880.

84. NA, RG393, LS, DAZ, Martin to Haskell, January 23, 1880.

85. Spence, *The Arizona Diary of Lily Fremont*, 143.

CHAPTER 8. NAICHE SPEAKS, AND FATE FINDS VICTORIO

Epigraph: NA, RG393, Field LR, DAZ, Carr to AAG, July 4, 1880.

1. NA, RG393, LS, DAZ, Willcox to Chaffee, January 12, 1880; Chaffee to Willcox, January 13, 1880.

2. NA, RG393, LS, DAZ, Willcox to AG, Division of the Pacific, February 13, 1880, February 17, 1880; Willcox to Chaffee, February 13, 1880.

3. Ibid., Willcox to Prieto, January 29, 1880, February 11, 1880.

4. Ibid., Willcox to Governor Fremont, April 3, 1880.

5. *Grant County Herald*, February 14, 1880.

6. Bret Harte, "The San Carlos Indian Reservation," 549.

7. Fort Bowie Records, Carr to CO, Fort Bowie, March 24, 1880.

8. NA, RG393, Field LR, DAZ, Martin to Carr, April 16, 1880.

9. Cruse, *Apache Days and After,* 82–83.

10. Salzman, "Geronimo," 226.

11. Thrapp, *Victorio*, 261–62; *Thirty-Four*, January 15, 1880.

12. Thrapp, Victorio, 261–62; *Thirty-Four*, January 21, 1880.

13. Laumbach, *Hembrillo*, 121–22.

14. Ibid.; *Grant County Herald*, January 28, 1880; Thrapp, *Victorio*, 261–62.

15. Thrapp, *Victorio*, 262.

16. NA, RG393, LS, DAZ, Martin to Chaffee, February 8, 1880.

17. Thrapp, *Victorio*, 264.

18. Mescaleros later admitted to their agent that fifty-three of their men were in the fight, with one fatality. *Thirty-Four*, June 2, 1880.

19. Laumbach's conclusions may be correct. Yet, I am inclined to believe that most of the scouting done by Chiricahuas against the Chihennes actually took place in the year after Victorio's death against his successor, Nana.

20. Laumbach, *Hembrillo*, 135–53.

21. *Thirty-Four*, April 28, 1880, May 5, 1880.

22. NA, RG123, Indian Depredation Claim 3657, *Maria Reniana Santillanes de Sanchez vs. the United States and Apache Indians*; *Thirty-Four*, May 12, 1880. Although the claim places the attack on April 25, 1880, contemporary reports give the date as April 28. NA, RG393, LR, DISTNM, Pollock to AAAG, District of New Mexico, May 8, 1880.

23. Manuelito was listed on Shaw's 1877 census with a wife and two children. He had gone to the Mescalero reservation with Tomaso Coloradas in February 1879.

24. *Thirty-Four*, May 5, 1880, May 12, 1880; Rakocy, *Mogollon Diary*, 81–85.

25. NA, RG393, LS, DAZ, Martin to Chaffee, May 4, 1880; Ridgway, *Mt. Graham Profiles*, 46.

26. AHS, San Carlos Microfilm, R1, Tiffany to CIA, August 10, 1881; *Globe Silver Belt*, May 15, 1880; Goodwin, *Western Apache Raiding and Warfare*, 116; Santee, *Apache Land*, 178; NA, RG393, LR, DAZ, Jeffords to Carr, May 25, 1880; Connell, "Apaches Past and Present," chapter 15.

27. NA, RG75, M234, R26, Chaffee to CIA, May 8, 1880; NA, M1495, R14, Stacey to AAG, Dept. of the Missouri, May 8, 1880.

28. Thrapp, *Victorio*, 276.

29. NA, RG393, LS, DAZ, Willcox to AG, Division of the Pacific, May 9, 1880.

30. NA, RG393, LS, DAZ, Willcox to Colonel Carr, Commanding in the field, Fort Lowell, May 8, 1880, May 9, 1880.

31. Ibid., Martin to Carr, May 11, 1880.

32. *Thirty-Four*, November 19, 1879.

33. *Weekly Arizona Miner*, May 14, 1880.

34. NA, RG393, Field LR, DAZ, Willcox to Carr, May 12, 1880; NA, RG393, LS, DAZ, Willcox to Carr, May 11, 1880, May 12, 1880.

35. NA, RG393, Field LR, DAZ, Willcox to Carr, May 12, 1880; NA, RG393, LS, DAZ, Willcox to Carr, May 11, 1880, May 12, 1880; NA, RG393, Field LR, DAZ, Carr to Willcox, May 12, 1880; Carr to Jeffords, May 14, 1880.

36. NA, RG393, Field LS, DAZ, E232, Carr to Stacey, May 12, 1880.

37. NA, RG393, Field LR, DAZ, Chaffee to Carr, May 14, 1880.

38. Ibid., Carr to Jeffords, May 14, 1880.

39. Ibid., Carr to Stacey, May 12, 1880; Carr to Willcox, May 19, 1880.

40. NA, RG393, Field LS, DAZ, Stacey to Carr, May 24, 1880; Carr to AG, DAZ, July 4, 1880; *Arizona Daily Star*, May 27, 1880.

41. Bret Harte, "The Strange Case of Joseph C. Tiffany," 383–404.

42. NA, RG75, M234, R26, Clum to Hoyt, December 20, 1879.

43. Spence, *The Arizona Diary of Lily Fremont*, 143.

44. NA, RG75, M234, R26, Fremont to Schurz, January 23 [24], 1880, January 25, 1880.

45. NA, RG393, LS, DAZ, Willcox to Secretary of the Interior, February 26, 1880.

46. Howard Papers, Guy Howard to father, February 17, 1880.

47. Bret Harte, "The Strange Case of Joseph C. Tiffany," 385.

48. Spence, *The Arizona Diary of Lily Fremont*," 163; Bret Harte, "The San Carlos Indian Reservation," 549.

49. *Arizona Daily Miner*, March 23, 1880.

50. NA, RG393, Field LR, DAZ, Carr to AAG, DAZ, July 4, 1880, July 5, 1880.

51. NA, RG94, M1495, R14, Tiffany to CIA, July 20, 1880.

52. NA, RG393, LS, DAZ, Martin to Carr, July 8, 1880.

53. NA, RG75, M234, R27, Tiffany to CIA, July 12, 1880; NA, RG393, Field LR, DAZ, Carr to AG, DAZ, July 10, 1880, July 20, 1880; NA, RG393, LS, DAZ, Martin to Carr, July 13, 1880.

54. *Arizona Weekly Star*, July 22, 1880.

55. NA, RG393, Field LS, DAZ, Carr to Hatch, July 10, 1880; NA, LS, DAZ, Willcox to AG, Division of the Pacific, September 11, 1880.

56. *Grant County Herald*, June 5, 1880, June 12, 1880; Thrapp, *Victorio*, 277–81.

57. *Grant County Herald*, June 12, 1880.

58. Thrapp, *Victorio*, 280–81.

59. *Grant County Herald*, June 12, 1880; Thrapp, *Victorio*, 282.

60. For his activities between June 1880 and October 1880, see Thrapp *Victorio*, 275–92.

61. Ibid., 290–91.

62. Opler, *Apache Odyssey*, 81–82; NA, RG94, M666, R528, Conrad to Post Adjutant, Fort Sumner, December 1, 1880. See Thrapp, *Victorio*, 293–307, and *Encyclopedia*, 3:1483–85, for American and Mexican accounts of the battle. For the Chiricahuas' perspective see, Ball, *In the Days of Victorio*, 88–99, S. Robinson, *Apache Voices*, 17–26, and *Oficial Periodico*, February 12, 1881.

CHAPTER 9. SUSPICION AND FEAR LEAD TO OUTBREAK

Epigraph: OP, box 35, folder 4, Chatto interview.

1. AHS, Connell, "Apaches Past and Present," chapter 15; AHS, San Carlos Microfilm, R1, Tiffany to CIA, February 28, 1881.

2. Opler, *Life-Way*, 475.

3. AHS, San Carlos Microfilm, R1, Tiffany to CIA, February 28, 1881.

4. Connell, "Apaches Past and Present," chapter 15.

5. Ball, *Indeh*, 9.

6. Leckie, *The Buffalo Soldiers*, 230; Floyd, *Chronological List*, 73.

7. NA, RG393, LS, DAZ, Willcox to Price, December 6, 1880; information from Berndt Kuhn, July 19, 2003.

8. NA, RG393, LR, DAZ, Price to Willcox, January 24, 1881.

9. Altshuler, *Cavalry Yellow and Infantry Blue*, 326; NA, RG393, LS, DAZ, AAG to Price, December 6, 1880 (two letters); Willcox to Price, December 6, 1880; Tassin, "Reminiscences of Indian Scouting," 169.

10. NA, RG393, LS, DAZ, Benjamin to Willcox, January 8, 1881.

11. *Grant County Herald*, January 22, 1880; Couchman, *Cooke's Peak*, 204; NA, RG393, LR, DAZ, Benjamin to Ward, January 15, 1881; Dudley to Willcox, January 15, 1881; Price to Benjamin, January 17, 1881; NA, RG393, LS, DAZ, Benjamin to Price, January 15, 1881.

12. NA, RG393, LR, DAZ, Price to Benjamin, January 23, 1881; Lekson, *Nana's Raid*, 6; Couchman, *Cooke's Peak*, 205; D. A. Miller, *Captain Jack Crawford*, 92.

13. NA, RG393, LR, DAZ, Biddle to AAG, DAZ, February 20, 1881; information from Berndt Kuhn, July 19, 2003.

14. *New York Times*, March 23, 1881; *Thirty-Four*, March 23, 1881.

15. For a short biography on him, see Sweeney, "Chihuahua of the Chiricahuas," 24–28, 67.

16. NA, RG94, Registers of Enlistments in the United States Army, 1798–1914, M233, R71, Indian Scouts, 1878–1914.

17. Ball, *Indeh*, 47–49; Ball, *In the Days of Victorio*, 80–81; Ball, "The Apache Scouts," 313–28. In this article, based mainly on the views of Asa Daklugie, Ball implies that the Chiricahuas scorned those who served as scouts. Actually, a very small minority of the tribe held that opinion, for, as we shall see, in the final campaign, most of the able-bodied men on the reservation served as scouts against Geronimo.

18. AHS, San Carlos Microfilm, R1, Tiffany to CIA, December 31, 1880, January 31, 1881; Bret Harte, "The Strange Case of Joseph C. Tiffany," 386.

19. Betzinez, *I Fought with Geronimo*, 56–57.

20. Connell, "Apaches Past and Present," chapter 16. The weekly rations per person were 5 ½ pounds of flour, 4 ounces of beans, 8 pounds of sugar per 100 rations, 4 pounds of coffee per 100 rations, 1 pound of salt per 100 rations, and beef.

21. Ibid., AHS, San Carlos Microfilm, R1, Tiffany to CIA, undated, "Report of Indians arrested and confined at the San Carlos Agency during the first quarter of 1881"; "Report of Police services performed during the second quarter of 1881."

22. GP, Peaches interview.

23. Collins, *Apache Nightmare*, 14–15.

24. Connell, "Apaches Past and Present," chapter 16; NA, RG393, LR, DAZ. Biddle to AAG, DAZ, June 23, 1881.

25. Collins, *Apache Nightmare*, 17–18.

26. Ibid., 18–20. AHS, San Carlos Microfilm, R1, Tiffany to CIA, August 10, 1881.

27. For complete accounts of Nana's famous raid, see Lekson, *Nana's Raid*, and H. Miller, "Nana's Raid of 1881," 51–70; Thrapp, *The Conquest of Apacheria*, 211–16.

28. *Army and Navy Journal*, September 10, 1881. Thrapp, *Encyclopedia*, 2, 597–98;

Rio Grande Republican, October 15, 1881; NA, RG393, M1088, R45, Llewellyn to CO, Fort Stanton, January 4, 1882.

29. Ball's informants differed about the circumstances. James Kaywaykla, whose stepfather was Kaetenae, claimed that Kaetenae had insulted Chihuahua's party for their "treacherous hearts"; Ball, *In the Days of Victorio*, 80. Eugene Chihuahua heard a different version from his father, Chief Chihuahua. According to him, the scouts knew where Kaetenae was hiding but "pretended they couldn't find him." Ball, *Indeh*, 48–49.

30. Thrapp, *Dateline Fort Bowie*, 158.

31. *Rio Grande Republican*, July 23, 1881.

32. Ibid., August 20, 1881; Lekson, *Nana's Raid*, 19; H. Miller, "Nana's Raid in 1881," 60.

33. V. Sanchez, "Robert H. Stapleton," 22–27.

34. NA, RG123, Indian Depredation Claims 4584, *Joseph Ware vs. United States and Apache Indians*; *Claim 3838, Francisco Gallegos vs. United States and Apache Indians*.

35. This derisive cliché, which whites for many years have applied to the hereafter for American Indians, is actually not far from the mark, at least as far as the Chiricahuas were concerned. They believed that the spirit of a deceased relative, restored to good health and vigor, would lead one to a village in the afterlife to live in eternal happiness. Opler, *Life-Way*, 472–78.

36. *Army and Navy Journal*, September 10, 1881.

37. *Albuquerque Evening Review*, April 2, 1882.

38. Lekson, *Nana's Raid*, 32; Thrapp, *Conquest of Apacheria*, 215–16.

39. AHS, San Carlos Microfilm, R1, Tiffany to Carr, August 10, 1881; Collins, *Great Escape*, 34.

40. NA, RG393, LR, DAZ, Carr to Willcox, August 22, 1881.

41. NA, RG393, LR, DAZ, Egbert to AAG, DAZ, December 10, 1881; Collins, *Apache Nightmare*, 45–60, has the most complete account of the Cibecue affair. The army tried three of the scouts who deserted, found them guilty, and hanged them at Fort Grant on March 3, 1882. Collins, *Apache Nightmare*, 201.

42. Collins, *Apache Nightmare*, 95.

43. NA, RG393, LR, DAZ, Egbert to AAG, DAZ, December 10, 1881; Tiffany to Willcox, September 2, 1881. Tiffany believed that Chenah (She-neah) was a brother of Bonito, but Betzinez notes that he was Bonito's cousin. Betzinez, *I Fought with Geronimo*, 95.

44. Chuck Collins, who has done extensive research on Cibecue and the events leading to the Chiricahua outbreak that followed, states, "No contemporary documentation, memoirs, or historical papers of any kind, suggest that Chiricahuas participated in the hostilities that followed the fight or planned to join their revolt." Collins, *Great Escape*, 37.

45. Ball, *Indeh*, 53. In fact, Geronimo, Jason Betzinez, Sam Haozous, Kinzhuna, and Fatty fail to mention any Chiricahua involvement at Cibecue or with Nock-ay-det-klinne in their autobiographical accounts.

46. Connell , "Apaches Past and Present," chapter 15.

47. OP, box 37, folder 28, Perico interview.

48. NA, RG393, LR, DAZ, Haskell to Willcox, September 1, 1881; Viven to Haskell, September 1, 1881; *Arizona Weekly Star*, September 8, 1881.

49. *Weekly Arizona Miner*, September 16, 1881; NA, RG393, LR, DAZ, Haskell to Arnold, September 8, 1881; Collins, *Great Escape*, 37.

50. Collins, *Apache Nightmare*, 102–120.

51. AHS, San Carlos Microfilm, R1, Tiffany to CIA, September 3, 1881.

52. Collins, *Great Escape*, 21–41.

53. Ibid., 160.

54. OP, box 35, folder 4, Chatto interview.

55. NA, RG123, Claim 9695, *Jeffords vs. United States and Apache Indians*.

56. NA, RG393, Records of the San Carlos Agency, Statement of Chihuahua, November 19, 1883; Statement of Naiche, November 5, 1883; Statement of Geronimo, March 21, 1884; Connell, "Apaches Past and Present," chapter 16.

57. Barrett, *Geronimo's Story*, 134.

58. *Arizona Weekly Citizen*, October 9, 1881; AHS, San Carlos Microfilm, R2, Tiffany to CIA, October 1, 1881.

59. AHS, San Carlos Microfilm, R2, Tiffany to CIA, October 1, 1881, October 24, 1881; NA, RG393, Records of the San Carlos Agency, Statement of Naiche, November 5, 1883.

60. AHS, San Carlos Microfilm, R2, Tiffany to CIA, October 1, 1881, October 24, 1881; Charles Lummis, *The Land of Poco Tiempo*, 181.

61. NA, RG393, Records of the San Carlos Agency, Statement of Chihuahua, November 19, 1883.

62. According to the latest census, Naiche had 160 Chokonens (24 men); Juh had 86 Nednhis (17 men); Chatto, who had replaced Esquine upon the latter's death in 1880–81, had 78 Chokonens and Bedonkohes (18 men); and Bonito, 93 Bedonkohes, Chokonens, and a few White Mountain Apaches (16 men). Total of these four bands was 417. Some 30 Chiricahuas from Bonito's band under the old chief Chiva did not leave or later returned to the agency with Tom Jeffords. NA, RG75, LR, CIA, Tiffany to CIA, March 4, 1881. Estimates vary as to the number of Chiricahuas who left. Charles Connell said 309; "Apaches Past and Present," chapter 16; The *Arizona Weekly Citizen* on October 2, 1881, reported 346.

63. *Arizona Weekly Star*, June 1, 1882; AHS, Bourke diary, October 30, 1882, April 7, 1883.

64. OP, box 35, folder 4, Fatty biography.

65. NA, RG393, Records of the San Carlos Agency, Statement of Naiche, November 5, 1883.

CHAPTER 10. JUH TAKES CHARGE

Epigraph: OP, box 35, folder 5, Perico interview.

1. Ball, *Indeh*, 73.

2. Barrett, *Geronimo's* Story, 134–35; Larry L. Ludwig and James L. Stute, *The Battle of K-H Butte*, 77. Tom Jeffords, who was in the Chiricahua camps shortly before

the breakout, said that their fighting men numbered ninety-six. It was well established that seventy-four adult males left the reservation. NA, Indian Depredation Claims, Number 9695, *Tom Jeffords vs. United States.*

3. Collins, *Great Escape*, 41.

4. Ibid., 44–45, 53; Accounts differ as to the number who deserted and to which bands they belonged. One version reported that five Chihenne scouts returned to Loco's camp at the main agency and four Chokonens went to the subagency to look for their families. *Arizona Weekly Citizen*, October 9, 1881, October 16, 1881. The second account, by Erza Hoag, the Chiricahuas' agent who was in a position to know the facts, reported that six Chihennes and two Chokonens deserted. NA, RG393, LR, DAZ, Hoag to Corlis, October 7, 1881. One of the Chokonens was referred to as Magazi, who was probably Na-guji, a member of Bonito's band.

5. Collins, *Great Escape*, 59–73; NA, RG123, Claim 1520, *Mariano Samaniego vs. United States and Apache Indians.*

6. Ludwig and Stute, *The Battle of K-H Butte*, 9–10; Collins, *Great Escape*, 78–81.

7. Betzinez, *I Fought with Geronimo*, 49.

8. Ludwig and Stute, *The Battle of K-H Butte,* 10–11; Collins, *Great Escape*, 73–86, has a comprehensive account of the fight; Mazzanovich, *Trailing Geronimo*, 166–75, a trooper with Overton's command, describes the fight from an enlisted man's point of view.

9. Collins, *Great Escape*, 122.

10. *Army and Navy Journal*, October 15, 1881; Geronimo recalled they lost one man in the fighting, Barrett, *Geronimo's Story*, 134–35.

11. Collins, *Great Escape*, 144–45.

12. Ibid., 200n3.

13. Mazzanovich, *Trailing Geronimo*, 185. Collins, *Great Escape*, 137; *Arizona Weekly Star*, October 13, 1881. Bernard gave one girl to Merejildo Grijalva, who took her home to his wife to raise.

14. Collins, *Great Escape*, 116.

15. NA, RG393, LR, DAZ, Smith to Mackenzie, November 19, 1881, forwarded to AAG, DAZ.

16. *Rio Grande Republican*, October 22, 1881; NA, RG123, Number 1508, *Jose García vs. United States,* and Number 4050, *Placida Romero vs. United States*; *Albuquerque Evening Review*, April 26, 1882. One American, Van Smith, who was at Janos in late October, reported that the two captives were taken to San Buenaventura or Carrizal, Chihuahua. They remained at San Buenaventura. She finally arrived home, "broken down in health and penniless," in early April 1882.

17. S. Robinson, *Apache Voices*, 57.

18. NA, RG393, M1088, R44, Bradley to Smith, October 13, 1881; Thrapp, *Encyclopedia*, 1337.

19. *Arizona Weekly Citizen*, December 18, 1881; *Grant County Herald*, November 5, 1881; NA, RG393, M1088, R44, Carroll to AAG, October 31, 1881.

20. On August 19, 1881, Nana's band ambushed a mixed group of soldiers and miners at Gavilan Canyon, fifteen miles west of Lake Valley. They killed five men, including Lieutenant George W. Smith and George W. Daly, the superintendent of

the Lake Valley Mining Company, and wounded several others. Nana escaped without loss, taking many of their horses and pack mules, some loaded with ammunition. Lekson, *Nana's Raid*, 29–31. NA, RG393, M1088, R45, McDonald to Post Adjutant, Fort Cummings, January 23, 1882.

21. *Arizona Weekly Citizen*, December 16, 1881.

22. NA, RG393, M1088, R44, Zimpleman to CO, District of New Mexico, October 31, 1881.

23. Ball, *In the Days of Victorio*, 121–28.

24. Almada, *Biografía Chihuahuenses*, 273.

25. Jose Carlos Chavez, "Indio Ju," 11; NA, RG393, LR, DAZ, Smith to Mackenzie, November 10, 1881; Lister and Lister, *Chihuahua* 165–66.

26. Chavez, "Indio Ju," 11; F. T. Sanchez, *La Guerra Apache En Mexico*, 152–54; Lister and Lister, *Chihuahua*, 165–66.

27. NA, RG393, M1088, R44, Zimpleman to Mackenzie, November 16, 1881; Smith to Mackenzie, November 19, 1881, December 14, 1881.

28. AHS, SA, R20, Barcelo to Governor, December 19, 1881.

29. NA, RG393, M1088, R45, Macdonald to Post Adjutant, Fort Cummings, January 23, 1882.

30. Fort Bowie Records, Telegrams Received, AAG, DAZ to CO, Fort Bowie, December 14, 1881; NA, RG393, LR, DAZ, Smith to AAG, DAZ, December 14, 1881.

31. NA, RG393, Field LR, DAZ, Special Order 14, October 17, 1881; *Arizona Weekly Citizen*, October 2, 1881, October 30, 1881; NA, RG393, LS, Fort Thomas, Smith to Chaffee, October 19, 1881.

32. *Arizona Weekly Citizen*, October 2, 1881.

33. AHS, San Carlos Microfilm, R2, Tiffany to CIA, October 3, 1881.

34. *Arizona Citizen*, December 1, 1881.

35. Barrett, *Geronimo's Story*, 105–106.

36. Ball, *In the Days of Victorio*, 136–39.

37. Shapard to author, February 2, 2004; Western History Collections, Betzinez, "My People," 88.

38. Thrapp, *General Crook*, 61–62; *Grant County Herald*, January 14, 1882, January 21, 1882.

39. Opler, "The Geronimo Campaign of 1886," 369.

40. AHS, SA, R22, Valencia to Secretary of State, December 17, 1881; R20, Quiroz to Governor, December 30, 1881.

41. Ibid, R20, Barcelo to Governor, December 22, 1881, December 28, 1881.

42. Ibid., R22, Valencia to Sec. of State, December 17, 1881, December 23, 1881, December 30, 1881.

43. *Tombstone Epitaph*, February 13, 1882.

44. *Periodico Oficial del Gobierno del Estado de Chihuahua*, January 25, 1882; *Grant County Herald*, February 25, 1882.

45. C. C. Smith, *Emilio Kosterlitzky*, 72.

46. AHS, SA, R20, Barulo to Governor, February 18, 1882; *Arizona Weekly Star*, March 9, 1882.

47. *Arizona Daily Star*, January 12, 1882.

48. NA, RG393, LS, Fort Thomas, Morton to Reynolds, Post Adjutant, May 27, 1882.

49. Ibid.

50. NA, RG393, LS, DAZ, Willcox to CO, Fort Thomas, February 8, 1882; LS, Fort Thomas, CO, Fort Thomas to AAG, DAZ, February 15,1882.

51. Thrapp, *General Crook*, 63.

52. NA, RG393, LR, DAZ, Benjamin to Perry, February 17, 1882; NA, RG75, M1070, R45, Howard to Kirkwood, March 25, 1882.

53. Thrapp, *General Crook*, 72–73; NA, RG393, LS, DAZ, Benjamin to Perry, March 22, 1882; *Tombstone Epitaph*, February 13, 1882.

54. NA, RG393, LR, DAZ, Otero to Willcox, November 15, 1881.

55. NA, RG393, M1088, R45, McDonald to Post Adjutant, Fort Cummings, January 23, 1882; Fuero to Mackenzie, January 13, 1882; *Grant County Herald*, January 21, 1882.

56. NA, RG393, M1088, R45, McDonald to Post Adjutant, Fort Cummings, January 23, 1882; Smith to Mackenzie, January 13, 1882.

57. NA, RG393, M1088, R45, Mackenzie to Fuero, January 21, 1882; Pierce, *The Most Promising Young Officer*, 215.

58. *Grant County Herald*, March 11, 1882.

59. *Periodico Oficial*, March 25, 1882; *Grant County Herald*, April 15, 1882; NA, RG393, M1088, R45, Hudson to Mackenzie, March 27, 1882; NA, RG123, Claim 8246, *Corralitos Stock Company vs. the United States and the Apache Indians*.

60. *Periodico Oficial*, March 25, 1882; *Grant County Herald*, April 15, 1882; NA, RG393, M1088, R45, Hudson to Mackenzie, March 27, 1882; NA, RG123, Claim 8246, *Corralitos Stock Company vs. the United States and the Apache Indians*.

61. NA, RG393, M1088, R45, Hudson to Forsyth, March 28, 1882.

62. Ibid.; *Periodico Oficial*, April 8, 1882.

63. *Periodico Oficial*, April 8, 1882.

64. Ball, *In the Days of Victorio*, 112.

65. NA, RG393, M1088, R45, Forsyth to AAG, District of New Mexico, April 12, 1882; Fuero to CO, District of New Mexico, April 5, 1882.

66. NA, RG393, M1088, R45, Zimpleman to Mackenzie, April 5, 1882.

67. *Periodico Oficial*, April 15, 1882; F. T. Sanchez, *La Guerra Apache en Mexico*, 154–55; Joaquin Terrazas, *Memorias*, 127–28.

68. *Periodico Oficial*, April 29, 1882; *New Southwest and Grant County Herald*, April 29, 1882.

CHAPTER 11. LOCO HAS NO CHOICE

1. Estimates range from sixty to as high as ninety-three warriors. I favor the lower number, mainly because of the statements made by Peaches and by Loco's daughter, both present, who placed the Chiricahuas at sixty men. Bourke diary, April 7, 1883; NA, RG94, M689, R97, Sheridan to AG, Washington, May 19, 1882. The acting agent at San Carlos, S. D. Pangburn, also reported their numbers at sixty on the

afternoon of Geronimo's appearance at San Carlos. NA, RG393, LR, DAZ, Pangburn to AAG, DAZ, April 19, 1882. Lieutenant Charles Morton investigated the outbreak and concluded that they numbered between 60 and 70; NA, RG393, LS Fort Thomas, Morton to Reynolds, May 30, 1882. John Walker, based on a conversation he had with a White Mountain woman who was at the sheep ranch, said there were sixty-eight men present; NA, RG94, M689, R97, Brackett to AG, DAZ, May 30, 1882. Jimmie Stevens told Ross Santee that seventy-six Chiricahuas were at his father's camp at Ash Springs; Santee, *Apache Land*, 168. George Stevens reported that Geronimo's party numbered ninety-three; *Arizona Weekly Citizen*, April 23, 1882.

2. NA, RG94, LR, AGO (Washington), M689, R96, McDowell to AG, April 22, 1882.

3. Connell, "Apaches Past and Present," chapter 16.

4. NA, RG94, M689, R97, Sieber to Willcox, June 8, 1882.

5. NA, RG393, LS, Fort Thomas, Walker to Brackett, May 13, 1882.

6. NA, RG94, LR, AGO, M689, R97, Forsyth to AAG, Dept. of the Missouri, May 18, 1882.

7. My primary source for this story is Jimmie Stevens, whose sorrel horse Geronimo killed for food. He heard the details from Bylas. Santee, *Apache Land*, 167–170. Contemporary accounts can be found in the *Arizona Weekly Citizen*, April 23, April 30, 1882; *New Southwest and Grant County Herald*, April 29, 1882; AHS, Connell, "Apaches Past and Present, chapter 16.

8. *Arizona Weekly Citizen*, April 23, 1882; NA, RG393, LS, Fort Thomas, Scully to Perry, April 19, 1882; Scully to Perry, April 20, 1882.

9. Goodwin, "Experiences of an Indian Scout," 2, 46.

10. S. Robinson, *Apache Voices*, 39.

11. Connell, "Apaches Past and Present," chapter 16; AHS, Gatewood Collection (hereafter GC), Charles Hatfield, "Expeditions," 1; NA, RG393, LR, DAZ, Pangburn to Benjamin, April 19, 1882.

12. Betzinez, *I Fought with Geronimo*, 55.

13. NA, RG94, M689, R96, Sheridan to AGO, May 19, 1882.

14. NA, RG94, M689, R175, Crawford to Crook, January 2, 1884.

15. Author's correspondence with Bud Shapard, May 11, 2003.

16. Betzinez, *I Fought with Geronimo*, 56.

17. OP, box 37, folder 36, Sam Haozous account.

18. Peaches interview in Bourke diary, April 7, 1883.

19. NA, RG393, LR, DAZ, Pangburn to Benjamin, April 19, 1882. There has been much confusion about the numbers of Loco's party. Acting Agent Pangburn's report should set the record straight. Loco arrived at San Carlos in November 1878 with 172 people. Zele and some eighty Bedonkohes, Chokonens, and Chihennes who had remained at San Carlos in September 1877 (part of the 145 Chiricahuas with Geronimo) later joined Loco's band. Births between 1878 and 1881 brought the total to 270, which was the population of Loco's and Zele's band at San Carlos in December 1880. Pangburn's total of 300 must have included Chiva's group of 30. And his count of 40 warriors seems correct. On October 20, 1881, Tiffany did a count of men at the agency and reported that the Warm Springs numbered 32 men, but this did not

include the 7 warriors serving as scouts or the 4 with Chiva's group at the subagency. RG393, LR, Post at San Carlos (hereafter PSC), Tiffany to CO, October 20, 1881; NA, RG393, M1088, R46, Richards to CO, Fort Stanton, April 22, 1882.

20. Betzinez, *I Fought with Geronimo*, 56–57.

21. Connell, "Apaches Past and Present," chapter 16.

22. Ibid.

23. OP, box 37, folder 36, Sam Haozous account; Connell, "Apaches Past and Present," chapter 16; Goodwin, "Experiences of an Indian Scout," 2, 47; University of Arizona, Special Collections, Charles Lummis Papers, Lummis's notebook, 1886.

24. GP, Peaches interview.

25. Ball, *In the Days of Victorio*, 141.

26. Thrapp, *Conquest of Apacheria*, 236.

27. Goodwin, "Experiences of an Indian Scout," 2, 47; Connell, "Apaches Past and Present," chapter 16; *New Southwest and Grant County Herald*, April 29, 1882; GP, Peaches interview.

28. Thrapp, *Conquest of Apacheria*, 236.

29. Goodwin, "Experiences of an Indian Scout," 2, 47–48.

30. NA, RG393, LS, DAZ, CO, Fort Thomas to AAG, DAZ, April 20, 1882.

31. NA, RG393, LS, Fort Thomas, Scully to AAG, DAZ, April 20, 1882.

32. Betzinez, *I Fought with Geronimo*, 58.

33. AHS, Connell, "Apaches Past and Present," chapter 16; NA, RG393, LS, Fort Thomas, Scully to Haskell, April 21, 1882.

34. Betzinez, *I Fought with Geronimo*, 59–60; NA, RG393. LR, DAZ, Perry to AAG, DAZ, April 26, 1882; *New Southwest and Grant County Herald*, May 27, 1882, has the names of the men killed during these attacks.

35. Betzinez, *I Fought with Geronimo*, 59–60; NA, RG393. LR, DAZ, Perry to AAG, DAZ, April 26, 1882; *New Southwest and Grant County Herald*, May 27, 1882.

36. Connell, "Apaches Past and Present," chapter 16; Ridgway, *Mt. Graham Profiles*, 357; AHS, Dan Williamson Collection, ms. 870, box 2; Thrapp, *Conquest of Apacheria*, 236–37.

37. *New Southwest and Grant County Herald*, April 29, 1882.

38. Betzinez, *I Fought with Geronimo*, 60–61.

39. Ibid., 62; NA, RG393, M1088, R47, Smith to AAAG, District of New Mexico, May 22, 1882; Bradley to AAAG, District of New Mexico, May 30, 1882; RG393, LS, District of New Mexico, Dorst to AAG, Dept. of the Missouri, May 11, 1882; Dorst to CO, Fort Union, May 24, 1882.

40. Forsyth describes McDonald's exciting but deadly encounter in his autobiography, *Thrilling Days in Army Life*, 87–104.

41. Betzinez, *I Fought with Geronimo*, 63.

42. Vandenberg, "Forsyth and the 1882 Loco Outbreak Campaign," 182–83; Betzinez, *I Fought with Geronimo*, 65–66.

43. See for example, Al Sieber's comments in a letter written to the *Prescott Weekly Courier*, May 27, 1882, which is printed in full by Cozzens, *The Struggle for Apacheria*, 290–94. Forsyth's lack of initiative and faulty decisions earned him the scorn of Sieber, who said that Forsyth had conducted the campaign in a shameful manner.

44. Hoyt Sanford Vandenberg, Jr. "Forsyth and the 1882 Loco Outbreak Campaign," 182–83; Thrapp, *General Crook*, 80–84; Thrapp, *Conquest of Apacheria*, 241–48; Dixon, *Hero of Beecher Island*, 148–54. For Forsyth's account see, Forsyth, *Thrilling Days in Army Life*, 95–107, and NA, RG94, M689, R96, Sheridan to Drum, April 25, 1882, which contained Forsyth's first report.

45. Betzinez, *I Fought with Geronimo*, 65–66.

46. GP, Chiricahua Apache Place Names.

47. Alden Hayes, *A Portal to Paradise*, 136.

48. OP, box 37, folder 36, Haozous autobiography.

49. AHS, San Carlos Microfilm, R2, List of killed and wounded during Chiricahua outbreak of April 1882; NA, RG393, LR, DAZ, Madden to Perry, April 26, 1882.

50. *Arizona Weekly Star*, April 27, 1882.

51. Betzinez, *I Fought with Geronimo*, 65–66.

52. *Arizona Weekly Star*, May 4, 1882.

53. Betzinez, *I Fought with Geronimo*, 66–68.

54. Ibid., 67–70; NA, RG393, LR, DAZ, Perry to AAG, DAZ, April 25, 1882; Cozzens, *The Struggle for Apacheria*, 291; Thrapp, *Al Sieber*, 225–34; GP, Curley interview.

55. GP, Curley interview; Cozzens, *The Struggle for Apacheria*, 286–94; Thrapp, *Al Sieber*, 227–29.

56. Ball, *In the Days of Victorio*, 141; Debo, *Geronimo*, 147.

57. GP, Curley interview.

58. Ibid.; Ball, *In the Days of Victorio*, 141.

59. OP, box 37, folder 36, Haozous autobiography; Sam Haozous combined the Tupper fight of April 28 and the García fight on April 29, 1882, into one battle.

60. Betzinez, *I Fought with Geronimo*, 68–69; Thrapp, *Al Sieber*, 232–37; Thrapp, *General Crook*, 89–90; NA, RG393, LR, DAZ, Tupper to Perry, May 8, 1882, in appendix C, Headquarters Scouting Operations, Southeastern Arizona.

61. OP, box 37, folder 36, Haozous autobiography; GP, Curley interview; Betzinez, *I Fought with Geronimo*. 69.

62. GP, Curley interview; Ball, *In the Days of Victorio*, 141–42; S. Robinson, *Apache Voices*, 38; University of Chicago, Special Collections Research Center, Tax Papers, box 10, folder 17.

63. NA RG393, LR, DAZ, Tupper to Perry, May 8, 1882.

64. Ibid.; OP, box 37, folder 36, Haozous autobiography; GP, Curley interview; Ball, *In the Days of Victorio*, 141–42; Cozzens, *The Struggle for Apacheria*, 285–294; Thrapp, *General Crook*, 87–95.

65. Betzinez, *I Fought with Geronimo*, 70–71; GP, Curley interview.

66. Goodwin, "Experiences of an Indian Scout," 2, 42.

67. NA, RG393, LS, DAZ, Benjamin to CO, Fort Bowie, April 18, 1882; NA, RG393, M1088, R46, CO, Fort Bliss to AG, District of New Mexico, April 25, 1882; NA, RG94, LR, AGO, M689, R96, Sherman to AGO, April 29, 1882; AHS SA, R20 Reyes to Governor, April 19, 1882.

68. Neil Erickson, a soldier with Forsyth's command, mentioned that Forsyth sent a runner to Janos to warn García that Geronimo's party was heading their way.

Likely, he remembered that Forsyth had sent Lorenzo Carrasco, his guide, to Janos. But Carrasco reached Janos at 4:00 P.M. on April 30, 1882, the day after the battle. Erickson, "Trailing the Apache," 6; *Periodico Oficial*, May 13, 1882.

69. Unless noted, the principal sources for the battle at Alisos Canyon are the Apache accounts: Betzinez, *I Fought with Geronimo*, 72–74; S. Robinson, *Apache Voices*, 35–44; Ball, *In the Days of Victorio*, 142–44; Barrett, *Geronimo's Story*, 106–109; OP, box 37, folder 36, Haozous autobiography; Opler, "The Geronimo Campaign of 1886," 365–66; and the Mexican accounts: *Periodico Oficial*, May 13, 1882, June 17, 1882; AHS, SA, R20, Reyes to Governor, May 1, 1882; *Army and Navy Journal*, June 24, 1882. For published accounts, see Debo, *Geronimo*, 150–52; Thrapp, *General Crook*, 91–96; Thrapp, *Al Sieber*, 228–40.

70. GP, Peaches interview. Betzinez also mentioned that Peaches was wounded; Betzinez, *I Fought with Geronimo*, 75.

71. NA, RG393, LR, DAZ, Rafferty to Perry, May 15, 1882; AHS, GC, C. Hatfield, "Expeditions."

72. OP, box 35, folder 4. Dan Nicholas account.

73. Erickson, "Trailing the Apache," 6–7.

74. OP, box 35, folder 4, Nicholas account.

75. None of the famous Chiricahua raids from Mexico into the United States during the 1880s included women. This includes Nana's raid of 1881; Geronimo's and Naiche's raid at San Carlos of 1882; Chatto's and Bonito's of 1883; Geronimo's and Ulzana's raids, both in late 1885; and Naiche's raid at Fort Apache in May 1886. It has become fashionable by many writers to place Lozen, Victorio's sister, as an active participant in these conflicts. Morris Opler explains that the "Chiricahua raid and war complex was normally a male enterprise. It required a special vocabulary, to which only men were privy," He concludes that "despite repeated efforts, I could not uncover instances of Chiricahua women who joined war parties." OP, box 37, folder 21.

76. Opler, *Life-Way*, 192.

77. Choneska, a noted Chihenne warrior, was born in the early 1850s. His older brother, Showano, was Victorio's war chief. Choneska remained with the Mescaleros until his death in 1931 at the age of eighty. NA, RG393, M1088, R47, Llewellyn to AAAG, District of New Mexico, August 16, 1882; Sonnichsen, *The Mescalero Apaches*, 212–13; Ball, *Indeh*, 297; S. Robinson, *Apache Voices*, 119.

78. NA, RG393, M1088, R47, Llewellyn to AAAG, District of New Mexico, August 16, 1882; R20, Reyes to Governor, August 21, 1882. Debo, *Geronimo*, 38; García died on August 19, 1882.

79. Betzinez, *I Fought with Geronimo*, 70; S. Robinson, *Apache Voices*, 37; Cozzens, *The Struggle for Apacheria*, 291.

80. AHS, SA, R20, Reyes to Governor, August 21, 1882. When Captain Rafferty was in García's camp, he estimated the wounded at thirty to forty. according to the American doctor who looked after them. Perhaps García reported only those seriously wounded. NA, RG393, LR, DAZ, Rafferty to Perry, May 15, 1882. *Periodico Oficial*, June 17, 1882.

81. Shapard to author, February 1, 2004. Of the thirty-three captives, sixteen were boys or girls under the age of sixteen. García adopted one girl, and she was living with him as of June 1885. The other fifteen children were adopted by families from Bavispe, Bacerac, Guasabas, Granados, and Arizpe. Six of the sixteen captives died within the first three years; ten were still living as of June 12, 1885. The seventeen teenage girls and women were probably sold as slaves and servants. AHS, SA, R21, Sonora's governor to Secretary of the Interior, Mexico City, June 12, 1885.

82. NA, RG393, M1088, R46, Richards to CO, Fort Stanton, April 22, 1882.

Chapter 12. Life in the Sierra Madre

Epigraph: OP, box 39, folder 1, "Power from the Horned Snake."

1. Betzinez, *I Fought with Geronimo*, 74.

2. NA, RG393, LR, DAZ, Tupper to Perry, May 8, 1882; GP, Curley interview; GC, C. Hatfield, "Expeditions," 2.

3. GP, Curley interview.

4. GC, C. Hatfield, "Expeditions," 3.

5. Forsyth, *"Thrilling Days in Army Life,"* 116–20.

6. GP, Curley interview.

7. AHS, SA, R20, Tritle to Ortiz, May 9, 1882.

8. Forsyth, *Thrilling Days in Army Life*, 120; Mackenzie returned to Forsyth his official report that contained information about his incursion into Mexico and his meeting with García. As long as Mexico did not complain about Forsyth's action, Mackenzie decided he would bury the report.

9. Salas, *In the Shadow of the Eagles*, 60.

10. Alonso, *Thread of Blood*, 57–59.

11. Basehart, "Chiricahua Apache Subsistence," 76.

12. Betzinez *I Fought with Geronimo*, 75–77; Ingstad, *The Apache Indians*, 137–38.

13. Betzinez, *I Fought with Geronimo*, 75–77.

14. Hayes Library, George Crook Papers, Crook to AG, Dept. of the Pacific, March 28, 1883; Bourke diary, statement of Eskebenti to General Crook, October 30, 1882.

15. Betzinez, *I Fought with Geronimo*, 77–78; OP, box 37, folder 36, Haozous account; Terrazas, *Memorias*, 128.

16. Terrazas, *Memorias*, 128–29; Betzinez, *I Fought with Geronimo*, 78. Barrett, *Geronimo's Story*, 103.

17. Terrazas, *Memorias*, 128–29; NA, RG393, LR, DAZ, Perry to AAG, DAZ, May 22, 1882; Strother to Walker, May 24, 1882.

18. OP, box 37, folder 36, Haozous autobiography.

19. Betzinez, *I Fought with Geronimo*, 78.

20. Terrazas, *Memorias*, 128–130; *New Southwest and Grant County Herald*, June 17, 1882, June 24, 1882.

21. OP, box 37. folder 25, Kayitah's account; OP, box 39, folder 1, "Power from the Horned Snake."

22. Griswold, "Fort Sill Apaches," biographies on Ny-Ith-Shizeh (Nahilzay), 116; E-Nah-Dez-le, 35; Doaskada, 30.

23. Terrazas, *Memorias*, 130.

24. OP, box 48, folder 8, Martine's account.

25. OP, box 36, folder 20, Perico account.

26. Griswold, "The Fort Sill Apaches," 78.

27. Hayes Library, Crook Papers, Crook to AG, Dept. of the Pacific, March 28, 1883.

28. OP, box 37, folder 36, Haozous autobiography.

29. Terrazas, *Memorias*, 130. A wife of Geronimo, whose Mexican name was Mañanita, escaped from a Chihuahua City prison in the summer of 1883. When she had arrived there in February or March of 1883, the prison had housed twelve Chiricahuas, including seven women and five men, one of whom was a brother of Chihuahua, probably Is-pie-de. Mexicans had captured most of them near Casas Grandes in May 1882. NA, RG393, Records of the San Carlos Agency, "Statement of Mañanita, wife of Geronimo, formerly a captive among the Mexicans in Chihuahua," to Captain Crawford, March 21, 1884.

30. OP, box 37, folder 36, Haozous autobiography.

31. Betzinez, *I Fought with Geronimo*, 78.

32. Barrett, *Geronimo's Story*, 103–04; Betzinez, *I Fought with Geronimo*, 80; Bourke diary, statement of Eskebenti to Crook, October 28, 1882; Bourke diary, Peaches interview, April 7, 1883.

33. NA, RG393, Records of the San Carlos Agency, "Statement of Mañanita," March 21, 1884.

34. AHS, SA, R21, Vasquez to Governor of Sonora, May 25, 1885; Betzinez, *I Fought with Geronimo*, 80.

35. Betzinez, *I Fought with Geronimo*, 81, 144.

36. NA, RG393, M1088, R46, Richards to CO, Fort Stanton, April 22, 1882.

37. Ibid., Dorst to CO, Fort Stanton, May 2, 1882.

38. Ibid., Richards to CO, Fort Stanton, April 22, 1882.

39. NA, RG393, M233, R71, Register of Indian Scouts enlistments.

40. NA, RG393, LS, DAZ, Willcox to AAG, Division of the Pacific, September 2, 1882; *Arizona Weekly Citizen*, June 11, 1882; *New Southwest and Grant County Herald*, June 10, 1882; Betzinez, *I Fought with Geronimo*, 143.

41. Betzinez, *I Fought with Geronimo*, 82; *Oficial Periodico*, July 1, 1882, July 8, 1882.

42. Betzinez, *I Fought with Geronimo*, 81–84.

43. Opler, *Life-Way*, 333.

44. AHS, SA, R20, Haro to Sec. of the State, July 10, 1882, July 13, 1882; Betzinez, *I Fought with Geronimo*, 85–86.

45. Arizona State Library, Archives and Public Records, Arizona Secretary of the Territory correspondence with the Governor of Sonora, the U. S. Consul and Arizona Citizens, 1864–1893, Torres to Governor of Arizona, June 6, 1881.

46. *New Southwest and Grant County Herald*, July 22, 1882, July 29, 1882. Almada, *Biografia Sonorenses*, 696.

47. S. Robinson, *Apache Voices*, 46–48.

48. Betzinez, *I Fought with Geronimo*, 86–87; AHS, SA R20, Reyes to Governor, July 16, 1882; *Arizona Weekly Citizen*, August 20, 1882.

49. Betzinez, *I Fought with Geronimo*, 87–88; AHS, SA, R20, Reyes to Governor, July 28, 1882; Barcelo to Secretary of the State, July 29, 1882; Bailey, *The Devil Has Foreclosed*, 12.

50. Betzinez, *I Fought with Geronimo*, 88.

51. Ibid., 88; NA, RG393, LS, DAZ, Willcox to AAG, Division of the Pacific, September 2, 1882.

52. Betzinez, *I Fought with Geronimo*, 88.

53. Ibid., 89; Griswold, "Fort Sill Apaches," biography of Bonita, 12; AHS, SA, R20, Barreda to Secretary of the State, August 27, 1882, September 2, 1882.

54. AHS, SA, R20, Barreda to Secretary of the State, August 27, 1882; *Tombstone Epitaph*, September 9, 1882.

55. AHS, SA, R20, Barreda to Secretary of the State, September 12, 1882.

56. NA, RG393, LS, DAZ, CO, DAZ to AG, Division of the Pacific, September 1, 1882; NA, RG393, LR, DAZ, Evans to CO, Troop L, Sixth Cavalry at Morenci, August 28, 1882; *Tombstone Epitaph*, September 2, 1882.

57. *Tombstone Epitaph*, September 2, 1882, September 9, 1882.

58. Ibid.

59. Ibid.; Bailey, *The Devil Has Foreclosed*, 18–20.

60. AHS, SA, R20, Marreda to Secretary of State, September 12, 1882; Bailey, *The Devil Has Foreclosed*, 21–22;

61. *Tombstone Epitaph*, September 9, 1882; Betzinez, *I Fought with Geronimo*, 89.

62. Betzinez, *I Fought with Geronimo*, 89–91. A small party of White Mountain Apaches (one man and a few women) left Loco's camp to return to San Carlos on or about September 30, 1882. They knew that Geronimo's band had lost two men during the summer's raiding, probably hearing this information from Chihuahua. Bourke diary, October 30, 1882.

63. *Arizona Daily Star*, July 21, 1882; *New Southwest and Grant County Herald*, July 29, 1882; *Globe Silver Belt*, July 18, 1885; NA, RG393, LS, DAZ, Willcox to Mackenzie, July 20, 1882; Betzinez, *I Fought with Geronimo*, 90–92.

64. AHS, SA, R22, Valencia to Secretary of the State, July 6, 1882.

65. Ibid., Haro to Secretary of the State, July 31, 1882; Porchas to Governor, August 3, 1882; Valencia to Secretary of the State, August 11, 1882; *Arizona Weekly Citizen*, August 13, 1882, August 20, 1882.

66. AHS, SA, R22, Sotomayor to Municipal President, Onavas, July 27, 1882.

67. Betzinez, *I Fought with Geronimo*, 91.

68. AHS, SA, R22, Reyes to Governor, August 3, 1882.

69. Ibid., Reyes to Governor, August 22, 1882.

70. Connell "Apaches Past and Present," chapter 16, part 2; Bourke diary, October 30, 1882.

71. AHS, SA, R22, Lastroy to Secretary of the State, September 14, 1882; Valencia to the Secretary of the State, September 15, 1882; Haro to Secretary of the State, September 22, 1882; *Periodico Oficial*, October 22, 1882,

72. Betzinez, *I Fought with Geronimo*, 92–93.

73. Griswold, "Fort Sill Apaches," 23, writes that Cloh-neh "died or was killed" before 1886.

74. Betzinez, *I Fought with Geronimo*, 92.

75. *Periodico Oficial*, October 28, 1882; November 4, 1882.

76. Ingstad, *The Apache Indians*, 139–40.

77. Betzinez, *I Fought with Geronimo*, 93; Opler, *Life-Way*, 111–12.

78. Opler, *Life-Way*, 338.

79. Tax Papers, box 16, folder 15, Perico account.

80. Opler, "Chiricahua Apache Material Relating to Sorcery," 81–92; Opler, *Life-Way*, 208–09.

81. Terrazas, *Memorias*, 133–34.

82. Betzinez, *I Fought with Geronimo*, 93–95.

83. One informant of Opler declared "in a battle . . . the leader takes the front and the shaman the rear, urging their men forward." The flanking party employed this formation in the Mata Ortiz fight. Opler, *Life-Way*, 345.

84. University of Oklahoma, Western History Collections, Betzinez, "My People," 26.

85. Betzinez, *I Fought with Geronimo*, 95.

86. Opler, "Chiricahua Apache Material Relating to Sorcery," 81–92; Opler, *Life-Way*, 208–209.

87. Betzinez, *I Fought with Geronimo*, 95–96; *New Southwest and Grant County Herald*, December 2, 1882. For Mexican accounts of the battle, see Terrazas, *Memorias*, 133; Escarcega, *La Apacheria en Chihuahua*, 276–77; *Periodico Oficial*, November 25, 1882; AHS, SA, R20, Barcelo to Governor, November 29, 1882.

CHAPTER 13. JUH FALLS FROM GRACE

Epigraph: *Arizona Weekly Citizen*, June 23, 1883; OP, box 35, folder 4, Kayitah account.

1. Bret Harte, "The Strange Case of Joseph C. Tiffany," 390–91.

2. Collins, *Apache Nightmare*, 210–11.

3. Hayes Library, Crook Papers, Crook to AAG, Division of the Pacific, September 6, 1882.

4. Bourke, *On the Border with Crook*, 434–35; Thrapp, *General Crook*, 103–109, takes an insightful look at Crook's personality and methods.

5. Barnes, *Apaches and Longhorns*, 91.

6. Cruse, *Apache Days and After*, 179–80.

7. Bourke, *On the Border with Crook*, 433–43; Cozzens, *The Struggle for Apacheria*, 311–17.

8. *Arizona Weekly Citizen*, August 13, 1882.

9. Davis, *Truth*, 52–53.

10. Bret Harte discusses this unusual alliance in his excellent article "The Strange Case of Joseph C. Tiffany," 390–98.

11. Schmitt, *General George Crook*, 244.

12. Bret Harte, "Conflict at San Carlos," 27.

13. Collins, *Apache Nightmare*, 235–36.

14. NA, RG393, LS DAZ, Bourke to Crawford, September 28, 1882; Bourke to CO, Fort Thomas, September 28, 1882; Martin F. Schmitt, *Crook's Autobiography*, 243–44.

15. Cozzens, *The Struggle for Apacheria*, 321–23.

16. Bret Harte, "Conflict at San Carlos," 33–34.

17. *Arizona Weekly Citizen*, August 27, 1882.

18. Davis, *Truth*, 53.

19. Massai returned to the agency and was accepted without punishment after explaining that he had gone to Mexico simply to retrieve his family. S. Robinson, *Apache Voices*, 89.

20. Griswold, "Fort Sill Apaches," 101; Schwatka, *Among the Apaches*, 14, 18.

21. Thrapp, *General Crook*, 108–17; Connell, "Apaches Past and Present," chapter 16; Bourke diary, November 8, 1882; *Arizona Weekly Citizen*, December 17 1882.

22. Betzinez, *I Fought with Geronimo*, 96–97.

23. Bourke diary, Peaches interview, April 7, 1883. Peaches makes it clear that the Chiricahuas lived in two groups in the winter of 1883, and that he remained with Geronimo and Chihuahua, probably because of his friendship with Beneactinay, who was Chihuahua's son-in-law.

24. Ibid.

25. Betzinez, *I Fought with Geronimo*, 98, has a map of their raid.

26. AHS, SA, R22, Pardo to Secretary of the State, January 6, 1883; C. C. Smith, *Emilio Kosterlitzky*, 73.

27. Betzinez, *I Fought with Geronimo*, 98–99; AHS, SA, R21, Lopez to Governor, January 5, 2008; R22, Pardo to Secretary of the State, January 5, 1883.

28. Betzinez, *I Fought with Geronimo*, 98–99; AHS, SA, R22, Maldoñado to Secretary of the State, January 14, 1883; Panda to Secretary of State, January 14, 1883; Moreno to Prefect of Huepac, January 9, 1883; C. C. Smith, *Emilio Kosterlitzky*, 73–74.

29. Betzinez, *I Fought with Geronimo*, 99–102.

30. AHS, SA, R22, Porchas to Secretary of the State, December 15, 1882; Valencia to Governor, December 29, 1882, December 30, 1882.

31. OP, box 35, folder 1. Perico account.

32. Ball, *Indeh*, 70–73. Bourke diary, Peaches interview, April 7, 1883; Bonito testimony, May 8, 1884. Betzinez, *I Fought with Geronimo*, 101–102; *Periodico Oficial*, February 10, 1883, February 17, 1883; NA, RG393, Records of the San Carlos Agency, "Statement of squaw Mañanita, wife of Geronimo"; Thrapp, *Conquest of Apacheria*, 265; *Arizona Weekly Citizen*, June 30, 1883.

33. Opler, *Life-Way*, 355.

34. *Periodico Oficial*, February 10. 1883.

35. *Arizona Weekly Citizen*, June 30, 1883.

36. Betzinez, *I Fought with Geronimo*, 101–102.

37. *New Southwest and Grant County Herald*, June 27, 1883.

38. Opler, *Life-Way*, 470.

39. Bourke diary, Peaches interview, April 7, 1883.

40. Ball, *Indeh*, 73.

41. OP, box 35, folder 4. Kayitah interview.

42. C. C. Smith, *Emilio Kosterlitzky*, 74–75; AHS, SA, R21, Carbo to Governor, April 6, 1883; García to Governor, March 24, 1883.

43. Betzinez, *I Fought with Geronimo*, 102.

44. Contemporary evidence confirms that the leaders of this daring foray were Bonito and Chatto, as do Peaches and Betzinez. In recent years Asa Daklugie, who despised Chatto, told Eve Ball that Chihuahua led the raid and that Chatto accompanied him in a subordinate role. But it is clear from Jason Betzinez's account that Chihuahua was with Geronimo during their joint raid into Sonora. Ball, *Indeh*, 50–51; Bourke's diary, Peaches account, April 3, 1883, April 7,1883; Betzinez, *I Fought with Geronimo*, 102. Both Debo and Thrapp accept Betzinez's version. Debo, *Geronimo*, 166n21; Thrapp, *General Crook*, 116n17. Easily the best treatment of Chatto's raid is Marc Simmons, *Massacre on the Lordsburg Road*.

45. AHS, SA, R22, Molina to Pesqueira, March 20, 1883; Gomez to Secretary of the State, March 22, 1883, March 25, 1883; Bourke diary, Peaches account, April 7, 1883.

46. Thrapp, *Conquest of Apacheria*, 267–68, Simmons, *Massacre on the Lordsburg Road*, 90–91.

47. Bourke diary, Madden to Crook, March 30, 1883.

48. Simmons, *Massacre on the Lordsburg Road*, 91.

49. *Prescott Courier*, April 3, 1883.

50. *Arizona Weekly Citizen*, April 1, 1883; Simmons, *Massacre on the Lordsburg Road*, 91–92.

51. Simmons, *Massacre on the Lordsburg Road*, 92–93.

52. OP, box 36, folder 15, Chatto interview.

53. NA, RG393, LR, DAZ, Rafferty to AAG, DAZ, March 27, 1883.

54. Bourke diary, Peaches interview, April 7, 1883.

55. AHS, San Carlos Microfilm, R2, Wilcox to CIA, March 24, 1883; Crook to Secretary of the Interior, March 26, 1883.

56. Bourke diary, Peaches account, April 7, 1883.

57. GP, Peaches interview.

58. Betzinez, *I Fought with Geronimo*, 117–18.

59. NA, RG393, Field LR, PSC, Davis to AAG, DAZ, March 30, 1883.

60. AHS, San Carlos Microfilm, R2, Wilcox to Teller, April 1, 1883; Davis, *Truth*, 86–90.

61. Bourke diary, Peaches account, April 7, 1883.

62. NA, RG94, M689, R173, Mackenzie to Forsyth, March 27, 1883; AAG, Dept. of the Missouri to AG, Washington, March 28, 1883; Simmons, *Massacre on the Lordsburg Road*, 98–99.

63. OP, box 35, folder 5, Chatto account.

64. Simmons, *Massacre on the Lordsburg Road*, 109–12.

65. NA, RG393, Records of the San Carlos Agency, Naiche's statement to Captain Crawford, November 5, 1883.

66. Simmons, *Massacre on the Lordsburg Road*, 111–13.

67. O P, box 36, folder 17, Perico interview.

68. Simmons, *Massacre on the Lordsburg Road*, 121–22; *Arizona Weekly Citizen*, April 1, 1883.

69. AHS, M563, Charles Morton Papers, Crawford to Morton, April 7, 1883.

70. Simmons, *Massacre on the Lordsburg Road*, 120–25.

71. Betzinez, *I Fought with Geronimo*, 107.

72. AHS, SA, R22, Moreno to Gomez, March 21, 1883.

73. Ibid., Gomez to Secretary of the State, March 22, 1883.

74. Betzinez, *I Fought with Geronimo*, 102–103.

75. NA, RG393, LR, DAZ, unsigned telegram from Hermosillo to AAG, DAZ, March 22, 1883; *Arizona Weekly Citizen*, April 1, 1883, April 8, 1883, April 28, 1883.

76. AHS, SA, R22, Gomez to Secretary of the State, April 20, 1883, "Apache murders in the District of Moctezuma, 1883"; Betzinez, *I Fought with Geronimo*, 104–107.

77. Bourke diary, dispatch of April 11, 1883.

78. *Arizona Weekly Citizen*, April 28, 1883.

CHAPTER 14. COOL HAND CROOK

Epigraph: GP, Peaches interview.

1. Ibid. AHS, Morton Papers, Crawford to Morton, December 22, 1882, February 10, 1883; NA, RG393, LS, DAZ, Martin to Crawford, February 15, 1883; Goodwin, "Experiences of an Indian Scout," 2, 51; Goodwin, *Western Apache Raiding and Warfare*, 196.

2. AHS, Morton Papers, Crawford to Morton, December 22, 1882.

3. NA, RG393, LS, DAZ, Martin to Crawford, February 15, 1883.

4. Goodwin, "Experiences of an Indian Scout," 2, 51–54.

5. AHS, Morton Papers, Crawford to Morton, April 7, 1883.

6. Thrapp, *General Crook*, 118.

7. S. Hatfield, *Chasing Shadows*, 53–60.

8. NA, RG94, M689, R173, Schofield to AG, March 30, 1883; AG to Sheridan, March 31, 1883.

9. Salas. *In the Shadow of the Eagles*, 14–15; Ruiz, *The People of Sonora and Yankee Capitalists*, 7–12.

10. Thrapp, *General Crook*, 118–27.

11. Betzinez, *I Fought with Geronimo*, 110–11.

12. Simmons, *Massacre on the Lordsburg Road*, 158–60.

13. NA, RG393, LS, Fort Thomas, Evans to West, May 1, 1883.

14. Simmons, *Massacre on the Lordsburg Road*, 158–160; AHS, San Carlos Microfilm, R3, Wilcox to Teller, June 4, 1883.

15. AHS, SA, R22, Barela to Secretary of State, May 6, 1883; Betzinez, *I Fought with Geronimo*, 111–12; Thrapp, *General Crook*, 141–42; NA, RG94, M689, R173, Martin to AG, June 6, 1883; Bourke, *An Apache Campaign*, 85–88, 112.

16. This was Loco's seventeen-year-old son Dar-dis-pe-nay (Stands in That Place), who became known as Dexter Loco.

17. OP, box 35, folder 4, Sam Kenoi interview.

18. NA, RG393, LR, DAZ, West to Martin, May 29, 1883, May 30, 1883; NA, RG393, LS, DAZ, Martin to Dorst, May 30, 1883; AHS, San Carlos Microfilm, R2, Wilcox to CIA, June 6, 1883.

19. AHS, San Carlos Microfilm, R2, Wilcox to CIA, June 6, 1883; NA, RG393, LS, DAZ, Martin to Dorst, May 30, 1883.

20. For the seminal account of this fascinating operation, see Thrapp's *General Crook*, 128–75. For good primary accounts, see Bourke, *An Apache Campaign*, 54–128 and Goodwin, "Experiences of an Indian Scout," 2, 59–73.

21. Thrapp, *General Crook*, 128–29.

22. GP, Peaches interview.

23. Goodwin, "Experiences of an Indian Scout," 2, 58.

24. GP, Peaches interview; Curley interview; Goodwin, "Experiences of an Indian Scout," 2, 55–56.

25. Thrapp, *General Crook*, 124–26.

26. Ibid., 138–41; Bourke diary, May 11–14, 1883; Goodwin, "Experiences of an Indian Scout," 2, 58–59.

27. GP, Curley interview. He placed the rancheria at Bugatseka.

28. Ibid.

29. It is unclear how many of the dead were men, although Rope reports they killed one warrior. Goodwin, "Experiences of an Indian Scout." 2, 60–61.

30. GP, Curley interview; Goodwin, "Experiences of an Indian Scout," 2, 58–62; Thrapp, *General Crook*, 143–47; Bourke diary, May 15–16, 1883.

31. Goodwin, "Experiences of an Indian Scout," 2, 63–65.

32. Betzinez, *I Fought with Geronimo*, 118–20.

33. Thrapp, *General Crook*, 139–44; Rope, "Experiences of an Indian Scout," 2, 61–65.

34. Goodwin, "Experiences of an Indian Scout," 2, 64–65.

35. Bourke did his own informal survey of the first Apaches to surrender and discovered that sixty-four were Chokonens, eleven were Nednhis, four were Chihennes, and eight were White Mountain Apaches (part of Bonito's band). Bourke diary, May 19, 1883, May 20, 1883.

36. OP, box 35, folder 6, Fatty biography.

37. Goodwin, "Experiences of an Indian Scout," 2, 66.

38. Betzinez, *I Fought with Geronimo*, 114–15; Opler, "The Geronimo Campaign of 1886," 366–68; Opler, *Life-Way*, 100, 216; Opler's papers have several references on this subject; S. Robinson, *Apache Voices*, 182; Ingstad, *The Apache Indians*, 140.

39. *Oficial Periodico*, May 19, 1883. This report also mentions that Mexicans found the bodies of two men. They were both horribly mutilated. The Apaches had beheaded one man. This corroborated what the Mexican women later told Bourke. They described how Geronimo tortured these two men before the Apaches clubbed and speared them to death. Bourke diary, May 22, 1883.

40. Goodwin, "Experiences of an Indian Scout," 2, 66–67; Bourke diary, May 20, 1883; NA, RG94, M689, R187, Wrattan to AAG, Department of Texas, October 20, 1886.

41. Bourke diary, May 21, 1883.

42. NA, RG393, Misc. Records, 1882–1900, Post at San Carlos, Geronimo's interview, Crawford to Crook, March 21, 1884.

43. GP, Curley interview; Bourke, *An Apache Campaign*, 111–12; Bourke Diary, May 26–June 1, 1883; Goodwin, "Experiences of an Indian Scout," 2, 68–69.

44. Goodwin, "Experiences of an Indian Scout," part 2, 68–69.

45. Bourke diary, May 22–26, 1883.

46. Ibid., May 26–June 1, 1883; Goodwin, "Experiences of an Indian Scout," 2, 68–69.

47. The numbers are in a letter Crawford wrote on June 10, 1883, from Silver Creek, Arizona, to Captain Morton, and from San Carlos in a letter to Crook on June 26, 1883. AHS, Morton Papers, Crawford to Morton, June 10, 1883; NA, RG393, LR, DAZ, Crawford to Crook, June 26, 1883. Lieutenant Britton Davis, then at San Carlos during Crawford's absence, also put the Chiricahuas remaining in Mexico at "about two hundred, including most of the fighting men." Davis, *Truth*, 104.

48. Thrapp, *General Crook*, 166.

49. NA, RG393, LR, DAZ, Crook to AAG, Division of the Pacific, July 23, 1883.

50. AHS, Morton Papers, Crawford to Morton, June 10, 1883.

51. Goodwin, "Experiences of an Indian Scout," 2, 69.

52. NA, RG393, Records of San Carlos, Naiche's interview, Crawford to Crook, November 5, 1883; NA, RG94 M689, R175, Zele interview, Crawford to Crook, January 2, 1884; Chatto interview, Crawford to Crook, March 3, 1884; Davis, *Truth*, 115.

53. NA, RG94, M689, R173, Teller to Lincoln, June 18, 1883; AHS, San Carlos Microfilm, R2, Wilcox to Teller, June 15, 1883.

54. NA, RG393, LS, DAZ, Crook to Wilcox, June 15, 1883.

55. Schmitt, *Crook's Autobiography*, 249.

56. Hayes Library, Crook Papers, Crook to Teller, February 23, 1883, March 27, 1883; NA, RG393, LS, DAZ, Crook to Teller, March 5, 1883.

57. Bret Harte, "Conflict at San Carlos," 35–37; Bailey, *The Valiants*, 78–82.

58. NA, RG94, M689, R173, Teller to Lincoln, June 15, 1883; Lincoln to Teller, June 15, 1883. Captain Richard Pratt, superintendent of the Carlisle Indian School,

wired Lincoln that he could accommodate 50–75 children. He believed that "once here, they would be good hostages." Pratt to Lincoln, June 18, 1883. *Arizona Weekly Citizen*, June 23, 1883.

59. NA, RG94, M689, R173, Wilcox to Teller, June 16, 1883. AG to Crook, June 18, 1883.

60. Ibid. Schofield to Sherman, June 17, 1883; Crook to Schofield, June 20, 1883; Hayes Library, Crook Papers, Crook to Schofield, June 19, 1883.

61. Goodwin, "Experiences of an Indian Scout," 2, 71; NA, RG393, LS, DAZ, Crook to United States Consul to Mexico (Tucson), June 20, 1883; NA, RG94, M689, R173, Crook to AG, June 24, 1883.

62. NA, RG153, Records of the Office of the Judge Advocate General (Army), File RR-440 (hereafter Crawford inquiry).

63. NA, RG393, LR, DAZ, Crawford to Crook, June 26, 1883; Goodwin, "Experiences of an Indian Scout," 2, 72.

64. NA, RG393, LR, DAZ, Crawford to Crook, June 26, 1883. AHS, Morton Papers, Crawford to Morton, June 10, 1883; *Arizona Weekly Citizen*, June 23, 1883.

65. NA, RG393, LR, DAZ, Crawford to Crook, June 26, 1883.

66. OP, box 35, folder 4, Fatty biography.

67. NA, RG94, M689, R173, Crook to AG, June 26, 1883; AHS, San Carlos Microfilm, R2, Wilcox to Teller, June 25, 1883; Lincoln to Teller, June 27, 1883.

68. See Thrapp, *General Crook*, 174–75; C. Robinson, *General Crook and the Western Frontier*, 266–67.

69. NA, RG393, LR, DAZ, Schofield to Crook, June 17, 1883.

70. *Arizona Weekly Citizen*, June 30, 1883; NA, RG94, M689, R173, Willard to Hunter, June 16, 1883.

71. NA, RG393, LR, DAZ, Taylor to Sherman, June 16, 1883; NA, RG94, M689, R174, Romero to Davis, July 4, 1883.

72. NA, RG94, M689, R174, General Orders Number 10, June 20, 1883.

73. NA, RG393, LR, DAZ, Crawford to Crook, June 26, 1883.

CHAPTER 15. CROOK AND CRAWFORD PLAY THE WAITING GAME

Epigraph: Davis, *Truth*, 109.

1. Bret Harte, "Conflict at San Carlos," 37–38; Schmitt, *Crook's Autobiography*, 249–50.

2. NA, RG393, LR, DAZ, "Memorandum of the result of a conference between the Secretary of the Interior, Commissioner of Indian Affairs, the Secretary of War, and Brigadier General George Crook, July 7, 1883"; NA, RG94, M689, R174, General Orders Number 13, July 24, 1883.

3. Davis, *Truth* 46–47, 57–60; Charles P. Elliott, "An Indian Reservation under General George Crook," 95–96.

4. Davis, *Truth*, 49; Elliott, "An Indian Reservation under General George Crook," 102; Corbusier, *Verde to San Carlos*, 159; AHS, Connell, "Apaches Past and Present," chapter 17; Daly, "Scouts, Good and Bad," 70.

5. AHS, Morton Papers, newspaper account (about 1908) of remarks by Brigadier General Charles Morton.

6. Davis, *Truth*, 65.

7. Ibid., 65–67.

8. Ibid., 108.

9. *Arizona Weekly Citizen*, June 23, 1883.

10. NA, RG393, LR, DAZ, Taylor to Sherman, June 16, 1883.

11. NA, RG94, M689, R174, Terrazas to Romero, June 28, 1883; Crook to AG, August 7, 1883; Terrazas to Romero, September 11, 1883.

12. NA, RG393, LS, DAZ, Freberger to Chief Commissary of Subsistence, July 27, 1883; Crawford inquiry.

13. NA, RG393, LR, DAZ, Crawford to Crook, August 14, 1883; NA, RG393, LR, PSC, Crook to Crawford, August 4, 1883.

14. NA, RG393, LS, DAZ, Martin to Crawford, July 19, 1883.

15. Ibid., Crook to Crawford, July 20, 1883.

16. Ibid., Martin to Rafferty, August 7, 1883.

17. NA, RG393, LR, DAZ, Crawford to Crook, August 14, 1883, August 17, 1883; NA, RG393, LS, DAZ, Crook to Crawford, August 19, 1883; NA, RG94, M689, R174, Crook to AG, September 30, 1883.

18. Connell, "Apaches Past and Present," chapter 17; *Arizona Weekly Citizen*, September 15, 1883; *Southwest Sentinel*, November 3, 1883; RG94, M689, R174, Crook to AGO, September 30, 1883.

19. Davis, *Truth*, 115–16.

20. NA, RG393, LR, DAZ, Ware to Secretary of State, August 31, 1883.

21. NA, RG94, LR, AGO, M689, R174, Crook to AGO, September 30, 1883.

22. *Southwest Sentinel*, November 3, 1883.

23. Ibid.

24. NA, RG393, LR, DAZ, Crawford to Crook, September 23, 1883, October 3, 1883; Rafferty to Crook, September 28, 1883.

25. *Arizona Weekly Citizen*, September 15, 1883.

26. AHS, SA, R22, "List submitted by the Municipal President of Bavispe of Apache raids there between May 1883 and November 1883"; Barcelo to Secretary of the State, June 20 1883; *Indian Raids as Reported in the Silver City Enterprise*, 6–7.

27. NA, RG393, PSC, "Statement of Chihuahua," Crawford to Crook, November 19, 1883 (hereafter Chihuahua interview); NA, RG94, M689, R175, "Statement of Zele," Crawford to Crook, January 2, 1884 (hereafter Zele interview); M689, R176, "Statement of Chatto," Crawford to Crook, March 3, 1884 (hereafter Chatto interview).

28. John Rope incorrectly thought that the Chiricahuas had killed Jelikine because he refused to go along with their plans to attack the Western Apache scouts during the dance in the Sierra Madre. But he was wrong for Jelikine was undeniably killed in battle at Nácori Chico. Yahnozha admitted this to Ingstad in 1937, and several contemporary reports say the same thing. Goodwin, "Experiences of an Indian Scout," 2, 71; Ingstad, *The Apache Indians*, 120, 133; S. Robinson, *Apache Voices*, 47; C. C. Smith,

Emilio Kosterlitzky, 72–73; *Arizona Weekly Citizen*, July 28, 1883, August 18, 1883; Connell, "Apaches Past and Present," chapter 17; AHS, SA, R22, "Apache depredations in the District of Ures, June 1883–January 1884"; Barcelo to Secretary of State, July 8, 1883; R21, Aguirre to Secretary of State, July 17, 1883; Porchas to Secretary of State, July 6, 1883.

29. AHS, SA, R22, "Apache depredations in the District of Moctezuma and Arispe, June 1883–December 1883"; R23, Topete to Governor, August 17, 1883 (two letters); NA, RG393, LR, DAZ, Will Smith to Tom Smith, July 27, 1883; C. C. Smith, *Emilio Kosterlitzky*, 73.

30. NA, RG393, PSC, Mañanita interview, Crawford to Crook, March 21, 1884.

31. Zele interview; *Periodico Oficial*, September 22, 1883.

32. *Arizona Weekly Citizen*, September 15, 1883; Terrazas, *Memorias*, 135–36; F. T. Sanchez, *La Guerra Apache En Mexico*, 160.

33. NA, RG94, M689, R174, "The Captive Boy," *Deming Tribune*; R175, Crawford to Crook, January 2, 1884; Zele interview; RG393, Misc. Records, 1882–1900, PSC, Crawford to Crook, November 19, 1883; Chihuahua interview; AHS, Connell, "Apaches Past and Present," chapter 17.

34. Terrazas, *Memorias*, 135–36; Naiche interview; Chatto interview.

35. Chavez, "Indio Juh," 265–67; *Arizona Weekly Citizen* October 6, 1883; Naiche interview.

36. Chatto interview.

37. Ball, *Indeh*, 75–77.

38. Naiche interview; Kaetenae interview; Zele interview.

39. OP, box 37, folder 35, Perico account.

40. OP, box 40, folder 9, "The Western Tanager."

41. Naiche interview; Chihuahua interview.

42. Ball heard that Perico had made friends with a family at Casas Grandes when he was a boy. Ball, *Indeh*, 301.

43. NA, RG94, M689, R174, undated article from the *Deming Herald*.

44. Ibid.

45. NA, RG94, M689, R175, Martesinos to the Chief Clerk in charge of Foreign Relations, January 7, 1884.

46. *Rio Grande Republican*, August 2, 1884.

47. Chavez, "Indio Ju," 367; *Periodico Oficial*, October 30, 1883.

48. AHS, San Carlos Microfilm, R2, Rafferty to Crook, October 26, 1883.

49. Terrazas, *Memorias*, 136; NA RG393, Misc. Records, 1882–1900, PSC, Naiche interview, Geronimo interview, Kaetenae interview. Zele interview; Chatto interview.

50. Naiche interview.

51. Ibid.

52. Ibid.; NA, RG393, LR, DAZ, Parker to Crook, October 22, 1883; Fort Bowie Files, Parker to Hunter, October 22, 1883; Parker to CO, Fort Grant, November 4, 1883.

53. Opler, "Mountain Spirits," 130–31.

54. Naiche interview; AHS, SA, R22, Gomez to Secretary of State, October 27, 1883. Bonito was the only one of the three emissaries from San Carlos with Naiche. As mentioned, Frijole was then at Silver Creek, and Fatty had remained behind with Chatto and Zele.

55. NA, RG393, LR, DAZ, Crawford to Davis, October 3, 1883.

56. NA, RG393, LR, DAZ, Davis to Crawford, October 26, 1883; Rafferty to Crook, October 26, 1883.

57. NA, RG393, LR, DAZ, Rafferty to Davis, September 28, 1883; Davis, *Truth*, 57.

58. NA, RG393, LR, DAZ, Crawford to Crook, November 2, 1883; *Southwest Sentinel*, November 17, 1883.

59. NA, RG393, LR, DAZ, Rafferty to Crook, November 5, 1883; AHS, SA, R22, "Apache Depredations in the Districts of Arispe and Moctezuma, 1883."

60. AHS, SA, R22, "Apache Depredations in the Districts of Moctezuma, 1883"; R23, Arvizu to Secretary of the State, November 6, 1883.

61. NA, RG393, LR, DAZ, Rafferty to Crook, November 5, 1883; Crawford to Crook, November 15, 1883; Rafferty to Crook, February 8, 1884; NA, RG94, M689, R174, "The Captive Boy," *Deming Tribune*; Zele interview; Chihuahua interview; Connell, "Apaches Past and Present," chapter 17.

CHAPTER 16. NO CHIRICAHUAS ARE LEFT IN MEXICO

Epigraph: Chatto interview.

1. AHS, San Carlos Microfilm, R2, Crook to AAG, Division of the Pacific, November 3, 1883; Crawford to AAG, DAZ, October 25, 1883; Crawford inquiry.

2. AHS, San Carlos Microfilm, R2, Crook to AAG, Division of the Pacific, November 24, 1883.

3. Ibid.

4. Naiche interview.

5. NA, RG393, LR, DAZ, Crawford to Crook, November 17, 1883, November 18, 1883, November 19, 1883.

6. NA, RG393, LS, DAZ, Crook to Crawford, November 19, 1883.

7. NA, RG393, LR, DAZ, Crawford to Crook, November 17, 1883, November 18, 1883, November 19, 1883.

8. Ibid.

9. AHS, Morton Papers, Crawford to Morton, November 19, 1883.

10. NA, RG393, LR, DAZ, Crawford to Crook, November 19, 1883; LS, DAZ, Crook to Crawford, November 19, 1883.

11. NA, RG393, LR, DAZ, Wright to Crawford, December 15, 1883.

12. Ibid., Crawford to Crook, November 20 1883; *Indian Raids*, 8–9.

13. NA, RG393, LR, DAZ, Crawford to Crook, December 5, 1883; Davis, *Truth*, 110.

14. The War Department granted Crook's request to issue surplus and damaged clothing from the army depot in San Francisco to the Chiricahuas. These were 107 un-

made trousers, 195 frocks, 23 pair of boots, and 21 fur caps. Crawford issued them to the Chiricahuas in mid-February 1884. NA, RG94, M689, R175, Pope to AG, January 9, 1884, with second and third endorsements; NA, RG393, LR, DAZ, Crawford to AG, DAZ, February 11, 1884.

15. NA, RG393, LR, DAZ, Crawford to Crook, December 12, 1883, December 17, 1883; Crawford inquiry.

16. Ibid., Crawford to Crook, December 15, 1883.

17. Ibid.; NA, RG393, LR, PSC, Gatewood to Crook, December 22, 1883.

18. Ibid.

19. NA, RG393, LR, DAZ, Crawford to Crook, December 12, 1883; Rafferty to Martin, December 23, 1883.

20. Milton Edward Joyce, a prominent citizen of Tombstone, who had once owned the Oriental Salon, established this ranch in late 1882 or early 1883. For a biography on this colorful Cochise County character, see Bailey and Chaput, *Cochise County Stalwarts*, 1, 206–210.

21. NA, RG393, LR, DAZ, Rafferty to AG, DAZ, December 21, 1883 (two letters), December 22, 1883.

22. Ibid.; NA, RG393, LR, DAZ, Rafferty to AG, DAZ, December 23, 1883.

23. Zele interview; OP, box 35, folder 4, Fatty biography; RG393, LR, DAZ, Crawford to Crook, December 28, 1883.

24. NA, RG393, LR, DAZ, Crawford to Crook, August 14, 1883; Crawford inquiry.

25. NA, RG393, LR, DAZ, Crawford to Crook, September 23, 1883; AHS, San Carlos Microfilm, R3, Wilcox to Teller, September 12, 1883.

26. NA, RG94, M689, R175, Wilcox to Crawford, February 9, 1884.

27. Crawford inquiry.

28. Ibid.; NA, RG94, M689, R176, West to Crawford, March 10, 1884.

29. Lot Eyelash (1870–1950) was the son of a White Mountain man and a Chiricahua woman. Both parents had died, victims of the recent conflict in Mexico. A strong case can be made that his father was She-neah, the shaman who had predicted his own death in the Mata Ortiz fight in November 1882. Eyelash had an older brother, Binday, of whom we shall hear more during the last Geronimo War. Griswold, "Fort Sill Apaches," 36. This was the first definite news that Gordo, who had left the reservation in September 1881, had died in Mexico, probably in the García ambush. In all likelihood, Fatty eventually married one of Gordo's widows.

30. Crawford inquiry; NA, RG393, LR, DAZ, Crawford to Crook, January 10, 1884, January 23, 1884, Crawford's itemized List of Apache children attending Carlisle Indian School; NA, RG94, M689, R175, Pope to AG, Washington, January 8, 1884, January 24, 1884; Teller to Lincoln, February 2, 1884.

31. NA, RG94, M689, R175, Wilcox to Crawford, December 3, 1883; Crawford to Wilcox, December 3, 1883; Crawford to Crook, January 6, 1884.

32. He was not as inhibited during the court of inquiry, when he made that allegation. Crawford inquiry; AHS, Records of the San Carlos Agency, R2, Crawford to Crook, December 29, 1883.

33. Crawford inquiry.

34. AHS, Records of the San Carlos Agency, R1, copy of letter written by Wilcox on January 7, 1884, to the *Arizona Livestock Journal.*

35. *Globe Silver Belt,* September 18, 1886; AHS, Records of the San Carlos Agency, R2, Crawford to Hooker, December 5, 1883; Hooker to Crawford, December 5, 1883.

36. AHS, Records of the San Carlos Agency, R2, Hooker to Price, February 11, 1884.

37. NA, RG94, M689, R175, Teller to Lincoln, February 2, 1884; Wilcox to Price, February 9, 1884; Crawford inquiry.

38. NA, RG94, M689, R 175, Wilcox to CIA, February 9, 1884; Crawford inquiry.

39. NA, RG393, LR, DAZ, Crook to Lincoln, November 23, 1883; Crawford to Crook, December 5, 1883; Crawford to Wilcox, December 29, 1883; Wilcox to Crawford, January 4, 1884; NA, RG94, M689, R174, Teller to Lincoln, December 18, 1883.

40. *Arizona Weekly Citizen,* January 12, 1884.

41. Davis, *Truth,* 120–21; NA, RG393, Rafferty to Crook, February 8, 1884.

42. NA, RG393, LR, DAZ, Rafferty to Crook, February 8, 1884; Crawford to Crook, March 4, 1884.

43. Chatto interview.

44. NA, RG393, LR, DAZ, Davis to AG, DAZ, February 26, 1884.

45. Davis, *Truth,* 128–147; Radbourne "Geronimo's Contraband Cattle," 1–24. Radbourne's insightful study reveals that the customs officers' interpretation of the law was incorrect and their claim of jurisdiction highly dubious.

46. NA, RG393, LR, DAZ, Crawford to Crook, March 10, 1884.

47. Ibid.; Crawford to Crook, March 15, 1884, March 17, 1884; NA, RG393, LR, PSC, Crook to Crawford, March 15, 1884.

48. Radbourne, "Geronimo's Contraband Cattle," 17–18.

49. They were camped near the main agency, which did not have the mosquito-infested marshes that dominated the lowlands along their former homes near Camp Goodwin.

50. Geronimo interview.

51. *Indian Raids,* 10.

52. NA, RG393, LR, DAZ, Crawford to Crook, March 10, 1884, March 14, 1884; NA, RG393, LS, PSC, Crawford to Crook, June 28, 1884.

53. NA, RG393, LR, DAZ, Crawford to Crook, March 14, 1884.

54. Ibid., Crawford to Crook, March 17, 1884.

55. NA, RG393, LS, DAZ, Crook to Crawford, March 19, 1884; NA, RG393, LR, DAZ, Crawford to Crook, March 19, 1884.

56. NA, RG393, LR, DAZ, Crawford to Crook, March 14, 1884, April 20, 1884, April 23, 1884; NA, RG94, M689, R176, Kelton to Pope, May 15, 1884; Hayes Library, Crook Papers, Crook to AG, Division of the Pacific, May 17, 1884.

CHAPTER 17. NEW HOME, NEW AGENT, NEW HOPE

Epigraph: NA, RG393, LR, PSC, Crawford to Davis, June 25, 1884.

1. NA, RG393, LR, DAZ, Gatewood to Crook, February 10, 1884.

2. Ibid., Crawford to Crook, March 2, 1884.

3. *Globe Silver Belt*, March 8, 1884.

4. Geronimo interview.

5. NA, RG393, LR, DAZ, Crawford to Crook, March 21, 1884.

6. Geronimo interview. Grenville Goodwin notes that most of the mescal in Western Apache country grew south of the Gila on the slopes of Mount Turnbull and the Graham Mountains. North of the Gila, it grew in a few scattered areas along the southern face of the Nantanes Plateau. Goodwin, *Social Organization*, 156.

7. Geronimo interview; Chatto interview.

8. Cruse, *Apache Days and After*, 190.

9. Davis, *Truth*, 150.

10. NA, RG393. LR, DAZ, Crawford to Crook, March 2, 1884; NA, RG393, LS, DAZ, Crook to Crawford, March 19, 1884, April 5, 1884; NA, RG94, M689, R175, Teller to Lincoln, January 17, 1884; AGO to Pope, January 21, 1884; NA, RG94, M689, R176, Pope to AGO, April 7, 1884.

11. NA, RG393, LR, DAZ, Lincoln to Teller, April 16, 1884.

12. NA, RG94, M689, R176, Pope to AGO, April 18, 1884; NA, RG393, LR, DAZ, Crawford to Crook, April 23, 1884.

13. NA, RG393, LR, DAZ, Crawford to Crook, April 5, 1884, with enclosures dated October 26, 1883, and March 14, 1884.

14. Bourke diary, May 22, 1883.

15. NA, RG393, LR, DAZ, Crawford to Crook, April 5, 1884; NA, RG393, LS, DAZ, Crook to Crawford, April 4, 1884.

16. As quoted in Thrapp, *Al Sieber*, 291–92.

17. NA, RG153, Crawford inquiry.

18. Davis, *Truth*, 152–55; Betzinez, *I Fought with Geronimo*, 122–23.

19. He did have a son (who had gone to Carlisle) and a daughter, married to a White Mountain Apache. He was still mourning the loss of his cousin She-neah, who had perished in the Mata Ortiz fight, and his wife and other relatives in the January 1883 attack at Satachi Falls.

20. Betzinez, *I Fought with Geronimo*, 123–25; Porter, *Paper Medicine Man*, 167; Bourke diary, May 8, 1884.

21. Betzinez, *I Fought with Geronimo*, 122–25; Ball, *In the Days of Victorio*, 150; OP, box 35, folder 4, Kinzhuna biography.

22. Altshuler, *Cavalry Yellow and Infantry Blue*, 283.

23. NA, RG393, LR, PSC, Crawford to Gatewood, May 15, 1884; West to Crawford, May 27, 1884.

24. Ibid., West to Crawford, May 27, 1884, May 28, 1884.

25. Davis, "A Short Account of the Chiricahua Tribe."

26. NA, RG393, LR, PSC, West to Crawford, May 31, 1884. Zele's wives were Juana (1835–1904) and Tzis-tohn (1868–1956), who was the sister of Mithlo and

Astoya, two warriors in Zele's band. Zele was probably abusing the younger Tzis-tohn. In the case of polygyny, the older wife was typically the female head of house-hold. Griswold, "Fort Sill Apaches," 71, 142; Debo, *Geronimo*, 219; Opler, *Life-Way*, 416–20.

27. As noted earlier, the Chiricahuas made tiswin from corn sprouts. The Apaches could take these sprouts from the fields or grow it from shelled corn. The first method was the favored one because of potency and taste. Opler, *Life-Way*, 369–70.

28. NA, RG391, Muster Rolls, Indian Scouts, Company B.

29. Davis, *Truth,* 156–59.

30. Ibid., 157–58; Ball, *Indeh*, 49.

31. NA, RG393, LR, PSC, Davis to Crawford, June 25, 1884.

32. Davis, *Truth*, 179–80.

33. Ibid., 181–82.

34. NA, RG393, LR, PSC, Gatewood to Crawford, June 21, 1884.

35. Ibid., Gatewood to Crawford, June 22, 1884; Davis, *Truth*, 183–84.

36. NA, RG393, LR, PSC, West to Crawford, May 27, 1884; Davis to Crawford, June 25, 1884; Davis to Post Adjutant, San Carlos, July 8, 1884.

37. NA, RG393, LR, PSC, Davis to Crawford, June 22, 1884; Davis, *Truth*, 186–89.

38. Ibid. Years later, an officer who was with Smith's command met Davis at a West Point dinner and recalled how he'd reacted when he had seen Davis unbuckle Kaetenae's cartridge belt: "I thought you were the damnedest fool I had ever known, in the army or not." Davis, *Truth*, 189.

39. NA, RG393, LR, PSC, Davis to Crawford, June 23, 1884.

40. Ball, *In the Days of Victorio*, 162–67.

41. NA, RG393, LR, DAZ, Crawford to Crook, June 23, 1884; NA, RG393, LR, PSC, Crawford to Davis, June 25, 1884.

42. AHS, Morton Papers, Crawford to Morton, June 26, 1884.

43. NA, RG393, Misc. Records, 1882–1900, PSC, Trial of Kaetenae.

44. NA, RG393, LR, PSC, Crawford to Crook, June 28, 1884.

45. NA, RG393, LR, DAZ, Crawford to Crook, June 27, 1884; Betzinez, *I Fought with Geronimo*, 126.

46. Hayes Library, Crook Papers, Crook to Crawford, July 11, 1884; Crook to AG, Division of the Pacific, July 12, 1884, August 2, 1884; Bourke diary, July 17, 1884; NA, RG393, LR, PSC, Crawford to Crook, July 11, 1884.

47. NA, RG153, Crawford inquiry; NA, RG393, General Orders Number 13, DAZ, July 14, 1884.

48. Connell "Apaches Past and Present," chapter 17; Bret Harte, "Conflict at San Carlos," 40.

49. Davis, *Truth*, 190–93, 196–97.

50. OP, box 36, folder 1, Dan Nicholas biography. Nicholas, who knew Naiche at Fort Sill and Mescalero sat in on many discussions at Tah-ni-toe's home. Besides Naiche, Naiche's brother-in-law Kaydahzinne often reminisced about "the old days." Nicholas was surprised that they held "no resentment in their hearts against white men for how they had been treated."

51. Davis, *Truth,* 165–69.

52. NA, RG391, Muster Rolls, Indian Scouts, Company B.

53. Davis letter to Chief of Historical Section, Army War College, September 26, 1923, quoted by M. M. Quaife, in Davis, *Truth,* xxxii.

54. Opler, *Life-Way,* 363; Goodwin, *Social Organization,* 157.

55. NA, RG393, LR, PSC, Davis to Crawford, July 31, 1884.

56. Ibid., Daugherty to Crawford, August 7, 1884; Davis to Crawford, August 8, 1884, August 10, 1884; NA, RG92, Quartermaster Consolidated Files, box 901, Daugherty to AG, August 9, 1884; NA, RG393, LR, DAZ, Crawford to Crook, August 9, 1884.

57. NA, RG92, Quartermaster Consolidated Files, box 901, Davis to Daugherty, September 9, 1884.

58. Ball, *In the Days of Victorio,* 167.

59. NA, RG393, LR, PSC, Davis to Crawford, September 22, 1884.

60. Ibid., Davis to Crawford, October 6, 1884.

61. NA, RG393, LR, PSC, Crawford to AAG, DAZ, September 20, 1884; Davis to Crawford, September 19, 1884; Davis, *Truth* 190–91. A month later Robert Frazer, a member of the Indian Rights Association, examined their farms and reported seventy-five acres under cultivation. R. Frazer, *The Apaches of the White Mountain Reservation,* 7, 14.

62. Bud Shapard to author, August 1, 2005.

63. OP, box 36, Kenoi biography.

64. Bourke diary, October 12, 1884, October 13, 1884; R. Frazer, *The Apaches of the White Mountain Reservation,* 7; Hayes Library, Crook Papers, Crook to AG, Division of the Pacific, October 30, 1884.

65. NA, RG94, M689, R176, Crook to AG, Division of the Pacific, July 11, 1884; NA, RG393, PSC, Davis to Crawford, September 26, 1884.

66. R. Frazer, *The Apaches of the White Mountain Reservation,* 15.

67. Davis, *Truth,* 199.

CHAPTER 18. PRELUDE TO DISASTER

Epigraph: NA, RG303, LR, DAZ, Pierce to Roberts, August 4, 1885.

1. Davis, *Truth,* 193–96.

2. Ibid., 196–97.

3. Davis, "A Short Account of the Chiricahua Tribe," 26–27.

4. NA, RG393, LR, PSC, Davis to Crawford, December 8, 1884, December 24, 1884.

5. Davis, *Truth,* 201–202.

6. Bret Harte, "Conflict at San Carlos," 40–41; Bret Harte, "The San Carlos Indian Reservation," 763, 779–80.

7. Bret Harte, "Conflict at San Carlos," 41; Bret Harte, "The San Carlos Indian Agency," 781–84; NA, RG94, M689, R177, "Brief of Correspondence relative to the issue of annuity goods to Chiricahua Indians," Crook to Headquarters, Division

of the Pacific, March 5, 1885; NA, RG393, LR, PSC, Davis to Crawford, January 21, 1885.

8. NA, RG94, M689, R177, Ford to CIA, January 18, 1885; Price to Secretary of the Interior, January 20, 1885; Acting Secretary of the Interior to Secretary of War, January 21, 1885; Lincoln to AG, January 26, 1885.

9. Bourke, *On the Border with Crook*, 461.

10. Ibid.

11. NA, RG94, M689, R177, Crook to AG, January 29, 1885; AAG to Crook, February 14, 1885.

12. NA, RG94, M689, R178, Crook to Pope, June 3, 1885; Davis, "A Short Account of the Chiricahua Tribe, 26–27.

13. AHS, San Carlos Microfilm, R2, General Orders Number 7, DAZ, February 27 1885.

14. *Globe Silver Belt*, April 25, 1885.

15. NA, RG393, LR, PSC, Gatewood to Crawford, February 28, 1885. Hayes Library, Crook Papers, Crook to AG, Division of the Pacific, February 22, 1885. Louis Kraft, *Gatewood and Geronimo*, 57.

16. Thrapp, *Encyclopedia*, 1144; Heitman, *Historical Register*, 791; Bret Harte, "Conflict at San Carlos," 41–42.

17. Cruse, *Apache Days and After*, 205.

18. James Parker, *Old Army Memories*, 150–52; NA, RG393, LR, DAZ, Fisher to Roberts, October 27, 1885. The Chiricahuas used a fire drill to make fire. Opler, *Life-Way*, 393–94; See Sweeney, *Making Peace with Cochise*, 74, for Lieutenant Joseph Sladen's description of the Chiricahuas' use of the fire drill.

19. NA, RG393, LR, PSC, Davis to Crawford, February 6, 1885; Davis, *Truth*, 136–37; AHS, San Carlos Microfilm, R2, Crook to AG, February 19, 1885.

20. NA, RG393, LR, PSC, Gatewood to Crawford, February 28, 1885.

21. Betzinez, *I Fought with Geronimo*, 126–28, Davis, *Truth,* 192–93; Kraft, *Gatewood and Geronimo*, 57–58.

22. Connell, "Apaches Past and Present," chapter 17, writes that Geronimo became angry with Chatto in early 1885; Davis, "A Short Account of the Chiricahua Tribe," 25.

23. NA, RG94, M689, R177, Crawford to Crook, February 27, 1885; NA, RG393, LS, DAZ, Crook to AG, April 9, 1886.

24. NA, RG92, box 895, Price to the Secretary of the Interior, March 13, 1885; Endicott to Sheridan, March 21, 1885; Sheridan to Endicott, March 24, 1885.

25. NA, RG393, LS, DAZ Crook to Pierce, March 16, 1885. The list can be found in Sonora's State Archives, AHS, SA, R21, Secretary of State to Governor of Sonora, May 25, 1885, and in NA, RG94, M689, R177, Davis to Crook, April 5, 1885.

26. NA, RG94, M689, R177, Crook to AG, April 7, 1885.

27. AHS, SA, R21, Governor of Sonora to Secretary of State, Mexico, June 25, 1885.

28. Hayes Library, Crook Papers, Crook to Governor of Chihuahua, April 29, 1885; Governor of Chihuahua to Crook, May 2, 1885.

29. NA, RG393, LR, DAZ, Pierce to Crook, April 17, 1884.

30. United States Military History Institute (USMHI), Elliott, "Campaign Against the Chiricahua Apache Indians," 1.

31. NA, RG393, LR, DAZ, Pierce to Crook, May 5, 1885; *Globe Silver Belt*, November 21, 1885.

32. Davis, *Truth*, 211.

33. AHS, San Carlos Microfilm, R2, Ford to CIA, June 24, 1885; *Globe Silver Belt*, November 21, 1885.

34. A. Smith, "An Apache War Dance," 64, 442–43. Smith placed the dance on May 7, 1885, But it more likely took place on May 10, the evening that Davis issued the annuities. A statement made by Bish-to-yey, a warrior in Naiche's band, who was tending to crops and sheep at East Fork, confirms this. He had not seen Naiche "for a long time," not until the day the annuities were given out. So, the dance could not have occurred before the distribution of the annuities. NA, RG393, LR, DAZ, Pierce to Roberts, August 4, 1885.

35. Chino, probably born in the 1820s, had one wife (name not noted) and six children on Shaw's 1876 census at Ojo Caliente and is listed on the 1880 and 1885 censuses as married and a member of Loco's band. After the death of his first wife, he married Nah-go-tsieh, who had been married to Massai. Chino's Apache name was Esk-kel-lain or Ish-Kaa-lin. He died at Fort Sill in 1907. NA, RG75, M234, R572, Shaw's census, Shaw to CIA, September 3, 1877; NA, RG75, Connell's census, Tiffany to CIA, March 4, 1881, #5313; NA, RG393, Misc. Records, 1882–1900, PSC, Davis's census, compiled by Lt. Britton Davis, 1884–1885; Griswold, "Fort Sill Apaches," 22.

36. A. Smith, "An Apache War Dance," 442–43. The boy was probably Paul Naiche, whose mother was Nah-de-yole, daughter of Skinya.

37. Barnes, *Apaches and Longhorns*, 51.

38. NA, RG393, LR, DAZ, Pierce to Roberts, August 4, 1885.

39. Ibid.; Cruse, *Apache Days and After*, 205–206.

40. NA, RG393, LR, DAZ, Pierce to Roberts, August 4, 1885.

41. Unless noted otherwise, Lieutenant Davis was the source for the account of the events that occurred between May 14 and May 17. He wrote several contemporary reports and covered this period in his book *Truth*, 208–18, and in "A Short Account of the Chiricahua Tribe." NA, RG393, LS, DAZ, Crook to AG, Division of the Pacific. Davis wrote his most complete account from Fort Bowie on September 15, 1885. It was published in the *Army and Navy Journal*, October 24, 1885, and in Quiafe's edition of *Truth*, May 21, 1885, 344–56.

42. NA, RG393, LR, DAZ, Pierce to Roberts, August 4, 1885.

43. Ibid.

44. OP, box 36, folder 2, Sam Kenoi biography.

45. OP, box 35, folder 4, Chatto interview.

46. Goodwin, *Social Organization*, 663.

47. GC, interview with Perico in an identified newspaper.

48. Porter, *Paper Medicine Man*, 170, 197–98; Davis, *Truth*, 203.

49. Wood, *Lives of Famous Indian Chiefs*, 534.

50. Ball, *In the Days of Victorio*, 176–77.

51. Ball, *Indeh*, 49.

52. Davis, *Truth*, 206.

53. The unidentified man did leave the reservation when he found out that Naiche was leaving. NA, RG393, LR, DAZ, Pierce to Roberts, August 4, 1885.

54. NA, RG94, M689, R183, Smith to Crook, June 15, 1885.

55. Opler, *Apache Odyssey*, 49. Fifty years later, Charley's son told Morris Opler that Geronimo had tried to persuade his father to leave, but he had refused. Given that Charley was a scout who had always been loyal to Davis, and apparently was not in the Bonito Creek camp, it seems unlikely that Geronimo reached out to Charley.

56. The Indian scout register shows that Charley was discharged on March 16, 1885. It was customary to reenlist at that time, or the next day, but the record of his enlistment seems to be missing. This would appear to be an error; twenty-eight of the thirty scouts in Davis's company can be accounted for from the register of Indian scouts. Given that Davis positively stated that Charley was present the night of May 17, 1885, I have concluded that he was one of the two men who should have been listed in the register but were not.

57. Davis recalled that Perico was involved, but he mixed him up with Fun, Davis, *Truth*, 217–18; NA, RG393, LS, DAZ, Barber to Pierce, May 20, 1885.

58. Davis, *Truth*, 214.

59. Crook to Secretary of War, January 6, 1890, 31, in U.S. Congress, SED 83.

60. Morris Opler believed that Geronimo's followers were mainly blood relatives and kinfolk by marriage whom the Chiricahuas termed "friends we have become." Opler also felt that in the fighting between 1882 and 1886, Naiche was the military leader, or strategist, while Geronimo's contribution came from "ritual and ceremony." His followers believed that he could locate the enemy and predict their movements. University of Chicago, Fred Eggan Papers, Opler MS, "Mescalero and Chiricahua Social Organization"; Opler, "The Geronimo Campaign of 1886," 366–68.

61. NA, RG393, LR, DAZ, Pierce to Roberts, August 4, 1885.

62. *Globe Silver Belt*, May 30, 1885, July 4, 1885.

63. NA, RG94, M689, R177, Crawford to Crook, February 27, 1885.

64. *Globe Silver Belt*, May 30, 1885.

65. Ibid., November 21, 1885. Ford may have been upset because Pierce had succeeded him after a Crook power play during the summer of 1885. Pierce had nothing to do with the matter. And Ford had every reason to be bitter, for he was doing an excellent job as agent at San Carlos.

66. Ibid., May 30, 1885.

67. Kraft, *Lt. Charles Gatewood*. 7–9.

68. *Globe Silver Belt*, May 30, 1885.

CHAPTER 19. CROOK EMPOWERS CHATTO

Epigraph: OP, box 37, folder 35, Chatto interview.

1. *Weekly Arizona Miner*, June 12, 1885.

2. NA, RG393, LS, DAZ, Crook to AG, Division of the Pacific, May 21, 1885.

3. Ibid., Crook to AG, Division of the Pacific, May 29, 1885; NA, RG94, M689, R183, Smith to Crook, June 15, 1885; Ferguson, "Private Myers's First Scout," 965–66; Parker, *Old Army Memories*, 152–53.

4. In 1850, the four bands totaled about 2,000 people. In the summer of 1885, they numbered about 540, which included the recent arrivals of former captives from Fort Union and Mexico. Most of the significant fatalities were a result of many years of warfare and smallpox epidemics in Mexico. American troops and their allies, primarily Western Apache scouts, had a small role. Malaria outbreaks at San Carlos between 1878 and 1880 claimed at least 150 lives.

5. *Arizona Weekly Citizen*, April 30, 1885.

6. Ferguson, "Private Myers's First Scout," 965–66; Parker, *Old Army Memories*, 152–54; Davis, *Truth*, 218–19; NA, RG94, M689, R183, Smith to Crook, June 15, 1885.

7. Davis, *Truth*, 219–20, 347; *Army and Navy Journal*, October 24, 1885.

8. Davis assumed that Geronimo had headed this group, but as we shall see, he had remained with Mangas. NA, RG393, LR, DAZ, Davis to Roberts, June 7, 1885.

9. Davis, *Truth*, 218–19; NA, RG393, LS, DAZ, Crook to AG, Division of the Pacific, May 20, 1885, May 21, 1885. In the first report, Crook said Davis left Smith's command at sunrise, May 19, and in the second report, he said Monday afternoon, May 18. Private Myers noted that Davis and his scouts had remained the first twenty-four hours. Likely, Davis left when the pack train came up on May 18. Ferguson, "Private Myers's First Scout."

10. AHS, GC, Davis to Crook, May 17, 1885; NA, RG393, LS, DAZ, Davis to Crook, May 20, 1885; Crook to Governor's of Sonora and Chihuahua, May 19, 1885.

11. C. Robinson, *General Crook*, 274–75; NA, RG393, LS, DAZ, Crook to Governor of Sonora and Chihuahua, May 19, 1885; Crook to AG, Division of the Pacific, May 19, 1885, Crook to Sheridan, May 19, 1885.

12. NA, RG393, LS, DAZ, Crook to Davis, May 20, 1885; Crook to AG, Division of the Pacific, May 20, 1885.

13. NA, RG94, M689, R177, Schofield to AG, May 23, 1885; AAG, District of New Mexico to AG, May 20, 1885; NA, RG393, LS, DAZ, Crook to Bradley, May 21, 1885.

14. NA, RG393, LS, DAZ, Crook to AG, Division of the Pacific, May 21, 1885.

15. Thrapp, *Dateline Fort Bowie*, 62–63. After Chihuahua's surrender at Embudos Canyon, Charles Lummis quotes him as saying:, "I want nothing to do with him [Geronimo]. He told me so many lies I had to leave."

16. NA, RG393, LS, DAZ, Crook to Davis, May 21, 1885 (two letters).

17. Ibid., Crook to Pierce, May 20, 1885.

18. Opler, "The Geronimo Campaign of 1886," 368–69.

19. OP, box 36, folder 2, Kenoi autobiography.

20. Silas Cochise, a grandson of Naiche, said that his mother, Amelia Naiche, had told him that Chatto and her father were close friends. He said this in response to

my questioning the characterization of Chatto by Eve Ball's sources. Silas Cochise to author, July 4, 1997.

21. Dorst to AG, no date, 50–51, SED 83.

22. OP, box 35, folder 4, Kinzhuna biography

23. GP, Walter Hooke interview; Tassin, "Reminiscences of Indian Scouting," 151–69; Bourke, *The Apache Scouts*, 1–16.

24. NA, RG393, LS, DAZ, Crook to Bradley, August 22, 1885.

25. GP, Hooke interview.

26. Betzinez, *I Fought with Geronimo*, 55.

27. OP, box 36, folder 23, Chatto interview.

28. NA, RG393, LS, DAZ, Barber to CO, Fort Bowie, June 5, 1885.

29. For the majority of the time, the men in these groups remained with their leaders during the campaign of 1885–1886. Chihuahua and Naiche led the Chokonens; Geronimo, Mangas, and Nana led the few Chihennes, Bedonkohes, and Nednhis. The identity of those who followed Mangas, who eventually split from Geronimo, can be determined by noting those who surrendered with Mangas and those of his group captured at Casas Grandes later that year. Geronimo's followers are also easy to identify, for most were members of his band at Turkey Creek, several accompanied him on the raid to Fort Apache in September 1885 (they were identified by Santiago Mc-Kinn), and many surrendered with him in September 1886.

30. Parker, *Old Army Memories*, 156–67; Ferguson, "Private Myers's First Scout," 965–66; Smith's report is in NA, M689, R183, Smith to Crook, June 15, 1885; NA, RG393, LR, District of New Mexico, Chaffee to AAG, District of New Mexico, June 15, 1885; *Arizona Weekly Citizen*, June 13, 1885; *Indian Raids*, 14–15; USMHI, "Remarks of General James Parker, USA, at Banquet of the Order of Indian Wars of the United States."

31. Camp Vincent, located near the junction of Taylor and Beaver creeks, was a tent outpost of the Ninth Cavalry from Fort Bayard in the late 1870s. Giese, *Forts of New Mexico*, 19.

32. Julyan, *Place Names of New Mexico*, 152.

33. NA, RG393, M1088, R56, Biddle to AAG, District of New Mexico, June 14, 1885; Chaffee to AAG, District of New Mexico, June 15, 1885; NA, RG94, M689, R178, Bradley to AG, Dept. of the Missouri, June 22, 1885.

34. NA, RG393, M1088, R56, Biddle to AAG, District of New Mexico, June 14, 1885.

35. AHS, SA, R23, Aquiliar to Secretary of State, June 4, 1885. The miners were Fred Huntington, Peter McKurtan, and Peter Palma.

36. NA, RG393, M1088, R56, Biddle to AAG, District of New Mexico, June 14, 1885.

37. William Llewellyn (1851–1927) became agent of the Mescalero Reservation in the spring of 1881. He would remain for four years, bringing stability to the reservation until he resigned effective October 10, 1885. He was a tough but fair agent, respected by the Mescaleros. In the late 1880s, he became involved in Las Cruces politics. In the late 1890s, he was named captain of Troop G, in the Rough Riders of Teddy Roosevelt. Thrapp, *Encyclopedia*, 863–64.

38. *Rio Grande Republican*, May 30, 1885.

39. Ibid.; NA, RG94, M689, R178, Bradley to AG, Dept. of the Missouri, June 22, 1885; NA, LR, DINM, M1088, R56, Cruse to CO, Fort Stanton, June 28, 1885.

40. This was Davis's estimate, based on what Chatto had told him. NA, RG393, LR, DAZ, Davis to Roberts, June 7, 1885.

41. Ibid.; *Indian Raids*, 14–23.

42. NA, RG393, LR, DAZ, Davis to Roberts, June 7, 1885.

43. Crook to Secretary of War, January 6, 1890, 33, SED 83.

44. *Indian Raids*, 14–23.

45. *Black Range*, May 29, 1885; *Indian Raids*, 24–28.

46. Davis, *Truth*, 220–21; NA, RG393, LR, DAZ, Smith to Crook, May 29, 1885; NA, RG94, M689, R183, Smith to Crook, June 15, 1885.

47. *Weekly Arizona Miner*, June 5, 1885, June 12, 1885.

48. Parker, *Old Army Memories*, 166–67.

49. NA, RG393, LR, DAZ, Walsh to AAG, DAZ, May 30, 1885; Davis to Roberts, June 7, 1885; NA, RG393, LS, DAZ, Crook to Crawford, June 5, 1885. Ridgway, *Mt. Graham Profiles*, 144–45; *Indian Raids*, 24–28.

50. NA, RG393, LR, DAZ, Walsh to AAG, DAZ, May 30, 1885; Davis to Roberts, June 7, 1885; NA, RG393, LS, DAZ, Crook to Crawford, June 5, 1885. Ridgway, *Mt. Graham Profiles*, 144–45; *Indian Raids*, 24–28; McChristian, *Fort Bowie*, 192.

51. *Arizona Weekly Citizen*, June 13, 1885; Ridgway, *Mt. Graham Profiles*, 144–46; Thrapp, *Conquest of Apacheria*, 323; Ringold, *Frontier Days in the Southwest*, 78–83; S. Robinson, *Apache Voices*, 32–34. The boy was raised by a family in Duncan headed by Bill Adams, who gave him the name Sam "Doubtful" Adams. He attended school in Solomonville and as a young man became a miner and a cowboy. He died in 1913 from consumption.

52. Hayes, *A Portal to Paradise*, 154–55; Hooker, *Child of the Fighting Tenth*, 193–94; Bailey, *The Valiants*, 86–87; Bailey, *We'll All Wear Silk Hats*, 64; *Arizona Weekly Citizen*, June 13, 1885.

53. *Weekly Arizona Miner*, June 19, 1885; *Indian Raids*, 26–29; GC, C. C. Hatfield, "Expeditions"; C. Hatfield, "Geronimo Campaign, 1885–96," 6–9; NA, RG04, M689, R178, Barber to Pope, June 11, 1885; Henry P. Walker, "The Reluctant Corporal," 33–38; Sweeney, "Chihuahua," 67; Bigelow, *Bloody Trail*, 37–39; Davis, *Truth*, 221–22.

54. Bailey, *The Valiants*, 87–90; *Arizona Weekly Citizen*, June 13, 1885.

55. NA, RG393, LS, DAZ, Barber to Crook, June 9, 1885.

56. Davis, *Truth*, 342–343. Thrapp, *Dateline*, 122.

57. *Indian Raids*, 26.

CHAPTER 20. CROOK SENDS HIS "INDIAN MEN" INTO MEXICO

Epigraphs: GP, Hooke interview. LC, Scott Papers, box 70, conference dated September 27, 1911.

1. *Albuquerque Journal*, October 13, 1885.

2. NA, RG94, M689, R177, Mexican Consulate (Washington, D.C.) to Bayard, May 22, 1885; Crook to AG, Washington, May 23, 1885.

3. *Arizona Weekly Citizen*, May 30, 1885.

4. NA, RG393, LS, DAZ, Barber to Beaumont, May 29, 1885; NA, RG94, M689, R178, Crook to Sheridan, May 31, 1885.

5. NA, RG94, M689, R178, Pope to AG, Washington, June 6, 1885; Sheridan to Pope, June 9, 1885; Sheridan to Crook, June 11, 1885; NA, RG393, LS, DAZ, Crook to AG, Division of the Pacific, June 5, 1885.

6. NA, RG393, LS, DAZ, Roberts to Crawford, June 4, 1885.

7. *Arizona Weekly Citizen*, June 20, 1885.

8. Ibid.; NA, RG94, M689, R178, Pope to AG, June 19, 1885; AHS, GC, C. Hatfield, "Expeditions," 8.

9. OP, box 35, folder 5, Chatto interview; Basehart called this place Diltalecu. Basehart, "Chiricahua Apache Subsistence," 75.

10. Opler, *Life-Way*, 358–59; Opler and Castetter, "The Ethnobiology of the Chiricahua and Mescalero Apache," 37.

11. Bailey, *The Valiants*, 96–97; AHS, SA, R23, Arvizu to Secretary of State, June 15, 1885.

12. AHS, SA, R21, Robles to Arvizu, June 25, 1885.

13. Davis, *Truth*, 222–26.

14. Schmitt, *Crook's Autobiography*, 254–55; Thrapp, *Al Sieber*, 296–98; Davis, *Truth*, 222–26; Daly, "The Geronimo Campaign," 26–27; USMHI, Elliott, "Campaign Against the Chiricahua Apaches," 5–6; Hanna, "With Crawford in Mexico," 56–65. Daly remembered that the command entered Mexico by Agua Prieta, south of Douglas. He was confusing this with another campaign. Hanna and Elliott correctly recalled that they entered through San Luis Pass and made their first camp at the Enmedio Mountains. This route seems more likely given Crawford's objective to get south of the Chiricahuas. Besides, if Crawford had entered from Arizona, he would have cut the trail of Lawton's command that had followed Chihuahua's band to the northern bend of the Bavispe River.

15. OP, box 37, folder 35, Chatto interview.

16. The surgeon at Fort Bowie treated him. He reported the wound as coming from a Winchester rifle. On July 8, 1885, the scout left for Fort Apache. Fort Bowie Files, Medical Records.

17. Davis, *Truth*, 230–31. The shooter was an American named Robert Woodward, who had mistaken the scouts for hostiles. NA, RG393, LS, DAZ, Crook to AG, Division of the Pacific, June 28, 1885.

18. NA, RG393, LS, DAZ, Crook to Bradley, June 28, 1885; RG393, LR, DAZ, Crawford to Crook, June 25, 1885; NA, RG94, M689, R178, Crook to Pope, June 29, 1885; Dan R. Williamson, "Oskay de No Tah," 78–83; Elliott, "Campaign Against the Chiricahua Apaches," 6–7; Daly, "The Geronimo Campaign," 26–29; Hanna, "With Crawford in Mexico," 62–63; OP, box 37, folder 35, Chatto interview. Over seventy years later, Eugene Chihuahua gave his version to Eve Ball. Though inaccurate in many ways, he has a good description of his cousin's death and their flight to the

cave. He incorrectly recalls that "Negro" soldiers had captured them. Only Apache scouts were involved in the affair. Ball, *Indeh*, 98–99.

19. Elliott, "Campaign Against the Chiricahua Apaches," 7–8. Captain Kendall's troop was ordered to return to Fort Wingate. He stopped at Albuquerque, where a reporter from the *Albuquerque Journal* interviewed him. His appearance gave "every indication of hard and trying service." He thought that Mangas was the real leader and not Geronimo. *Weekly Arizona Miner*, August 14, 1885.

20. S. Hatfield, *Chasing Shadows*, 87.

21. Fort Bowie Medical Records; Hanna, "With Crawford in Mexico," 63–65; NA, RG393, LS, DAZ, Roberts to Roach, July 3, 1885, July 5, 1885; Roberts to Elliott, July 2, 1885; Crook to Pope, July 3, 1886.

22. NA, RG393, LS, DAZ, Roberts to Pierce, June 9, 1885; Crook to Gatewood, June 11, 1885, Crook to Bradley, June 12, 1885.

23. NA, RG94, M233, R71, Indian Scout enlistments, June 1885.

24. Kraft, *Gatewood and Geronimo*, 96–97; NA, RG393, LS, DAZ, Crook to Bradley July 1, 1885.

25. USMHI, Roach to Roberts, July 9, 1885.

26. NA, RG393, LS, DAZ, Roberts to Roach, July 9, 1885; Roberts to Gatewood, July 9, 1885.

27. NA, RG393, LR, DAZ, Carusi to Cleveland, June 15, 1885.

28. Thrapp, *Conquest of Apacheria*, 326–27.

29. GP, Hooke interview.

30. Goodwin, *The Social Organization*, 658. University of Arizona (UA), Special Collections, Documents relating to the Apache Campaign of 1885–86, Wirt Davis to Roberts, March 10, 1886 (from here on, noted as "Captain Davis's first campaign into Mexico"); GC, Walter Hooke interview.

31. Altshuler, *Cavalry Yellow and Infantry Blue*, 98–99; Thrapp, *Encyclopedia*, 382–83; Patch, *Reminiscences of Fort Huachuca*, 4–5; AHS, William L. Wardwell File, Letter to parents from Fort Thomas, December 21, 1885.

32. UA, Captain Davis's first campaign into Mexico.

33. AHS, SA, R23, Gomez to Secretary of State, July 25, 1885.

34. UA, Captain Davis's first campaign into Mexico.

35. GP, Chiricahua Apache Place Names; Basehart, "Chiricahua Apache Subsistence," 75.

36. GP, Hooke interview.

37. Ibid.; UA, Captain Davis's first campaign into Mexico.

38. GP, Hooke interview.

39. Ibid.; GP, Curley interview; UA, Captain Davis's first campaign into Mexico; NA, M689, R179, Davis to Crook, August 14, 1885; NA, RG393, LS, DAZ, Crook to AG, Division of the Pacific, August 17, 1885; Daly, "The Geronimo Campaign," 29; Williamson, "Oskay de No Tah," 81; *Rio Grande Republican*, September 12, 1885; *Lone Star*, October 31, 1885.

40. According to a report from Sonora, Captain Wirt Davis had told the prefect of Bacadéhuachi that his command had struck the rancheria of Geronimo and Mangas.

Of course, the capture of Mangas's wife Huera indicates that they were probably together. Chiricahua accounts say that Geronimo and Mangas had split in the rainy season, which means sometime in July or August. AHS, SA, R23, Guerra to Governor, August 17, 1885; see Chihuahua's statement published in Thrapp, *Dateline Fort Bowie*, 62.

41. Davis, *Truth*, 248–50.

42. OP, box 37, folder 35, Chatto interview.

43. Britton Davis explained that "the officers on Indian duty, following the General's [Crook] example, rode mules . . . [that] were surer footed, more enduring, less likely to stray, and able to sustain themselves on grass that would soon put a horse down and out." Davis, *Truth*, 253.

44. NA, RG393, LS, DAZ, Crook to AG, Division of the Pacific, August 17, 1885; Daly, "The Geronimo Campaign," 30; Fort Bowie Files, Fort Bowie Post Returns, September 1885; UA, Captain Davis's first campaign into Mexico.

45. NA, RG393, Roberts to Davis, August 18, 1885; UA, Captain Davis's first campaign into Mexico.

46. S. Hatfield, *Chasing Shadows*, 84–87; Captain Davis heard that Guerra had brought five hundred cavalry with him. NA, RG94, M689, R179, Davis to Crook, August 14, 1885.

47. GP, Hooke interview; UA, Captain Davis's first campaign into Mexico.

48. GP, Hooke interview; UA, Captain Davis's first campaign into Mexico.

49. AHS, SA, R21, Espina to Governor, July 23, 1885, July 25, 1885; *Arizona Weekly Citizen*, August 1, 1885.

50. Information from Berndt Kuhn to author, August 1, 2007; NA, RG393, Post Records, Fort Huachuca, Lawton to Post Adjutant, Fort Huachuca, August 28, 1885; NA, RG393, LS, DAZ, Roberts to AG, Division of the Pacific, July 30, 1885, Crook to Forsyth, August 1, 1885; GC, C. Hatfield, "Expeditions"; Bigelow, *Bloody Trail*, 27.

51. AHS, SA, R23, Arvizu to Secretary of State, August 4, 1885; Ahumada to Secretary of State, August 20, 1885; Aguirre to Secretary of State, August 22, 1885; *Arizona Weekly Citizen*, August 29, 1885.

52. GP, Hooke interview; UA, Captain Davis's first campaign into Mexico; NA, RG393, LS, DAZ, Crook to AG, Division of the Pacific, September 21, 1885.

53. AHS, SA, R23, Carbo to Governor, September 10, 1885; Aguirre to Secretary of State, September 22, 1885.

54. GP, Hooke interview; UA, Captain Davis's first campaign into Mexico.

55. Ibid.

56. This sentiment was shared by Berle Kanseah, spokesman and leader of the Chiricahuas on the Mescalero Reservation in the late twentieth century. Kanseah to author, October 11, 1998.

57. GP, Hooke interview; Nashkin interview; UA, Captain Davis's first campaign into Mexico.

58. GP, Hooke interview.

Chapter 21. "Moccasin Tracks Left in the Sand"

Epigraph and chapter title: Title quotation from *Globe Silver Belt*, September 26, 1885. Epigraph from NA, RG393, LS, DAZ, Roberts to Gatewood, September 30, 1885.

1. NA, RG94, M689, R183, Crawford to Crook, August 30, 1885; R179, Crook to Pope, September 6, 1885.

2. Debo, *Geronimo*, 245.

3. Forty-five years later, without the benefit of notes, Davis remembered that he took about "forty picked scouts." Davis, *Truth,* 252; Henry W. Daly recalled Davis taking fifty scouts. Daly, "The Geronimo Campaign," 31; Crawford's report of August 30, 1885, provides the exact numbers, which took into account the ten scouts that Davis had left behind at San Buenaventura with Lieutenant Elliott. NA, RG94, M689, R183, Crawford to Crook, August 30, 1885.

4. OP, box 37, folder 28, Perico interview.

5. Davis, *Truth*, 254–57.

6. Daly, "The Geronimo Campaign," 31.

7. Again, there was some confusion as to the number of scouts and packers sent with Elliott. Crawford said eighteen in his report dated August 30, 1885, but he was obviously counting the ten scouts that Davis had left behind with Elliott at San Buenaventura; NA, RG94, M689, R183, Crawford to Crook, August 30, 1885; Other accounts varied: Davis recalled five scouts; Elliott recalled eight; Sherman Curley, who was with Elliott, thought nine; and Henry Daly remembered twenty-five. Davis, *Truth,* 262; USMHI, Elliott, "Campaign Against the Chiricahua Apaches"; GP, Curley interview; Daly, "The Geronimo Campaign," 31.

8. Elliott, "Campaign Against the Chiricahua Apaches"; NA, RG94, M689, R183, Elliott's report, Elliott to AG, Washington, June 1886; GP, Curley interview.

9. The term "tame Apache" was one used throughout the Southwest and Mexico to distinguish Apaches who were no longer wild or warlike. It was usually applied to Apache scouts and to Apaches who had begun to live near Mexican settlements and had assimilated into Mexican culture.

10. GP, Curley interview; NA, RG94, M689, R183, Elliott's report to the AG; Elliott, "Campaign Against the Chiricahua Apaches."

11. GP, Curley interview; NA, RG94, M689, R183, Elliott's report to the AG; Elliott, "Campaign Against the Chiricahua Apaches."

12. GP, Curley interview.

13. Davis, *Truth*, 271.

14. GP, Curley interview.

15. Ibid; NA, RG94, M689, R183, Elliott's report to the AG; USAMH, Elliott, "Campaign Against the Chiricahua Apaches."

16. Davis, *Truth*, 263–65.

17. Ibid, 265–68; Charles, "The Old Scouts of the Mescaleros," 19.

18. GP, Curley interview.

19. NA, RG94, M689, R183, Elliott's report to the AG; Davis, *Truth*, 269.

20. Davis, *Truth*, 269.

21. GP, Curley interview.

22. Williamson, "Oskay de No Tah," 82.

23. Davis, *Truth*, 269.

24. NA, RG94, M689, R183, Crawford to Crook, August 30, 1885.

25. LC, Scott Papers, Toclanny statement, September 11, 1911.

26. Davis, *Truth*, 269–76.

27. NA, RG393, LSDINM, M1072, R7, Bradley to Hammond, September 9, 1885.

28. Ibid., AAG, District of New Mexico to AAG, Dept. of the Missouri, September 17, 1885.

29. Twenty years later, Geronimo recalled that his party consisted of six men and four women. In Santiago McKinn's earliest testimony, he placed the party at six men and a few women. He was more specific when he testified in 1893 to the Indian Claims Commission. Here he named the men and said Geronimo had five women with him; Barrett, *Geronimo's Story*, 140–41; NA, RG123, Claim 3109 (hereafter McKinn testimony). Colonel Bradley said that his troops (with Western Apache and Navajo scouts) patrolled the border daily from the Arizona line to Lake Palomas. Geronimo took advantage and easily avoided detection by crossing a few miles east of Palomas; NA, RG393. LRDINM, M1072, R7, AAG, District of New Mexico, to AG, Dept. of the Missouri, September 28, 1885.

30. McKinn testimony.

31. Barrett, *Geronimo's Story*, 140–41. Geronimo was confused in his chronology, placing this event during General Nelson Miles's tenure. But he never entered New Mexico during Miles's command of the Department of Arizona.

32. According to Frank Bennett, who followed Geronimo's trail, this was the route he had taken from Mexico. NA, RG393, LS, DAZ, Crook to Bradley, September 29, 1885.

33. NA, RG393, LRDINM, Headley (?) to Post Adjutant, Fort Bayard, September 12, 1885.

34. NA, RG393, LS, DAZ, Barber to Crook, September 5, 1885; NA, RG393, M1072, R7, LSDINM, Bradley to CO, Fort Stanton and Fort Wingate, September 12, 1885.

35. NA, RG393, LRDINM, Headley (?) to Post Adjutant, Fort Bayard, September 12, 1885; *Rio Grande Republican*, September 19, 1885; *Indian Raids*, 41–43.

36. Aranda, "Santiago McKinn, Indian Captive," 1–3; *Indian Raids,* 40–42, 71; *Globe Silver Belt*, April 17, 1886; *Rio Grande Republican*, September 19, 1885; Hudson, "Chief Geronimo's Captive," 354–55; McKinn testimony.

37. *Globe Silver Belt,* September 26, 1885, April 17, 1886; McKinn testimony; NA, RG94, M689, R179, Bradley to AG, Dept. of the Missouri, September 12, 1885.

38. *Indian Raids*, 40–41.

39. Ibid., 42; McKinn testimony; *Globe Silver Belt*, April 17, 1886; Hudson, "Chief Geronimo's Captive," 354–55.

40. McFarland, *Wilderness of the Gila*, 25.

41. Schmitt, *Crook's Autobiography,* 256–57; Faulk, *The Geronimo Campaign,* 69–70.

42. *Albuquerque Journal,* October 13, 1885.

43. NA, RG94, M689, R178, Crook to Pope, June 5, 1885.

44. NA, RG94, M689, R178, Pope to AG, July 27, 1885; NA, RG94, M689, R179, Lamar to Endicott, July 31, 1885; Pope to AG, August 1, 1885; AG to Pope, August 16, 1885; John Bret Harte suggests that Lamar, a Democrat, made little effort to save Ford's job because Ford was a Republican appointed by a previous administration. Bret Harte, "Conflict at San Carlos," 42–43.

45. NA, RG393, LS, DAZ, Crook to Bradley, September 11, 1885, September 12, 1885.

46. Wooster, *Nelson A. Miles,* 141–42.

47. NA, RG393, LS, DAZ, Crook to AG, Division of the Pacific, September 19, 1885; NA, RG94, M689, R179, Ross to President Cleveland, September 18, 1885; NA, RG94, M689, R180, Miles to AAG, Division of the Missouri, November 30, 1885.

48. NA, RG393, LS, DAZ, Crook to AG, Division of the Pacific, August 13, 1885; Roberts to Pierce, September 11, 1885.

49. NA, RG94, M689, R179, Crook to AG, Division of the Pacific, September 17, 1885.

50. Ibid., Pope to AG, September 30, 1885, first endorsement.

51. Ibid., Armstrong to Lamar, September 12, 1885.

52. Ibid., Sheridan to Endicott, September 30, 1885.

53. Ibid., Miles to Schofield, October 2, 1885 (third endorsement), Schofield to AG, October 9, 1885 (fourth endorsement), Sheridan to Endicott, October 13, 1885, (fifth endorsement).

54. NA, RG393, LS, DAZ, Roberts to Pierce, September 11, 1885; Crook to Bradley, September 12, 1885.

55. *Indian Raids,* 42–44.

56. NA, RG393, LS, DAZ, Crook to AAG, Division of the Pacific, September 22, 1885.

57. NA, RG393, LR, DAZ, Gatewood to Crook, September 22, 1885 (9:00 A.M.), September 23, 1885; Crawford to Crook, November 7, 1885; NA, RG393, LS, DAZ, Crook to AG, Division of the Pacific, September 22, 1885, September 23, 1885; *Globe Silver Belt,* September 26, 1885, October 3, 1885; *Arizona Weekly Citizen,* September 26, 1885.

58. NA, RG393, LS, DAZ, Crook to Davis, September 23, 1885; Crook to Gatewood, September 23, 1885 (three telegrams); Gatewood to Roberts, September 23, 1885.

59. Davis *Truth,* 276–78; *Arizona Weekly Citizen,* October 7, 1885; *Indian Raids,* 47.

60. NA, RG393, LR, DAZ, Davis to Roberts, September 23, 1885 (two telegrams, 4:30 P.M. and 10:15 P.M).

61. NA, RG393, LS, DAZ, Roberts to Davis, September 24, 1885; Roberts to Gatewood, September 25, 1885.

62. Ibid., Roberts to Davis, September 24, 1885; Crook to AG, Division of the Pacific, September 25, 1885; Roberts to Gatewood, September 25, 1885.

63. *Indian Raids*, 44; *Globe Silver Belt*, April 17, 1886.

64. Elliott, "Campaign Against the Chiricahua Apaches"; UA, Captain Davis's first campaign into Mexico.

65. Elliott, "Campaign Against the Chiricahua Apaches"; UA, Captain Davis's first campaign into Mexico.

66. Schmitt, *Crook's Autobiography*, 257.

67. NA, RG393, LS, DAZ, Roberts to Wade, September 29, 1885; Roberts to Gatewood, September 29, 1885.

68. Ibid., Roberts to Gatewood, September 30, 1885.

69. Ibid., Roberts to Gatewood, September 30, 1885; Schmitt, *Crook's Autobiography*, 257.

70. NA, RG393, LS, DAZ, Crook to Bradley, October 1, 1885; Elliott, "Campaign Against the Chiricahua Apache Indians; C. Hatfield, "Expeditions," 17–19; *Arizona Weekly Citizen*, October 10, 1885; Schmitt, *Crook's Autobiography*, 257.

71. *Arizona Weekly Citizen*, October 10, 1885; Bailey, *The Valiants*, 100–101; *Indians Raids*, 45.

72. *Arizona Weekly Citizen*, October 10, 1885; Bailey, *The Valiants*, 100–101; *Indians Raids*, 45.

73. Connell, "Apaches Past and Present," chapter 17.

74. Ibid.; Rockfellow, *Log of an Arizona Trail Blazer*, 112–17, has a good description of Noonan and the circumstances surrounding his death. *Arizona Weekly Citizen*, October 10, 1885; *Indian Raids*, 45.

75. NA, RG393, LR, DAZ, Roberts to Crook, October 2, 1885, October 3, 1885.

76. Ibid., Crook to AG, Division of the Pacific, October 9, 1885; Schmitt, *Crook's Autobiography*, 257–58.

77. NA, RG94, M689, R179, Crook to AG, Division of the Pacific, October 11, 1885; *Albuquerque Journal*, October 13, 1885.

78. Ibid., Crook to AG, Division of the Pacific, October 11, 1885, with endorsements by General John Pope and General Philip Sheridan.

Chapter 22. The Trail to Espinosa del Diablo

Epigraph: *Indian Raids*, quoting the *Wilcox Stockman*, October 23, 1885, 47.

1. NA, RG393, LS, DAZ, Crook to Bradley, October 6, 1885, October 8, 1885; NA, RG393, LSDINM, M1072, R7, Bradley to AG, Dept. of the Missouri, October 9, 1885; NA, RG94, M689, R179, Crook to Pope, October 10, 1885; AHS, SA, R21, Torres to Secretary of State, October 13, 1885.

2. NA, RG393, LS, DAZ, Crook to Bradley, October 8, 1885; NA, RG393, LRDINM, M1072, R7, Bradley to AG, Dept. of the Missouri, October 8, 1885; *Albuquerque Journal*, October 13, 1885; *Indian Raids*, 46; *Winners of the West*, December 30, 1925, has Grover's account.

3. University of Oregon (UO), Crook Papers, Crook to Pope, November 10, 1885; SA, R22, Guerra to Secretary of State, October 21, 1885; *Lone Star,* October 21, 1885.

4. NA, RG393, LS, DAZ, Roberts to Crook, October 2, 1885; USMHI, Crook diary, November 3, 1885; Ball, *Indeh,* 89–90, has Daklugie's version of his brother's captivity. Daklugie had forgotten that his brother had become lost at the time Mangas moved camp.

5. NA, RG393, LS, DAZ, Roberts to Gatewood, July 27, 1885. Crawford had learned that Shoie, Cathla, and Len-see had left their wives on the reservation. Tah-ni-toe had also left his spouse at Fort Apache. NA, RG393, LR, PSC, Roberts to Pierce, March 29, 1886. Moh-tsos had run off with another woman deserting his wife, Bash-da-le-hi, and three children. After the conclusion of the war, she was not too anxious to rejoin her husband. NA, RG94, M689, R188, Sinclair to AAG, Governor's Island, New York, August 18, 1887; NA, RG393, LR, PSC, Roberts to Pierce, March 29, 1886.

6. From piecing together various accounts, a good guess can be made of the identity of Ulzana's raiders. Crook stated that four of the men who surrendered with Chihuahua in March 1886 were members of the party. Cathla, who is mentioned as left behind with a broken leg before they reached Fort Apache, was one, along with Ulzana, and probably Shoie and Len-see. Perico was identified in one contemporary report. In addition, a woman whom he captured was with him at the final surrender. Perico's half-brother, Fun, according to Chiricahua oral history, was also with him. An informant of Morris Opler places Jaspar Kanseah with Ulzana. According to Chiricahua sources, Kanseah was the orderly for Yahnozha in the last campaign, so the latter was likely a participant. A White Mountain captive, Na-dis-ough, identified Atelnietze as her captor. That leaves three men to account for. Zachia, or Azariquelch, the only warrior killed during the foray, and likely Tah-ni-toe and Moh-tsos.

7. NA, RG393, LR, DAZ, Lockett to Roberts, November 25, 1885.

8. *Lone Star,* October 21, 1885, November 7, 1885; *Arizona Weekly Citizen,* October 31, 1885; NA, RG393, LS, DAZ, Crook to Governor of Chihuahua, October 27, 1885.

9. *Indian Raids,* 49–52; NA, RG393, LRDINM, Chaffee to Forsyth, November 12, 1885; Carter, *The Life of Lieutenant General Chaffee,* 111–12; Crook diary, November 11, 1885.

10. NA, RG94, M689, R180, Bradley to AG, Dept. of the Missouri, November 5, 1885; NA, RG393, LRDINM, Kendall to James, November 13, 1885.

11. Carter, *The Life of Lieutenant General Chaffee,* 111–12; NA, RG393, LRDINM, Chaffee to Forsyth, November 12, 1885; West to Field Adjutant, 6th Cavalry, Separ, November 7, 1885; UA, Special Collections, MS288, diary of Frank West, November 7, 1885, November 8, 1885.

12. NA, RG393, LRDINM, West to Field Adjutant, 6th Cavalry, November 7, 1885; UA, diary of Frank West, November 7, 1885. NA, RG123, Claim 7087, *John T. Shy vs. the United States and Apache Indians*; Claim 10156, *Francis M. Yeater vs. the United*

States and Apache Indians. Shy said that Ulzana's party numbered twelve men. My thanks to Apache historian Berndt Kuhn for providing me copies of these claims.

13. *Indian Raids,* 50–51; NA, RG123, Claim 7087; Claim 10156; *Lone Star,* November 14, 1885.

14. *Indian Raids,* 50–51; NA, RG123, Claim 7087; Claim 10156; *Lone Star,* November 14, 1885; Connell, "Apaches Past and Present," chapter 17.

15. The two men killed were George Hay and Jacob Hailing. Reports vary as to the location. One says near Mule Springs, another near Cow Springs, and a third on Berrenda Creek. *Indian Raids,* 50–52; NA, RG393, LRDINM, Kendall to Forsyth, November 13, 1885; UA, West diary, November 9, 1885.

16. *Indian Raids,* 52.

17. NA, RG94, M689, R180, Miles to AAG, Division of the Missouri, November 10, 1886; Schofield to AG, November 12, 1885.

18. Hutton, *Phil Sheridan and His Army,* 129.

19. NA, RG94, M689, R180, Sheridan to Crook, November 19, 1885; Crook to Sheridan, November 20, 1885; Endicott to Sheridan, November 20, 1885.

20. NA, RG393, LSDISTNM, Bradley to AG, Dept. of the Missouri, October 9, 1885; *Albuquerque Journal,* October 13, 1885; Crook diary, October 14, 1885.

21. AHS, GC, List of Scouts; NA, RG393, LR, PSC, Pierce to Roach, November 10, 1885; LR, DAZ, Crawford to Crook, November 7, 1885; LS, DAZ, Crook to Crawford, November 7, 1885.

22. Crook diary, November 7, 1885.

23. Ruby, also known as Tahyan, was on the 1880 census as To-yaj-in-sa and the 1885 census as Ro-wey. He married Bey-it-zhun, the only child Loco had with his first wife, Chiz-pah-odlee. It was his second marriage. Griswold, "Fort Sill Apaches," Tahyan biography, 131.

24. AHS, GC, List of Scouts; Shipp, "Crawford's Last Expedition," 346–49.

25. NA, RG393, LS, DAZ, Crook to Crawford, November 11, 1885; Crook to Pierce, November 14, 1885, November 22, 1885; Crook diary, November 13, 1885.

26. Crook diary, November 17, 1885; NA, RG393, LR, DAZ, Davis to Roberts, March 20, 1886; Maus to Roberts, April 8, 1886; Shipp, "Crawford's Last Expedition," 346–51.

27. *Clifton Clarion,* December 9, 1885, courtesy of Berndt Kuhn; AHS, Roberts Diary, November 24, 1885; Crook diary, November 24, 1885.

28. OP, box 37, folder 25, Chatto statement; Opler, *Life-Way,* 189.

29. NA, RG393, LR, DAZ, Lockett to Roberts, November 24, 1885, November 26, 1885.

30. Ibid.; NA, RG393, LS, DAZ, Roberts to Crawford, November 25, 1885; Crook to AG, Division of the Pacific, November 25, 1885; NA, RG393, LR, PSC, Pierce to Clum, January 6, 1886; Griswold, "Fort Sill Apaches," Perico biography, 118.

31. OP, box 36, folder 8, Sam Kenoi interview; Opler, *Life-Way,* 343.

32. Goodwin, *Social Organization,* 213, 578; Kraft, *Lt. Charles Gatewood,* 77.

33. OP, box 36, folder 8, Sam Kenoi interview; Opler, *Life-Way,* 343.

34. Kraft, *Lt. Charles Gatewood*, 76; NA, RG393, LS, DAZ, Crook to AG, Division of the Pacific, November 25, 1885; NA, RG94, M689, R180, Crook to Pope, November 27, 1885; *Weekly Arizona Miner*, January 13, 1886; NA, RG393, LR, PSC, Pierce to Clum, January 6, 1886; *Tombstone Epitaph,* January 6, 1886, February 20, 1886.

35. NA, RG393, LS, DAZ, Roberts to Lockett, November 26, 1885; November 27, 1885; Crook to AAG, Division of the Pacific, January 14, 1886.

36. Thrapp, *Conquest of Apacheria*, 336.

37. NA, RG393, LS, DAZ, Crook to Lockett, November 27, 1885; Crook to CO, Fort Apache, November 27, 1885; LR, DAZ, Lockett to Roberts, November 28, 1885.

38. NA, RG393, LR, DAZ, Lockett to Roberts, November 28, 1885.

39. Ibid., Roberts to Pierce, November 26, 1886 (two letters).

40. NA, RG393, LR, PSC, Pierce to Crook, November 29, 1885; Crook diary, November 29, 1885; *Tombstone Epitaph*, February 20, 1886.

41. Schmitt, *Crook's Autobiography*, 258; Roberts diary, November 27, 1885; NA, RG303, LR, DAZ, Lockett to Roberts, November 28, 1885; GP, Nashkin's interview.

42. Hutton, *Phil Sheridan and His Army*, 364–66; Roberts diary, November 29, 1885; Crook diary, November 29, 1885; C. Robinson, *General Crook*, 277.

43. Wooster, *Nelson A. Miles*, 142.

44. Horn, *Life of Tom Horn*, 169–70.

45. NA, RG393, LR, DAZ, Sieber to CO, Post at San Carlos, December 9, 1885; Graham County Historical Society, Wright Brothers File, Ray D. Crandall manuscript, "The Wright Brothers."

46. NA, RG94, M689, R181, Crawford to Crook, December 24, 1885. Crawford reported that Chihuahua came in a week before the capture of Juh's sons, which occurred about December 2, 1885. Britton Davis was more specific. In a letter to Crook dated November 24, 1885, he said that he had received word from Mexican officials at Casas Grandes that "some hostile bucks" were in Casas Grandes "requesting peace." This was Chihuahua after returning from his raid into New Mexico. NA, RG393, LS, DAZ, Roberts to Crawford, December 5, 1885.

47. A raiding party killed two men in the district of Ures on November 23 and two days later ambushed and killed three men from Suaqui, about fifteen miles south of Tepache. AHS, SA, R21, Guerra to Governor, November 26, 1885; Armijo to Governor, December 4, 1885.

48. NA, RG94, M689, R191, "Report of Remarks Made to Captain Maus," August 29, 1894; NA, RG393, LR, DAZ, Davis to Roberts, March 20, 1886. Escarcega, *La Apacheria en Chihuahua*, 255–59; Chavez, "Indio Juh," 365–67, 376–77.

49. Escarcega, *La Apacheria en Chihuahua*, 255–59; Chavez, "Indio Juh," 365–67, 376–77; NA, RG393, LR, DAZ, Davis to Roberts, March 20, 1886.

50. Escarcega, *La Apacheria en Chihuahua*, 255–59; Chavez, "Indio Juh," 365–67, 376–77; NA, RG393, LR, DAZ, Davis to Roberts, March 20, 1886; GC, Pettit to Roberts, December 30, 1885; Davis to Roberts, March 20, 1886.

51. NA, RG393, LR, DAZ, Davis to Crook, March 20, 1886; NA, M689, R181, Davis to Crook, January 2, 1886

52. U.S. Department of State, House Executive Doc. 302, 49th Congress, Second Session, 600, 610–12.

53. NA, RG393, LR, DAZ, RG94, Davis to Crook, March 20, 1886; NA, RG94, M689, R181, Davis to Crook, January 2, 1886

54. Hooker, *Child of the Fighting Tenth*, 183–84.

55. NA, RG94, M689, R181, Crawford to Crook, December 24, 1885; Horn, *Life of Tom Horn*, 170–71.

56. NA, RG94, M689, R181, Crawford to Crook, December 24, 1885.

57. Shipp, "Crawford's Last Expedition," 346.

58. Horn, *Life of Tom Horn*, 173.

59. NA, RG94, M689, R181, Crawford to Crook, December 28, 1885; M689, R182, Crawford to Kelton, January 1, 1886; Miles, *Personal Recollections*, 452; Shipp, "Crawford's Last Expedition," 349–51. Daly remembered that Crawford took eleven pack mules; Day, "The Geronimo Campaign," 82.

60. OP, box 35, folder 4, Kinzhuna biography. Kinzhuna placed the dance the night before the attack on Geronimo's camp but this was simply a product of a faulty memory. The dance occurred the evening of January 2, 1886. Maus and Shipp both mentioned that it occurred the night before they left for the Aros River. Miles, *Personal Recollections*, 453; Shipp, "Crawford's Last Expedition," 349.

61. AHS, GC, Pettit to Roberts, December 30, 1885.

62. Miles, *Personal Recollections*, 453–54; Shipp, "Crawford's Last Expedition," 350–51; Daly, "The Geronimo Campaign," 83.

63. Miles, *Personal Recollections*, 451–52.

64. Shipp, "Crawford's Last Expedition," 347–48.

65. Unless noted otherwise, the primary sources for the remainder of Crawford's campaign are Shipp, "Crawford's Last Expedition" 343–361; Miles, *Personal Recollections*, 450–71; NA, RG393, LR, DAZ, Maus to Roberts, April 8, 1886. Charles Lummis collected Maus's and Shipp's statements after the campaign. They are published in Thrapp, *Dateline Fort Bowie*, 163–70, 179–83; UO, Crook Papers, Maus to Roberts, January 23, 1886; February 6, 1886. They will be referred to as "Consolidated accounts."

66. Consolidated accounts

67. Horn, whose account of this affair was garbled, probably because he wrote it some twenty years later, claimed that Crawford had instructed him to kill Geronimo if he got the chance. Horn, *Life of Tom Horn*, 175–83. No doubt this outcome would have pleased Crawford.

68. Horn, *Life of Tom Horn*, 175; GP, Nashkin interview.

69. Consolidated accounts.

70. Ibid. Most accounts say that only one woman came in and talked to Crawford. But Maus told Charles Lummis that there were two messengers, "one after the other." Naiche had evidently sent both; Thrapp, *Dateline Fort Bowie*, 166. Some accounts say that Geronimo had sent his sister in, but this was apparently at a later time.

71. Consolidated accounts; Horn, *Life of Tom Horn*, 177; OP, box 37, folder 28, unidentified Apache statement; Berle Kanseah to author, October 14, 1998. Kanseah echoed Maus and Shipp's comments to me.

72. Consolidated accounts; OP, box 37, folder 26, Jim Miller account.

CHAPTER 23. THE ROAD TO EMBUDOS CANYON

Epigraph: UO, Crook Papers, Maus to Roberts, January 23, 1886.

1. GP, Nashkin interview.

2. Consolidated accounts.

3. Ibid.

4. GP, Nashkin interview.

5. Opler, "The Geronimo Campaign of 1886," 373–74. His sources heard this conversation from several scouts who were present.

6. OP, box 35, folder 6, Fatty biography.

7. Consolidated accounts.

8. Ibid. Scott Papers, conference dated September 27, 1911, 19–20.

9. Consolidated accounts. Thrapp, *Dateline Fort Bowie*, 180, contains what Shipp told Lummis. Lummis, *General Crook*, 18.

10. OP, box 36, folder 8, Kenoi interview; Horn, *Life of Tom Horn*, 186–87.

11. Opler, "The Geronimo Campaign of 1886," 374.

12. Consolidated accounts; UO, Crook Papers, Maus to Roberts, January 23, 1886.

13. Sweeney, *Cochise*, 324.

14. Shipp, "Crawford's Last Campaign," 361.

15. Consolidated accounts; Hooker, *Child of the Fighting Tenth*, 211.

16. Consolidated accounts.

17. Ibid.

18. UO, Crook Papers, Maus to Roberts, January 23, 1886; NA, RG393, LR, DAZ, Maus to Roberts, April 8, 1886; Debo, *Geronimo*, 251–52.

19. Consolidated accounts.

20. Ibid.

21. Ibid.

22. Shipp, "Crawford's Last Expedition," 361.

23. *Weekly Arizona Miner*, February 10, 1886.

24. NA, RG393, LS, DAZ, Roberts to AG, District of New Mexico, December 8, 1885; *Indian Raids*, 55–56.

25. NA, RG94, M689, R181, Fountain to AG, District of New Mexico, December 12, 1885; *Indian Raids*, 56, 58; Mazzanovich, *Trailing Geronimo*, 307–308.

26. NA, RG94, M689, R181, Fountain to AG, District of New Mexico, December 22, 1885; Fountain's second account, written forty years later at the request of Anton Mazzanovich, was published in *Trailing Geronimo*, 301–314. This account, though less accurate than Fountain's original reports, adds colorful anecdotes. I have relied heavily on Fountain's original reports, filed three days after each encounter;

McFarland, *Wilderness of the Gila*, 29–31; Bryan, *True Tales of the American Southwest*, 18; Geronimo Springs Museum, Keith Humphries Papers, *Mogollon Mines*, 1915, has McKinney's account.

27. Mazzanovich, *Trailing Geronimo*, 312–13. According to Jaspar Kanseah, Yahnozha "never wasted a bullet"; Robinson, *Apache Voice*, 54.

28. Ibid., 56–61; Thrapp, *Conquest of Apacheria*, 337–39; Hayes, *A Portal to Paradise*, 160–61; *Tombstone Epitaph*, January 15, 1886.

29. Roberts diary, December 31, 1885; NA, RG123, Claim 2535, *Harrington vs. United States and Apache Indians*; *Tombstone Epitaph*, January 1, 1886.

30. *Tombstone Epitaph*, January 7, 1886; *Weekly Arizona Miner*, January 13, 1886; Hayes Library, Crook Papers, Crook to AG, Division of the Pacific, January 7, 1886.

31. Hayes Library, Crook Papers, Crook to AG, Division of the Pacific, January 11, 1886.

32. *Tombstone Epitaph,* January 3, 1886, January 8, 1886.

33. For details on this battle, see Sweeney, *Mangas Coloradas,* 210–12.

34. AHS, SA, R23, Torres to Secretary of State, January 11, 1886, January 21, 1886; R24, Aguirre to Secretary of State, January 9, 1886, January 10, 1886, January 11, 1886.

35. NA, RG94, M689, R180, Sheriff James Wood to President Cleveland, December 14, 1885; Crook to Sheridan, December 30, 1885; *Indian Raids*, 58; Schmitt, *Crook's Autobiography*, 259.

36. Schmitt, *Crook's Autobiography*, 259; Robert's diary, January 14, 1886; *Tombstone Epitaph*, January 6, 1886, February 5, 1886.

37. Schmitt, *Crook's Autobiography*, 259; Robert's diary, January 14, 1886; *Rio Grande Republican*, February 6, 1885; Bigelow, *Bloody Trail*, 116–17.

38. UO, Crook Papers, Maus to Roberts, February 6, 1886.

39. Ibid.

40. Porter, *Paper Medicine Man*, 251. Nowhere was this more evident than in Crook's refusal to help his former staff officer, Captain John G. Bourke, gain promotion in the late 1880s. The erudite Bourke had been Crook's loyal supporter, press agent, and publicist. Crook's betrayal, as Bourke considered it, hurt him, for he had done much to support the general.

41. UO, Crook Papers, Maus to Roberts, February 6, 1886; NA, RG393, LR, DAZ, Maus to Roberts, March 14, 1886; Hooker, *Child of the Fighting Tenth*, 212–13.

42. UO, Crook Papers, Maus to Roberts, February 6, 1886; Miles, *Personal Recollections*, 467; Roberts diary, January 28, 1886; *Tombstone Epitaph*, February 16, 1886.

43. Ibid.; Miles, *Personal Recollections,* 467; Roberts diary, March 25, 1886.

44. UO, Crook Papers, Roberts to Maus, February 6, 1886; NA, RG94, M689, R181, Sheridan to Crook, February 1, 1886; Crook to Pope, February 10, 1886.

45. Hayes Library, Crook Papers, Crook to AG, Division of the Pacific, February 19, 1886; NA, RG393, LS, DAZ, Roberts to Lockett, February 15, 1886; NA, RG393, LS, Fort Thomas, Mills to Pierce, February 19, 1886.

46. NA, RG393, LR, Fort Thomas, Pierce to Read, February 8, 1886; LS, Fort Thomas, Mills to Roberts, February 9, 1886; NA, RG393, LS, DAZ, Roberts to Lockett, February 1, 1886 (two letters); Roberts to Pierce, February 2, 1886.

47. Hayes Library, Crook Papers, Crook to Judge, First District of Arizona, February 19, 1886; *Tombstone Epitaph*, February 20, 1886; Crook diary, February 21, 1886.

48. Lynn R. Bailey and Don Chaput, in their two-volume work *Cochise County Stalwarts*, 2:155–58, argue that any one of four Tribolet brothers could have been involved. Two sources, packer Henry Daly, who was with Maus the entire time, and George Parsons, a resident of Tombstone, who had visited White's ranch in Sulphur Springs on March 29, 1886, pointed the finger at Charles. Bailey, *The Devil Has Foreclosed*, 200–201; Daly, "The Geronimo Campaign," 94–95.

49. NA, RG393, LR, DAZ, Maus to Roberts, March 11, 1886; Thrapp, *Dateline Fort Bowie*, 75–76.

50. AHS, SA, R25, Porchas to Secretary of State, February 1, 1886; Torres to Secretary of State, February 15, 1886; Guerra to Governor, February 10, 1886.

51. *Tombstone Epitaph*, February 20, 1886.

52. AHS, SA, R23, Torres to Secretary of State, February 15, 1886; Aguirre to Secretary of State, February 20, 1886; Aguirre to Secretary of State, February 21, 1886, March 1, 1886; R24, Kosterlitzky to Guerra February 18, 1886, February 19, 1886; Torres to Secretary of State, February 22, 1886, March 30, 1886; R25, Guerra to Governor, February 10, 1886.

53. AHS, SA, R24, Aguirre to Secretary of State, March 9, 1886, March 10, 1886, March 13, 1886; *Globe Silver Belt*, March 20, 1886, March 27, 1886, November 13, 1886. Santiago McKinn identified the slain Apache as Chinco, an obvious reference to Chinche; *Indian Raids*, 71. Charles Connell thought that Chinche was related to Mangas; Ball heard that he was a brother of Ponce; Connell, "Apaches Past and Present," chapter 18; Ball, *In the Days of Victorio*, 133.

54. AHS, SA, R24, Aguirre to Secretary of State, March 10, 1886, March 20, 1886.

55. Crook diary, March 12, 1886; NA, RG393, LR, DAZ, Sheridan to Crook, March 12, 1886; Hayes Library, Crook Papers, Crook to Sheridan, March 12, 1886.

56. NA, RG393, LR, DAZ, Maus to Roberts, March 11, 1886.

57. *Tombstone Epitaph*, February 4, 1886, March 9, 1886, March 19, 1886, March 23, 1886, March 25, 1886.

58. NA, RG393, LR, DAZ, Maus to Roberts, March 14, 1886, March 19, 1886.

59. Roberts diary, March 16, 1886, March 17, 1886; Crook diary, March 16, 1886; Hayes Library, Crook Papers, Crook to Sheridan, March 16, 1886; Crook to AG, Division of the Pacific, March 16, 1886.

60. NA, RG393, LR, DAZ, Maus to Roberts, March 19, 1886.

61. Bourke, *On the Border with Crook*, 473–74; Daly, "The Geronimo Campaign," 93.

62. NA, RG393, LR, DAZ, Maus to Roberts, March 22, 1886; Daly, "The Geronimo Campaign," 93; *Arizona Daily Citizen*, April 2, 1886.

63. Daly, "The Geronimo Campaign," 93; NA, RG393, LR, DAZ, Maus to Roberts, March 22, 1886; *Globe Silver Belt*, March 27, 1886.

64. NA, RG393, LR, DAZ, Maus to Roberts, March 22, 1886.

65. Bourke, *On the Border with Crook*, 473.

66. Ibid., 472. Crook diary, March 22, 1886.

67.Roberts diary, March 24, 1886; Crook diary, March 24, 1886; Bourke, *On the Border with Crook*, 478.

68. Miles, *Personal Recollections*, 467–68; Daly, "The Geronimo Campaign," 93–94.

69. NA, RG94, M689, R182, Crook to Sheridan, March 26, 1886; Crook diary, March 25, 1886; Roberts diary, March 25, 1886; Daly. "The Geronimo Campaign," 93–94; Bourke, *On the Border with Crook*, 474–79; Thrapp, *Dateline Fort Bowie*, 28–29; *Arizona Weekly Citizen*, April 2, 1886; *Tombstone Epitaph*, April 2, 1886, April 3, 1886; AHS, MS288, James Benton Glover recollections.

70. Crook diary, March 26, 1886; Roberts diary, March 26, 1886; Bourke, *On the Border with Crook*, 474–79; NA, RG94, M689, R182, Crook to Sheridan, March 26, 1886.

71. *Tombstone Epitaph*, April 2, 1886; Thrapp, *Dateline*, 30–32.

72. NA, RG393, LR, PSC, Roberts to Pierce, March 29, 1886; Fort Bowie Files, Roberts to CO, Fort Bowie, March 29, 1886.

73. Bourke, *On the Border with Crook*, 480; Connell, "Apaches Past and Present," chapter 18; Daly, "The Geronimo Campaign," 101.

74. Crook diary, March 28, 1886; Porter, *Paper Medicine Man*, 177.

75. Daly, "The Geronimo Campaign," 247–48.

76. Ibid.; NA, RG393, LR, DAZ, Maus to Roberts, March 29, 1886; NA, RG94, M689, R183, Maus to Roberts, April 8, 1886.

77. NA, RG393, LR, DAZ, Maus to Roberts, March 29, 1886.

78. Daly, "The Geronimo Campaign," 249–50; NA, RG393, Maus to Roberts, March 29, 1886.

79. Daly, "The Geronimo Campaign," 250–51.

80. NA, RG94, M689, R187, Stanley to Drum, September 30, 1886; Crook to Secretary of War, January 6, 1890, 33, SED 83.

81. NA, RG94, M689, R187, Stanley to Drum, September 30, 1886.

Chapter 24. General Miles to the Rescue

Epigraph: Thrapp, *Dateline Fort Bowie*, 33.

1. UMHI, Crook diary, March 29, 1886; AHS, Roberts diary, March 29, 1886; NA, RG393, LS, DAZ, Crook to Sheridan, March 27, 1886.

2. NA, RG393, LR, DAZ, Sheridan to Crook, March 30, 1886; Schmitt, *Crook's Autobiography*, 262–65.

3. Roberts diary, March 30, 1886; Thrapp, *Dateline Fort Bowie*, 20; NA, RG393, LR, DAZ, Sheridan to Crook, March 30, 1886; LS, DAZ, Crook to Sheridan, March 30, 1886.

4. NA, RG393, LR, DAZ, Sheridan to Crook, April 1, 1886; NA, RG393, LS, DAZ, Crook to Sheridan, April 1, 1886.

5. Crook diary, April 2, 1886; Roberts diary, April 2, 1886; NA, RG393, LR, DAZ, Drum to Roberts, April 2, 1886, forwarding copy of General Orders Number 15, Adjutant General's Office, Washington.

6. Bailey, *The Devil Has Foreclosed*, 202; Thrapp, *Dateline Fort Bowie*, 32–33, 54–55, 61; Roberts diary, April 2, 1886; Crook diary, April 2, 1886.

7. Porter, *Paper Medicine Man*, 209; McChristian, *Fort Bowie*, 199; Roberts diary, April 2, 1886; Crook diary, April 2, 1886.

8. Thrapp, *Dateline Fort Bowie*, 33, 53; NA, RG393, LS, DAZ, Crook to Sheridan, April 2, 1886.

9. NA, RG393, LR, DAZ, Roberts to Smith, April 3, 1886; Crook to Sheridan, April 4, 1886; Crook diary, April 3, 1886; Roberts diary, April 3, 1886; Thrapp, *Dateline Fort Bowie*, 33.

10. NA, RG393, LR, DAZ, Crook to Sheridan, April 4, 1886; Sheridan to Crook, April 5, 1886; Schmitt, *Crook's Autobiography*, 265–66.

11. Thrapp, *Dateline Fort Bowie*, 35, 57–58; *Indian Raids*, 71.

12. Thrapp, *Dateline Fort Bowie*, 63–65; NA, RG393, LR, DAZ, Muir to Crook, April 6, 1886; NA, RG393, LR, PSC, Crook to Pierce, April 5, 1886; NA, RG393, LR, Fort Thomas, Crook to Mills, April 5, 1886. According to Eugene Chihuahua, the boy's name was Osolo. S. Robinson, *Apache Voices*, 53.

13. Thrapp, *Dateline Fort Bowie*, 35–37; Crook diary, April 7, 1886; Roberts diary, April 7, 1886; *Arizona Weekly Citizen*, April 10, 1886; *Rio Grande Republican*, April 10, 1886; *Winners of the West*, June 1924; NA, RG94, M689, R182, Field Orders Number 22, DAZ, April 6, 1886; Schofield to AG, April 14, 1886.

14. Crook diary, April 8–12, 1886; Roberts diary, April 11–12, 1886; Thrapp, *Dateline Fort Bowie*, 68. Miles later recalled that he reached Bowie on April 12, but he clearly arrived a day earlier. Miles, *Personal Recollections*, 477.

15. *Tombstone Epitaph*, April 4, 1886.

16. Miles, *Personal Recollections*, 476–77; NA, RG94, M689, R182, Sheridan to Miles, April 3, 1886; Thrapp, *Dateline Fort Bowie*, 70–71.

17. NA, RG94, M689, R182, Miles to AG, Washington, April 18, 1886; Sheridan to Miles, April 19, 1886.

18. Miles, *Personal Recollections*, 485–86.

19. Lane, *Chasing Geronimo*, 13.

20. Davis, *Truth*, 309.

21. Miles, *Personal Recollections*, 481–87; Thrapp, *Conquest of Apacheria*, 351; Wooster, *Nelson A. Miles*, 145–47; Roberts diary, April 15, 1886. Miles, in an article written in 1916, "How U.S. Troops Caught Geronimo," failed to mention the heliograph as a factor in the victory. Instead, he praised the perseverance and tenacity of Lawton's command. *Frontier Times*, February 1932. Rolak, "General Miles Mirrors," 145–60.

22. AHS, SA, R24, Aguirre to Secretary of State, April 7, 1886 (two letters), April 11, 1886, April 12, 1886; *Tombstone Epitaph*, April 16, 1886; Connell, "Apaches Past and Present," chapter 18; Stout, "Soldiering and Suffering," 212.

23. AHS, SA, R24, Rivero to Torres, April 24, 1886; Rivero to Secretary of State, April 24, 1886, May 2, 1886; Torres to Corral, April 27, 1886; Beach to Scott, April 27, 1886; C. C. Smith, *Emilio Kosterlitzky*, 79–80. *Weekly Arizona Miner*, May 5, 1886; *Tombstone Epitaph*, April 28, 1886, May 23, 1886; *Arizona Weekly Citizen*, June 26, 1886; McCarty and Sonnichsen, "Trini Verdin," 158; Bigelow, *Bloody Trail*, 222.

24. AHS, SA, R24, Beach to Scott, April 27, 1886.

25. McCarty and Sonnichsen, "Trini Verdin," 149–63; Connell, "Apaches Past and Present," chapter 18; *Indian Raids*, 72–73; *Weekly Arizona Miner*, May 5, 1886; Lane, *Chasing Geronimo*, 32; Bigelow, *Bloody Trail*, 183; Margaillan, "The Story of My Great-Great Grandmother and Geronimo," 29–30; *Arizona Weekly Citizen*, May 8, 1886, July 3, 1886; UA, Special Collections, Peck Family Papers, A. M. Peck manuscript, "In the Memory of a Man"; NA, RG123, Claim 7237, *A. L. Peck vs. the U.S.*.

26. For a thorough examination of the events in late April through mid-May, see Radbourne's "Geronimo's Last Raid," 22–29, and "Captain Hatfield," 71–81; McCarty and Sonnichsen, "Trini Verdin," 154–58.

27. McCarty and Sonnichsen, "Trini Verdin," 154–58; Gale, "Lebo in Pursuit," 11–24; Lane, *Chasing Geronimo*, 28; Miles, *Personal Recollections*, 489–90; Bigelow, *Bloody Trail*, 164; Schubert, *Voices of the Buffalo Soldier*, 139–40, has Lieutenant Clarke's version of the fight; *Arizona Weekly Star*, May 13, 1886.

28. Benson, "The Geronimo Campaign," 552–53; Lane, *Chasing Geronimo*, 28–30.

29. AHS, SA, R24, Walker to Torres, May 11, 1886; Miles to Torres, May 14, 1886; *Arizona Weekly Citizen*, May 15, 1886; McCarty and Sonnichsen, "Trini Verdin," 155.

30. AHS, SA, R24, Rivera to Torres, May 11, 1886; Pravadi to Torres, May 14, 1886; Walker to Torres, May 14, 1886; Rivero to Sec. of State, May 15, 1886; *Indian Raids*, 75–76.

31. Radbourne, "Captain Hatfield," 75–78; Gale, "Hatfield Under Fire," 447–68; *Tombstone Epitaph*, May 23, 1886; GC, C. Hatfield, "Expeditions"; NA, RG94, M689, R183, Miles to Howard, May 16, 1886; Barrett, *Geronimo's Story*, 142, quotes Geronimo as saying he lost three men in this fight. But this was either a faulty translation or a faulty memory. The Chiricahuas did not lose one warrior in battle during Miles tenure.

32. Miles, *Personal Recollections*, 490; NA, RG94, M689, R183, Howard to AG, May 10, 1886; Lane, *Chasing Geronimo*, 35; *Tombstone Epitaph*, May 22, 1886.

33. Miles, *Personal Recollections*, 490, 506. Miles identified this man as Kayitah, but he was wrong, for Kayitah had remained on the reservation and served as a scout for Britton Davis. As we shall see, this man was Tah-ni-toe, a member of Naiche's band; NA, RG393, LR, PSC, Crook to Pierce, March 29, 1886.

34. Bailey, *The Devil Has Foreclosed*, 220; *Tombstone Epitaph*, May 19, 1886, May 20, 1886; AHS, SA, R24, Rivera to Secretary of State, May 22, 1886; *Indian Raids*, 79.

35. AHS, SA, R24, Walker to Torres, May 19, 1886; Lane, *Chasing Geronimo*, 37–38; Bigelow, *Bloody Trail*, 181.

36. McCarty and Sonnichsen, "Trini Verdin," 155.

37. Ibid.; Crook to Secretary of War, January 6, 1890, 33, SED 83.

38. NA, RG94, M689, R183, Miles to Howard, May 22, 1886; Berndt Kuhn correspondence, September 9, 2007; AHS, GC, Wade to Miles, May 24, 1886; *Globe Silver Belt*, May 29, 1886; *Arizona Weekly Citizen*, May 29, 1886; Kitt, "Reminiscences," 85–89.

39. NA, RG94, M689, R183, Howard to AG, May 23, 1886.

40. NA, RG393, LR, PSC, Miles to Pierce, May 20, 1886; GC, Pierce to Miles, May 20, 1886; Wade to Miles, May 28, 1886.

41. NA, RG393, LR, PSC, Miles to Pierce, May 24, 1886; *Weekly Arizona Miner*, June 2, 1886; RG92, Kimball to Perry, September 14, 1886; Bigelow, *Bloody Trail*, 187.

42. NA, RG92, Kimball to Perry, September 14, 1886; NA, RG94, M689, R184, Hackett to Secretary of War, August 1, 1886; *Weekly Arizona Miner*, May 26, 1886.

43. Gale, "An Ambush for Nachez," 32; NA, RG393, LS, PSC, Pierce to Miles, June 20, 1886; AHS, GC, Bradley to Miles, May 29, 1886.

44. AHS, GC, Wade to Miles, May 23, 1886, May 24, 1886; Miles to Wade, May 26, 1886; NA, RG393, LR, PSC, Pierce to Miles, May 2, 1886.

45. *Tombstone Epitaph*, May 30, 1886; AHS, GC, Wade to Miles, May 29, 1886; Griswold, "Fort Sill Apaches," 12.

46. Gale, "An Ambush for Nachez," 35–37; *Globe Silver Belt*, May 29, 1886, June 12, 1886.

47. AHS, GC, Wade to Miles, May 29, 1886; Wade to Miles, September 1, 1886.

48. AHS, GC, Wade to Miles, May 29, 1886; Lawton to AAAG, DAZ, June 1, 1886; *Globe Silver Belt*, June 5, 1886.

49. AHS, GC, Walsh to Lawton, June 7, 1886; *Arizona Weekly Citizen*, June 12, 1886; *Globe Silver Belt*, June 12, 1886; Cozzens, *The Struggle for Apacheria*, 554; Bigelow, *Bloody Trail*, 200–209; NA, RG94, M689, R184, Howard to AG, June 8, 1886; LC, Lawton Papers, Lawton to wife, June 22, 1886; Rolak, "General Miles Mirrors," 151.

50. NA, RG94, M689, R183, Howard to AG, May 30, 1886.

51. NA, RG94, M689, R184, Howard to AG, June 8, 1886, June 15, 1886; Sheridan to Howard, June 18, 1886.

52. Allan Radbourne correspondence; AHS, GC, *Arizona Star*, May 17, 1886.

53. McCarty and Sonnichsen, "Trini Verdin," 155–61; AHS, SA, R24, Ruiz to Secretary of State, May 28,1886.

54. McCarty and Sonnichsen, "Trini Verdin," 155–63; AHS, SA, R24, Aguirre to Secretary of State, June 18, 1886.

55. AHS, GC, Lawton to AAAG, DAZ, June 1, 1886.

56. Lane, *Chasing Geronimo*, 49–56; LC, LP, Lawton to wife, June 22, 1886.

57. McCarty and Sonnichsen, "Trini Verdin," 154–63; SA, R24, Rivera to Secretary of State, June 19, 1886. Debo, *Geronimo*, 384, has an anecdote about Geronimo's accuracy with a rifle in a shooting contest with Elbridge Burbank in Oklahoma.

58. SA, R24, Rivera to Secretary of State, June 19, 1886; *Arizona Weekly Citizen*, June 26, 1886; LC, LP, Lawton to wife, June 21, 1886; Lane, *Chasing Geronimo*, 54–56.

59. AHS, SA, R24, Aguirre to Secretary of State, June 23, 1886 (two letters), June 26, 1886.

60. LC, LP, Lawton to wife, June 22, 1886.

CHAPTER 25. ALL CHIRICAHUAS ARE CREATED EQUAL

Epigraph: Lane, *Chasing Geronimo*, 104.

1. LC, LP, Lawton to wife, June 21, 1886.

2. Lane, *Chasing Geronimo*, 55–60; LC, LP, Lawton to wife, June 24, 1886, June 26, 1886 (2 letters).

3. LC, LP, Lawton to wife, June 30, 1886, July 1, 1886, July 2, 1886; Lane, *Chasing Geronimo*, 63–65.

4. LC, LP, Lawton to wife, July 7, 1886; LC, Leonard Wood Papers, Wood to Miles, September 8, 1886; SA, R25, Torres to Secretary of State, July 6, 1886.

5. LC, LP, Lawton to wife, July 7, 1886; Lane, *Chasing Geronimo*, 65–66.

6. AHS, SA, R24, Aguirre to Secretary of the State, June 23, 1886, June 26, 1886.

7. LC, LP, Lawton to wife, July 11, 1886; Lane, *Chasing Geronimo,* 67–68.

8. LC, LP, Lawton to wife, July 14, 1886; Lane, *Chasing Geronimo*, 68–70.

9. LC, LP, Lawton to wife, July 14, 1886; Lane, *Chasing Geronimo*, 69–72. Wood's version, which he apparently inserted in his diary years later, had the battle plan different from Lawton. He remembered that once Brown's Apache scouts were in position, Lawton and he were to lead the infantry on a frontal assault of the village and thus drive the Indians into Brown's scouts. I favor Lawton's version because he described the strategy in a letter to his wife the next day. Stout, "Soldiering and Suffering," 217–18." Trooper Laurence Jerome has a garbled account of this affair, but he was not there.

10. *Arizona Weekly Citizen*, September 11, 1886; Lane, *Chasing Geronimo*, 72; AHS, GC, Gatewood to Miles, October 15, 1886.

11. LC, LP, Lawton to wife, July 14, 1886; Lane, *Chasing Geronimo*, 73–76.

12. LC, LP, Lawton to wife, July 31, 1886, August 1, 1886.

13. Miles, *Personal Recollections*, 495.

14. Ibid.; AHS, GC, Wade to Miles, May 5, 1886; Wade to Miles, May 31, 1886; Bud Shapard correspondence, June 15, 2006.

15. Miles, *Personal Recollections*, 496; *Globe Silver Belt*, July 3, 1886, July 17, 1886; AHS, GC, Wade to Miles, May 31, 1886; Thompson to Pierce, June 23, 1886; Wooster, *Nelson A. Miles*, 149.

16. *Globe Silver Belt*, July 3, 1886, July 17, 1886; Miles, *Personal Recollections*, 496–97.

17. AHS, GC, Wade to Thompson. July 12, 1886; Miles to AG, U.S. Army, July 3, 1886; Miles to AG, Washington, July 5, 1886; Crook to Secretary of War, January 6, 1890, 2–3, 34–35, SED 83; Miles, *Personal Recollections*, 496–97.

18. Several sources, including Wade, identify the man who surrendered as Tah-ni-toe; AHS, GC, Wade to Thompson, June 27, 1886; NA, RG393, LR, PSC, Gibson to Pierce, June 27,1886; *Globe Silver Belt*, July 10, 1886.

19. Betzinez, *I Fought with Geronimo*, 136; OP, box 37, folder 36, Haozous interview.

20. AHS, GC, Wade to Miles, September 7, 1886.

21. NA, RG393, LR, PSC, Beaumont to Pierce, July 3, 1886; Opler, "The Geronimo Campaign of 1886," 372–77.

22. NA, RG94, M233, R71, Register of Enlistments in the United States Army; Quaife, in Davis, *Truth*, xxxiii, cites the letter written from Fort Apache; Kraft, *Gatewood*, 133.

23. Kraft, *Gatewood*, 134.

24. Ibid., 137–39; Gatewood "Surrender of Geronimo."

25. Kraft, *Gatewood*, 140–45.

26. LC, LP, Lawton to wife, August 3, 1886, August 4, 1886; USMHI, "Remarks of General James Parker"; Lane, *Chasing Geronimo*, 88; Gatewood, "Surrender of Geronimo," 56.

27. Lane, *Chasing Geronimo*, 88; LC, LP, Lawton to wife, August 5, 1886, August 6, 1886.

28. Lane, *Chasing Geronimo*, 93; LC, LP, Lawton to wife, August 9, 1886; GC, Lawton to AG, District of Huachuca, August 8, 1886.

29. *Alta California*, September 20, 1886; SA, R23, Aguirre to Secretary of State, July 30, 1886.

30. *Alta California*, September 20, 1886; AHS, SA, R24, Aguirre to Secretary of State, August 16, 1886 (three letters); Montano to Secretary of State, August 10, 1886; C. C. Smith, *Emilio Kosterlitzky*, 81; LC, LP, Benson to Lawton, August 17, 1886.

31. C. C. Smith, *Emilio Kosterlitzky*, 81–82; S. Hatfield, *Chasing Shadows*, 107; *Arizona Weekly Citizen*, August 21, 1886; AHS, GC, Torres to Miles, August 18, 1886.

32. Crook to Secretary of War, January 6, 1890, 33, SED 83.

33. AHS, SA, R24, Aguirre to Secretary of State, August 21, 1886; Aguirre to Governor, August 31, 1886; Torres to Pesqueira, August 24, 1886.

34. AHS, SA, R24, Torres to Pesqueira, August 24, 1886; Aguirre to Benitez, August 22, 1886.

35. C. C. Smith, *Emilio Kosterlitzky*, 82; GC, Forsyth to Thompson, August 21, 1886; Kraft, *Gatewood*, 151–52.

36. C. C. Smith, *Emilio Kosterlitzky*, 82.

37. Ball, *Indeh*, 107. In the last forty years Lozen, sister of Victorio, has become a legendary icon as a woman warrior, whose accomplishments border on the mythical. Many readers have probably wondered about her absence in this narrative, especially given the spate of recent hagiographical books and articles extolling her achievements as a warrior, her supernatural powers, and her clairvoyant abilities during the Victorio and Geronimo periods. Some writers suggest that she was behind Victorio's success. It is an indisputable fact that all of Lozen's remarkable exploits originate with Eve Ball, whose primary source was James Kaywaykla. Ball's book *In the Days of Victorio* relies on his recollections, a boy of three or four years old when the events he talked about took place. Yet, somehow he remembered conversations and events with clarity.

It is quite conceivable that Lozen was with her brother, Victorio, between 1879 and 1880. In June 1883, she returned to the San Carlos Reservation with Loco after Crook's expedition. From this point forward, she remained on the reservation, at San Carlos, Turkey Creek, and Fort Apache, until their removal to Florida in 1886. Thus,

Ball's accounts (deriving from Kaywaykla, who stayed on the reservation with Loco) that place Lozen with Geronimo in 1885–86 would seem to be mistaken. She was not in the final outbreak, not with Geronimo or Mangas, not part of the final surrender, and not pictured in the famous photo of Geronimo's group sitting on the embankment in front of the train. No Chihennes were with Geronimo at the final surrender, and every one of the ten women at the final surrender was with her husband. It is a well-known fact that Lozen never married. In fact, those writers who assert that Lozen participated in the final campaign disregard the words of James Kaywaykla himself. He stated that Lozen was with him on the train that left from Holbrook, thus precluding any possibility that she was with Geronimo.

Even contemporary Chiricahuas and Americans fail to mention her. We can start with Jason Betzinez's *I Fought with Geronimo*, Geronimo's own autobiography *Geronimo's Story of His Life*, and John Bourke's several books and articles. Bourke was fascinated with Apache shamans. He wrote one book exclusively on that subject, *The Medicine Men of the Apache*. In his writings, he referred to two women, both Chihennes, but said not one word about Lozen. Britton Davis, in *The Truth About Geronimo*, wrote about a medicine woman named Huera, but he never mentioned Lozen.

Now I am not suggesting that Lozen was a figment of someone's imagination. In my research of literally thousands of documents in the National Archives and other depositories, I found one reference to her. It confirms the genealogical account of Gillett Griswold that Lozen "probably died in Alabama." In the National Archives, Register of Indian Prisoners at Mount Vernon, there appears a note dated June 17, 1889, "female Lozen died."

Morris Opler's collection of materials, which is housed at Cornell, contains accounts of the interviews that became the source material for his anthropological books and articles on the Chiricahua Apaches. Because his informants were silent on Lozen as a woman warrior, he was skeptical of Ball's characterizations. In a response to a friend's inquiry about Lozen, Opler agreed with Gillett Griswold's findings. Ball's identification of Lozen in the celebrated photo in front of the train particularly disturbed him. According to him, Lozen remained on the reservation and was not a part of the final outbreak. He further explained:

> I have many accounts of Chiricahua women who were notable for one thing or another but no one named Lozen is involved. I also ran through the 900 pages of two unpublished Chiricahua autobiographical accounts that carry the Chiricahua story from the pre-American period through the Florida, Alabama, Fort Sill, and Mescalero reservation phases, without encountering tales of the exploits of Lozen. I have a good deal of material from informants and other sources regarding the events in which she [Ball] claims Lozen took a prominent or crucial part but [nothing on] Lozen. . . . I worked with Charlie Istee, the youngest of Victorio's four sons and the only one to survive the Victorio Wars, without hearing about warrior status in regard to Lozen.

Eve Ball was truly a remarkable woman, who was an inspiration to a host of writers, including me. Like Opler, I remain skeptical of Lozen's exploits during the Victorio Wars, and I am certain that she had no role in the final Geronimo War of 1885–86. Ball, *In the Days of Victorio*, 10–11, 14–15, 76–77; S. Robinson, *Apache Voices*, 13; OP, box 37, Folder 2; NA, RG393, Register of Indian Prisoners at Mount Vernon.

38. Kraft, *Gatewood*, 152–155; OP, box 37, Folder 36, Haozous autobiography; AHS, GC, Wrattan's statement as recorded by S. M. Huddleson, "An Interview With Geronimo and His Guardian, Mr. G M. Wrattan and the Story of the Surrender of Geronimo as told by Mr. Wrattan to Dr. S. M Huddleson."

39. Kraft, *Gatewood,* 156–58; AHS, GC, Martine and Kayitah's account.

40. Kraft, *Gatewood*, 158–163; AHS, GC, Martine and Kayitah's account; Gatewood, "Surrender of Geronimo," 58–63; GC, Wrattan's statement; S. Robinson, *Apache Voices*, 49–54; Debo, *Geronimo*, 287.

41. NA, RG94, M689, R184, "The President's Dispatch," August 24, 1886; Miles to AAG, Division of the Pacific, July 3, 1886, July 7, 1886; Sheridan to Secretary of War, July 30, 1886.

42. Ibid., Sheridan to Miles, July 15, 1886.

43. Shapard, "Chief Loco," 280–86.

44. "Transcript of Stenographers Notes of a Conference between Honorable William C, Endicott, Secretary of War, and Chatto," July 26, 1886, 41, SED 83.

45. NA, RG94, M689, R184, Miles to AG, Division of the Pacific, July 7, 1886. In his contemporary reports, Miles described the overall situation of the Chiricahuas at Fort Apache in much milder terms than he did in his book *Personal Recollections*. In this account, he went overboard to justify his recommendation to remove the Chiricahuas from Fort Apache: "The entire camp was an arsenal, the breeding place, the recruiting depot, the hospital, the asylum of the hostiles." The only truthful part of this characterization was that the reservation Chiricahuas were armed. The rest of this self-serving and exaggerated statement suggesting an active cooperation between the hostiles and the reservation Chiricahuas was pure hogwash. Miles, *Personal Recollections*, 504.

46. Sheridan to Secretary of War, July 30, 1886, 5, SED 83.

47. Porter, *Paper Medicine Man*, 215–16.

48. Sheridan to Miles, July 31, 1886, 8–9; Miles to Sheridan, August 1, 1886, 9, SED 83.

49. Miles to Sheridan, August 2, 1886, 9–10, SED 83.

50. NA, RG94, M689, R184, Lamar to Endicott, August 10, 1886; Cleveland's decision was contained in "The President's Dispatch," August 24, 1886; M689, R186, Ross to Cleveland, August 14, 1886; Drum to Dorst, August 16, 1886; Miles to AG, August 20, 1886; Drum to AG, August 24, 1886; Lamar to Secretary of War, August 25, 1886; Sheridan to Miles, August 25, 1886; SED 83, 16–19; GC, Wade to Miles, August 14, 1886.

51. NA, RG94, M689, R186, Miles to Sheridan, August 26, 1886; NA, RG393, LS, DAZ, Miles to AG, September 29, 1886.

52. NA, RG94, M689, R184, Miles to AG, Washington, August 28, 1886.

53. Miles, *Personal Recollections*, 503–504; Cooney's and Toclanny's accounts are in Crook to Secretary of War, January 6, 1890, SED 83, 34–35; Opler, "The Geronimo Campaign," 381; Betzinez, *I Fought with Geronimo*, 140–41.

54. Goodwin, "Experiences of an Indian Scout," 2, 72; GP, Curley interview, 43–45; Betzinez, *I Fought with Geronimo*, 140–41, 144; Opler, "The Geronimo Campaign," 382.

55. AHS, GC, Wade to Miles, September 7, 1886.

56. LC, LP, Miles to Lawton, August 23, 1886; NA, RG94, M689, R186, Miles to Sheridan, August 26, 1886.

57. LC, LP, Miles to Forysth, August 29, 1886.

58. Kraft, *Gatewood*, 176–78; Lane, *Chasing Geronimo*, 106–107.

59. LC, LP, Miles to Lawton, August 31, 1886 (three letters).

60. Kraft, *Gatewood*, 183–87, presents a complete account of this affair.

61. LC, LP, Lawton to wife, September 2, 1886; Miles to Lawton, September 3, 1886; GC, Lawton to Miles, September 2, 1886.

62. Kraft, *Gatewood*, 190–96; Miles, *Personal Recollections*, 519–32.

63. Kraft, *Gatewood*, 190–96; Miles, *Personal Recollections*, 519–32.

64. Lane, *Chasing Geronimo*, 111. In a telegram dated September 8, 1886, to the commanding officers at Fort Grant, Fort Apache, and the post at San Carlos, Captain Thompson clears up the identity of the man referred to as Naiche's brother. He warned them to be on the lookout for the seven Chiricahuas (two men, three women, one teenage boy, and one child) who had escaped from Lawton's command. The two men were Natculbaye and the "brother" of Naiche, otherwise known as Atelnietze. GC, Thompson to CO, Fort Grant, San Carlos, Fort Apache, September 8, 1886.

65. Faulk, *The Geronimo Campaign*, 170, quotes Miles's report of September 24, 1886.

66. Lane, *Chasing Geronimo*, 112; Wooster, *Nelson A. Miles*, 151–56.

67. Debo, *Geronimo*, 295–98.

68. Lane, *Chasing Geronimo*, 112; Wooster, *Nelson A. Miles*, 151–62. Wooster has an objective and thorough account of the circumstances surrounding Miles's decision and the ensuing controversy between Miles and Howard, Sheridan, Drum, and President Cleveland.

69. NA, RG393, LR, PSC, Jones to Pierce, September 7, 1886; GP, Curley interview; Noskin account; AHS, GC, Miles to Wade, September 1, 1886; Wade to Miles, September 7, 1886; Strover, "The Apaches' Last Trek,"16–18.

70. Bud Shapard correspondence. Strover, "The Apaches' Last Trek," 6, 18.

71. Schubert, *Voices of the Buffalo Soldier*, 146–47.

Epilogue

1. Debo, *Geronimo*, 304–309.

2. East, "Apache Prisoners in Fort Marion," 2, 17–18.

3. Ibid., 3, 4.

4. Debo, *Geronimo*, 317–18; Shapard, "Chief Loco," 417–18.

5. Porter, *Paper Medicine Man*, 226–33.

6. Ibid.

7. Skinner, *The Apache Rock Crumbles*, 159–61.

8. Ibid., 164–65.

9. Ibid., 175–80.

10. Ibid., 220, 268–69.

11. Debo, *Geronimo*, 344–45; Shapard, "Chief Loco," 448, 454–55.

12. Debo, *Geronimo*, 363–68.

13. LC, Scott Papers, box 70, "Conference with Apache Prisoners of War on Fort Sill Reservation," September 21, 1911.

14. Debo, *Geronimo,* 447–50.

15. GP, Curley interview.

BIBLIOGRAPHY

MANUSCRIPT MATERIALS, UNPUBLISHED DOCUMENTS, COLLECTIONS

Archivo Historico de Sonora, Hermosillo, Sonora.
Arizona Historical Society
    Bourke, John, diary
    Connell, Charles T. Papers
    Devers, William, File
    Gatewood, Charles, Collection: Charles Hatfield, "Expeditions Against the Chiricahua Apaches, 1882–1883"; "Geronimo campaigns, 1885–86"
    Glover, James Benton, MS288, Recollections
    Hughes, Fred, Papers
    Morton, Charles, Papers
    Roberts, Charles, diary
    San Carlos Apache Reservation, Letterbooks, MS 707San Carlos Apache Reservation, Microfilm Collection, three rolls
    Sonora State Archives, Rolls 19–25
    Wardwell, William L., File
Arizona State Library. Arizona Secretary of the Territory correspondence with the Governor of Sonora, the U. S. Consul and Arizona Citizens.
Arizona State Museum, Grenville Goodwin Papers
Arizona State University Library. Copy of Hubert Howe Bancroft scraps, a collection of Arizona items clipped from California newspapers.
Bowdoin College, Brunswick, Maine. Oliver Otis Howard Papers.
Cornell University, Division of Rare and Manuscript Collections. Morris Edward Opler Papers, no. 14/25/3238.
Fort Bowie National Historic Site. Fort Bowie Files: Medical Records.
Geronimo Springs Museum, Truth or Consequences, New Mexico. Keith Humphries Papers.

Graham County Historical Society. Wright Brothers File.

Field Artillery Museum, Fort Sill, Oklahoma. Gillett Griswold. "The Fort Sill Apaches: Their Vital Statistics, Tribal Origins, Antecedents."

Kuhn, Berndt. Correspondence 1998–2008.

Library of Congress:
    Lawton, Henry, Papers
    Scott, Hugh, Papers
    Wood, Leonard, Papers

Museum of New Mexico, Santa Fe, New Mexico. Benjamin Thomas Papers.

Rutherford B. Hayes Library, Fremont, Ohio. George Crook Papers.

United States Congress
    49th Congress, 2nd session, House Executive Documents 301, 302.
    51st Congress, 1st session, Senate Executive Document 83.

U.S. Army Military History Institute, Carlisle Barracks, Pa. George Crook diary, 1885–1886; Remarks of General James Parker, USA; Charles Elliott, "Campaign Against the Chiricahua Apache Indians, Geronimo and others, 1885–1886."

U.S. Department of the Interior. Annual Reports of the Commissioner of Indian Affairs, 1871–1877.

U.S. National Archives and Records Administration
    Record Group 48, Records of the Indian Division of the Office of the Secretary of the Interior.
    Record Group 75, Records of the Bureau of Indian Affairs. Microcopy 234, Letters Received, 1824–80. Arizona Superintendency, 1863–1880, rolls 3–28; Letters Received, New Mexico Superintendency, 1824–1880, R546–582; microcopy 734, Records of the Arizona Superintendency of Indian Affairs, 8 rolls; T21, Records of the New Mexico Superintendency of Indian Affairs, 1849–1880, 30 rolls; microcopy 574, Special Files of the Office of Indian Affairs, roll 74, file no. 270, Investigation of the San Carlos Agent by Inspector J. H. Hammond. Records of Inspection of the Field Jurisdiction of the Office of Indian Affairs, 1873–1900, M1070, rolls 1–2, 29, 45.
    Record Group 92, Quartermaster Consolidated Files. Expenditures Relating to Indian Wars.
    Record Group 94, Records of the Adjutant General's office, 1780s–1917. M233, Registers of Enlistment in the United States Army, R70–71, Indian Scouts 1866–1914; M666, R123, Correspondence Relating to the treaty between Cochise and General Howard; R265, Correspondence relating to the removal of the Chiricahua Apache Indians to the San Carlos Reservation, 1876–77; R366, Correspondence relating to Military operations against the Warm Springs Indians who fled from the San Carlos Reservation in 1877–79. M689, R96–97, Papers relating to the outbreak of violence by the Chiricahua Apaches who escaped from San Carlos in September 1881; R173–202, Papers relating to the Chiricahua Apaches, 1883–1906, M1495, Special Files of the Headquarters Division of the Missouri, R14, Victorio campaign.

Record Group 123, Records of the United States Court of Claims, Indian Depredation Claims.

Record Group 153, Records of the Office of the Judge Advocate General (Army). Case File of Military Courts and Commissions, file RR-440, Investigation and trial of Captain Emmet Crawford.

Record Group 217, Records of the U.S. General Accounting Office.

Record Group 391, Records of United States Regular Army Mobile Units, 1821–1942. Records relating to Indians as Soldiers. Descriptive Roll of Warm Springs and Chiricahua Apache Indian bands, 1884–85.

Record Group 393, Record of United States Army Continental Commands, 1821–1920. Department of Arizona, Letters Received, 1879–1886, Letters Sent, 1874–1886; Unregistered Letters Received, District of Arizona, 1863–1871; New Mexico, LR, District of New Mexico, M1088, R27–60; M1072, LS, District of New Mexico, R4–7. Miscellaneous Records, Department of New Mexico. Miscellaneous Records, Department of Arizona, 1876–1879. Brief of Affairs at San Carlos, 1877–78; Miscellaneous Records, 1882–1900, Post at San Carlos; Field Letters Sent and Received, Department of Arizona, 1878–1881; Letters Sent, Fort Thomas; Post Records, Fort Bowie, Fort Craig, Fort Huachuca, Camp Rucker, Post at San Carlos. Letters Sent Fort Cummings, Fort Tularosa. Returns from Military Posts, Fort Bowie; Register of Indian Prisoners at Mount Vernon, Alabama.

University of Arizona, Special Collections.

Documents relating to the Apache Campaign of 1885–86

Lummis, Charles, Papers

Peck Family Papers

West, Lt. Frank, diary MS 288

University of Chicago, Special Collections Research Center.

Eggan, Fred, Papers

Tax, Sol Papers

University of Oklahoma, Western History Collections. Jason Betzinez, "My People: A Story of the Apaches."

University of Oregon, Eugene. George Crook Papers.

University of Texas, El Paso. Janos Archives, 1700–1899.

Yale University, New Haven, Conn., Beinecke Rare Book and Manuscript Library. John Vance Lauderdale Papers, WA MSS, S-1317.

AMERICAN NEWSPAPERS

Albuquerque Evening Review
Albuquerque Journal
Army and Navy Journal
Clifton Clarion
(El Paso) *Lone Star*
Globe Silver Belt

Las Cruces Borderer
(Las Cruces) *Rio Grande Republican*
(Las Cruces) *Thirty-Four*
Mesilla News
New York Times
(Prescott) *Arizona Miner*
(Prescott) *Weekly Arizona Miner*
(San Francisco) *Alta California*
Santa Fe New Mexican
(Silver City) *Grant County Herald*
(Silver City) *New Southwest and Grant County Herald*
(Silver City) *Southwest Sentinel*
Tombstone Epitaph
(Tucson) *Arizona Citizen*
(Tucson) *Arizona Daily Star*

MEXICAN NEWSPAPERS

SONORA

(Ures) *Boletin Oficial*
Estrella de Occidente
La Era Nueva

CHIHUAHUA

Oficial Periodico del Gobierno del Estado de Chihuahua

BOOKS, ARTICLES, AND PAPERS

Acuña, Rodolfo F. *Sonoran Strongman: Ignacio Pesqueira and His Times.* Tucson: University of Arizona Press, 1974.

Almada, Francisco R. *Diccionario de Historia, Geografia, y Biografia Chihuahuenses.* Chihuahua: Talleres Graficos del Gobierno del Estado, 1927.

———. *Diccionario de Historia, Geografia, y Biografia Sonorenses.* Hermosillo: Instituto Sonorense de Cultura, 1990.

Alonso, Ana Maria. *Thread of Blood: Colonialism, Revolution, and Gender on Mexico's Northern Frontier.* Tucson: University of Arizona Press, 1995.

Altshuler, Constance Wynn. *Cavalry Yellow and Infantry Blue: Army Officers in Arizona Between 1851 and 1886.* Tucson: Arizona Historical Society, 1991.

———. *Starting with Defiance: Nineteenth Century Arizona Military Posts.* Tucson: Arizona Historical Society, 1983.

Aranda, Daniel D. "Apache Depredations in Doña Ana County: An Incident in Victorio's War." *Southern New Mexico Historical Review* 3 (January 1996): 3–8.

———. "Josanie: Apache Warrior." *True West,* 23 (May–June 1976): 38–39, 62.

————. "Santiago McKinn, Indian Captive." *Real West* 24 (June 1981): 41–43.

Bailey, Lynn R., ed. *The Devil Has Foreclosed: The Private Journal of George Whitwell Parsons: The Concluding Arizona Years, 1882–1887.* Tucson: Westernlore Press, 1997.

————. *A Tenderfoot in Tombstone: The Private Journal of George Whitwell Parsons: The Turbulent Years, 1880–1882.* Tucson: Westernlore Press, 1996.

————. *The Valiants: The Tombstone Rangers and Apache War Frivolities.* Tucson: Westernlore Press, 1999.

————. *We'll All Wear Silk Hats: The Erie and Chiricahua Cattle Companies and the Rise of Corporate Ranching in the Sulphur Springs Valley of Arizona, 1883–1909.* Tucson: Westernlore Press, 1994.

Bailey, Lynn R., and Don Chaput. *Cochise County Stalwarts: A Who's Who of the Territorial Years.* 2 vols. Tucson: Westernlore Press, 2000.

Ball, Eve. "The Apache Scouts: A Chiricahua Appraisal." *Arizona and the West* 7 (Winter 1965): 315–28.

————. *In the Days of Victorio: Recollections of a Warm Springs Apache,* Tucson: University of Arizona Press, 1970.

Ball, Eve, with Nora Henn and Lynda Sanchez. *Indeh: An Apache Odyssey.* Provo, Utah: Brigham University Press, 1980.

Barnes, Will C. *Apaches and Longhorns: The Reminiscences of Will C. Barnes.* Tucson: University of Arizona Press, 1982.

————. *Arizona Place Names.* Revised and enlarged by Byrd H. Granger. Tucson: University of Arizona Press, 1979.

Barrett, Stephen M. *Geronimo's Story of His Life.* New York: Garrett Press, 1969.

Barrick, Nora, and Mary Taylor. *The Mesilla Guard, 1851–1861.* El Paso: Texas Western Press, 1976.

Basehart, Harry W. "Chiricahua Apache Subsistence and Socio-Political Organization." A report of the Mescalero-Chiricahua Claims Project. Contract research no. 290-154. University of New Mexico, 1959.

Basso, Keith H., and Morris E. Opler, , eds. *Apachean Culture History and Ethnology.* Tucson: University of Arizona Press, 1971.

Benson, Harry C. "The Geronimo Campaign. " In *Eyewitnesses to the Indian Wars: The Struggle for Apacheria,* ed. Peter Cozzens, 552–56. Mechanicsburg, Pa.: Stackpole Books, 2001.

Betzinez, Jason, with Wilbur Sturtevant Nye. *I Fought with Geronimo.* New York: Bonanza Books, 1959.

Biddle, Ellen McGowan. *Reminiscences of a Soldier's Wife.* Mechanicsburg, Pa.: Stackpole Books, 2002.

Bigelow, John. *On the Bloody Trail of Geronimo.* Foreword, introduction, and notes by Arthur Woodward. Tucson: Westernlore Press, 1986.

Billington, Monroe Lee. *New Mexico's Buffalo Soldiers, 1866–1890.* Niwot: University Press of Colorado, 1991.

Bourke, John G. *An Apache Campaign In the Sierra Madre.* New York: Charles Scribner's Sons, 1958.

————. *The Apache Scouts*. Bisbee, Ariz.: Frontera House Press, 1995.

————. *On the Border with Crook*. New York: Time-Life Books, 1980.

Boyer, Ruth McDonald, and Narcissus Duffy Gayton. *Apache Mothers and Daughters*. Norman: University of Oklahoma Press, 1992.

Bret Harte, John. "Conflict at San Carlos: The Military-Civilian Struggle for Control, 1882–1885." *Arizona and the West* 15 (Spring 1973): 27–44.

————. "The San Carlos Indian Reservation, 1872–1886." Ph.D. dissertation, University of Arizona, Tucson, 1972.

————. "The Strange Case of Joseph C. Tiffany: Indian Agent in Disgrace." *Journal of Arizona History* 16 (Winter 1975): 383–404.

Bryan, Howard. *True Tales of the American Southwest: Pioneer Recollections of Frontier Adventures*. Santa Fe: Clear Light Publishers, 1998.

Calvin, Ross, ed. *Lieutenant Emory Reports: Notes of a Military Reconnaissance*. Albuquerque: University of New Mexico Press, 1968.

Carmony, Neil B. *Apache Days and Tombstone Nights: John Clum's Autobiography*. Silver City, N.Mex.: High-Lonesome Books, 1997.

————. *Whiskey, Six-Guns and Red-Light Ladies: George Hand's Saloon Diary. Tucson. 1874–1878*. Silver City, N.Mex.: High-Lonesome Books, 1994.

Carpenter, John A. *Sword and Olive Branch: Oliver Otis Howard*. Pittsburgh, Pa.: University of Pittsburgh Press, 1964.

Carroll, John, comp. and ed. *The Papers of the Order of Indian Wars*. Fort Collins, Colo.: Old Army Press, 1975.

————. *The Unpublished Papers of the Order of Indian Wars*. Book 6. New Brunswick, N.J.: Privately published, 1977.

Carter, William H. *From Yorktown to Santiago: With the Sixth U. S. Cavalry*. Austin, Tex.: State House Press, 1989.

————. *The Life of Lieutenant General Chaffee*. Chicago: University of Chicago Press, 1917.

Charles, Tom. "The Old Scouts of the Mescaleros." *New Mexico Magazine* 19 (August 1931): 17–19.

Chavez, Jose Carlos. "Indio Ju." *Tomo* 11 (April 15, 1938): 365–67, 376–77.

Clendenen, Clarence C. *Blood on the Border: The United States Army and the Mexican Irregulars*. London: Macmillan Company, 1969.

Clum, Woodworth. *Apache Agent: The Story of John P. Clum*. Lincoln: University of Nebraska Press, 1978.

Collins, Charles. *Apache Nightmare: The Battle at Cibecue Creek*. Norman: University of Oklahoma Press, 1999.

————. *The Great Escape: The Apache Outbreak of 1881*. Tucson: Westernlore Press, 1994.

Colyer, Vincent. *Peace With the Apaches of New Mexico and Arizona: Report of Vincent Colyer, Member of Board of Indian Commissioners, 1871*. Tucson, Ariz.: Territorial Press, 1964.

Corbusier, William T. *Verde to San Carlos: Recollections of a Famous Army Surgeon and His Observant Family on the Western Frontier, 1869–1886*. Tucson: Dale Stuart King, 1968.

Couchman, Donald Howard. *Cooke's Peak—Pasaron Por Aqui: A Focus on United States History in Southwestern New Mexico*. Santa Fe, N.Mex.: Bureau of Land Management, 1990.

Cozzens, Peter. *Eyewitnesses to the Indian Wars: The Struggle for Apacheria*. Mechanicsburg, Pa.: Stackpole Books, 2001.

Cruse, Thomas. *Apache Days and After*. Lincoln: University of Nebraska Press, 1987.

Daly, Henry W. "The Geronimo Campaign." *Journal of the United States Cavalry Association* 19 (July 1908): 68–103; (October 1908)" 247–76.

———. "Scouts, Good and Bad." *American Legion Monthly* 5 (August 1928): 24–25, 66–70.

Davis, Britton. "A Short Account of the Chiricahua Tribe of Apache Indians and the Causes Leading to the Outbreak of May 1885." In *The Unpublished Papers of the Order of Indian Wars, book 6, ed*. John Carroll, 23–27. New Brunswick, N.J.: Privately published, 1977.

———. *The Truth About Geronimo*. Ed. Milo Milton Quaife. Chicago: Lakeside Press, 1951.

Davisson, Lori. "Fort Apache Arizona Territory: 1879–1922." Tucson Corral of the Westerners' *Smoke Signal* 33 (Spring 1977): 62–80.

———. "New Light on the Cibecue Fight: Untangling Apache Identities." *Journal of Arizona History* 20 (Winter 1979): 423–44.

Debo, Angie. *Geronimo: The Man, His Time, His Place*. Norman: University of Oklahoma Press, 1976.

Dixon, David. *Hero of Beecher Island: The Life and Military Career of George A. Forsyth*. Lincoln: University of Nebraska Press, 1994.

Dunlap, H. E. "Clay Beauford—Welford C. Bridwell." *Arizona Historical Review* 3 (October 1930): 44–66.

East, Omega G. "The Apache Prisoners at Fort Marion, 1886–87." 6 (January 1969): 11–27; (April 1969): 2–23; (July 1969): 4–23; (October 1969): 20–38.

Eggan, Fred, ed. *Social Anthropology of North American Tribes*. Chicago: University of Chicago Press, 1937.

Elliott, Charles P. "An Indian Reservation under General George Crook." *Journal of the American Military Institute* 12 (Summer 1948): 91–102.

Ellis, Richard N. *General Pope and U.S. Indian Policy*. Albuquerque: University of New Mexico Press, 1970.

Erickson, Neil. "Trailing the Apache." *Old Army* (August 1931): 6–7, 43.

Escarcega, Alfonso. *La Apacheria en Chihuahua*. Chihuahua City, Chihuahua, Mexico: Privately printed, 1975.

Etulain, Richard W., ed. *New Mexican Lives: Profiles and Historical Stories*. Albuquerque: University of New Mexico Press, 2002.

Farish, Thomas Edwin. *History of Arizona*. 8 vols. San Francisco, Calif.: Filmer Brothers Electrotype, 1915–1918.

Faulk, Odie B. *The Geronimo Campaign*. New York: Oxford University Press, 1969.

Ferguson, Lewis. "Private Myers's First Scout." *Harpers Weekly*, April 13, 1894, 965–66.

Floyd, Dale E. *Chronological List of Actions, etc. with Indians from January 15, 1837, to January 1891*. Fort Collins, Colo.: Old Army Press, 1979.

Fontana, Bernard L., ed. *An Englishman's Arizona: The Ranching Letters of Herbert R. Hislop 1876–1878*. Tucson: Overland Press, 1965.

Forsyth, George A. Introduction by David Dixon. *Thrilling Days in Army Life*. Lincoln: University of Nebraska Press, 1994.

Frazer, Robert. *The Apaches of the White Mountain Reservation, Arizona*. Philadelphia, Pa.: Indian Rights Association, 1885.

Frazer, Robert W. *Forts of the West*. Norman: University of Oklahoma Press, 1977.

French, William. *Recollections of a Western Ranchman*. Silver City, N.Mex.: High-Lonesome Books, 1990.

Gale, Jack C. "An Ambush for Natchez." *True West* 27 (July–August 1980): 32–37.

———. "Hatfield Under Fire, May 15, 1886: An Episode of the Geronimo Campaigns." *Journal of Arizona History* 18 (Winter 1977): 447–68.

———. "Lebo in Pursuit." *Journal of Arizona History* 21 (Spring 1980): 13–24.

Gatewood, Charles. "The Surrender of Geronimo." In *Geronimo and the End of the Apache Wars*, ed. C. L. Sonnichsen, 53–70. Tucson: Arizona Historical Society, 1987.

Giese, Dale F. *Forts of New Mexico: Echoes of the Bugle*. Silver City, N.Mex.: Privately printed, 1991.

Goff, John S. *Arizona Biographical Dictionary*. Cave Creek, Ariz.: Black Mountain Press, 1983.

———. *Arizona Territorial Officials: The Governors 1863–1912*. Cave Creek, Ariz.: Black Mountain Press, 1978.

Goodwin, Grenville, ed. "Experiences of an Indian Scout." *Arizona Historical Review* 7 (January–April 1936): 31–68, 31–72.

———. *The Social Organization of the Western Apache*. Tucson: University of Arizona Press, 1969.

———. *Western Apache Raiding and Warfare*. Edited by Keith Basso. Tucson: University of Arizona Press, 1971.

Graves, Laura. *Thomas Varker Keam: Indian Trader*. Norman: University of Oklahoma Press, 1998.

Grover, Sylvester. "Statement of Private Sylvester Grover." *Winners of the West* 3 (December 30, 1925).

Hanna, Robert. "With Crawford in Mexico." *Arizona Historical Review* 6 (April 1935): 56–65.

Hart, Herbert M. *Old Forts of the Far West*. New York: Bonanza Books, 1965.

Hatfield, Shelley Bowen. *Chasing Shadows: Apaches and Yaquis Along the United States-Mexican Border, 1876–1911*. Albuquerque: University of New Mexico Press, 1998.

Hayes, Alden. *A Portal to Paradise*. Tucson: University of Arizona Press, 1999.

Heitman, Francis B. *Historical Register and Dictionary of the United States Army*. Urbana: University of Illinois Press, 1965.

History of Monticello Canyon: Centennial Celebration. Monticello, N.Mex.: Privately printed, April 1984.

Hodge, Frederick Webb, ed. *Handbook of American Indians North of Mexico.* 2 vols. Totowa, N.J.: Rowman and Littlefield, 1975.

Hooker, Forrestine C. *Child of the Fighting Tenth: On the Frontier with Buffalo Soldiers.* Ed. Steve Wilson. New York: Oxford University Press, 2003.

Horn, Tom. *The Life of Tom Horn: Government Scout and Interpreter.* Norman: University of Oklahoma Press, 1986.

Howard, Oliver Otis. *My Life and Experiences Among Our Hostile Indians.* New York: Da Capo Press, 1972.

Hudson, G. B. "Chief Geronimo's Captive." *Frontier Times* 5 (June 1928): 354–55.

Hutton, Paul Andrew. *Phil Sheridan and His Army.* Norman: University of Oklahoma Press, 1999.

Indian Raids as Reported in the Silver City Enterprise. Silver City, N.Mex.: William H. Mullane, 1968.

Ingstad. Helge. *The Apache Indians: In Search of a Missing Tribe.* Translated by Janine K. Stenehjem. Lincoln: University of Nebraska Press, 2004.

Jones, Daniel W. *Forty Years Among the Indians.* Salt Lake City: Bookcraft, 1960.

Julyan, Robert. *The Mountains of New Mexico.* Albuquerque: University of New Mexico Press, 2006.

———. *The Place Names of New Mexico.* Albuquerque: University of New Mexico Press, 1996.

Kitt, Mrs. George F. "Reminiscences of Juan I. Tellez." *Arizona Historical Review* 7 (January 1936): 85–89.

Kraft, Louis. *Gatewood and Geronimo.* Albuquerque: University of New Mexico Press, 2000.

———, ed. *Lt. Charles Gatewood and His Apache Wars Memoir.* Lincoln: University of Nebraska Press, 2005.

Kvasnicka, Robert M., and Herman J. Viola. *The Commissioners of Indian Affairs, 1824– 1977.* Lincoln: University of Nebraska Press, 1979.

Lane, Jack C., ed. *Chasing Geronimo: The Journal of Leonard Wood May–September, 1886.* Albuquerque: University of New Mexico Press, 1970.

Laumbach, Karl W. *Hembrillo: An Apache Battlefield of the Victorio War.* Tularosa, N.Mex.: Human Systems Research, 2000.

Leckie, William H. *The Buffalo Soldiers: A Narrative of the Negro Cavalry in the West.* Norman: University of Oklahoma Press, 1967.

Lekson, Stephen H. *Nana's Raid: Apache Warfare in Southern New Mexico, 1881.* El Paso: Texas Western Press, 1987.

Lister, Florence C., and Robert H. Lister. *Chihuahua: Storehouse of Storms.* Albuquerque: University of New Mexico Press, 1966.

Lockwood, Frank C. *The Apache Indians.* New York: Macmillan, 1938.

———. *Arizona Characters.* Los Angeles: Times Mirror Press, 1928.

Ludwig, Larry L., and James L. Stute. *The Battle of K-H Butte: Apache Outbreak—1881: Arizona Territory.* Tucson: Westernlore Press, 1993.

Lummis, Charles F. *General Crook and the Apache Wars*. Flagstaff, Ariz.: Northland Press, 1966.

———. *The Land of Poco Tiempo*. Albuquerque: University of New Mexico Press, 1966.

Margaillan, Cynthia. "The Story of My Great-Great Grandmother and Geronimo." *Cochise Quarterly* 24 (Spring 1885): 29–30.

Mason, Joyce Evelyn. "Indians Scouts in the Apache Wars, 1870–1886." Ph.D. thesis, Indiana University, 1970. Mazzanovich, Anton. *Trailing Geronimo*. Los Angeles: privately printed, 1931.

McCarty, Kieran, and C. L. Sonnichsen. "Trini Verdin and the Truth of History." *Journal of Arizona History* 14 (Summer 1973): 149–64.

McChristian, Douglas C. *Fort Bowie, Arizona: Combat Post of the Southwest, 1858–1894*. Norman: University of Oklahoma Press, 2005.

McFarland, Elizabeth. *Wilderness of the Gila*. Albuquerque: University of New Mexico Press, 1974.

McKenna, James A. *Black Range Tales*. Glorieta, N.Mex.: Rio Grande Press, 1984.

Meketa, Charles, and Jacqueline Meketa. *One Blanket and Ten Days' Rations: 1st Infantry New Mexico Volunteers in Arizona 1864–1866*. Globe, Ariz.: Southwest Parks and Monuments, 1980.

Miles, Nelson A. "How U.S. Troops Caught Geronimo." *Frontier Times* 9 (February 1932): 193–96.

———. *Personal Recollections of General Nelson A. Miles*. New York: Da Capo Press, 1969.

Miller, Darlis A. *The California Column in New Mexico*. Albuquerque: University of New Mexico Press, 1982.

———. *Captain Jack Crawford: Buckskin Poet, Scout, and Showman*. Albuquerque: University of New Mexico Press, 1993.

Miller, Harold. "Nana's Raid of 1881." *Password* 19 (Summer 1974): 51–70.

Myers, Lee. "New Mexico Volunteers, 1862–1866." Tucson Corral of the Westerners *Smoke Signal* 37 (Spring 1979): 138–52.

Nentvig, Juan, S. J. *Rudo Ensaya: A Description of Sonora and Arizona in 1764*. Translated, clarified, and annotated by Alberto Francisco Pradeau and Robert R. Rasmussen. Tucson: University of Arizona Press, 1980.

Ogle, Ralph H. *Federal Control of the Western Apaches, 1848–1886*. Albuquerque: University of New Mexico Press, 1970.

Opler, Morris Edward. *An Apache Life-Way: Yhe Economic, Social, and Religious Institutions of the Chiricahua Indians*. Chicago: University of Chicago Press, 1965.

———. *Apache Odyssey: A Journey Between Two Worlds*. New York: Holt, Rinehart, and Winston, 1969.

———. "A Chiricahua Apache's Account of the Geronimo Campaign of 1886." *New Mexico Historical Review* 13 (October 1938): 360–86.

———. "Chiricahua Apache Material Relating to Sorcery." *Primitive Man* 19 (July–October 1946), 81–92.

————. "Mountain Spirits of the Chiricahua Apache." *Masterkey* 20, no. 4 (1946): 125–31.

————. *Myths and Tales of the Chiricahua Apache Indians*. American Folklore Society, 1942.

————. "Some Implications of Culture Theory for Anthropology and Psychology." *American Journal of Orthopsychiatry* 18 (October 1948): 611–21.

Opler, Morris Edward, and Edward F. Castetter. *The Ethnobiology of the Chiricahua and Mescalero Apache*. Albuquerque: University of New Mexico Press, 1936.

Ortiz, Alfonso. *Handbook of North American Indians*. Vol. 10. Washington: Smithsonian Institution, 1983.

Parker, James. *The Old Army Memories*. Philadelphia: Dorrance, 1929.

Patch, Joseph Dorst. *Reminiscences of Fort Huachuca, Arizona*. Privately printed, no date.

Perry, Richard J. *Western Apache Heritage: People of the Mountain Corridor*. Austin: University of Texas Press, 1991.

Pierce, Michael D. *The Most Promising Young Officer: A Life of Ranald Slidell Mackenzie*. Norman: University of Oklahoma Press, 1993.

Porter, Joseph C. *Paper Medicine Man: John Gregory Bourke and His American West*. Norman: University of Oklahoma Press, 1986.

Radbourne, Allan. "Captain Hatfield and the Chiricahuas." In *Ho, For the Great West*, ed. Barry C Johnson, 70–81. English Westerners' Society Special Publication 6A (1980).

————. "Geronimo's Contraband Cattle." *Missionaries, Indians, and Soldiers*, English Westerners' Society Special Publication 8A (1996): 1–24.

————. "Geronimo's Last Raid into Arizona." *True West* 41 (March 1994): 22–29.

————. "The Juh-Geronimo Surrender of 1879." *English Westerners' Society Brand Book* 21 (1983): 1–18.

————. *Mickey Free: Apache Captive, Interpreter, and Indian Scout*. Tucson: Arizona Historical Society, 2005.

Rakocy, Bill. *Mogollon Diary Number 2*. El Paso, Tex.: Bravo Press, 1988.

Ridgway, Rider. *Mt. Graham Profiles*. Vol. 2. Safford, Ariz.: Graham County Historical Society, 1988.

Ringold, Jennie Parks. *Frontier Days in the Southwest: Pioneer Days in Old Arizona*. San Antonio, Tex.: Naylor Company, 1952.

Robinson, Charles M. *General Crook and the Western Frontier*. Norman: University of Oklahoma Press, 2001.

Robinson, Sherry. *Apache Voices: Their Story of Survival as Told to Eve Ball*. Albuquerque: University of New Mexico Press, 2000.

Rockfellow, John A. *Log of an Arizona Trail Blazer*. Tucson: Arizona Silhouettes, 1955.

Rolak, Bruno. "General Miles Mirrors: The Heliograph in the Geronimo Campaign of 1886." *Journal of Arizona History* 16 (Summer 1975): 145–60.

Ruiz, Ramon Eduardo. *The People of Sonora and Yankee Capitalists*. Tucson: University of Arizona Press, 1988.

Salas, Miguel Tinker. *In the Shadow of the Eagles: Sonora and the Transformation of the Border during the Porfiriato.* Berkeley: University of California Press, 1997.

Salzman, M., Jr. "Geronimo: The Napoleon of Indians." *Journal of Arizona History* 8 (Winter 1967): 215–47.

Sanchez, Filberto Terrazas. *La Guerra Apache en Mexico.* Mexico: Veinte de Octobre, 1977.

Sanchez, Victoria. "Robert H. Stapleton of Socorro." *Herencia* 7 (October 1999): 22–27.

Santee, Ross. *Apache Land.* New York: Charles Scribner and Sons, 1947.

Schellie, Don. *Vast Domain of Blood: The Story of the Camp Grant Massacre.* Los Angeles: Westernlore Press, 1968.

Schmitt, Martin F., ed. *General George Crook: His Autobiography.* Norman: University of Oklahoma Press, 1946.

Schubert, Frank N. *Black Valor: Buffalo Soldiers and the Medal of Honor, 1870–1898.* Wilmington, Del.: Scholarly Resources, 1997.

———, ed. *Voices of the Buffalo Soldier: Records, Reports, and Recollections of Military Life and Service in the West.* Albuquerque: University of New Mexico Press, 2003.

Schwatka, Frederick. *Among the Apaches.* Palmer Lake, Colo.: Filter Press, 1974.

Shapard, John (Bud). "Chief Loco." Norman: University of Oklahoma Press, in press.

———. "A Federally Funded Wedding and Honeymoon." *Arizona Magazine,* July 15, 1879.

Shipp, William E. "Captain Crawford's Last Expedition." *Journal of the United States Cavalry Association* 5 (December 1892): 343–61.

Simmons, Mark. *Massacre on the Lordsburg Road: A Tragedy of the Apache Wars.* College Station: Texas A&M University Press, 1997.

Skinner, Woodward B. *The Apache Rock Crumbles: The Captivity Of Geronimo's People.* Pensacola, Fla.: Skinner Publications, 1997.

Smith, Allen, Jr. "An Apache War Dance." *Truth's Companion* 44 (August 13, 1891): 64, 442–43.

Smith, Cornelius C., Jr. *Emilio Kosterlitzky: Eagle Of Sonora And The Southwest Border.* Glendale, Calif.: Arthur H. Clark, 1970.

Sonnichsen, C. L. *Geronimo and the End of the Apache Wars.* Tucson: Arizona Historical Society, 1987.

———. *The Mescalero Apaches.* Norman: University of Oklahoma Press, 1973.

Spence, Mary Lee, ed. *The Arizona Diary of Lily Fremont, 1878–1881.* Tucson: University of Arizona Press, 1997.

Stout, Joe A. "Soldiering and Suffering in the Geronimo Campaign: Reminiscences of Lawrence R. Jerome." *Journal of the West* 11 (January 1972): 206–24.

Strover, William. "The Apaches' Last Trek." *Arizona: The State Magazine* 10 (May 1919): 6, 18.

Sweeney, Edwin R. "Chihuahua of the Chiricahuas." *Wild West* 13 (August 2000): 24–28, 67.

———. *Cochise: Chiricahua Apache Chief.* Norman: University of Oklahoma Press, 1991.

———. "Cochise and the Prelude to the Bascom Affair." *New Mexico Historical Review* 64 (October 1989): 427–46.

———, ed. *Making Peace with Cochise: The 1972 Journal of Captain Joseph Sladen.* Norman: University of Oklahoma Press, 1997.

———. *Mangas Coloradas: Chief of the Chiricahua Apaches.* Norman: University of Oklahoma Press, 1998.

———. *Merejildo Grijalva: Apache Captive, Army Scout.* El Paso: Texas Western Press, 1992.

Tassin, Augustus Gabriel de Vivier. "Reminiscences Of Indian Scouting." *Overland Monthly* 14 (August 1889): 151–69.

Terrazas, Joaquin. *Memorias La Guerra Contra Los Apaches.* Chihuahua: Centro Libero La Prensa, S.A. de C.V., 1994.

Thompson, Jerry D. *Desert Tiger—Captain Paddy Graydon and the Civil War in the Far Southwest.* El Paso: Texas Western Press, 1992.

Thrapp, Dan L. *Al Sieber: Chief of Scouts,* Norman: University of Oklahoma Press, 1964.

———. *The Conquest of Apacheria.* Norman: University of Oklahoma Press, 1967.

———. *Dateline Fort Bowie: Charles Fletcher Lummis Reports on an Apache War.* Norman: University of Oklahoma Press, 1979.

———. *Encyclopedia of Frontier Biography.* 4 vols. Glendale, Calif.: Arthur H. Clark, 1988.

———. *General Crook and the Sierra Madre Adventure.* Norman: University of Oklahoma Press, 1972.

———. "The Indian Scouts, with Special Attention to the Evolution, Use, and Effectiveness of the Apache Indian Scouts." In *Military History of the Spanish American Southwest,* 14–166. Ft. Huachuca, Ariz.: US Army Commo. Cmd., 1976.

———. *Juh: An Incredible Indian.* El Paso: Texas Western Press, 1992.

———. *Victorio and the Mimbres Apaches.* Norman: University of Oklahoma Press, 1974.

Turcheneske, John Anthony, Jr. *The Chiricahua Prisoners of War: Fort Sill, 1894–1914.* Niwot: University Press of Colorado, 1997.

Turner, Katharine C. *Red Men Calling on the Great White Father.* Norman: University of Oklahoma Press, 1951.

Ungnade, Herbert E. *Guide to the New Mexico Mountains,* Albuquerque: University of New Mexico Press, 1977.

Utley, Robert M. *Frontier Regulars: The United States Army and the Indians, 1866–1891.* New York: Macmillan Publishing, 1973.

Vandenberg, Hoyt Sanford, Jr. "Forsyth and the 1882 Loco Outbreak Campaign." Tucson Corral of the Westerners' *Smoke Signal* 60 (Fall 1993).

Voss, Stuart F. *On the Periphery of Nineteenth-Century Mexico: Sonora and Sinoloa 1810–1877.* Tucson: University of Arizona Press, 1982.

Walker, Henry P., ed. "The Reluctant Corporal: The Autobiography of William Bladen Jett—Part 1." *Journal of Arizona History* 12 (Spring 1971): 1–50.

Wallace, Andrew. "General Augustus V. Kautz in Arizona, 1874–1878." *Arizoniana* 4 (Winter 1963): 54–65.

The War of the Rebellion: A Compilation of the Official Records of the Union and Confederate Armies. Series 1, 53 vols. Washington, D.C.: Government Printing Office, 1880–1901.

Wasserman, Mark. *Capitalists, Caciques, and Revolution: The Native Elite and Foreign Enterprise in Chihuahua, Mexico, 1854–1911*. Chapel Hill: University of North Carolina Press, 1984.

Wharfield, H. B. *Alchesay: Scout With General Crook*. El Cajon, Calif.: Privately printed, 1969.

————. *Apache Indian Scouts*. El Cajon, Calif.: Privately printed, 1964.

Williamson, Dan R. "Story of Oskay de No Tah: The Flying Fighter." *Arizona Historical Review* 3 (October 1930): 78–83.

Wood, Norman. *Lives of Famous Indian Chiefs*. Aurora, Ill.: American Indian Historical Publishing Company, 1906.

Wooster, Robert. *Nelson A. Miles and the Twilight of the Frontier Army*. Lincoln: University of Nebraska Press, 1993.

INDEX